Government and Binding The
the Minimalist Program

Generative Syntax

General Editor David Lightfoot

Recent work in generative syntax has viewed the language faculty as a system of principles and parameters, which permit children to acquire productive grammars triggered by normal childhood experiences. The books in this series serve as an introduction to particular aspects or modules of this theory. They presuppose some minimal background in generative syntax, but will meet the tutorial needs of intermediate and advanced students. Written by leading figures in the field, the books will also contain sufficient fresh material to appeal at the highest level.

1 *Government and Binding Theory and the Minimalist Program*
Edited by Gert Webelhuth

Forthcoming

2 *Logical Form*
Norbert Hornstein

Government and Binding Theory and the Minimalist Program

Principles and Parameters in Syntactic Theory

Edited by Gert Webelhuth

BLACKWELL
Oxford UK & Cambridge USA

First published 1995
Reprinted 1995

Blackwell Publishers Inc.
238 Main Street
Cambridge, Massachusetts 02142
USA

Blackwell Publishers Ltd
108 Cowley Road
Oxford OX4 1JF
UK

Library of Congress Cataloging-in-Publication Data
Government and binding theory and the minimalist program: principles and parameters in syntactic theory / edited by Gert Webelhuth.
p. cm. — (Generative syntax)
Includes bibliographical references and index.
Contents: X-bar theory and case theory / Gert Webelhuth — Theta theory / Edwin Williams — Logical form / C.-T James Huang — Binding theory, control, and *pro* / Wayne Harbert — The empty category principle / Norbert Hornstein and Amy Weinberg — Morphosyntax / Randall Hendrick — The minimalist program / Alec Marantz — Bare phrase structure / Noam Chomsky.
ISBN 0-631-18059-1. — ISBN 0-631-18061-3 (pbk.)
1. Grammar, Comparative and general—Syntax. 2. Generative grammer. 3. Government-binding theory (Linguistics) 4. Principles and parameters (Linguistics) I. Webelhuth, Gert. II. Series.
P291.G68 1995
415—dc20 94-34963
CIP

British Library Cataloguing in Publication Data

A CIP catalogue record for this book is available from the British Library.

Typeset in 11 on 13 pt Palatino
by Graphicraft Typesetters Limited, Hong Kong
Printed and Bound in Great Britain by Hartnolls Limited, Bodmin, Cornwall.

This book is printed on acid-free paper

Contents

Introduction by the Editor

Contents

Preliminary Remarks

Linguistics is concerned with explaining what natural languages are, what it is about human beings that makes them *know* a language, and how they are able to acquire and use their specific linguistic abilities. According to Generative Grammar, on the observable level natural languages are the visible result of speakers putting to use their grammatical knowledge in uttering structured sounds which are systematically related by the grammar to structured meanings. To know a language, then, means to know (largely unconsciously) how to construct the mental representations of sound and meaning and the possible interrelations between the two types of representations. Generative Grammar is founded on the specific hypothesis that sound and meaning are only indirectly related in that they are mediated by *syntactic representations.* The claim that these three types of representations exist in any natural language, statements about the permissible relationships among them, and the principles governing their construction and use make up what Chomsky calls *Universal Grammar* (*UG*). UG, hypothesized to be an innate property of the human mind, can thus be thought of as a general theory of grammar and language; it is the set of assumptions about what is a possible grammar, and hence a possible natural language, that all language learners bring to the analysis of the primary linguistic data they are exposed to in the environment in which they grow up. If the learners are stimulated with data that can be analyzed with the conceptual categories of UG, they will proceed along a path at the end of which stands a system of grammatical statements that determines which of the universally available categories exist in this language, what their allowable meanings and surface expressions are in this language, and how they may be combined. Being able to construct these representations, we say that the speaker *knows* or *speaks* the language in question.

Natural languages are different from artificial mathematical or logical languages, created for a certain purpose, e.g. for programming a computer, testing mathematical theorems, etc. These artificial languages share with natural languages their vastness in that there are far too many different structures in each of them for the individual components (sentences, formulas) to be stored in a finite human memory individually. Because natural languages allow for lexical and structural ambiguities and because they show many irregularities, it was long thought to be impossible to characterize them in terms of systems that are as explicit as the recursive syntaxes of formal languages. And yet, we humans have judgments ranging from very sharp to very elusive about which strings of words and phrases are grammatical in our language and we can draw logical inferences from the meanings of natural language sentences.

Generative Grammar was developed as a program to characterize the knowledge of a native speaker about his/her natural language as a *formal and explicit* set of rules to generate all and only the representations that underlie the grammatical sentences in a natural language (cf. Chomsky (1965, 4)). A *Generative Grammar* is thus nothing more than a formally precise grammar whose empirical predictions follow mechanically from its rules and postulates. Given the problems mentioned earlier with regard to the vastness and irregularity of natural language, the earliest versions of Generative Grammar focused on the task of making it initially plausible that a formal, coherent, explicit, and complete rule system could be developed with the property that it made mechanically derivable correct predictions about the judgments of native speakers about their language. Among these judgments are the abilities to label certain sentences as clearly grammatical, others as clearly ungrammatical, to recognize certain sentences as ambiguous, pairs of sentences as synonymous, etc. Given that we can apply these abilities to expressions we have certainly never heard before, they are to be characterized in terms of a computational system rather than some kind of list in human memory about which sentences enter into the various relationships. This means that the rules underlying these abilities do not apply to sentences directly but rather to recurrent sentence patterns or as we prefer to call them, *sentence structures.*

While the American structuralists pursued the goal of developing a theory of *discovery procedures* that would make it possible to mechanically detect *the* grammar for a recorded corpus of utterances in what they considered the only permissible scientific manner, Generative Grammarians try to explicate the notion of grammar. This is done by proposing answers to such questions as: What is the form of a language-particular grammar? How many rule types are there and what can these rules do? What substantive categories such as noun, verb, subject, sentence, segment, etc. may be referred to in these rules? Once we have formulated hypotheses concerning these issues, the sentences that make possible utterances can be analyzed as strings of units that receive an analysis in several levels of grammatical representation, e.g. phonology and syntax.

The resulting grammar should characterize a language in a completely precise and mechanical fashion: a string is in the language only if the grammar makes a full grammatical representation available for it on every level of analysis.

In earlier versions of generative grammar the descriptive burden of the syntactic component rested on two types of syntactic rules, phrase structure rules (PS) and transformational rules. Examples of PS rules are given in (1):[1]

(1) S → NP VP
NP → Det N
VP → V NP
Det → *the*
N → *man, ball,* etc.
V → *hit, took,* etc.

These phrase structure rules can be applied to generate part of the structural description of the sentence *the man hit the ball* in a mechanical and stepwise fashion. Its structure can be represented by a *labeled bracketing* as in (2) or a *tree diagram* as in (3):

(2) $[_{S}\,[_{NP}\,[_{Det}\ \textit{the}\ ]\ [_{N}\ \textit{man}\ ]]\ [_{VP}\,[_{V}\ \textit{hit}\ [_{NP}\,[_{Det}\ \textit{the}\ ]\ [_{N}\ \textit{ball}\ ]]]]$

(3)

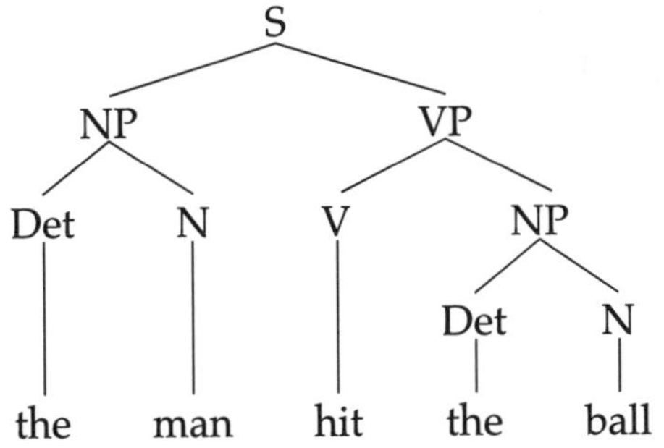

The structural description in (3) is created by the phrase structure rules until a point is reached where no more rules can be applied. The structure is referred to as an *underlying representation* or in later years as a *Deep Structure,* because it serves as the input to the second type of grammatical rule available, *transformations.* Each member of this latter rule type maps an underlying representation/Deep Structure or a transform of such a representation into a new tree structure.

Transformations are composed of elementary operations that do such things as rearranging the categories in a tree, deleting categories, adding new ones, etc. In addition, transformations are allowed to introduce and delete morphemes.

(4)–(8) illustrate some typical transformational formulations cited from the textbook by Akmajian and Heny (1976):[2]

(4) *Passive* (Optional)

SD:	NP	–	Aux	–	V	–	NP
	1		2		3		4
SC:	4		2 be en		3		by 1

(5) *Reflexivization* (Obligatory)

SD:	NP	–	Aux	–	V	–	X	–	NP
	1		2		3		4		5
SC:	1 2		3		4				5 [+REFLEXIVE]

Condition: Term 1 must be identical with term 5.

(6) *Affix Hopping* (Obligatory)

SD: $\underset{1}{\left\{\begin{array}{c}\text{pres}\\ \text{past}\\ \text{ing}\\ \text{en}\end{array}\right\}} - \underset{2}{\left\{\begin{array}{c}\text{Modal}\\ \\ \\ \text{V}\end{array}\right\}}$

SC: 2 # 1

(7) *Subject–Auxiliary Inversion* (Obligatory)

SD: $\underset{1}{\text{Q}} - \underset{2}{\text{NP}} - \text{Tense} \quad \underset{3}{\left(\left\{\begin{array}{c}\text{Modal}\\ \text{have}\\ \text{be}\end{array}\right\}\right)}$

SC: 1 3 2

(8) *Wh- Fronting* (Obligatory)

SD:	Q	–	X	–	[+WH]
	1		2		3
SC:	1 + 3		2		ø

(4) might relate such active–passive pairs as *John admires Mary* and *Mary is admired by John.* It transforms active into passive structures by moving the active subject to the end of the sentence following the inserted preposition *by.* Furthermore, the postverbal NP is moved into the subject position and the auxiliary *be* and the participial ending *en* are inserted into the passive string. (5) creates sentences with reflexive pronouns in them. It transforms the structures for strings like *You like you* into *You like yourself.* (6) attaches affixes to verbs and (7) inverts

subjects with auxiliaries in the formation of, among others, Yes–No and constituent questions. Finally, (8) moves a *wh*-element leftward to the beginning of a sentence. It might convert *Bill knows John saw who* into *Bill knows who John saw.*

Akmajian and Heny discuss many more transformations in their book. They point out that not only is it necessary to specify for each transformation whether it applies optionally or obligatorily and to add special conditions to certain transformations (e.g. (5)), but the system also requires that the transformations be applied in a certain order to operate correctly. (9) reproduces the ordering they impose on the transformations they introduce:

(9)
1 Dative Movement (Optional)
2 Equi NP Deletion (Obligatory)
3 Raising to Object (Obligatory)
4 Raising to Subject (Obligatory)
5 *For* Deletion (Obligatory)
6 Passive (Optional)
7 Agent Deletion (Optional)
8 Reflexivization (Obligatory)
9 Extraposition (Optional)
10 *It* Deletion (Obligatory)
11 Number Agreement (Obligatory)
12 *There* Insertion (Optional)
13 Tag Formation (Optional)
14 Negative Placement (Obligatory)
15 Contraction (Optional)
16 Subject–Auxiliary Inversion (Obligatory)
17 *Wh-* Fronting (Obligatory)
18 Affix Hopping (Obligatory)
19 *Do* Support (Obligatory).

Once we extend our analysis beyond the simplest transitive and intransitive sentence types, phrase structure description becomes much more complex as well. Chomsky (1965, 106ff) presents the following "illustrative fragment of the base component":

(10)
(i) S $\rightarrow$ NP Predicate-Phrase
(ii) Predicate-Phrase $\rightarrow$ Aux VP (Place) (Time)
(iii)
$$\text{VP} \rightarrow \left\{ \begin{array}{l} \text{Copula Predicate} \\ \text{V} \left\{ \begin{array}{l} \text{(NP) (Prep-Phrase) (Prep-Phrase) (Manner)} \\ \text{S}' \\ \text{Predicate} \end{array} \right\} \end{array} \right\}$$

(iv) $\text{Predicate} \rightarrow \left\{ \begin{array}{l} \text{Adjective} \\ \\ (\textit{like})\ \text{Predicate–Nominal} \end{array} \right\}$

(v) Prep-Phrase → Direction, Duration, Place, Frequency, etc.

(vi) V → CS

(vii) NP → (Det) N (S′)

(viii) N → CS

(ix) [+Det _] → [±Count]

(x) [+Count] → [±Animate]

(xi) [+N, +_] → [±Animate]

(xii) [+Animate] → [±Human]

(xiii) [–Count] → [±Abstract]

(xiv) [+V] → CS/α Aux _ (Det β), } where α is an N

(xv) Adjective → CS/α . . . _ } and β is an N

(xvi) Aux → Tense (M) (Aspect)

(xvii) Det → (pre-Article *of*) Article (post-Article)

(xviii) Article → [±Definite]

Some of these phrase structure rules only mention syntactic categories (i, vii), others mention specific lexical items of English (iv, xvii), again others refer to semantic categories like "Time," "Place," "Manner." As in transformations, reference is made to obligatory and optional expansions.

Quite apart from the issue of whether these rules are descriptively adequate, the complexity of this genre of phrase structure rules and transformational rules raises the question of how language learners go about finding their correct formulation. The models of Universal Grammar from this period emphasized the descriptive utility and versatility of the rule devices in relating sentences that were either intuitively felt to be related or showed similar grammatical behavior in some respect. The rule types they made available to the analysis of individual languages and constructions were thus very general and imposed only very weak conditions on the use of rules in terms of substantive linguistic categories and relations. It is open to doubt whether all language learners are systematically exposed to the data that are crucially needed to establish the exact rule statements including the special conditions that appear in some of the rules. As Baker (1979) pointed out, many transformations of the general format (4)–(8) require that the language learner know for certain that specific sentence types are systematically ungrammatical. Learners are thus typically confronted with the dilemma of deciding whether a given sentence type is accidentally absent from the corpus of utterances they have been exposed to or whether it is ungrammatical.

The format of the rules in (4)–(8) and (10) poses another serious problem. Given the weak substantive constraints on the rules, many other ones could be formulated in the same language of rules and each one is predicted to be a possible rule of some natural language. Given the *wh*-movement rule in (8) and the reflexivization rule in (5), for instance, what would prevent us from writing a *wh*-movement rule that incorporates the condition on the reflexivization rule? We might require that prepositional phrases are *wh*-moved only if there are two identical NPs in the sentence. Or, putting together the information in the passive transformation (4) and the *wh*-movement transformation (8), we could easily write a rule that restricts passivization only to those sentences that contain a *wh*-phrase. Consider the additional possibilities that arise when we incorporate into our model other grammatical properties necessary for syntactic description, such as case, gender, number, relative pronounhood, stress, clitichood, definiteness, quantification, referential inclusion, etc. There being no substantive constraints on which features can co-occur in the same rule, the number of potential rule hypotheses available to the language learner is huge.

The remedy to this situation lies in an attempt at what might be called *modularization* and *localization*. The properties and distribution of each given grammatical feature must be universally allowed to interact only with those other features that it shows interdependencies with in some language, i.e. we must settle the empirical question of what is a possible feature co-occurrence restriction. If the features of passive constructions may not refer to the feature [+*wh*], then there cannot be a rule to the effect that passivization is only possible in sentences with a *wh*-phrase. In determining such legitimate feature interactions, we are likely to be provided with natural alliances of features, i.e. groups of categories whose properties and distribution typically covary. Perhaps we may be able to find further restrictions, i.e. in exactly how the features may be related, etc. In this case we have achieved a measure of "modularization," i.e. we have a specific set of concepts and conditions on their co-occurrence that can be viewed as a subpart of the grammatical system as a whole. In Government–Binding Theory there are several such *modules*. The module of binding-theory, for instance, deals with "binding theory–compatible indexings" among such referentially different types of NPs as pronouns, anaphors, R-expressions, operators, etc. The theta module, in contrast, deals with the distribution of arguments and expletives and arguably makes no reference to binding-theoretic features, etc.

Highly modularizing grammatical information has the crucial advantage that it allows us to isolate those grammatical properties from each other that our empirical syntactic studies show do not interact directly in any language. It also allows for partial isolation in that our modules can act as filters on *how* two or more grammatical properties can interact. A case in point is the interaction of the theories of *wh*-movement and agreement. While complementizers and verbs sometimes agree with fronted *wh*-operators, such phenomena are typically restricted to elements occurring in the same sentence at some point in the derivation. The agreement facts in clauses lower than the starting site of the *wh*-phrase or higher than its final landing site are irrelevant to the wellformedness of *wh*-movement. Parceling *wh*-movement and agreement into two different modules allows us to control the amount and type of information that can flow from one domain into the other and hence to adjust the options made available by the rule system to those required by the empirical generalizations.

Localizing grammatical information is another powerful means for bounding the richness of descriptive devices. I am referring to constraints on where in the representational system specific information and wellformedness conditions are located and how they apply. Obviously, for this to be possible there must be different stages in a derivation or several levels of representation to begin with. Government–Binding theory standardly makes use of three syntactic levels of representation and the level of Phonological Form (PF).[3] In addition, a lexicon is postulated. Many important proposals crucially rely on localization: in Chomsky (1981), structural Case is assigned at S-structure but not at D-structure and the binding theory does not apply before S-structure either. Parasitic gaps must be licensed at S-structure but not at LF. In one version of the theory of proper government, some licensing clauses for empty categories are placed in PF, others in LF.

One of the central constraints of the theory is the Projection Principle. It is in a sense an "everywhere" principle in that it ties together the information in lexical entries with all syntactic representations. It entails trace theory and the existence of phonologically unexpressed subjects (i.e. PRO and *pro*) and imposes very strict constraints on how much a derivation is allowed to 'deform' an initial syntactic representation. In combination with other principles of the grammar it profoundly limits possible rule applications and hence the inventory of syntactic rules in natural languages as well.

This book provides an overview of the attempts within Government–Binding Theory (or, the Principles and Parameters approach, as it is now often called) to develop universal concepts of representation, derivation, and wellformedness that answer the objections to the postulation of rules like (4)–(8) and (10). While it discusses many different and often mutually incompatible approaches, they all share the goal of equipping Universal Grammar with maximally rich constraints on grammar formulation that minimize the amount of learning of language-particular constraints necessary for the formulation of individual grammars. Optimally, Universal Grammar is designed so as to present the language learners with a finite and small number of Yes–No decisions ("parameters") that can be made on the basis of the types of example sentences these learners are guaranteed to encounter in their language-learning environment. By limiting from the start in this manner the kinds of hypotheses the learners bring to the languages to be learned, we have the core of an explanation of why languages have the form they do and why they are acquired the way they are.

There are several appropriate ways in which the truly massive amount of material to be covered in an overview of the Principles and Parameters approach could be grouped into chapters. The grouping in this book is the result of many considerations and circumstances, the details of which the reader is better spared. Some topics fit equally well into several chapters but are discussed only in one to avoid too much redundancy. The readers are advised to use the tables of contents for the book as a whole and for the individual chapters as well as the index to quickly locate the topics they are particularly interested in. The sections called "Prelude" and "Related Material in Other Chapters" (written by the editor) which introduce and close each chapter may provide additional orientation.

The Concept of This Book

The contributors to this book were invited to write chapters on their areas of specialization in GB/Principles and Parameters theory that describe the history of a module of the theory, the core data it deals with, the major competing approaches within the module, and the most important literature discussing it. The chapters were to be written so as to address the typical needs of both teachers and graduate students of linguistic theory. Teachers should be enabled to use the core data and theory in introductory courses and should have the option of leaving more exotic or advanced topics to seminars or self-study. Thorough literature reviews of even advanced material should allow teachers to build seminars around the individual chapters and should also function as guides to the literature for students who ask for references on a particular topic. For the material covered in this book, it should no longer be necessary for the teacher to provide the student with a long list of papers and books from memory.

Students at every level should profit from reading this book. They should keep in mind, however, that this book is special in several respects. It was written by a number of different authors who did not communicate with each other during writing. Therefore the chapters are largely self-contained and autonomous. Unlike with most other handbooks, therefore, the material here is not developed in a step-by-step fashion from less difficult to more difficult. The sequence of the chapters was designed to ensure that basic concepts from X-bar theory, Case theory, and theta theory would be covered early in the book but it may still be necessary for the student to reread certain sections of one chapter after other chapters have been covered. Also, the reader should be aware that due to coordination difficulties the individual papers were completed over a span of time.

Due to the conditions just described, a certain measure of redundancy between the individual chapters could not be avoided, even though the editor has made an effort to reduce these to a minimum. Since the authors were encouraged to bring unresolved problems out in the open rather than ignore them, it was felt in a number of cases that the benefit to the reader from seeing two different discussions of the same sub-topic from different perspectives would outweigh the nuisance of a slight redundancy.

While the readers must be the ultimate judges, I feel that the difficult experiment of bringing nine busy authors together to write on the current state of the Principles and Parameters Approach was a full success. With the chapters coming in successively, I was reminded of what attracted me to linguistics originally: the contributions authentically reflect the intellectual excitement of being a linguist at the frontiers of syntactic research, and with each chapter I read I instantly wanted to go off and be a part of this interesting research myself. Since the authors did not cut out discussion of unsolved problems or present the illusion that there is only one solution to the problems discussed, they directly invite the reader to participate in real-world syntactic research: to weigh the advantages and disadvantages of alternative explanations and explore potential explanations for recalcitrant data.

Several authors have expressed regret that the space and time limitations they had to operate under did not allow them to discuss all the material they wanted, or to go into the amount of detail that they wanted. Every chapter in this book refers the reader to additional writings on some topic. The students should take this to be a reflection of real-world linguistics as well. The literature on syntax, especially within GB theory, is so large that no review could possibly be complete. This book, therefore, can be no more than a guide, and it remains the responsibility of the student to explore the primary literature for him/herself, especially those works that have appeared too recently to be considered here. While a reading of the works cited in the bibliography to each chapter will undoubtedly keep a student busy, there are many additional books and papers that could and, perhaps, should have been recommended.

Acknowledgments

First and foremost I would like to thank the contributors of this book for their faith in its concept and their great efforts in realizing it.

Case Theory and *pro*-drop were originally supposed to be treated in their own chapters by other authors, but these manuscripts never materialized. These topics were therefore incorporated into chapters 1 and 4 respectively. I would like to thank Wayne Harbert for volunteering to add a section to his chapter.

I also owe special thanks to Alec Marantz for offering to write on the Minimalist Program at very short notice, and to Randy Hendrick for generously agreeing to adjust the organization of his chapter in the service of an optimal coverage of the material in the book. I would like to thank Noam Chomsky warmly for permitting us to incorporate his paper "Bare Phrase Structure," which brings the volume fully up to date with the current research in the field.

In a work that puts such heavy emphasis on the review of the literature the accuracy of the bibliographical references is particularly important. Barbara Levergood volunteered to check for correctness every single published reference in this book where this was possible, and to make sure that the citations are complete and consistent across chapters. This was a huge and often thankless task which entitles her to a good part of the credit for this project.

Gunsoo Lee from the Department of Linguistics at the University of Wisconsin–Madison has helped me with the editing of various chapters. This was a big and laborious task as well, since the chapters were composed on different word processors and had to be made stylistically consistent. Gunsoo spent many hours doing this very thoroughly and dependably, and deserves my special recognition.

I used the manuscript in teaching Linguistics 530 at the University of Wisconsin–Madison in the spring of 1993 and would like to thank the participants of this class for their cooperation. Gina Suh from this class read a part of the manuscript carefully and provided me with a list of necessary corrections.

David Lightfoot, the editor of the series in which this book will appear, was very generous and allowed me to follow my own instincts. Thanks for your confidence in me! Philip Carpenter and Steve Smith from Blackwell publishers have followed the project and offered their help when it was necessary. It has been a pleasure to work with them.

Finally, it is with great pleasure that I thank the members of my home base, the Department of Linguistics at the University of North Carolina, and in particular Randy Hendrick who was its chair during most of the production of the book. It is no secret among my acquaintances that I often refer to Randy as the best mentor and colleague I could imagine. I am deeply grateful for the opportunity to work on a daily basis with someone who not only is an outstanding linguist but a wonderful human being as well. I have never seen him compromise the highest standards of academic integrity or the professionalism with which he drives our department towards excellence in research and teaching. In almost every aspect of my professional career I have relied on his experienced advice and have turned to him many times in the process of editing this book and writing my own chapter. May every reader have a role model like him!

NOTES

1 These rules are presented in Chomsky (1957). Their format has been slightly modified for the exposition here.

2 "SD" stands for "Structural Description" and "SC" for "Structural Change." The former is a set of conditions that a structure must fulfill to undergo a transformation; the latter specifies the changes brought about by the application of the transformation.

3 Chomsky (1992) has proposed a model with only two distinguished levels of representation, Logical Form and Phonological Form. This model is discussed in chapters 7 and 8 of this book.

1

X-bar Theory and Case Theory

Gert Webelhuth
University of North Carolina at Chapel Hill

Contents

The basic relations that can obtain between elements of a grammatical theory and the corresponding relations in the language described by the grammar are surprisingly few. The bewildering variety encountered in any real language results from the interplay of these logically simple relations.

Bach (1964, 103)

Prelude

Chapter 1 introduces the concepts that underlie the theories of phrase structure and abstract Case. The first half of the chapter deals with the development of these theories in the late 1960s through the 1970s and their canonical formulations in Chomsky's (1981) book *Lectures on Government and Binding*. The second half of the discussion is reserved for a description of the major modifications of the two modules after 1981, especially the incorporation of Comp, Infl, and Det into X-bar theory, the VP-Internal Subject Hypothesis, and questions relating to the projection of functional heads and the status of the A/A-bar distinction.

X-bar theory (and to some extent Case theory as well) is intimately related to other modules of the theory and for that reason is discussed early. Its structural distinctions (e.g. specifier vs. complement vs. modifier positions) are made use of practically everywhere else in the theory: theta theory uses the distinctions for the purpose of argument realization (which ensures, among others, that *the cat ate the mouse* does not mean the same as *the mouse ate the cat*); the theories of government and binding formulate the definitions of such core-structural notions as *c-command, govern, bind, governing category, minimality* on the basis of primitive X-bar-theoretic notions, etc. Because of this strong information flow between X-bar theory and the remainder of the grammar, X-bar theory is almost always affected as well when some other module is redefined.

1 Introduction[1]

X-bar theory is a central module of the Principles and Parameters approach to syntactic theory. All other modules in one way or another draw on the basic structures it makes available together with the lexicon and the projection principle in defining their own concepts.

In this chapter we will ask how X-bar theory came to occupy such a central place in syntactic theory and what contributions it has made to descriptive and explanatory adequacy.

The theory of Case strongly interacts with X-bar theory, the lexicon and the projection principle and will be discussed in this chapter as well.

2 "Remarks on Nominalization"

We will begin with an analysis of a monumentally important work, Chomsky's (1970) "Remarks on Nominalization." This paper was a contribution to what has probably been the most acrimonious debate among generative grammarians in the history of this approach to language, that between two groups of generative linguists, the *Interpretive Semanticists* and the *Generative Semanticists.* This split in convictions, as the names of the two camps suggest, relates to assumptions about the role of meaning in grammars.

Towards the end of their very influential book *An Integrated Theory of Linguistic Descriptions,* Katz and Postal (1964, 157) propose the following heuristic principle:

> Given a sentence for which a syntactic derivation is needed; look for simple paraphrases of the sentence which are not paraphrases by virtue of synonymous expressions; on finding them, construct grammatical rules that relate the original sentence and its paraphrases in such a way that each of these sentences has the same sequence of underlying P-markers. Of course, having constructed such rules, it is still necessary to find *independent syntactic justification* for them.

Katz and Postal propose that any two surface structures which are nonlexically synonymous should be reduced to the same underlying structure. This heuristic led to a picture of the relationship between form and meaning that many linguists found extremely appealing, namely, that a large class of synonymous sentences had identical representations at the semantically significant deepest level of analysis, and that it was the function of transformations to create the possible surface structures that express these meanings. Pursuing this idea meant that it was not necessary to rely solely on vague and often subjective notions of simplicity and elegance in choosing which surface structures are derived transformationally from the same deep structures. Justifying underlying structures in terms of their semantic content seemed more principled and satisfactory and, in fact, even simpler in many cases. For example, Lakoff (1968), in a paper on instrumental phrases, argued that in (1) and (2) the three NPs are subject to the same selectional restrictions in the presence of the verb *slice* and that a theory that derives both from the same deep structure is preferable to one that does not because the selectional restrictions would have to be stated only once:

(1) Seymour$_1$ *sliced* the salami$_2$ with a knife$_3$
(2) Seymour$_1$ used a knife$_3$ to *slice* the salami$_2$

This required the postulation of a more abstract underlying structure for (1) than in earlier Generative approaches, for instance *Syntactic Structures* (Chomsky (1957)) and *Aspects of the Theory of Syntax* (Chomsky (1965)).

Chomsky had used this same type of argument for transformational relationships in his own work. Now, this argument from simplicity, paired with the attractive concept that deep structure should be the level of representation at which non-lexically synonymous sentences are represented identically and non-synonymous sentences differently, led many linguists to postulate more abstract deep structures and to rely on the power of transformations to produce the widely varying surface structures that can express these meanings.[2]

Some linguists thus started working on a model of grammar, dubbed "Generative Semantics," that would realize the appealing conception of syntactic rules operating on underlying semantic representations.

But by the end of the 1960s, Chomsky began to argue forcefully against the generative semantics model. "Remarks on Nominalization" was the first in a trilogy of articles designed to reestablish the interpretivist conception of the relationship between syntax and semantics which holds that the semantic component is non-generative and its role is restricted to the interpretation of the forms created by the syntactic component.[3]

Chomsky (1970) takes a position against the view that surface structure makes no contribution to semantic interpretation (a position known as the *Katz–Postal Hypothesis*) and rejects the a priori assumption that every two semantically related surface structures must be derived transformationally from the same underlying representation. The latter argument lies at the center of "Remarks" and concerns the relationships between sentences such as (3) and the two types of nominals in (4)–(5) which Chomsky terms, respectively, *derived* and *gerundive nominals*:

(3) The enemy destroyed the city
(4) The enemy's destruction of the city "derived nominal"
(5) The enemy's destroying the city "gerundive nominal"

Chomsky objects to a transformational derivation of (4) from the structure underlying (3) motivated on semantic grounds and claims that a much more economic and elegant grammar results if derived nominals are listed as such in the lexicon and enter into no transformational relationships with their semantically related sentences at all. The gerundive nominals as in (5), however, would still have the same deep structure as their sentential counterparts.

Derived nominals, then, are morphologically rather than transformationally derived. Chomsky points to a cluster of properties that distinguish the two types of nominals that would be immediately explained if the derived nominals are listed in the lexicon but the gerundive ones are produced by a structural transformation from an underlying sentence built on the same verb.

First, listing the derived nominals one by one allows for there to be gaps. In fact it is not unusual for morphological paradigms to be defective. On the other hand, the evaluation measure requires that syntactic transformations express structurally regular and productive relationships between expressions.[4] We would therefore not expect there to be irregular gaps in the formation of the transformationally generated gerundive nominals. Chomsky argues that the expected difference in productivity indeed obtains. There are sentences for which gerundive nominals exist even though corresponding derived nominals are lacking:

(6) John is easy (difficult) to please
(7) John's being easy (difficult) to please
(8) *John's easiness (difficulty) to please

(9) John is certain (likely) to win the prize
(10) John's being certain (likely) to win the prize
(11) *John's certainty (likelihood) to win the prize

Second, the meaning of derived nominals like that of other listed expressions should be able to drift, leading to differences in meaning between the morphological base and the derived noun that cannot be predicted by a general rule. Such changes in meaning are disfavored by the evaluation metric on transformational operations. Hence, the relationship in meaning between gerundive nominals and their related verbs ought to be transparent. (12) shows that this is the case as well:

(12) try, trying, trial
marry, marrying, marriage
revolve, revolving, revolution
construct, constructing, construction

Revolution in *political revolution* has a meaning quite distinct from the verb *revolve,* and *construction* has taken on a technical meaning in linguistics that the verb *construct* lacks. The corresponding gerundive nominals do not arbitrarily differ in meaning from their base verbs in this manner.

Third, Chomsky points out that derived and gerundive nominals have very different distributions. Derived nominals have the syntax of basic nouns, whereas gerundive nominals display the properties of verbs. Thus, only derived nominals can appear with articles:

(13) the book
the proof of the theorem
*the proving of the theorem

Derived nominals are modified by adjectives, whereas gerundive nominals resist such modification:

(14) John's yellow hat
John's unmotivated criticism of the book
*John's unmotivated criticizing the book

Nouns, unlike verbs, cannot co-occur with aspect:

(15) *the have/ing book
*John's have/ing criticism of the book
John's having criticized the book

Many derived nominals but no gerundives take plural morphology and can occur with number adjectives:

(16) the three books
John's three proofs of the theorem
*John's three provings the theorem

Chomsky (1972c, 161) contains the clearest formulation of why these paradigms argue against a transformational derivation of both types of nominals from a semantically motivated sentential source:

> If . . . we were to suppose that each nominal, gerundive or derived, is generated from an initial phrase-marker representing its semantic interpretation, we would fail entirely to explain why the gerundive nominals, with a regular semantic relation to the associated sentence, have the formal properties of sentences, whereas the derived nominals, which would have a variety of different sources, exhibit the convergence of formal properties just noted (i.e., in essence, the properties of noun phrases), differing from gerundive nominals in this respect. All of this would be simply a remarkable accident from this point of view . . . Notice that the failure is one of explanatory, not descriptive adequacy. There is no doubt that the facts noted can be described in a grammar that derives all of the these forms by transformation.

That generative grammars with excessive descriptive devices would not be able to attain explanatory adequacy was of particular concern to Chomsky at the time, cf. Chomsky (1972c, 124ff):

> The gravest defect of the theory of transformational grammar is its enormous latitude and descriptive power. Virtually anything can be expressed as a phrase marker, i.e., a properly parenthesized expression with parenthesized segments assigned to categories. Virtually any imaginable rule can be described in transformational terms. Therefore a critical problem in making transformational grammar a substantive theory with explanatory force is to restrict the category of admissible phrase markers, admissible transformations, and admissible derivations . . .

This is what Chomsky set out to do in the 1970s. In "Remarks," he concentrated on X-bar theory, in its two companion papers (1972a, b) he pursued the question of how deep and surface structure each contribute to semantic interpretation. Starting with his 1973 paper "Conditions on Transformations," he built on the work in Ross (1967) in developing ever more general ways of restricting the power of transformations.

What made X-bar theory possible was the separation of the lexicon from the phrase structure rules and the introduction of *syntactic features* in *Aspects*. "Remarks" generalizes the treatment of lexical categories as sets of features to all categories, both lexical and phrasal (Chomsky (1970, 48ff)):

> In the earliest work in generative grammar it was assumed that the elements of the underlying base grammar are formatives and categories; each category corresponds to a class of strings of formatives. This assumption was carried over from structuralist syntactic theories . . . For reasons discussed in Chomsky (1965, Chapter 2), it was soon found necessary to depart from this assumption in the case of lexical categories . . . We might just as well eliminate the distinction of feature and category, and regard all symbols of the grammar as sets of features.

Classifying expressions not in terms of unanalyzed categories but as bundles of features allows verbs and nouns to be non-transformationally related just by virtue of sharing important features. That is the idea underlying X-bar theory and a category-neutral base component.

Recall from our earlier discussion that derived nominals posed the following problems for a transformational derivation:

(17)
- there are unsystematic lexical gaps, i.e. not every verb has a corresponding nominal and vice versa;
- there is semantic drift, i.e. the meaning of a derived nominal can often not be predicted from the meaning of its morphologically related base;
- derived nominals have the internal structure of basic NPs rather than sentential structures, i.e. they can contain determiners, adjectival modifiers, the head can take plural morphology, etc.

Gerundive nominals pose none of these problems, or at least not systematically. All these difficulties disappear if derived nominals are base-generated on the basis of listed nouns in the lexicon and their relationship with existing morphological bases is expressed through syntactic and semantic features.

To capture the relationship between *destroy* and *destruction*, we postulate one lexical entry *destr-* with two branches, one leading to the verb, the other to the noun. Whatever features are shared by the verb and the noun are listed at the root of the entry that is shared by both. The differences between the two, however, are encoded on each separate branch in terms of features. To the extent that there are regularities across pairs of related nominals and their base, these can be expressed by lexical redundancy rules, a mechanism that is needed independently of derived nominals. Since the lexicon is not subject to the strict productivity and regularity requirements on syntactic transformations, we expect to find some lexical gaps, semantic drift, and morphological irregularities; since the derived nominals are inserted into noun positions in deep structure, they should appear in phrases that have the internal structure of noun phrases and not sentences. These are precisely the properties in (17). Gerundive nominals, on the other hand, are derived transformationally from underlying sentential bases and therefore are correctly predicted to have a much more regular relationship to verbs and to display the internal syntax of sentences.

What is left to do is to establish a relationship between the syntactic features of lexical entries and the categorial configurations in which the entries occur. This is the *configurational* aspect of X-bar theory which is often identified with the module as a whole.

We will express non-transformationally that the preverbal/nominal and postverbal/nominal NPs satisfy the same semantic restrictions of the head in the sentence (18) and the noun phrase (19):

(18) [$_{S}$*John* [$_{V}$ proved] *the theorem*]
(19) [$_{NP}$*John's* [$_{N}$ proof] (of) *the theorem*]

For the purposes of selectional restrictions we must somehow identify the respective positions. Chomsky accomplishes this in "Remarks" by building a categorial asymmetry into noun phrases in analogy with the subject–object asymmetry on the sentential level. Specifically, he postulates a hierarchy of syntactic expressions of category X. The lowest category is X^0, the category of the lexical item. X″ (X-double-bar) is the maximal projection. X′ (X-bar) is an intermediate phrasal category. He distinguishes sets of selectional restrictions in terms of at what level the targeted category combines with the head of a phrase. The sister constituents of an X^0 (e.g. the V^0 *destroy,* the N^0 *destruction,* the A^0 *proud*) that form an X′ with the head (e.g. the V′ *destroy the city,* the N′ *destruction of the city,* or the A′ *proud of Mary*) are referred to as **complements** of the head. Expressions that combine with such an X′ to form the maximal projection X″ (e.g. the N″ *the destruction of the city,* the A″ *very proud of Mary*) are termed **specifiers** of the head. The following diagram from Chomsky (1970) shows the analysis of the noun phrase *several of John's proofs of the theorem* within this system of representation:

(20)

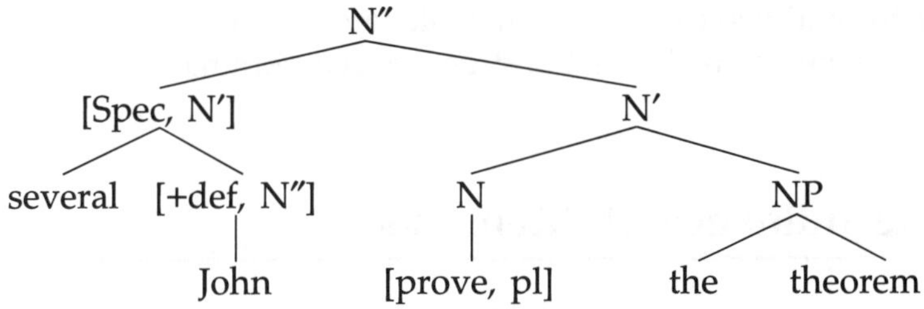

Once we can refer to specifiers and complements across heads of different syntactic categories, it is easy to assign a constituent structure to the sentence in (18) from which the identity in semantic selection between the noun in (19) and the verb in (18) will follow:

(21)

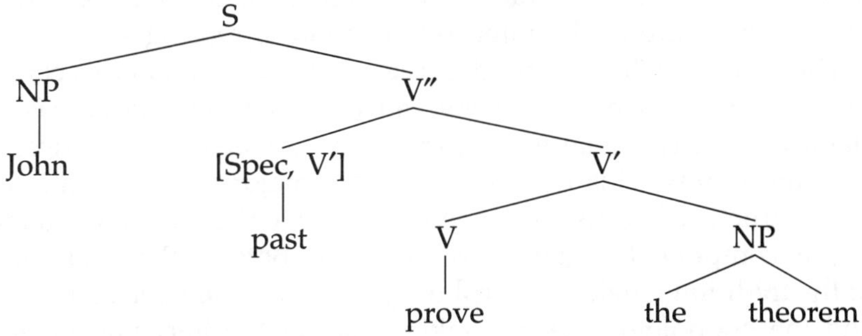

Chomsky writes (1970, 53ff): "The internal structure of the nominal . . . mirrors that of the sentence . . . The strict subcategorization features of the lexical item *prove* take account of the phrases V′ and N′ dominating the category to which it is assigned . . . Its selectional features refer to the heads of the associated phrases, which are the same in both cases." In other words, the selectional relation of the complements to their head verbs/nouns remains constant and for selectional purposes the specifier of N′ is identified with the sentential subject position. To ensure this across different verb/noun pairs, Chomsky requires that (1970, 38) "in the simplest case, all of the contextual features of the items that appear as verbs in verb phrases and as derived nouns in derived nominals will be common to the two types of context." Given this requirement on branching lexical entries, we expect morphologically derived items to have many selectional and subcategorizational properties in common with their underlying morphological bases while allowing for the exceptions and idiosyncrasies made possible by lexical listing. In Chomsky's view, this is the only treatment of derived nominals which is flexible enough to be descriptively adequate and constrained enough (in that it does not undermine the productive and regular role of transformations) to serve as an explanatory account of the systematic differences between derived and gerundive nominals.

3 The Influence of "Remarks"

The theoretical influence of "Remarks on Nominalization" cannot be overstated. In many respects the development of the study of syntax after this paper is highly ironic. Due in large part to the new mechanisms the interpretivists led by Chomsky introduced into the study of syntax, generative semantics eventually collapsed.[5] But several of these new ideas quickly developed a life of their own and now began to split the camp of the interpretivists into opposing subgroups.

Three ideas of "Remarks" deserve special mention in this connection. The first one is what Chomsky called the *lexicalist hypothesis,* i.e. the claim that derivational word formation happens in the lexicon rather than the syntax. This idea represented a major shift in thinking about word structure because it opened the door to the creation of a morphological component in generative grammar. Before "Remarks," the tasks of the traditional field of morphology were divided between the syntax and the phonology, the first taking care of the linear arrangement of the parts of words, the second dealing with allomorphy. Once certain word formation operations were excluded from the syntax, an analytic vacuum was created that could only be filled with an independent theory of morphology. Work on this new component began quickly with Halle (1973), Siegel (1979), Aronoff (1976), Allen (1978), and a large number of other works continuing on to the present day (see chapter 6).

This new work in morphology quickly began to yield insights into word structure and the relationship between morphology and syntax on the one hand and morphology and phonology on the other. Some of these insights have consequently had profound impacts on the study of syntax. For instance, Halle (1973) – the seminal work on the new generative morphology – observed that derivational and inflectional morphological processes make use of exactly the same set of morphophonological operations, e.g. suffixation, infixation, reduplication, ablaut, etc. Based on this evidence he went beyond Chomsky's position on morphology in "Remarks" which is now referred to as the *weak lexicalist hypothesis* (i.e. derivational morphology is in the lexicon, inflectional morphology in the syntax) and postulated the *strong lexicalist hypothesis* (i.e. both derivational and inflectional morphological operations apply exclusively in the lexicon). The strong lexicalist hypothesis became the cornerstone of the most influential grammatical theories since the late 1970s besides Government–Binding Theory: it is utilized in Bresnan's Lexical–Functional Grammar, Kiparsky's Lexical Phonology and Morphology, Generalized Phrase Structure Grammar / Head-Driven Phrase Structure Grammar, and many versions of Categorial Grammar.

The second idea introduced in "Remarks" which has taken off is the conception of categories as bundles of features. As we have seen, it is this innovation that made the lexicalist hypothesis possible to begin with and led to much fruitful work in morphology. But the idea proved irresistible to syntacticians as well and in some corners features and conditions on feature bundles have taken the central role in syntactic theory. This is particularly true of the very influential theories of Generalized Phrase Structure Grammar and Head-Driven Phrase Structure Grammar.

The irony referred to at the beginning of this section is that "Remarks" introduced syntactic features and the lexicalist hypothesis to reunite generative grammar behind the interpretivist conception of grammar. While the paper ultimately succeeded in that Generative Semantics was abandoned, the paper's new ideas were the source of strong lexicalist and phrase-structural approaches to grammar which established themselves as credible alternatives to Chomsky's position within the interpretivist group. The adherents of these competitors argued, often completely parallel to Chomsky's strategy in "Remarks," that many other, and, in the end, all other, syntactic relationships are better expressed without transformations and that the most explanatory theory of grammar is *monostratal*, i.e. it contains exactly one categorial representation reflecting the surface constituent structure and word order that can be directly observed or justified through general constituency tests. Recent representative work on Lexical–Functional Grammar can be found in Bresnan and Kanerva (1989) and Mohanan (1990). Head-Driven Phrase Structure Grammar is presented, among others, in Pollard and Sag (1987).

The third crucial component of "Remarks," the close relationship between lexical properties and syntactic configurations, is the one we are now going to pursue here because it leads to Government–Binding Theory and the Principles and Parameters Approach.

4 *Lectures on Government and Binding* (LGB)

4.1 *The Role of X-bar Theory*

The research following "Remarks" and leading up to LGB (= Chomsky (1981)) concentrates mostly on the transformational component and makes few changes to X-bar theory that are incorporated into LGB. The major work on X-bar theory that appeared in that period was Jackendoff (1977) whose study of English phrase structure represents the most systematic and comprehensive empirical application of the X-bar theoretic ideas of "Remarks" in the Extended Standard Theory and its successors. Jackendoff's system brings a wide variety of English structures under a system of rules restricted by the X-bar schema, many of which have not been analyzed in comparable depth elsewhere within Government–Binding theory. Unfortunately, however, Jackendoff's innovations were overshadowed by the attempt within the LGB framework to reduce the base component to a small number of phrase structure parameters (configurationality, directionality, the *wh*-movement parameter, pro drop), and much of the data Jackendoff (1977) had discussed did not lend itself easily to such an analysis and has ultimately been largely ignored since.[6]

We will now turn our attention to LGB. This work represents presumably the most ambitious research project in the history of Generative Grammar, perhaps of all linguistic theorizing to date. *Syntactic Structures* and *Aspects* had been concerned mostly with making it plausible that rule systems as formal as those that had been developed for artificial languages could also be made to generate all and only the grammatical sentences of natural languages. All such language-specific rule systems were supposed to be different instances of one and the same universal schema for grammars laid down in Universal Grammar. To countenance the wide variety of surface forms found in the world's languages, the original proposals for Universal Grammar imposed few substantive constraints on rules UG made available and hence allowed a wide variety of individual grammars. By the end of the 1960s when the descriptive devices of generative grammars were generally considered powerful enough to describe natural languages the field became dominated by the concern for explanatory adequacy, as comes out in the quotation from Chomsky (1972c, 124ff) which we encountered earlier (see p. 22). Ross's (1967) constraints on transformations, the X-bar theory of phrase structure worked out in "Remarks," and the work on constraints on filters that occupied generative syntacticians in the 1970s all served to approach this goal. LGB now tries to put together these strands of research into one coherent system of grammatical organization that is qualitatively different from the early approaches in generative syntax. The goal has become to reduce the language-particular options in grammars to the absolute minimum necessary to achieve descriptive adequacy. This is done through the imposition of very strict substantive constraints on the system of rules and representations that make up individual grammars. Ross's idea of a skeleton rule is brought to full bloom in the form of universal principles of grammar which allow language-particular options only in the form of a very small number of *parameters,* preferably in the form of Yes–No decisions that can be made by language learners on the basis of actually occurring example sentences they are likely to encounter at the critical moments of language acquisition.[7]

Many of the substantive components of the LGB system can be viewed as universal instances of the concept of output condition that Ross had introduced as well. In particular, the level of *Logical Form* (LF), the final level of syntactic derivation, must meet the theta criterion and subcategorization restrictions; since the *Projection Principle* ensures that this information remains constant throughout all syntactic levels, these constraints on the output of the syntactic derivation impose very powerful constraints on the nature of the derivation as a whole. We look at this important feature of the LGB system in some more detail, against the background of the system of lexical and syntactic representations assumed in Chomsky (1981):[8]

```
(22)            Lexicon
                   |
              D-structure
                   |
              S-Structure
               /        \
            PF            LF
     (Phonological    (Logical
          Form)          Form)
```

The lexicon is still conceptualized as the repository of the information associated with lexical items that cannot be predicted on the basis of universal principles or category-wide language-particular parametric choices. (23) contains a representative example of the syntactically relevant aspects of a lexical entry:

(23) kill, [+V, –N] (Category information)
(Ag, Pt) (Thematic information)
[NP, V′] (Subcategorication information)

Entries specify information about category membership, thematic roles, and strict subcategorization. The decomposition of categories had in the meantime yielded a system where the formerly atomic category symbols N, V, A, and P now have the status of abbreviatory labels for sets of more primitive features:[9]

(24) N = [+N, –V]
A = [+N, +V]
V = [–N, +V]
P = [–N, –V]

The thematic information (or *theta grid)* associated with lexical items specifies the number of theta roles the item assigns and usually classifies each role in terms of a theta role name.[10] In addition, following Williams (1980, 1981a), a distinction is drawn between an *external* and the *internal* arguments of a head, where – as suggested by the terminology – the external argument is generated outside the predicator's maximal projection and the remaining arguments internal to it.[11] Following "Remarks," lexical entries are in principle allowed to differ from each other in these properties in unpredictable ways, with lexical subgeneralizations being captured through lexical redundancy rules.[12] Recall, however, that "Remarks" also postulated that lexically related items should have similar lexical entries. This is a leading idea in LGB as well, even though it is not formalized there. We can assume, then, that the analyses in LGB are guided by something like the following principle, which in the following we will refer to as "lexical regularity":

(25) *The Doctrine of "Lexical Regularity"*
The degree of markedness of a stem S increases to the extent that (i) the argument structures and (ii) the subcategorization frames of the lexical items containing S are distinct and cannot be related by a general rule.

Thus, it is assumed that while the lexicon allows for the listing of unpredictable information, lexically related items in the best case have maximally similar features or at least that they belong to classes of expressions whose features can be related by a general rule or principle. Examples of the latter might include general affixation rules that produce the passives, causatives, impersonals or gerunds that are found in many languages of the world.

The crucial relationship between the lexicon and the syntactic levels of representation depicted in (22) is now established by the *projection principle*. Informally stated, the projection principle ensures that lexical items at all syntactic levels of representation appear in configurations that are in accordance with their lexical properties. Technically that means the following. The theory draws distinctions between the members of a set of configurationally defined grammatical functions:

(26a) Argument grammatical functions ("A-GFs"): [NP, S], [NP, NP], [XP, Y′]
(26b) Non-argument grammatical functions ("A-bar GFs"): all other positions, in particular [XP, S′] (the "clausal operator position")

(26) establishes a positional typology and is part of X-bar theory. The distinction between so-called *A* and *A-bar positions* is exploited by theta theory and binding theory. For now, we will only discuss theta theory.

Theta theory requires that every *theta position* bear an A-GF, or – in different parlance – be an A-position. The external argument is always associated with the clausal subject position [NP, S], the internal arguments with A-positions linked to the argument in the lexical entry of the theta marker. We may postulate general principles about the mapping from theta role names to grammatical functions that are able to predict the subcategorization frame of a typical verb like *kill* in (23):

(27) *The Doctrine of "Universal Thematic Alignment"*
(27a) If a head's theta grid contains an agent argument, then this argument is the external argument;
(27b) if a head's theta grid contains a patient argument, then this argument is associated with [YP, X′].

(27a) universally makes agents into subjects and patients into direct objects.[13]

The projection principle should now state that at LF a head is licensed only if there is an appropriate A-position linked to an argument for each theta role in the head's theta grid, where "appropriate" of course means that the external theta role is associated with [NP, S] and the internal theta roles with the positions internal to the head's maximal projection specified in the head's lexical entry. Secondly, if these positions exist at LF then they should exist at D-structure and S-Structure as well and should be associated with the same argument expressions as at LF. Chomsky (1981, 38) states these parts of the projection principle as follows:

(28a) If α selects β in γ as a lexical property, then α selects β in γ at L_i;
(28b) if α selects β in γ at L_i, then α selects β in γ at L_j.

Unlike our immediately preceding statement, the formulation in (28a) does not refer specifically to "LF," but elsewhere in Chomsky (1981) it is made clear that lexical properties are foremost checked at LF and projected from there to D-structure and S-structure. Take the following statement for instance (cf. Chomsky (1981, 39ff):

> the subcategorization frames at every syntactic level must be exactly those that appear at LF and . . . they correspond to θ-marking in head-complement constructions, and . . . when the subject is a θ-position at LF it appears as a θ-position at every syntactic level.

It is important to note that β ranges over different types of information in (28a) and (28b): in the former it refers to a grammatical function (= syntactic position), because a head's subcategorization frame contains only information about syntactic categories but not what expressions fill them. Thus while *kill* requires an NP for its *Pt* role, it does not require a specific NP, e.g. the expression *John.* (28b), however, is intended to ensure that if an expression is associated with a function (= position) at one syntactic level, then it will be so associated at all levels. This constraint would rule out a derivation where at D-structure, S-structure, and PF the object position of *kill* is occupied by the argument *John,* but between S-structure and LF *Mary* is substituted for *John.* If that were not prohibited, a sentence might be generated with a PF for *You killed John* and an LF for *You killed Mary.* Since the same problem would arise if optional meaning-bearing expressions such as modifying adjectives, adverbs, and auxiliaries could be deleted or added in the course of a syntactic derivation, (28b) must presumably be given an interpretation wide-ranging enough to exclude such cases.

Before proceeding, we sum up the import of (28). These parts of the projection principle establish relationships between the lexicon and X-bar theoretically defined configurations at LF (via 28a) and between configurations at LF and the other two levels of syntactic representation, D-structure and S-Structure (via 28b). The lexicon lists the syntactically atomic elements. Lexical redundancy rules establish paradigmatic relations within the lexicon. By enforcing configurational and thematic co-occurrence restrictions associated with lexical heads at LF and throughout the syntax, we say that the projection principle *projects* lexical properties into syntactic representations. In this sense it is responsible for establishing syntagmatic relationships in the syntax.

Against the background of earlier generative theories, we recognize that the close relationship between the lexicon, X-bar theory, theta theory, and the projection principle carries much of the descriptive weight of the base components of these earlier approaches, while being explanatorily superior. This can be illustrated with the following set of phrase structure rules for English which would have been part of the base components of these earlier more rule-based frameworks:

(29)	VP → V	AP → A	NP → N
	VP → V NP		
	VP → V PP	AP → A PP	NP → N PP
	VP → V S	AP → A S	NP → N S
	VP → V NP PP		
	VP → V NP S		
	VP → V PP S	AP → A PP S	NP → N PP S

This set of rules exhibits clear patterns both regarding linear order and dominance which could not be captured in *Syntactic Structures* or *Aspects* because these theories lacked mechanisms to capture generalizations across phrase structure rules. What is worse, because these generalizations remain unexpressed, the theory has no way of explaining why phrase structure rules like (29) appear in many languages but rules like (30) are uninstantiated (or at the very least, highly marked):

(30a) *VP → A PP
(30b) *VP → V′ N
(30c) *V′ → NP V PP

Stowell (1981, 70), based on the groundwork laid in "Remarks", proposes the following conditions on phrase structure that extract the generalizations from (29) and rule out (30):

(31)
- Every phrase is endocentric.
- Specifiers appear at the XP-level; subcategorized complements appear within X′.
- The head always appears adjacent to one boundary of X′.
- The head is one bar level lower than the immediately dominating phrasal node.
- Only maximal projections may appear as non-head terms within a phrase.

The endocentricity constraint rules out (30a), the maximality constraint on non-head terms excludes (30b), and the peripherality condition on heads takes care of (30c).

The rules in (29) are now seen to contain a lot of information that is redundant: the number of categories that co-occur with a head and their identity is predictable from the lexical subcategorization frames of the heads. Unlike the rules in (29), these subcategorization frames cannot be eliminated from the grammar because they are item-specific and cannot be predicted on general grounds (recall in this connection the group *dine/devour/eat* mentioned in note 12 which are respectively intransitive, transitive, and transitive/intransitive). Since the bar level of the head raises by one upon combination with a complement or specifier, the lexical information about the grammatical function of the element combined with will suffice to predict the bar levels. Finally, given that all phrases have to be endocentric, once we know the category of the head, the categories of the phrasal constituents it heads are known as well.

It is now easy to see in what sense syntactic representations can be *projected* on the basis of lexical information and a few category-wide phrase structure parameters, i.e. how it is possible as argued by Stowell (1981), to reduce language-particular base components to the setting of a few simple X-bar-theoretic parameters. Recall, once more, what information lexical entries typically contain:

(32) kill, [+V, –N] (Category information)
(Ag, Pt) (Thematic information)
[NP, V′] (Subcategorication information)

At this point we know already that *kill* is a verb and requires an NP complement. Given (31) and the projection principle, we can predict that at LF *kill* will co-occur under a V′ with an NP and that the V′ will be dominated by a maximal projection VP. Additionally, by the projection principle and (27), we know that *kill*'s sister-NP is interpreted as the patient of killing and the NP-subject of the sentence minimally containing *kill*'s maximal projection is interpreted as the agent of killing. Finally, we can be sure that if these facts hold at LF, then they will hold at D-structure and S-structure as well.

What we don't know at this point is whether *kill* will precede its complement within the VP or follow it and what is the relative order of the VP and the subject. This is the residue that must be stipulated on a language-particular basis and that is what the *directionality parameter* is designed to do. For a language like English, it would specify that the subject precedes the VP and that all heads precede their complements. Language learners will have plenty of overt evidence to fix the values of these parameters.[14]

While Stowell (1981) formulated X-bar theory as a set of conditions, Webelhuth (1992) states a set of recursive construction principles that build syntactic constituents in accordance with X-bar theory and parametric values. The universal principle for projecting heads and specifiers is the following one:

(33) *Projection of the Specification Relation*
If • α is a member of category YP,
• β is a member of category X′, and
• α can specify members of category X′,
then [α β] is a member of category XP if the direction of specification of α is "Right" and [β α] is a member of category XP if the direction of specification of α is "Left."

In this system, all internally complex categories are created by the application of construction principles like (33) that contain variables whose values are contributed either by the lexicon (e.g. the category variables *X* and *Y* above) or by parameters (e.g. the direction of specification). The goal of this approach is to find X-bar-theoretically implemented locality constraints over parameters that predict which aspects of language-particular constituent structures can be lexically idiosyncratic or parametrically defined and to use X-bar theory to prevent individual grammars from stating parametric relationships between items that are too "distant" from each other in phrase structure. The proposed constraints are tested against several constructions from the modern Germanic languages, including directionality, pro-drop, pied-piping, the distribution of argument clauses, and various free word order constructions.[15]

We still have to tie down a few loose ends in connection with the projection principle. Chomsky includes a third clause under this principle beyond the two parts of (28):

(34) If β is an immediate constituent of γ . . . at L_i, and γ = α′, then α θ-marks β in γ.

This principle has profound conceptual consequences. Informally, it states that a head must theta-mark each of its configurational complements. GB is the only theory of grammar which accepts (34), and as such the principle is controversial. Its major consequence is that it rules out "raising to object" analyses of constructions where a verb determines the form but not the theta role of an NP internal to its maximal projection:

(35) John [$_{VP}$ considers *him* to have insulted Mary]
(36) John [$_{VP}$ believes *him* to have lied]

The objective case on the italicized NPs in these sentences must be governed by the higher verb, since infinitives do not govern the case of their subjects, and secondly because the objective case changes to nominative when the higher verb is passivized:

(37) *He* is considered to have insulted Mary
(38) *He* is believed to have lied

And yet, the NP under consideration depends semantically on the lower verb alone:

(39) #He considered *the rock* to have insulted Mary
(40) #He believed *the rock* to have lied

Compare (39)–(40) with (41)–(42):

(41) He considered *the rock* to be heavier than the candle
(42) He believed [*the rock* to have lain outside the window]

The relevant NP behaves like an object of the higher verb also with respect to the binding theory. We illustrate this here with principle B, but the same point can be made on the basis of principle A:

(43) *John$_i$ believes *him$_i$*
(44) John$_i$ believes that *he$_i$* can win the race
(45) *John$_i$ believes *him$_i$* to have won the race

The pronoun in (45) behaves like the object in (43) rather than the subject in (44).

In LGB, *believe*-type sentences like (42) are referred to as "exceptional Case-marking constructions" (ECM). The bracketed constituent which was generated at D-structure as an S′ was rewritten in the course of the syntactic derivation as S on the basis of a lexical stipulation associated with the entries of the verbs that can appear in the construction. This being a marked operation (among others, because its status with respect to the projection principle was less than clear), this type of construction was predicted to be rare cross-linguistically. Indeed, languages like German and French have no equivalent of this sentence type. Deleting the maximal projection S′ between the higher verb and the subject of the embedded clause allowed for a government relationship between these elements to be established and for Case to be assigned exceptionally across a clause boundary as well as for subject traces to be properly governed. In this way, by reference to the notion "government" it was possible to capture the many similarities in behavior between the subjects of such clauses and bona fide direct objects even though they appear in X-bar-theoretically different configurations.

Constructions involving a secondary predicate are assimilated to ECMs:

(46) John considers [Bill a liar]
(47) John finds [that argument interesting]

The bracketed constituents above are referred to as *small clauses,* since they are assumed to have a propositional semantics more or less parallel to (42). Many aspects of such postulated small clauses are controversial, however, including the questions of whether they uniformly belong to the category "Sentence" or are projections of the embedded predicate (which would make the bracketed constituent in (46) an NP and that in (47) an AP), whether they contain inflectional elements, whether they are scope domains, etc. Empirical evidence for or against different positions on these issues is hard to come by and often depends on theory-internal assumptions that have fallen by the wayside as GB theory has progressed in recent years. The interested reader is referred to section 6 in chapter 2 and to the following works: Williams (1975, 1983), Stowell (1978, 1983, 1991), Schein (1982), Safir (1983), Hoekstra (1984, 1988), Kayne (1985), Kitagawa (1985), Hornstein and Lightfoot (1987) and Hoekstra and Mulder (1990).

Traditional grammar classifies the relevant NPs in (35)–(36) and (46)–(47) as objects of the higher verb and there is evidence from case marking, passivization, and binding theory in support of this view. Yet this classification is precisely what (34) forbids.

The major motivation for bracketing the accusative NPs with the lower predicate derives from *lexical regularity* in (25) and from the behavior of subjects. Since the stem *believe* occurs in both (44) and (45) we would like to unify these two uses of the verb as much as possible: in both cases, the verb is a two-place predicate that denotes a relation between a believer and a proposition; the two uses differ only in the finiteness of the complement sentence. Since *he/him* in both sentences bears the external theta role of the embedded verb, it would be desirable to project this role in uniform structural configurations, i.e. if the NP forms a constituent with the lower VP in (44), then the same should be true in (45). Similar considerations apply in the case of small clauses.

The second major reason for projecting *him* in (45) as a subject rather than an object has to do with the "Specified Subject Condition (SSC)."[16] Note that (49) is as ungrammatical as (48):

(48) *Mary believes that **John** has scratched *herself*
(49) *Mary believes **John** to have scratched *herself*

In (48) *John* is uncontroversially a subject and the sentence is ruled out by the SSC. If *John* is analyzed as a subject in (49) as well, then we have a uniform way of accounting for the ungrammaticality of both sentences.[17]

To sum up our discussion of ECMs and small clauses, (34) has the function of tying together X-bar theory and theta theory in the complement domain. This immediately forces the constituency illustrated in (42) and (46). The theoretical costs associated with this move are the following: a marked complementation option must be admitted into the grammar ("S-bar deletion") and neither principles A, B of the binding theory nor Case marking can be limited in their domains of application to simple clauses. Instead, the notion of government must be so defined that it can cross clause boundaries and treats complements of a verb in a manner identical to the subjects of small clauses embedded under a verb (or some other exceptional governor).

(34) has a second important consequence: since it disallows non-theta-marked complements, it rules out expletive expressions in all object positions. All apparent instances of expletive objects must therefore be analyzed either as idiomatic expressions (which by definition do not fall under the theta criterion) or as subjects of ECMs/small clauses.[18] For (50) an analysis as idioms is not implausible and the examples in (51)–(53) indeed have the trappings of small clauses:

(50) beat it; blow it; can it; cheese it; cool it; cut it out . . .
(51) We kept **it** a secret that Jerome was insane
(52) I make **it** my business to know what is going on
(53) Elmer regards **it** as suspicious that no primitives are defined

The sentences below, however, do not seem to fall into either category:

(54) They never mentioned **it** to the candidate that the job was poorly paid
(55) We demand **it** of our employees that they wear a tie
(56) I blame **it** on you that we can't go

In each of these examples the expletive can be replaced by a referential NP which is inconsistent with an idiomatic analysis:

(57) They never mentioned **the low salary** to the candidate
(58) We demand **absolute commitment** of our employees
(59) I blame **our problems** on you

With respect to the prospects of analyzing (54)–(56) as small clauses, Postal and Pullum (1988, 643) write:

> This belies the relationship of subcategorization between the ditransitive verb *mention* and its indirect object *to the candidate.* Other examples we have cited are similarly intractable to small clause analyses. Strings like *it of our employees that they wear a tie . . .* or *it my business to know what is going on . . .*, for example, are highly implausible constituents to begin with. But in addition, the [small clause] analysis in [54] falsely implies that a verb like *mention* does not select a prepositional phrase with *to,* wrongly claims that the (semantic) relationship between *that the job was poorly paid* and *to the candidate* is one of subject and predicate, and so on.

In an interesting paper, Authier (1991) discusses this data from the point of GB theory and concludes that a theoretical revision is necessary that will allow "not only θ-role assignment but also Case assignment to project syntactic positions" (p. 724). That move, if widely accepted, would effectively eliminate the distinguished relationship that (34) creates between complements and argumenthood. This would have severe consequences for the justification of the clausal analysis of ECM and small clause constructions.[19]

From the discussion of expletives in subcategorized positions let us now move to the topic of how the positions occupied by expletives are projected in the first place. This will conclude our discussion of the relationship between X-bar theory, theta theory, and the projection principle.

Recall that (28) guarantees the existence of all those positions at every syntactic level that a head needs to satisfy its subcategorization and thematic requirements. Since (34) ties together complementhood with argumenthood, it follows (with help from the theta criterion) that one distinct complement position must exist for each of the head's internal arguments. If the head assigns an external theta role, then a position for this theta role must exist as well. This close relationship between theta marking and X-bar theory fails to guarantee the existence of a subject position for sentences whose thematic head does not assign an external theta role:

(60) **It** is likely that Mary will be elected treasurer
(61) Mary thought that **it** seemed that Bill was nervous
(62) **It** was widely believed that the election had been thrown

Interestingly, there are languages where under precisely these circumstances no overt subjects need appear. Cf. the following German sentences:

(63) weil mir scheint daß Hans krank ist
because me (DAT) seems that Hans sick is
"Hans seems to me to be sick"

(64) weil getanzt wurde
because danced was
"because dancing was going on"

(63) is a case of raising and (64) instantiates the impersonal passive construction. Only when the verb has no external argument does German allow sentences without an overt subject.

The data in (63)–(64) is directly predicted by the projection principle, but something additional is needed to account for (60)–(62). In LGB Chomsky assumes that universally sentences expand into three categories:

(65) S → NP INFL VP

This rule makes [NP, S] obligatory. To draw the distinction between German and English, we now invoke the *pro*-drop parameter which is independently necessary to generate Italian sentences like (66):

(66) *pro* ho telefonato
have telephoned
I have telephoned

Assuming that *telephone* has the same argument structure in Italian and English, the projection principle requires the presence of a subject position for its external argument. Yet, no overt subject appears in (66). To save the projection principle from immediate falsification by (66), we postulate an empty subject *pro,* in accordance with the theory of *pro*-drop (on details of this, see chapter 4). If (65) is correct, then we must assume that German allows *pro*-drop to a limited degree, namely precisely when there is no external argument. This will account for (63)–(64). Assuming that English never licenses *pro,* the non-thematic subject positions in (60)–(62) have to be filled by an overt non-argument: not projecting the position would violate (65), projecting it but filling it with *pro* would violate the *pro*-drop parameter, and filling it with an argument would violate the theta criterion.

Chomsky (1982) explicitly formulates a clause that all sentences must have subjects and this principle, along with the projection principle, is known as the "Extended Projection Principle."[20]

4.2 *Case Theory within the LGB Framework*

Let us discuss the status of the sentences in (67)–(68) and their passive counterparts in (69)–(70) in the LGB system with respect to the principles we have encountered so far:

(67) Everybody believed the rumor
(68) Everybody believed that the rumor was true

Based on (25), the verb *believe* is assumed to have a uniform theta grid of the form (<u>Believer</u>, Believed) with the internal argument expressible either as an NP as in (67) or a sentence as in (68). That the postverbal NP and sentence in these examples are objects is confirmed by their passivizability:

(69) [The rumor]$_i$ was widely believed t$_i$
(70) [That the rumor was true]$_i$ was widely believed t$_i$

The existence of a postverbal trace in the passive counterparts of (67)–(68) is guaranteed by the interaction of the principles discussed earlier: the passive participles in (69)–(70) are obviously lexically related to their active morphological bases and as such should be both thematically as similar to them as possible and occur in the same structural environments (cf. (25)). In the LGB system the argument structure of the participle *believed* differs from that of the active verb merely in the absence of an external argument: *believed, V,* (Believed).[21] A head with this argument structure must have an object position at every syntactic level to be able to discharge its internal theta role. The necessity of arguments leaving behind traces under movement thus follows from assumptions about the lexicon and the projection principle (or, in the case of expletives, the extended projection principle).

The structures under discussion also show, however, that these principles do not provide an explanation for the contrast between (71) and (72). (72) is unremarkable from their point of view, but the ungrammaticality of (71) is unexpected. Why should the argument *the rumor* not be able to occupy the theta position whose existence is guaranteed by the theory of the lexicon and the projection principle (and which (72) clearly shows to exist anyway)?

(71) *It was widely believed *the rumor*
(72) It was widely believed *that the rumor was true*

Passives are not the only constructions where an overt NP cannot appear in a position projected by the projection principle.[22] This problem arises in thematic subject positions as well, as can be illustrated with the complement of a raising verb:

(73) It appears that Mary walked to the board
(74) [Mary]$_i$ appears [t$_i$ to have walked to the board]
(75) *It appears *Mary* to have walked to the board

In (73)–(75) *Mary* is interpreted as the agent of walking. While the NP can appear in the position where this theta role is assigned when the complement clause is finite in (73) and can raise to the main clause subject position in (74), it is barred from the theta position of the infinitival complement clause in (75). Non-finite complements embedded under control verbs only allow the equivalent of (73), since the movement of the lower subject into the subject position of the control verb would of course violate the theta criterion:

(76) Mary$_i$ persuaded John [PRO$_i$ to leave]
(77) *Mary$_i$ persuaded John [she$_i$ to leave]
(78) *She$_i$ persuaded John [t$_i$ to leave]

For our current concerns, it is the impossibility of the overt NP *she* in (77) that binds this paradigm together with the examples from passive and raising that we saw immediately above in (71) and (75).

Overt NPs thus seem to be barred from the following positions in ways which cannot be predicted by the (extended) projection principle:

(79)
- the object position of passive verbs;
- the subject position of non-finite complements to raising verbs;
- the subject position of controlled complements.

Not all infinitives disallow overt NPs in their subject positions however. Recall from our discussion of (34) that the bracketed non-finite constituent in (80) is analyzed as a clause:

(80) John believes [Mary to be a genius]

The thematic similarity between (81) and (82) suggests that (82) contains a non-finite clause with an overt subject as well:

(81) John heard [that Mary was singing]
(82) John heard [Mary sing]

And, assuming that the verbs in the main clauses below each denote two-place relations between an individual and a proposition, then their non-finite complement clauses also have overt subjects:

(83) John let [his son ride the car]
(84) John made [his son mow the lawn]
(85) The boy caused [the vase to fall to the ground and break]

The complementizer *for* can co-occur with subjects in infinitives as well:

(86) [For Mary to have gotten this job] was illegal

Jean-Roger Vergnaud (apparently in a personal communication to Chomsky) proposed the leading idea that the grammar be enriched by a *Case module*. He connected the inability of overt NPs to occur in certain positions with the independent requirement that the grammar specify which case form of NPs can appear in which positions. That is, we need principles to predict that in most languages only nominative NPs can appear in the subject positions of finite clauses and direct objects are restricted to accusatives:

(87) *He/*him* is sleeping
(88) I admire **she/her*

Vergnaud also suggested that the theory incorporate the conception of case being *governed* in the sense that certain prepositions in a language like Latin require their thematic object to appear in the dative while others require the ablative or some other case. Chomsky (1980, 25) incorporates these ideas in the following form:

(89a) NP is oblique when governed by P and certain marked verbs;
(89b) NP is objective when governed by V;
(89c) NP is nominative when governed by Tense.

It is crucially assumed that from a syntactic point of view all NPs bear these features under the conditions specified in (89) no matter whether the features are morphologically visible or not. Government is defined as follows (Chomsky (1980, 25; a footnote at the end of the definition is omitted here)):

(90) α is governed by β if α is c-commanded by β and no major category or major category boundary appears between α and β.

The syntactic features referred to in (89) are known as *abstract Case* ("Case" is always capitalized in this usage of the term). Assuming that the morphological nominatives and accusatives are realizations of the abstract features "nominative" and "objective" specified in (89), the starred options in (87)–(88) are excluded.

With this, let us return to the problem posed by (67)–(86). Some of the problematic examples now fall out since they contain morphologically realized NPs that appear in positions for which (89) makes no Case feature available. Assuming that the only way for the heads of these NPs to receive a Case feature is through inheritance from their maximal projections, the following restriction, known as the *Case Filter*, will rule out the appropriate examples:

(91) *N, where N has no Case

(77), repeated below, is predicted to be ungrammatical, because the italicized NP is not governed by any Case assigner: non-finite Infls cannot assign Case according to (89) and the major category boundary S′ separates the NP from the verb *persuade*:

(92) *Mary persuaded John [$_{S'}$ *she* to leave]

To distinguish (71) and (75) from the grammatical examples (82)–(85), we need a further assumption, namely that the verbs in the former sentences are not Case assignors. This is stipulated in Chomsky (1980) but was later argued in Burzio (1986) to be derivable from a principle relating argument structure and Case assignment. The principle has come to be known as "Burzio's Generalization":

(93) A verb that governs an NP Case-marks this NP structurally[23] iff the verb has an external argument.

Observe that the main verb in (75) is a raising verb and the one in (71) is a passive participle. According to the projection principle and the theta criterion, neither type of verb can have an external theta role because they both allow argument movement into their subject positions, and such movement would lead to double theta-marking of the moved NP if the landing site were theta-marked. Given (93), it follows that precisely these types of verbs are unable to assign structural Case to an NP internal to their maximal projection.[24]

In contrast, all the verbs in (82)–(85) have external arguments and on this basis are predicted to be possible Case assigners.

This leaves (86) as the only example of an infinitive with a lexical subject that our principles do not cover yet. For this case, Rouveret and Vergnaud (1980, 132) propose that the possible Case governors should be characterized as the class of categories that is non-distinct from the X-bar-theoretic feature [–N] (cf. (24) above), and that the complementizer *for* has retained this feature from its use as a preposition. This assumption predicts the following paradigm:

(94) John *likes* her
(95) John is *for* her
(96) John is *proud* *(of) her
(97) the *destruction* *(of) the city

While the [–N] categories V and P can license NP complements through Case, the [+N] categories N and A need the help of a preposition to combine with NP arguments.

Making the natural assumption that the complementizer *for* can govern across a sentence boundary in analogy with such exceptional Case-marking verbs as *believe* or *cause* predicts the grammaticality of (86).

Much of this Case theory is retained in LGB, but one important modification is made in connection with problems that can be illustrated with the group of examples below:

(98) It was widely acknowledged *that Kennedy had made a big mistake*
(99) *That Kennedy had made a big mistake* was widely acknowledged
(100) *It was widely acknowledged *Kennedy's big mistake*
(101) *Kennedy's big mistake* was widely acknowledged
(102) *It was widely acknowledged *Kennedy's having made a big mistake*
(103) *Kennedy's having made a big mistake* was widely acknowledged

(98)–(99) are unremarkable: when the theme argument of the passivized verb *acknowledge* is realized as a sentence, then it can move into subject position (which has been dethematized by the passive affix), or it can remain in the object position as in (98), given that sentences are not headed by a word in need of Case. The next two sentences are predicted by Case theory as developed so far as well. (100) violates the morphological requirement in (91) because the noun *mistake* cannot inherit any Case feature from its maximal projection since the latter is not in a position where Case can be assigned. (101) is grammatical, since movement of the internal argument into the Cased subject position is allowed by the principles of grammar.

The last pair of sentences is problematic, however. The italicized constituent has the external distribution of an NP, e.g. it can appear as a subject (103), an object (104), the subject of a small clause (105) and the object of a preposition (106). In addition, it can be coordinated with other NPs (107) and undergo NP-movement (108):

(104) Everybody regretted *Kennedy's having made a big mistake*
(105) They considered *Kennedy's having made a big mistake* unfortunate
(106) They talked about *Kennedy's having made a big mistake*
(107) *Kennedy's having made a big mistake* and the recent unrests have left the country shaken
(108) *Kennedy's having made a big mistake* does not seem to bother anyone

Given that the italicized expression in (102)–(103) shows the external distribution of an NP, it is not surprising that these two sentences pattern with (100)–(101) and not with (98)–(99). However, the principle in (91) is unable to account for these correlations, because it is a morphological principle (i.e. it restricts the distribution of an X^0 and not a maximal projection) and (102) does not contain a head noun that lacks Case! Recall that "Remarks" drew a distinction between gerundive and derived nominals and that gerundives are assumed to be transforms of sentential structures, in contrast to base-generated derived nominals. Hence, the expression *Kennedy's having made a big mistake* will have a structure like the following: [$_{NP}$ [Kennedy]'s [$_{VP}$ having made a big mistake]].[25] Under this analysis *Kennedy* gets genitive Case internal to the NP and the only other NP, *a big mistake,* is governed by the transitive verb *make* internal to the NP as well.

In order to solve this problem and others for the morphologically motivated principle in (91), Rouveret and Vergnaud (1980), Aoun (1979), and LGB assume the existence of a second Case requirement principle. This principle is syntactically motivated and applies to noun *phrases* and not nouns. Maintaining the well-motivated assumption that the gerunds in (102)–(103) are NPs, it is explained why they pattern with the NPs in (100)–(101) rather than the sentential complements in (98)–(99).

The specific idea pursued in LGB is that proposed in Aoun (1979): arguments are made "visible" for theta role assignment by Case. In this conception, the Case Filter becomes a condition on theta role assignment and hence a part of the theta criterion. The clearest formulation of this suggestion can be found in Chomsky (1986b, 96ff):

(109) A position P is visible in a chain if the chain contains a Case-marked position.

(110) Each argument A appears in a chain containing a unique visible theta position P, and each theta position P is visible in a chain containing a unique argument A.

Hence, theta roles are technically assigned to chains which are sets (possibly singletons) of A-positions. The passive sentence (111), for instance, satisfies (110) because the chain (subject position, direct object position) contains a theta position of *kill* (namely, the direct object position) and the chain is visible for theta-marking by virtue of the subject position's being Case-marked through the tensed INFL:

(111) $John_i$ INFL $[_{VP}$ was killed t_i]

Conversely, the only argument of (111), the NP *John,* appears in a chain with a visible theta position (again, the direct object position).

The visibility version of the Case Filter solves problems associated with the morphological version in (91) and is conceptually attractive in that it adds to the network of relationships the grammar establishes between argument structures and "spell-out." Recall that the grammar already has other such principles, notably (27), the principle of Universal Thematic Alignment, Grimshaw's principles of Canonical Structural Realization mentioned in note 12, and (93), Burzio's Generalization. Yet, the LGB version of the Case Filter is not without problems of its own. Some of these will be spelled out in the next paragraphs.

First, note that the formulation in (110) requires Case on all *arguments,* not just NPs. NPs used as predicates (112) or adjuncts (113) no longer fall under the filter even though their heads of course show morphological case forms. The examples come from German.

(112) Er nannte ihn einen Idioten
he called him(ACC) an idiot(ACC)
"He called him an idiot"

(113) Ich habe den ganzen Tag gelesen
I have the whole day(ACC) read
"I read during the whole day"

This is not that much of a problem, but the connection between the distribution of case forms and the positions in which NPs with overt nominal heads can occur that was established by the morphological version of the filter is partially broken.

The extension of the Case Filter to all arguments is also problematic for PP and sentential arguments. Within the logic of the LGB system, the italicized expressions in the sentences below should appear in non-Case marked environments:

(114) It seems *that Rose has a lot of influence on the boss*
(115) It was predicted *that Rose would have a lot of influence*
(116) It seems *to me that Rose has a lot of influence on the boss*
(117) The book was put t *on the table*

(114) and (116) contain non-NP arguments to raising verbs, and (115) and (117) analogous arguments of passive participles. Of course, the Case Filter can be restricted so as to require only NP arguments to have Case, but then there is no general visibility requirement on all arguments.[26]

Thirdly, there are open questions concerning the status of PRO with respect to the thematic version of the Case Filter. Since the PRO theorem of LGB requires PRO to be ungoverned, it should not be in a position to get Case.[27] And yet, according to (110) it would need Case to receive a theta role. LGB does not propose a solution to this problem and simply exempts PRO from the Case Filter by stipulation. Under the morphological Case Filter, in contrast, it was natural for PRO not to need Case, since it does not enter into visible paradigmatic contrasts.[28]

Finally, expletives pose an obvious problem for the thematic Case Filter that did not arise under the morphological version. Note the examples below:

(118) Lydia believed [*it* to have appeared that John was hurt]
(119) *It was believed [*it* to have appeared that John was hurt]
(120) *It* was believed [t_i to have appeared that John was hurt]
(121) It is likely [*it* appeared that John was hurt]
(122) *It is likely [*it* to have appeared that John was hurt]
(123) *It*$_i$ is likely [t_i to have appeared that John was hurt]

In (118) and (121) the expletive in the embedded clause is assigned Case exceptionally by the verb *believe* and by the finite inflection internal to its clause. When we take away the Case on the position occupied by the expletive by passivizing the verb in (118) and making the inflection non-finite in (121), then the expletives have to raise into the main clause in (120) and (123). If they remain in situ, we obtain the ungrammatical examples (119) and (122).

The ungrammaticality of the structurally identical examples (124)–(125) involving argument NPs follows directly from the thematic Case Filter but the judgments of (119) and (122) do not:

(124) *It was believed [*John* to have overslept]
(125) *It is likely [*John* to have overslept]

Chomsky (1986b, 1991) contains an interesting attempt to get around this problem. Discussing examples like (126)–(127) he notes that the English expletive *there* requires an NP associate and that the distribution of *there* + associate is very similar to that of an NP-moved argument and its traces in that the expletive must be in a position from which it can c-command and bind the associate (also, no specified subject may intervene between the two):

(126) There is/*are a man in the room
(127) There seems to be a unicorn in the garden

Most importantly, under the assumption that the post-copular argument is not Case-governed,[29] the expletive–argument pair satisfies the general requirement of chains that their heads be Case positions (or PRO) and their feet theta positions.

Recent proposals concerning the analysis of agreement provide further motivation for associating the expletive with the argument. Assume that we allow an argument to agree with the verb only if the two expressions stand in an X-bar-theoretic Spec-Head relationship (cf. Koopman (1987), Chomsky (1992), Aoun, Benmamoun, and Sportiche (1992), and references cited there). The agreement in (126) between the finite verb and the argument NP then requires that at some level of representation the argument appear in the Spec position of Infl. Which level could this be?[30] Chomsky suggests that the most natural solution is LF. He invokes a *Principle of Full Interpretation* which entails that at LF every expression contributes to the interpretation of the sentence. In Chomsky (1986b) this was interpreted to mean that all expletives had to be eliminated at LF; this was achieved by moving the argument into the position of the expletive. In Chomsky (1991) a slightly different version of this idea appears: here the expletive turns into an "LF-affix" and shares its position with its associate at LF.[31]

According to this hypothesis, the sentence in (126) has the following LF:

(128) A man-there$_i$ is t$_i$ in the room

(128) solves the problems with respect to expletives and Case theory and quite a few others, as is easy to see. Expletives at S-structure must appear in Case-marked positions because their position must be

occupied by an argument at LF. The chain headed by that argument will be theta-marked only if the head of the chain is a Case-marked position. This is an ingenious way of bringing expletives under the thematic version of the Case Filter. Secondly, that the expletive–argument pair satisfies the other conditions on chains follows directly from the necessity of the argument to move to the position of the expletive at LF. Since the expletive occurs in an A-position, the resulting movement has to form an A-chain, and hence the structural relation between the expletive and the argument must meet all conditions on A-chains. Also, we can maintain that all agreement takes place between specifiers and heads.[32] Since expletives are only allowed in specifier positions, the argument can agree with the verb after expletive replacement from this position, or we can require that the argument must check its features against those of the expletive which in turn directly agrees with the verb.

Lastly, we have a solution to the problem we left open in connection with examples (54)–(56) and the projection principle. These examples contain sentences that have been extraposed from a complement position that is occupied by an expletive. Recall that one clause of the projection principle bans expletives from complement positions and these sentences appeared to be counterexamples to this claim. Once we make the assumption that the relevant expletives are replaced at LF by the argument sentences, the projection principle ought to be satisfied at that level, and a suitable statement of the remainder of the projection principle should allow for the appearance of expletives in complement positions under just those circumstances.[33]

The expletive replacement hypothesis thus is well-motivated conceptually by the Principle of Full Interpretation and also does quite a bit of work empirically. There are problems with it as well, however, some of which appear to be serious.[34]

First, the hypothesis would appear to rule out the expletives that appear in impersonal constructions in many languages, e.g. German or Icelandic:[35]

(129) Es wurde getanzt
it was danced
"There was dancing going on"

According to LGB assumptions, the only argument of the participle *getanzt* has been "absorbed" by the passive morphology. This leaves no argument to replace the expletive at LF.

Secondly, while in many of the examples that Chomsky discusses the argument can overtly appear in the position of the expletive,

(130) There is a man in the garden
(131) A man is in the garden

this is not always the case. Take (132) and (133):

(132) It seems that the car is in need of repair
(133) There is a god

Replacement in each case yields the ungrammatical (134)–(135):[36]

(134) *That the car is in need of repair seems
(135) *A god is

As Lasnik (1992, note 9) points out, it is mysterious why the derivation of the latter two forms should be ruled out at S-structure but allowed at LF to achieve expletive replacement.

Third and finally, there are cases where the verb makes available an argument to replace the expletive, but the replacement would violate principles of grammar needed to make the theory work. We can illustrate this with examples from German and French:[37]

(136) *Es* ist *uns* kalt
it is us(Dat) cold
"We feel cold"
(137) Il est arrivé *trois filles*
there is arrived three girls
"Three girls arrived"

The problem is the following: if the italicized NP does not move at LF to replace the expletive, the LF would be ruled uninterpretable. On the other hand, if the NP does move, then the LF should be ruled out due to a number clash: in each case the verb appears in the singular but the respective NP is plural. In either case, a plural verb is ungrammatical. We thus must assume that the verb in these cases agrees with the expletive exclusively. This suggests that the assumption of expletive replacement at LF is by itself not sufficient to account for why the verb in (126) agrees with the postverbal NP.

5 Some Major Developments After 1981

We now turn to the major departures from the treatment of X-bar and Case theory that followed LGB up to the present. In some areas, especially the treatment of functional heads, there have been so many divergent and highly speculative developments, that it is not possible to cover the details of all of them within the space allotted to this chapter. Many ideas are only sketched briefly. Chapters 7 and 8 are dedicated exclusively to an analysis of the innovations presented in connection with Chomsky's "Minimalist Program."

5.1 The Incorporation of Comp, Infl and Det into X-bar Theory

In LGB and earlier work after "Remarks," the categories S, S′, Infl, and Comp had a peculiar status with respect to X-bar theory. Essentially, these categories were introduced by the following rules:

(138) S′ → Comp S
(139) S → NP Infl VP

Note that S and S′ are related by the bar notation which X-bar theory of course reserves for the relationship between heads and their first-level categorial projections. (138) expresses that when a sentence combines with a complementizer, then we get an extended sentence in some sense. But this suggests that S is the head of S′, which is peculiar since in all other such cases the head of an X′ is an X^0 item pulled from the lexicon. (139), however, shows that sentences have obligatory internal syntactic structure that makes them very different from listed X^0 elements. From this point of view, S and S′ – not being lexical – would lose their exceptionality with respect to the X-bar schema if they were analyzed as phrasal categories projected from X^0 heads.

The status of Comp and Infl is exceptional as well. Both are typically filled with X^0 expressions from the lexicon, in the first case lexical complementizers such as *that, if, for, whether*, and in the second modal auxiliaries such as *would, might*, or *can*. Further evidence for the X^0 status of both of these categories comes from the fact that they are fruitfully analyzed as serving as landing sites for X^0 movement. For example, Emonds (1970, 1976, 1978), Jackendoff (1972), and others assume that under certain circumstances auxiliaries (as well as main verbs in French) move out of their VP into the Infl constituent. Den Besten (1983) makes a strong case that the verb-second phenomenon that characterizes several Germanic languages and certain inversion constructions in French are best analyzed as involving movement of a verb to Comp.

Given these analyses, we would like to characterize Comp and Infl as X^0 heads in X-bar theory. Putting together the considerations in the last two paragraphs, we have S and S′ as phrasal constituents which are in search of X-bar-theoretic heads and Infl and Comp as X^0 constituents in search of maximal projections. It is a natural step to conclude that Comp should be analyzed as the head of S′ and Infl as the head of S.[38] In Chomsky (1986a) this is precisely what is proposed. Here Infl (I^0) is projected as an X^0 element with a VP complement and an NP specifier which acts as the subject of the sentence. Comp (C^0) projects a phrase of category *CP*. The specifier of CP acts as a clausal operator position that is targeted by moved *wh-* and relative clause operators (and, perhaps, topicalized elements). The complement of C^0 is the maximal projection of I^0, which is IP:

(140) $[_{CP}\ XP_{Operator}\ [_{C'}\ C^0\ [_{IP}\ NP_{Subj}\ [_{I'}\ I^0\ VP\ ]]]]$

The operator position is classified as an A-bar position and the subject position as an A-position. The restriction of a single operator position and a single Comp position have been fruitfully exploited in accounting for second position[39] and complementarity effects.[40]

The further stratification of the sentential categories has led to similar developments within the noun phrase and other categories. Two main considerations played a role in this. First, Abney (1987) provided evidence from several languages that possessive NPs and determiners can co-occur within the same NP, incompatible with the assumption in "Remarks" that both of these constituent types are instances of specifiers of NP. (In English they are in complementary distribution, hence **John's the book.*) Second, Abney (1987) reminded us of the difficulty of incorporating gerundive NPs into a strict version of X-bar theory (already pointed out earlier):

(141) $[_{NP}$ John's $[_{VP}$ quietly having read the book$]]$

Quietly having read the book has all the trappings of a VP and in "Remarks" the possessor is analyzed as a specifier. The whole phrase has the external distribution of an NP despite the lack of a suitable noun that could act as its head.

Abney (1987) consequently proposed that noun phrases should be reanalyzed as *determiner phrases* (DP), i.e. that nominals are really headed by determiners which typically take a noun phrase complement and a specifier which can be occupied by a possessor. This makes enough positions available to allow for the co-occurrence of a possessor and a determiner within one NP. Analyzing the possessive morpheme of (141) as the head of the DP and optionally allowing this determiner to combine with a VP complement brings these gerundive structures under the umbrella of headed structures as well.[41]

The analysis of Comps, Infls, and Dets as X-bar-theoretic heads is by now generally accepted.

5.2 *The Concepts of Case Assignment and Case Realization*

The reader will recall from our prior discussion of X-bar theory and the projection principle that the theory since "Remarks" is designed to establish a "category-neutral" base. Predicate–argument structures should be projected into maximally similar configurations independent of the category of the theta-marking head. Differences in the appearance of the arguments should follow from other principles.

The most important principles in that regard are those of the theory of Case. Recall that certain verbs and non-finite inflection are incapable of assigning Case.

The systematic similarities and differences between the internal structure of sentences and that of noun phrases are approached in the same manner:[42]

(142) $[_{IP}$ The enemy $[_{I'}$ I^0 $[_{VP}$ destroyed the city$]]]$
(143) $[_{NP}$ The enemy's $[_{N'}$ destruction of the city$]]$

The configurational assumptions in (142)–(143) are those of "Remarks" and LGB: the complement of the verb/noun appears within the first projection of the head and the subject outside. In both cases the specifier is defined as a subject and creates binding-theoretic domains. These similarities follow from X-bar theory, the projection principle, and the concepts of the binding theory. The differences in appearance of the arguments fall out from universal principles of Case theory: transitive verbs but not nouns are able to assign objective Case, hence only the verbal object appears as a bare NP. The subject of the sentence is assigned nominative Case by Infl containing agreement, and the specifier of NP is assigned genitive Case by virtue of the configuration in which it appears.[43]

Chomsky (1986b) points to a number of additional differences between the structure of sentences and that of NPs that the previous assumptions are not sufficient to derive. Maintaining the strategy of predicting the relevant distinctions from Case theory, he proposes a sharpening of the principles of that module.

We will describe three such differences between sentences and noun phrases. First, the nominative–genitive alternation of the subjects we saw in (142)–(143) breaks down when the subject is an expletive. Genitive expletives are barred throughout:[44]

(144) *There* has been too much rain last year
(145) **There's* having been too much rain last year

Second, we do not find exceptional Case marking within NPs:[45]

(146) John believes [*Mary* to be intelligent]
(147) *John's belief (of) [*Mary* to be intelligent]

Third, there is no raising within NPs:

(148) *Mary* seems [*t* to be intelligent]
(149) **Mary's* semblance [*t* to be intelligent]

Chomsky (1986b) establishes Case-theoretic assumptions that tie these three observations together and rule out (145), (147), and (149). Following Travis (1984) and Koopman (1984) he assumes that all Case markers in a language have to assign Case in the same direction. In English, Case assignment is to the right. That means that even genitive Case within NPs now has to be assigned postnominally. Secondly, he draws a distinction between Case *assignment* and Case *realization*. An NP can be assigned its Case in one position while realizing it in another (Chomsky (1986b, 193)):

(150) Both Case-assignment and Case-realization fall under government: At D-structure, N governs and θ-marks its complement and assigns Case to it; at S-structure N governs both the complement and the subject, so that Case can be realized in either position.

In prenominal position genitive Case is realized by *'s*, postnominally by the preposition *of*. Now we need only one further assumption to account for the paradigm above. Assume that, contrary to the assumptions in LGB, we allow [–N] categories, i.e. nouns and adjectives, to assign Case after all, but we impose the restriction that they can only assign *inherent* Case.[46] The special properties of inherent Case will now be able to draw the distinctions between the sentences in (144)–(149):

(151) *The Uniformity Condition on Case Marking*[47]
If α is an inherent Case marker, then α Case-marks NP if and only if α theta-marks the chain headed by NP.

Thus, inherent Case necessitates a thematic dependence of the NP receiving the Case on its Case assigner. Structural Case is not subject to such a condition. Note the consequences of this distinction for the examples under discussion.

(145) is ungrammatical since the prenominal expletive bears inherent genitive Case. Since the only source of this Case is the head noun, (151) forces the N to theta-mark the expletive, which is of course impossible. In (144), the expletive bears the structural nominative Case assigned by Infl which does not entail theta-marking, and the sentence is grammatical.

The differences between nouns and verbs with respect to exceptional Case marking and raising fall out as well. In both (147) and (149), the NP *Mary* is an argument of an infinitive incapable of assigning Case. Its only potential source of Case is thus the noun preceding it in (147) and following it in (149). The only Case this noun has to assign is classified as inherent, however, and there is no thematic relationship between the noun and the respective NPs. The verbal equivalents in (146) and (148) contain structural Case assigners in each Case and the sentences are both grammatical.

Problems with (151) arise in two areas: oblique subjects and the notion "inherent" Case. These issues will be discussed in turn.

Note the following sentences drawn from Icelandic:[48]

(152) Ólafur er bóndi
Olaf(NOM) is a farmer
"Olaf is a farmer"

(153) Drengina vantar mat
the boys(ACC) lacks food(ACC)
"The boys lack food"

(154) Hennar var saknað
her(GEN) was missed
"She was missed"

(155) Hana virðist vanta peninga
her(ACC) seems to lack money(ACC)
"She sems to lack money"

(156) Ég vonast til að PRO vanta ekki einan í tímanum
I(NOM) hope toward to lack not alone in class
"I hope not to be the only one missing from class"

(152) contains a nominative subject, (153) an active verb with an oblique subject, and (154) a passive sentence with an oblique subject. The last two examples illustrate two tests for subjecthood in Icelandic that support this grammatical function assignment. In (155), the oblique NP has undergone raising and in (156) it appears as a non-overt PRO in the infinitive complement ((153), (155) and (156) all contain the verb *lack* which requires an accusative subject).[49]

Note that (153)–(156) all violate the conditions in (150) and (151) under standard GB assumptions. The most glaring case is (156). Since the inherent case on the PRO subject of the embedded clause is verb-specific (other verbs require other cases), it must have been assigned under government internal to the VP. Being inherent, the Case is assigned at D-structure where PRO is allowed to be governed.[50] But at S-Structure where (150) requires Case to be realized under government, government of PRO would violate the standard binding theory. Hence the theory predicts (156) to be ungrammatical.

(153)–(155) all violate the constraint that the oblique phrase is governed at S-Structure by its theta-marker. In all three examples the subject is governed by the matrix Infl but not its theta-marking verb.

Perhaps it is possible to protect the Uniformity Condition against examples like (153)–(156). Observe that all the advantages of the condition we have stated are concerned with the syntax of NPs, whereas the problems seem to occur in the syntax of sentences. If we were to restrict the application of (150)–(151) to inherent Cases assigned by nouns (and perhaps adjectives), the paradigm (144)–(149) would find a uniform explanation that remains untouched by examples involving oblique sentence-level subjects.[51]

The second problem for the Uniformity Condition derives from the uncertainty of the criteria for separating structural from inherent Cases. Recall the standard assumption that inherent Case, unlike structural Case, is linked to a theta role (cf. for instance Chomsky (1986b, 193)). As such, we would expect that NPs bearing a theta role linked to an inherent Case would never show Case alternations like the accusative–nominative alternation produced by passivization. Haegeman (1991, section 3.5.4) uses this criterion on the examples below to decide that the dative Case is inherent in German but the accusative is structural:

(157)	Sie	sieht	ihn	
	she	*sees*	*him(ACC)*	
	"She sees him"			
(158)	Er/*ihn	wird	gesehen	
	he(NOM)/him(ACC)	*is*	*seen*	
	"He is seen"			

(159) Sie hilft ihm
she helps him(DAT)
"She helps him"

(160) *Er/ihm wird geholfen
he(NOM))/him(DAT) is helped
"He is helped"

Haegeman accounts for the change from accusative to nominative in (158) and the retainment of the dative in (160) as follows:

> apparently only the ACCUSATIVE is absorbed: DATIVE and GENITIVE survive under passivization. In order to explain this property of German we shall use our hypothesis . . . that the DATIVE and GENITIVE in German . . . are instances of inherent Case.
>
> Passivization alters the theta grid for the verb in that it absorbs the external theta role. But, crucially, this need not affect the properties of the internal theta role. We assume that inherent Case, which is associated with the internal theta role, is unaffected by passivization. If DATIVE is inherent Case then the pattern . . . is accounted for.

Contrast this with the situation that arises in the sentences below taken from Webelhuth and Ackerman (1993):

(161) weil Maria dem Mann die Blumen schenkt
because Maria the man(DAT) the flowers(ACC) gives
"because Maria gives the man the flowers"

(162) weil der Mann die Blumen geschenkt **bekommt**
because the man(NOM) the flowers(ACC) given gets
"The man is given the flowers"

(162) is an instance of a German passive construction based on the auxiliary *bekommen* (note that the construction discussed by Haegeman involves the passive auxiliary *werden).* As argued at length in Webelhuth and Ackerman (1993), Reis (1985a), and Wegener (1985), the *bekommen* construction has all of the properties conventionally associated with passive with the exception that it promotes the *indirect* object of the base verb to the subject function instead of the direct object. As can be seen from a comparison of (161) and (162), the indirect object has changed its case from dative to nominative in the process of *bekommen* passivization. (Also, although not visible from (162) alone, the nominative governs the agreement on the verb.) No other case distribution is allowed.

It is clear that under Haegeman's assumptions we are now faced with an analytic paradox. The retainment of the dative Case in (160) was derived from its classification as inherent but the Case alternation in (161)–(162) necessitates the assumption that dative is structural. The same paradox arises with respect to accusative.

These data thus suggest that "inherent" and "structural" Case are not absolute notions but must be relativized, because which Cases are allowed to alternate is dependent on the construction. Since this problem, like the Icelandic difficulty raised above, seems to pertain only to the syntax of sentences and not to NPs, a restriction of the applicability of the Uniformity Condition to Cases assigned by nouns would find additional support.

5.3 Further Revisions and Extensions

Much of the appeal of the LGB framework derived from its assumptions about lexical organization and the nature of its structure-building apparatus, i.e. theta theory, X-bar theory, and the projection principle. Recall that X-bar theory and the projection principle convert the theta-theoretic distinction between external and internal arguments into a structural asymmetry that groups a head together with its complements into a phrase that is predicated of the external argument. This fundamental structural asymmetry between subjects and objects facilitated the statement of simple and relatively intuitive principles that accounted for the differential properties of subjects and objects that in earlier theories had to be captured through elaborate language-particular rules. To repeat a few examples: the most frequently encountered distribution of nominative and objective cases which was stipulated in individual grammars with transformations in the *Aspects* framework requires no language-specific statement in LGB. By referencing the local configuration of subjects and objects created on thematic grounds by the projection principle in the concept of government required for Case assignment, the appearance of nominative on the subjects of tensed sentences and objective on direct objects could be predicted universally. Excluding non-finite Infls but not verbs from the class of governors derives the distribution of PRO, i.e. the prohibition against PRO complements at S-structure. Excluding Infls from the class of proper governors predicts many ECP effects. Finally, by imposing a c-command requirement on anaphora, many binding-theoretic asymmetries between subjects and objects do not have to be stated in rules specific to individual languages but fall out from principles of Universal Grammar. Similarly, by postulating a sentence-external Comp position that makes an A-bar landing site available for operators derives not only word order generalizations but such effects as weak crossover, the *wh*-island condition, etc.

As a result of the strong universal constraints on the existence of positions and their properties that were predicted by the various modules of grammar, the amount of language-particular stipulation was considerably less than that found in the earlier rule-based systems.

After 1981, many attempts were made to extend the data coverage of the theory. Some of this work revealed that certain of the restrictions and assumptions of the LGB framework were successful because they were tailored closely to the data discussed there, and that the theory consequently was hard to apply to additional data without modification of some of the restrictive LGB assumptions. In this section, we will discuss a number of efforts to equip the theory with more flexibility than the 1981 version allows for. We will treat the VP-internal subject hypothesis, the A/A-bar distinction, and functional heads.

5.3.1 *The VP-Internal Subject Hypothesis (VISH)*

We begin by asking what analysis the LGB framework would make available for the sentence below from Breton drawn from Hendrick (1991, 183):

(163) Ar merc'hed a lavare e wele Yann Mona
the women PRT say-IMPERF PRT see-IMPERF Yann Mona
"The women said that Yann saw Mona"

Note that the subordinate clause has VSO order. Hendrick points out that the embedded clause is introduced by the overt complementizer *e* which typically appears when nothing is topicalized.

The standard analysis of verb fronting in the Germanic languages had involved movement to an empty complementizer position. One of the many good arguments for this view is based on the fact that the verb-second constraint in most Germanic languages is restricted to main clauses. The following two German sentences help to illustrate this:

(164) Johanna **liest** das Buch
Johanna reads the book
"Johanna is reading the book"

(165) **daß** Johanna das Buch **liest**
that Johanna the book reads
"that Johnna is reading the book"

(165) is assumed to show the verb in its D-structure position (or, perhaps, in a sentence-final Infl). Main clauses typically do not contain

lexical complementizers and thus in (164) the verb can move from its sentence-final position into Comp. Afterwards, one phrase can move to the left of the verb and adjoin to Comp or occupy its specifier position, depending on what assumptions are made with respect to the headhood of Comp. Embedded sentences with overt complementizers prevent the verb from fronting since its landing site is already filled. This accounts for the difference between main and subordinate clauses concerning verb-second.

Returning to (163) we see that no equivalent analysis is possible for VSO languages because verb fronting occurs in the embedded clause even in the presence of an overt complementizer, i.e. there is no main–subordinate clause asymmetry.[52]

What other options do we have? We could postulate an additional Comp position in these languages but many syntacticians object to this on the grounds that it fails to explain why at most one lexical complementizer can appear per clause and why in clauses with both a complementizer and a fronted verb the former always precedes the latter. We might allow verb fronting to be an adjunction operation between the complementizer and S/IP but most researchers prefer a substitution operation so as to minimize the number of non-structure-preserving operations in the sense of Emonds (1970, 1976). These desiderata all seem to converge on the following analysis which is possible under LGB assumptions:

(166) $[_{S'}$ Comp $[_{S}$ Infl NP VP]]

(166) is an instance of the universal expansion for sentences in (65) with the directionality parameter set such that Infl precedes both NP and VP. Assuming that in VSO languages the verb moves out of the VP to Infl, the surface order in (163) falls out naturally.[53]

With the integration of Comp and Infl into the X-bar system, the proposal above ran into problems. The analysis of (166) depends on Infl, the subject and the VP being sisters and therefore easily reorderable. The new system in contrast makes Infl and VP sisters and the subject the specifier of this new I′ constituent:

(167) $[_{CP}$ Comp $[_{IP}$ NP $[_{I'}$ I^0 VP]]]

Now we have no easy way of getting Infl to the left of the subject unless we want to postulate a double Comp or non-structure preserving verb movement after all.

This problem has been one central argument for a revision of the structure-building apparatus assumed in LGB. Koopman and Sportiche

(1991) propose that subjects may appear in [Spec, IP] but are base-generated within the maximal projection of the VP.[54] The structure created by the projection principle and X-bar theory is then the following:[55]

(168)

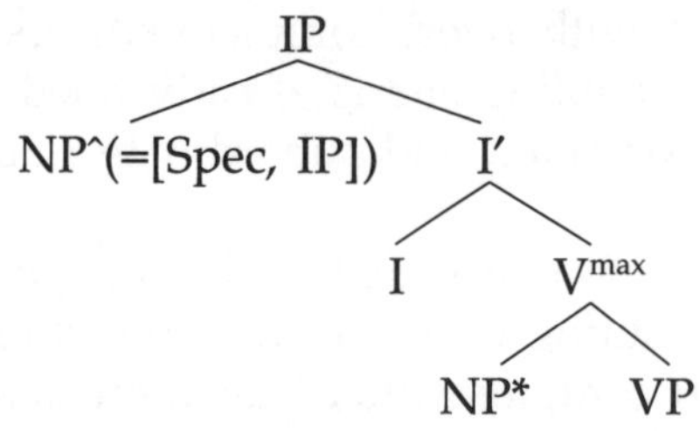

(168) is compatible with the arguments that Irish (see Chung and McCloskey (1987)), Welsh (cf. Harlow (1981), Sproat (1985b), Koopman (1984)), and Arabic (Ouhalla (1991), Benmamoun (1992)) sentences contain the substructure *Infl NP VP.* Assuming that the hierarchical structure in (168) is universal, it is possible for the main verb to move to Infl and the subject to move to [Spec, IP]. If the subject moves and the verb appears in $Infl^0$ or in V^0, the resulting order will be SVO. If only the verb moves and the subject remains within the VP, then we will derive a VSO order that is compatible with the presence of an overt complementizer as in our original example (163).

What determines whether the subject moves out of the VP (as in English-type languages) or stays in situ (as in VSO languages)? Koopman and Sportiche (1991) suggest that nominative Case can be assigned in two configurations: (i) the relevant NP can appear in the specifier position of a tensed Infl or (ii) it can be governed by Infl where government is defined so that a head cannot govern its specifier. Languages then differ from each other in how nominative Case is assigned. If it is always assigned under specifier–head agreement, then the subject must move out of the VP into the specifier of Infl to get Case. On the other hand, if Infl assigns its nominative only under government, then the subject must remain lower than Infl to receive Case. If Infl appears to the left of the VP and the verb is attracted to Infl, the result is a VSO order.

As evidence for tying only the preverbal position to agreement, Koopman and Sportiche refer to the fact that in S-Infl-VO languages like English and French the subject agrees with the finite verb whereas in the Infl-V-SO languages Irish and Welsh there is no subject–verb agreement.[56]

Sportiche (1988) presents an interesting empirical argument from French for the VISH. Note the positions in which a floating quantifier can appear in (169)–(170):[57]

(169) Les enfants (*tous) verront (tous) ce film
the children all see-FUT this movie
"The children will all see this movie"

(170) Les enfants (*tous)ont (tous) vu (*tous) ce film
the children all have seen this movie
"The children have all seen this movie"

Why is the quantifier barred from the starred positions? The following assumptions provide an elegant explanation: (1) at D-structure the quantifier is immediately to the left of the NP it quantifies over; (2) in D-structure, the subject is the first NP within the VP; (3) in finite clauses the finite verb moves to Infl; and (4) the subject moves to [Spec, IP], optionally taking along the quantifier. The first and third assumptions are justified by other data, and the last assumption is probably not controversial. The second assumption is the one we are seeking to support, namely VISH.

(169)–(170) are now predicted. In (169), the quantifier was stranded by the subject and remains at the left periphery of the VP. Since the main verb is finite, it must move to Infl and in the process cross over the quantifier and appear to its left.

The quantifier in (170) cannot appear between the subject and the finite verb either, for the same reason as in (169). It is banned from the position following the non-finite verb because the movement to Infl is restricted to finite verbs. The only position left is the one between the finite auxiliary and the non-finite main verb. Had the subject not stranded the quantifier, it should precede the NP in [Spec, IP]. This is indeed the case:

(171) Tous les enfants ont vu ce film
all the children have seen this movie
"All the children have seen this movie"

Sportiche explicitly discusses putative attempts to derive this distribution from analyzing floating quantifiers as adverbs but rejects this move on the basis that these quantifiers do not behave like any of the adverb classes in French. This paradigm thus finds an elegant explanation that crucially depends on the correctness of VISH and thus supports this hypothesis.

Other authors have argued for VISH on conceptual grounds. Among these are Kuroda (1988) and Kitagawa (1986) who both depart from Koopman and Sportiche in that they assume that the subject is base-generated in the specifier position of VP rather than adjoined to the VP. Kuroda points out that although X-bar theory predicts the existence of a VP-specifier the theory had actually not utilized this position. The VISH fills this gap. Kitagawa sees as an advantage that all theta-marked positions of a head are now projected within the maximal projection of the head which according to him constitutes a more natural characterization of theta domains than a theory which projects some theta roles inside and one outside the predicator's maximal projection.

The VISH is by now generally accepted. Few objections have been raised against it; Williams presents one problem for it in chapter 2 of this book. As already mentioned, it is controversial exactly where the subject is generated within the VP and exactly what principles force it to move out. The status of [Spec, IP] with respect to the A/A-bar distinction is also unsettled. Some authors argue that the position is always an A-position, others support the view that it can sometimes be an A-bar position as well. Since the various researchers make different additional assumptions, the respective theories have to be evaluated against each other as a whole, leading us beyond the discussion of the VISH here. The interested reader is referred to the following additional works for further discussion of the VISH: Zagona (1982), Manzini (1983b), Fukui and Speas (1986), Contreras (1987), Pesetsky (1989), Speas (1990), Guilfoyle, Hung, and Travis (1990), Woolford (1991), and Huang (1993).

5.3.2 *Scrambling and Mixed Positions*

Up to this point in our discussion we have only dealt with languages that have relatively fixed word and phrase order. We have deliberately avoided the question of how the many languages with freer constituent order, e.g. Warlpiri, Latin, German, Japanese, and Korean, fit into this picture. The latter three are free phrase-order languages in that under certain circumstances they allow the order of phrases within a sentence to be syntactically free. Warlpiri and Latin go even further and under the right conditions allow the parts of phrases to be discontinuous.

For most of the history of Generative Grammar, free constituent languages have been considered somewhat of an anomaly whose properties were claimed not to be fully describable with the mechanisms of core grammar or at the least to require powerful and exceptional syntactic mechanisms for analysis. Chomsky (1965, 126ff) takes the first road and denies the relevance of the free word order phenomenon for the justification of grammars:

(172) the free word order phenomenon is an interesting and important one, and much too little attention has been given to it. First of all, it should be emphasized that grammatical transformations

> do not seem to be an appropriate device for expressing the full range of possibilities for stylistic inversion . . . In general, the rules of stylistic reordering are very different from the grammatical transformations, which are much more deeply embedded in the grammatical system [footnote omitted; GW]. It might, in fact, be argued that the former are not so much rules of grammar as rules of performance . . . In any event, though this is surely an interesting phenomenon, it is one that has no apparent bearing, for the moment, on the theory of grammatical structure.

Ross (1967) proposed that free word order is brought about by a *Scrambling* rule that was ordered late in the block of transformations and followed the ordinary phrase structure rules, case marking, agreement, reflexivization, and pronominalization transformations that free and rigid word order languages were assumed to have in common. In that way, free constituent order languages would only differ from rigid order languages in terms of order, but with respect to other grammatical properties such as case marking and binding they were predicted to be similar or alike, i.e. subjects bear nominative case, objects accusative, and subjects can bind objects but not vice versa. Ross (1967) explicitly proposed the existence of a *stylistic* component, an idea that was incorporated into Chomsky and Lasnik (1977) and Rochemont (1978), among others. It was generally assumed that the rules in this component were exempt from at least some of the wellformedness conditions on core syntactic rules.

Chomsky (1981), following the fascinating study of the Australian aboriginal language Warlpiri in Hale (1978, 1983), admitted free constituent order languages into the syntax. But again they were treated as exceptional. Since this approach is now generally thought to be superseded within GB-type approaches we will not sketch it here, although Hale's studies are still strongly recommended for reading. Suffice it to say that this approach involved the postulation of a *Configurationality Parameter* one of whose settings allowed languages to suspend most of the consequences of the projection principle and X-bar theory. The orphan status of this concept is revealed by the fact that only eight consecutive pages out of the 346 text pages of LGB are dedicated to this problem.[58]

Given the monumental role of the projection principle and X-bar theory in creating similar configurations across languages which underlie the notions used by the theories of government, Case, binding, etc., it is not surprising that attempts were made to find arguments that the structure of free word order languages is not really radically different from that of languages with rigid constituent order.

Saito and Hoji (1983) was very influential in that regard.[59] They argue that the grammaticality contrast between the following two sentences should be seen as a *Weak Crossover Effect*:

(173) [[Hanako-ga zibun$_i$-o kiratteiru koto] -ga [Ziroo$_i$-o
Hanako(NOM) self(ACC) dislike fact NOM Ziroo(ACC)
yuuutu-ni siteiru]]
depressed make
"The fact that Hanako dislikes himself$_i$ has depressed Ziro$_i$"

(174) ??Ziroo-o$_i$ [[Hanako-ga zibun$_i$-o kiratteiru koto] -ga t$_i$
Ziroo(ACC) Hanako(NOM) self(ACC) dislike fact NOM
yuuutu-ni siteiru]]
depressed make
"Ziro$_i$, the fact that Hanako dislikes himself$_i$ has depressed t$_i$"

In both sentences we find the expression *zibun* which can in principle corefer with names. But whereas coreference is possible in (173) it is not in (174). Saito and Hoji (1983) pin this difference to a difference in structure between the two sentences. In the first sentence, there is no c-command relation in either direction between *zibun* and the intended antecedent *Ziroo-o*. This is different in (174), however. Here the intended antecedent has moved to the left into a position from which it c-commands the expression with variable reference. Assuming in accordance with the projection principle that the moved expression leaves a trace and lands in an A-bar position, the typical weak crossover configuration is established: an expression in an A-bar position c-commands both its trace and a variable and there is no c-command between the latter two expressions. Such sentences typically have a degraded status as can be seen from the following English example:

(175) ??Who$_i$ does [$_{IP}$ [$_{NP}$ his$_i$ mother] [$_{VP}$ like t$_i$]]

If (174) indeed instantiates a weak crossover effect, the theoretical consequences would be profound. Saito and Hoji's weak crossover explanation of the contrast between (173) and (174) crucially depends on the existence of a trace in the object position of *depressed.* But the presence of this trace is only guaranteed if *Ziroo-o* cannot be base-generated in the initial position in (174). Such base generation is precisely what the projection principle and X-bar theory would prohibit because they would force *Ziroo-o* to be generated adjacent to its theta marker and leave a trace after movement. This paradigm thus was taken as a powerful argument against relaxing the projection principle and X-bar theory.

In Saito and Hoji's theory, the difference between English and Japanese was minimal. Assume that the projection principle and X-bar theory operate identically in English and Japanese. Also, assume the following definition of *A-position* from Chomsky (1981, 47):

(176) An A-position is a potential θ-position.

Potential theta positions are the subject positions of NPs and sentences and all complement positions. It now follows that the moved object in (174) has to occupy an A-bar position from which it may bind at most one variable.[60] (173) contains no A-bar binder and there is no problem, but (174) violates the condition.

LGB contains a rule schema *Move-α* which allows free and recursive adjunction to A-bar positions unless some other condition is violated. Potential adjunction sites for scrambling thus exist in both English and Japanese. Assuming the existence of a parameter that allows languages to make use of these adjunction sites to varying degrees will suffice to derive the differences in word order freedom between English-type and Japanese-type languages. This is a much more minimal and hence more desirable theory of degrees of word order freedom than an approach that allows for a parametrization of the projection principle. It does not necessitate a revision of the projection system or the A/A-bar distinction assumed in LGB.

Unfortunately, however, things are not that simple. Later work on other languages (and, in fact, Japanese as well, cf. Saito (1992, n. 5)), showed that the examples (173)–(174) are not representative and that scrambling does not necessarily lead to weak crossover violations. Webelhuth (1987, 1992, 1993) illustrates this with examples from German:

(177) *Er hat seinem$_i$ Nachbarn jeden Gast$_i$ vorgestellt
he has his neighbor every guest introduced
"He introduced every guest to his neighbor"

(178) Er hat jeden Gast$_i$ seinem$_i$ Nachbarn t$_i$ vorgestellt
he has every guest his neighbor introduced
"He introduced every guest to his neighbor"

While (177) is ungrammatical because the pronoun *seinen* is not c-commanded by the intended quantified antecedent *jeden Gast*, the example (178) is grammatical even though *jeden Gast* has moved around the NP containing the bound pronoun. Structurally, (178) instantiates the weak crossover configuration as much as (174). Yet, the sentence is uncontroversially grammatical!

(178) creates a problem for the LGB projection principle and X-bar theory that is similar to the difficulties that arose from VSO languages for the X-bar system where Infl projects its own phrase. The problem

is that we do not have "enough" positions with the right properties available in the tree to account for all the properties of the respective constructions. In (178), we need a position between the subject and the VP from which scrambled objects can A-bind. The LGB system makes no such position available.

Webelhuth (1987, 1992, 1993) proposes the following solution to this problem. (178) shows that scrambled elements are in principle capable of A-binding. We recall, however, that there is considerable evidence that scrambling shares properties with A-bar movement (cf. the evidence referred to in note 59). For instance, in German scrambling licenses parasitic gaps, a phenomenon exclusively associated with A-bar movement:

(179) ?Peter hat *die Gäste*$_i$ [ohne PRO e_i anzuschauen] dem Pfarrer t_i
Peter has the guests without looking-at the priest
vorgestellt
introduced
"Peter introduced the guests to the priest without looking at them"

In fact, scrambled elements can A-bind and A-bar bind in one and the same sentence, as shown in (180):

(180) ?Peter hat *die Gäste*$_i$ [ohne PRO e_i anzuschauen] einander t_i
Peter has the guests without looking-at each other
vorgestellt
introduced
"Peter introduced the guests to each other without looking at them"

If we maintain with Saito and Hoji (1983) that scrambling is uniformly movement to an A-bar position as suggested by the strong parallelism between *wh*-movement and scrambling with respect to movement constraints, then our problem is the following: we do not need to create more positions, since the option of recursive adjunctions provides for slots in all positions where scrambled elements can appear: to the left of subjects, in-between adverbs and between the subject and the left periphery of the VP. Rather, what we need is more positions from which A-binding is possible. To this end, Webelhuth (1987, 1992, 1993) proposes to put a ternary positional system into the place of the binary distinction between A and A-bar positions in LGB. The properties of the positions are fixed as follows:[61]

(181)

Type of Position	Definition	Binding Potential
A(rgument)-position	[Spec, IP], [Spec, NP], [Compl, X^0]	A-binding
O(perator)-position	[Spec, CP]	A-bar binding
U(nrestricted)-position	adjoined positions	A & A-bar binding

Note that the first two types of positions are those found in the classical system. The third type is added. Whereas the LGB system classifies adjoined positions with operator positions binding-theoretically, (181) makes them into a class by themselves with the unique property of being positions from which both A-binding and A-bar binding is possible. (181) thus captures the data presented in this section but it requires a modification of the LGB system, albeit a very minimal one.[62]

Other attempts have been made to handle the binding paradoxes created by scrambling languages for the positional system of LGB. Since they involve functional heads, we will describe them in the next section of this chapter.

5.3.3 *Functional Heads*

We will now describe a third argument that the assumptions about sentence structure of LGB are too inflexible and need to be revised.

The evidence comes from Pollock (1989) and is based on the comparative word order of adverbs and verbs in French and English. We will discuss French first. Pollock finds two types of alternations, one depending on the type of adverb involved, the other on whether the clause is finite. In finite clauses, all finite verbs must precede both sentence adverbs like the negation and VP-adverbs.[63] (182)–(183) show this for main verbs, (184)–(185) for an auxiliary:

(182) Jean n' *aime* <u>pas</u> Marie
Jean ne likes not Mary
"Jean does not like Mary"

(183) Jean *embrasse* <u>souvent</u> Marie
Jean kisses often Mary
"Jean often kisses Mary"

(184) Jean n' *est* <u>pas</u> heureux
Jean ne is not happy
"Jean is not happy"

(185) Jean *est* <u>complètement</u> malheureux
Jean is completely unhappy
"Jean is completely unhappy"

Infinitives, interestingly, behave differently and that is what Pollock's argument is based on. Here we find that the auxiliaries *avoir "have"* and *être "be"* do not behave like main verbs with respect to certain adverb classes. The two auxiliaries can appear on either side of both types of adverbs:

(186) N' *être* pas heureux est une condition pour écrire
ne be not happy is a condition for writing
"Not being happy is a condition for writing"
(187) Ne pas *être* heureux est une condition pour écrire
ne not be happy is a condition for writing
"Not being happy is a condition for writing"
(188) *Etre* complètement malheureux est dangereux
be completely happy is dangerous
"Being completely happy is dangerous"
(189) Complètement *être* malheureux est dangereux
completely be happy is dangerous
"Being completely happy is dangerous"

Main verbs, on the other hand, can appear on either side of VP adverbs but must follow sentence adverbs like the negation:

(190) *Perdre* complètement la tête est dangereux
lose completely the head is dangerous
"Completely losing one's head is dangerous"
(191) Complètement *perdre* la tête est dangereux
completely lose the head is dangerous
"Completely losing one's head is dangerous"
(192) Ne pas *sembler* heureux est une condition pour écrire
ne not seem happy is a condition for writing
"Not to seem happy is a condition for writing"
(193) *Ne *sembler* pas heureux est une condition pour écrire
ne seem not happy is a condition for writing
"Not to seem happy is a condition for writing"

It is now easy to see that under the assumption that the position of adverbs is fixed we are facing the same type of problem we already encountered in the previous two sections: the LGB X-bar theory and projection principle do not make enough positions with the right properties available to account for all the possible word orders we find in French. Only one position appears between the subject and the adverbs which could serve as a landing site for verb movement, namely Infl. But the data above requires at least two different landing sites.

Assume that the finite verbs in (182)–(185) have moved to Infl. Then we must assume that Infl precedes both sentence adverbs and VP-adverbs. This is not problematic for the auxiliaries in (186)–(189). We may say that movement to Infl is optional in infinitives, thus predicting all four sentences to be grammatical. However, while this is consistent with the first two sentences of the non-finite main verb paradigm in (190)–(193), it incorrectly predicts that non-finite main verbs should be able to precede or follow sentence adverbs. (193) shows that this is not the case.

There is no easy solution to this problem within the LGB framework. Since (190) shows that non-finite main verbs *can* move out of the VP, the only landing site there is available in this theory is Infl. And since the negation is assumed to occur between Infl and the VP, we predict that if main verbs can occur to the left of a VP-adverb as in (190) they will also be able to precede the negation as in (193).

Pollock proposes to solve this problem by creating an additional landing site for verb movement in-between sentence adverbs and VP-adverbs. He suggests that the Infl node which in LGB houses both tense and agreement features be "split" or "exploded," into two heads, called "Tense (T)" and "Agreement (AGR)" respectively and each projects its own maximal projection, "TP" and "AGRP." The order of embedding of TP, AGRP, and VP is as follows:

(194)

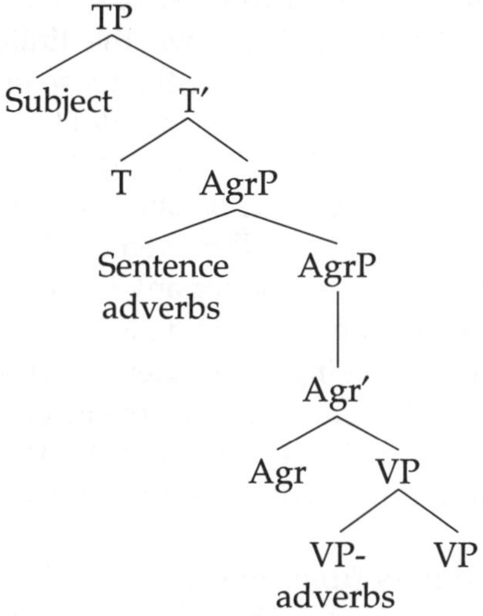

As shown in diagram (194), sentence adverbs are assumed to be generated between T and Agr and VP-adverbs between Agr and V. Now, Pollock argues, we have enough positions to describe the whole paradigm in (182)–(193) with the positions filled as follows ("MV" = main verb):

(195)

	$\mathbf{T^0}$	**AGRP-Adv**	$\mathbf{AGR^0}$	**VP-Adv**	$\mathbf{V^0}$
Finite:	{MV, *avoir*, *être*}				
Non-finite:	{*avoir*, *être*}		{MV, *avoir*, *être*}		{MV, *avoir*, *être*}

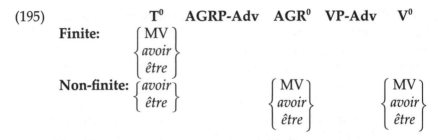

Whereas in finite clauses all finite verbs must move to the head of TP, only the two auxiliaries can reach this position in infinitives. Non-finite main verbs, like auxiliaries, have the option of staying in the VP, moving to AGR, but they are not allowed to move all the way to T.

Pollock forces the finite verbs to move by claiming that finite tense is an operator and has to bind a verb trace as a variable. The movement of the finite verbs creates this variable. Movement of non-finite verbs is optional where allowed at all. A diacritic is created to distinguish between "strong" and "weak" AGRs and Ts.[64] The strong versions of these heads have the ability to transfer the theta grid of an adjoined head to the head's trace, but weak heads lack this ability. Thus, adjoining a thematic verb to a weak head will lead to a violation of the theta criterion: the verb's thematic roles cannot be assigned. Pollock assumes that non-finite T^0 is universally weak in this sense but that the strength of AGR is parametrized. In French it is said to be strong.

With these assumptions, the data in (195) follow: the finite verbs must move all the way to T^0 to create a variable for the tense operator. The verb movement is successive-cyclic to satisfy the *Head Movement Constraint* from Travis (1984, 131).[65] Since finite T^0 and AGR^0 in French are strong, both auxiliaries and main verbs will be able to move without violating the theta criterion. In infinitives, all movement is optional since no verb trace need be created as a variable for any tense operator. However, since non-finite T^0 is universally weak and AGR in French is strong, in infinitives only non-theta-marking auxiliaries are allowed to move around sentence adverbs to T^0. The AGR is strong enough to transfer a non-finite main verb's theta grid but the non-finite tense is not. This means that the (optional) movement of non-finite main verbs cannot extend beyond AGR^0.

Pollock assumes that English differs from French in that its AGR is weak in both finite and non-finite clauses. This allows auxiliaries to move out of the VP through AGR to T, this movement being obligatory in finite clauses but optional in infinitives:

(196) John (is) not/completely (*is) happy
(197) John hopes to (be) not/completely (be) happy

Main verbs, however, cannot get to AGR without violating the theta criterion and hence can never leave the VP. As a result, they are not allowed to precede the adverbs under discussion:

(198) *John opened not/quickly the door
(199) *John was believed to open not/quickly the door

Do-support must apply in finite clauses under conditions predicted by a mechanism that Pollock proposes but which we will skip here. Sentences such as (200) thus argue for the existence of AGRP in English as well:

(200) John is believed to <u>not</u> *be* <u>completely</u> happy

Here the auxiliary has not moved over the sentence adverb to Tense but occurs to the left of the VP-adverb. AGR serves as a landing site here as well.

There are many problems with Pollock's argument that splitting Infl into two independent projections, TP and AGRP, leads to an optimal analysis of the word order of French and English. We will now turn to Iatridou (1990) who claims that Pollock's data and additional considerations favor the view that there is only one landing site for verb movement, namely one integrated Infl, and that all word orders that cannot be captured in this manner are due to choices of adverb placement that Pollock disregards.

Iatridou concedes that all verbs obligatorily move to Infl in French finite clauses and that the auxiliaries *have* and *be* and their French equivalents optionally move to Infl in non-tensed environments. No AGRP projection is necessary for these cases. This leaves only two types of examples unaccounted for, the French (190) where a non-finite main verb precedes a VP-adverb and the English (200) [and its French equivalent] where a non-finite auxiliary intervenes between a sentence adverb and a VP-adverb.

For the second case, Iatridou argues that no movement of the auxiliary is involved at all and that the relevant structure is base-generated. She shows that adverbs differ from each other in their ordering privileges relative to non-finite auxiliaries, which is unexpected under Pollock's theory where all movement of non-finite verbs is optional where allowed at all:

(201) I believe John to (deliberately) be (deliberately) sarcastic
(202) I believe John to (*tolerably) be (tolerably) sarcastic

In her view, when the adverb is adjacent to the adjectival predicate it forms a constituent with the adjective and the semantic compatibility of the two expressions determines whether this constituency is possible. Strong independent evidence for her assumptions about constituency comes from the following examples:

(203) ?I consider John [often sarcastic]
(204) [Often sarcastic] though John is, he is still very popular
(205) I believe John to have been [often sarcastic]

The bracketed constituent in (203) is an adjectival small clause that does not contain a VP that could serve as an adjunction site for the adverb *often* that is required within Pollock's framework of assumptions. (204) shows that the adverb and the adjective can be topicalized as one constituent, suggesting again that the adjacency of certain adverbs and adjectival predicates is a function of their constituency and does not require an intervening auxiliary to move out of the way. In (205), *often sarcastic* is preceded by two auxiliaries in the same clause. According to standard assumptions at most one auxiliary should be able to move around an adverb, suggesting that at least one of the auxiliaries preceding the adverb in (205) is base-generated there and does not need to get into that position by movement. (201)–(205) thus all point in the same direction, namely that infinitives should not be analyzed in terms of movement of auxiliaries. This eliminates one of the two arguments for an AGR projection in Pollock (1989).

With respect to the remaining case, the "short movement" of a main verb around a VP-adverb in French (cf. (190)), Iatridou points out that Pollock's analysis cannot be extended to cover the full range of data and that a more liberal theory of adverb placement is presumably the correct answer to this problem as well. In this connection she discusses Pollock's proposal to deal with (206)–(207):

(206) Pierre a à peine vu Marie
Pierre has hardly seen Marie
"Pierre hardly saw Mary"
(207) Pierre a vu à peine Marie
Pierre has seen hardly Marie
"Pierre hardly saw Mary"

The first example fits into Pollock's theory unproblematically. The perfective auxiliary moves around the adverb adjoined to its VP into AGR and finally into T (the sentence being finite). (207) cannot be handled in that way, however, because here both the finite verb and the participle *vu* precede the adverb. Pollock handles this data by creating a second AGR as a landing site for the participle and base-generating the adverb adjoined to the lower VP, i.e. in-between the base position of the perfective auxiliary and the main verb. The main verb then moves around the adverb into the lower AGR and the auxiliary moves into the higher AGR and on to tense.

Iatridou points out that this way of handling (207) undermines Pollock's previous arguments for the existence of AGR and AGRP as a landing site for auxiliary movement. Since the structure Pollock assumes for (207) allows auxiliaries to be base-generated already in the correct surface order relative to adverbs, movement and hence an additional landing site other than Infl are superfluous.

The most damaging evidence against movement to an intermediate AGR comes from the following examples, however (Iatridou (1990, 567)):

(208) Souvent mal *faire* ses devoirs – c' est stupide
frequently badly make poss homework that is stupid
"To frequently do one's homework badly is stupid"
(209) *Faire* souvent mal ses devoirs . . .
(210) Souvent *faire* mal ses devoirs . . .

These examples involve a non-finite main verb and two VP-adverbs. Movement of such verbs to AGR is optional, allowing for the generation of (208) where *faire* has stayed in situ and (209) where it has moved out of the VP and hence precedes both adverbs adjoined to the VP. (210), however, is grammatical as well and even with the explosion of Infl, Pollock's theory does not have enough landing sites for verb movement to generate this word order. The logic of his theory requires that non-sentence adverbs can only be adjoined to VP and do not move sentence-internally. Under these assumptions the two adverbs in (210) are adjoined to the same VP and there is no X^0 landing site between them.[66]

Most commentators have not rejected Pollock's Split Infl Hypothesis and have either suggested modifications or extensions of it. Belletti (1988b, 1990), reviewed in Pollock (1992), and Mitchell (1991), based on Finnish (on which see also Malatin (1991)), postulate separate Tense and AGR nodes as well but generate them in the opposite order proposed by Pollock. Ouhalla (1991), finally, postulates that the order of embedding of these categories must be parametrized, since some languages allow tense morphemes to be closer to the stem than agreement affixes and others prefer the inverse order:

(211)	sa-	y-	ashtarii	Zayd-un	darr-an
	will(TNS)	*3MS(AGR)*	*buy*	*Zayd-NOM*	*house-ACC*
	"Zayd will buy a house"				
(212)	Mtsuko	u-	na-	gw-	a
	waterpot	*SP(AGR)*	*PAST(TNS)*	*fall*	*ASP*
	"The waterpot fell"				

(211) is from Arabic and shows the order TNS–AGR–V; (212) is a Chichewa example cited from Baker (1988a) and instantiates AGR–TNS–V. Assuming with Baker (1985) that the order of morphemes in a word mirrors the order of application of syntactic rules that combines the verb with the affixes, we are forced to conclude that there is no universal sentence structure with an invariant embedding of tense and agreement.

Once the idea of an integrated Infl node is given up, there is of course no reason to limit the "splitting" of this node to two resulting heads, Tense and Agreement. It is thus natural that other inflectional information has been presented in the form of heads projecting their own syntactic projection. The table below contains a list of some such new categories that have been proposed in the field during the last few years:

(213)

Proposed Category	**Source**
AGR_A	Chomsky (1992)
Agr_{IO}	Mahajan (1990)
AGR_N	Johns (1992)
AGR_V	Johns (1992)
Aspect	Hendrick (1991)
Aux	Mahajan (1990)
Clitic voices	Sportiche (1992)
Gender	Shlonsky (1989)[67]
Honorific	Kim (1992)
μ	Pesetsky (1989), Johnson (1991)
Neg	Pollock (1989), Benmamoun (1992)
Number	Shlonsky (1989), Ritter (1991)
Person	Shlonsky (1989)
Predicate	Bowers (1989)
Tense	Pollock (1989)
Z	Stowell (1992)

Space considerations forbid us to examine all of these proposals, so that we will restrict ourselves to choosing a few representative examples to give the reader some idea of the basis on which the existence of these new functional heads is argued for.

Benmamoun (1992) is one of the few works so far that embeds the analysis of specific functional heads in a general discussion of the necessary and sufficient conditions on the postulation of new heads. The work contains very interesting analyses from various dialects of Arabic whose behavior with respect to word order, agreement, and case marking bears heavily on a correct theoretical explication of these notions in Universal Grammar. Benmamoun follows Pollock (1989) in postulating that the sentence negation is a syntactic head with its own projection.[68] His argument is simple and intuitive. The author starts out his discussion by pointing to two differences between the English negation word *not* and the negative affix *un-*:

(214) He is not happy
(215) He is unhappy

First, while the negative free form can license negative polarity items, the affixal negation cannot:

(216) He is not happy with any of his paintings
(217) *He is unhappy with any of his paintings

Secondly, whereas the free form negation shows scope ambiguities with quantificational NPs, quantificational NPs always have scope over an affixal negation within the same clause:

(218) He is not happy with many of his paintings (ambiguous)
(219) He is unhappy with many of his paintings (unambiguous)

Turning now to Arabic, Benmamoun points out that the sentence negation in this language is expressed as a bound form, the affix *ma*:

(220) ma-xraj-š
Neg-exit-s
"He did not go out"

However, even though this negation is expressed affixally, it behaves like the free form negation in English and not the affixal one with respect to the licensing of negative polarity items (221) and quantifier scope (222):

(221) ma-gra Hatta ktaab
(he)Neg-read any book
"He did not read any book"

(222) ma-gra-š bezaaf d-le-ktuba (ambiguous)
(he)Neg-read-s many of-the-books
"He did not read many books"

This paradigm thus shows that there have to be two different grammatical representations for negative elements but that the relevant difference cannot be tied to the syntax–morphology split. Benmamoun suggests that both licensing of negative polarity items and quantifier scope require the interaction of syntactically "visible" categories in the sense that each is represented in the syntactic X-bar theory, i.e. is an X^0 or a projection of one. The English negation *not* (and its contracted counterpart) and the Arabic negation would qualify as independent heads by this criterion but the affix *un-* in English would not.

Hendrick (1991) argues for the existence of "Aspect" as an independent functional head on the basis of a detailed comparison of Breton and Welsh. What is interesting in light of the argument just described is that Hendrick derives several important differences between these two languages by taking into account the different morphosyntactic spell-outs of aspect in the languages. In Welsh, the perfective is expressed analytically, with the particle *wedi* (the tense is carried by a form of the verb *be*):

(223) Mae e **wedi** canu
be-PRES he PRT sing
"He has sung"

Breton, in contrast, expresses its perfect much like English, with an aspectual verb and an additional affix *-et* on the main verb:

(224) Dec'h **en deus** Yann gwel**et** Mona
yesterday have-PRES-3SNG-MASC Yann seen Mona
"Yann saw Mona yesterday"

Hendrick postulates an aspect phrase (ASPP) in both languages:

(225)
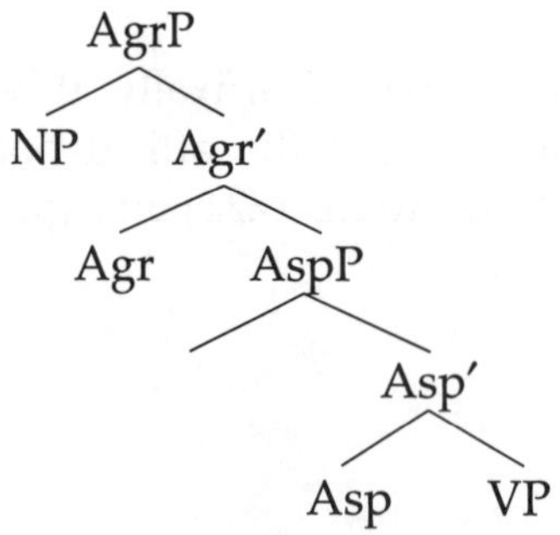

A crucial contrast between the two languages now arises because verb movement must apply to the head of ASPP in Breton or otherwise the affix occupying this position would not be attached to a head.[69] In Welsh, however, the free form *wedi* occupying ASP^0 blocks the potential landing site of the main verb and verb raising out of the VP is impossible in these structures in this language. Hendrick assumes that in both languages ASP^0 is incapable of L-marking its complement by itself but that after the aspectual affix is supported by the lexical verb in Breton, V-ASP L-marks the VP and allows free extraction of the object. This means that in Breton both the head of the VP and its object can leave the VP but in Welsh neither one can. This provides an elegant explanation of the following paradigms. In Breton (226), but not Welsh (227), the main verb can move to the left to a position preceding the subject:

(226) **Gwelet** en deus Yann Mona
seen be-PRES-3SNG-MASC Yann Mona
"Yann saw Mona yesterday"

(227) *Dim **golchi** mae John wedi y car
not wash be-PRES John PRT the car
"John has not washed the car"

(227) falls victim to the ECP, since the verb *wash* cannot properly govern its trace contained in a non-L-marked VP.

Secondly, whereas Breton allows the object of the verb to leave its L-marked VP and *wh*-move directly to the beginning of the sentence (228), the object in Welsh can leave its non-L-marked VP only by first moving through the specifier of an object agreement phrase (229). In this way it is predicted that *wh*-moved objects must agree with the verb in Welsh but that this is not necessary in Breton:[70]

(228) Setu ul levr he deus Mona lennet
here a book have-3SNG-FEM Mona read
"Here's a book that Mona read"

(229) Beth mae e 'n *(ei) ddarllen
what be-PRES he PRT AGR read
"What is he reading?"

The postulation of an independent ASP phrase thus allows Hendrick to tie together several differences between Breton and Welsh in an interesting manner.

We now turn to Scrambling which we had promised to return to in the section on "mixed positions." Recall from our discussion there that the absence of weak crossover effects requires the postulation of additional A-binding possibilities. Webelhuth had proposed to create these new binding possibilities through the postulation of mixed positions from which both A-binding and A-bar binding is possible.

In the wake of functional head theory, several authors have proposed to use specifiers of functional heads rather than mixed positions as the mechanism to create more positions from which A-binding is possible, among them Déprez (1990) and Mahajan (1990, chapter 1) whose argument we will describe here.

Mahajan argues on the basis of Hindi data that mixed positions are not the correct mechanism to account for the weak crossover data in connection with Scrambling. His argument is based on a difference between weak crossover repair in short-distance scrambling (within a clause) and long-distance scrambling (across a clause boundary). (230) shows that a base-generated object quantifier cannot bind a pronoun contained in a subject it does not c-command:

(230) *uskii$_i$ bahin kis-ko$_i$ pyaar kartii thii
his sister(SUB) who(DO) love do-imp-f be-pst-f
"Who$_i$ did his$_i$ sister love?"

In (231), where the object has been scrambled around the subject, the weak crossover violation of (230) disappears:

(231) kis-ko$_i$ uskii$_i$ bahin t$_i$ pyaar kartii thii
who(DO) his sister(SUB) love do-imp-f be-pst-f
"Who$_i$ did his$_i$ sister love?"

When an object scrambles out of a subordinate clause, however, then it is not able to bind a pronoun in the main clause:

(232) *kisko$_i$ uskii$_i$ bahin-ne socaa [$_{CP}$ ki raam-ne t$_i$ dekhaa thaa]
who(EDO) his sister(SUB) thought that Ram(ESUB) seen be-past
"Who$_i$ did his$_i$ sister think that Ram had seen?"

In Mahajan's view, this contrast in weak crossover repair between short- and long-distance scrambling should be explained as follows. In principle, there are two types of landing site for Scrambling, specifier positions of certain functional heads (e.g. object agreement, indirect object agreement, auxiliary phrases, etc.) which count as A-positions, and adjoined positions which count as A-bar positions. Scrambling into adjoined positions is possible in both short- and long-distance movement[71] but Scrambling into an A-position is only possible under short-distance movement since A-chains cannot be formed across sentence boundaries. This predicts the absence of weak crossover effects in short-distance scrambling like (231), since there the moved NP has available specifier landing sites from which A-binding is possible. The inability of NPs to scramble to sentence-external A-binding specifier positions forces them to adjoin there and to be A-bar binders. It is predicted that this will always lead to weak crossover effects.[72]

Asymmetries in weak crossover repair do not follow directly from an analysis in terms of mixed positions (but could be incorporated into one if the data required it) but are predicted if Scrambling is split into two operations: substitution for a specifier and adjunction. The latter approach requires as many specifier positions as there are different Scrambling sites that display crossover repair effects. According to Mahajan, the evidence for these specifiers is thus indirect evidence for the functional heads themselves.

Sportiche (1992) proposes the existence of a whole class of new functional heads which he refers to as "clitic voices." This is done in an attempt to reconcile the two standard treatments of Romance clitics, the base-generation analysis (which generates the clitic in its surface position) and the movement analysis (which moves the clitic from a complement position to its surface slot). The author begins by summing up the arguments for each position which include the movement approach's ability to derive the strict locality conditions on cliticization from general movement conditions (e.g. the Specified Subject Condition) and the advantage of base generation that it predicts the phenomenon of clitic doubling illustrated in (233):

(233) Lo vimos a Juan
him saw-we Juan
"We saw Juan"

In this sentence, the preverbal clitic and the postverbal phrase share a theta role. This is on the face of it problematic for the movement analysis, since the position from which the clitic is supposed to have moved is occupied by another phrase.

Sportiche proposes an ingenious method for capturing both the base generation and movement effects at the same time, similar in style to Chomsky's (1986b) attempt to explain why expletives need Case. He assumes that the clitic is a base-generated head that projects its own maximal projection. This aspect of the analysis is meant to capture the base generation effects. Clitic doubling, for instance, ceases to be a problem, because the clitic never moves from a postverbal position. To account for the movement effects, the author assumes that the postverbal NP is licensed by moving into the specifier position of the clitic phrase. Languages differ from each other in whether this movement is overt or covert and in whether the specifier of the clitic phrase tolerates overt expressions (which determines whether clitic doubling is allowed). As a result of this movement, the clitic and the postverbal NP are predicted to agree in features such as person, number, gender, etc. That the clitic appears to satisfy movement constraints such as the Specified Subject Condition and Huang's (1982) Condition on Extraction Domains falls out from the movement of the postverbal NP into the specifier position of the clitic. For the case of non-doubled clitics it is assumed that the postverbal position is occupied by *pro* which has to be licensed by movement to a specifier position like any overt phrase doubling the clitic.

Sportiche's idea of having the clitic license a phrase in its specifier position follows a trend in recent work that puts more emphasis on specifier positions than the LGB theory which was complement-focused due to its emphasis on the concept of head government. We have already encountered the idea that all Case marking and agreement is checked in the specifier position of a functional head specialized for that purpose. Rizzi (1994) has argued for an extension of this concept to *wh*-movement, based on the assumption of Chomsky (1986a) that *wh*-movement lands in the specifier of Comp. Rizzi postulates the "*wh*-Criterion" as a licensing mechanism for *wh*-operators in close analogy to the theta criterion as a licensing mechanism for arguments:

(234) *The Wh-Criterion*

(234A) A *wh*-operator must be in a Spec-head configuration with an X^0 marked [+*wh*].

(234B) An X^0 marked [+*wh*] must be in a Spec-head configuration with a *wh*-operator.

This principle, an adaptation of a similar one originally proposed in May (1985), is parametrized as to whether it applies only at LF or both at LF and S-structure to account for the difference between languages with overt and covert *wh*-movement.

It is likely that the trend of postulating specialized functional heads that license such features as *wh*, Case, Specificity, *pro*-drop, and agreement will continue.[73]

The postulation of functional heads is a relatively recent phenomenon and very little consensus has been attained with respect to their properties. Questions for which no widely agreed on answers have been found include the following:

(235)
- Is there a universally closed list of functional heads?
- Do all functional heads exist in all languages?
- If not, what are the necessary and sufficient conditions for the postulation of functional heads?
- Must all functional heads be spelled out overtly?
- Does it matter whether a head is realized as a free form or an affix?
- Can functional projections be recursive? All of them or just particular ones?
- Is the order of embedding of functional projections fixed universally? If not, are there any constraints on parametrization?
- Is parametrization restricted to functional heads or can it affect lexical heads as well?
- What is the barrier/minimality status of functional heads? Are there universal principles or is it a matter of parametrization whether a functional head blocks movement?
- Is the A/A-bar distinction relevant to functional heads, i.e. are some A-positions and others A-bar positions?[74]
- What positional typology is imposed on the specifiers of functional heads? Is this typology universal or open to parametrization?

The answers to these questions will have to take into account questions of learnability,[75] in particular if functional heads are allowed to be covert and/or associated with diacritical properties that cannot be detected on the head itself (e.g. a weak/strong AGR distinction in a language without morphological agreement). The current practice of postulating much covert structure also leads to the problem of analytical indeterminacy, e.g. if the subject can in principle appear in several parametrically determined specifier positions, then several different versions of SVO or SOV languages are predicted to exist, depending on where the subject and the verb end up in the tree. This situation did not arise in the LGB framework whose very restrictive positional system allowed for practically only one structural analysis of these language types. Within that system the language learner could use easily accessible evidence from simple sentence types to fix the parameters whose consequences were supposed to project the grammaticality judgments for data that the language learner might not be systematically exposed to (the "poverty of stimulus" argument). In a system with rich covert structure and many diacritics the learners might instead be forced to use subtle alternations in relatively complex constructions to fix the parameter values responsible for simple generalizations of the language, e.g. the correct analysis of its basic word order. It must be guaranteed that all postulated parameter values remain learnable under the conditions typically encountered by the language learner.

If covert structure is allowed, this also raises the question of the relationship between syntax and morpho-phonological spell-out. Until now the work on functional heads has almost exclusively concentrated on making it initially plausible that additional heads have benign consequences. Few authors have addressed the problems with explanatory adequacy that a drastic enrichment of descriptive devices always brings with it. A theory is always as weak as its weakest component: its syntactic component may be made elegant and explanatory by postulating the same functional projections in each language, but if this requires the morpho-phonological component to contain a large number of unprincipled and unconstrained spell-out stipulations, then no close relationship between the grammatical strings in a language and their syntactic analysis is predicted. For the sake of illustration, let us compare how many grammatical statements are necessary in a simple phrase structure grammar and in Chomsky's (1992) Minimalist Program (see chapter 7) to capture the basic word order of an SVO language, and how many elements are overt in a simple sentence (thus, we ignore what shape the overt elements appear in, this would require additional statements in both). In a phrase structure grammar, a language learner will only postulate categories that can be filled by overt constituents, hence the problem of which of the elements listed in a rule are overt or covert does not arise. To capture the order of elements, typically no more than two rules will be necessary: S → NP VP and VP → V NP . . . In contrast, in a system like Chomsky's, the following decisions have to be made:

(236)
- Do Agr_S, T, Agr_O, and V precede or follow their complements?
- Do the specifiers of these heads precede or follow their sister?
- Are the head features of these heads weak or strong?
- Are the Spec features of these heads weak or strong?
- Is the functional head morpho-phonologically overt or covert?

The new descriptive devices thus bring with them many additional decisions to be made by the language learners, even in a system like

Chomsky's that involves only three functional heads of the many listed in (213) in an invariant order of embedding.

In light of this, recall that one of the motivations of the X-bar-theoretic program was the elimination of the stipulativeness of phrase structure grammars in favor of a few phrase structure parameters whose values could be acquired on the basis of simple and overt evidence. We have discussed in this chapter that the LGB system with its beautiful elegance seemed to come close to this ideal but that more and more evidence has been presented in recent years that it is too restrictive in many ways to be descriptively adequate. Functional head theory with its new devices holds the promise of overcoming these difficulties but at the same time brings into focus the tension between descriptive phrase structure parameters and explanatory adequacy more sharply than it has been since the problem was originally discussed in "Remarks on Nominalization." We hope that the proposals and considerations analyzed in this chapter will be helpful in deciding these vitally important questions in future syntactic research.

Related Material in Other Chapters

The reader may want to read this chapter in connection with topics in later chapters that are particularly closely related to the material covered here. Chapter 2 deals with *arguments* and the *Projection Principle* as well as the passive and raising constructions where the principles of Case theory play an important role. It also contains a discussion of *small clauses*. The treatment of *scope and locality constraints* at the level of Logical Form in chapter 3 touches on X-bar theory as well. Binding theory and *pro*-drop, discussed in chapter 4, are based on featural distinctions among different types of NPs and define wellformedness conditions on the NP types countenanced by the theory in terms derived from structural notions. Chapter 5, i.e. the treatment of the *Empty Category Principle,* intersects with X-bar theory due to the structural nature of *government* in GB theory. The current chapter was designed so that its content would be complemented by chapters 6 and 7 of the volume. The chapter on morphosyntax deals with X-bar and Case-theoretic aspects of the theory that pertain directly to morphology. It discusses *clitics, agreement, compounding,* and *derivational morphology*. Chapter 7, finally, discusses Chomsky's *Minimalist Program* and analyzes the functions of X-bar theory and Case theory in that latest version of the Principles and Parameters approach.

NOTES

1 Some topics that might fall under the rubric of X-bar theory and Case theory are discussed in other chapters and are not dealt with here in detail or not at all. These include small clauses (see chapter 2), passive morphology (see chapters 2 and 6), agreement (see chapter 6), double objects (see chapter 6) and Chomsky's Minimalist Program (see chapters 7 and 8).

2 At times Chomsky himself seemed sympathetic to this view, cf. Chomsky (1965, 158):

> we might raise the question whether the functions of the semantic component as described earlier should not be taken over, *in toto*, by the generative syntactic rules. More specifically, we may ask whether the cycle of interpretive rules that assign readings to higher nodes (larger constituents) of the underlying generalized Phrase-marker should not be made to apply before some of the syntactic rules, so that the distinction between the two components is, in effect obliterated . . . It is clear from this fragmentary and inconclusive discussion that the interrelation of semantic and syntactic rules is by no means a settled issue, and that there is quite a range of possibilities that deserve serious exploration.

See also in this connection the discussion in Chomsky (1965, 172ff).

3 The articles I am referring to are Chomsky (1970, 1972a, b). They have been published collectively as Chomsky (1972c). Other linguists who contributed arguments in favor of interpretive semantics that Chomsky refers to and cites in his papers include Jackendoff (e.g. (1969, 1972)) and Fodor (e.g. (1970)).

4 Wasow (1977) will later use a productivity argument of this sort to claim that there are two types of passive in English, a transformational and a lexical one.

5 In turn, many of the innovations of the generative semanticists became standard tools in the interpretivist conception, e.g. the use of referential indices and the concept that at the semantic level (or, in interpretivist terms, the semantically relevant syntactic level), quantificational expressions appear sentence-externally and are related to sentence-internal variables. Many of today's most hotly debated issues date back to observations by the generative semanticists as well, for instance, the crossover phenomenon discussed initially by Paul Postal. In fact, even abstract syntax made a reappearance which in retrospect has to be seen as an unlikely event given the powerful arguments that were marshaled against it in the early 1970s.

6 Also, it did not help that whereas Jackendoff (1977) postulates V as the head of S (like Marantz (1979)), LGB is committed to attributing that function to the category INFL (see in this connection Hornstein (1977)). Since INFL plays important roles in the treatment of subjects (tensed INFL assigns nominative Case, non-tensed INFL tolerates PRO as a subject, INFL interacts with subject *pro*-drop), this made Jackendoff's approach less desirable. Finally, whereas LGB favors a uniform two-level approach to X-bar theory, Jackendoff proposed a different system. All this drew attention away from his careful study. Alternatives to the standard X-bar system are also proposed in Muysken (1982). For further detailed discussion of these and related questions, see Bresnan (1977), Hornstein and Lightfoot (1981), Stuurman (1985), and Radford (1988).

7 In this connection, Baker (1979) was very influential in proposing a constraint against grammatical analyses that in order to be learned presuppose the ability of the language learner to conclude that sentences containing certain structures are

ungrammatical rather than being accidentally absent from the corpus of utterances they have been exposed to. The "no-negative-evidence" problem is further discussed in Wexler and Manzini (1987) and Manzini and Wexler (1987).

8 This organization of grammar is known as the *T-model* or the *Y-model,* due to the fact that the derivation splits after S-structure into the "LF branch" and the "PF-branch." Other organizations have been proposed, including the linear model of Riemsdijk and Williams (1981). Williams (1986) argues for a model that eliminates D-structure and LF in favor of a syntactic system made up of an "NP structure" and "S-structure."

9 See Chomsky (1972c, 160ff, n. 32). While in Chomsky's original system, P was not an X-bar theoretic head, Jackendoff (1977) and Riemsdijk (1978) argued for its incorporation. Webelhuth (1992, chapter 4) discusses the role of P in the categorial and percolation system in the light of the pied piping phenomenon. With the exception of the necessary condition that Case markers must be [−N], relatively little explanatory usage has been made of categorial cross-classification. Other categorial compositions have been proposed in Jackendoff (1977), Reuland (1986), and Holmberg (1986), but (24) remains dominant. See also the contributions to Muysken and Riemsdijk (1986).

10 The idea that the participants in the events denoted by predicators can be classified into a number of case roles dates back to the Sanskrit grammarians and was introduced into Generative Grammar in Gruber (1976), Fillmore (1968), and Jackendoff (1972). Since then it has played a role in one form or another in virtually every influential generative theory so that the references are too numerous to cite. For more on thematic roles, see chapter 2.

Given that there have always been controversies about the identification of theta roles across predicators and the development of a closed list of theta role names, some linguists have felt that syntactic rules and principles should not refer to names of theta roles (cf. for instance Hoekstra (1984)). The *theta criterion,* for example, does not depend on naming theta roles. Several theories in the literature depend on theta role names, however. For instance, at the core of Baker's (1988a) theory of incorporation lies a "Uniformity of Theta Assignment Hypothesis" (UTAH) which identifies specific phrase-structural configurations with individual theta role names. The association of the agent role with the subject function in active sentences found in Chomsky (1981, 10) is standard. Role names have also been invoked to restrict the type of argument that can appear in the prenominal genitive position in English (cf. Anderson (1979) and Rozwadowska (1988)) and to account for the choice of controller of PRO (cf. Růžička (1983), Nishigauchi (1984) and Culicover and Wilkins (1986)).

11 By convention, the external argument is underlined in theta grids. As will be seen in connection with passive, raising, and unaccusative verbs below, not every predicator must have an external argument. This is discussed in more detail in chapter 2.

12 See Jackendoff (1975) for further discussion. Grimshaw (1979) argues that subcategorized categories in lexical entries are largely predictable on the basis of *Canonical Structural Realization* rules, once the arguments of a predicator are also identified as denoting individuals vs. propositions, etc. For example, the patient of the verb *kill* in its literal meaning would denote an individual but that of *regret* would be a proposition. If individuals are canonically realized as NPs and propositions as either NPs or sentences, then the subcategorizational differences between the two verbs follow from their semantic differences. Pesetsky (1982b) went beyond Grimshaw's proposal and claimed that subcategorization can be eliminated

altogether. There are many empirical difficulties with this proposal, however. Webelhuth (1992, chapter 1), for instance, points to the impossibility of predicting the choice of prepositions in the head position of many complements on semantic grounds and the failure to predict the differences between the subcategorization frames of such semantically similar minimal groups as *eat/dine/devour* or *probable/likely*. The latter work proposes the use of canonical realization rules together with the marked option of categorially pre-specifying subcategorization frames that bleed the more general canonical rules in accordance with an elsewhere condition.

13 These associations only hold for basic lexical items and can be altered through lexical operations such as passive or dative shift. While LGB allows for such lexical function changes, other versions of GB which have become very influential in recent years do not, most notably those of Marantz (1984) and Baker (1988a).

14 In the early 1980s there was much hope that further aspects of the serialization system could be predicted on universal grounds. Stowell (1981), for instance, proposed that the adjacency of verbs and NP direct objects in English could be derived from an adjacency requirement on Case marking. This principle was dogged by many counterexamples, however, some of which Stowell himself pointed out (see Johnson (1991) for further discussion). More recent theories of Case marking that depend on Spec-head configurations make it very hard to derive the adjacency effect from Case theory. Koopman (1984) and Travis (1984) propose that Case markers should uniformly assign their Cases in the same direction which is plausibly the consequence of a markedness statement, since individual exceptions have been reported to this as well.

15 This system incorporates Kayne's (1984) assumption that all syntactic structure is at most binary-branching. Kayne's idea is now generally accepted, even though it is challenged by Carrier and Randall's (1992) powerful arguments for a ternary analysis of resultatives.

Attempts to find constraints on parameters have been made elsewhere. Thus, Borer (1984a), Manzini and Wexler (1987), Wexler and Manzini (1987), and Déprez (1990) countenance the "Lexical Learning Hypothesis" (actually also espoused in Webelhuth (1992)) which holds that all parameters are associated with lexical properties. Lebeaux (1988) and Ouhalla (1991) narrow the hypothesis to restrict all parametric variation to the properties of so-called "functional heads" which will be discussed in more detail later in this chapter.

Wexler and Manzini assume furthermore the "Subset Principle" which is actually not a principle of grammar but a learning principle that says that a learning theory orders parameter values according to a specific inclusion hierarchy.

16 It is also sometimes claimed that the relevant NPs behave like subjects with respect to certain movement constraints. These data are controversial, however, and we will not pursue this angle here.

17 Williams (1980) uses his theory of predication to account for why the accusative NP in (46)–(47) triggers binding-theoretic opacity effects. In his theory, the higher verb, the accusative NP, and the secondary predicate would all be sister constituents in a ternary branching tree. This allows the NP to act simultaneously as the object of the head verb and the external argument of the secondary predicate. Binding theory then makes reference to predication.

18 This issue has been debated among others in Rosenbaum (1967), Postal and Pullum (1988), and Authier (1991). Most of the examples in this section are taken from Postal and Pullum's paper which also contains references to the heated debate about the status of "raising to object." Postal has been a strong critic of the view that such raising does not exist, cf. Postal (1974). In Chomsky (1992), after almost

20 years, Chomsky has finally dropped his opposition and now also adopts the view that the accusative NP in ECM and small clause constructions raises into the higher clause (for reasons of Case).

19 Below we will discuss a proposal in Chomsky (1986b) that all expletives need to be "replaced" at LF by an argument. There might be a formulation of the projection principle that allows expletives to occur in complement positions as long as at LF the position is occupied by an argument associated with the expletive. The problematic examples in (54)–(56) would then be taken care of.

20 Rothstein (1983) proposes that the extended projection principle can be derived from a theory of syntactic predication. She views the category VP as syntactically incomplete and in need of saturation by an NP constituent, the subject.

21 Hence the slogan that passive morphology "absorbs" the external theta role of the verb. The post-LGB period has seen proposals that the external argument in passive is not absorbed but assigned to a constituent other than the subject, e.g. the passive affix itself (Jaeggli (1986)) or INFL (Baker, Johnson, and Roberts (1989), Baker (1988a)). See section 4 of chapter 6 for further discussion.

22 So-called "unaccusative" verbs, i.e. verbs analyzed as having surface subjects that appear as (direct) objects at D-structure, sometimes behave like passives but the data here are murky:

(i) *While John had been lying in the garden, there suddenly collapsed *a wall*
(ii) After it had been nice all day, there suddenly arose *a storm*

Both of these verbs have the thematic characteristics of unaccusative verbs. The distinction between "unergative" and "unaccusative" verbs was originally drawn within Relational Grammar in Perlmutter (1978) on the basis of empirical evidence from impersonal passives. Evidence from auxiliary selection, extraction, word order, and morphology has been adduced in favor of the distinction as well. Upon incorporation of the idea into GB in Burzio (1986), the class of "unaccusative" verbs was referred to as "ergative."

23 "Structural" Case marking refers to the assignment of nominative and accusative Case and excludes oblique Cases.

24 While Burzio's Generalization is quite successful in predicting which verbs can assign Case both within languages and cross-linguistically, there are exceptions and counterexamples as well. This suggests that it has the status of a markedness principle, as proposed in Marantz (1984). The English verb *object*, for instance, shows the following pattern:

(i) Mary objected [that the water did not have the right temperature]
(ii) Mary objected *(to) the temperature of the water

It assigns an internal theta role that can be realized as a sentence and a PP but not an NP. Yet, its theta grid contains an external theta role.

Exceptions in the other direction are found in languages where passivization does not "absorb" the objective Case of the verb, i.e. where the patient argument in passives appears in accusative Case even though the external argument has been removed. This phenomenon does not occur infrequently. Examples can be found in Sobin (1985), Baker (1988a) and in chapters 2 and 6 of this book.

25 This structure is actually problematic for (31), since it violates the endocentricity constraint of X-bar theory. Abney (1987) has proposed that in general noun phrases are headed by determiners and should be more properly referred to as determiner

phrases (DPs). Analyzing the possessive marker as a determiner allows gerunds to be analyzed as headed with the possessor appearing in a specifier position and a VP in the complement of the determiner. The DP hypothesis is now generally agreed upon, but it requires the postulation of many empty heads, e.g. in English plural indefinites or German possessive NPs like *Peters Buch "Peter's book"* without a syntactically separate possessive element.

26 In this connection, it is interesting to note that when PPs occur in subject position they require Case. Take the sentence *[$_{PP}$ Under the bed] is a good place to hide.* It can be embedded under the active verb *believe* (*I believe under the bed to be a good place to hide*) but not under its non-Case assigning passive counterpart: **It was believed under the bed to be a good place to hide.* Moving the PP into the main clause subject position which is Case-marked by Infl saves the latter structure: *Under the bed is believed to be a good place to hide.* It appears that PPs with NP meanings (*under the bed* could be replaced by *the location under the bed*) can appear in subject position and then fall under the Case-theoretic requirements for subject NPs. For further comments, see Chomsky (1986b, n. 122).

27 Empirical problems arise in this connection as well. Icelandic, for instance, allows its subjects to bear verb-governed oblique case and subject modifiers normally agree with them in case. There are examples where the modifier in control infinitives appears in an oblique case, strongly suggesting that the PRO of these clauses bears the morphological case as well; see Andrews (1982b, examples (66)–(67)). This would be excluded in principle under the LGB theory, however. See also, among others, Andrews (1976, 1982a, b), and Sigurðsson (1991).

28 Chomsky (1986b, 104) suggests that "PRO has an inherent Case," commenting that "this decision conceals a problem rather than solving it." Chomsky and Lasnik (1991) have recently taken a different approach to the licensing of PRO but it also requires a stipulation restricted to this one element.

29 This falls out from the assumption that the copula is an unaccusative verb that combines with a small clause complement. Not having an external argument, the verb is predicted not to assign Case by Burzio's Generalization. Recently, Belletti (1988a) has argued that unaccusative verbs are in general able to assign Case, in particular *partitive* Case which is classified as inherent and hence is exempt from Burzio's Generalization. Taking as a point of departure the restrictions on partitive NPs in Finnish (but see the caveats in her footnote 6), the author claims that universally all partitive NPs must be indefinite. Assuming that, among others, the copula, unaccusative and passive verbs are assignors of partitive, it is predicted that the relevant arguments typically must be indefinite; compare *There is a unicorn in the garden* with **There is the/every unicorn in the garden.* Many linguists find the proliferation of abstract Cases without widespread morphological realization bothersome, but the partitive Case idea has been adopted for example in Lasnik (1992) and Raposo and Uriagereka (1990). The latter authors suggest that the grammar should contain both the morphological and the thematic Case Filter, unlike Safir (1985b) and Borer (1986a) who favor the morphological version exclusively.

30 In the sixties and seventies, it was assumed that the relevant level is deep structure.

31 The notion of LF affix is not further explicated, i.e. it is not clear exactly what the complete set of properties is of these elements, which other expressions can change their status in such a way from one representation to the next, etc.

32 Perhaps this hypothesis should be restricted to cases where one of the agreeing elements is a verb. Otherwise there are apparent counterexamples: in a language

like German, adjectives and determiners agree with their head nouns and relative pronouns agree with the heads they modify.

33 For a typology of expletives, see Travis (1984). Important further work on expletives occurs in Safir (1985b) and Bennis (1986).

34 Chomsky (1986b, 212, n. 70) points out that expletive–argument pairs do not appear in one typical A-chain environment, namely raising across a clause boundary. Thus, even though we find *A unicorn seems [e to be in the garden]*, the expletive equivalent **There seems [a unicorn to be in the garden]* is ungrammatical. One approach to this problem has been to assume that the argument in the expletive–argument pair must be Case-marked independently of the expletive after all. In accordance with Belletti (1988a) the only Case that can be assigned by a raising verb would be partitive. Given that this Case is inherent and linked to theta-marking, the argument in the problematic sentence above does not qualify since it is not theta-marked by the raising verb.

35 In German, the expletive is usually assumed to occupy the topic position, cf. for instance den Besten (1983). Nevertheless, a nominative argument of the verb must be indefinite. The Icelandic expletive is presumably a subject. See Platzack (1983) and Rögnvaldsson (1984).

36 Webelhuth (1992, chapter 3) discusses sentences like (134) and what might be responsible for their ungrammaticality.

37 (137) is drawn from Belletti (1988a, 4).

38 Chomsky (1981) actually frequently toys with this idea but stops short of fully endorsing it.

39 For instance in Evers (1981), den Besten (1983), Koopman (1984), Haider (1986), Platzack (1986), Holmberg (1986), Diesing (1990), Webelhuth (1992), and the contributions to Haider and Prinzhorn (1986). Déprez (1990), however, argues for a positional system where only subjects use the specifier of Comp for *wh*-movement and other *wh*-extractions occur via adjunction to CP.

40 Thus den Besten's classical argument for postulating Comp as the landing site of verb movement in Germanic verb second clauses is based on the complementary distribution of overt complementizers and verbs in second position in these languages. Kayne (1983a), in contrast, assumes that fronted verbs can be adjoined to the sentence.

The complementarity between *wh*-movement, relative clause formation, and topicalization in the verb-second languages also is elegantly accounted for if all these constructions make use of the operator position and there is only a single such position.

On the other hand, not all languages display the required complementarity. Icelandic (see Zaenen (1985), Platzack (1986), and Holmberg (1986)) and Yiddish (see Diesing (1990)) show verb-second effects also in embedded contexts, i.e. in the presence of an overt complementizer. Various proposals have been made to account for this, among them the postulation of a recursive complementizer projection (for a recent proposal along these lines, see Iatridou and Kroch (1992)) and the assumption that verb-second movement is not always movement to Comp but instead to Infl (cf. Travis (1984), Diesing (1990)). For further discussion of these and related issues in several languages, see Reis (1985b), Scherpenisse (1986), den Besten and Moed-van Walraven (1986), Thráinsson (1986a, 1986b), Holmberg (1986), Platzack (1986), Santorini (1989), Rögnvaldsson and Thráinsson (1990), Vikner (1990), Vikner and Schwartz (1994), and references cited there.

41 Other early works in support of the DP hypothesis were Hellan (1986) and Bowers

(1987). For much further discussion, see Giorgi and Longobardi (1991) and references cited there.

42 The innovations about to be described are taken from Chomsky (1986b) which antedates the DP Hypothesis in Abney (1987). Nominals at this point are thus still assumed to be headed by nouns and analyzed as noun phrases.

43 These are the assumptions of the LGB Case assignment rules. Cf. Chomsky (1981, 170).

44 The "ACC-ing" version of this example is grammatical, however (as observed by Mark Baker): *There having been too much rain last year*... Here the expletive bears structural accusative Case. For further discussion and analysis of the various *-ing* constructions, see, among others, Reuland (1983) and Johnson (1988).

45 This and the next observation to be discussed were originally analyzed in Kayne (1984). In that theory it is the inability of nouns to govern across sentence boundaries that rules out the nominal equivalents to the verbal constructions. In (147), the noun cannot Case-mark the embedded subject because it cannot govern into the clause and in (149) it cannot properly govern the trace left by movement for the same reason and an ECP violation results.

46 That adjectives can assign Case had been argued for already by Riemsdijk (1983) on the basis of German and Platzack (1982/1983) with data from Swedish.

47 In Chomsky (1986b, 194) the statement of the condition is followed by the explanation that "Case-marking" in the definition includes Case-assignment and Case-realization.

48 The sentences are quoted from Andrews (1982b) and Zaenen, Maling, and Thráinsson (1985).

49 See Zaenen, Maling, and Thráinsson (1985) for much further systematic evidence that oblique NPs can be subjects in Icelandic. The same is argued for Hindi in Mohanan and Mohanan (1990).

50 Recall that the PRO theorem derives from the binding theory and the principles of that module apply at S-structure in the LGB framework (and to some extent at LF). PRO thus can be governed at D-structure and in passive infinitives it would be, cf. *John hates [PRO$_i$ to be interrupted t$_i$]* whose D-structure is *John hates [e to be interrupted PRO]*.

51 There is a huge literature on the problem of case marking and agreement in Icelandic that we lack the space to review in this chapter. See, among others, Andrews (1976, 1982a, 1982b), Thraínsson (1979), Marantz (1984, 1991), Zaenen, Maling, and Thráinsson (1985), Zaenen (1985), Holmberg (1986), Platzack and Holmberg (1989), Sigurðsson (1989), Ottósson (1989), Zaenen and Maling (1990). Of particular concern is that in certain sentences the properties that GB predicts to co-occur on one NP are borne by separate NPs, e.g. there are sentences with an oblique and a theme where the oblique appears in subject position and drops out in infinitives but the VP-internal theme bears nominative case and agrees with the main verb or auxiliaries. Also, in infinitives where the oblique is non-overt the theme may retain its nominative case, which is impossible under the standard assumption that neither verbs nor non-finite Infls assign nominative.

Frameworks like LFG that reject the notion of abstract Case and instead invoke principles for the distribution of morphological case that depend on grammatical functions rather than tree-geometric government provide relatively simple accounts of the Icelandic data. None of the many GB-based theories of this data that I have seen seem able to achieve the elegance of the LFG-based approach in Zaenen, Maling, and Thráinsson (1985).

Marantz (1991), discussing Icelandic and other similarly problematic languages, is led to the conclusion that abstract Case theory should be eliminated from GB and replaced by theories of positional licensing and morphological case realization respectively.

52 In fact, even in the SVO languages Icelandic (Zaenen (1985)) and Yiddish (Diesing (1990)) we find verb-second effects in embedded clauses with overt complementizers.

53 See Emonds (1980) for a detailed discussion of VSO languages against the background of Greenbergian word order universals. See also McCloskey (1979) and Hendrick (1988).

54 See also Koopman and Sportiche (1985, 1988). This section is based on the 1991 work because it is published in an easily accessible location.

55 This structure is reminiscent of two proposals relating to sentence structure in earlier versions of Generative Grammar. Fillmore (1968), a paper which led to *Case Grammar*, proposed that sentences are basically split into two parts, modality and proposition. The modality part can be roughly equated with Infl and the proposition with a complete thematic domain, which under the VISH would be dominated by the category VP. McCawly (1970a) proposed within *Generative Semantics* that English is underlyingly a VSO language.

56 Pronominal subjects trigger agreement in these languages, however. The authors refer to McCloskey and Hale's (1984) treatment of Irish which they take to be compatible with their assumptions.

In addition, the authors mention that in Arabic both SVO and VSO orders are found. They assume that Infl can assign Case either under specifier-head agreement or government. This predicts that subject–verb agreement is possible only in the SVO order. The authors claim that this expectation is fulfilled but the data actually do not bear this out. According to Benmamoun (1992, 116ff [and reconfirmed in a personal communication]) the correct generalization for Arabic is that when the verb precedes the subject, agreement is in gender and person; in the SVO order, agreement is in gender, person, and number. The Arabic data would thus actually be problematic for Koopman and Sportiche's theory. Aoun, Benmamoun, and Sportiche (1992) reconsider Arabic agreement in an interesting paper that concludes that the data is consistent with the view that "agreement is to be analyzed as a structural relation between a head and its specifier."

57 Sportiche mentions that quantifiers can marginally appear sentence-finally, which we will gloss over in our discussion.

58 In general, less attention is paid in GB and the Principles and Parameters framework to free than rigid word order languages although things have loosened up somewhat in the last few years. The interested reader may consult the following works and references cited therein to get a foothold in this arena. On Japanese: Saito and Hoji (1983), Farmer (1984), Saito (1985), Hoji (1985), Saito (1992); on Korean: Kim (1992), Lee (1993); on German: Haider (1981a, b, 1985), Thiersch (1982), Webelhuth (1984/5, 1987, 1990, 1992, 1993), Lee and Santorini (1990), Diesing (1992), and the papers in Grewendorf and Sternefeld (1990); on Hungarian: Horvath (1986), Kiss (1987), Marácz (1989); on Dutch: Haan (1979), Bennis and Hoekstra (1984/5), Koster (1987b); on Scandinavian: Holmberg (1986), Vikner (1990); on Bengali: Sengupta (1990). Also see the collection of papers in Marácz and Muysken (1989). This list is necessarily selective since there are now many more works on this topic.

59 See also Saito (1985) and Hoji (1985). While these authors relied mainly on binding-theoretic tests to show that certain "scrambled" word orders in Japanese behave as if they are derived by movement, Webelhuth (1990, 1992) tried to find

evidence from Ross-style movement constraints since those often yield stronger grammaticality judgments. The latter work establishes a catalog of altogether 14 diagnostics that show certain word orders in German to be subject to exactly the same conditions as *wh*-movement and hence to be a powerful argument for the movement analysis of the free word order phenomenon in this language. Saito (1992) points to Harada (1977) for similar evidence from Japanese.

60 According to the *Bijection Principle* of Koopman and Sportiche (1982/3). Other accounts of weak crossover are proposed in Safir (1984) and Reinhart (1983a) but they all lead to the same consequence for the matter at hand.

61 The "unrestricted" positions are also sometimes called "mixed" positions, hence the title of this section.

62 Saito (1992) and Rizzi (1994) recently have suggested the existence of A-bar positions without operator properties as well.

63 Pollock argues that *pas* and not *ne* is the counterpart of the English negation *not.* The morpheme *ne* is taken to be a clitic whose position is an unreliable indicator of the position of the negation. Hence all statements in this section concerning the behavior of negation in French should be interpreted as applying to *pas.*

64 This diacritic is usually applied in the theory of *pro*-drop (see chapter 4) but Pollock (1989, n. 47) appears to dispute its role there and instead claims it as a trigger for verb movement. Apparently, in Pollock's theory there is no requirement for any observable reflex of the "strength" of AGR or T in morphologically visible inflection. In contrast, Platzack and Holmberg (1989) and I. Roberts (1985) require overt person and number inflection for verb movement to the inflectional nodes.

65 "An X may only move into the Y which properly governs it."

66 Pollock's approach is open to several other criticisms. Recall that instead of referring directly to the auxiliaries *have/avoir* and *be/être* he claims that it is the thematic status of these items that sets them apart from main verbs in terms of verb movement to strong/weak AGR/Tense. (This idea is also pursued in Chomsky (1992).) We would thus expect that all non-thematic auxiliaries behave alike, but this is not the case as the copula *be* behaves differently from the copulas *become* and *remain.* Only the former shows the signs of moving out of the VP such as lack of *do*-support, participation in subject–auxiliary inversion, etc. If all copulas are non-thematic, as seems plausible, then no binary stipulation distinguishing between "weak" and "strong" inflectional heads is sufficient to classify those verbs correctly which do and don't move out of the VP.

Secondly, Pollock's statement that [–Tense] is universally a "weak" head that cannot support thematic verbs runs into potential counterexamples from the Germanic languages where both finite and non-finite verbs may appear on the same side of the negation. In Icelandic, for instance, both types may precede the negation under the right circumstances, in German and Dutch both follow (in subordinate clauses). It would thus appear that for Tense as well a strength parameter has to be invoked and that, as in the case of AGR, the setting of this parameter does not correlate with any observable morphological property of the head.

67 Reported in Benmamoun (1992, 167, n. 5).

68 Laka (1990) and Zanuttini (1991) also contain extensive discussion on negation and other sentence operators and their relationship to functional head theory.

69 See Baker (1988a). Different positions have been taken on the mechanism that combines stems and inflectional affixes (verb raising vs. affix lowering) and at what level of representation the relevant operation(s) apply (SS vs. PF). See Chomsky (1981) [in connection with "Rule R"], Pollock (1989), and Chomsky (1991). Chomsky (1992) assumes that no stray affixes can be generated in the syntax but that the

features of inflectional affixes still have to be checked via head movement of the head they are a part of. Such checking is allowed in the syntax but not in PF.

70 A similar argument for the existence of an object agreement phrase had previously been presented in Kayne (1989a) on the basis of French data.

71 Modulo a language-particular ban against adjunction to certain heads under short-distance Scrambling that the author imposes.

72 The Hindi data concerning binding and Scrambling is very controversial. Srivastav (to appear) claims that many important grammaticality judgments of Mahajan (1990) are not representative of what she refers to as the "majority dialect." She refers to similar reports in Jones (1993a, b). In Srivastav's view, for Hindi "a binary classification of movement types is insufficient" and "a third type of movement is needed to describe the phenomenon of scrambling" (pp. 24, 28).

There are dialects of Japanese without differences in weak crossover between short- and long-distance Scrambling (Saito (1992, n. 8) refers to Ueyama (1990)). Korean (Lee (1993) and Soon-Hyuck Park (personal communication)) and German fail to instantiate this difference as well. On the latter see Webelhuth (1993).

73 In fact, Rizzi (1994) postulates a structurally similar "Negative Criterion" which is exploited in the context of negative concord in Romance and Germanic in Haegeman and Zanuttini (1990).

74 Or some other positional typology, e.g. the difference between lexically related and non-lexically related heads discussed in Chomsky (1992) or the extent to which diacritical distinctions between "strong" and "weak" heads are necessary.

75 Positions on this have been taken among others in Lebeaux (1988) and Poeppel and Wexler (1993). See these works for further references.

2

Theta Theory

Edwin Williams
Princeton University

Contents

Prelude

In this chapter we turn our attention to predicates, argument structures, and arguments. It is discussed how the argument structure of a predicate might be determined and how the different arguments of a predicate are best distinguished, i.e. in terms of ordered argument lists (where arguments are individuated according to their position in the list) or "keywords" (which function as distinctive names like "Agent" and "Patient" for arguments). The keyword approach allows for the identification of argument types across different predicates whereas the former may or may not.

The chapter proceeds to a discussion of whether all arguments of a predicate must be obligatorily realized, an issue that is relevant for the relationship between lexical and syntactic properties which is largely defined by the *Projection Principle.* Issues that arise in that connection are whether certain arguments can remain unexpressed altogether or whether they must be represented structurally but in an invisible manner (through some empty category, e.g. *pro*).

The important question of the locality conditions of theta-role assignment is discussed next, together with the distinction between internal and external arguments. This discussion leads naturally to an analysis of the GB approach to passive and raising which are handled in terms of an interplay of conditions on argument structures and conditions on argument realization.

The chapter concludes by further discussing the relationship between argument structures and argument realization in connection with so-called *small clauses* and the interaction between theta theory and binding.

1 Introduction

Theta theory is the linguist's development of the intuitive logical notion of "argument of"; of the relation of *John* and *Mary* to *loves* in *John loves Mary*. In this chapter we review the structural conditions on the relation, on the representation of the *argument structure* of predicates, and the interaction of the conditions on argumenthood with the other parts of grammar, notably movement and binding.

On many important questions there is not unanimity, and so wherever appropriate we will outline alternative approaches to problems.

Since Panini, linguists have had some means of classifying or counting the relations a verb bears to its arguments. Fillmore's (1968) *case relations* and Gruber's (1965) *thematic relations* are the basis of the ideas in current theory.

2 What is an Argument?

The notion "argument" has an intuitively clear content, though the boundaries of the concept and the correct characterization are not only not agreed upon, but seldom discussed. *Love* is intuitively a two-place relation, taking two arguments, and *give*, three; but is *cut* a two-place relation, which can be modified by *with a knife*, or is *cut* a three-place relation with an optional instrumental argument? For that matter, is *love* a two-place relation which can be modified by a time adverbial, or is it a three- (or more) place relation with an optionally specified time element? These are difficult questions to answer in the abstract, though theory can force choices in particular cases.

For example, what can we make of the difference between (a) and (b) below?

(1a) *Where did you wonder [why John danced t]?
(1b) Who did you wonder [why John liked t]?

What is the difference between *where* and *who* that makes this difference? A possible answer is that *where* is not an argument of the embedded verb, and that *who* is. Difficult and vague questions are always sharpened and sometimes answered by considering how the subtheories within which they arise interact with other subtheories. For more on the relation of the "argument of" relation to syntactic movement, see chapters 3 and 5 of this handbook.

Since verbs apparently differ in the number of arguments that they require, some means of indicating this must be devised. The simplest means would be to assign to each lexical item a digit which represented its "adicity"; however, the evidence for some further structure will become apparent as we proceed. A delicate question is how the arguments are distinguished from each other. We have already used such terms as "patient" and "goal" and "dative," but their use was incidental, and their role in the theory remains to be determined. As a matter of fact, the core of theta theory can get by without the descriptive content that these labels come with; all that is required is a number of distinguishable items in a list ((a, b, c, d . . .)). The arguments must be distinguished – *John recommended Bill to Mary* does not mean the same as *John recommended Mary to Bill.* Clearly some sort of "realization conditions" distinguish the arguments from one another.

At a minimum, we might consider that each argument of each verb was annotated as to its realization conditions; for example, the *b* argument of *recommend* is annotated as "NP"; the *c* argument of *recommend* is annotated as "PP" headed by *to*, etc. This is obviously the worst case, failing to acknowledge the redundancies that hold here – goals are always realized by *to* in English, etc., and so some room for improvement, or perhaps even insight, remains. But for the discussion that is to follow, we will assume essentially what we have just outlined: that there are a number of distinguishable arguments, $A_1 \ldots A_n$, for each verb. This is "bare" theta theory. It is worthwhile to distinguish the proposals which can be embedded in "bare" theta theory, from those that cannot. The Theta Criterion itself, to be discussed shortly, can, but the original proposals of Gruber (1965) and Jackendoff (1972) (see below) cannot.

3 Obligatoriness and Locality

Although we speak of a Noun Phrase as "having a theta role" it is important to realize that the "argument of" relation is a relation, a relation between a verb and a Noun Phrase, and it is this relation that the theory characterizes, not the "having of a theta role." Three features of the relation stand out; first, the relation is "obligatory" in a couple of senses. Second, the relation is "unique" in a couple of senses. And third, the relation is structurally local, very local.

3.1 Obligatoriness

There are two senses of obligatoriness that are relevant here. First, an NP in a sentence must be an "argument of" some verb. There are obvious exceptions to this: vocatives, for example. There are more subtle exceptions, such as the "subjects" of pseudocleft constructions, or the topics of certain topicalization structures:

(2a) What John saw was Bill
(2b) Sakana wa tai ga ii
fish TOP red snapper NOM good
"As for fish, red snappers are good"
(Shibatani (1990))

The topic in (b) is not the argument of any verb, but it clearly fills a function in the sentence – it is the topic of the following comment. This obligatoriness probably reduces to such a requirement of "full interpretation" – every NP must have some business being in the sentence in the first place, and being an argument of a verb is one business.

The other "obligatory" aspect of the "argument of" relation is that at least in certain circumstances, there must be an NP to fill a certain "argument of" relation. As mentioned earlier, verbs take multiple arguments and some of these arguments are obligatorily specified:

(3a) John tried
(3b) *John attempted

It is not clear what the difference between (3a and b) amounts to, and we will outline a couple of alternatives below. But there is one circumstance in which there is no choice in the matter, namely, the subject argument:

(4) *(*It) hit Bill

The subject argument must be specified. Although the subject is sometimes inaudible, as in "*pro*-drop" languages, we will assume nevertheless that it is always present in S-structure; see chapter 4 for further details.

The non-subject arguments present a different picture. The two possibilities are first, that non-subject arguments are just like subject arguments, in that they are always obligatorily present, only sometimes inaudibly so; or second, that they are simply optionally specified. Both possibilities have been investigated – the first, in Rizzi (1986a), in a study of differences between English and Italian, as illustrated in the following:

(5a) *A serious doctor visits nude
(5b) Un dottore serio visita nudi
a doctor serious visits nude

Italian, but not English, seems to permit a direct object controller to be missing, although both languages permit direct objects in general to be missing, as idiosyncratically specified by particular verbs.

Rizzi's proposal is that the direct object is present always, but in Italian, as opposed to English, the direct object can be realized as "small *pro*," the same empty category that is used for missing subjects in *pro*-drop languages. The opposing idea, developed somewhat in Williams (1987a), is that these arguments are simply optional. The issue is complex, as there are some signal differences between missing subjects and objects, which makes an extension of a theory of the one to the other not straightforward. First, the interpretation is different: missing objects are interpreted as generic in some sense, whereas missing subjects are generally, though not always, interpreted as definite. Secondly, the missing objects must be directly arguments of the matrix verb, and not "subjects" of small clauses, but there is no corresponding thematic restriction on missing subjects. We leave the issue open, but for concreteness assume that these arguments are optional, and that verbs idiosyncratically specify whether their arguments are obligatory or not.

We are left then with a lopsided "theta criterion," which includes at least the following:

(6a) Every NP must get some sort of interpretation in the sentence, and bearing an "argument of" relation to some verb is one way.
(6b) The "subject argument" of every verb must be assigned to some NP.

Theta roles are also unique. An NP can receive only one theta role, and a theta role can be assigned to only one NP. For the purposes of counting, a chain consisting of an NP and a trace counts as a single NP; so the uniqueness requirement prevents the following:

(7) *John hit t

Where *John* is assigned the subject theta role of *hit*, and *t* is assigned the object theta role, rendering this as "John hit himself."

The original notions of obligatoriness and uniqueness are from Freidin (1978), whose **Functional Uniqueness** and **Functional Relatedness** principles required that every NP get at most one theta role, and that they get at least one. Chomsky (1981) added to this the requirement that every theta role be uniquely assigned, and dubbed the resulting principle the **Theta Criterion**. The principle (6) above is from Williams (1989).

3.2 Locality

The structural locality of the "argument of" relation is the tightest of all grammatical relations. It is essentially as tight as you can get – that is, immediate sister nodes may enter in the relation, and nothing else. So, for example, while there is a close parallel between Case marking and the "argument of" relation, there is no analogue of "exceptional Case marking" in the theta system; that is, there is no verb which can assign a theta role to the subject of an embedded clause:

(8) V $[_S$ NP VP]

The exact formulation depends on a couple of independent decisions about grammatical structure; we will here examine some alternatives. In this section we will examine the non-subject arguments.

Many verbs take more than one non-subject argument; *give*, for example, takes a theme and a goal argument (*John gave the money to Mary*). In one possible structure, these two arguments are both sisters of the verb:

(9) $[_{VP}$ give $[_{NP}$ the money] $[_{PP}$ to Mary]]

If this is the correct structure, the narrowest possible structural relation, strict sisterhood, can be imposed on the "argument of" relation:

(10)

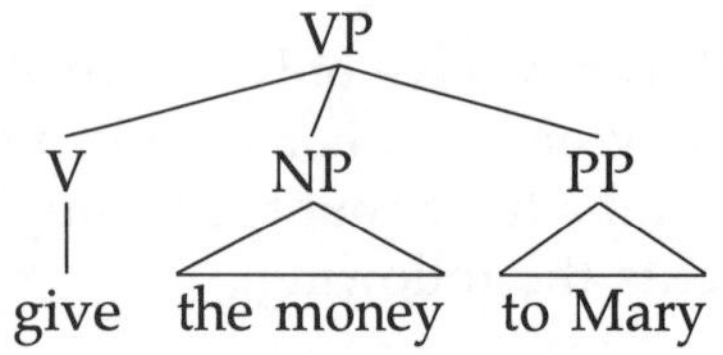

However, if one holds that phrase structure is strictly binary branching, then the VP must have a structure like that in (11). In such a structure, the first argument is a sister of the verb, but the second is not. Here, the notion of locality must be somewhat looser. Although sisterhood is not required, some other relation nearly as tight must be imposed. A likely candidate is *m-command*: a verb and its arguments must be dominated by all the same maximal projections (VP in (11)). Higginbotham (1987b) has introduced a notation and rule which captures just such a relation. In his conception, the verb's argument structure is passed up the X-bar projection. At any level, the "argument of" relation can hold between the projection at that level and one of its sisters. This gives exactly the effect of m-command, since every non-head in the projection is the sister of one of the projections of the lexical head:

(11)

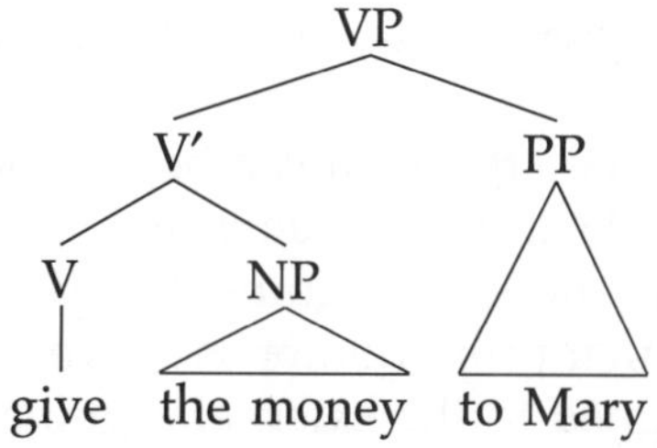

Either assumption – strict sisterhood or binary branching – will suffice for the discussion that follows.

A different sort of challenge to locality comes from a closer consideration of the prepositional phrase *to Mary* in (11) – if *Mary* is the argument of the verb *give* in (9) (or in (11)), then we have a case of an argument that is not a sister to (a projection of) the verb. On the other hand, if *to Mary* is the argument of the verb, then no such problem arises. The question is, is there any reason to consider one or the other of these the argument of the verb? Clearly, at this point, we would prefer to consider the PP the argument, just to preserve the notion of locality. There are in fact some important generalizations at stake, and sorting out the possibilities is a delicate matter we will take up in section 5.

4 The External Argument

The subject argument has a special status. It is not a sister of the verb, but is in fact a sister of the maximal projection of the verb. For this reason, we may call this argument the "external argument" of the verb – it is located external to the maximal projection of the verb, whereas the other arguments are internal to the verb. Underlining is used to indicate this argument in the list of a maximal projection of the verb's arguments:

(12) give (<u>A</u>, B, C)

The external argument has a further distinction – there can be only one external argument, whereas there can be an indeterminate number of internal arguments.

The external argument of the verb is not "local" to the verb, since it is outside of its maximal projection; however, there is still a locality restriction – namely, the external argument of the verb must be a sister of the maximal projection of the verb. Thus, for example, a verb cannot take as its subject the object of a higher clause, since this condition would not be met.

The locality restriction on the external argument can be rationalized by viewing the external argument as bearing the same relation to the maximal projection of the verb as the internal arguments bear to the verb itself. This means that the maximal projection of the verb bears a theta role, and that theta role is assigned to the external argument. So the maximal projection of the verb is a predicate, in fact a one-place predicate. The theta role it assigns is the external theta role of the verb which is its head.

One way to implement this idea – the idea that the VP is a one-place predicate based on the external argument of its head verb – is to assign to the VP an operator that binds an argument of the head V, like a lambda operator. Since there can be no more than one such operator (there is never more than one argument outside the VP) we would want a non-recursive operator. If we assume that every maximal projection can have exactly one index – the referential index of referential expressions – we may use this index as the operator, as follows:

(13)

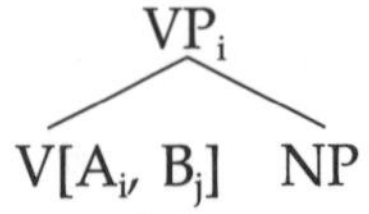

The coindexation of the VP and the *A* argument of the V indicates that the VP is a one-place predicate by virtue of binding the A role of the head verb. The VP, interpreted now as a one-place predicate, can now bear the "argument of" relation to an NP, the subject.

The theory just outlined is a theory of the "subject of" relation. It proposes that the "subject of" relation has two components; first, there is the binding of the external argument of the head by the index on the projection of the head; and second, there is the ordinary "argument of" relation holding between the projection of the predicate and an NP. The second relation is already familiar; the first, however, requires some further specification.

In fact, the second relation can be seen as a derivative of the notion of head in X-bar theory. The binding of the external argument of the verb by the maximal projection is simply the (X-bar) projection of the index of the external argument:

(14)

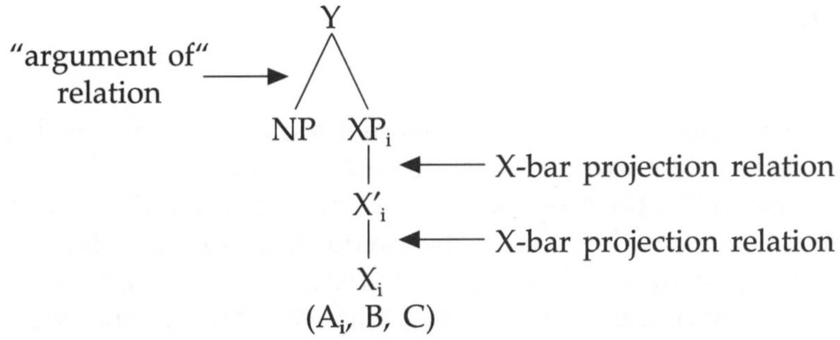

In fact, we may explain why it is the index of the external argument which percolates if we assume further that the argument structure itself has an X-bar structure with a head and non-head component, with the external argument in head position and the rest of the arguments as non-head. Since X-bar projection is "local" in that it relates only immediate constituents in a tree, the "subject of" relation, while it appears non-local, is actually composed of linking relations each of which is as local as any relation can be: the "argument of" relation, and the X-bar projection relation.

Any major category, not just verbs, can project a predicative expression, as we see in the following absolutive constructions:

(15a) With John happy . . .
(15b) With John a judge . . .
(15c) With John in the Netherlands . . .

In particular note that a noun like *judge* must have at least one argument, an external argument, which ultimately is assigned to *John* in (b). Since this argument is not one of the usual verbal arguments (agent, theme, etc.,) this nominal external argument is designated *R*, so *judge* is represented as (a), and the projected NP as in (b):

(16a) judge (R̲) (16b) $[_{NP\text{-}i}$ a judge]

Hence, every category has external arguments. What happens to the external argument when a lexical item does not project a one-place predicate, as in the "normal" referential use of nouns? Why is there not a Theta Criterion violation, since the external argument is apparently unassigned? This issue can be clarified by comparing the two possible uses of the same NP, one predicative and the other referential. A noun like *father* has two arguments, the parent argument and the child argument ("x is the father of y"), and is clearly asymmetric:

(17) father
(P, C)

The parent argument (P) is the external argument, since, in *John is a father, John* is described as a parent, not a child. Now, when *father* is used referentially, the reference is to the parent end of the parent–child relation, just as in the case of the predicative use. Clearly, then, the external argument, which defines the predicative use, is involved in the referential use of the projected phrase as well. This is what we would expect, if the syntax of the two uses is identical: in both cases, the external argument of the head is bound by the dominating maximal projection.

So, when one says, *I saw a father,* one is saying that one has seen an individual on the parent end of the parent–child relationship. In logic, this might be expressed as,

for some x, I saw x and father(x,y)

In other words, the external argument of the head noun is *bound to* an argument of the verb. In our X-bar notation, we will indicate this by coindexation:

(18)

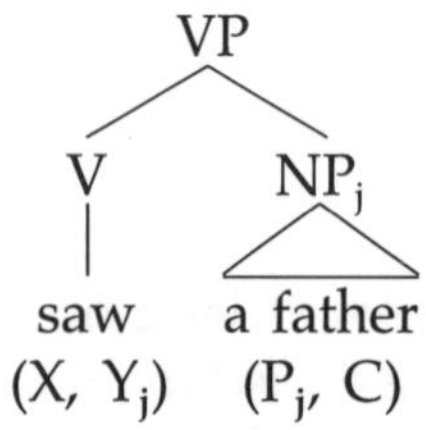

Here, the *j* index of the *P* argument of *father* ascends to the top of the NP by X-bar theory; the NP is coindexed with the *Y* argument of *saw*; and thereby the external argument of *father* winds up coindexed with the Y argument of *saw*.

Now, the scheme just outlined is one means of achieving the locality of theta role assignment. There are some related proposals that differ in details.

The first concerns the notion "external argument." In the conception here, the external argument is an absolute thing – something is it, or is not. In the work of some, notably Grimshaw (1990) and Higginbotham (1987b), the notion "external" is a relative notion. In their conception, the arguments form a hierarchy, and any given argument is "more external" or "less external" than another. The entire argument structure is inherited at each X-bar level, with saturation occurring under a sisterhood condition (the following is based on Higginbotham's notation, where the asterisk indicates saturation):

(19)

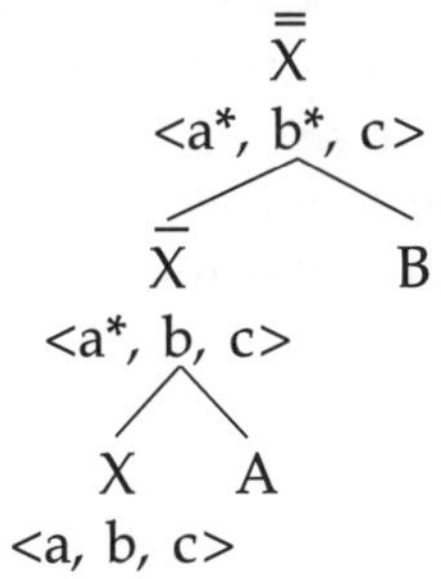

Of course, in their conception, there is still a "most external" argument, and it coincides with the external argument in the sense defined here. Differences arise in the definition of forms with no external argument, to be discussed in the next section. Another difference is that in principle such theories permit more than one external argument. If the argument structure of the head is inherited by the maximal projection with more than one unsaturated argument, then that phrase is not a one-place property.

A somewhat different theory of the subject argument is the "VP internal subject hypothesis" (Koopman and Sportiche (1988)). Under this hypothesis, the subject argument is generated internal to the VP in D-structure. It is then moved, either obligatorily or optionally, depending on the theory and on the construction, to the VP external subject position, the SPEC of IP:

(20)

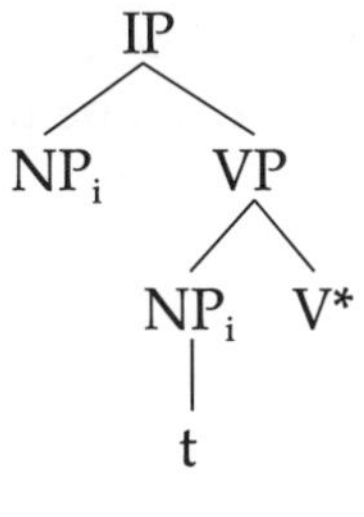

The advantage of this theory is that it reduces the theory of the subject argument to the theory of NP movement. The subject, like all of the other arguments, is generated in a VP-internal position, and is assigned under sisterhood, or, with binary branching, under m-command. The relation of the S-structure subject to the verb is thus a compound of internal theta role assignment and NP movement.

We will not explore these alternatives, but will continue to develop our main line. The differences in prediction are surprisingly subtle.

The above-mentioned theories are theories in which *all* subjects are generated in VP-internal subject position. Besides these, there are a number of proposals that the subjects of *some* verbs are generated in VP-internal position, specifically, in object position. This has been proposed for "psych" predicates, and for "unaccusative" verbs.

The principal reason to generate the surface subject of "psych" predicates in VP-internal position has to do with the following sort of binding facts:

(21) Pictures of himself$_i$ [$_{VP}$ frightened John$_i$]

Here, because it is contained in the VP, *John* does not c-command the reflexive. However, if the following were the structure, as proposed by Belletti and Rizzi (1988), then of course c-command holds:

(22) NP [$_{VP}$ frightened John pictures of himself]

NP movement is then required to move the object *John* to surface subject position. This solution is not without problems, since it is required that the binding be established before NP movement, a questionable stipulation, as it is known from other facts that binding theory applies to the output of NP movement.

A related sort of case, but with somewhat stronger evidence and theoretically sounder analysis, are the "unaccusative" intransitive motion (and some other) verbs (*go*, etc.). Here the evidence is from Romance (e.g. Burzio (1986)), where a number of phenomena point to a VP-internal position for the surface subject of these predicates. Particularly revealing is the behavior of the partitive clitic *ne* in Italian or *en* in French. The general feature of this clitic is that it can be moved from objects, but not from subjects:

(23a) *Trois en ont vu Pierre
"Three of them saw Pierre"
(23b) Pierre en a vu trois
"Pierre saw three of them"

This applies to a variety of intransitive subjects as well:

(24) *Trois en ont téléfoné
"Three of them telephoned"

However, with the special class of motion verbs, the *en* clitic is moved from subject position:

(25) "Trois en est arrivés"
Three of them arrived

In other words, the surface subjects of these verbs are acting like the objects of other verbs. One way to capture this is to assume that these verbs take their subjects as deep structure objects, and that NP movement moves the objects to subject position. In order for this to explain the phenomena just illustrated, it is necessary that the distribution of *en* be determined prior to NP movement, or that the trace of NP movement play a role in determining the wellformedness of *en* moved from surface subject. See Burzio for an exploration of the possibilities.

5 Passive and Raising

The analysis of passive and raising structures involves theta theory in a direct way; just how is a matter of debate. We will examine two theories of this interaction, the NP movement theory and the "relative head" theory of these constructions.

The theory of these constructions must respond to the following questions which arise more or less independent of theory, but we will assume for the moment that in these constructions the postverbal NP moves to the subject position, for the purpose of stating the questions:

1 Why is it possible for the object to move to the subject?
2 Why is it necessary for the object to move to the subject?
3 Why does (can) the subject move to the *by* phrase, and why is it a prepositional phrase?
4 Why is a form of the verb *to be* inserted?
5 Why can a preposition optionally intervene between the verb and the object?
6 Why is there an affix on the verb?
7 Why are there strict locality conditions on the rule?
8 Why are only subject and object involved?

Some of these questions are answered by theta theory and the interaction of theta theory and the rest of the grammar.

We will begin with the aspects of the analysis that the two theories have in common. The passive and raising constructions are characterized by two properties: first, the theta role that is normally assigned to the subject is not assigned to the subject; second, the direct object, if there is one, does not get Case. The consequences of these two features are the constellation of derivative properties that is associated with the raising and passive constructions. Just how these derivative properties flow from the fundamental two properties of Case and theta role assignment is how the two views differ.

The lexical entry for the passive and raising verbs is different from the entry of ordinary active verbs. If the representation of the active verb is as in (a), then the passive verb is as in (b):

(26a) saw ($\underline{A}$, B)
(26b) seen (A, B)

That is, the external argument, indicated by underlining, has been internalized, and must be expressed internal to the VP. The verb in fact has no external argument. Similarly for the raising verb.

The second aspect of these constructions is the absence of accusative Case for the direct object. This too is a lexical property of the governing verb, and plays a crucial role in determining the forms of the passive and raising constructions. We will assume the absence, but will not focus on it, as it is treated in chapter 1.

First we will treat the movement theory of these constructions. The properties of the typical passive construction follow from the retraction of accusative Case and subject theta role in the following way. The direct object will fail to be licensed by the verb, since the verb cannot assign it Case. Therefore, the structure in (27) is ungrammatical:

(27) NP . . . [$_{VP}$ seen [$_{NP}$ the boy]]

However, the object can move to the subject position, where it will get Case from the inflectional system of the matrix S:

(28) The boy . . . [$_{VP}$ seen t]

The movement is not permitted for transitive verbs; for transitive verbs, the theta criterion will be violated, as the resulting S-structure would assign two theta roles to the same NP (the *A* theta role to *John,* and the *B* theta role to the trace of *John,* which is the same as assignment to *John*):

(29) John [saw t]
(A̲,B)

Thus, it is only in the special case of the passive verbs, which have no external argument, that the movement is possible. In sum, then, the movement in (28) is made necessary by the absence of accusative Case, and is made possible by the absence of a subject theta role. Thus the passive construction is explicated by Case theory and theta theory jointly. And since movement is involved, movement theory will limit the possible kinds of passives that are available as well.

In fact, as we will see in the following, it is the internalization of the subject theta role that is most fundamental, and the absence of Case that characterizes the English passive is not universal.

As we noted, the passive morpheme induces two changes in the verb to which it attaches: internalization of the subject theta role, and removal of the Case-assigning property of the verb. A strong confirmation of the correctness of the views outlined would be the discovery of circumstances in which one or the other of the induced changes was isolated. Now, suppose that the verb did not have the Case-assigning property in the first place. Then, the sole change in the outcome would be the internalization of the subject argument.

The simplest example is the passive of an intransitive, which English does not have, but which is attested in other languages, for example German:

(30a) Hans fragte ob getanzt wurde
Hans asked whether danced was
"Hans asked whether there was dancing"
(30b) Gestern wurde getanzt
yesterday was danced
"Yesterday there was dancing"
(30c) Es wurde getanzt
it was danced
"There was dancing"

Here there is no object, and the subject position is left empty; the adverb in (b) and the expletive in (c) are both in Topic position (see den Besten (1981)). In each of these constructions, the subject position is not associated with any theta role.

English lacks this possibility, as the passive morpheme is restricted to transitive verbs, a restriction which the German cases show is not intrinsic to the change induced by the morpheme.

The passive morpheme in French likewise does not require a direct object, although it does require a complement of some kind, thereby falling somewhere between English and German; if that complement is not a direct object, then it will not require Case, and will not move; again, as in German, the subject will in such a case be filled with an expletive:

(31) Il a été tiré sur le bateau (French)
**it was fired upon the boat*
from: NP a tiré sur le bateau

So far, we have looked at cases where the direct object needed a Case from the verb, or where there was no direct object. Imagine a case where there is a direct object, it needs a Case, but can get it from somewhere other than from the verb; in that kind of case again we might expect a passive where nothing moves. This we find in Spanish (from Jaeggli (1986)):

(32) En la fiesta fue presentada (*a) Maria por su padre
at the party was presented Maria by her father
"Maria was presented by her father at the party"

Here the direct object *Maria* has not moved. The verb does not assign accusative Case, but Spanish has a means of assigning nominative Case inside the VP, which English lacks. That *Maria* is marked as nominative can be seen from the fact that it does not take the usual *a* prefix for accusative animates. And finally in English there is a set of cases in which the "direct object" does not have to move: when it is an S:

(33) It was reasoned that Bill had left

If S does not need Case, it can stay in the VP.

This brief survey isolates the "retraction of the theta role from subject position" as an atomic element in the passive and raising constructions, common to all of the constructions considered. We have seen that no two languages are the same in the details of the passive construction. Part of the variation can be located in the restrictions on the attachment of the passive morpheme: in English, it attaches only to verbs with direct complements (NP or S); in French, it attaches only to verbs with some sort of complement; and in German, it attaches to any verb with an external argument.

There is one obvious case we have not considered: suppose that the passive morpheme retracted the theta role from the subject, but did not alter the verb's accusative Case-assigning property. Then we would expect a passive like:

(34) *(It) was eaten the meat by John

where the subject was internalized, but the direct object remained in place, and received accusative Case. Not only does such a case not exist in English, but not in general, though this is not understood. It does though seem to be part of a slightly broader pattern, known as Burzio's Generalization: a verb which does not assign an external theta role cannot assign accusative Case.

It appears though, that Russian has a construction, the impersonal passive construction, which has just the form of (34):

(35) It was hit John(acc)
(L. Babby, pers. comm.)

If this is indeed the correct analysis, then Burzio's Generalization is in fact false; it remains to be explained, however, why such passives are quite rare.

In the preceding discussion, we have assumed that the passive and raising constructions were derived by syntactic movement. However, an articulation of the method of theta role assignment provides an alternative. At issue is not really whether there is "movement" or not, but rather how the locality and other properties of the relation are to be explained. The movement theory says that at least some of the properties derive from the general theory of movement, i.e. the theory of *wh*-movement; the alternative to be outlined below suggests rather that theta theory determines these properties.

Consider the "small clause" raising construction, below:

(36) John seems sad

At a minimum, one wants it to come out that (a) *John* is an argument of *sad*, and (b) *John* is an argument of *seems sad. Seems* itself has no external argument; hence, *seems sad* is a one-place predicate by virtue of the fact that it contains the one-place predicate *sad*. This is reminiscent of the fact that an ordinary VP is a one place predicate by virtue of the fact that it dominates a verb with an external argument. What is needed is a means of "transferring" the external argument of *sad* to the VP *seems sad*.

One means of achieving this transferral is the same means by which the external argument is "transferred," that is by feature percolation provided by the definitions of X-bar theory. However, in this case at hand, the source of the external argument, *sad*, is not the head of *seems sad*, so the normal X-bar theory does not work. But a modification in the definition of head will achieve the result: in the special circumstance where the head of a phrase is not marked for a category, we might let the phrase take its marking from the non-head. Since *seems* itself has no external argument, then the external argument of its complement will, under this arrangement, become the external argument of the whole under the definition of Relativized Head (Williams (1982b), Di Sciullo and Williams (1987), Williams (1994)):

(37) $[_{VP\text{-}i}$ seems sad$_i$]

In a sense, *sad* is the head of the VP *seems sad* for the purpose of determining the external argument, while *seems* is the head for all other purposes. Since a head is a head only with respect to a given feature or marking or category, we will refer to such-and-such as the "head-wrt-X," and to the theory that incorporates this principle as the "Relative Head" theory.

This mechanism just outlined can of course be extended to cover all cases of NP movement to subject position. So, for example, suppose we give a passive VP the following representation:

(38) $[_{VP\text{-}i}$ seen t_i]
(A, B_i)

The *B* argument is assigned to the trace, so the trace "has" this argument. The trace cannot satisfy this argument; however, the argument can be bound by the VP, because the head of the VP does not have an external argument. So the "trace" is the head with respect to the external argument. How the trace got there is of little consequence at this point – just to emphasize what is important, suppose we say that it was movement. The matter of importance is how to explain the locality of NP movement: is it via the theory developed to explain *wh*-movement phenomena, or is it via the theory developed to explain theta role assignment? The "relativized head" theory of raising and passive constructions explains directly why the moved NP can never be extracted from a phrase which contains a head with an external argument, but can be extracted from indefinitely many phrases which do not.

So, for example, if *not* heads a phrase, with VP as its complement, it is transparent to raising, since *not* lacks an external argument.

The same mechanism can be used to solve the problem that PPs pose for the locality of the assignment of theta-roles posed earlier. There, the problem was that a layer of structure, the PP, seemed to intervene between a verb and one of its arguments:

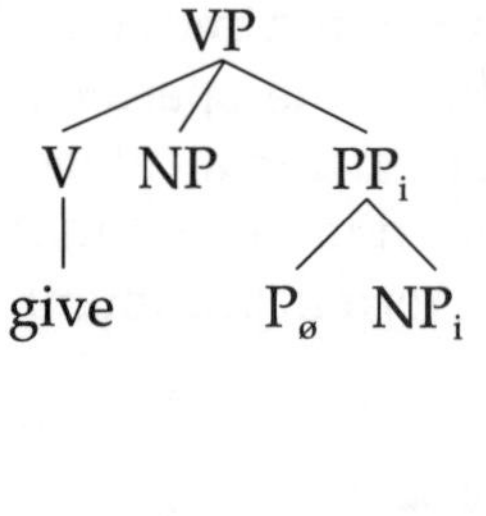

But, as this diagram illustrates, suppose that the P itself did not have an external argument; then the argument of the NP could be passed up to the PP, where it is available for assignment to the GOAL argument of the V in a completely local way.

6 Small Clauses

We have so far ignored an important controversy, the controversy surrounding the notion of "small clause." If the generalized "small clause" theory is correct, then the environments of predication may well reduce to a single one, clausal predication, $[\text{NP VP}]_S$.

The issue is not whether there are "small clauses." Jespersen settled that issue in (1924) when he observed the *nexus of deprecation,* as illustrated below:

(39) Me dance? [How ridiculous]
Jespersen (1924, 130)

Here we have a clause with no tense, no agreement, just a subject and a predicate.

The issue is rather what is stated above: do all cases of predication reduce to clausal structures?

6.1 *The Projection Principle and the Theta Criterion*

The small clause hypothesis says that there is only one instance of predication, and that is in some clausal structure YP. All others reduce to this.

(40) $[_{\text{YP}}$ NP XP]

So, for example, the complement to *consider* cannot be (a), but must be (b), for some YP:

(41a) John [considers Bill silly]
(41b) John [considers $[_{\text{YP}}$ Bill silly]]

Why would the small clause hypothesis be true? Chomsky (1981, 29–30) pins it on what he calls the Extended Projection Hypothesis. The Projection Principle insists that lexical properties be satisfied in the same way at all levels of representation: DS, SS, LF. Given this, and given that *seems,* for example, is a monadic predicate taking a propositional argument (as (c) suggests), Chomsky argues that (a) must be represented as (b):

(42a) John seems sad
(42b) John [seems [t sad]]
(42c) It seems that John is sad
(42d) John [$_{VP}$ seems sad]

His argument rests on a notion of uniformity across different uses of a lexical item: if (d) is the correct S-structure analysis, and not (b), then *seems* in this usage must be dyadic in S-structure, and with a new strange notion of S-structure argument, such that *John* and *sad* wind up in LF as a single argument, violating the projection principle (p. 106).

I think though that the notion of Relativized Head we have developed here will permit the uniformity that Chomsky seeks and permit (d) to be the correct structure. *Seems* is a propositional operator; in the case where the proposition is closed, as in (c), the result of adding *seems* to it is closed as well; however, when the propositional element is open, that is, when it is a one-place predicate, such as *sad,* then the result of applying *seems* to it will be open as well. In other words, *seems* uniformly applies to propositional objects, and preserves their state of closure.

Under this view, there is then no need to construct a proposition *John sad* in the LF of (a). It is enough to derive the complex property, *seem sad* and apply it to *John*.

Chomsky (1981) eliminates structures like (3a) in another way; he suggests that they violate not only the Projection Principle, but also a principle which says that if an item is in the VP then it is assigned a theta role by the verb ("subcategorization entails theta-marking," pp. 39–40). This would require that *Bill* in (41a) receive a theta role from *consider,* which it clearly doesn't. This would leave only (41b) as an admissible structure.

Such a principle meets some difficulty in adjunct modifiers of direct objects, since, by ordinary tests, these are in the VP, and they are not assigned theta roles by the verb:

(43a) and [eat the meat raw] he did t
(43b) *and [eat the meat] he did t raw

(43) is an example of VP fronting, which clearly indicates that the adjunct modifier *raw* is in the VP, but it is not assigned a theta role by *eat*.

6.2 *Opacity*

The debate about small clauses boils down to whether predication is syntactically "trivial," in that it is always a reflex of something else, specifically, the configuration $[NP\ VP]_S$. Some subject opacity effects we will look at in this section bear on the issue.

In Williams (1980) it was proposed that the opacity ordinarily attributed to subjects was actually a fact about 1-place XP predicates:

(44a) Predicate Opacity Condition (POC) : α cannot occur free in XP, if XP is a predicate.
(44b) $John_i$ considers $Mary_k$ [mad at $himself_{*i/*k}$]
(44c) $John_i$ considers $Mary_k$ [mad at $herself_{*i/k}$]

When the reflexive is contained in a VP and not bound within it or by it, it violates the POC. In the special case when it is related to the subject of the predicate, it will be bound by the index on the predicate itself, and thus not be free in it. For almost all cases, this matches the ordinary Subject Opacity Condition (as in Chomsky (1973), or principle A of the Binding Theory of Chomsky (1981)).

Under the POC subject-bound reflexives can occur in a predicative XP if they are bound to the subject that the XP is predicated of, because they will then be coindexed with the predicative XP itself, and that counts as being bound in the XP, since the external argument index on VP is a binder:

(45) John $[_{VP\text{-}i}$ saw $himself_i$]

Here, *himself* is bound in VP because it is coindexed with VP. It should be easy to see why the Predicate Opacity Condition matches the Subject Opacity Condition so closely in empirical prediction: wherever there is a subject, there is a predicate. So it might seem difficult to distinguish the two ideas.

Recently, though, some evidence favoring the Predicate Opacity Condition has come to light. The difference between the following pair, observed by D. Lebeaux (personal communication) and K. Johnson, follows from the Predicate Opacity Condition, but not from the Subject Opacity Condition:

(46a) $John_i$ wondered [which picture of $himself_i$] Mary would like
(46b) *John wondered $[_{AP\text{-}i}$ how mad at $himself_i$] $Mary_i$ would be

In the (a) case, the reflexive occurs in no predicative XPs except the one predicated of its antecedent, so the reflexive satisfies the POC; in (46b), however, the reflexive occurs in the AP predicated of *Mary* and so must be bound in that AP; coindexation of the reflexive with the AP would satisfy the POC but would give the wrong meaning, for then the reflexive would be bound by *Mary*. So the POC correctly discriminates between the two cases, the important difference being that the *wh*-fronted XP is not predicative in the (a) example, but in the (b) case it is.

The Subject Opacity Condition cannot discriminate these – in both cases, the reflexive has been moved out of the domain of the subject. It is not clear what prediction the Subject Opacity Condition makes here – it depends on whether it applies to the pre- or post-*wh*-movement structure – but whatever the prediction, it should be the same for the two cases, and so incorrect for one.

The subject opacity condition can mimic the effect of the POC by including a "subject" inside the AP; this subject – clearly not the surface subject – can then induce opacity effects. In (b), we would have:

(47) *John$_k$ wondered [$_{AP}$ t$_k$ how mad at himself] Mary$_i$ would be

Since the surface subject is not in the AP subject position, movement must have taken place – hence, the trace. The opacity effect can be attributed to the trace.

We have here one of the "VP-internal subject" theories – theories in which subjects are in VP in D-structure. These subject theories overlap in motivation and mechanism with small clause theories. In connection with the present topic, one danger in the VP-internal subject theories is that the VP-internal subject must be endowed with all the same properties as the VP-external subject, and so one winds up reconstructing the clause inside of the VP, with no gain. Such is the case here, where the VP-internal subject is not simply another verbal argument, but has the opacity-inducing effects of a VP-external subject, including *derived* VP-external subjects, such as the subjects of passives. So both positions have this property.

I believe that there is no version of these theories that answers to all that they must. In this version, essentially Stowell's (1983), the category of the predicate matches the category of the predicate it dominates. Paradox arises when one attempts to determine the internal structure of the small clause. The question is, is the predicate of the small clause a maximal projection or not?

If we look at the *consider* complement, alleged to be clausal, it would seem that the predicate is a maximal projection, since it is frontable, without its subject, by *wh*-movement:

(48) [How tall] do you consider John

But in order for (47) to work, the predicate cannot be a maximal projection, for if it were, then we could derive (22):

(49) *$John_k$ wondered $[_{A?P}$ how mad at himself] $Mary_i$ would be $[_{A?P}\ t_k$ –]

Here, the predicate has been fronted, leaving behind the trace; but this should lead to a canceling of the opacity effect, just as in (46a), but it does not.

In sum, in one kind of structure, the predicate is a maximal projection, and in another, it is not.

One could perhaps evade paradox by analyzing the *consider* complement as consisting of two subject positions, one inside of an AP, and another higher subject, in some category different from AP:

(50)

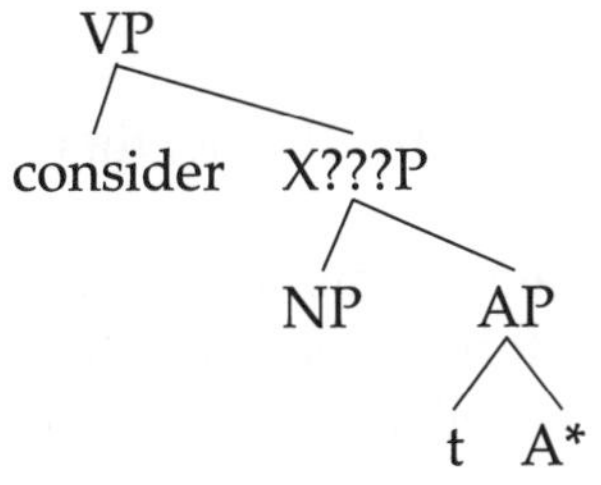

In this theory, A* is not a maximal projection, that is, not frontable without it. This theory maintains a distinction between XP internal subjects (the *t* in AP in (50)) and small clause subjects (the NP under X???P). There are a couple of problems with this theory. First, nothing forces the extra layer of structure (X???P), since AP is in fact already propositionally closed. Second, X???P, since it is categorically different from AP, and must be, will prevent selection of the type of the predicate, but such selection does take place:

(51) *I consider John in the garden

Again, I believe we have a paradox: selection suggests that some projection of AP is directly the argument of *consider*; on the other hand, the opacity facts suggest that there must be some category different from AP intervening between the verb and the maximal projection of AP.

7 Theta Theory and Binding Theory

Theta roles have been implicated in binding theory since the beginning. The question remains open, however, just what the relation is. In this section we will explore some of the possibilities.

Jackendoff (1972) showed that theta roles determined in part the wellformedness of anaphoric relations. In his conception, theta roles form a hierarchy, and binding must respect the hierarchy, in that the antecedent of an anaphor must be higher on the hierarchy than the anaphor itself.

Jackendoff's hierarchy is

(52) Agent, Goal, Theme . . .

So, for example, we have the following:

(53) John talked to Bill_i about himself_i
*John talked about Bill_i to himself_i

If *Bill* is the Goal argument and the *about* NP is the Theme, then (a) but not (b) respects the hierarchy.

There are two important things to note about this theory. First, this proposal, unlike, for example, the Theta Criterion, relies on the "cognitive" identity of the various theta roles, and relies on the possibility of identifying, across verbs, various instances of such argument types as "agent," "theme," etc. Thus, it lies outside of the narrow notion of "theta theory" that we have chosen to expose here. This is not to say, of course, that the proposal is wrong. The second thing is that the proposal expresses a "surprising" connection between two subtheories, binding theory and theta theory – why should binding care about the nature of the theta roles of the NPs it is connecting? If one were designing an artificial language, one would not think to add this in, though one might add in some analog of the Theta Criterion.

The binding theory is standardly taken to be a theory about certain relations (coindexation, linking, "coreference," disjointness of reference, etc.) that hold among the A-positions of a sentence; that is, among the NPs of a sentence that occupy the argument positions of predicates. There is another possibility, though – rather, it is a theory of certain relations that hold among the theta roles in a sentence. In this conception, one thinks of the theta roles as referring, and the NPs that they are assigned to as "conditioning" that reference. Coreference, "linking," and the other binding theory relations would be relations among theta roles.

Some preliminary evidence for this is the existence of "implicit" arguments – exactly in these cases, there is no NP to enter into the binding theory relation, and still we find binding theory effects:

(54) To see oneself as others do is dangerous

Here, *dangerous* is a two-place relation, "x is dangerous to y," and the *y* argument is implicit; however, it is the understood subject of *see,* and so enters into the control relation. So the expression of the argument is not required for its role in Binding Theory. Of course, the argument can be expressed (just add "for one" to the end of this example), but it does not change the binding relations. This suggests that the binding theory is not looking at the expression of the arguments anyway, but rather at the arguments (theta roles) themselves.

The alternative is to have inaudible, or deleted, expressions of arguments for these cases. So, for example, the D-structure representation of (54) might be:

(55) To see oneself as others do is dangerous for one

with deletion following control.

Related Material in Other Chapters

Theta theory as a theory of argument structures and the realization of arguments is closely related to the modules of the grammar that contribute conditions on the representation of predicates and arguments. Among them are X-bar theory which deals with the representation of heads and their specifiers, complements, and modifiers. These issues are the major topics of chapter 1. Also discussed there is Case theory which plays a role in the licensing of most kinds of arguments. Chapter 3 on Logical Form deals with selection and the representation of quantificational and interrogative arguments in the course of a syntactic derivation. The binding theory, discussed in chapter 4, is connected to theta theory since it deals with constraints on the distribution of arguments that follow from their referential type. The issue has been raised occasionally whether the relational properties of arguments which are now handled by theta theory and their referential properties which are currently handled by binding theory should be dealt with by one and the same module instead. The theory of *pro*-drop, also outlined in chapter 4, directly affects the realization conditions of arguments and is intimately connected with theta theory as well.

The topic of chapter 5, the Empty Category Principle, in many of its versions makes reference to a distinction between theta-marked and non-theta-marked elements or between those expressions which are theta-marked by a lexical head and those which are not. The same issues arise in chapter 6 in connection with the properties of passive, compounding, and the behavior of noun incorporation, causatives, and applicatives which are typically analyzed as involving movement and hence the Empty Category Principle. Theta theory is directly involved in the question of whether and, if yes, what kinds of argument structure and grammatical function-changing operations Universal Grammar makes available, an issue that is covered in chapter 6 as well. Chapter 7 provides an overview of the projection mechanism in the Minimalist Program which determines the condition on the realization of arguments.

3

Logical Form

C.-T. James Huang
University of California at Irvine

Contents

Prelude

This chapter deals with the conception of the syntax–semantics interface in the Principles and Parameters framework and in particular the role of the level of Logical Form (LF) in mediating between the syntactic form of a sentence in terms of its tree structure and its truth conditions and entailments.

The chapter focuses on the differential LF representations of quantificational (including interrogative) expressions as opposed to nonquantificational ones. The processes of *quantifier raising* (QR) and *wh-movement* at LF are discussed in detail, and several versions of these leading ideas are compared and evaluated. The relative adequacy of restrictive as opposed to unrestrictive quantification as the representation of the semantics of quantificational sentences is provided as one of the arguments for the existence of QR and LF as a level of representation. Other arguments for this conception come from the similarity between constraints on overt movement and restrictions on the scope of elements which have not undergone visible movement.

The chapter also covers the behavior of various types of pronouns in connection with crossover phenomena and so-called "donkey" sentences and discusses competing analyses of these phenomena.

A discussion of *wh*-in-situ elements, the role at LF of general locality conditions from the theories of bounding and binding, and the contributions of the assumptions about LF to a general theory of comparative semantics conclude the chapter.

1 The Syntax–Semantics Interface

The relationship between syntax and semantics, or between linguistic form and logical form, has been a persistent issue of central concern to modern linguistic theory. How is the meaning of a sentence, where one talks about its truth conditions and entailment properties, etc., determined by its syntactic form, where elements of the sentence are presented in one constituent structure or another? In GB theory, the answer to this question is that grammar and meaning are mediated through a linguistic level of Logical Form. This is an abstract level of representation derived from the level of S-Structure through transformational operations (e.g. the rule Move α), operations which are also responsible for mapping D-structure to S-Structure representations. It is assumed that semantic interpretation rules apply to representations at this level of mediation, but not directly to S-Structure representations, to derive the appropriate semantic interpretations. LF is thus the interface between grammar and the conceptual-intentional properties of language, just as the level of Phonetic Form (PF) is an interface between grammar and the audio-perceptual properties of utterances. LF is not to be equated with the level of semantic structure any more than PF is to be treated as a level specifying the sound waves of any given utterance. It expresses only aspects of semantic structure that are syntactically expressed, or that are contributed by grammar.

The supposition that the meanings of sentences are not directly "read off" from their surface forms is based to a large extent on the combination of the following three facts: (a) that sentences with quantifiers and question words exhibit special *semantic* properties which distinguish them from non-interrogative, non-quantificational sentences; (b) that these properties reflect *syntactic* generalizations that are best captured by reference to their structure at LF; and (c) that the derivation of LF representations from S-Structure involves little or no extra cost other than what is already made available by a proper theory of overt syntax.

A simple difference between quantificational and referential sentences can be seen by comparing a pair like (1)–(2):

(1) John flunked
(2) Every student flunked

The mapping of a non-quantificational sentence to its logical structure is relatively straightforward. The predicate in (1) says something about the individual named John, and a simple rule will interpret this sentence to be true if and only if this individual, John, flunked, and false otherwise. For our present purposes, the logical structure of (1) does not differ from its linguistic structure in any essential way. The situation with (2) is different, however. Here the predicate cannot be said to be predicated of an individual named "every student," and the truth of (2) cannot be determined in the same way. The truth conditions of (2) are more appropriately captured by the logical formula (3) or (4):

(3) $\forall x$ ((x is a student) $\rightarrow$ (x flunked))
(4) ($\forall x$: x is a student) (x flunked)

That is, (2) is more appropriately interpreted through a quantification. The subject of the VP *flunked* occurs in the form of a variable bound by a universal quantifier, either one that ranges over all elements in the domain of discourse as in (3), or one that ranges over the restricted domain defined by the set of x such that x is a student as in (4). The appropriate semantic rule can apply to either (3) or (4) to yield the correct semantics of the sentence. In set-theoretic terms, these logical structures yield truth iff the intersection of the set X comprising all students and the set Y comprising all students who flunked equals the former set X, and falsehood otherwise. More informally, (3)–(4) are interpreted as true just in case they are true on every assignment of the value of x, x a student, that x flunked.

To interpret quantificational sentences properly, then, S-Structure representations need to be mapped to semantic structures like (3)–(4). In GB, it is assumed that this mapping from syntax to semantics is mediated through LF. Following May (1977), quantificational sentences are subject to the rule QR (Quantifier Raising), which Chomsky-adjoins a quantified NP to IP, leaving a trace A′-bound by the adjoined NP. This operation gives (2) the LF-Structure (5):

(5) $[_{IP}$ Every student$_i$ $[_{IP}$ t_i flunked]]

A structure of this sort already has the form of a restrictive quantification structure as given in (4). The A′-bound trace corresponds to the variable x in (4). The QP specifier of *every student* corresponds to the universal quantifier, and the N′ *student* corresponds to its restriction, specifying that the universal quantifier ranges over individuals who are students. Everything that is contained in (4) is already provided in (5). Much of the mapping that is required to relate a linguistic structure to its logical structure is achieved in the domain of syntax already, i.e. in the syntax of LF. Given LF as a syntactic level of representation, the mapping between syntax and semantics is relatively trivial in this case.

An LF representation like (5) captures one distinctive property of quantificational sentences: they convey a sense of generality which referential sentences do not. Another property of quantificational sentences is that they exhibit the phenomena of scope. Thus (6) below is ambiguous as to whether the existence of someone is true to the speaker or only in the mind of the matrix subject:

(6) John believes that someone is in the cellar

A common view holds that these two readings differ in whether the existential quantifier has scope over the matrix or the embedded clause. Their simplified logical structures are given in (7)–(8):

(7) (∃x: x a person) (John believes that x is in the cellar)
(8) John believes that (∃x: x a person) (x is in the cellar)

These logical structures are, again, directly obtainable at LF by applying QR, depending on which IP the QNP *someone* is adjoined to:

(9) $[_{IP}$ Someone$_i$ $[_{IP}$ John believes that $[_{IP}$ t_i is in the cellar$]]]$
(10) $[_{IP}$ John believes that $[_{IP}$ someone$_i$ $[_{IP}$ t_i is in the cellar$]]]$

Another kind of ambiguity arises from the difference in relative scope among QNPs. In (11) the universal quantifier may have a distributive or a collective reading, meaning, respectively, either that everyone loves someone or other, or that there is someone that everybody loves.

(11) Everyone loves someone

The distributive and collective readings are the readings one gets when the universal quantifier is interpreted as having wide or narrow scope, respectively, with respect to the existential quantifier. The appropriate representations for these readings are directly derived by QR:

(12) $[_{IP}$ Everyone$_i$ $[_{IP}$ someone$_j$ $[_{IP}$ t_i loves $t_j]]]$
(13) $[_{IP}$ Someone$_j$ $[_{IP}$ everyone$_i$ $[_{IP}$ t_i loves $t_j]]]$

Note that the two facts that distinguish QNPs from referential NPs, with respect to generality and scope ambiguities, are semantic facts and, by themselves, do not argue for the existence of a syntactic level of LF. Since LF structures are subject to interpretation, one may as well devise mapping rules that convert S-Structure representations directly into semantic structure, without the mediation of LF. No appeal to semantics per se can provide a real argument for the existence of this level of syntactic representation. In spite of common misunderstandings, LF is not motivated merely as a level of disambiguation.

One argument for LF lies in the fact that representations at LF are derivable through syntactic means at little or no cost to the grammar. Since LF more faithfully represents the semantics of certain sentences than overt syntax, postulation of this level reduces the burden of mapping from syntax to semantics. If LF structures are derived at little or no cost, a grammar that incorporates such a level is a simpler grammar than one that does not. For example, notice that the LF structures (5) and (9)–(10) have the syntactic form of A′-binding, commonly observed with *wh*-questions in overt syntax:

(14) [Who$_i$ [t_i flunked]]
(15) [What$_i$ [do you think [Bill will buy t_i]]]
(16) [I wonder [what$_i$ [Bill will buy t_i]]]

Other examples of overt A′-binding include topicalization in various languages, and Scrambling in certain "order-free" languages. These structures are derived by a process of movement from A to A′ position, some involving adjunction to IP, others involving movement into Spec of CP. All of these are but special instances of the single rule Move-α, α any category. The rule QR is also an instance of Move-α, so its postulation does not add to the burden of grammar. The mapping of S-Structure to LF is thus fundamentally an extension of overt syntax, of the mapping from D-structure to S-Structure.

The more important arguments for the existence of LF as a linguistic level come from the fact that quantificational sentences exhibit properties that are best captured by principles and constraints that have been independently motivated in overt syntax. Arguments of this form can be found in various areas, in discussions of constraints on quantifier scope, on the possibility of interpreting pronouns as bound variables, on the syntax and interpretation of constituent questions, and so forth.

The idea that there is a linguistic level with representations resembling formulas of Predicate Calculus can be found in early generative literature, most notably in the works of generative semanticists (see Lakoff (1971), Bach (1968), and McCawley (1970b)). In Lakoff's work, for example, quantifiers are represented as higher predicates in underlying structure, and lowered to their surface syntactic position through a lowering process. But the notion of Logical Form as an independently motivated level of syntax, derived by syntactic rules and defined by generalizations and principles governing syntax, was not crystallized until Chomsky (1976) presented his well known arguments from weak crossover which show that the conditions governing the use of pronouns as bound variables are defined at the level of LF. The case for LF was considerably strengthened with May's (1977) formal proposal of the rule QR, and his analysis of "inversely linked quantification" and of other matters of scope. The significance of this level gained widespread recognition in the early 1980s when weak crossover and the syntax of scope became the subject matter of several highly influential publications, and when the notion of LF was extended to the syntax of *wh*-in-situ, as in Aoun, Hornstein and Sportiche (1981), Jaeggli (1982), and to the syntax of *wh*-questions in languages without *wh*-movement, as in Huang (1982). Although some of the crucial facts that were used to motivate the existence of LF have been reanalyzed in one way or another (see, for example, Lasnik and Saito (1984, 1992), Rizzi (1990),

Cinque (1990b), Aoun (1986), Aoun, Hornstein, Lightfoot, and Weinberg (1987), Pesetsky (1982b, 1987), and May (1985)), the level of LF has continued to play a crucial role in these recent accounts.

Three areas of research constitute the core of the syntax of LF: (a) quantifier scope, (b) variable binding, and (c) the grammar of *wh*-in-situ.[1] In sections 2, 3 and 4, I take up each of these in some detail, and review the major achievements in these areas. In section 5, I will discuss a few current issues in the theory of LF that have gained prominence in more recent years. Section 5.1 touches on the status of Subjacency in LF and the issue of pied-piping in LF. Section 5.2 discusses recent developments in Binding Theory. In section 5.3, several issues of "comparative semantics" are broached, concerning cross-linguistic variations in superiority violations, scope ambiguities, bound variable pronouns, and the typology of *wh*-questions.

2 The Syntax of Scope

2.1 *Inverse Linking*

One of the strongest arguments for the existence of QR, hence also of LF, was put forth by May (1977) in his analysis of "inversely linked quantification," illustrated below:

(17) [$_{NP1}$ Somebody from [$_{NP2}$ every California city]] owns a Porsche
(18) [$_{NP1}$ Every senator on [$_{NP2}$ a key congressional committee]] voted for the amendment

Each of these sentences contains two QNPs, one properly contained in another. In both cases, NP2 is contained in a PP that is itself part of NP1. In both sentences, NP1 has scope over the sentence of which it is the subject. NP2, on the other hand, may be interpreted as having scope either internal to NP1, or over the entire sentence. According to the internal reading, NP2 has scope over the clause that provides the restriction of NP1's domain, so (17) means that somebody who comes from every California city owns a Porsche; and (18) means that every senator who comes from a key congressional committee or another voted for the amendment.[2] On the external, sentential-scope reading of NP2, (17) may be paraphrased as "every California city is such that there is someone from it who owns a Porsche," and (18) means that there is a congressional committee such that every senator on that committee voted for the amendment.

The relevant property of interest here is that, when both the QNPs have sentential scope, the less inclusive NP2 must have wider scope than the more inclusive NP1. Thus the sentences have the meanings just indicated, but (17) cannot be paraphrased as "for some person x, every California city is such that x owns a Porsche." (18) does not mean "for every senator there is a congressional committee such that he voted for the amendment." That is, more generally, for two QNPs one of which contains the other, the relative scope of these QNPs is "inversely linked" to their relation of domination, so that the smaller, contained NP must have wider scope than the larger, containing NP. May (1977) argues that this otherwise rather surprising fact is readily explained under QR by the independently motivated conditions of (a) Proper Binding (PB), which requires all variables to be properly A′-bound, and (b) Non-Vacuous Quantification (NVQ), which requires all quantifiers to each properly bind a variable. Assuming that QR affects whole QNPs, (17) may be turned into the structure (19) in which the smaller NP2 has wider scope, or the structure (20), in which the larger NP1 has wider scope:

(19) $[_{IP}$ [every California city]$_i$ $[_{IP}$ [somebody from t_i]$_j$ $[_{IP}$ t_j owns a Porsche]]]

(20) $[_{IP}$ [somebody from t_i]$_j$ $[_{IP}$ [every California city]$_i$ $[_{IP}$ t_j owns a Porsche]]]

In (19) *every California city* properly binds the variable t_i, and the larger NP *somebody from* t_i properly binds the variable t_j. The LF structure is well-formed with respect to both PB and NVQ, so (17) is predicted to have the interpretation according to which the smaller QNP has scope over the larger QNP containing it. In (20), however, although the larger QNP and its trace are in a proper binding relationship obeying both PB and NVQ, the variable t_i is unbound, in violation of PB, and the quantifier *every California city* does not bind a variable, in violation of NVQ. The structure is ill-formed, and (17) is predicted not to have a reading with the subject having wider scope than the smaller NP it contains. The same explanation applies to (18).

Note that PB and NVQ are independently motivated in overt syntax, to ensure, among other things, that movement of a *wh*-phrase moves it upward into a position c-commanding the movement site. Thus a D-structure like (21a) can be turned into a grammatical S-Structure by moving the embedded *wh*-phrase upward as in (21b), a D-structure like (22a) cannot be turned into a grammatical S-Structure by lowering the matrix *wh*-phrase as in (22b):

(21a) John wonders you bought what
(21b) John wonders what$_i$ you bought t$_i$
(22a) Who wonders John bought the book
(22b) *t$_i$ wonders who$_i$ John bought the book

The ill-formedness of (22b) as opposed to the well-formedness of (21b) is accounted for by PB and NVQ. The restriction on inversely linked quantification also falls out in the same way at no additional cost once QR is assumed to apply to sentences like (17) and (18). Inverse-linking thus provides strong support for QR, and hence for the existence of LF.

May's treatment of inverse-linking also provides an important argument against earlier treatments of quantifier scope by generative semanticists. Although the rule QR might be thought of as simply the EST translation of Lakoff's of Quantifier Lowering, this is not the case. For one thing, QR is an upward movement rule, which makes it an instance of Move-α, whereas Quantifier Lowering does not conform to the general pattern of movement and is not independently motivated. Secondly, once lowering rules are allowed, the requirement of inverse-linking cannot be explained without recourse to some ad hoc mechanisms. A Quantifier Lowering analysis would be justified only by appeal to semantics, and in this case there is little evidence for an abstract syntactic level of scope representation distinct from the level of "real semantics."

2.2 *Opacity in NP*

As noted above, sentences like (17) and (18) have, in addition to the inversely linked reading, a reading according to which the smaller QNP has scope internal to the NP containing it. Two more examples are given below:

(23) Pictures of everybody are on sale
(24) Every professor from two areas of social science was elected to membership in the academy

According to the inversely linked interpretation, (23) says that everybody is such that his/her pictures are on sale, and (24) that there were two areas of social science from which every professor was elected to membership in the academy. According to the internal-scope reading,

(23) says that pictures that have everybody on them (group pictures) are on sale, and (24) that all those who specialize in two areas of social science were elected to academy membership.

The inversely linked interpretation becomes unavailable, however, if the containing NP is definite or specific. Thus in contrast to (23)–(24), the following sentences have only the internal reading of the quantifiers:

(25) This picture of everybody is now on sale
(26) Those professors from two areas of social science were elected to membership in the academy

Fiengo and Higginbotham (1981) propose that the absence of inverse-linking follows from the Specificity Condition (cf. also the Name Constraint in May (1977)).

(27) No specific NP may contain a free variable.

Fiengo and Higginbotham propose that a QNP has NP-internal scope when it is adjoined to N′ at LF, and sentential scope if adjoined to IP. In (25), N′-adjunction of *everybody* yields (28), and IP-adjunction gives (29):

(28) $[[_{NP}$ This $[_{N'}$ everybody$_i$ $[_{N'}$ picture of $t_i]]]$ is now on sale]
(29) $[_{IP}$ Everybody$_i$ $[_{IP}$ $[_{NP}$ this picture of $t_i]$ is now on sale]]

(28) is well-formed, because the variable t_i is bound in the definite subject NP; (29) is ruled out, because the variable is free in the NP. Note that the Specificity Condition is independently observed in overt syntax, accounting for patterns like the following:

(30a) Who did you see pictures of t?
(30b) Who did you see many pictures of t?
(30c) Who did you see three pictures of t?
(30d) *Who did you see this picture of t?
(30e) *Who did you see those pictures of t?

2.3 Wh–*QP Interaction*

Another kind of support for LF turns on the fact that scope interpretation appears to be constrained by established syntactic constraints. One of these had to do with the contrast brought to light by May (1985), concerning the relative scope of *wh*-phrases and quantifiers:

(31) What did everyone buy for Max?
(32) Who bought everything for Max?

Sentence (31) is ambiguous, admitting both a collective and a distributive reading of the universal quantifier. In the former case it is a singular question, to which one may answer with "They bought a Nintendo set for Max." In the distributive reading, (31) is a family of questions, asking for each person x, what x bought for Max. In this case an answer like "John bought a Nintendo set, Bill bought a Monopoly, and Mary bought a pair of tennis shoes for him" would be more appropriate. In contrast, (32) is not ambiguous. It has only the collective reading, so an answer like "John did" would be appropriate, but not a pair-list sentence like the one just given.

May argues that this contrast manifests an effect of the Path Containment Condition (PCC) proposed in Pesetsky (1982b). Pesetsky shows that an array of grammatical contrasts observed in overt *wh*-movement can be naturally accounted for by observing the interaction of paths that such movement creates. An A′-path is a set of successively dominating nodes leading from a trace to its c-commanding A′-binder. The PCC provides that if two A′ paths intersect, then one must be properly contained in the other. Overlapping but non-nesting paths are ill-formed. May shows that the contrast between (31) and (32) can be seen as an effect of the PCC at LF if quantifiers are subject to QR. The result of applying QR to (31) is (33):

(33) $[_{CP}$ What$_j$ did $[_{IP}$ everyone$_i$ $[_{IP}$ t_i buy t_j for Max]]]

The path connecting *what* and its trace t_j consists of {VP, IP, IP, CP}, and the path connecting *everyone* and its LF trace is {IP, IP}. The latter path is properly contained in the former, so the path structure of this LF representation is well-formed with respect to the PCC. May further assumes that in such a structure as (28), where *what* and *everyone* are in a mutual government relation, either operator may be interpreted as having wider scope than the other, whence the ambiguity of (31) arises. In the case of (32), however, the result of adjoining *everyone* to IP gives (34):

(34) $[_{CP}$ Who$_j$ $[_{IP}$ everyone$_i$ $[_{IP}$ t_j bought t_i for Max]]]

The path connecting *who* and its trace is {IP, IP, CP}, and the path connecting *everyone* and its trace is {VP, IP, IP}. The two paths overlap, but neither contains the other, in violation of the PCC, so the structure is excluded at LF. To obtain a grammatical LF structure, *everyone* needs to adjoin to VP, yielding (35):

(35) $[_{CP}$ Who$_j$ $[_{IP}$ t$_j$ $[_{VP}$ everyone$_i$ $[_{VP}$ bought t$_i$ for Max]]]]

Here the two paths {IP, CP} and {VP, VP}, do not overlap, so the structure is well-formed with respect to the PCC. In this structure *everyone* does not govern *who*, and so cannot have scope wider than *who*. (32) is predicted to be unambiguous. Since the PCC makes crucial reference to syntactic trees, and is itself motivated independently as a constraint on overt syntax, this account provides evidence for LF as a syntactic level of grammar.

2.4 *Restrictive Quantification*

An indirect argument for QR, and hence for LF, comes from the relative adequacy of restrictive quantification (RQ) over non-restrictive quantification (UQ) as a more faithful representation of the semantics of quantificational sentences. Consider the two logical formulas (3)–(4) again:

(3) ∀x ((x is a student) → (x flunked))
(4) (∀x: x is a student) (x flunked)

There are reasons that the RQ schema (4) is to be preferred over the UQ schema (3). For one thing, a sentence like (2) makes a claim about (a set of) students, as indicated by the RQ, but not about humans or objects in general, as implied by the UQ. Secondly, as pointed out by J. Higginbotham (personal communication), a UQ does not adequately distinguish the normal *Which man is a bachelor?* and the semantically odd *Which bachelor is a man?*, since on the existential interpretation of a *wh*-NP (see Karttunen (1977), among others), the two sentences would have the same semantic structure: (Which x) ((x is a man) & (x is a bachelor)), the left-to-right order of the two conjuncts being irrelevant to the semantics of the coordinate structure. On the other hand, the oddity of a sentence like *which bachelor is a man?* follows readily from the RQ formula *for which x, x a bachelor, x is a man?*, since every x such that x is a bachelor is necessarily a man. Thirdly, and most importantly, the semantics of quantifiers like *most, two thirds of*, etc., cannot be described within the vocabulary of the Predicate Calculus and a UQ, even if new operators like *Most x, Two thirds of x*, etc. are introduced. *Most students flunked* means neither *Most x ((x a student)→ (x flunked))* nor

Most x ((x a student) & (x flunked)), but its meaning is faithfully represented in the RQ *(Most x: x a student) (x flunked)*. (See Higginbotham and May (1981), Barwise and Cooper (1981).)

If RQ is to be preferred over UQ, an argument for QR derives itself from the fact that the RQ schema is directly obtainable from the result of applying QR at LF, as explained above, the mapping from LF to semantic representation being quite trivial. In fact, given general constraints on Move-α, the theory of LF is simply unable to turn a simple sentence like (2) into a complex conditional sentence. The fact that the syntax of LF forces the choice of RQ over UQ lends important support to the QR rule, and hence to LF itself.

3 Pronouns as Bound Variables

3.1 *Weak Crossover*

Anaphoric pronouns may take referential or quantificational antecedents. In the former situation they are used in coreference, or overlapping reference, with their referential antecedents, whereas in the latter situation they are used as bound variables, their referential values varying with the value-assignment of their quantificational antecedents. These two uses of pronouns are not independent of each other. In particular, the indexing possibilities of a pronoun as a bound variable constitute a proper subset of the indexing possibilities of a pronoun taking a referential antecedent. Thus all impossible cases of pronouns in coreference are also impossible for pronouns as bound variables, but the reverse is not true.

(36) John$_i$ thinks that Bill$_j$ will praise him$_{i/*j}$
(37) Everyone$_i$ thinks that no one$_j$ will praise him$_{i/*j}$
(38a) John$_i$ loves his$_i$ mother
(38b) John$_i$'s mother loves him$_i$
(38c) His$_i$ mother loves John$_i$
(38d) *He$_i$ loves John$_i$'s mother
(39a) Everyone$_i$ loves his$_i$ mother
(39b) Everyone$_i$'s mother loves him$_i$
(39c) *His$_i$ mother loves everyone$_i$
(39d) *He$_i$ loves everyone$_i$'s mother
(40a) Someone$_i$ loves his$_i$ mother
(40b) Someone$_i$'s mother loves him$_i$

(40c) *His$_i$ mother loves someone$_i$
(40d) *He$_i$ loves someone$_i$'s mother

The ungrammatical indexings in both (36) and (37) are ruled out by condition B. The ungrammatical indexings in (38d), (39d), and (40d) are ruled out by condition C. Neither condition B nor condition C, however, rules out the ungrammatical (39c) and (40c). In other words, Binding Theory provides necessary, but not sufficient, conditions on the use of bound variable pronouns. The following examples illustrate the same point.

(41a) John$_i$ loved the woman who left him$_i$
(41b) The woman who left him$_i$ loved John$_i$
(42a) Everyone$_i$ loved the woman who left him$_i$
(42b) *The woman who left him$_i$ loved everyone$_i$

All of these sentences satisfy Binding Theory, but that is not sufficient to make (42b) grammatical.

Chomsky (1976) proposed to assimilate the paradigm in (39)–(40) to that of *wh*-questions:

(43a) Who$_i$ loves his$_i$ mother?
(43b) Whose$_i$ mother loves him$_i$?
(43c) *Who$_i$ does his$_i$ mother love t$_i$?
(43d) *[Whose$_i$ mother]$_j$ does he$_i$ love t$_j$?

(43d) is a case of "strong crossover," where an R-expression has moved across a c-commanding coindexed pronoun. (43c) involves "weak crossover," in which an R-expression has moved across a non-c-commanding coindexed pronoun. The strong crossover case can be ruled out by condition C,[3] along with the (d) sentences of (38)–(40). But the weak crossover case (43c) is unaccounted for by Binding Theory, as are the (c) examples of (39)–(40). Intuitively, whatever principle accounts for (43c) should also account for (39c) and (40c). A unified structural account is not available at S-Structure, since (43c) and (39c)–(40c) have very different structures at this level. No appeal to pre-movement levels (where the sentences have identical structures) is likely to work either, since pronominal anaphora is affected by movement:

(44a) John$_i$'s mother saw him$_i$
(44b) *He$_i$ was seen by John$_i$'s mother
(45a) *He$_i$ likes several pictures that John$_i$ took
(45b) How many pictures that John$_i$ took does he$_i$ like?

A unified account is available at LF, however. After QR applies to (39c) and (40c), the resulting LF structures are essentially identical to the structure of (37c):

(46) *[$_{IP}$ everyone$_i$ [$_{IP}$ his$_i$ mother loves t$_i$]]
(47) *[$_{IP}$ someone$_i$ [$_{IP}$ his$_i$ mother loves t$_i$]]

The common property of these sentences, then, is that they all involve a weak crossover configuration at the level of LF. To exclude all cases of weak crossover, Chomsky proposed the following "Leftness Principle," applied at LF:

(48) A variable cannot be the antecedent of a pronoun to its left.

The argument for LF comes from the fact that it makes possible a unified account of weak crossover observed across different surface constructions.

3.2 *Scope and Binding*

Although the Leftness Principle excludes weak crossover configurations at LF, it is not a sufficient condition for a pronoun to be used as a bound variable. For example, both of the following sentences are well-behaved with respect to the Leftness Principle and Binding Theory, but (50) is ill-formed:

(49) The woman who loved John$_i$ decided to leave him$_i$
(50) *The woman who loved every man$_i$ decided to leave him$_i$

(50) is not unlike the following sentences with a pronoun following the QNP (hence its trace at LF), but these are all well-formed:

(51) Every man$_i$'s mother loves him$_i$
(52) A report card about every student$_i$ was sent to his$_i$/her$_i$ parents

There is a crucial difference, however. In (51)–(52), the QNP binding the pronoun has scope over the entire sentence which contains the pronoun, but in (50) the QNP *every man* can only have scope over the relative clause containing it, but does not have scope over the matrix clause containing the pronoun. The relevant principle is that, even though the QNP may not c-command the pronoun at S-Structure (as in all of (50)–(52)), it must c-command, i.e., have scope over, that pronoun at LF:

(53) A pronoun P may be bound by a quantified antecedent Q only if Q c-commands P at LF.

The distinction between (50) and (51)–(52) then follows from the fact that, at LF, the QNP is adjoined to the relative clause in (50), where it does not c-command the pronoun, but to the root IP in (51)–(52), where it does. The requisite distinction can be made at LF, but not at S-Structure.

Recall that a sentence like *A report about every student was sent out* is ambiguous between an inversely linked reading and an internal-scope reading. According to the former reading, every student is such that a report about him was sent out (five reports for five students); according to the latter, a report which contains information about every student was sent out (only one report). The principle (53) predicts, correctly, that (52) is not ambiguous under the bound variable reading of the pronoun, having only the interpretation according to which different reports were issued to different parents. A group reading would entail adjunction of *every student* to the N′ containing it, leaving the pronoun unbound at LF:

(54) $[_{IP}$ Every student_i $[_{IP}$ $[_{NP}$ a report card about $t_i]$ was sent to $\text{his}_i/\text{her}_i$ parents]]

(55) *$[_{IP}$ $[_{NP}$ A $[_{N'}$ every student_i $[_{N'}$ report card about $t_i]]]$ was sent to $\text{his}_i/\text{her}_i$ parents]

If the inversely linked reading is unavailable for some reason (e.g. the Specificity Condition), then a bound variable interpretation of the pronoun is impossible:

(56) *This report card about every student_i was sent to $\text{his}_i/\text{her}_i$ parents

The cases we have examined should be distinguished from "donkey sentences" like the following, where the pronoun apparently can be related to the existential quantifier even though the quantifier does not have scope over the matrix sentence:

(57) Everybody who owns a donkey beats it
(58) Every student who found a cheap book bought it

(57) does not mean that there is a donkey such that everyone who comes to own it will beat it. A donkey pronoun should be distinguished from a true bound variable pronoun. As Evans (1980) puts it, a donkey pronoun (his "E-type" pronoun) is more like a definite description (therefore a referential expression),[4] deriving its reference from a preceding text containing the quantifier. *It* in (57) and (58) can be paraphrased as "the donkey that he owns" and "the book," respectively. But a true bound pronoun cannot be paraphrased in the same way.[5]

Two other properties of donkey pronouns distinguish them from true bound pronouns. First, when a donkey pronoun is used in connection with a universal quantifier, it must be in plural form, whereas either the plural or the singular may be acceptable for a true bound pronoun:

(59) Every student thinks she/they is/are smart
(60) If you see everyone, tell them/*him/*her to come here
(61) That report about every student shocked their/*his/*her parents

Secondly, a negative QNP like *nobody* cannot antecede a donkey pronoun, since the text containing it will derive no reference for the donkey pronoun to refer to. This is not the case with true bound pronouns, which do not refer at all:

(62) Nobody thinks he/she is smart
(63) *Everyone who owns no donkey will beat it
(64) *If you see nobody, tell him/her to come here

Summarizing, putting aside donkey pronouns, the use of pronouns as bound variables is subject to the following two conditions at LF: (a) that they occur in the scope of their antecedent QNP's, (b) that they respect the Leftness Principle.

3.3 *Alternatives to the Leftness Principle*

As stated in (48), Chomsky's Leftness Principle is given in linear terms. Conceptually, such an account is somewhat unsatisfactory, since abstract LF principles otherwise operate in hierarchical terms only. Empirically, furthermore, the Leftness Principle turns out to be too strong in certain cases and too weak in others. Reinhart (1983a, 129) points out the following contrasts:

(65a) Near his_i child's crib $nobody_i$ would keep matches
(65b) *Near his_i child's crib you should give $nobody_i$ matches

(66a) For his_i birthday, each of the $employees_i$ got a Mercedes
(66b) *For his_i birthday, we bought each of the $employees_i$ a Mercedes

In both the (a) sentences here, the pronoun precedes the quantifier antecedent (and hence its trace at LF). The bound interpretation is available in both cases, but it is incorrectly ruled out by the Leftness Principle.

Some examples indicating that the Leftness Principle is also too weak were pointed out by Higginbotham (1980a, 1980b):

(67a) Which pictures of which man_i please him_i?
(67b) *Which pictures of which man_i does he_i like?
(68a) Everybody in some California $city_i$ hates its_i climate
(68b) *Its_i climate is hated by everybody in some California $city_i$

The problem is how the ungrammatical cases can be ruled out. In (67b), the pronoun does not precede a trace of *which* man at S-Structure (where there is no such trace), or at LF (where it follows the trace). Therefore the Leftness Principle is unable to rule out the bound construal. In the case of (68b), application of QR to both *everybody in some California city* and to *some California city* gives the following LF structure:

(69) $[_{IP}$ some California $city_i$ $[_{IP}$ [everybody in $t_i]_j$ $[_{IP}$ its_i climate is hated by $t_j]]]$

In this structure, the pronoun follows the variable t_i and the Leftness Principle fails to rule out the non-existing bound construal.

Reinhart's alternative to Chomsky's account is formulated in terms of *c-command* (p. 122):

(70) Quantified NPs and *wh*-traces can have anaphoric relations only with pronouns in their c-command syntactic domain.

This condition sufficiently rules out all the weak crossover cases reviewed in the previous sections. It also successfully distinguishes the (a) and (b) sentences of (65) and (66), under a slightly modified notion of *c-command* independently defended in Reinhart (1981), according to which a preposed complement PP is c-commanded by a subject (though a sentence-initial topic is not). The examples follow because the preposed PP falls within the c-domain of the subject in (a), but not within the c-domain of the object in (b).

A proposal similar in spirit is made by Koopman and Sportiche (1982/3) in the form of the Bijection Principle (BP), as a condition on LF:

(71) There is a bijective correspondence between variables and A′ positions.

That is, a variable is locally bound by one and only one A′ position, and an A′ position locally binds one and only one variable. Koopman and Sportiche assume the functional definition of variables, according to which α is a variable iff it's locally A′-bound, whether α is an overt pronoun or a trace. The cases of weak crossover are excluded by the BP because they involve an A′ position locally binding two variables at LF (an overt pronoun and a trace):

(72) $[_{CP}$ Who$_i$ does $[_{IP}$ his$_i$ mother love t$_i$]]?
(73) $[_{IP}$ Everyone$_i$ $[_{IP}$ his$_i$ mother loves t$_i$]]
(74) $[_{IP}$ No one$_i$ $[_{IP}$ the woman he$_i$ loved betrayed t$_i$]]

In the permissible cases of bound pronouns below, the BP is obeyed at LF, with the A′ category locally A′-binding the trace, which in turn locally A-binds the pronoun:

(75) [Who$_i$ [t$_i$ loves his$_i$ mother]]?
(76) [Everyone$_i$ [t$_i$ thinks [he$_i$ is smart]]]

The same account also rules in (65a) and (66a), under Reinhart's modified version of *c-command*. In both cases, at LF, the trace of the subject quantifier locally A-binds the pronoun in the preposed PP and is in turn locally A′-bound by the quantifier. A bijective relationship is maintained throughout.[6]

Although they overcome certain difficulties of the Leftness Principle, both Reinhart's and Koopman and Sportiche's proposals still fail to account for the contrasts pointed out by Higginbotham, in (67)–(68). They also incorrectly exclude the bound pronoun in each of the following sentences below:

(77) No one's mother loves him
(78) The election of no president will please his or her opponents
(79) You should blame no one without letting him or her speak first
(80) No attempt by any student will succeed without his parents' help

These sentences also show that any attempt to attribute a pronoun in these contexts to its donkey pronoun use is bound to fail, since as we just saw, a donkey pronoun cannot be used in the context of a negative QNP. In the same way, the following sentences with singular pronouns indicate that they are true bound variables but not donkey pronouns:

(81) Applications from every student should be accompanied by his/her signature
(82) Under our blind review policy, the name of every author must be kept apart from the manuscript that he or she submitted

Higginbotham's (1980a, 1980b) treatment turns out to be more adequate in dealing with these problems. Essentially his solution consists of the condition that in order for a pronoun β to take α, α a QNP or an empty category, as its antecedent, α must be accessible to β. His definition of accessibility is paraphrased below:[7]

(83) α is accessible to β iff:
 (a) α is an empty category c-commanding β, or
 (b) α is coindexed with a category accessible to β, or
 (c) α is contained in an NP accessible to β.

In cases where a QNP c-commands a pronoun at S-Structure, accessibility obtains straightforwardly. The QR trace of the QNP is accessible by (83a), and hence the QNP is also accessible, by (83b). For a permissible case of a bound pronoun where the QNP does not c-command the pronoun, consider the LF structure of (68a):

(84) $[_{IP}$ some California city$_i$ $[_{IP}$ [everybody in $t_i]_j$ $[_{IP}$ t_j hates its$_i$ climate]]]

Neither the QNP *some California city* nor its trace t_i is accessible to *its* by (83a) or (83b) alone. However, the trace t_i is contained in NP_j, and this NP is accessible to the pronoun by (83b), since it is coindexed with t_j, which is accessible to the pronoun by (83a). Therefore, by (83c) the trace t_i is accessible, and in turn by (83b) the QNP is also accessible. However, in the LF structure of (68b):

(85) $[_{IP}$ some California city$_i$ $[_{IP}$ [everybody in $t_i]_j$ $[_{IP}$ its$_i$ climate is hated by t_j]]]

NP_j containing t_i is not accessible to the pronoun by any of (83): not by (a) because it's not an empty category, not by (b) because the only category with which it is coindexed does not c-command the pronoun, and not by (c) because it is not contained in any NP. Thus the trace t_i contained in NP_j is not accessible, hence also the QNP_i. The contrast between (67a) and (67b) follows in the same way, assuming that the QNP *which man* raises in LF, adjoining to CP:

(86a) $[_{CP}$ which man_i $[_{CP}$ which pictures of $t_i]_j$ $[_{IP}$ t_j please $him_i]]]$?
(86b) $[_{CP}$ which man_i $[_{CP}$ [which pictures of $t_i]_j$ $[_{IP}$ does he_i like $t_j]$?

Note that according to the accessibility account, a non-empty category cannot be directly accessible to a pronoun by simply binding it, but must derive its accessibility through a coindexed empty category. This is because NP_j c-commands the pronoun in (86b) as much as it does in (86a). In other words, we cannot save Reinhart's condition by simply allowing a QNP to be contained in some NP that c-commands the pronoun at S-Structure, or the contrast in (67) would be unaccounted for. This means, in turn, that an account of (68) must refer crucially to LF, after QR has created empty categories on the basis of which accessibility is determined.

Another non-linear theory of bound variable pronouns is given in May (1985, 1988b) in terms of Pesetsky's (1982b) Path Containment Condition (PCC). May proposes a theory of adjunction which allows for a QNP adjoined to a subject NP to be directly interpreted as c-commanding the IP containing the subject. Thus the inversely linked readings of (68) of a QNP contained in another are obtained by simply adjoining it to the containing QNP:

(87)

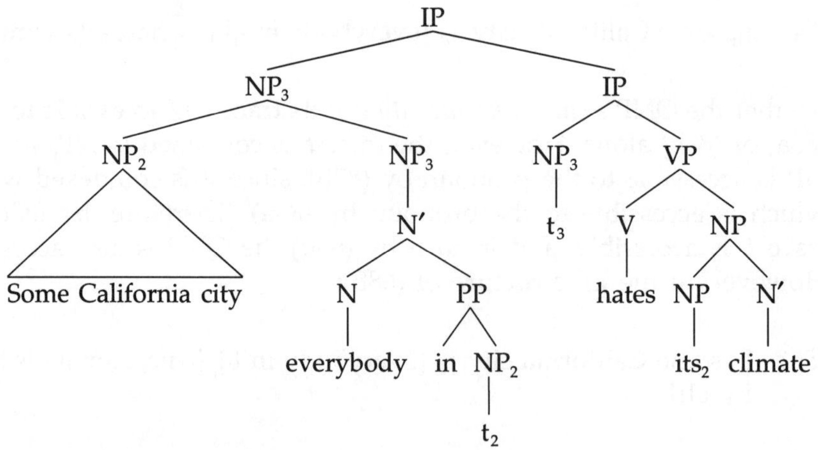

(88)

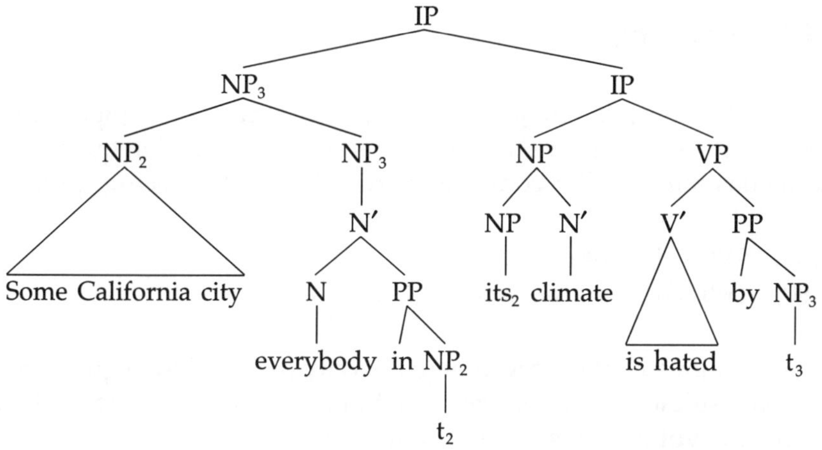

In both (87) and (88), NP_2 adjoined to NP_3 c-commands both its trace t_2 and the pronoun *its*. In (87), there are three A′-paths. Path (t_3) starts from the lowest IP dominating it and consists of {IP, IP, NP_3}. Path (t_2) starts from PP and includes {PP, NP_3, NP_3}. These two paths meet at the top at NP_3 but do not overlap, so the PCC is irrelevant. Path (*its*) starts from the pronoun and consists of {NP, VP, IP, IP, NP_3}, again meeting the other paths at NP_3 without overlapping with either. The LF structure (87) is thus well-formed. In (88), Path (t_3) consists of {PP, VP, IP, IP, NP_3}, Path (t_2) consists of {PP, NP_3, NP_3}, and Path (*its*) consists of {NP, IP, IP, NP_3}. Path (t_3) and Path (*its*) overlap at three points, i.e. IP, IP, and NP_3. However, there is one link, namely the link between NP and IP in Path (*its*) which is not properly contained in path (t_3). Thus the LF structure (88) is ill-formed. The contrast between (68a) and (68b) thus follows from the PCC at LF.[8]

4 *Wh*-in-situ

That *wh*-phrases are also quantifiers is a relatively old idea and has been widely used in the generative literature (especially since Chomsky (1976)). Like ordinary quantificational NPs, they are non-referential. In standard semantic treatments, *wh*-questions are represented in quantificational schemas which denote possible or actual answers to them (cf. Karttunen (1977), Higginbotham and May (1981), Engdahl (1986) and the references cited there). In GB, *wh*-phrases are operators binding variables at LF, like other QNPs.

4.1 Selection

In English-type languages, *wh*-phrases are moved to [Spec, CP] at S-Structure, so at this level *wh*-questions are represented in quantificational schemas already, the conversion from (89) to (90) being quite trivial:

(89) Who$_i$ did John see t$_i$?
(90) (Which x: x a person) (did John see x)?

The *wh*-movement observed here not only provides for a quantificational schema suitable for interpretation, but also fulfills a selectional requirement in syntax. Consider the following:

(91a) What does John think Mary bought t?
(91b) *John thinks what Mary bought t
(92a) *What does John wonder Mary bought t?
(92b) John wonders what Mary bought t
(93a) What does John remember Mary bought t?
(93b) John remembers what Mary bought t

These sentences have almost identical D-structure representations:

(94) John thinks Mary bought what
(95) John wonders Mary bought what
(96) John remembers Mary bought what

However, whereas (96) may be mapped into a direct question or a statement containing an indirect question at S-Structure, (94) must surface as a direct question, and (95) as a statement containing an indirect question. The differences in grammaticality among (91)–(93) are clearly to be attributed to the selectional properties of the matrix verbs: *think*-type verbs select declarative clauses, *wonder*-type verbs select questions, and *remember*-type verbs select either, as their complements. These differences are not directly observable in (94)–(96) at D-structure, since in each of these sentences the *wh*-phrase *what* is contained in the embedded clause, but the relevant generalization is captured at S-Structure by the requirement that each verb either requires, prohibits, or permits a question phrase in the Spec of its complement CP, i.e. *think*: +___[–wh], *wonder*: +___[+wh], and *remember*: +___[±wh]. In other words, *wh*-movement provides for a level of representation where the relevant selectional requirements may be stated.

Now consider *wh*-questions in languages of the Chinese type, where the *wh*-words are not moved at S-Structure.

(97) Zhangsan yiwei Lisi mai-le shenme?
Zhangsan thinks Lisi bought what
"What does Zhangsan think Lisi bought?"

(98) Zhangsan xiang-zhidao Lisi mai-le shenme
Zhangsan wonder Lisi bought what
"Zhangsan wonders what Lisi bought"

(99) Zhangsan jide Lisi mai-le shenme (?)
Zhangsan remember Lisi bought what
(99a) "Zhangsan remembers what Lisi bought"
(99b) "What does Zhangsan remember Lisi bought?"

Despite their similar appearance at S-Structure, these sentences nevertheless are interpreted very differently: (97) must be interpreted as a direct question to which an answer is needed, (98) as a statement containing an embedded question, and (99) as either. These restrictions are clearly the same restrictions just observed with the English sentences (91)–(93). The only difference is that whereas the restrictions are observed as a matter of *form* (i.e. grammaticality) in English, they present themselves as a matter of *interpretation* (e.g. presence vs. absence of ambiguity) in Chinese. A unified account of the relevant generalization is clearly desirable across *wh*-questions of these language types. In Huang (1982), it is proposed that such a unified account is readily available if it is assumed that *wh*-phrases in Chinese-type languages, even though they do not move in overt syntax, nevertheless undergo movement in LF. Assuming that *wh*-phrases move to [Spec, CP] in LF as they do in overt syntax, the structures below may be derived from (97)–(99):

(100a) [shenme$_i$ [Zhangsan yiwei [[Lisi mai-le t$_i$]]]]
for which x: x a thing, Zhangsan thinks Lisi bought x
(100b) [[Zhangsan yiwei [shenme$_i$ [Lisi mai-le t$_i$]]]]
Zhangsan thinks [for which x: x a thing, Lisi bought x]
(101a) [shenme$_i$ [Zhangsan xiang-zhidao [[Lisi mai-le t$_i$]]]]
for which x: x a thing, Zhangsan wonders Lisi bought x
(101b) [[Zhangsan xiang-zhidao [shenme$_i$ [Lisi mai-le t$_i$]]]]
Zhangsan wonders [for which x: x a thing, Lisi bought x]
(102a) [shenme$_i$ [Zhangsan jide [[Lisi mai-le t$_i$]]]]
for which x: x a thing, Zhangsan remembers Lisi bought x

(102b) [[Zhangsan jide [shenme$_i$ [Lisi mai-le t$_i$]]]]
Zhangsan remembers [for which x: x a thing, Lisi bought x]

Assuming that the selectional restrictions that account for (91)–(93) apply also at the level of LF, (100b) and (101a) are ruled out as ill-formed LF structures. This leaves (100a), (101b) and (102a)–(102b) as well-formed, representing the only possible interpretations of (97)–(99).

A typological view that emerges under this treatment of *wh*-in-situ is that languages do not differ in whether they have a rule of *wh*-movement or not. Rather, all languages have *wh*-movement as an instance of Move-α, but they differ in where *wh*-movement applies, if not in overt syntax then in LF.

4.2 Scope

In addition to accounting for question selection, *wh*-movement also serves to automatically fix the scope of *wh*-phrases *qua* quantifiers. It is commonly assumed that *wh*-phrases are existential quantifiers with interrogative features (*who* being *wh*- + *someone*). These two components of a *wh*-phrase can be taken apart by considering the presupposition of a question and its focus. Thus in uttering *who came?* the speaker presupposes that someone came and demands to know the identity of the one(s) who did come. Similarly, both the questions in (93) (repeated below) may be said to have the sentence (103) as their presupposition.

(93a) What does John remember Mary bought t?
(93b) John remembers what Mary bought t
(103) John remembers Mary bought something
(103a) There is something that John remembers that Mary bought
(103b) John remembers that there is something that Mary bought

Significantly, however, although as a sentence in isolation (103) allows *something* to have wide or narrow scope, as the presupposition clause of (93a) or (93b) it must be interpreted as in (103a) and (103b), respectively. This, of course, follows from the fact that it is impossible to do *wh*-movement without also doing "QR" at S-Structure in English. A similar restriction is observed with (99) in Chinese. Thus LF movement not only accounts for selection but also correctly fixes the scope of interpreted *wh*-phrases *qua* quantifiers.

The properties of *wh*s-in-situ in Chinese-type languages are also observable in multiple questions in English-type languages. A multiple question like (104) has one *wh*-phrase moved to [Spec, CP] and the other in situ:

(104) Who bought what?

A multiple question typically asks for the exact pairings of members from two or more restrictive domains defined by the occurring *wh*-phrases. A possible answer to (104) is (105):

(105) John bought the book, Mary the pencil, and Bill the pen

That is, the sentence is suitably interpreted by a restrictive quantification that ranges over possible ordered pairs, as given in the informal schema: [which pairing <x,y> : x a person and y a thing] [x bought y]. This schema can be obtained, following Higginbotham and May (1981), first by moving the unmoved *what* and adjoining it to *who* at [Spec, CP], thus forming a constituent with multiple operators, and then by invoking the rule of "absorption" which turns a string of unary operators into a single n-ary operator: $[Qx, Qy, \ldots] \rightarrow [Q_{<x,\, y,\ldots>}]$. Each unary operator ranges over individuals, but an n-ary operator ranges over ordered pairs.

One fact about English multiple questions, well known since Baker (1970), is that a sentence like (106) is ambiguous, admitting either (107) or (108) as an appropriate answer:

(106) Who remembers where we bought what?
(107) John remembers where we bought the books, Bill remembers where we bought the pencils, and Mary remembers where we bought the pens
(108) John does. John remembers where we bought what

(107) is an appropriate answer to (106) as a direct multiple question regarding the pairing <x,y> : x a person, y a thing, such that x remembers where we bought y. (108) is an appropriate answer to (106) as a singular question containing an embedded multiple question, where the matrix operator ranges over individuals and the embedded operator ranges over pairings of places and things. The ambiguity is one of scope, and it arises, under the LF movement hypothesis, out of the possibility of moving the unmoved *what* to the matrix or to the embedded CP.

4.3 Locality Constraints in LF

Although the facts surrounding scope ambiguities and the like are in themselves of considerable significance, the most important evidence for the LF movement hypothesis again comes from the fact that the interpretation of syntactically unmoved *wh*-questions is subject to independently motivated syntactic constraints.

One of these well-known syntactic constraints is the Empty Category Principle (ECP) proposed in Chomsky (1981) and further developed in later works (see chapter 5 for details). In its original version, the ECP requires a trace to be properly governed, i.e. either lexically governed or antecedent-governed. A complement to a lexical category is lexically governed, but a subject is not, so a subject trace needs to be antecedent-governed but an object trace need not. Hence long extraction of a subject gives considerably worse results than long object extraction:

(109a) ??What did you wonder why I bought t?
(109b) *Who did you wonder why t bought the book?
(110a) ??This is the book that I wonder why you bought t
(110b) *This is the person that I wonder why t bought the book

Huang (1982) observes that long extraction of adjuncts exhibits severe locality effects on a par with long subject extraction, indicating that there is a more general asymmetry between complements on the one hand and non-complements on the other.

(111a) ??What did you wonder why I bought t?
(111b) *Why_i did you wonder [what I bought t_i]?
(112a) ??This is the book that I wonder why you bought t
(112b) *This is the reason why_i I wonder [what you bought t_i]
(113a) ?Of which city did you witness [the destruction t]?
(113b) *On which table did you buy [the books t]?

These contrasts also follow from the ECP. The trace in each of the (b) sentences is not lexically governed in VP or NP; hence it must be antecedent-governed and cannot be moved out of the *wh*-island or NP containing it. The severe locality effects of adjunct extraction are also clear in other island violations:

(114) *How_i do you like the man [who fixed the car t_i]?
(115) *How_i did you feel satisfied after [he fixed the car t_i]?
(116) *How_i would [for him to fix the car t_i] be nice?

This account of adjunct extraction under the ECP has been refined in various ways over the years, most notably in Lasnik and Saito (1984,

1992), Chomsky (1986a), and Rizzi (1990), but the point to be made below about LF remains essentially unaffected.

The relevance of the ECP to LF *wh*-movement was first pointed out in Jaeggli (1982), Aoun, Hornstein, and Sportiche (1981), and Chomsky (1981), concerning the superiority phenomenon first discussed in Chomsky (1973).[9]

(117a) $[_{CP}$ Who$_i$ $[_{IP}$ t_i bought what]]?
(117b) *$[_{CP}$ What$_j$ did $[_{IP}$ who buy t_j]]?

The contrast illustrates a subject/object asymmetry – suggesting an ECP account – though paradoxically the situation is precisely the opposite of the ECP effects observed in (109)–(110), where a sentence is good with an object trace and bad with a subject trace. The paradox disappears, however, if we look at the asymmetry as holding of the unmoved *wh*-phrases: an object *wh*-in-situ is allowed but a subject *wh*-in-situ is not. Given the LF movement hypothesis, the asymmetry now holds of the traces created in LF, and this can be reduced to the ECP. Assume that the Spec of CP carries the index of the first *wh*-phrase moved into it, then the LF structures of (117) are as in (118):

(118a) $[_{CP}$ [What$_j$ Who$_i$]$_i$ $[_{IP}$ t_i bought t_j]]?
(118b) *$[_{CP}$ [Who$_i$ What$_j$]$_j$ did $[_{IP}$ t_i buy t_j]]?

The object trace of *what* is lexically governed in both (118a) and (118b), and the subject trace is not in either. In (118a) the subject trace t_i is antecedent-governed by the Spec of CP whose index is *i*. But in (118b) the subject trace t_i is not antecedent-governed by the Spec of CP whose index is *j*. (118b) is therefore ruled out by the ECP.

Huang (1982) points out that adjuncts also exhibit superiority effects like subjects:

(119a) Why did you buy what?
(119b) *What did you buy why?
(120a) Tell me how John fixed which car
(120b) *Tell me which car John fixed how

These are again reducible to the ECP at LF. The (b) sentences are excluded by the ECP because the LF-created traces of *why* and *how* fail to be properly governed. A similar account will explain the ungrammaticality of (121)–(123):

(121) *Who likes the man [who fixed the car how]?
(122) *Who drove away the car after [John fixed it how]?
(123) *Who said that [for John to fix the car how] would be nice?

The relevance of the ECP at LF receives strong support from the presence of a whole range of adjunct locality effects in Chinese (and other *wh*-in-situ languages). Thus, the following sentence in Chinese can have the interpretation (124a) as a direct question about the object bought, but not the interpretation (124b) as one about the reason for buying:

(124) ni xiang-zhidao [wo weishenme mai shenme]?
you wonder I why buy what
(124a) "What is the x such that you wonder why I bought x?"
(124b) Not: "What is the reason x such that you wonder what I bought for x?"

This complement/adjunct contrast mirrors the contrasts illustrated in (111)–(112) with respect to overt extraction out of *wh*-islands. Furthermore, direct questions with *weishenme* "why" contained in a relative clause, an adverbial clause, or a sentential subject are entirely unacceptable:

(125) *ni zui xihuan [weishenme mai shu de ren]?
you most like why buy book Comp person
"*Why do you like [the man who bought the books t]?"
(126) *ta [zai Lisi weishenme mai shu yihou] shengqi le?
he at Lisi why buy book after angry Prt
"*Why did he get angry [after Lisi bought the books t?]"
(127) *[wo weishenme mai shu] zui hao?
I why buy book most good
"*Why is [that I buy the books t] best?"

These restrictions mirror those observed with (114)–(116), and are accountable for under the ECP account, but only if the relevant *wh*-phrases are assumed to move in LF.

Other restrictions on question interpretation have been observed that also argue for an LF syntactic account. Huang (1982, 1991) observed a similar paradigm with the so-called A-not-A question in Chinese. This restriction may be reduced to the Head Movement Constraint of Travis (1984), or the ECP. Larson (1985) showed that the syntax of disjunction scope, as manifested by the properties of *whether* and *either*, is constrained by the ECP at LF. Baltin (1991) cites additional cases for head-movement in LF. (In section 5.2 below, two cases of head-movement in LF will be presented in more detail.)

Summarizing, the postulation of LF as a syntactic level of representation has provided a very useful tool for the investigation of the nature of linguistic meaning and of the relationship between syntax and semantics. In particular, the notion that meaning is determined by form is amply demonstrated by the fact that many properties of quantificational sentences which are generally thought of as matters of interpretation are to a large extent seen to pattern on a par with matters of form and are explainable as such at little or no additional cost to the grammar. LF is a syntactic level because it is a level defined crucially by such syntactic entities as c-command, dominance, adjunction, binding, Move α, weak crossover, accessibility, paths, superiority, the Head Movement Constraint and the ECP.

Before we turn to the next section it should be noted that the account just described of the various locality effects of *wh*-in-situ represents only one version of the syntactic approach in GB. In addition to the ECP account represented by the works of Chomsky (1981, 1986a), Huang (1982), Lasnik and Saito (1984, 1992), and Rizzi (1990), at least two other approaches have been proposed in the literature to deal with roughly the same range of facts. One of these is the theory of Generalized Binding proposed by Aoun (1985, 1986) and developed in subsequent works (cf. Aoun, Hornstein, Lightfoot, and Weinberg (1987), Aoun and Li (1988), Hornstein and Weinberg (1991), etc.). In Generalized Binding, the requirement of antecedent government is recast as one of local A′-binding. The other approach that has gained considerable support in the literature considers the fundamental explanation for the movement constraints to lie in a theory of paths, defined over hierarchical syntactic structures, of the sort proposed in Kayne (1983b), Pesetsky (1982b) and developed in May (1985, 1988b). Among other things, Pesetsky (1982b) argues that the PCC, a condition independently motivated by constraints in overt syntax, also explains certain important facts about the distribution and interpretation of *wh*-in-situ. In addition, as we saw above, the PCC was employed in May (1985, 1988b) to account for weak crossover and certain constraints on *wh*–QP interactions.

Although these various approaches to the observed phenomena differ in non-trivial ways both conceptually and in their empirical coverage, they share the important common property of making crucial reference to the syntactic level of LF. In the concluding section of this chapter, I shall address three areas of current research concerning questions and issues which have become meaningful only as a result of recent research on LF.

5 Some Current Issues

5.1 Bounding Theory in LF

We have seen that LF movement exhibits the effects of syntactic constraints on overt movement, including most significantly the ECP or its counterpart in Generalized Binding or the Path Theory. As is well-known, overt syntactic movement is also constrained by conditions of Bounding Theory, including Subjacency (the *wh*-Island Condition (WIC) and the Complex NP Constraint (CNPC)), the Condition on Extraction Domains (CED) (which subsumes the Subject Condition (SC) and the Adjunct Condition (AC)), and the Coordinate Structure Constraint (CSC). If LF movement is constrained by the ECP, the question arises whether it is also subject to these bounding conditions.

Earlier inquiry into the nature of LF showed that the construal of quantifier scope is restricted by the CNPC (see Lakoff (1971), Rodman (1976)), and May (1977) suggested that LF mappings are constrained by Subjacency. Although this assumption works by and large in the cases involving QR, a problem arises when one considers the LF movement of *wh*-phrases from argument positions. Although, as we saw, LF extraction of an adjunct from an island is impossible, LF extraction of an argument appears to be completely free of island effects:

(128a) Who remembers why we bought what?
(128b) Who likes books that criticize who?
(128c) Who thinks that pictures of who are on sale?
(128d) Who got jealous because I talked to who?
(128e) Who bought the books on which table?
(128f) Who saw John and who?

These sentences also contrast sharply with cases where an argument is extracted at S-Structure:

(129a) *What do you remember why we bought t?
(129b) *Who do you like books that criticize t?
(129c) *Who do you think that pictures of t are on sale?
(129d) *Who did you get jealous because I talked to t?
(129e) *Which table did you buy the books on t?
(129f) *Who did you see John and t?

Singular questions in Chinese also exhibit an adjunct/argument asymmetry in LF. An example of this is already shown in (124), repeated below:

(124) ni xiang-zhidao [wo weishenme mai shenme]?
you wonder I why buy what
(124a) "What is the x such that you wonder why I bought x?"
(124b) Not: "What is the reason x such that you wonder what I bought for x?"

The sentence can have the reading (124a), though not the reading (124b). This means that whereas the adjunct *weishenme* "why" cannot be LF-moved across a *wh*-island headed by *shenme* "what," the latter can be LF-moved across a *wh*-island headed by the former. Similarly, in contrast to the ungrammatical (125)–(127) with an adjunct in an island, the following are perfectly grammatical when an argument is involved:

(130) ni zui xihuan [shei mai de shu]?
you most like who buy Comp book
"Who is the x such that you like the books that x bought?"
(131) ta [yinwei shei mai shu] shengqi le?
he because who buy book angry Prt
"Who is the x such that he got angry because x bought the books?"
(132) [wo mai shenme] zui hao?
I buy what most good
"What is it best [that I buy t]?"

These also contrast with those involving overt extraction of an argument (e.g. relativization):

(133) *[wo zui xihuan [t_i mai de shu]] de ren lai-le
I most like buy Comp book Comp person come-Prt
"*The person x such that you like the books that x bought has come"
(134) *[ni [yinwei t_i mai shu] shengqi] de neige ren zou-le
you because buy books angry Comp that person leave-Asp
"*The person x such that you got angry because x bought the book has left"

In other words, extraction of an adjunct shows locality effects both in overt syntax and in LF, whereas extraction of a complement exhibits such effects only under overt movement, not under LF movement. This led Huang (1982) to conclude that Bounding Theory is a condition on overt movement only, but that the ECP applies at both S-Structure and LF. Although the conclusion is not implausible, it raises the question of what makes overt movement and LF movement differ in this way. This hypothesis remains a stipulation as long as it is not related to other, independently established differences between the two components of grammar. Empirically, furthermore, certain languages exhibit LF island effects that are not attributable to the ECP. In their study of "internally headed relative clauses" in Navajo, Barss, Hale, Perkins, and Speas (1991) (BHPS) argue that such constructions are best analyzed as involving a head-raising rule in LF. Internally headed relative clauses are "relatives-in-situ" constructions, on a par with *wh*-in-situ constructions, which undergo relativization in LF. BHPS further show that it is impossible to relativize an argument within a relative clause (both internally headed) and they suggest that this is a Subjacency effect. (See also Itô (1986) and Cole (1987) on the analysis of similar constructions in Japanese and Imbabura Quechua, respectively and other references cited.) Similarly, Longobardi (1991) shows that the interpretation of certain QNPs, for example the negative quantifier *nessuno* and *only*-phrases in Italian is systematically constrained by Subjacency, the CED and the CSC.

One sort of solution to this question comes from the LF pied-piping hypothesis proposed by Nishigauchi (1990), Choe (1987), and Pesetsky (1987). The idea is that, for some reason, LF movement of a *wh*-phrase is capable of pied-piping a larger chunk of material than overt movement. In the particular cases of apparent island violations observed here, LF movement of a *wh*-phrase in fact pied-pipes the whole island containing the phrase. Since the *wh*-phrase does not move out of the island, no bounding condition has been violated. On the other hand, assuming that adjunct *wh*-phrases cannot pied-pipe, movement must cross syntactic islands. Given this hypothesis, one can maintain that Bounding Theory applies in LF as much as it does in overt syntax, although its effects are generally invisible in LF due to the possibility of pied-piping. This solves the conceptual problem that has arisen under Huang's stipulation.

Fiengo, Huang, Lasnik, and Reinhart (1988) (FHLR) also appeal to the idea of pied-piping, but claim that pied-piping only occurs with *wh*-phrases *qua* quantifiers, not when they move into [Spec, CP] *qua* question words. That is, only QR may pied-pipe. Just as *everyone* is a quantifier ranging over individuals, *pictures of everyone* is also a quantifier, ranging over pictures of individuals. Thus any indefinite phrase containing a quantifier is also subject to QR.[10] The fact that pied-piping occurs more extensively in LF than in overt syntax reduces to the fact that QR is a rule of LF, not of overt syntax. FHLR further adopt the theory of adjunction proposed in May (1985), and the theory of barriers of Chomsky (1986a), according to which adjunction of a category to a barrier has the effect of debarrierizing the barrier. Thus a *wh*-phrase contained in a syntactic island XP may be moved out of XP after the entire XP is pied-piped to an adjoined position under QR. As in Nishigauchi, Choe, and Pesetsky's proposal, Bounding Theory applies to LF as much as it does in syntax.

Pesetsky (1987) proposes an additional explanation for certain apparent island violations in terms of the notion of "D(iscourse)-linking". Certain *wh*-phrases are used in discourse in which the range of their reference is somewhat transparent. These are assumed not to move in LF, but are simply "unselectively bound" by an appropriate [+*wh*] C^0, as originally suggested in Baker (1970). This explains contrasts like the following, and other apparent island violations:

(135a) What did which man buy?
(135b) *What did who buy?

Adjunct *wh*-phrases are never D-linked, whereas *which*-phrases are always D-linked. And argument *wh*-phrases like *who* and *what* may in some circumstances be D-linked. Thus adjunct extraction always exhibits island effects, but argument extraction need not.

If all apparent island violations in LF are explainable away in terms of either pied-piping (under *wh*-movement or under QR) or D-linking, then all bounding conditions apply in LF as they do in syntax. However, none of these proposals are entirely free of problems, and other authors have taken other directions to explain apparent island violations. For example, Hornstein and Weinberg (1991) propose that LF movement may affect a smaller part of a phrase than syntactic movement does (exactly the opposite of pied-piping), assuming with Huang (1982) that Subjacency does not apply in LF. In (135a), movement may affect only the determiner *which,* leaving a trace properly governed by the head noun *man.*[11] Watanabe (1992) also claims that Subjacency does not apply in LF, arguing that some island effects observed in LF are in fact effects caused by the invisible movement of an abstract operator at S-Structure. The most important evidence comes from the fact that Comparative Deletion in Japanese, which is formed by S-Structure movement as shown by Kikuchi (1987), cannot apply across embedded questions:

(136) *[minna-ga [naze Paul-ga e yonda ka] siritagatteiru
everyone-Nom why Paul-Nom read Q know-want
yori(mo)] John-ga takusan-no hon-o yonda
than John-Nom many-gen book-Acc read
"*John read more books than everybody wants to know why Paul read"

However, at S-Structure an embedded question is still not an island since the *wh*-word has not moved at this level. Watanabe concludes from this and similar considerations that there is an invisible movement that fills the relevant [Spec, CP] at S-Structure, and that it is this movement that forms a *wh*-island, rendering Comparative Deletion impossible in (136). Watanabe also suggests that the LF island effects observed with internally headed relative clauses in various languages and with negative and *only*-phrases in Italian actually arise from S-Structure movement of an invisible operator. Watanabe's analysis, if correct, has important consequences for parametric theory and the theory of LF, which will no doubt interest other researchers in this area.

5.2 *Binding Theory in LF*

A second recent issue concerning the theory of LF has to do with the treatment of Binding Theory at this level. Earlier investigations of LF centered around the properties of quantificational sentences only, including the properties of quantificationally bound pronouns. An exception is Aoun's work on Generalized Binding, which requires Binding Theory (including A-binding and A′-binding) to apply at LF, thus letting LF play an important role in the theory of A-binding as well. More recently, more linguists have relied increasingly on LF as the level where Binding Theory applies.

One line of research originates with Lebeaux's (1983) and Chomsky's (1986b) treatment of nominative anaphors involving an LF process of anaphor raising, which inspired considerable work on long-distance anaphora, among them the work of Pica (1987), Battistella (1987), Huang and Tang (1991), Cole, Hermon, and Sung (1990), and Katada (1991), among many others. It has been well known that in many languages reflexives may have long-distance antecedents. However, long-distance binding is subject to various restrictions, thus casting doubt on solutions that simply parametrize binding categories across languages. For example, in Chinese the bare reflexive *ziji* can have a long-distance antecedent, but only when the remote antecedent agrees with all closer potential antecedents in their phi-features.

(137) Zhangsan$_i$ juede Lisi$_j$ zongshi piping ziji$_{i/j}$
Zhangsan feel Lisi always criticize self
"Zhangsan said that Lisi always criticized him/himself"

(138) Zhangsan$_i$ juede wo$_j$ zongshi piping ziji$_{*i/j}$
Zhangsan feel I always criticize self
"Zhangsan said that I always criticized *him/myself"

(139) ni$_i$ juede Lisi$_j$ zongshi piping ziji$_{*i/j}$
you feel Lisi always criticize self
"Zhangsan said that Lisi always criticized *you/himself"

Huang and Tang propose that the facts surrounding long-distance *ziji* can be accounted for nicely if *ziji* is assumed to undergo IP-adjunction, i.e. QR, in LF, and if Binding Theory applies at LF, in addition to S-Structure. Since the bare reflexive does not contain phi-features, the first pass of Binding Theory enables the reflexive to inherit the phi-features, but not referential features from the local antecedent. In LF, adjunction of *ziji* to IP enables it to be locally bound by a higher antecedent, as long as the antecedent matches the phi-features that *ziji* now possesses. Long-distance anaphora is blocked in (138) and (139) because the reflexive has received phi-features from the local antecedent prior to LF movement, making it incompatible with the remote antecedent.

Katada (1991) also offers an LF analysis of long-distance *zibun* in Japanese. She shows that *zibun* behaves more like an operator than other forms of the reflexive pronoun, suggesting that it should appear in A′ position in LF. A common property of Katada's and Huang and Tang's proposals is, then, the view that the bare reflexives are both operators and anaphors, and hence they undergo QR (*qua* operators) and are subject to condition A (*qua* anaphors) at LF, which combine to derive their long-distance properties.

The accounts proposed by Pica, Battistella, and Cole, Hermon, and Sung treat the long-distance anaphors more in line with the Lebeaux–Chomsky proposal, taking the movement involved to be one of head-movement of the bare reflexive to I^0. Though these accounts differ non-trivially from the XP-movement account, they share the spirit of reducing apparent long-distance anaphora to successive links of local anaphora, relying on the level of LF. For more details of these analyses, see chapter 4 in this volume, and the references cited.

Although, in contrast to reflexives, reciprocals are typically locally bound, Higginbotham (1981) and Lebeaux (1983) show that they may also exhibit long-distance binding.

(140) John and Mary think they like each other

This sentence is ambiguous, meaning either (a) that John and Mary think that they, John and Mary, like each other, or (b) that John thinks he likes Mary and Mary thinks she likes John. As Higginbotham indicates, this ambiguity is a matter of scope, the first reading instantiating the narrow scope reading of *each other*, and the latter its wide scope reading. An important contrast with (140) is observed in the following sentences:

(141) John and Mary think that we like each other
(142) *John and Mary think that I like each other

(141)–(142) cannot have the wide scope reading. Thus (141) cannot have the reading that John thinks that we like Mary and Mary thinks that we like John. As Lebeaux (1983) indicates, the wide scope reading is available only when the local subject is understood anaphorically, as in the wide scope paraphrase of (140).

Now the standard Binding Theory does not provide an adequate way to represent the two readings, since the standard indexing system gives only the following representation for both readings of (140):

(143) John and $Mary_i$ think $they_i$ like each $other_i$

The theory also fails to explain why the wide scope reading disappears in (141)–(142).

In a recent paper, Heim, Lasnik, and May (1991) (HLM) take up this problem and show that the relevant facts fall together naturally under an LF account they propose, modifying an earlier proposal by Lebeaux (1983). Specifically, in LF a reciprocal sentence has the element *each* adjoined to an NP:

(144) [[John and Mary] $each_2$] like [e_2 other]

The NP to which *each* is attached is then interpreted distributively. The ambiguity of (140) concerns which NP is interpreted distributively, i.e. an ambiguity concerning the scope of *each*:

(145) [[John and Mary] $each_2$] think they like [e_2 other]
(146) John and Mary think that [[they] $each_2$] like [e_2 other]

To account for the locality or "blocking effects" illustrated in (141) and (142), HLM propose that in a representation like (144), (a) the trace e_2 of *each* in *[e_2 other]* is an anaphor, and (b) the phrase *[e_2 other]* is an R-expression. (Furthermore, both the [NP-*each*] phrase and the *[e_2 other]* phrase are quantificational, subject to QR.) As an anaphor, the e_2 must be bound in its governing category. In both (145) and (146), this requirement is fulfilled, and the sentence is ambiguous, just in case the embedded subject *they* has index 2 and binds e_2. The sentence (141) has only the narrow scope reading because *we* must locally bind the trace of *each,* and *we* cannot be coindexed with *John and Mary.* (142) is ill-formed because the singular embedded subject cannot have a distributive interpretation.

HLM note that the same proposal also solves the "grain puzzle" discussed by Higginbotham (1985), as illustrated in (147), which poses another serious problem to the classical binding theory:

(147) John and Mary told each other that they should leave

This sentence has at least the following three readings: John and Mary told each other: (a) "I should leave," (b) "You should leave," or (c) "We should leave." The LF representation after *each* is adjoined to *John and Mary* is (148):

(148) [[John and Mary]$_1$ each$_2$ told [e$_2$ other]$_3$ that they should leave

The three readings are simply those according to which *they* takes (a) the distributed sense of *John and Mary,* (b) the R-expression *[e$_2$ other],* and (c) the group sense of *John and Mary* as its antecedent.

Note that there is a striking similarity between the Huang–Tang–Katada account of long-distance reflexives and the HLM treatment of "long-distance reciprocals." In both cases long-distance binding is subject to some local blocking effects. In both accounts the relevant categories are treated as having a dual status, both as an anaphor and as an operator. And the interactions of Binding Theory and QR give the result that long-distance reciprocals and reflexives are limited in the way they are.[12]

Other principles of Binding Theory have also begun to play an increasing role in LF. For example, within the Generalized Binding framework, Aoun and Li (1988) and Aoun and Hornstein (1991) show that bound variable pronouns are subject to not only an A-disjointness requirement (Principle B), but also an A′-disjointness requirement, at LF. As for Principle C, the idea that it can apply in LF has been around for several years, but it has also been generally assumed that it must also apply at S-Structure. The most important evidence comes from the contrast below:

(149) Which picture that John$_i$ took did he$_i$ like t?
(150) *He$_i$ liked every picture that John$_i$ took
(151) *Who knows he$_i$ likes how many pictures that John$_i$ took?

The distinction between (149) and (150)–(151) is drawn if Principle C applies at S-Structure. At LF, (150) and (151) have their object phrases preposed, yielding structures which do not differ from (149) as far as Principle C goes:

(152) *[[Every picture that John$_i$ took] [he$_i$ liked t]]
(153) *[[How many pictures that John$_i$ took] who] [t knows he$_i$ likes t]]?

A different possibility is considered in Chomsky (1992), and in Hornstein and Weinberg (1991), who propose that the LF movement may affect only the QP or determiner of a QNP, but need not pied-pipe. (See also Dobrovie-Sorin (1992), who discusses both the determiner-raising and the NP-raising possibilities.) Suppose that there is actually an anti-pied-piping requirement (perhaps based on economy considerations), then in (150) and (151) only *every* and *how many* (or merely *how*) will be moved in LF. The LF structures of these sentences can be ruled out at this level. This makes it possible to require Binding Theory to apply at LF only, trivializing the role of S-Structure, and has other consequences for the general theory of grammatical design.

5.3 *Comparative Semantics*

As indicated in section 4.1, the LF movement hypothesis of *wh*-in-situ has the consequence that languages do not differ in whether they have a rule of *wh*-movement, but in where the rule applies, if not in overt syntax then in LF. The conception of grammar embodying this and other assumptions of LF has led to numerous fruitful studies on a diverse range of languages in the past decade with results that form the basis of a field of "comparative semantics," or typology of LF, as part of comparative syntax. Variations across languages in the interpretive properties of their sentences are reduced to certain parameters of Universal Grammar whose values may be fixed on the basis of primary linguistic data. For example, we noted earlier that although in the Chinese–Japanese type of languages a sentence like (99) (repeated below) is ambiguous, the corresponding English sentences are not, as in (93):

(99) Zhangsan jide Lisi mai-le shenme (?)
Zhangsan remember Lisi bought what
(99a) "Zhangsan remembers what Lisi bought"
(99b) "What does Zhangsan remember Lisi bought?"
(93a) What does John remember Mary bought t?
(93b) John remembers what Mary bought t

This difference in ambiguity is a fact of comparative semantics reducible directly to the parameter of where *wh*-movement takes place. The scope of a *wh*-phrase is fixed once it moves to an A′-position binding a variable. Chinese and English *wh*-questions have the same D-structure representations; in English they are disambiguated in the mapping from D-structure to S-Structure, but in Chinese they are disambiguated in the mapping from S-Structure to LF.

5.3.1 *Quantifier Scope*

A similar cross-linguistic contrast in scope ambiguity of quantifiers is observed by Kiss (1991). Kiss shows that in Hungarian non-interrogative quantifiers may be adjoined to VP at S-Structure, unlike quantifiers in English, or they may stay in their base positions, as in English. One may think of this as meaning that QR may apply in overt syntax in Hungarian, though in English it only applies in LF. What is interesting is that quantifiers that are A′-moved this way do not exhibit scope ambiguities, whereas those that stay in their base positions often display such ambiguities, as quantifiers in English typically do. The difference between Hungarian and English with respect to QR is thus on a par with that between English and Chinese with respect to *wh*-movement. Thus, another fact of comparative semantics follows from the parameter of where a particular instance of Move-α applies in the grammar.

There are other cross-linguistic differences in quantifier scope ambiguities. For example, although in English a sentence like (154) is now generally considered to be ambiguous between a distributive and a collective reading, it has been observed that similar ambiguities are often not found in Chinese or Japanese (S. Huang (1981), Huang (1982); Hoji (1985)). In contrast to (154), (155) does not have a *purported* collective reading:

(154) Every student bought a book (ambiguous)
(155) mei-ge xuesheng dou mai-le yi-ben shu
every student all bought one book
"Every student bought one book or another" (unambiguous)

Huang (1982) proposed that the non-ambiguity of (155) follows from a general correspondence principle which says that if QNP1 c-commands QNP2 at S-Structure then there is a representation at LF in which the same c-command relationship is preserved. In fact, the correspondence principle, which has been dubbed the Isomorphic Principle in Aoun and Li (1989) (A&L), has its origin in earlier works on quantifier scope in English (Lakoff (1971), Reinhart (1976); cf. also a linear version given in Kroch (1974) and S. Huang (1981)). The essence of the principle is also found in current work (e.g., the Rigidity Condition of Lasnik and Saito (1992), and the principle of "Relation Preservation" in Watanabe (1991).) A&L proposed a modification of the Isomorphic Principle to allow the trace of a QNP to play a role in determining quantifier scope. That is, for two QNPs α and β, α may have scope over β if α c-commands β or a trace of β. This offers a simple account of the contrast between (31) and (32) highlighted in May (1985):

(31) What$_i$ did everyone buy t$_i$ for Max?
(32) Who$_i$ t$_i$ bought everything for Max?

In (31), *what* c-commands *everyone,* and *everyone* c-commands the trace of *what,* so the sentence exhibits scope ambiguity. In (32), *everything* c-commands neither *who* nor the *wh*-trace, so the sentence has only a collective reading.

The necessity of some version of the Isomorphic Principle appears to be beyond doubt then. Its incorporation into the theory of grammar is also quite natural, and conceptually fits into the general considerations of economy of derivation (Chomsky (1991, 1992)). The question that remains is, how the cross-linguistic difference illustrated in (154)–(155) is to be explained. One cannot, of course, account for the difference by parametrizing the Isomorphic Principle itself; this move is excluded not only on learnability grounds, but also on grounds of examples in English (e.g. (31)–(32)) which show the relevance of the principle. Therefore this fact of comparative semantics must be explained in some other way. Attempts at an explanation were made in Huang (1982) and A&L (1989). Huang's proposal was that the English–Chinese difference should follow from the head-directionality parameter which characterizes the surface word order differences between the two languages, and a concomitant difference in the possibility, or lack thereof, of vacuously extraposing one quantifier above the other.[13] A&L's was to relate the difference to a difference in the D-structure position of the subject in these two languages, which amounts to parametrizing the VP-internal Subject Hypothesis. Both accounts are somewhat incomplete (see A&L and Huang (1993) for discussion), however, and a thorough explanation of this contrast is still yet to come.

5.3.2 *Bound Variable Pronouns*

The properties of bound variable pronouns also show considerable variation among languages. One of the earliest observations in this area was made by Higginbotham (1980b), who showed that, although sentences like *Whose mother loves him?* admit a bound reading of the pronoun, corresponding sentences in Chinese are generally judged to have no bound reading. An important fact of variation was brought to light in Saito and Hoji's (1983) study of weak crossover in Japanese, where it is reported that overt pronouns only have a referential use, and that only zero pronouns or reflexives can take quantificational antecedents in this language. The following sentences are ungrammatical under a bound construal, but become grammatical once the overt pronoun is replaced by *zibun* "self" or a zero pronoun:

(156) *daremo-ga [kare-ga atamaga ii to] omotteiru
everyone-Nom he-Nom smart-be Comp think
"Everyone thinks he is smart"

(157) *daremo-ga [John-ga kare-o nagutta to] omotteiru
everyone-Nom John-Nom he-Acc hit Comp think
"Everyone thinks that John hit him"

Montalbetti (1984) observes that there is also a ban on using overt pronouns as bound variables in Spanish, but only when they appear as subjects. So sentences corresponding to (156) are also ill-formed in Spanish, though those corresponding to (157) are well-formed. Aoun and Li (1988) also observe a similar but somewhat different restriction on overt pronouns in Chinese.

The question raised by these facts for comparative semantics is how the differences among these languages can be reduced to independent, learnable parametric differences among them. Montalbetti (1984) observed that the environments in which overt pronouns are excluded from bound variable interpretations are those in which an empty pronoun is available. English does not allow *pro*-drop, so overt pronouns may be used as bound variables. Spanish allows *pro*-drop in subject positions, but not in object positions, so only in the subject position are overt pronouns prohibited from having bound interpretations. And Japanese disallows overt bound pronouns in both subject and object positions, because zero pronouns are allowed in both positions, etc. Montalbetti proposed the Overt Pronoun Constraint (OPC), which prohibits an overt pronoun to be linked to a variable just in case the overt/empty alternation obtains. The explanation provided by the OPC appears to be quite natural; in fact, it may simply be a formal statement of the informal "Avoid Pronoun" principle suggested in Chomsky (1981) which accounts for the following:

(158) John_i enjoys PRO_i reading these books

(159) ??John_i enjoys his_i reading these books

Although (159) is not nearly as bad as (156)–(157), this is probably due to the fact that although binding is prohibited in (159), the sentence may nevertheless be acceptable under accidental coreference. With a non-referential antecedent, the Avoid Pronoun effect is clear:

(160) Who enjoys PRO reading these books?
(161) *Who enjoyed his reading these books?

Aoun and Li (1988) and Aoun and Hornstein (1991) take the restriction on overt bound pronouns to be a reflection of their A′-disjointness principle, which requires an overt pronoun to be A′-free in its minimal governing category with a subject. For some of the speakers they consulted, the following facts obtain:

(162) *shei shuo ta kanjian-le Lisi?
who say he see-Perf Lisi
"Who said that he saw Lisi?"
(163) shei shuo Lisi kanjian-le ta?
who said Lisi see-Perf he
"Who said that Lisi saw him?"
(164) shei zhidao ni shuo ta kanjian-le Lisi?
who knows you say he see-Perf Lisi
"Who said that you said that he saw Lisi?"

That is, an overt pronoun in an embedded clause cannot be quantificationally bound in the immediate clause up if it occurs as a subject (162), but binding is possible if it occurs as an object (163), or in a further embedded clause (164). This locality effect is accounted for by their principle, in effect a "condition B" of A′-binding. In (162), the minimal CP containing the overt pronoun and a distinct subject is the root clause, so the pronoun cannot be A′-bound in this clause. In both (163) and (164), the minimal CP containing the pronoun and a distinct subject is embedded under the main verb, so the pronoun may be A′-bound in the main clause.

The A′-disjointness theory accounts for certain contrasts that Montalbetti's OPC account does not. For example, although the subject/object asymmetry between (162) and (163) is explained by the OPC under the assumption that Chinese has subject *pros* but no object *pros* (Huang (1984)), the well-formedness of (164) is unexpected with an overt subject pronoun.[14] Furthermore, the following seems to obtain for some speakers of English:

(165a) ?*The election of no president_i will please him_i
(165b) The election of no president_i will please his_i critics

The ameliorating effect of further embedding observed here may be explained under some appropriate version of the A′-disjointness principle (on a par with the contrast **John saw him* vs. *John saw his mother*), but the OPC has nothing to say here since English is not a *pro*-drop language.

The theory of A′-disjointness is not without its problems, however. For example, Japanese disallows overt bound pronouns regardless of their depth of embedding, and Italian/Spanish excludes overt bound pronouns from embedded subject position even though the embedded clause is the disjointness domain in this language (with Agr). Furthermore, it is not clear why zero pronouns are not subject to the A′-disjointness principle given that they are obviously subject to the A-disjointness principle, though this question does not arise in the OPC account. Finally, for the speakers who accept all of (162)–(164), neither the OPC nor the disjointness theory provides an account for these sentences. So the issue surrounding variations in bound variable pronouns is still open.

5.3.3 Wh-*in-situ*

An issue of variation that has emerged since Huang's (1982) and Lasnik and Saito's (1984) investigation of *wh*s-in-situ is that, although the complement/adjunct asymmetry with respect to *wh*-extraction evidently holds universally of all languages, and of both overt and covert movement, languages like Chinese and Japanese do not display the familiar subject–object asymmetry observed in English and other languages. Thus, although the following sentences cannot be interpreted as a direct *why*-question or a direct A–not-A question, they can be easily interpreted as direct questions regarding the embedded subject *shei* "who":

(166) ni xiang-zhidao [shei weishenme mai shu]?
you wonder who why buy book
"Who is the x such that you wonder why x bought the books?"

(167) ni xiang-zhidao [shei you-mei-you mai shu]?
you wonder who have-not-have buy book
"Who is the x such that you wonder whether x bought the books?"

The absence of subject-ECP effects under overt *wh*-movement in certain "free inversion" languages is, of course, familiar since Rizzi (1982), but their absence in Chinese–Japanese crucially cannot be accounted for along Rizzi's well known solution in terms of inversion, since the issue concerns *wh*-in-situ and since these languages do not allow free inversion.

The account for this variation suggested by Huang (1982) was that the subject is somehow properly governed internally in Chinese. The specific execution of this idea was to simply stipulate that I^0 is a proper governor in this language. A more satisfactory execution of the idea was proposed by Koopman and Sportiche (1991) (K&S), under the VP Internal Subject Hypothesis. K&S propose, in essence, that although in all languages the subject is base-generated in [Spec, VP], languages differ as to where the subject is at S-Structure. In particular, in English-type languages the subject raises from [Spec, VP] to the [Spec, IP] position, binding an NP trace, prior to *wh*-movement, whereas in Chinese-type languages raising to [Spec, IP] is not required. Hence, *wh*-movement of a subject must always take place from the [Spec, IP] position in English, whether it takes place at S-Structure or in LF, but in Chinese extraction may directly take place from the [Spec, VP] position. The lack of subject ECP effects in Chinese thus follows from the fact that its subjects are lexically governed in [Spec, VP] and need not be antecedent-governed.[15]

K&S's account works as far as the above facts go. It has been observed recently, however, that even in English a subject *wh*-in-situ may fail to display locality effects (see May (1985), Lasnik and Saito (1992), Tiedeman (1990)). Consider English multiple questions corresponding to (166)–(167):

(168) Who remembers why who bought the books?
(169) Who remembers whether who went to the movies?

These sentences are in fact well-formed if the embedded subject is paired with the matrix subject, but not if it is paired with the embedded *wh*-phrase (cf. **Why did who buy the books?*, **What did who buy?*). On the matrix paired-list reading, the embedded subject does not exhibit any ECP effect. English and Chinese do not differ, then, in allowing subject long extraction in LF. The real difference seems to lie between overt movement, where long extraction of the subject is excluded, and LF movement, where it is not. Tiedeman (1990) suggests that the difference stems from the nature of proper government, which should be defined in linear terms at S-Structure (*à la* Kayne's (1983b) notion of canonical government), but in pure structural terms at LF. This has the effect that subjects are properly governed by I^0 at LF but not at S-Structure, since I^0 occurs to the right of subjects. Huang (1993), on the other hand, proposed that the possibility of long subject extraction follows from the assumption that the LF-created trace in [Spec, IP] can be deleted freely in the presence of a trace in VP-internal subject position, in accordance with general considerations of economy of representation. Because of the possibility of deletion, an LF-created subject trace will not cause any ECP violations.[16]

A final issue of variation has to do with the very fact that languages vary in whether or not they exhibit (overt) *wh*-movement. The theory of LF states this variation in terms of where *wh*-movement takes place in grammar, but deeper questions concerning this typology have not been addressed. For example, why is it that in Chinese and Japanese, but not in English, *wh*-phrases move only in LF? And why is it that in Polish but not, say, in French, all *wh*-phrases have to be fronted in overt syntax? One plausible answer to the first question may be derived from Nishigauchi's (1990) and Li's (1992) recent studies concerning the various uses of *wh*-phrases. It is well known that *wh*-words in Chinese and Japanese, in addition to their uses as question words, may also be used as existential or universal quantifiers, though in English they are used as question words only. Thus depending on different contexts the phrase *shenme* may have an interrogative, universal, or existential reading:

(170) ni xiang mai shenme (ne)?
you want buy what Q
"What do you want to buy?"

(171) wo shenme dou mai
I everything all buy
"I will buy everything"

(172a) wo bu xiang mai shenme
I not want buy anything
"I don't want to buy anything"

(172b) ni xiang mai shenme ma?
you want buy something Q
"Would you like to buy something?"

(172c) ta dagai mai-le shenme le
he probably buy-Perf something Part
"He probably bought something"

In brief, a *wh*-word is interpreted as an existential quantifier in a negative or affective context (172a–b), or minimally a context where the truth of a proposition is not positively asserted (172c); as a universal quantifier in the context of the adverb *dou* "all"; and as a question word otherwise. The exact quantificational force of a *wh*-word is therefore not inherently fixed, but determined by its context. This reminds one of a similar property of indefinite NPs, as treated in Lewis (1975) and Heim (1982), whose quantificational force seems to vary depending on the types of adverbs of quantification that "unselectively" bind them. One natural answer to why *wh*-phrases in Chinese and Japanese must stay in situ may then be that they must be in the domain of some appropriate binder at S-Structure in order to be interpreted as interrogative phrases. If they were moved to [Spec, CP] at S-Structure outside of the domain of an unselective binder, they would be left uninterpreted. One way to execute this idea is to invoke a rule that assigns a *wh*-phrase the features of a universal, existential, or interrogative quantifier at S-Structure under an appropriate binder. Once the appropriate features are assigned, the *wh*-phrases may then be subjected to the appropriate LF-movement process (QR or *wh*-movement).

Cheng (1991) observes that the lack of syntactic *wh*-movement in a given language generally correlates with the availability of question particles in that language. For example, in Mandarin Chinese yes/no questions require the final particle *ma*, and direct *wh*-questions, disjunctive questions, and A–not-A questions may optionally take the particle *ne*. In Japanese the question particle *ka* or *no* is routinely required of all questions. And these languages employ the in-situ strategy of forming questions. English, on the other hand, does not have question particles, and *wh*-movement is obligatory in this language. Cheng proposes a theory of Clausal Typing to account for this correlation. According to this theory, all interrogative clauses must be typed as such by some marking within the CP constituent, and languages may type a clause as a *wh*-question by base-generating a question particle under CP, or by moving a *wh*-phrase into its Spec. Question particles in Chinese and Japanese thus not only unselectively bind *wh*-words and give them their interrogative force, but also serve to type clauses as interrogatives. The lack of syntactic *wh*-movement in Chinese-type languages then comes from the existence of question particles in them, and from the principle of economy of derivation. Economy considerations also prohibit English-type languages (or any language) from overtly moving more than one *wh*-phrase into [Spec, CP]. Movement of the second *wh*-phrase, like that of all *wh*-phrases in Chinese, must be delayed until LF, where it is motivated by other considerations (scope, the *wh*-Criterion, the ECP, etc.). As Cheng shows, her proposal has significant implications for the analysis of other languages, some of which she discusses in detail, including those with apparent cases of optional movement and multiple fronting, and it has other theoretical consequences yet to be fully addressed.

Related Material in Other Chapters

Given that the linguistic level of Logical Form most directly represents the contribution of the syntactic structure to the meaning of a sentence, practically every other chapter contains material that in one way or the other relates to the theory of LF. The treatment of X-bar theory and Case theory in chapter 1 as well as the theory of the structural conditions on the assignment of thematic roles and the realization of arguments from chapter 2 complement the conditions on the representations of quantified arguments, selection for different clause types, and the treatment of scope and various pronoun types in the present chapter. The remarks on binding at LF overlap with the discussion of anaphors and LF movement in chapter 4 and hence with the conditions the ECP imposes on movement, the topic of chapter 5. Chapter 7 details the strengthened role that the level of LF plays in the Minimalist Program.

NOTES

1 Other topics that have figured prominently in the syntax of LF include the syntax of "antecedent-contained deletion" (widely discussed since May (1985); see Baltin (1987), Larson and May (1990), Clark (1992)), Ellipsis (Reinhart (1991)) and the problem of reconstruction (Barss (1986) among others). Due to space limitations, these will not be addressed in this chapter. It should also be noted that even the existence of LF is not entirely uncontroversial among linguists working within the GB framework. For some recent exchanges of opposing views, see Williams (1977, 1988), May (1988a), Hornstein and Weinberg (1991) and references cited there.

2 That this reading of (17) seems difficult to get is presumably due to pragmatic factors, since there is no possibility for there being anybody who has every California city as his/her place of origin.

3 On a par with **Who$_i$ did he$_i$ say I saw t$_i$?* and **John$_i$, he$_i$ said I saw t$_i$*, where a variable (as an R-expression) is A-bound. (43d) is actually not readily excluded by condition C, as it stands, because the trace is the trace of *whose mother*, not that of *whose*. Several proposals have been made to bring (43d) under condition C. Chomsky's proposal (1976) is to convert, or reconstruct, (43d) into the structure (i) or (ii) at LF:

(i) Who$_i$ does he$_i$ love t$_i$'s mother?
(ii) For which x: x a person, he loves x's mother?

The ill-formedness follows if condition C is made to apply at LF. Other proposals to deal with such problems of reconstruction include the "layered traces" hypothesis discussed in Riemsdijk and Williams (1981) and the approach of Barss (1986), who modified the notion of binding by incorporating into it the relevance of chains.

4 A definite description (including anaphoric epithets) should probably be classified as both a referential expression and a pronominal, as Lasnik (1989a) has argued. The donkey pronoun is clearly *also* a pronoun, in addition to being an R-expression.

5 The pronoun in *Everybody thinks he is smart* cannot have a donkey pronoun reading. This illustrates an anti-c-command requirement of the donkey pronoun. This requirement follows from the donkey pronoun's being an R-expression, which cannot be A-bound.

6 The BP, as given, fails to account for an important difference between weak crossover and permissible parasitic gap constructions like the following:

(i) What $book_i$ did you buy t_i without reading e_i?

In this construction the A′-phrase locally A′-binds both its trace and the empty category in violation of the BP, but the sentence is quite good. Safir (1984) explains this by a parallelism condition that allows an A′ category to bind more than one variable, as long as the variables are of the same type (all overt pronouns or all empty categories).

7 Higginbotham in fact took accessibility as a condition on an LF re-indexing rule that changes the index of a pronoun to that of a QNP or its variable.

8 It has been observed that weak crossover effects are considerably weaker in relative and topic structures and other null-operator constructions. Thus examples like *the man who his mother saw* and *John, his mother saw* are quite acceptable with bound variable readings. Chomsky (1982) attributed this ameliorating effect to a post-LF predication rule. See Lasnik and Stowell (1991) for detailed discussions.

9 The relevance of the ECP to QR was first demonstrated by Kayne (1981), on the basis of the following distribution of the negative polarity item *ne . . . personne* in French:

(i) ?je n'exige que tu vois personne
I (neg)-require that you see nobody
"There is nobody that I require that you see"

(ii) *je n'exige que personne vienne
I (neg)-require that nobody come
Intended: "There is nobody that I require to come"

Kayne shows that the scope interpretation of *personne* depends on the position of *ne*. So, in sentences like the above with *ne* occurring in the matrix clause, the embedded *personne* is required to have matrix scope. As illustrated, however, although *personne* can occur in the object position, it cannot occur as a subject. Kayne argues that this is a subject/object asymmetry to be attributed to the ECP at LF. In particular, after QR applies to *personne* in LF, the subject trace in (ii) will not be properly governed and will be ruled out by the ECP.

10 That QR can pied-pipe an entire phrase like *pictures of everybody* or *everyone's friend's mother* was already shown to be a necessary assumption by Higginbotham (1980b) for his accessibility account of weak crossover.

11 The operator can then be interpreted as a restrictive quantifier ranging over determiner meanings (i.e., {this, that, the one you met yesterday, etc.}).

12 HLM show that long-distance reciprocals exhibit clear island effects. This follows because the trace of *each*, though an anaphor, occurs in an adjunct position, and thus is subject to antecedent government in addition to local binding. Huang and

Tang (1991) show, on the other hand, that long-distance *ziji* in Chinese does not exhibit island effects. Thus a bare reflexive contained in a relative clause may have as its antecedent an NP outside the relative clause. This again is expected because *ziji* is an argument, and as indicated already in the discussion above, LF movement of a *wh* argument does not show Subjacency effects.

13 That is, English (as a head-initial language) allows the object to be vacuously extraposed to the right to a position where it can c-command a preceding argument, but Chinese (being essentially head-final) does not. This possibility is quite natural and is in line with Fukui's (1993) hypothesis that the difference between English and Japanese with respect to the existence of scrambling also follows from the head-directionality parameter, under the hypothesis that the economy of derivation principle allows for free optional movement where the movement does not change the head-directionality pattern of a given language. (Leftward Scrambling is possible for head-final languages, and rightward Scrambling possible for head-initial languages.)

14 Actually the difficulty presented by (164) for the OPC may be solved given the fact that, even though the most deeply embedded subject may be a *pro*, it needs to take the immediate superordinate subject as its antecedent under some minimal distance requirement. In other words, the OPC applies only when the overt/empty alternation obtains under the same interpretation.

15 In fact, K&S's account is formulated in terms of the Condition on Long Extraction, instead of antecedent government. The theory of proper government has undergone substantial development since it was first proposed in Chomsky (1981), as can be seen from chapter 5 in this volume and references cited there. But I will keep to the classical version where differences from recent formulations are irrelevant to our discussion.

16 This account has the consequence that the Superiority Condition cannot be subsumed under the ECP, but may be reformulated in terms of economy of derivation. Thus, the contrast between *Who bought what?* and **What did who buy?* obtains because the principle prefers shorter moves than longer moves. *Who* has to be moved first at S-Structure, and the longer move of *what* is postponed until LF by the principle "Procrastinate" (Chomsky (1992)). See also Lasnik and Saito (1992) for a restatement of the Superiority Condition.

4

Binding Theory, Control, and *pro*

Wayne Harbert
Cornell University

Contents

Prelude

The topic of the current chapter is the Binding Theory, i.e. the set of conditions on the co-occurrence of different types of NPs, both overt and covert. The chapter begins with an introduction to the paradigm the canonical version of the Binding Theory was based on and a discussion of the evolution of the binding principles. This discussion is followed by a detailed examination of several binding-theoretic phenomena which require modifications to the version of the Binding Theory in Chomsky (1981). Among these are long-distance anaphors which raise the important question of whether the notion of *governing category* needs to be parametrized and, if yes, how this is best done. The chapter presents a number of different approaches to this topic some of which treat anaphor binding in terms of movement while others do not. Discussed as well are logophors and the special descriptive problems they pose as well as a peculiar anti-anaphor.

We also find a discussion of the status of the disjoint reference principles, in particular whether principle C of the binding theory might be dropped from the grammar in favor of a treatment of the phenomena it is supposed to cover by pragmatic principles. The arguments for and against both views are compared.

The final section of the chapter contains a detailed presentation of the relationship between binding theory and empty categories, in particular the treatment of PRO and *pro*, the two pronominal empty categories whose main function it is to serve as the subjects of non-tensed and tensed clausal structures. Different approaches to the licensing of each of these elements are discussed.

A discussion of the relationship between binding theory and traces concludes the chapter.

1 Introduction

Binding Theory is the subtheory of Government and Binding Theory which deals with indexing relationships between nominal expressions.[1] We will begin our examination of it by looking in a very sketchy way at some of the properties of these elements which it attempts to account for, and establishing some basic concepts and definitions. We will then proceed to a more detailed consideration of a number of core problems to which investigators of these properties have addressed themselves. Consider the examples in (1).

(1a) *I hurt himself
(1b) He_i hurt himself_i

English has a set of nominal elements, including reflexives like *himself,* which are referentially dependent on an antecedent in the same sentence, which they must match in such grammatical features as number and gender. (1a) is ill-formed because the sentence contains no such antecedent. (1b), on the other hand, is well-formed, because there is an antecedent – the pronoun *he*. We understand the reflexive to corefer with *he* here, and we represent this by assigning them identical indices.[2] Reflexives and similar elements, such as reciprocals, which are required to be coindexed with antecedents in this way are known collectively as *anaphors.*

There are restrictions on the admissible structural relationships between anaphors and their antecedents. The first of these has to do with the relative position of the two elements within the syntactic tree. Compare (2a) with the ill-formed (2b):

(2a) John and Mary_i $[_{VP}$ saw each other's_i children]
(2b) *Each other's_i children $[_{VP}$ saw John and $\text{Mary}_i]$

These examples show that, while a subject phrase is a suitable antecedent for an anaphoric element contained within the object of the verb (in this instance, a reciprocal), the object is not a suitable antecedent for an anaphor contained in the subject phrase. This asymmetry in the anaphor–antecedent relationship can be captured by claiming that anaphors must be c-commanded by their antecedents, where *c-command* is defined as in (3):

(3) α c-commands β iff α does not dominate β and every phrase γ dominating α also dominates β.

This c-command requirement is satisfied in (2a), but not in (2b), where the VP dominates the intended antecedent but not the anaphor. Thus, anaphors appear to have to be coindexed with c-commanding antecedents. We will say that an element α which is coindexed with a c-commanding element β is *bound* by β.[3]

Other restrictions on the binding relation between anaphors and antecedents have to do with *locality*. Anaphors have to be bound within specific syntactic domains. So, for example, while an English reflexive may be bound to the subject of its own clause, as in (4a), it may not be bound to the subject of a higher clause, across the subject of its own clause, as seen in (4b):

(4a) She thinks [$_D$ he$_i$ hurt himself$_i$]
(4b) *He$_i$ thinks [$_D$ she hurt himself$_i$]

In (4a), the anaphor is bound within its *local domain*, D, and therefore satisfies the locality requirement. In (4b), on the other hand, the intended antecedent occurs outside the local domain of that anaphor, and therefore the locality requirement is not satisfied.

A quite different type of behavior is exhibited by elements like *she, her*. Unlike anaphors, these elements do not have to be bound, as shown in (5a). They can be bound, as in (5b), but, as (5c) shows, only by a binder outside of their local domains. The relationship between a pronoun and a c-commanding nominal within the same local domain, as in (5c), is one of obligatory *disjoint reference*.

(5a) I$_i$ like her$_k$
(5b) She$_i$ thinks [$_D$ I like her$_i$]
(5c) *She$_i$ likes her$_i$

These properties are captured by claiming that these elements represent a second type of nominal element, *pronouns*, which must be *free* in their local domain, where free means "not bound."[4] (These local domains are sometimes known as domains of *opacity*, since they are "opaque" to the processes of anaphor binding and disjoint reference interpretation of pronouns.)[5]

Full noun phrases like *the man in the hat* – that is, those headed by lexical nouns – exhibit yet a third type of behavior. Like pronouns, they require no antecedents within the sentence. Unlike pronouns, they may not be coindexed with any c-commanding argument, no matter how distant.[6] Compare (6) with (5b):

(6) *He$_i$ thinks [$_D$ I like [the man in the hat]$_i$]

Corresponding to these three types of nominals, it has been assumed since Chomsky (1980) that Binding Theory contains three Principles – one for anaphors, one for pronouns and one for *Referring Expressions* – which determine in each case which indexings are allowed and which are prohibited. The latter category, along with full NPs (*"names"*) like the one in (6), also includes the variables left behind by *wh*-movement. The assumption that these share with names the property of having to be free in all domains allows us to derive the so-called *strong crossover* effect in (7a) from Binding Theory.[7]

(7a) *The man who$_i$ she thinks he$_i$ believes [I like [vbl]$_i$] is over there
Cf.
(7b) The man who$_i$ [vbl]$_i$ thinks she believes [I like him$_i$] is over there

(7a) is ill-formed on the interpretation under which *he* and the relative pronoun corefer. This can be accounted for if we assume that the trace left behind by *wh*-movement has the same status for Binding Theory as a full NP. (7a) is then out for the same reason as (6) – because an R-expression is coindexed with a c-commanding nominal. Note, however, that this requires a modification of our claims about referring expressions; they cannot be required to be free with respect to all c-commanding elements. (7a) becomes good if the pronoun and the variable are differently indexed, even though the variable is still coindexed with a c-commanding antecedent, the relative pronoun *who*. (Cf. the well-formed (7b).) There is a difference in the status of the relative pronoun and the subject pronoun *he* in (7a), though; the former, but not the latter, is in an A-bar position. Therefore, we could get the right result (and in fact insure that *wh*-movement is a movement to A-bar positions) by restricting our binding principles to *A-Binding*.[8] With this modification, our Binding Theory may be stated schematically as in (8):

(8) *Principle A* An anaphor must be A-bound within its local domain D.
Principle B A pronoun must be A-free within its local domain D.
Principle C An R-expression must be A-free.[9]

Against the background of this rudimentary sketch of the basic concepts of Binding Theory, we can now turn to a systematic consideration of the central issues which have been a concern to investigators working in this area. It should be noted from the outset that the relevant literature is by now very extensive, and it is impossible to do any more than give a cursory survey of it here. For expository purposes, we can identify a number of central problems which emerge repeatedly in that literature.

The first problem is the *domain problem* – the problem of the proper definition of the local domain D in (8). This question has probably been the focus of the largest amount of attention in the literature on Binding Theory. It is made the more interesting by the fact that there is at least the appearance of considerable cross-linguistic variation in the domains in which anaphors must be bound and pronouns must be free. In Chinese, for example, the equivalent of the ungrammatical English (4b) is well-formed, as we will see. One of the current hot topics in Binding Theory is whether the definition of local domain must be assumed to be parameterized in order to accommodate this variation, or whether there is an invariant definition, with apparent variation arising from interaction between binding and other grammatical operations, e.g. abstract movement. Section 2 examines the domain problem. 2.1 briefly traces the development of the characterization of local domains for binding. Section 2.2 reviews a number of recent approaches to the phenomenon of apparent "long-distance" binding and cross-linguistic variation in binding domains (the *variation problem*). This discussion also touches tangentially on two problems fairly closely related to the domain problem. These are the *level problem* – the problem of the level(s) of representation at which binding principles hold[10] – and the *antecedent problem*. At issue in the latter is the proper characterization of the fact that while some languages, like English, allow non-subjects to antecede anaphors, many other languages, including Gothic, for example, allow only subjects as binders. This is illustrated by the examples in (9).

(9) guþ$_i$ hauheiþ ina$_k$ in sis$_{i/*k}$
(John 13:32)
God$_i$ glorifies him$_k$ in self$_{i/*k}$

As we will see below, Gothic also differs from English with respect to the domain in which anaphors must be bound. Under some accounts, these two differences are claimed to be linked.

Aspects of the *classification problem* – the problem of the number of different types of nominals the theory must account for, and how they fit under the principles of Binding Theory – are considered at various points in this study. Suppose we take as our starting point the assumption that the three principles in (8) correctly and exhaustively partition nominal expressions with respect to their referential properties – that is, that every nominal may be characterized as either an anaphor, a pronoun or an R-expression. There are three possible ways in which this initial assumption might be modified, and each of these has been proposed in individual cases. First, it has been envisioned since early in the development of Binding Theory that a single element may simultaneously fall under more than one principle. Chomsky (1981) uses this assumption to derive the distribution of the null pronominal PRO – in particular, the fact that it is restricted to ungoverned positions. According to Chomsky, this is because PRO is subject to both Principle

A and Principle B.[11] The conflicting requirements of these two principles can be satisfied (vacuously) only when PRO occurs in contexts not satisfying the definition of D. Given the definition for local domain which he adopts, this requirement is satisfied only in ungoverned contexts. Similarly, in his theory of *Generalized Binding,* Aoun (1985) claims that *wh*-traces fall under both Principle A and Principle C. These two cases are discussed in section 5, which consists of some brief, primarily bibliographical remarks on the question of how the principles of the Binding Theory apply to various types of empty categories. The possibility that an element may fall under more than one principle also arises in connection with the overt elements discussed in section 3. The converse possibility – that there are nominal elements which have no status at all with respect to Binding Principles – is discussed briefly in section 5.2.2 in connection with traces.

Second, it is possible that the inventory of principles in (8) is insufficiently rich, and does not provide an exhaustive typology of nominal types. Suggestions along these lines are mentioned in 2.2.2 and subsequent sections, and in section 3. Finally, section 4 reviews some proposals that (8) can be reduced through the elimination of one or more of the principles requiring disjoint reference, since disjoint reference effects are claimed to be derivable in a more general way.

Due to lack of space, virtually no mention will be made of the *acquisition problem* – the problem of how native speakers acquire their knowledge of the binding properties of individual nominal elements. It is probable that more attention has been paid to this aspect of syntactic acquisition than any other, making even the sketchiest review of the relevant literature impossible in the present chapter.

2 Specific Problems in Binding Theory

2.1 *The Evolution of Binding Principles*

By way of introducing our discussion of local domains, it will be useful perhaps to illustrate some of the behavior of anaphors and pronouns in English, a language in which these elements appear to observe fairly restricted domain conditions. The basic cases are listed in (10).

(10a) $They_i$ helped *each* $other_i$/$*them_i$
(10b) $They_i$ expected [*each* $other_i$/$*them_i$ to win]
(10c) $They_i$ expected [me to help $them_i$/*each* $*other_i$]

(10d) They$_i$ expected [**each other$_i$/they$_i$* would win]
(10e) They$_i$ expected [I would help **each other$_i$/them$_i$*]
(10f) They$_i$ read [books about *each other$_i$/??them$_i$*]
(10g) They$_i$ read [Mary's books about **each other$_i$/them$_i$*]
(10h) They$_i$ sold [*their$_i$/each other's$_i$* books]
(10i) They$_i$ put the books [beside *them$_i$/each other$_i$*]
(10j) They$_i$ thought that [[books about *each other$_i$/them$_i$*] would be on sale]

We observe that in the first several examples, proximate pronouns and anaphors (reciprocals, in the present case) are in complementary distribution: where an anaphor can be coindexed with the subject, a pronoun cannot be, and vice versa. This near complementarity led to the view in early work that the domains for Principle A (the domains in which anaphors must be bound) and the domains for Principle B (the domains in which pronouns must be free) are identical. A consideration of the rest of the paradigm, however, shows that complementary distribution does not hold throughout. We will return to the question of whether this observation requires us to abandon the assumption of identical domain specifications.

Contrasting (10f) and (10g), we see that the subject of the containing clause can count as a local binder for an anaphor occurring in complement position within a noun phrase if the noun phrase has no subject, but not if the noun phrase has a subject. Furthermore, an anaphor occurring in subject position of an infinitive clause can be locally bound to the subject of the main clause, as in (10b), but the object of an infinitive clause cannot be bound to the subject of the main clause, across the subject of its own clause, as (10c) shows. In both cases, then, the presence of a closer c-commanding subject appears to define a local domain, D, for the anaphor; an anaphor c-commanded by a subject cannot be bound to a higher subject. This role of subjects in defining domains for anaphor binding has been recognized since Chomsky (1973), and I follow the terminology of that work in referring to this as the *Specified Subject Condition* (SSC) case, as is still done in much recent work.

(11) D (in (8)) = the c-command domain of a subject NP (the SSC case).

(11) by itself, however, does not provide a completely adequate characterization of local domains. If we replace the infinitive complement of (10b) with a finite complement, as in (10d), we see that an anaphor in embedded subject position can no longer be bound to the higher clause subject, even though the higher clause is the minimal domain-satisfying

definition (11). A further locality requirement must be assumed, therefore, to cover this case. There are at least three differences between (10b) and (10d) to which their difference with respect to binding might be linked. The verb in (10d) is inflected for both agreement and tense, while the one in (10b) is not. Moreover, the subject of the complement clause in (10d) is in a context of nominative Case assignment, while the one in (10b) is not. Chomsky (1973) proposed that tense is the relevant factor here, and formulated a *Tensed S Condition* (TSC), which prevented anaphors from being bound across the boundaries of tensed clauses.[12] In the terms of our Binding Theory in (8), then, we arrive at the following two-part definition of local domains:

(12a) D = the c-command domain of tense (the TSC case).
(12b) D = the c-command domain of a subject NP (the SSC case).

This characterization goes a fair way toward accounting for the paradigm in (10). In the one instance, (10b), in which an anaphor occurs within an embedded clause but is not c-commanded by either tense or a subject within that clause, it is allowed to be bound by an antecedent in the higher clause.

There are some problems with this account, however. First, in (10e), the anaphor is free within the c-command domain of both the subject and the tense of the embedded clause, yet this example does not exhibit the additive effect in relative ill-formedness that one might expect to result from the violation of two independent conditions. Second, a characterization of local domains like (12) would predict, contrary to fact, that the version of (10j) with the reciprocal should be ill-formed, since that reciprocal is free in the c-command domain of the tense of the embedded clause. Chomsky (1980) proposes an alternative characterization of local domains which addresses both of these problems. This version keeps the SSC essentially as in (12b), but rejects the TSC in favor of a quite different principle, the *Nominative Island Condition* (NIC), which prevents a nominative anaphor from being free within the minimal clause containing it.

(12′a′) A nominative anaphor may not be free in S′ (the NIC)
(12′b′) (=12b)

The NIC duplicates the effect of the TSC in the one case, (10d), in which that principle does not overlap with the SSC. Under this account, the anaphor is excluded in (10d) because, as a nominative anaphor, it cannot be free in its clause. Unlike the TSC, however, the NIC does not overlap with the SSC in the case of (10e): the anaphor is ruled out here by the SSC alone, since it is not nominative, hence not covered by the NIC. Finally, the version of (10j) with the anaphor is correctly predicted to be well-formed under this account. The anaphor is neither nominative nor c-commanded by the subject of the embedded clause (since it is contained within that subject). Hence, nothing prevents it from being free in the embedded clause.

Both of these models of Binding Theory, the SSC/TSC model and the SSC/NIC model, have more or less direct successors in later work. The idea of the former that finite clauses and the c-command domain of subject nominals are the two binding domains is continued in a general way in the LGB model of Chomsky (1981), for instance, in which the *Governing Category* (=local domain) for an anaphor or pronoun is characterized as the domain of an *accessible SUBJECT*, as defined in (13a):[13]

(13a) β is a Governing Category for α iff β is the minimal category containing α, a governor for α, and a SUBJECT accessible to α.[14]
(13b) SUBJECT = AGR where present, a subject NP otherwise.
(13c) α is accessible to β iff α is in the c-command domain of β and the assignment to α of the index of β would not violate (13d).
(13d) $*[_{\delta} \ldots \gamma \ldots]$, where δ and γ bear the same index.

This characterization of local domains differs from the one in (12) in three basic ways. First, it takes AGR(eement), rather than Tense, to be the component of "finiteness" responsible for the PIC effect – a claim for which there seems to be substantial cross-linguistic evidence.[15] This in turn makes possible a partial conflation of the two clauses of (12), by means of the notion SUBJECT defined in (13b). While this notion is defined disjunctively, the two elements which are potential SUBJECTS are not unrelated. AGR(eement) is a label for the features of INFL licensed by subject–aux agreement, and these phi-features are shared with the coindexed subject NP through the agreement relationship. We may therefore conceive of SUBJECT as the highest, or most prominent, occurrence of subject features in a phrase, where AGR, as the head of the phrase, counts as more prominent when present. Collapsing the two parts of the definition of local domain in this way eliminates the theoretically undesirable overlap between the two provisions of (12) with respect to example (10e). Only AGR constitutes a SUBJECT within the lower clause, given the disjunctive definition in (13b), and this example therefore involves only a single violation of the locality requirement on anaphor binding.

Finally, (13) differs from (12) in including the *accessibility provision* (13c). This provision is introduced to address the class of facts represented by (10j). Here, AGR c-commands the anaphor (satisfying half of the definition of accessibility). However, AGR is related by subject agreement to the phrase containing the anaphor. If we assume that subject agreement involves coindexation, then coindexation between the anaphor and AGR as well would result in the prohibited *i-within-i* configuration in (13d), in which a phrase and a non-head constituent contained within it share the same index.[16] Thus, the AGR of the embedded clause fails to satisfy the second half of the accessibility provision. It is therefore not an accessible SUBJECT, and the anaphor is allowed to be free within its domain. AGR in the main clause is accessible to the anaphor, however, and it must be bound within that domain.[17]

Note, however, that (10j) is one of the contexts in which the usual complementarity between pronouns and anaphors breaks down.

(10j) They$_i$ thought that [[books about *each other$_i$/them$_i$*] would be on sale]

Either the pronoun or the reciprocal can be used to refer back to the subject. Another such context is the position of the possessor in (10h) (repeated).

(10h) They$_i$ sold [*their$_i$/each other's$_i$* books]

In both of these, the indexing possibilities indicate that the main clause must count as the local domain for the anaphor, since it need not be bound in any smaller domain, but that the bracketed constituent must be the local domain for the pronoun, since it need not be free in any larger domain. Huang (1983) observes comparable instances of non-complementary distribution in Chinese, and points out that they can be accommodated by assuming that only anaphors, not pronouns, require the presence of an *accessible* SUBJECT. In (10j), the embedded clause contains a SUBJECT (AGR), but that SUBJECT is not accessible to the italicized position, because of the i-within-i provision. Under Huang's modification, the embedded clause counts as a GC for the pronoun, but not for the anaphor. Similarly, in (10h), the NP contains a SUBJECT, but it is not accessible to the italicized position.[18] Thus, the NP is a GC for the pronoun, but not for the anaphor, and non-complementarity in these contexts is accommodated.

This insight is incorporated into the version of Binding Theory presented in Chomsky (1986b), though in a rather different way, which avoids stipulating different domains for the two types of elements in the individual binding principles themselves. Chomsky (1986b, 169) proposes that the local domain for a pronoun or an anaphor is its minimal Governing Category, where the definition of Governing Category is reformulated as in (14):

(14) A Governing Category for α is a maximal projection containing both a subject and a lexical category governing α (hence, containing α).[19]

Note that (14) contains no reference to AGR (it specifies subject, not SUBJECT), and no Accessibility provision. The effect of the latter is incorporated into the account by assuming that a particular convention is observed in evaluating potential local domains for binding. In order for a phrase β to constitute a Governing Category for some element α, (a) it must satisfy the definition in (14), and (b) there must be some possible indexing of elements within β on which the relevant Binding Principle **could** be satisfied for α within β. That is, there must be some possible assignment of indices which is *BT-Compatible* with α in β. Consider the case of (10h). The bracketed NP satisfies (14) for both of the italicized elements, since it contains a subject, and a lexical governor for those elements (the head N). For the pronoun, moreover, there is a possible indexing on which the relevant Binding Principle, Principle B, can be satisfied within NP. In fact, any indexing will suffice. The pronoun is not c-commanded by any prospective binder within NP, and will therefore be free within NP no matter what indices are assigned. The BT-Compatibility requirement is therefore satisfied, and NP counts as a GC for the pronoun. For the anaphor, however, the computation leads to a different result: since there is no possible binder for the anaphor within NP, there is no possibility that Principle A could be satisfied for that anaphor within NP – i.e., there is no possible BT-compatible indexing for that anaphor within NP, and NP therefore does not count as a GC for the anaphor. The asymmetry between pronouns and anaphors in (10h) is predicted. The "accessible subject" requirement reduces to a "potential binder" requirement (at least for most cases), and this in turn permits the elimination of a certain redundancy in the model. The two components of the definition of accessibility – c-command and non-violation of the i-within-i provision – are also requirements on binders. An NP must c-command an anaphor in order to bind it, and it must be coindexed with it in a legal way (cf. note 16).

Consider next how the "NIC"-case, (10d), is treated under this account.

(10d) $They_i$ expected [*each $other_i$/$they_i$ AGR_i would win]

For the pronoun, there is no problem here; the bracketed phrase has a governor for the pronoun, and a subject, and the BT-Compatibility requirement is satisfied since there is a possible indexing on which the pronoun is free in that domain. By the same token, a problem does arise with the anaphor in (10d). Since it is not c-commanded by any potential binder within the embedded clause which could allow potential satisfaction of Principle A, the BT-Compatibility Requirement is not satisfied within that clause, which should therefore not constitute a GC for the anaphor, just as the NP in (10h) does not. Rather, the matrix clause should be the relevant GC, and the version of (10d) with the anaphor would be predicted, incorrectly, to be good.

Chomsky considers the possibility that it is AGR in (10d) which serves as a potential binder for the anaphor, thereby satisfying the BT-Compatibility requirement within the lower clause, but rejects this as somewhat artificial. IF AGR can't be an actual binder for an anaphor, there is no reason to assume that it can count as a potential binder for purposes of BT-compatibility. Chomsky proposes instead that the version of (10d) with the anaphor is not ill-formed with respect to BT at all. Rather, we can derive its ill-formedness from the theory of Government, under certain assumptions about LF movement. In particular, suppose that anaphors raise at LF, and are adjoined to a higher INFL node. An S-structure (SS) string like (15a) will then correspond to an LF string like (15b). (Chomsky, and, preceding him, Lebeaux (1983), note that this makes the LF structure of such English sentences resemble their SS counterparts in French, where clitic movement of the reflexive to INFL takes place in the syntax.)

(15a) John INFL hurt himself
(15b) John $himself_i$-INFL hurt t_i

Since the trace left by the hypothesized LF movement is subject to the ECP, it must be properly governed. The position of subject of IP is not a properly governed position. The inadmissibility of the reflexive in (15c, d) is then simply a particular case of the general ECP-based prohibition against extraction from nominative subject position which is also in evidence in the "*that*-trace" effect illustrated in (15e):[20]

(15c) *John INFL thought that heself would win
(15d) John $heself_i$-INFL thought that t_i would win
(15e) *Who do you think that t_i would win

The resulting theory of binding is similar in spirit to the SSC/NIC model, in that it eliminates a special role for AGR, and divides responsibility for restricting the distribution of anaphors between a principle requiring that they be bound in the domain of the subject and a principle excluding them from nominative positions. The latter, though, is no longer a part of Binding Theory, but of Government Theory. (Others have attempted a reduction in the opposite direction – i.e. the derivation of the *that*-trace effect from Principle A of the Binding Theory, as we will see in the discussion of Generalized Binding in section 5.2.)

The characterization of local domains in this model is quite basic: a GC for an anaphor or a pronoun α must contain a governor for α, and a subject. Asymmetries in distribution between the two result from the BT-Compatibility computation. However, still more minimal formulations can be envisioned. Consider first the role of subject in this characterization. Hestvik (1990, 269) points out that the SSC effect for anaphors in such cases as (10f) and (10g) (repeated) follows, without stipulation, from BT-Compatibility; the bracketed NP can count as a GC for the pronoun only in (10g), not in (10f), even if the specification of a subject is omitted, since only in (10g) is there a potential binder within NP, allowing satisfaction of BT-Compatibility:

(10f) They$_i$ read [books about each other$_i$]
(10g) *They$_i$ read [Mary's books about each other$_i$]]

For pronouns, the force of the specification that GCs contain a subject is to insure that NP and S (or DP and IP, under more recent views of phrase structure) are the two possible GCs, since these are the two maximal phrases which may have subjects. Pronouns occurring within phrases of these types, but not within VPs or APs, for example, may satisfy Principle B within those phrases, and may therefore be bound outside of them, as seen in (16).

(16a) They$_i$ sold [$_{DP}$ their$_i$ pictures]
(16b) They$_i$ said [$_{IP}$ they$_i$ were sick]
(16c) *They$_i$ [$_{VP}$ saw them$_i$]
(16d) *They$_i$ were [$_{AP}$ proud of them$_i$]

In fact, however, it is not clear that the empirical generalization is quite correct. In English (and in several other languages), locative and directional PPs also apparently constitute GCs for pronouns, since pronouns they contain may be bound to arguments outside, as in (16e):

(16e) They$_i$ put the books [$_{PP}$ beside them$_i$]

The pronoun here is not required to be free in any domain larger than the PP, yet the PP has at least no apparent subject. Nor does the correct solution seem to be to posit a covert subject (i.e. PRO) controlled by *the books*, since anaphors may also appear in this context, and be bound by the clausal subject, as in (16f):

(16f) They$_i$ put the books [$_{PP}$ beside each other$_i$]

Thus, it appears reasonable to look for some other property than the presence or absence of a subject to distinguish those maximal phrases (e.g. DP, IP, and some PPs) which function as GCs for pronouns from those (e.g. VP and AP) which don't. One likely property is the following: VPs like the one in (16c) take an external argument, the clausal subject, to which their head Vs assign a theta-role. Heads of IPs and DPs, on the other hand, do not assign a θ-role to an argument outside their maximal projections. Similarly, the preposition in (16e) (arguably) assigns no external theta-role, but discharges its sole theta-role to its object. Hestvik (1990, 271ff) claims accordingly that the GC for an element α is the minimal "θ-Domain" containing it, where a theta-domain is the smallest domain in which all of the theta-roles associated with some independent θ-assigning head are discharged. (See Freidin (1986) for a similar proposal for pronouns.) In (16a, b) the pronoun is required to be free only in DP or IP respectively, because all of the theta-roles associated with the theta-assigner in those domains (N and V respectively) are discharged within those phrases.[21] In (16e), the pronoun is required to be free only in PP, since the sole theta-role assigned by P, the θ-assigning head in that domain, is discharged within PP. (PPs headed by prepositions like the one in (16g), with purely grammatical functions, are not independent theta-role assigners, and therefore do not define theta-domains.)

(16g) *They$_i$ looked [$_{PP}$ at them$_i$]

On the other hand, in (16c), it is not sufficient that the pronoun be free in VP, since VP does not contain all the θ-roles assigned by V, the theta-assigner for the relevant theta-domain.

GCs for anaphors are similarly characterized in terms of θ-domains, but considerations of BT-Compatibility once again produce some overlap. For instance, while the PP in (16f) is the minimal θ-domain containing the anaphor, it contains no possible binder for that anaphor, and therefore does not qualify as a GC.[22]

2.2 *Long-Distance Binding*

2.2.1 *The Problem*

Reflexives, reciprocals and pronouns in English appear to observe relatively restricted local domains, relative to some other languages. For example, the SSC effect for anaphors illustrated for English by example (10c) appears not to hold for reflexives in Icelandic, Danish, Gothic, or Russian, as shown in (17a–d).

(17a) Pétur$_i$ bað Jens um að raka sig$_i$
Peter$_i$ asked Jens to shave himself$_i$
(Thráinsson (1987))

(17b) at Peter$_i$ bad Anne$_k$ om [PRO$_k$ at ringe til sig$_i$]
that Peter$_i$ asked Ann (for) to ring to self$_i$
(Vikner (1985))[23]

(17c) Þai$_i$-ei ni wildedun [$_S$ mik þiudanon ufar sis$_i$/(*im$_i$)]
*who$_i$ not they-wanted me to-rule over selves$_i$/*them$_i$*
"who didn't want me to rule over them"
(Luke 19:27)

(17d) On$_i$ ne razrešaet mne proizvodit' opyty nad soboj$_i$
He$_i$ not permitted me to-perform experiments on self$_i$
(Rappaport (1986))

In each of these cases, the reflexive is bound across the subject of the infinitival complement clause. (In general, this is possible only for reflexives: reciprocals do not admit this type of long-distance binding.)

Other languages appear to allow reflexive binding of a yet more nonlocal sort, as in the Icelandic and Italian examples in (18), where a reflexive has been bound across the boundary of a finite (subjunctive) clause, in apparent violation of the TSC (as well as the SSC).

(18a) Jón sagði að ég hefði svikið sig$_i$
John$_i$ said that I had betrayed self$_i$
(Thráinsson (1987))

(18b) Gianni pensava che quella casa appartenesse ancora
Gianni$_i$ thought that this house belonged still
alla propria famiglia
to self's$_i$ family
(Giorgi (1983–4, 316))

Additional restrictions obtain in these cases of apparent long-distance (LD) binding, some of which will be discussed below.

Apparent LD binding of reflexives is also possible in Chinese, Japanese and Korean, as illustrated in (19).

(19a) Zhangsan$_i$ renwei Lisi hai-le ziji$_i$
Zhangsan$_i$ thought Lisi hurt-Asp self$_i$
(Huang and Tang (1991))

(19b) John$_i$-wa [Bill-ga zibun$_i$-o nikunde iru]-to omotte iru
John$_i$-Top Bill-Nom self$_i$-Acc hates that thinks
"John$_i$ thinks that Bill hates him$_i$"
(Manzini and Wexler ((1987))

(19c) John$_i$-in Bill-i Mary-ka [Tom-iy caki$_i$ tæhan
John-TOP Bill-Nm Mary-Nm Tom's self toward
thæto]-lɨl silhəhantako sængkakhantako mitninta
attitude-Acc hates thinks believes
(Yang (1983))
"John$_i$ believes that Bill thinks that Mary hates Tom's attitude toward self$_i$"

It is not immediately clear whether to classify these with (17) or (18). In each case, the clauses across whose boundaries the reflexive is bound here are finite, as evidenced by the fact that they have overt subjects (which are identifiably nominative in some of these languages). However, these languages systematically lack morphological realizations of AGR(eement), and the examples in (19) may therefore be classified with the cases in (17), if the component of finiteness relevant to binding is the presence of AGR. It is perhaps significant that LD reflexives occur with a high degree of frequency in languages lacking agreement morphology (cf. Progovac (1991)).

Apparent LD application of Principle B – cases in which a pronoun is apparently required to be free in a domain larger than the minimal GC/CFC containing it – is less frequent across languages, and more restricted. While Danish and Russian as well as Icelandic and Gothic allow long binding of complement reflexives to the matrix subject, across infinitive clause boundaries, as in (17), only Icelandic and Gothic, not Danish or Russian, require pronouns in such positions to be free with respect to the matrix clause subject. This is illustrated in (20).

(20a) Pétur$_i$ bað Jens að raka hann$_i$ (Thráinsson (1987))
Peter$_i$ asked Jens to shave him$_i$

(20b) Þai$_i$-ei ni wildedun [$_S$ mik þiudanon ufar sis$_i$/(*im$_i$)]
*who$_i$ not they-wanted me to-rule over selves$_i$/*them$_i$*
"who didn't want me to rule over them"
(Luke 19:27)

(20c) at Susan$_i$ bad Anne$_k$ om [PRO$_k$ at ringe til hende$_i$]
that Susan$_i$ asked Anne (for) to ring to self$_i$
(Vikner (1985))

(20d) Student$_i$ poprosil reportera vzjat' svoj$_i$/ego$_i$ stakan
The student$_i$ asked the reporter to take self's/his$_i$ glass
(Yokoyama (1980))

None of the languages in (19) has long-distance disjoint reference for pronouns either. In all of them, pronouns must be free only in their minimal GCs/CFCs. That is, languages which have long-distance Principle B effects appear to be a relatively small subset of those allowing LD binding of reflexives.

I am also aware of no clear cases in which Principle B observes a domain larger than the minimal finite clause containing it. That is, there seem to be no instances of LD disjoint reference operating across the boundaries of subjunctive clauses, analogous to (18).

The question of how this phenomenon of apparent LD binding is to be reconciled with a restrictive theory of locality for anaphors and pronouns is surely the most extensively discussed question in Binding Theory.[24] Primarily at issue is the following question: does the observed variation require the assumption that the definition of local domain is parameterized, and that individual languages may choose different values, or does it result from interaction between an invariant definition of local domains and independent differences in the grammars involved? If the former, how are the individual values of the parameter to be characterized, what is the relation among them, and how do language learners arrive at the appropriate value of the parameter for their own language? The literature on this *variation problem* is far too voluminous to be accorded more than superficial treatment here. This section will therefore limit itself to cataloguing (rather uncritically) the main approaches which have been suggested. The reader is referred to the works cited for detailed discussion.

There have been three major types of approach to the variation problem. The first involves the proposal that the characterization of binding domains is simply parameterized – underspecified in certain ways by UG – and that different values may be chosen for individual languages (or, in the view of some investigators, individual lexical items within languages). Such an approach is advocated, e.g. in Yang (1983), Harbert (1986, 1991), Koster (1987a), Manzini and Wexler (1987), and much other work. As an illustration, consider the five-valued definition of Governing Category in (21), from Manzini and Wexler (1987):

(21) (= M&W 29)
γ is a governing category for α iff γ is the minimal category that contains α and a governor for α and

(a) can have a subject, or, for α=anaphor, has a subject β, $\beta \neq \alpha$; or
(b) has an INFL; or
(c) has a Tense; or
(d) has a "referential" Tense; or
(e) has a "root" Tense
(if, for α anaphoric, the subject β' ($\beta' \neq \alpha$) of γ, and of every category dominating α and not γ, is accessible to γ).

The English reflexive observes value (21a), according to Manzini and Wexler. It must therefore be bound in the domain of an accessible subject. The Danish reflexive *sig*, on the other hand, observes domain (21c): it must be bound in the minimal tense domain, but may be free in the domain of the subject of an infinitive clause. Icelandic reflexives, as in (18a), are claimed to observe domain (21d). Adopting an analysis originating with Anderson (1982a), Manzini and Wexler propose that such reflexives may be bound across the boundary of a subjunctive complement clause because those clauses, though containing tense marking, have "anaphoric," not "referential" tense; they are dependent on the main clause for their tense interpretation.[25] Finally, the Japanese reflexive *zibun* in (19b) observes value (21e) and therefore need be bound only in the root clause.

This type of approach to the variation problem identifies the definition of local domains as the locus of variation. Since variation results directly from different choices for local domains for anaphors and pronouns, it is not predicted to correlate with other syntactic differences between the languages in question. The fact that a grammar assigns a particular local domain to a particular anaphor is not predicted to follow from other properties of that grammar (nor in any general way from other properties of the anaphor in question).[26] This, however, is contrary to the general expectation that different choices in parameter values should have widespread effects throughout the grammar. See Hermon (1990).

Two other approaches to the variation problem have gained currency in the past few years. The first of these, to be discussed in section 2.2.2, involves the view that the problem is in part simply a result of the misclassification of non-anaphors as anaphors. A more restricted definition of local domains can be maintained if the forms in, e.g., (18a) are not anaphors in the sense of the Binding Theory. The second approach, to be discussed in section 2.2.3, maintains an invariant characterization of binding domains by relocating variation to other parts of the grammar. A very prominent line of inquiry in this category holds that apparent long-distance binding is in fact the product of abstract movement of the anaphor into a higher domain, followed by local binding. Some anaphors exhibit apparent long-distance binding because they are subject to successive cyclic movement at LF. Others do not exhibit apparent LD binding because they do not admit such LF movement, or are more restricted in their possibilities for movement. These differences in turn, are claimed to follow from independent differences, either in the forms of the anaphors themselves (for example, whether they are eligible for head-movement), or in other aspects of the grammars involved.

2.2.2 *A Fourth Type of Nominal Element?*

It is likely that not all members of the traditional category of reflexive pronouns are to be considered anaphors in the sense of the Binding Theory, and therefore that not every observation about the behavior of reflexives need be accommodated by the Binding Theory. So, for example, (22) would clearly seem to involve a non-anaphoric use of the reflexive, since there is no c-commanding antecedent.[27]

(22) This paper was written by Ann and myself

However, the boundary between anaphors and non-anaphoric reflexives is not fixed in any pretheoretical way. There is no pretheoretical way of knowing, for example, that the elements involved in the type of non-local binding discussed in the preceding section are anaphors. Some investigators have responded to the problem posed by such cases by claiming that they are in fact not anaphors subject to Principle A, but belong to a different category, subject to a different principle. Anderson (1982a, 17) distinguishes between anaphors, which must be bound in their Governing Categories, and reflexive pronouns, which must be bound in the domain of the subject of an (independently) Tensed S. The Icelandic reflexive in (17a, 18a) is of the latter type. Its failure to observe the SSC in (17a) follows, as does its failure to be bound in the subjunctive complement in (18a), given the assumptions about tense dependencies mentioned above.[28]

Along similar lines, Giorgi (1983–4) classifies anaphors into two types – [+B(inding) T(heory)] anaphors – those subject to Principle A, and therefore required to be bound in their GCs – and [–BT] anaphors, including the Italian *proprio* and the Icelandic long-distance *sig*, which are not required to be bound in their GCs. [–BT] anaphors are subject to an independent binding condition – presumably also a part of Binding Theory – which requires that they be bound within the P-domains of their antecedents. α is in the P-Domain of β if it is (contained in) a coargument of β (and β is the thematically most prominent argument in the relevant thematic domain).[29] The P-Domain requirement is intended in part to capture an interesting restriction on LD anaphors in at least some languages, which we may illustrate with Icelandic data. While a reflexive in a subjunctive complement clause can be bound "long distance" to the higher clause subject, as in (18a), a reflexive in a subjunctive adverbial clause cannot, as shown in (23a).

(23a) *Jón$_i$ væri glaður ef María kyssti sig$_i$
John$_i$ would be glad if Mary kissed self$_i$
(Thráinsson (1976a))

This follows because the adverbial clause, as a non-argument, is not in the P-domain of the main clause subject. Strikingly, however, when the whole sentence in (23a) is further embedded as a subjunctive complement of a verb, as in (23b), the subject of the topmost clause (though still not the subject of the intermediate clause) *is* a possible binder for the reflexive in the adverbial clause.

(23b) Jón$_i$ sagði að hann væri glaður ef María kyssti sig$_i$
John$_i$ said that he would be glad if Mary kissed self$_i$
(Thráinsson (1976a))

According to Giorgi, this is because the reflexive is now within the P-domain of that topmost subject, being contained in one of its coarguments (the object complement).

Giorgi proposes that the P-domain requirement is a default requirement, which holds for [+BT] anaphors too, when these are contextually exempted from Principle A by virtue of not having a GC. Thus, an English reciprocal contained in the subject of an embedded complement clause can be bound to the matrix subject – a coargument of that clause – as in (23c), but a reciprocal contained in the subject of an adjunct clause may not be so bound, as in (23d):

(23c) They believe that pictures of each other are on sale
(23d) ??They will arrive before pictures of each other are put on sale

2.2.3 *Logophors*

Possible empirical support for treating some instances of long-distance reflexives as representatives of a nominal type distinct from local anaphors, rather than simply classifying them as anaphors and assuming a multivalued characterization of local domain, is provided by the fact that they differ from local anaphors not only in allowing binding within larger domains, but also in requirements imposed on their antecedents. It has been demonstrated by Sigurðsson (1986) and Thráinsson (1991) for Icelandic and by Kameyama (1984) for Japanese that the long-distance reflexives in fact need not be bound by a c-commanding binder at all, but may pick up their reference from a discourse antecedent as in (24), where the reflexive does not refer to Maria or Olaf but to the individual whose thoughts are being reported, or from a non-c-commanding antecedent.[30]

(24a) María$_i$ var alltaf svo andstyggileg. Þegar Ólafur$_k$ kæmi, segði hún sér$_k$ áreiðanlega að fara
"Maria was always so nasty. When Olaf$_k$ came she would certainly tell himself$_k$ to leave"
(Thráinsson (1991))

In view of this, it is not clear that they are anaphors in the sense of Principle A after all. The investigators in question identify them instead as *logophors* – members of a class of elements described in detail for Ewe, a Niger–Congo language, by Clements (1975). Ewe has forms distinct from both the strict reflexives and the personal pronouns of that language which are used "to distinguish reference to the individual whose speech, thoughts, or feelings are reported or reflected in a given linguistic context, from reference to other individuals" (1975, 141). Clements notes that constraints on coreference with these forms seem to involve primarily such discourse notions as point of view, rather than syntactic requirements such as c-command. Thus, the logophor *ye* can, for some speakers, be anteceded by *Kofi* in (24b) but not by *Komi,* even though the latter is a c-commanding subject, while the former doesn't c-command the logophor at all. This is because *Kofi,* not *Komi,* is the individual whose speech is being reported.

(24b) kɔmi$_k$ xɔ agbalẽ tso kofi$_i$ gbɔ be wò-a-va me kpe
Kwami receive letter from Kofi side that Pro-T-come cast block
na **yè**$_{i/*k}$
for LOG
"Kwami got a letter from Kofi$_i$ saying that he should cast some blocks for him$_i$"

Similarly, he points out (1975, 170) that (as is the case with Japanese and Icelandic reflexives) the discourse antecedents for these logophors need not even co-occur with them in the same sentence, but may appear several sentences earlier in the discourse. Thus, the antecedence requirements of Ewe logophors appear at least not to belong to the syntactic theory of binding at all, but to the discourse component.

It has been recognized for a long time that the occurrence of long-distance reflexives in Japanese and Icelandic is also linked to point-of-view considerations of this type (cf. Oshima (1979) and Thráinsson (1976a)), and identifying them as logophors, rather than anaphors, provides a basis for accounting for a number of their properties. We have already observed that they may have discourse antecedents and (in the case of Japanese, at least) non-c-commanding antecedents. Further, as Maling (1984) notes, the striking contrast between (23a) and (23b) can be derived from the assumption that the reflexive here is a logophor. Only in the acceptable (23b) does it "refer back" to the source of the reported speech, as required. Sigurðsson (1986) argues further that the apparent requirement that the complement clauses in Icelandic be in the subjunctive (for those dialects in which that condition holds) can also be accounted for under the logophoric analysis. Subjunctive is the mood used in indirect reporting of speech and beliefs to indicate that the speaker is not assuming responsibility for the truth of the report, but reporting it from the viewpoint of the source of that speech or belief. It therefore reflects a semantic, rather than a syntactic condition. (For detailed discussion of the rather complex semantics of logophors, see Sigurðsson (1986), Sells (1987).) If instances of long-distance anaphora like the ones illustrated in (18) involve logophors, not anaphors, then the variation problem is potentially reduced. Some investigators, including Reinhart and Reuland (1989), Hestvik (1990) propose that only local binding within CFCs and (apparent) binding into infinitival complements fall within the domain of Binding Theory. All instances of apparent binding across the boundaries of finite clauses involve logophors.

If the antecedence requirements for these forms are in fact discourse requirements, rather than following from the syntactic Binding Theory, then it remains to be determined what their status is with respect to Binding Theory. Assuming that the three principles of Binding Theory exhaustively partition nominals, the only possibility would appear to be that they are pronouns. If they were anaphors, then they would be syntactically bound, and the discourse antecedent possibility would be ruled out. If they were R-expressions, then they would disallow c-commanding argument antecedents. In fact, the conclusion that they are pronouns finds some potential support in Japanese. According to McCawley (1972), sentences like (25), in which *zibun* is bound in a local domain, are marginal or ungrammatical. (Katada (1991) also finds such sentences less than well-formed, but assigns them only a question mark).

(25) *Yazuka$_i$-ga zibun$_i$-o korosita
gangster-Nom self-Acc killed

This is as would be predicted by Principle B if *zibun* were a logophoric *pronoun*. Such sentences are well-formed in Icelandic, however, where we would have to conclude (as does Maling (1984)) that the logophoric pronoun is homophonous with a local, anaphoric reflexive.

The study of the behavior of logophors is in its early stages, as might be expected of an element so recently identified, and there are still a number of outstanding problems in their analysis. In particular, if the conditions imposed on their antecedents are not a part of the theory of syntax but of the theory of discourse, then we would expect them to be expressed exclusively in terms of the notions appropriate to that theory, and not in terms of syntactic notions. It is not clear that this is true in all cases. In some of these languages there are facts which suggest that the relation between logophoric pronouns and their antecedents must satisfy certain structural conditions when the latter do occur in the same sentence, and some investigators (e.g. Clements (1975), Maling (1984)) have posited that logophors have undergone a partial "grammaticization" in these languages.[31] Therefore, it is not clear at this point that the antecedence requirements of these forms can be claimed to fall wholly outside of the syntactic theory of binding. Two recent accounts, Enç (1989) and Koopman and Sportiche (1989), attempt to derive the referential properties of logophors primarily from a syntactic Binding Theory, under the assumption that they are operator-bound anaphors.

2.2.4 Core and Non-Core Anaphora

Standard versions of the Binding Theory have assumed that constructions like the one in (26a) are to be accommodated as core cases of anaphor binding – that both here and in (26b) the reflexive is bound in its local domain.

(26a) They$_i$ bought [those pictures of themselves$_i$]
(26b) They$_i$ hurt themselves$_i$

However, Bouchard (1982) and Lebeaux (1983, 1984–5) have pointed out that *"picture-noun reflexives"* like the one in (26a) seem to have properties which are different from those of still more local reflexives like (26b), involving the syntactic requirements imposed on the binder. As (27a) shows, the former but not the latter admit *split antecedents.*

(27a) John$_i$ showed Mary$_k$ these pictures of themselves$_{[i, k]}$
(27b) *John$_i$ told Mary$_k$ about themselves$_i$

Moreover, as (28) shows, the former, but not the latter, allow non-c-commanding antecedents:

(28a) John's$_i$ campaign required that pictures of himself$_i$ be placed all over town
(28b) *John's$_i$ campaign exhausted himself$_i$ (Lebeaux (1984–5))

They also differ with respect to their interpretation in VP-ellipsis contexts, where core anaphors allow only a *sloppy identity* interpretation, while non-core anaphors also allow a *strict identity* reading. These contrasts have been variously interpreted. If uniqueness of antecedents and c-command are conditions on anaphor binding, then they would seem to indicate that picture-noun reflexives are not strict anaphors after all. This is the position taken by Bouchard (1982). Bouchard proposes that the local domain for anaphors is the minimal maximal projection containing it, and claims that reflexives such as the one in (26a) which are bound in larger domains are "false anaphors," in fact belonging to the category of pronouns. If they are not anaphors, it remains to be explained why they nonetheless require an antecedent, since that requirement can no longer follow from Principle A. Reinhart and Reuland (1989), adopting a position similar to Bouchard's, answer this question by identifying them as logophors, of the type discussed in the preceding section, or, more accurately, as logophoric uses of the reflexive. When an anaphor is an argument of a syntactically saturated predicate, it must be bound within the theta domain of that predicate, as in (26b).[32] Where it is not the argument of such a predicate, as in (26a) the reflexive need not be bound, but may pick up reference as a logophor in case the language in question allows logophoric use of reflexives. The relaxation of the strict c-command and other requirements characteristic of local binding are due to the fact that no syntactic binding is involved.

A second approach, advocated in Lebeaux (1984–5), assumes that both types of reflexives in (26) are anaphors, and that therefore the c-command and uniqueness-of-antecedent requirements are not a part of the definition of binding. To satisfy Principle A, anaphors are only required to be referentially dependent within their local domain – not necessarily coindexed with a unique, c-commanding antecedent. The stricter requirements in evidence in (27b), (28b) are due to Predication Theory: when the minimal maximal phrase containing an anaphor is a predicate predicated of the antecedent of the reflexive, as is the case in

(26b), then the anaphor is not only bound, but "bound by predication," and, in addition to satisfying Principle A, it must satisfy the stricter requirements of predication coindexing. These include c-command and uniqueness of antecedent. On the other hand, when not contained within such a predicate, as in (26a), an anaphor must meet only the less restrictive coindexation requirement imposed by Binding Theory.

The reader is referred to Hestvik (1990) for further interesting discussion of the contrast between *core* and *non-core binding*. The characterization of core domain in Bouchard (1982) differs from that in Hestvik (1990) and Reinhart and Reuland (1989). Bouchard characterizes it in terms of government, while Hestvik and Reinhart and Reuland characterize it in terms of θ-grids. The two approaches make different predictions about the status of binding in the ECM case in (29):

(29) They believed [themselves to have won]

Bouchard would predict that this is an instance of core binding. The reflexive is bound in the matrix clause – the domain containing its governor. However, the other accounts would predict, all other things being equal, that it is an instance of non-core-binding, since the embedded IP is the complete theta-domain defined by the embedded verb. Reinhart and Reuland negate this result by claiming that the matrix and the embedded predicates in such constructions are amalgamated into a complex predicate, of which the ECM subject is an argument. Hestvik (1990, 222), on the other hand, accepts the result, and presents an argument based on VP-ellipsis interpretation that (29) does involve non-core binding.

2.2.5 *Anaphors and LF-Movement*

As we have seen, the idea that anaphors raise to higher positions (in particular, to INFL) was advanced by Lebeaux (1983) and Chomsky (1986b) to account for certain restrictions on anaphors in specifier positions, including the NIC case for reflexives. It was proposed that such abstract anaphor movement leaves traces which are subject to the ECP, and are therefore precluded from occurring in non-properly governed positions. Another effect of such movement, however, is that it reduces the distance between the anaphor and potential antecedents in higher domains. This raises the possibility that some apparent instances of long-distance binding might be reinterpreted as local binding, under the assumption that locality between the anaphor and the binder is established by such abstract movement.

The first to explore this possibility was apparently Pica (1987), and the idea has been extended by a number of investigators. Pica started out from two observations about the typological properties of anaphors which may be long-distance bound – i.e. bound in apparent violation of the SSC. First, they seem in general to be subject-oriented – that is, they do not allow object antecedents (a fact also noted in Giorgi (1983–4), Chomsky (1986b)). Second, as noted, they tend to be monomorphemic. So, for example, the Danish reflexive *sig*, which can be bound across the subjects of infinitive clauses, as in (30a), is morphologically simple, and allows only subject antecedents, as shown in (30b).

(30a) Peter$_i$ hørte [Anne$_k$ omtale sig$_i$]
Peter$_i$ heard Anne mention self$_i$
(Vikner (1985))

(30b) *Jag fortæller Hans$_i$ om sig$_i$
I tell Hans$_i$ about self$_i$
(Pica (1987))

(Interestingly, *sig* also cannot be bound to a subject within its own clause either, as seen in (30c):

(30c) *Peter$_i$ fortalte Michael om sig$_i$
Peter$_i$ told Michael about self$_i$

Possible accounts for this disjoint reference property will be taken up in section 3.1.)

On the other hand, the reciprocal of Danish is bimorphemic, allows object antecedents, as in (30d), and does not allow binding in violation of the SSC.

(30d) Jeg fortæller dem$_i$ om hinanden$_i$
I tell them$_i$ about each other$_i$

Similarly, Danish has a compound reflexive, consisting of *sig* plus the morpheme *selv*, which does not admit long-distance binding, as seen in (30e):[33]

(30e) *Peter$_i$ bad Michael$_k$ om [PRO $_k$ at barbere sig selv$_i$]
Peter$_i$ asked Michael to shave self

Pica proposes an account for this apparent clustering of properties along the following lines: all anaphors, he claims, raise at LF. The landing site for this movement, however, is dictated by the internal structure of the anaphor. He claims that *sig* and similar monomorphemic anaphors can be viewed as X^0s directly dominated by X^{max}, and proposes (note 5) that a maximal phrase exhaustively dominating its lexical head is able to assume the status of its head – i.e. to move by head-to-head movement. Thus, reflexives of this type can raise to an INFL adjunction position, by head-to-head movement, and in fact must do so in order to be interpreted.[34] The subject-orientation of these anaphors is partially accounted for by this assumption: only subjects are possible binders for them because, having moved to INFL they are now c-commanded only by [Spec I], the subject position – not by object NPs within VP.

On the other hand, morphologically complex anaphors, like the Danish reciprocal and the compound reflexive are viewed as phrasal – as XP anaphors. As such, they are unable to undergo head-to-head movement. When moved, they can only adjoin to the phrase containing them. This accounts for the fact that they are not necessarily subject-oriented, since after adjunction to VP (or PP) the reciprocal in (30d), for example, is still c-commanded by the object NP, given an appropriately modified definition of c-command.

Pica also proposes that the observed restriction of LD binding to "simple" reflexives can be derived under this account as well, in the following way: X^0 anaphors, having been moved to the INFL of an embedded clause, are still in the domain of the subject of that clause, which is therefore their only possible binder.[35] However, if the C^0 position governing the embedded IP is empty – a condition satisfied just in case the embedded clause is subjunctive or infinitival – then the X^0 reflexive can continue to move up by head-to-head movement from I to C. This step removes it from the domain of the embedded subject, and makes it accessible to other potential binders. These do not include the object of the matrix clause, however; since the X^0 anaphor must be interpreted in INFL, it cannot stop in C^0, but must continue to move, into the matrix I^0 (by way of adjunction to the matrix verb), where it is c-commanded only by the matrix subject. The derivation involved is represented schematically in (31):

(31) [NP_i $REFL_i$-I^0 V^0 NP_j [C^0 NP_k I^0 t_i]

From this it follows that long-distance binding is possible only out of subjunctive or infinitive clauses (since only these have empty C^0s), that long-distance anaphors are subject-oriented, and that long-distance binding is possible only for X^0 anaphors. No similar escape route from embedded CPs is allowed for XP anaphors.

Pica notes, however, that there are anaphors meeting all of the criteria for X^0 anaphors which nonetheless do not allow long-distance binding. So, for example, the reflexive *se* of the Romance languages is subject-oriented, monomorphemic and, in fact, undergoes overt adjunction to INFL in the syntax, yet it cannot be long-bound. Like all X^0 anaphors, according to Pica, it undergoes head-movement to the lower clause INFL. However, further movement to C^0 – the crucial step for long-distance binding – is not available, Pica speculates, because it is only possible for elements which are in some sense "pronominal" as well as anaphoric. *Se* does not qualify, and is therefore only locally bound. Pica claims that this explains why long-distance anaphors, like the Danish *sig*, exhibit such non-core properties as strict identity interpretation under VP-ellipsis, which Pica identifies as pronominal properties.

Numerous investigators have pursued Pica's suggestion that apparent long-distance binding can be reduced to local binding in the wake of LF movement. See the references in section 2.2.6, for example. A particularly systematic and detailed development of these ideas is found in Hestvik (1990). Hestvik claims that XP-anaphors move to the Specifier position of their governors, rather than adjoining to the projections of those governors. From this assumption, the SSC effect observed by such anaphors, illustrated in (10g) (repeated) is accounted for directly: these anaphors cannot move out of the containing phrase, and therefore out of the domain of the subject of that phrase, since the subject, as a specifier, blocks movement.[36]

(10g) $They_i$ read [Mary's books about *each $other_i$/$them_i$]]

He also points out that the assumption of LF movement of anaphors obviates the need for extending the local domain for anaphors beyond the minimal CFC by means of such provisions as the Accessibility condition or the BT-Compatibility provision. Suppose that the domain of an anaphor (or pronoun) is simply the minimal CFC containing it. In (10h) (repeated), the pronoun satisfies Principle B in situ, and therefore need not move farther. The anaphor cannot satisfy Principle A at S-Structure, since there is no possible binder in its minimal CFC. However, at LF, it can raise to a higher Spec – the Spec of VP, where it can be locally bound to the clausal subject. If anaphors can undergo abstract movement in this way, and be bound after movement, the BT-Compatibility computation is no longer needed.

(10h) $They_i$ sold [$their_i$/each $other's_i$ books]

Hestvik points out that the LF movement analysis can be extended to cover cross-linguistic differences in disjoint reference domains for pronouns, as well. Consider the contrast between English and Norwegian illustrated in (32):

(32a) John$_i$ likes [his$_i$ toys]
(Hestvik (1990))
(32b) *John$_i$ liker [hans$_i$ leker]

In (32a), the pronoun, since free in the minimal CFC containing it, can corefer with the clausal subject. In the Norwegian example (32b), however, *hans* cannot corefer with *John*. This can be explained, according to Hestvik, if we take *hans* (unlike *his*) to be an X^0 pronoun which obligatorily raises to INFL at LF. Such movement has the effect of extending the domain in which it must be free, since after movement it is no longer separated from the clausal subject by a CFC boundary. This will also account for the "anti-subject" orientation exhibited by long-distance *hans*. As (32c) shows, *hans* need only be disjoint in reference with the subject, not the object, of the containing clause.

(32c) John$_i$ fortalte Ola$_k$ om [hans$_{*i/k}$ kone]
John$_i$ told Ola$_k$ about his$_{*i/k}$ wife

Having raised to INFL, *hans* is only c-commanded by the subject, not the object, and therefore only coindexing with the subject will result in illicit binding of the pronoun within its domain.

Note, however, that *his* and *hans* do not differ in terms of their morphological structure. Both are monomorphemic. Therefore, as Hestvik points out, extending the XP/X^0 typology to these cases will require the identification of different criteria for distinguishing the two types. Hestvik proposes that XP pronouns and anaphors are *pro*-XPs – pronouns exhaustively and directly dominated by an XP node, which lacks internal structure, while X^0 pronouns are X^0 elements which head XP phrases. The contrast is represented in (33):

(33a) $[_{XP}$ he$]$
(33b) $[_{XP}$ $[_{X'}$ $[_{X^0}$ han$]]]$

While the Norwegian pronoun is available to X^0 movement, since there is an X^0 level of structure, X^0 movement cannot apply to the English pronoun in (33a) in principle, since there is no X^0 on which it could operate. Hestvik supports this claim of different internal structure for the two types of pronouns by noting that the English pronoun, but not the Norwegian one, strongly resists modification, as shown in (34):

(34a) Han med røtt hatt
(34b) ??He with the red hat

Given the absence of internal structure in (33a), there is no place for such modifiers. There is an apparent problem with the account offered by Hestvik for long-distance disjoint reference, however. As we have noted, the pronoun in (32c) need not be disjoint in reference with the object, because it is not c-commanded by the object after LF movement to INFL. The question arises whether in some constructions disjoint reference with higher subjects might not similarly be avoided by "jumping over" the subject in question, so that it no longer c-commands the pronoun at LF. Such a case might arise in a structure like (35), for example, where all of the INFL's are infinitival.

(35) [NP_i $INFL_1$ . . . [NP_j $INFL_2$ . . . [NP_k $INFL_3$ . . . pron . . .]]]

All other things being equal, it would appear that the pronoun could successive-cyclically raise to the highest INFL, $INFL_1$. It would then be required to be free only with respect to NP_i, since this is the only NP which c-commands it. This result is incorrect, however. In such cases the pronoun may not corefer with NP_j or NP_k, either. To prevent this outcome, Hestvik (1990, 181) suggests that pronouns cannot move successive-cyclically at LF, but only to the first possible landing site, and proposes a possible way of deriving this condition. This, too, however, makes a problematic prediction. In such a case, the pronoun would stop in $INFL_3$, the lowest functional head in which it can be interpreted. The CFC containing it would be the most deeply embedded clause, and the effect of long-distance disjoint reference of the type found, e.g. in (20a) (repeated) from Icelandic, would be lost:

(20a) Pétur$_i$ bað Jens að raka hann$_i$ (Thráinsson (1987))
Peter$_i$ asked Jens to shave him$_i$

2.2.6 *Long-Distance Binding in Chinese*

An LF-Movement analysis was independently suggested by Battistella in preliminary versions of the work published as Battistella (1989) for apparent long-distance binding in Chinese, and the idea has subsequently been pursued by a number of investigators, including Cole, Hermon, and Sung (1990), Cole and Sung (1991b), Huang and Tang (1991). The Chinese case has some properties, pointed out in Tang (1985), which make it particularly interesting. As (36a) shows, Chinese has two reflexives – *ziji* and the compound *ta-ziji*. The latter consists of *ziji* plus the third person pronoun *ta*. *Ta-ziji* can be bound only by the subject of the lower clause. *Ziji*, however, can be bound either by that subject or by the subject of the topmost clause (though interestingly not by the subject of the intermediate clause).

(36a) Zhangsan$_i$ yiwei Lisi$_j$ zhidao Wangwu$_k$ bu xiangxin
Zhangsan think Lisi know Wangwu not believe
ziji$_{i/*j/k}$ / ta-ziji$_{k/*j/*i}$
self
(Battistella (1989))

Significantly, however, as noted by Tang (1985, 1989), for many speakers the possibility of long binding of *ziji* is blocked if any intervening clause has a subject distinct in person from the binder. In (36b), for example, *ziji* cannot be bound to *Zhangsan* because the intermediate clause has a non-third-person subject.

(36b) *Zhangsan$_i$ zhidao wo (ni) juede Lisi dui ziji$_i$ mei
Zhangsan knows I (you) think Lisi toward self not
xinxin
confidence
"Zhangsan knows I (you) think that Lisi has no confidence in himself"
(Tang (1985))

Tang and Battistella point out that the existence of these *Blocking Effects* argues strongly against assuming that *ziji* is simply a long-distance anaphor, i.e. one which observes a very unrestricted value for a hypothesized Governing Categories parameter. It is not clear why a truly long-distance anaphor should be sensitive to the person features of intervening subjects. They propose, rather, that the observed blocking effects are evidence of successive-cyclicity. Tang develops a successive-cyclic reindexing account for these facts. Battistella argues that *ziji* undergoes successive cyclic raising into the matrix clause, followed by local binding to the matrix subject. In Battistella's account, the person features of *ziji* are permanently fixed at D-structure. It is then raised successive-cyclically through INFL-to-INFL movement, leaving traces in each INFL through which it passes. These traces share the person features of *ziji*, since they are a part of the same chain. As nominal features in INFL, the person features of these traces are in turn treated as Agreement features and become involved in abstract agreement between INFL and its Specifier. The blocking effects follow from this.

If an anaphor with third-person features has been raised successive-cyclically into the topmost clause, where it can be locally bound by the subject of that clause, then all of the INFL positions through which it has passed contain copies of its person features, and the feature matching required by subject–INFL agreement prevents the subjects of those INFLs from bearing non-third-person features.[37] Battistella also notes that the INFL-raising analysis predicts the general subject orientation of *ziji,* as discussed in the previous section. To insure that the binders of LD *ziji* are root subjects, not intermediate subjects, however, he is required to stipulate that INFL-to-INFL movement, if it applies at all, is obligatory.

This line of analysis is pursued in Cole, Hermon, and Sung (1990), and other papers by Cole and Sung (1991a, 1991b) which are concerned with the typological properties of the languages allowing such successive cyclic movement of anaphors.[38]

Huang and Tang (1991), however, take a somewhat different approach to the LF-movement analysis of *ziji.* In their account, too, locality is established between the reflexive and its antecedent by abstract successive-cyclic movement at LF, but they claim that the movement involved is XP-movement – in particular, adjunction to IP. As noted by Barss (1986), overt IP-adjunction of anaphors (or phrases containing them) in English creates new binding possibilities. Thus, in (37a) but not (37b), *John,* as well as *Bill,* is a possible antecedent for the reflexive.

(37a) John knows that [$_{NP}$ pictures of himself] Bill likes t
(37b) John knows Bill likes [pictures of himself]

The former interpretation is the one of immediate concern here.[39] Since the reflexive has been moved out of the domain of the lower subject, the higher subject comes into consideration as a potential binder. Huang and Tang claim that the possibility of binding *ziji* to higher subjects results in essentially the same way, except that the IP-adjunction takes place at LF, and is therefore invisible.

It remains to be established why *himself* in (37b) cannot similarly undergo LF adjunction to IP, giving the appearance of long-distance binding. Huang and Tang claim that it is because *himself,* unlike *ziji,* has overt phi-features (in this case, person and gender). *Ziji* has no inherent person/number features, but depends on its antecedent for those features, as well as its referential features. Huang and Tang exploit this difference in the following way: They claim that an anaphor must be bound at S-Structure with respect to at least some set of features. *Himself* is not dependent on an antecedent for its phi-features; they are an inherent part of its lexical form. It must therefore be bound with respect to its referential features, in order to satisfy the S-Structure binding requirement. *Ziji*, on the other hand, is dependent on binding for both sets of features. It can therefore satisfy the S-Structure binding requirement by having its phi-features determined at S-Structure, through binding to the local subject. Its referential features remain free to be fixed by binding at LF after successive-cyclic movement. Thus, the crucial difference between *ziji* and *himself* is claimed not to be that one is phrasal and the other is non-phrasal, but rather that one has overt number/person/gender features while the other does not. The claim that the phi-features of *ziji* are fixed by binding at S-Structure also plays a role in the explanation of blocking effects, in Huang's and Tang's analysis.

Cole and Sung have defended the head-movement account against this alternative XP-movement account in two recent papers (1991a, 1991b). Space does not permit us to review the details of the debate here, and the interested reader is referred to those two papers, as well as Huang and Tang (1991).

Katada (1991) has also advanced a successive-cyclic XP-movement analysis for Japanese *zibun*. He notes that Japanese has three "reflexives," each with distinct properties. *Zibun* is subject-oriented, and may be bound long distance. *zibun-zisin* is subject-oriented, but may only be locally bound. *kare-zisin* is non-subject-oriented and locally bound. This system is parallel in its properties to the three-member system *seg, seg selv, ham selv* found in Norwegian, as well as three-member systems found in other languages, and Katada proposes a common account for all of them, based on a distinction between *operator* and *non-operator anaphors*. *Zibun* is an operator anaphor, which must be moved at LF to an A-bar position, assumed to be a VP-adjunction position. Since Katada assumes subjacency not to apply at LF, and takes lexical government to be sufficient to satisfy the ECP at LF (both controversial assumptions), *zibun* may adjoin directly to any higher VP, resulting in subject-orientation (given an appropriate definition of c-command) and the appearance of long-distance binding. *Kare-zisin* is a non-operator anaphor, which does not move at all, and is therefore locally bound, and not subject oriented. It is suggested that this difference is connected with the fact that *zibun*, but not *kare-zisin*, is invariant, lacking overt phi-features. The *zibun* element of *zibun-zisin* is an operator anaphor and must therefore raise. It can only raise to the lowest VP, though, since (a) its trace is in a non-lexically governed position, and therefore requires antecedent government, and (b) successive-cyclic movement is not allowed at LF. (Local) subject orientation follows from the fact that after VP-adjunction it is not c-commanded by any NP but the local subject.

2.2.7 *Some Non-Movement Approaches*

As seen in the preceding sections, the prevailing approaches to the variation problem and the locality problem have been (a) the assumption of a multivalued "free-choice" Governing Category parameter, and (b) the assumption of an invariant characterization of Governing Category, coupled with the assumption that locality can be established through abstract movement of the anaphor in some cases. These have not been the only proposals, however. I will mention here a few others.

Progovac (1991) agrees with Battistella and others that only monomorphemic reflexives admit long-distance binding, and she adopts their position that this is connected with the possibility of construing these as X^0s, while polymorphemic reflexives can only be interpreted as XPs. However, she proposes that certain apparent problems with the movement analysis can be avoided if, instead of attributing different possibilities for movement to the two types of reflexives, we relativize the definition of local domains to the type of anaphor involved. SUBJECT, as defined in (13b) above, has two possible realizations: AGR – an X^0 element – or a subject nominal ([NP,XP]) – a phrasal element. Progovac proposes that the phrasal instance of SUBJECT counts as a potential SUBJECT only for phrasal (XP) anaphors. Thus, no X^0 anaphor should be subject to the SSC effect. Conversely, she argues that AGR, the X^0 instance of SUBJECT should not count as a potential SUBJECT for XP anaphors, but only for X^0 anaphors. The former therefore do not observe the TSC / PIC effect. This assumption makes it possible to eliminate the i-within-i provision.[40]

Everaert (1988) maintains an invariant characterization of local domains, defined in terms of Government Chains. In order to be bound, the anaphor and its binder must be contained in the same Government Chain, where Government Chains may be approximately identified with the G-Projections of Kayne (1983b), with additional licensing and identification requirements between the links in the chain. Phrase structure differences between languages affect the possibility of defining such Government Chains for anaphor / antecedent pairs, yielding the appearance of variation in binding domains.

3 Some Further Types of Pronominals

3.1 *Pronominal Anaphors*

As illustrated by the examples in (30), Danish *sig* must be bound. In this respect, it behaves as an anaphor. Significantly, however, its binder not only may but must occur outside of the minimal CFC/minimal subject domain containing it. In this respect, as Vikner notes, it behaves like a pronoun, since there is a minimal domain in which it must be free. Cross-linguistically, elements exhibiting this seemingly exotic behavior are not infrequent. They have been claimed to occur, for example, in Malayalam (Mohanan (1982)), Greek (Iatridou (1986)), and Dutch (Huybregts (1979)).[41] As noted above, Japanese *zibun* too seems to exhibit obviative behavior within minimal domains for some speakers. The question that arises is what the status of these elements is with respect to the Binding Theory. Some investigators (e.g. Huybregts, Iatridou) have suggested that they represent a distinct category of nominal, to be covered by a separate binding principle. In fact, though, it is not clear that this is necessary, since the properties they exhibit, viz. the requirement that they be bound in some domain and the requirement that they be free in some domain, are after all the definitional properties of anaphors and pronouns respectively. Suppose that they are simply anaphors and pronouns simultaneously. This is of course the status Chomsky (1981) attributed to the element PRO, to insure that it would occur only in ungoverned positions. Since it cannot be both free and bound in the same domain, it can satisfy these conflicting requirements only vacuously, by occurring in a position in which no local domain can be defined for it. On the other hand, if the domains for Principle A and Principle B have variable values, then the possibility arises that a pronominal anaphor could be free in some domain, satisfying the latter, and at the same time bound in a larger domain, satisfying the former under the choice of a less restricted domain. This would describe the behavior of the elements under discussion in this section. As will be seen in section 5.1, such a possibility would have serious consequences for the PRO theorem, however, and it is ruled out under a strict interpretation of the Binding Theory of Chomsky (1986b).

An interesting alternative characterization of these elements is developed in Hestvik (1990). Hestvik proposes that the pronoun/anaphor distinction (±p, ±a) should be replaced by a categorization based on the feature [±b(ound in local domain)], where the definition of local domain, as noted, is assumed to be invariant. Anaphors are [+b], while pronouns are [–b]. All pronominals are specified for two values for this feature – one for S-Structure and a second for LF. The two specifications, moreover, need not coincide. It is possible for an element to be specified [–b] at S-Structure, for example, but [+b] at LF. Such a specification would characterize pronominal anaphors. An element with these feature values could not have a local binder at S-Structure, so it would have to be free in its local domain. At LF, however, it would have to acquire a local binder through movement into a higher domain.

3.2 *The Dogrib Anti-Anaphor*

Dogrib, an Athabaskan language of Canada, as described by Saxon (1984 and later work), contains a pronominal form, *ye*, with unusual referential properties. *ye* must be disjoint in reference with a c-commanding clausemate subject, as in (38a), though it may corefer with the subject of a higher clause.

(38a) John$_i$ ye$_k$-hk'è ha
John him-3.shoot FUT
"John is going to shoot him"

With respect to its disjoint reference property, therefore, *ye* behaves like a pronoun. Unlike pronouns, however, it requires the presence of a local c-commanding argument, like *John* in (38a), even though it is not bound by that argument but interpreted as disjoint in reference with it. (38b), in which *ye* occurs without such an "anti-antecedent," is ill-formed:

(38b) *ye-zha shèeti
his son ate

Therefore, *ye* also resembles anaphors in that it requires the presence of a c-commanding local argument. Enç (1989) argues that we can capture this resemblance only by abandoning the idea that the local antecedence requirement imposed by Principle A is a binding requirement. The local licensing of anaphors, in her view, involves a strictly syntactic relationship, and is independent of any particular semantic content (cf. also C. Roberts (1985) for a similar suggestion). Both reflexives and *ye* are syntactic anaphors, subject to Principle A. Both must therefore be licensed by a local "antecedent" in an argument position. The relationship between the licenser and the anaphor, however, does not involve reference. Coreference properties result from additional specifications with respect to two other features – [±B_α], which determines whether the form is semantically (A or A-bar) bound, and [±ID], which determines whether the licenser and the binder of the form are identical. A redundancy rule insures that licensed elements are also [+B_α]; they must be bound either by an argument in A position or by an operator in A-bar position.[42] Reflexives are specified as A-bound, and, further, as [+ID]. The binder and the local licenser are therefore identical. The fact that the syntactic licenser is also the semantic binder for reflexives follows indirectly from positive specifications for these two features. The Dogrib anti-anaphor, on the other hand, is specified as [+L, +$B_{A'}$,

–ID]. In (38a), the subject *John* is required as a local licenser for *ye*. *John* is not the binder of *ye*, however, since it is not in an A′ position; the binder of *ye* is an empty operator in [Spec C]. This operator, moreover, must be contra-indexed with *John*; otherwise, *ye* would be A-bound by *John*, rather than A′-bound, as required, taking the binder of an element to be the most locally c-commanding element with which it is coindexed. Enç proposes that local disjoint reference requirements ("Principle B effects") arise in this way in general: pronouns which exhibit such effects are A′-bound elements. They count as bound by A′-elements only if not coindexed with more local binders in A-positions, and therefore they must be A-free in the minimal domain containing a possible A′-operator position.

Enç observes that her feature system yields seven non-contradictory possible combinations, and argues that all of these are attested. Pronominal anaphors of the type discussed in the preceding section, as well as logophors, are integrated into this system. The reader is referred to her paper for discussion, as well as arguments for the particular features proposed.

4 Some Notes on the Status of Disjoint Reference Principles

Under Enç's analysis the local disjoint reference property of pronouns is not directly stipulated, but derives instead from the definition of binding. They are A-bar bound, as required, only if their most local binder is in an A-bar position. Other proposals for deriving disjoint reference requirements from independent considerations have been advanced in Reinhart (1986), Burzio (1988) and Fanselow (1989). Reinhart proposes that Principle C can be eliminated from the theory of grammar since its effects are derivable from Grice's Maxim of Manner, requiring utterances to be as explicit as conditions permit. Her claim is that "when syntactically permitted, bound anaphora [construed to include bound pronouns – WEH] is the most explicit way . . . to express coreference," and failure to use it where possible leads to the pragmatic inference that coreference was not intended. Thus, the ill-formedness of (39a, b) in the indicated readings is a matter of pragmatics, rather than grammar.

(39a) *He$_i$ thinks that John$_i$ is crazy
(39b) *John$_i$ thinks that John$_i$ is crazy

This proposal is criticized in Lasnik (1991) on a number of grounds, including the observation that Principle C effects hold even in cases where fully equivalent sentences with bound pronouns are not possible, as in the case of the anaphoric epithet in (40a) and cases of overlapping reference like (40b):

(40a) *John$_i$ thinks I admire the idiot$_i$
(40b) They told John to visit Susan

In (40a), coreference is precluded even though no semantically equivalent bound anaphor can substitute for *the idiot*. In (40b), *they* cannot be understood as including either *John* or *Susan*, even though neither can be replaced by a bound anaphor.

Some of these arguments would seem to apply as well to the more recent attempt by Burzio (1988) to derive disjoint reference effects from a principle of Morphological Economy (ME), requiring that a bound NP be maximally unspecified. Reflexives are claimed to be underlyingly featureless, and therefore less morphologically marked than pronouns.[43] ME requires that they, rather than pronouns, be used where the relevant locality principle on reflexives allows. Burzio's proposal is intended in part to capture the observation (also remarked upon by Thráinsson (1976b)) that pronouns are subject to disjoint reference requirements just in case there exists a corresponding reflexive. Thus, the use of the pronoun yields a Principle B violation in (41a), but not in (41b) from Icelandic, which has no distinct reflexive forms in the first or second person.

(41a) *I like me
(41b) Ég$_i$ hata mig$_i$
I hate me
(Thráinsson (1976b))

Under this proposal, Principle B effects arise only when a less specified alternative than the pronoun (i.e. a reflexive) is available.[44] Again, however, if disjoint reference requirements followed entirely from this principle, we would expect that bound pronouns should be possible wherever reflexives are prohibited. This appears not to be correct. As Lasnik notes, both reflexives and bound pronouns are excluded in sentences like (42a,b).

(42a) *We like me/myself
(42b) *John and Mary like him/himself

Such examples again serve to show that disjoint reference principles cannot simply be viewed as "elsewhere" conditions.

As a further argument against the reduction of Principle C to a pragmatic principle, Lasnik notes that the equivalent of (39b) is well-formed in some languages, including Thai and Vietnamese. If the ill-formedness of this sentence in English is a matter of pragmatics, this would be an unexpected result, given the presumed universal applicability of pragmatic principles. On the other hand, if grammatical principles are involved, it can be accommodated by assuming that the relevant principle is parameterized in the appropriate way.

(39a) remains ill-formed in Thai, and Lasnik proposes on that account that Principle C effects are the result of a complex of two overlapping principles. One of these is the (apparently parameterized) requirement that names be R-free, which rules out English (39b) but not its Thai equivalent. The second is a prohibition against binding of more referential expressions by less referential ones, which rules out (39a) in both languages.

5 Binding Theory and Empty Categories

In a highly modular theory, questions about how to delimit the domain of responsibility of individual subtheories arise as a matter of routine. They have been very much in evidence in connection with the role of Binding Theory in determining the distribution and interpretation of empty categories. The following sections provide a brief outline of selected debates concerning the status of null elements with respect to Binding. Section 5.1 treats the base-generated null arguments PRO and *pro*, and section 5.2 treats traces – empty elements arising through movement.

5.1 Binding Theory and Null Pronominals

5.1.1 PRO

Sentence (43a) contains two verbs – the matrix verb *try* and the embedded verb *win* – each of which assigns a subject theta-role. It follows from the Projection Principle, which requires a one-to-one mapping between arguments and theta-roles at all levels, that both subject positions be occupied by arguments at D-Structure. Since the infinitival subject position is not occupied by an overt argument, we are led to posit a covert base-generated nominal element there. This null element, conventionally labeled PRO, exhibits fairly complex referential and distributional properties. PRO, unlike other types of nominals, is restricted in its distribution to the position of subject of an infinitive, as in (43a). It may not occur, for example, in object position (43b), nor as subject of a tensed clause (43c). In some contexts, PRO is obligatorily coindexed with a designated c-commanding NP in the higher clause, as in (43a, d–e). The former two examples illustrate coindexation with the subject argument, and the latter illustrates coindexation with the object argument. In other contexts, including infinitival subject clauses (43f) and interrogative object clauses (43g), coindexation with a higher clause argument is not required. In such cases PRO lacks specific reference, and is understood instead as arbitrary.

(43a) [$_\beta$ John$_i$ AGR$_i$ tried [PRO$_i$ to win]]
(43b) *Mary hoped for [the president to appoint PRO]
(43c) *I believe that [PRO will stay home]
(43d) Mary$_i$ promised me [PRO$_i$ to be home early]
(43e) John forced me$_i$ [PRO$_i$ to stay late]
(43f) [PRO$_{arb}$ to leave early] AGR would be inexcusable
(43g) John doesn't know [how PRO$_{arb}$ to behave oneself at parties]

As noted earlier, Chomsky (1981, 191 and later work) has proposed that the distribution of PRO follows from Binding Theory, under the assumption that PRO is both a pronoun and an anaphor and therefore subject to both Principle A and Principle B. Given the uniform definition of Governing Category in (13a), PRO can satisfy the conflicting demands of these two principles only vacuously, by appearing in contexts where it lacks a governor, and therefore a Governing Category. If infinitival INFL is assumed not to govern its subject, then (43a) but not (43b,c) will satisfy the Binding Theory. This proposal might appear to become somewhat problematic in the framework of Chomsky (1986b), in which the BT-Compatibility computation is introduced, allowing pronouns and anaphors to have overlapping distribution. As noted, the BT-Compatibility provision allows either the pronoun or the reciprocal to appear, for example, in the italicized position in (44).

(44) [$_\alpha$ They sold [$_\beta$ *their$_i$/each other's$_i$/*PRO$_i$* books]]

Here, β constitutes a GC for the pronoun, since β is a CFC and there is an indexing within β which is BT-Compatible with the pronoun. It may therefore be coindexed with the matrix subject. However, β does not constitute a GC for the reciprocal, since there is no indexing within β which is BT-Compatible with it, and the reciprocal may also be bound by the matrix subject. Why therefore can PRO not also occur in this position, satisfying Principle B within domain β and Principle A within domain α? In fact, as the discussion in Chomsky (1986b, 183) makes clear (cf. also Lasnik (1989b, 32)), this possibility is precluded under a strict interpretation of the licensing principle in Chomsky (1986b, 172), under which the licensing requirements for a given element must be satisfied within precisely one domain. This interpretation would also rule out the rather attractive account of overt pronominal anaphors sketched in section 3.1, however.

The principles of Binding Theory are employed under this standard account to capture the *distribution* of PRO by insuring that it can occur only in positions where the relevant binding principles apply to it vacuously; it follows that its *referential* properties – for example, the fact that it is obligatorily coindexed with the matrix subject in (43a) – must be determined outside of Binding Theory. Chomsky (1981) proposes that such facts fall under a separate subtheory of Control, which specifies possible antecedents for PRO. *Control Theory* appears to overlap extensively with Principle A of the Binding Theory, since both require coindexing of an element with a local, c-commanding argument. Partly because of this perceived redundancy, other investigators, including Bouchard (1982), Sportiche (1982), Manzini (1983a), Koster (1984), and Hestvik (1990), have pursued a different approach, under which the referential properties of (controlled) PRO follow from Principle A of the Binding Theory, while its distributional properties follow from other provisions (e.g. a requirement that PRO lack Case). The particular implementations of this idea vary substantially. In the account of Manzini, for example, PRO is a pure anaphor, which is restricted by Case requirements to the position of subject of infinitive, in which position it lacks a GC since it is ungoverned.[45] However, the embedded CP in which PRO occurs is itself governed in the higher clause, and therefore does have a Governing Category – the β of (43a). In such cases Manzini's extended Principle A requires the anaphor PRO to be bound within β, the Governing Category of the CP containing PRO, just in case β also contains a SUBJECT accessible to PRO, as accessibility was defined above. If β meets this condition, it is said to be a *Domain Governing Category* for PRO. Anaphors lacking Governing Categories must be bound in their Domain Governing Categories. Thus, obligatory control in instances like (43a) is due to Principle A. The matrix clause is a Governing Category for the embedded CP, and it contains a SUBJECT (AGR) accessible to PRO. It is therefore a DGC for PRO. In (43f), on the other hand, the matrix clause (the Governing Category for the CP containing PRO) does not contain a SUBJECT accessible to PRO. AGR is not accessible, due to the i-within-i provision.

PRO thus lacks a DGC here, and need not be bound. Because it is an anaphor, it is incapable of specific independent reference, and is therefore assigned an arbitrary interpretation by default. For discussion of other cases, the reader is referred to Manzini.

In spite of the similarities between anaphor binding and control of PRO, certain differences remain which bear on the prospect of collapsing the two theories. First, as noted by Chomsky and Lasnik (1991), there are languages in which lexical anaphors are subject-oriented but which nonetheless exhibit object control of PRO, as well as subject control. Whether this is in fact a problem for the potential unification of the two theories depends on the correct account of subject orientation on the part of lexical anaphors. If it results from the LF raising of certain anaphors, as some have suggested, then we might expect that PRO will not be exclusively subject-oriented in any language, since raising from the position of PRO would result in an improperly governed trace. Potentially more problematic is the fact that the controllers of PRO appear to be subject to restrictions not holding for binders of lexical anaphors. Chomsky (1981, 76) suggests that possible controllers are specified in terms of particular theta-roles (see also Růžička (1983), Chomsky and Lasnik (1991)). It may be, though, that a purely structural characterization is available, at least for core cases. With most control verbs, such as *try* in (43a) and *force* in (43e), the controller is chosen in accordance with the *Minimum Distance Principle* of Rosenbaum (1967); in each case, it is the NP most closely c-commanding PRO which serves as controller. In the case of *promise,* as in (43d), control seems to violate the MDP; the controller is the subject, not the object argument. Larson (1991) argues that here too, the MDP may be satisfied at the level of D-structure, since there is evidence that the object of *promise* fails to c-command the position of PRO at that level. He concludes (1991, 115) that controllers may in all cases be simply the closest c-commanding arguments at the relevant level. If so, there is still nonetheless a difference between control and binding of lexical anaphors, which appear not to be subject to such a closeness condition.

Finally, of course, alternative accounts of PRO which do not derive its distributional restrictions from Binding Theory remain responsible for showing that they follow naturally from other principles. Another approach to the control problem will be introduced in the following section.

5.1.2 pro

As observed in the preceding section, English does not allow non-trace null subjects in finite clauses. There are, however, other languages, the so-called *pro-drop languages,* which do allow such subjects. Spanish is a language of this type, as illustrated in (45b).[46]

(45a) *He said that [e] would come tomorrow.
(45b) Dijo que [e] vendría mañana (=45a)
(45c) *Yo hablé con [e]
I spoke with

The *pro*-drop phenomenon has been the subject of a very extensive literature within the GB framework, which cannot be reviewed adequately in the space available here. In the following, we will confine ourselves to a summary of selected attempts at answering two of the core questions addressed by this literature: what is the nature of the *pro*-drop subject, and what property or properties must a language have in order to admit *pro*-drop?

Chomsky (1981) identified the null subject of Spanish and similar languages with the pronominal anaphor PRO discussed above. Note that, like PRO, it does not occur freely in non-subject positions, as demonstrated by (45c). This identification requires that the subject position count as ungoverned even in finite clauses in *pro*-drop languages. Accordingly, Chomsky proposed the following account: the attachment of inflectional affixes to the verb is effected by a rule of affix movement ("Rule R"), which lowers inflectional features from INFL to the verb. The point of application of Rule R determines whether or not a language exhibits the *pro*-drop property. If Rule R applies in the syntax, as in Spanish, then INFL, lacking feature content at S-structure, will not be a governor for PRO in subject position. If it applies at PF, as claimed for English, then the subject position in finite clauses will still be governed at the point of application of Binding Theory, thus excluding PRO. This account is abandoned in Chomsky (1982) (and is unavailable in principle under current assumptions, since the verb in Spanish and like languages is now generally agreed to be raised into INFL in the syntax). The earlier identification of the *pro*-drop subject as PRO was rejected in large part because of differences in referential properties: the former does not share the latter's lack of independent reference. Rather than being assigned reference through control or receiving an arbitrary interpretation, the *pro*-drop subject has definite specific reference (when not pleonastic).[47] It functions, in other words, as a pure pronominal. Thus, Chomsky (1982) concludes that it is not [+a, +p] (i.e. PRO) but [–a,+p] – simply the null counterpart of overt pronouns.[48] This new element in the typology of empty categories is labeled *pro.*

As we have seen, though, the null pronoun *pro* does not share the distribution of overt pronouns. In particular, it is largely restricted to subject positions, where it may occur in some languages but not in others. Having abandoned the claim that it is a pronominal anaphor, we can no longer link its occurrence there to the special property of subject positions which is relevant for PRO – their potential ungovernedness. In fact, however, this is not an undesirable result, since there turns out to be an abundance of evidence that the admissibility of *pro* in subject positions is related in some way to another property of those positions – the fact that they are typically involved in an agreement relation with the inflectional head. The evidence that *pro*-drop is somehow linked to agreement morphology includes the following. First, it has long been noted that *pro*-drop tends to occur in languages with rich subject-agreement morphology, such as Spanish and Italian, but not in languages such as French and English, which have relatively impoverished agreement morphology (see Taraldsen (1980)). Second, pronouns may have a null realization even in non-subject positions in some languages, where those non-subject positions are associated with agreement morphology. So, for example, as noted by Huang (1989, 195), in perfect aspect sentences in Pashto, where there is object agreement morphology on the verb, object pronouns may be null (46a). Similarly, in the Celtic languages, as observed, e.g. by McCloskey and Hale (1984), prepositional object pronouns may be null just in case the preposition is one which agrees with its object. This is illustrated for Welsh in (46b).

(46a) ma [pro] wə-xwar-a
I *PRF-eat-FSg*
"I ate it"

(46b) Roedd car yn aros amdano [pro]
was *car PRT wait for-MSg*
"A car was waiting for him"

Considerations like these have led many investigators to conclude that the licensing of *pro*-drop somehow involves richness of agreement morphology, and that the usual restriction of *pro*-drop to subject positions results from the fact that in many languages only subjects are coindexed with agreement morphology. It has also been recognized at least since Perlmutter (1971, 102) that more is involved than the mere ability to recover the feature content from the agreement affix. In non-*pro*-drop languages like English and French, *pro* is disallowed even when the particular agreement ending allows for unambiguous recovery of its content, as in (46c).

(46c) *[pro] avons travaillé toute la journeé
"(We) worked all day long"
(Perlmutter (1971, 102))

Rather, to the extent that the "rich agreement" generalization holds at all, it must be characterized in terms of the overall richness of whole paradigms, rather than particular endings.

In the account of Chomsky (1982) the connection between rich agreement morphology and *pro*-drop was in fact an indirect one. *Pro* in subject position is licensed, under that account, just in case INFL determines its content through nominative case assignment under strict feature matching. This is possible, in turn, only in languages where INFL is generated with nominative case features in the base. In other languages, presumably, nominative case is not assigned through feature matching but simply under structural government, which is not sufficient for content recovery. The apparent association between *pro*-drop and rich agreement results from the fact that languages in which INFL contains nominative case features tend strongly to spell out the full feature content of INFL in Phonological Form, perhaps in consequence of the Visibility Condition. Most subsequent accounts have implemented the connection more directly; empty elements must be identified – i.e. their phi-feature content (categories such as person, number, gender) must be recoverable from their syntactic surroundings. In the case of *pro*, this is accomplished through coindexation with a sufficiently rich AGR (see Rizzi (1986a), Borer (1986a)).

There are certain facts, however, which prevent us from simply translating the observed general association between *pro*-drop and rich agreement into an exhaustive theory of *pro*. On the one hand, as noted, e.g. in Rizzi (1986a), there are languages with fairly rich systems of morphological agreement, such as German and Icelandic, where *pro*-drop is nonetheless not fully general. In these languages, referential pronouns may not have a null realization, as shown in (47a) from German. Pleonastic, non-argument subjects, however, may occur, in contrast to English. This is shown in (47b, c):

(47a) *[pro] will zu Hause bleiben
want at home to-stay
("I (*pro) want to stay home")

(47b) [pro] ihm scheint geholfen worden zu sein
him seems helped PASS-AUX to be
"He seems to have been helped" (lit "(It) seems to have been helped him")

(47c) [pro] klar ist, daß er nicht kommen wird.
clear is that he not come will
"(It) is clear that he will not come"

(For arguments that there are in fact null pleonastic subject elements in such sentences, see Safir (1985a).)

Thus, we must distinguish between degrees of *pro*-drop. Languages like English do not allow "dropping" of either thematic or pleonastic pronouns. Languages like Spanish allow dropping of both kinds of pronouns. Languages like German allow omission of pleonastic but not referential pronouns.[49] This typological difference is pointed out in Safir (1985b), who attempts to derive it from the claimed presence or absence of (abstract) subject clitics. Since Rizzi (1986a), it has been generally taken to reflect the existence of two distinct conditions on *pro* – a *Licensing* condition, to which all instances of *pro* are subject, and a more restrictive *Identification* requirement holding of referential/argumental *pro*s. (Rizzi notes that this distinction brings *pro* into line with other empty elements, which are subject to separate formal licensing and identification (content recovery) requirements. In the case of trace, the head-government provision of the ECP imposes a formal licensing requirement and the obligatory presence of a c-commanding antecedent represents the identification requirement. In the case of PRO, the requirement that it be ungoverned may be construed as a structural licensing condition, and identification is satisfied by Control.) The grammar of German, therefore, presumably satisfies the requirements for the *pro*-licensing but not identification, and therefore admits only those *pro*s which are not argumental. Specific proposals concerning the content of these two principles will be advanced shortly.

On the other hand, there are languages in which *pro* occurs in contexts where it is not linked to rich agreement morphology. We may distinguish two cases. Rizzi (1986a) argues that null objects must be posited in the syntactic representation of sentences like (48a) in Italian; their presence is demonstrated by the behavior of such sentences with respect to binding, control, and predication. By process of elimination, the null nominals in question must be *pro*, since they do not satisfy the conditions on any other empty category.

(48a) Il bel tempo invoglia [pro] a [PRO restare]
the good weather induces to stay

Second, a number of languages, including Japanese and Chinese, routinely allow *pro* in subject position even though they have no agreement morphology at all. This is illustrated in the Chinese example (48b), from Huang (1989):

(48b) Zhangsan$_i$ shuo [[pro$_i$] lai le]
Zhangsan say he come ASP

(Huang (1984) also observes that Chinese allows null objects, but argues that these are variables bound by null topic operators, which are subject to Principle C. The subject null elements, however, are pronominal, and may therefore be coindexed with a subject outside their Governing Categories, as in the present instance.)

Having laid out the core explicanda confronting any attempt at a comprehensive theory of *pro*, we can review briefly some of the major attempts at constructing such a theory. The work of Rizzi (1986a) is fundamental to much of the subsequent research on this problem. Rizzi, as noted, distinguished between a Licensing requirement, applying to all instances of *pro*, and an Identification requirement, applying to argumental *pro* (*pro* in a chain with a theta-role or a quasi-theta-role, as in the case of meteorological *it* – cf. note 49). *Pro* is licensed if Case-governed by a head belonging to a designated class of licensing heads, which can vary from language to language. In languages with *pro*-drop in subject position, INFL is a licensing head. In Italian, V is also a licensing head, opening the way for *pro* in object positions, such as (48a). In English, no head counts as a licensing head, and therefore *pro*-drop is disallowed in all contexts.

In addition to being licensed, argumental *pro* must be identified. Identification may be accomplished in more than one way. In the usual case, it is effected through binding by grammatical features on the licensing head. In order to be referential, an NP must be specified for person/number features. In the case of *pro*, therefore, it must be coindexed with features of person/number on its Case-governing head. Thus, the presence of rich agreement morphology is a necessary condition for this mode of identification. It is not a sufficient condition, however; languages with rich agreement morphology may opt not to exploit identification through head-binding. The grammar of German does not choose this option, and therefore, in spite of its rich morphology, German has no referential *pro*-drop. In the case of the *pro* in (48a), identification is accomplished by other means – specifically, through a rule which assigns the referential index *arb* to object *pro*s.

Rizzi notes that the case of Chinese poses a serious problem for his proposal, since subject *pro* is allowed there even though there is no agreement morphology to identify it. He notes, however, that agreement features play no role in other aspects of the grammar of Chinese (or like languages) either, and suggests that perhaps such languages make use of different mechanisms for *pro*-Identification, given the systematic irrelevance of agreement features in their grammars. Other investigators, however, have attempted to develop theories of *pro*-drop which provide a unitary characterization of the phenomenon in both language types, and capture the apparent generalization that *pro*-drop tends to occur in languages with very rich agreement (e.g. Italian) or with no agreement at all (e.g. Chinese), but not in languages with partial agreement paradigms, such as English and French. Jaeggli and Safir (1989) propose that it is not the richness of inflectional paradigms, but rather their morphological uniformity, which plays a role in *pro*-theory, where morphological uniformity is defined as in (49):

(49) *Morphological Uniformity*: An inflectional paradigm P in a language L is morphologically uniform iff P has either only underived inflectional forms or only derived inflectional forms.

Spanish and Japanese are morphologically uniform, under this definition; the former has inflectional endings throughout the paradigm, and the latter has no inflectional endings at all. English, on the other hand, is not, since some forms have endings (*he run-s*) while others do not (*I run*). *Pro* is licensed, according to Jaeggli and Safir, only in those languages with morphologically uniform paradigms.

German and like languages again emerge as potentially problematic, since German, too, has uniform paradigms (in the present tense), with inflectional endings on each form, as in (50), but it differs from Japanese and Spanish with respect to *pro*-drop, in that it lacks *pro*-drop of arguments.[50]

(50)	komm-e	komm-en
	komm-st	komm-t
	komm-t	komm-en

Jaeggli and Safir, as well as other investigators, including Adams (1987) and Gilligan (1987), have attempted a more deterministic solution to this problem than the one originally advanced by Rizzi. In particular, they have suggested that this difference indicates that German does not satisfy the Identification Requirement, and have proposed that its failure to do so is connected with yet another salient syntactic property of German (as well as Icelandic) – the Verb-Second property. German exhibits a subordinate/main clause asymmetry in verb position. In embedded clauses with initial complementizers, the verb is last, but in main declarative clauses, the verb is obligatorily second, preceded by (at most) a single topicalized constituent. This alternation is standardly assumed to reflect obligatory movement of the verb to the COMP position, in case that position is not occupied by a complementizer. Numerous accounts have been advanced for the obligatoriness of such verb movement. Jaeggli and Safir adopt a quite standard view, that verbs must move to COMP in German because Tense features are generated there (unlike English), and the verb must move there to support them. They then implement the claimed link between the V-2 property and the lack of argumental *pro*-drop by claiming that, for Identification as a null pronominal *pro*, an empty category must be governed by TENSE / AGR(eement) features occurring together under a single X^0 node. This is satisfied in non-V-2 languages, in which both TENSE and AGR are generated under INFL, but not in V-2 languages, like German where, by hypothesis, the AGR features but not TENSE features, originate under INFL. Thus, in German *pro* can be licensed by morphological uniformity but it cannot be identified. As evidence for this view of the claimed link between V-2 and *pro*-drop, they cite the fact that in Flemish, a language with complementizers which optionally inflect for person, null subjects can occur just in case the complementizer does exhibit person agreement – as in (51a, b), from Bennis and Haegeman (1984); AGR arguably does co-occur in COMP with TENSE in such instances, allowing Identification.[51] (See also Bavarian (Bayer (1983)).):

(51a) dase (pro) komt
that-3sg.fem comes
"that she comes"

(51b) *da (pro) komt
"that he / she comes"

Adams (1987) also relates the absence of referential *pro*-drop in German to the V-2 property, in a quite different way, having to do with directionality of government.

A very different approach to the problem posed by Chinese and similar languages is pursued by Huang (1989). Huang proposes the abolishment of the distinction between PRO and *pro* originating in Chomsky (1982). PRO and *pro* are in fact the same entity, according to Huang, and the Identification requirement for *pro* and the Control requirement holding of PRO reduce to a single principle – the *Generalized Control Rule.* Huang starts out by noting that the general connection between the occurrence of *pro* and rich agreement appears to be correct in some way, in view of, e.g., the facts of Pashto. Yet Chinese has no subject agreement to identify its missing subjects as *pro.* He notes further that the only missing subjects occurring in English – namely, PRO subjects – are in infinitive clauses, which also have no agreement. That is, null subjects are allowed in Chinese, which has no AGR, and they are allowed in English just in those clauses that lack AGR. This similarity suggests the possibility that the two elements might in fact be identical. Huang assumes that they are, and proposes that both are subject to the Generalized Control Rule in (52):

(52a) Generalized Control Rule: an empty pronominal is controlled in its control domain (if it has one)
(52b) Control Domain: α is the control domain for β if it is the minimal category satisfying (i) and (ii):
 (i) α is the lowest S or NP containing
  (a) β, or
  (b) the minimal maximal category containing β;
 (ii) β contains a SUBJECT accessible to α.

In the English example in (43a), there are two potential Control Domains for PRO. The embedded clause is a potential Control Domain since it is the minimal S containing PRO, but, lacking an accessible SUBJECT (AGR), it is not an actual Control Domain. The matrix clause is also a potential Control Domain, under clause (52b, i(b)), since it is the lowest S containing the minimal X^{max} containing PRO (the embedded CP).[52] Moreover, it is an actual Control Domain, since it does contain an accessible SUBJECT (AGR). PRO must therefore be controlled within the matrix clause. In (43f), the matrix clause is also a potential, but not an actual Control Domain, since it contains no accessible SUBJECT. The matrix AGR is disqualified by the i-within-i provision. Hence, PRO need not be controlled here.

Huang notes that the distribution of PRO – its restriction to subject position – falls out from the GCR, under the assumption that PRO/*pro* is a (pure) pronominal. If PRO/*pro* were to occur in object position, then it would have to be controlled within its minimal clause, since it is in the domain of an accessible SUBJECT (either the clausal AGR or the subject NP) within that clause. But coindexing an object PRO/*pro* with the subject NP of the clause in question (or any other c-commanding argument) would give rise to a Principle B violation. As a pronoun, PRO/*pro* must be free within its GC. These conflicting requirements can be satisfied when PRO/*pro* occurs in the position of subject of an infinitive, as in (43a), where it can be controlled within its Control Domain (the main clause) without being bound in its GC. PRO/*pro* is therefore restricted to subject positions in the usual case. Object PRO/*pro* is allowed where there is sufficiently rich object agreement morphology, as in (46a), since this agreement can serve as the controller for the null pronominal without giving rise to a Principle B violation. The pronoun will not be A-bound in such a case, agreement being non-argumental.

In the Spanish example (45b), the null pronominal element ("*pro*") must be controlled in the embedded clause, since that clause does have a SUBJECT (AGR) which is accessible to *pro*. Moreover, since Spanish AGR is "strong" (i.e. morphologically rich), it can serve as the controller for *pro*. Thus, *pro* satisfies the GCR by virtue of being controlled by strong AGR within the Control Domain defined by AGR. It may be free outside that domain. In the ill-formed English sentence (45a), the null pronominal (*pro*) must similarly be controlled in the embedded clause, since the embedded clause again contains a SUBJECT (AGR) accessible to *pro*. In English, however, since AGR is weak, it cannot serve as a controller for *pro*. Both types of AGR constitute (accessible) SUBJECTS, and so define Control Domains for a null pronoun occurring in their respective clauses. However, strong agreement, but not weak agreement, can serve as the controller of a coindexed null pronoun occurring within that domain. Thus, the correlation between strong and weak agreement with respect to *pro*-drop is captured. In the case of the infinitive construction in (43a), there is no AGR at all in the embedded clause. Thus no Control Domain is defined, leaving the null pronominal free to satisfy the GCR within the matrix clause.

In Chinese, AGR is systematically absent even in tensed clauses. These are therefore predicted to behave like English infinitive constructions for the purpose of the GCR. Huang argues that this is correct for at least some cases. In sentences like (53), the null subject needn't be controlled in the embedded clause, since, lacking AGR, that clause is not a potential Control Domain. It is, however, obligatorily understood as coreferring with a main clause argument, just as in cases of Control in English, since the main clause does contain a SUBJECT accessible to it (the subject NP).

(53a) Zhangsan qi ma qi de [[pro] hen lei]
Zhangsan ride horse ride til very tired
"Zhangsan rode the horse until he was very tired"

(53b) Lisi$_i$, Zhangsan ku de [ta$_i$/*[pro$_i$] hen shangxin]
Lisi Zhangan cried til he very sad
"Lisi$_i$, Zhangsan cried until he$_i$ was very sad"

There are, however, other cases in which the null pronominal subject of an object complement clause in Chinese does not behave like the PRO in English control contexts – i.e. in which it is not obligatorily coindexed with a matrix clause argument. This is true, in particular, of complements of "say" and "believe" in Chinese, as in (53c):

(53c) Zhangsan shuo [*pro* mingtian bu bi lai]
Zhangsan$_i$ says he$_{i/k}$ tomorrow not need come
"Zhangsan$_i$ says that he$_i$/he$_k$ need not come tomorrow"

Since it is not controlled here, the null pronominal must lack a control domain. Huang notes that we can achieve this result if we take complements of verbs of this type not to be just CPs but rather CPs contained in NPs, following an idea suggested by Rosenbaum in early work. If this is the case, then there will be two potential control domains for *pro* – the embedded CP, which contains *pro* (case 52b, i(a)) or NP, which contains the minimal maximal projection (CP) containing *pro* (case 52b, i(b)). Neither of these, however, contains a SUBJECT accessible to *pro*, so *pro* lacks a Control Domain. Huang sees as a desirable side effect of this analysis the fact that it predicts, apparently correctly, the absence of obligatory control operating "down into" NPs in general. Consider (53d):

(53d) He recognized [the need [PRO to approve of oneself]]

Huang adduces independent arguments, primarily from English, for the claim that complements of *believe*-type verbs, which do not exhibit obligatory control in Chinese, are in fact NPs.

5.1.3 Diary Drop

Even though it is generally a non-*pro*-drop language, English does allow the omission of subjects in such sentences as (54a) in certain (primarily written) styles, such as letters and diaries.

(54a) Came home after the party, got undressed and went to bed

These missing subjects have been investigated by Haegeman (1990) and Rizzi (to appear), who have observed that they are subject to some syntactic restrictions. They are, in particular, limited to root clauses in which no element has been fronted, as illustrated in (54b, c):

(54b) *He asked if _____ arrived yesterday
(54c) *What should _____ do?

Rizzi identifies this null element not as *pro*, but as a null constant – of the same category as traces of topicalization ([–a, –p, –v]), and claims that this element can be free, picking up discourse-identification, just in case it is not within the domain of a potential binder (i.e. a c-commanding [Spec, C] position). Assuming that the CP projection is optionally missing in root clauses when no part of it is instantiated (e.g. through movement), the restriction of diary drop to root clauses without fronted constituents is accounted for.

5.2 *Binding Theory and Traces*

5.2.1 **Wh-*Trace***

Apparent parallels like those in (55) led to the conclusion in early work on the Extended Standard Theory (EST) (e.g. Chomsky (1973, 1976, 1977b)) that movement rules are subject to the SSC and the TSC, just as the construal rules involved in the interpretation of anaphora are.

(55a) *John is expected for Mary to like
(55b) *John expects Mary to like *himself*
(55c) *Who do you think that ____ won?
(55d) *They think that *each other* won

With the introduction of trace theory, it became possible to reduce these conditions entirely to conditions on interpretation (cf. Chomsky (1976)). Thus, both (55c) and (55d) can be interpreted as violating the TSC (or the NIC, under an alternative characterization of local domains) because they contain anaphoric elements which are free in the relevant domain. At the same time, it was recognized (cf. Chomsky (1976, 1977b)) that *wh*-traces behave like names with respect to crossover phenomena.

The claimed parallelism between lexical anaphors and *wh*-traces was called into question, however, by the observation (originating with Rizzi (1982)) that *wh*-traces fail to exhibit SSC effects where expected. This is most clearly seen in the Romance languages, where subjacency (presumably because of a choice of bounding nodes different from that in English) does not prevent extraction from embedded questions. (56), in which a relative pronoun has been extracted from the embedded object position, skipping over the already occupied *wh*-landing site in the embedded clause, is well-formed even though the trace of that movement is free in the domain of the subject of the lower clause, in violation of the SSC. On the other hand, the NIC effect does hold, preventing similar extractions out of the preverbal subject position (cf. Aoun (1985, 17)).

(56) Questo è il libro che [mi chiedo [perchè [pro] ho
this is the book which I wonder why Aux
comprato [t]]]
bought

Chomsky (1980, 37) points out that the same asymmetry can be demonstrated for English; extraction from the object position of an embedded question, as in (57a), yields only mild ill-formedness, such as might result from a subjacency violation alone, while extraction from the subject position, as in (57b), is much worse.

(57a) ??What$_k$ did you wonder who$_i$ t_i saw t_k?
(57b) *Who$_k$ did you wonder what$_i$ t_k saw t_i?

The failure of *wh*-traces to observe the SSC led Chomsky (1979) to conclude that such traces are not anaphors after all, but only R-expressions, subject to Principle C but not requiring binding in any local domain. This leaves the ill-formedness of (55c, 57b) unaccounted for, however. If *wh*-traces are not anaphors, these examples no longer fall under the NIC case of Principle A, which presumably is what rules out (55d). Chomsky proposes that they are ruled out by a separate subtheory, the theory of Government – specifically, by the Empty Category Principle (ECP), which requires traces to be properly governed. The ECP is the subject of chapter 5 in the present volume. I will limit myself here to pointing out again that the apparent inelegance of this state of affairs, in which two separate subtheories – Binding Theory and Government Theory – single out the position of nominative subjects, has not gone unaddressed; reductions in both directions have been proposed. As we observed above, Chomsky (1986b) claimed that the NIC case for lexical anaphors can be reduced to the ECP if anaphors move at LF, leaving traces. The opposite approach has been suggested by Aoun (1985). Aoun claims that *wh*-traces are in fact anaphors, required to be bound in the domain of an accessible SUBJECT (where binding is now "generalized," to cover A-bar as well as A-binding). (57b) violates Principle A, since the (anaphoric) *wh*-trace is free in the domain of an accessible SUBJECT – the AGR of the embedded clause. The apparent parallelism between (55c) and (55d) is restored. The failure of *wh*-traces to observe the SSC effect is captured through a modification of the definition of accessibility, given in (58):

(58) α is accessible to β iff β is in the c-command domain of α and coindexing of (α, β) would not violate any grammatical principle.

Wh-traces are not only (A-bar) anaphors but R-expressions, subject to Principle C. They must be bound by an antecedent in A-bar position, because of Principle A, but because of Principle C they must be A-free in all domains. If a *wh*-trace in object position were to be coindexed with the subject of its clause (or any higher clause), a violation of Principle C (a Strong Crossover Violation) would result. Because of this, neither those subjects nor the AGR elements coindexed with them can constitute accessible SUBJECTS for *wh*-traces, as accessibility is defined in (58), and they therefore do not define opaque domains for *wh*-traces. This *Generalized Binding Theory* and its contribution to "ECP effects" are discussed further in Aoun (1986) and Aoun, Hornstein, Lightfoot, and Weinberg (1987).

5.2.2 *NP-Trace*

(55a), once held to be ill-formed because it violates the SSC effect of Principle A (parallel to (55b)), is no longer analyzed in this way. The trace here is in a Cased position – hence, a *wh*-trace. It falls under Principle C, not Principle A, in the standard Binding Theory. The sentence is therefore ungrammatical not because the trace is A-bound outside its local domain, but because it is A-bound in the first place. In the version of the theory outlined in Chomsky (1981), only Caseless traces are (A–) anaphors, and therefore subject to the SSC. In fact though, as pointed out by Bouchard (1982, 199), Chomsky (1986b, 180), the claim that Caseless traces are subject to Principle A seems to have very little if any predictive content (cf. also Harbert (1984)). It is not at all clear that it is possible to construct examples which are ill-formed only because an NP-trace is free in its local domain; the imaginable violations of the locality effects of Principle A that could arise through NP movement apparently in all cases also violate another principle or principles. A possible way of avoiding this rather extensive redundancy would be to claim that NP-traces are not subject to Principle A. They are clearly not subject to the other two Binding Principles, either, so this would amount to placing them outside of Binding Theory.[53] It is not clear, though, why only NP-traces, not *wh*-traces, should fall outside of Binding Theory. Yoon (1991) develops the interesting proposal that traces in general have no status with respect to the Binding Theory, which regulates only relations between chains, not chain-internal relationships.

Related Material in Other Chapters

Theta theory, X-bar theory, and Case theory interact to determine which positions in a tree can be occupied by NPs and by arguments in particular. Binding theory overlays this system of conditions on the occurrence of NPs with its own conditions on the *co-occurrence* of NPs. Binding theory also relies on principles from other modules in the treatment of crossover phenomena, for instance X-bar theory and theta theory which constrain the occurrence of syntactic operators. The X-bar-theoretic distinction between A and A-bar positions described in chapter 1 is of great importance to the theory of binding in general.

The wellformedness conditions on the occurrence of operators at LF is discussed in detail in chapter 3 where the reader will also find more discussion of crossover, the relationship between scope and binding, and the treatment of bound pronouns.

The presentation of the Empty Category Principle in chapter 5 is directly relevant to the movement approaches to long-distance anaphora discussed in the current chapter. Since empty categories are generally assumed to fall under the binding theory, there has been some controversy as to the extent that the Binding Theory and the ECP are responsible for constraining the distribution of empty categories. These issues are discussed in chapter 5. Chapter 6 discusses binding-theoretic approaches to agreement morphology and how an appeal to binding-theoretic notions might allow us to distinguish between incompatible theories of clitics. The Minimalist Program contains aspects of a binding-theoretically motivated theory of reconstruction which are discussed in chapter 7.

NOTES

1 See, however, Richards (1993) for a proposal that the principles of Binding Theory in fact regulate relations between syntactic heads rather than nominals, and are therefore only indirectly connected with referential dependencies among nominal expressions.

2 For reasons of space, I ignore here a number of important questions about the relationship between coindexing and coreference, and non-coindexing and non-coreference. The advanced reader is referred to Evans (1980), Higginbotham (1980b), Reinhart (1983b), C. Roberts (1985), Sells (1986) for some discussion.

I also ignore a number of arguments that simples indices are not adequate for the representation of referential dependencies. Lasnik (1981) argues that the index of a nominal should be a set of integers. Higginbotham (1983) proposes that referential dependencies should be represented as asymmetrical, directional linking relationships (cf. also Evans (1980)).

3 Alternatively, it might seem that the asymmetry could be captured by a linear condition, requiring that the antecedent precede the anaphor. However, that alternative would fail to account, e.g. for ungrammatical cases like (i), in which the intended antecedent, while not c-commanding the anaphor, does precede it:

(i) *[$_{NP}$ John's and Mary's$_i$ children] saw each other$_i$

In general, there is little evidence that linear order plays a role in binding relationships.

There are some instances in which the c-command requirement on anaphor binding is apparently not observed. Two cases are given in (ii) and (iii).

(ii) [Which picture of himself$_i$] do you think that he$_i$ likes t$_i$?
(iii) [Stories about each other$_i$] pleased the boys$_i$.

However, in (ii) the bracketed phrase containing the anaphor is linked to a trace which is c-commanded by the antecedent, and these cases have standardly been reconciled with the c-command requirement by claiming that Binding Theory makes reference to a level at which the bracketed phrase is in its pre-movement position – either before movement, or at LF, after the operation of "Reconstruction" has replaced the trace of movement with the bracketed phrase. For an alternative to reconstruction, the advanced reader is referred to Barss (1986). It has also been proposed, e.g. by Belletti and Rizzi (1988), that the apparent violation of c-command in (ii) can be explained by appeal to movement.

4 Throughout, I will use "pronoun" only in this technical sense. The term pronominal will be used when necessary to refer to reflexives, reciprocals and pronouns together.

5 The term "opacity" is assigned a narrower technical definition in Chomsky (1980), in which it is roughly equivalent to the Specified Subject Condition (SSC) (see below).

6 Again, there is abundant evidence that c-command, and not precedence, is the relevant notion. Consider:

(i) After he$_i$ left, we made fun of the old man in the hat$_i$

7 For an alternative derivation of Strong Crossover effects, see Huang (1982, 377ff).

8 Notice that this modification also achieves a desirable result for reflexives and reciprocals, which may only be bound by A-antecedents, not A-bar antecedents:

(i) They$_i$ bought pictures of themselves$_i$
(ii) *Which boys$_i$ did pictures of themselves$_i$ convince Mary that she shouldn't date t$_i$?

9 In Chomsky (1986b) the following modification is proposed:

(i) An R-Expression must be A-free (within the domain of its operator).

This allows the trace t in (ii) to be coindexed with *John*, since *John* is outside the domain of the null operator which is argued to locally (A-bar-)bind that trace:

(ii) John$_i$ is tough [OP$_i$ [PRO to please t$_i$]

10 For discussion of various aspects of this issue see Barss (1986), Huang and Tang (1991), Belletti and Rizzi (1988), Lasnik and Uriagereka (1988, 157ff).

11 This is implemented in Chomsky (1982) by eliminating "pronoun," "anaphor," and "R-expression" as primitive categories and replacing them with the features [±a], [±p]. PRO is [+p, +a]. R-expressions are [–p, –a].

12 In later work the TSC was replaced by the Propositional Island Condition (PIC), a parameterized version, which, although not precisely formulated, was intended to accommodate the fact that marking of tense is not involved in all languages in the realization of finiteness. For discussion, see Chomsky (1977b, 75).

13 The model of Chomsky (1981) also differs from its predecessors in other important respects. Unlike Chomsky (1980), for example, it holds that indices are assigned at random, rather than stipulated by rules of coindexing and contraindexing, after which the resulting indexed structure is evaluated by the Binding Principles. For a more detailed review of the development of local domains between Chomsky (1973) and Chomsky (1981), the reader is referred to Sinclair (1982), Lasnik (1989b).

14 The role of governor in this formulation is marginal, as Chomsky (1981, 221) points out; reference to it could be omitted, as far as overt pronouns and anaphors are concerned, without any clear empirical consequences. However, it must be retained for PRO, given the standard assumption that PRO is a pronoun as well as an anaphor. Consider (i):

(i) John$_i$ tried [PRO$_i$ to win]

If reference to the governor were omitted, then PRO here would have a GC (the main clause), in which it would have to be both free and bound. See section 5.1 for further discussion of PRO and the Binding Theory.

15 Turkish (George and Kornfilt (1981)) and Portuguese (Zaring (1985)), among other languages, provide evidence that Agreement has an opacity-inducing effect even in the absence of Tense marking. Further, the NIC effect for anaphors is systematically lacking in languages such as Chinese, Korean, and Khmer, which do not have subject–verb agreement, again suggesting that it is AGR which is responsible for this effect. Cf., however, Picallo (1984–5), Raposo (1985–6), who claim, on the basis of obviation facts in Romance subjunctive complements, that tense does play a role in the determination of binding domains for pronouns.

16 The i-within-i principle is independently needed to exclude referential circularity of the sort found in *[$_{NPi}$ the owner of his$_i$ boat]. Here, however, the indices all encode intended coreference, while the subject-INFL agreement coindexing in (10j) encodes another type of relationship entirely. It is not clear why this type of indexing should interact with referential indexing in the manner claimed.

17 A further default provision like (i) is necessary to prevent anaphors from being completely free when there is no accessible SUBJECT in any higher domain, as in example (ii):

(i) A root sentence is a GC for a governed element.
(ii) *[$_{IPi}$ For each other to win] AGR$_i$ would be unfortunate.

18 According to the analysis of Huang (1983), it is the head N^0 which counts as SUBJECT within NP, since it is the most prominent nominal element in NP.

However, because of the i-within-i provision, it is not an accessible SUBJECT for any element within its projection.

19 A maximal phrase containing a subject is, in Chomsky's terms, a *"Complete Functional Complex (CFC)"*. Hence, an anaphor must be bound in the least CFC containing a lexical governor for that anaphor.

20 Note that the two differ in terms of the effect of the omission of the *that*. Only (15e) is improved by such omission. This is perhaps to be linked to the fact that (15e) involves movement of an operator phrase to Spec, while (15c) is claimed to involve head movement. The idea of LF-movement of anaphors, leaving traces which are subject to the ECP, had been suggested by Lebeaux (1983), who employed it to account for certain asymmetries in the distribution of reciprocals and reflexives. (Little is said in either work about why such movement should be required. See note 34 for a suggestion.) These proposals should be compared to Kayne (1983b), which also suggests that the NIC effect for lexical anaphors might reduce to an ECP effect, although in a rather different way. As we will see, the assumption of LF movement of reflexives has also been exploited extensively in accounting for cases of apparent long-distance binding.

21 Hestvik notes that some problems remain with this characterization. Among them is the fact that non-specific NPs appear not to constitute GCs for pronouns:

(i) *He$_i$ found a picture of him$_i$

22 In fact, Hestvik eliminates the BT-Compatibility computation as a means of extending the binding domains for anaphors in such cases, in favor of LF-movement of those anaphors, as described in the next section. Hestvik (1990) also proposes that the notion of governor can be eliminated from the characterization of GCs. The arguments are too involved to be reproduced here. The advanced reader is referred to Hestvik (1990) for interesting discussion of these and related issues.

23 As we will see below, Danish has another reflexive, *sig selv*, which does observe the SSC.

24 For Russian see Yokoyama (1980), Rappaport (1986), Bailyn (1991). For Norwegian, see Hellan (1988), Hestvik (1990). For Danish, see Vikner (1985). For Gothic, see Harbert (1984, 1991). For Chinese, see Tang (1985, 1989), Pica (1987), Cole, Hermon, and Sung (1990), Huang and Tang (1991). For Icelandic, see Anderson (1982a), Thráinsson (1976a, 1987), Maling (1984), Sigurðsson (1986). For Italian, see Napoli (1979), Giorgi (1983–4). For Japanese, see Oshima (1979). For Korean, see Park (1986), Yoon (1989).

25 The choice of Tense, rather than Agreement, as the relevant element in defining domain (21c), appears to be dictated in part by this analysis of (18a), in conjunction with Manzini and Wexler's claim that the values for the parameter stand in a subset relation to one another. Domains with referential tense are a subset of domains with tense, but not of domains with agreement.

26 The last part of this criticism does not hold for all of the proposals listed. Manzini and Wexler note, as have others, that in general LD reflexives are monomorphemic. Polymorphemic reflexives and reciprocals, such as English *himself, each other*, and Danish *sig selv*, do not seem to admit LD binding. They claim that this follows from three general assumptions: first, (21a) is picked out by the Subset Principle as the unmarked, default value for anaphoric binding domains – the one assumed in the absence of contrary positive evidence. Second, parameters are associated with individual lexical items (the Lexical Learning Hypothesis), and can only be reset for individual lexical items. Finally, polymorphemic forms, like the English

reflexive and reciprocal, are phrasal, not lexical. Since they are not lexical items, and since the Lexical Learning Hypothesis allows resetting of parameter values only for lexical items, it follows that they must observe the default value, (21a). The idea that monomorphemic reflexives can be construed as X^0 elements while polymorphemic reflexives behave as XP elements also figures prominently in some other approaches to the variation problem, to be discussed below.

27 Even here, however, it was proposed in some earlier accounts that *myself* is in fact bound – by the covert subject of a higher performative predicate.

28 This idea that tense plays a role in the characterization of binding domains in such cases and that indicative and subjunctive clauses differ with respect to the status of their tense features has figured relatively prominently in the literature on LD binding. It is incorporated, for example, into the accounts of Giorgi (1983–4), Picallo (1984–5), Raposo (1985–6), and, as noted, Manzini and Wexler (1987).

29 The last provision captures the observation that in general LD anaphors may be bound only to subjects – an observation which will be brought up again below. Objects in higher clauses may not antecede [–BT] anaphors in more deeply embedded clauses because they are not the thematically most prominent elements in those higher clauses (the higher clauses' subjects being more prominent), and therefore do not have P-Domains.

30 The latter possibility exists only in Japanese. In Icelandic, aside from the highly restricted type of exception mentioned by Sigurðsson (1986, 38), when there is an antecedent in the same clause, that antecedent must be a subject.

31 We need not include here the fact that in Icelandic only subjects may antecede long-distance reflexives, nor the fact pointed out by Kang (1988) that in Korean, subjects may antecede LD reflexives regardless of their thematic role. Sells (1987) has proposed that the notion subject has theoretical status in Discourse Representation Structure.

32 The specification of a syntactically saturated predicate is intended to account for the contrast in (i) and (ii).

(i) The city watched the destruction of itself.
(ii) *The city watched the aliens' destruction of itself.

In (i), the agent theta-role of the predicate *destruction* is *lexically* satisfied. That predicate therefore does not define a local domain for the reflexive, which is free to function as a logophor. On the other hand, in (ii) the predicate is syntactically satisfied, since all of its theta-roles are assigned to syntactic positions, and the anaphor must therefore be bound in its domain. The SSC effect is captured in this way without direct reference to subjects.

33 *Sig selv* is also subject-oriented, though, indicating that the association between subject-orientation and the possibility of long-distance binding holds only in one direction. (However, see Cole and Sung (1991b), who claim that at the level of universal principles only LD anaphors are subject-oriented, and who attribute subject-orientation on the part of local anaphors to analogy).

34 Pica's account for the obligatoriness of this movement to INFL is in fact not particularly explicit. A concrete suggestion is offered in Reinhart and Reuland (1989), who note that "X^0 anaphors" like the Danish *sig* and the Chinese *ziji* are typically morphologically defective in that they lack phi-features such as number and person. On the other hand, "XP anaphors" like English *himself*, Chinese *ta-ziji*, and Danish *hinanden* are overtly marked for person and/or number. Reinhart and Reuland propose that the former must move to INFL to acquire phi-features,

through Subject–INFL agreement. Under an account of this type, what is important in determining the behavior of a reflexive is not its complexity, but whether or not its morphology encodes intrinsic phi-features. Note that this predicts reflexives like Danish *sig selv*, too, even though polymorphemic, should have to move to INFL to get phi-features, since they do not have them inherently. This accords well with the subject-orientation of these forms.

35 Pica argues later in the paper (following Chomsky (1986b)) that the relationship between the subject and the anaphor is not one of binding but of antecedent government.

36 Hestvik also differs from Pica in denying that the difference between infinitive and indicative clauses with respect to long binding has to do with whether C^0 is empty or not. He notes that in some languages, e.g. Norwegian, LF anaphor movement can apply across the boundaries of infinitival relative clauses, which arguably must have [–*wh*] C^0s. (This is not true of all LD binding languages (cf. Rappaport (1986) on Russian.) Hestvik concludes (1990, 38) that LF anaphor movement is simply prohibited out of tensed clauses. Thus, the TSC is reinstated in his account, as a condition on movement.

37 As Tang (1985) noted, higher clause experiencer nominals also trigger blocking effects – a fact claimed in Huang and Tang (1991) to be problematic for accounts like Battistella's, which link these effects to Subject–INFL agreement. Cole and Sung (1991a) argue, however, that these NPs are subjects at LF.

38 Cole, Hermon, and Sung (1990), the most accessible of these works, claims that INFL-to-INFL raising of anaphors is available in Chinese and typologically similar languages but not in English, for example, because Chinese INFL, unlike English INFL, is lexical (as suggested in Huang (1982)). It is thus able to debarrierize the matrix VP by L-marking, allowing the anaphor to move from the lower INFL to C^0, and from there to the matrix I^0, across the matrix VP. This claim is given up in later work, however. Cole and Sung (1991b) claims, among other things, that in languages with INFL-to-INFL movement of anaphors, blocking effects arise just in case INFL has no intrinsic agreement features, and therefore acquires its person features from the (trace of) the reflexive. In languages where INFL does have intrinsic person features, these take precedence, and the features of the trace of the anaphor do not enter into subject–INFL agreement. Thus, while Chinese *ziji* exhibits these effects, Italian *proprio* does not.

39 As pointed out in note 3, the other reading, in which *Bill* is the antecedent, would at one time have been handled by allowing binding to be satisfied after LF reconstruction of the bracketed phrase into the position of its trace. Barss (1986) dispenses with reconstruction in favor of an account making crucial use of the notion of chains.

40 The "NIC" case in (15c) is ruled out for her, as for Chomsky, by the ECP.

41 But see Everaert (1980) for a different characterization of *zich.*

42 However, the converse is not true. Japanese *zibun* is claimed to instantiate the feature combination [–L, +B]. It therefore must be bound, but is not necessarily licensed within a local domain. Enç's analysis therefore offers yet another approach to long-distance anaphora.

43 Burzio supports this by noting that in many languages reflexives are invariant in form. The locality requirement on anaphors is held to result not from a Binding Principle, but from the fact that they need to acquire their features through local agreement with an antecedent. Locality conditions therefore belong to the theory of agreement, rather than anaphora, and a total elimination of Binding Theory is envisioned.

44 This would seem to predict that pronouns are possible only when reflexives are not, and that there is therefore no overlap in their distribution. As we have seen, this is not correct in languages such as Chinese, in which there is long-distance binding of reflexives, but in which pronouns observe a local domain. Burzio accounts for such cases by claiming that the markedness of choosing the pronoun here in violation of ME is offset by the markedness of non-local binding of the reflexive.

45 However, cf. Chomsky and Lasnik (1991) for arguments that a characterization of the distribution of PRO in terms of Case is insufficient.

46 The *pro*-drop property appears to correlate with other features of grammars. As noted by Perlmutter (1971), languages with *pro*-drop seem, in general, to lack the complementizer-trace effect. See Safir (1985b) for discussion.

47 For a discussion of other differences between PRO and the *pro*-drop subject, see Jaeggli and Safir (1989).

48 Even apart from the restrictions imposed on the null pronoun by the Licensing and Identification theories to be discussed below, however, null and overt pronominals do not have the same distribution. For a discussion of one of the major differences, see Montalbetti (1984).

49 In fact, the typology of *pro*-drop is even richer than this. Icelandic and Yiddish agree with German in allowing expletive *pro*-drop and disallowing referential *pro*-drop. However, unlike German, they also allow dropping of "meteorological *it*." For discussion, see Rizzi (1986a).

50 There is also a problem with mainland Scandinavian which, as Jaeggli and Safir note, is morphologically uniform if imperative is left aside, yet does not allow even expletive *pros*.

51 It is not clear what prospects a solution along these lines might have under the assumption of recent, widely accepted proposals that Agreement and Tense are projected as separate heads universally.

52 Note that, as was the case with Manzini's proposal, the embedded CP, rather than the embedded IP, must be taken to be the category referred to in (b(ii)).

53 Only the locality provisions of Principle A are without independent consequences for NP traces. The requirement that they be bound still insures that NP movement is always to positions which c-command the original positions, as Chomsky (1986b) notes, and not, e.g., "sideways." Giving up the idea that traces fall under Principle A would entail stipulating this property separately. Note, however, that c-command conditions are already observed in other presumably independent subtheories, such as the theory of control.

5

The Empty Category Principle

Norbert Hornstein and Amy Weinberg
University of Maryland at College Park

Contents

Prelude

This chapter discusses an element of the theory which has taken a more and more central place over time, conditions on the occurrence of empty categories. The chapter starts off with a discussion of the binding theoretic connections of the Empty Category Principle (ECP) and in that connection presents the core data analyzed in terms of the principle. Following that we encounter various versions of the ECP, including an approach in terms of connected paths that was very influential in the mid-1980s, and the gamma marking and barriers conceptions of the ECP which have had the strongest influence on the most recent versions of the theory. In that connection approaches to the positioning of X^0 items, in particular, verbs are presented.

The chapter goes on to review so-called *conjunctive* versions of the ECP which aim to eliminate the classical disjunctive formulation of the principle. One of these conjunctive approaches states a lexical government condition on empty categories at the level of Phonological Form and combines it with a generalized binding theory that applies to empty categories in the LF component. An influential second approach of this kind, "Relativized Minimality," is presented in detail as well and compared with the other approaches.

1 Introduction: Binding Theory and the ECP

In the early 1970s, Chomsky and others argued that empty categories (i.e. traces) should be included in the inventory of category types found in natural language. This meant that a variety of constructions formerly treated as involving one position came to be seen as relations involving antecedents and empty categories (ec). In particular, it was argued that both *wh-* and NP-traces should be treated as anaphors. This claim had the major advantage of allowing the binding principles independently needed to govern the distribution of overt antecedent/anaphor pairs to govern the distribution of covert categories as well. In this way, the addition of traces provided for theoretical simplification.

To see the appeal of this idea, consider the following paradigms:

(1) *The men_i believed that $themselves_i$ were smart
The men_i believed $themselves_i$ to be smart
*The men_i were believed e_i were smart
The men_i were believed e_i to be smart
(2) *The $girl_i$ expected John to like $herself_i$
The $girl_i$ expected $herself_i$ to like John
*The $girl_i$ was expected John to like e_i
The $girl_i$ was expected e_i to like John

In the first case, we see that neither reflexives nor the trace of NP-movement can appear in the domain of the nominative case assigner (the agreement marker in the embedded clause) and in the second set, we see that neither an anaphor, nor the trace of NP movement can appear if there is a subject intervening whose reference is distinct from the anaphor's antecedent. Thus, traces of passive are also subject to Principle A of Chomsky's Binding Theory.[1] This theory leaves a residue of cases even with respect to NP movement as can be seen in (3).

(3a) It was illegal for the men to compete
(3b) *The men_i were illegal $[_{S'}$ $[_S$ e_i to compete]]
(3c) The women were told $[_{S'}$ how $[_S$ PRO to kiss the men]]
(3d) *The $women_i$ were known $[_{S'}$ how $[_S$ e_i to kiss the men]]

The trace in the ungrammatical examples in (3) is neither in the domain of agreement and is coreferential to the first SUBJECT and so is licensed by Principle A of the Binding Theory. The trace violates no other principles (it is licensed by the projection principle, it receives a theta-role, and it does not need Case). An independent principle is needed.

Wh-traces also seem to be recalcitrant in the sense that they can appear in places where NP-traces and lexical anaphors cannot, as shown in (4). It was claimed that this non-conformity was only apparent and that a category could land in the complementizer position and thus be bound in the domain specified by Principle A as formulated in (5)

(4) Who_i do the men believe e_i is smart
Who_i do the men believe the women to like e_i
(5) An anaphor must be bound in the smallest NP or S′ in which it is governed and there is a SUBJECT (NP or AGR).

Further inspection suggested however that *wh*-traces were in fact recalcitrant. The first piece of evidence came from cases of long movement from object position over a specified subject. In these cases, the intermediate COMP cannot serve as an escape hatch, as it houses another *wh* element and thus the structure violates even the reformulated Principle A.

(6) C'est à [mon cousin$_j$ [que$_j$ [je$_k$ sais [lequel$_i$ PRO$_k$ offrir e$_i$ e$_j$]]]]
"It is to my cousin that I know what to offer"

A final blow to the binding-theoretic account of the distribution of *wh*-traces came from Freidin and Lasnik's (1981) demonstration that *wh*-traces pattern like names rather than like anaphors with respect to strong crossover effects.

(7a) *He$_i$ thinks Mary likes Fred$_i$
(7b) Fred$_i$ thinks Mary likes him$_i$
(7c) *[Who$_i$ does [he$_i$ think [e$_i$ [Mary likes e$_i$]]]]
(7d) [Who$_i$ [e$_i$ thinks [Mary likes him$_i$]]]

If the traces in (7) are treated like names, and thereby subject to Principle C of the Binding Theory, we explain why they cannot refer to the pronouns in (7). The lack of coindexation is simply a subcase of the prohibition against a name being bound to anything in an A-position. From the data presented so far, one might conclude that *wh*-traces would simply be exempt from locality restrictions. However, empty categories are unlike names in the sense that they must be in the local domain of their antecedents where "local domain" now cannot be cashed out with respect to locality principles imposed by the binding theory or by subjacency. Cases like (8), instances of the Fixed Subject Constraint (Bresnan (1972) and Perlmutter (1971)), illustrate this point.

(8a) *Who$_i$ do you think [$_{S'}$ [COMP e$_i$ that] [$_S$ e$_i$ left the present on the table]]
(8b) What$_i$ do you think [$_{S'}$ [COMP e$_i$ that] [$_S$ Mary left e$_i$ on the table]]
(8c) *C'est mon cousin que$_i$ je sais [lequel$_j$ [e$_i$ a offert e$_j$ à Jean]]
"It is my cousin that I know what offered to John"
(8d) C'est le cadeau$_i$ que$_i$ je sais [quand [mon cousin a offert e$_i$ à Jean]]
"It is the present that I know when my cousin offered to John"
(8e) ?What$_i$ do you recall [$_{S'}$ whether [$_S$ Bill bought e$_i$]]
(8f) *Who$_i$ do you recall [$_{S'}$ whether [$_S$ e$_i$ bought a book]]

The contrast between (8c) and (8d) and (8e) and (8f) cannot be subsumed under subjacency. The grammaticality of (8d) shows that S′ is a bounding node in French as argued in Sportiche (1981). The same number of nodes separate the ec from its antecedent in both (8c) and (8d). The effect of the ECP can even be seen in the English example (8f) despite the interference of the subjacency condition. (8f) is considerably less acceptable than (8e). The additional unacceptability displayed by (8f) is attributable to the ECP.

(8a) is an instance of the *that-t* effect. The subject cannot be separated from its immediate antecedent by an overt complementizer. However, this is possible for an object trace.[2] Assuming that *wh*-traces are only subject to Principle C leaves us with no account of this fact. We also have the facts in (3) to account for.

2 The ECP and Some More Core Data

Chomsky (1981) proposed to reconcile these facts with the theory while maintaining that the distribution of empty categories should be subsumed under notions of locality that are independently needed. He proposed the *Empty Category Principle* (ECP), which postulated that empty categories need to satisfy an identification condition over and above the ones imposed on overt categories by the binding theory. As such, empty categories were singled out by the grammar and their distribution was not entirely handled by principles independently needed for lexical categories. However, the domain for identification was determined by the government relation in the core cases and so even though an independent principle was needed, the *government domain* was crucial for determining the distribution of empty and lexical categories alike. A working definition of the ECP is given in (9)

(9) An empty category must be:
(9a) Lexically/head governed: governed by a lexical X^0; or,
(9b) Antecedent governed: bound by (coindexed with and c-commanded by) a category that governs it.

If an ec meets (9) we say it is properly governed.

We will assume the Aoun and Sportiche (1981) definition of government given in (10):

(10) A governs B iff for all X, X a maximal projection, X dominates A iff X dominates B

Let us see how the ECP works by considering the recalcitrant Fixed Subject Condition cases that we discussed above. In general, subject/object asymmetries are handled by claiming that a complement can be head-governed as it is in the government domain of a verb. A subject can only be licensed by antecedent government, because it is separated from the potential verbal head-governor by the VP maximal projection. If the antecedent is too far away or in a non-governing position with respect to the ec, the sentence is ruled out.

In (8b), the object trace is head governed by the verb, and therefore the ECP places no restriction on the relationship between the ec and the intermediate trace in COMP. By contrast, the subject in (8a) is not lexically governed by the verb and so it must be antecedent-governed. However, neither the trace in COMP, nor the matrix *who* are possible antecedent governors; the former does not c-command the subject position and the latter does not govern it.

(8d) is like (8b) in that the trace of the moved object is lexically governed by the verb. In (8c) however, the subject trace is not properly governed. The *wh*-element in the governing COMP is not coindexed with it and the category with which it is coindexed is separated from it by too many maximal projections to govern it.[3]

In addition to Fixed Subject Effects, subsequent work showed that this version of the ECP provided insight into a host of other phenomena to which we now turn. This body of data, coupled with the data just reviewed, constitute the core cases that subsequent revisions of the theory have been tested against.

Huang (1982) observed that adjuncts pattern like subjects with regard to long extraction out of *wh*-islands. Adjunct traces left by *how* and *why* result in severe violations when pulled out of islands.

(11a) [Which problem_i did [you wonder [how_j [PRO to [$_{VP}$ solve e_i] e_j]]]]

(11b) *[How_j did [you wonder [which problem_i [PRO to [$_{VP}$ solve e_i] e_j]]]]

Note, the *how* in (11b) must be read as coming from the main clause, not the embedded one. Huang assumed that the object appeared within the VP with the adjunct outside. Thus, the object trace is head-governed by the verb in (11a) and the ECP imposes no locality restrictions on the relation between the trace and its antecedent. The adjunct, by contrast needs to be antecedent-governed, but the immediately adjacent complementizer does not contain a coindexed category.

Kayne (1981) made the important observation that both the subject/object asymmetries and the adjunct/complement asymmetries are found in cases of LF movement. He observes that in French *ne–personne* examples we can detect such an asymmetry.[4]

(12a) Je n'ai exigé qu'ils arrêtent personne
(12b) *Je n'ai exigé que personne soit arrêté
(12c) For no x_i [I demanded [that they arrest e_i]
(12d) For no x_i [I demanded [that e_i be arrested]

Kayne argues that *personne* raises to the clause where *ne* indicates scope. In (12c) the resulting trace position is properly governed by the verb *arrest*. In (12d), the subject is not head-governed and the antecedent is separated from its trace by the intervening S′, and so antecedent government also fails.

Similar remarks apply to the analysis of multiple questions. In English, multiple questions are interpreted as absorbed structures with all of the interrogation markers moved to a position that has independently been specified as +*wh* through movement of a question word at S-Structure. We further assume that the S-Structure-moved trace is the only one that c-commands the rest of the clause.[5] Thus, LF moved categories will not c-command their traces and cannot therefore serve as antecedent governors. This implies that multiple questions involving LF-movement of a subject or an adjunct should result in ungrammaticality, while movement from the object position should be fine.[6]

(13a) Who believes that John dropped what
(13b) *Who believes that what fell
(13c) *Who believes that John dropped the ball why

Aoun, Hornstein, and Sportiche (1981) and Kayne (1983b) suggested that the "superiority effects" noted in Chomsky (1973) could also be subsumed under the ECP. In (14a) the subject moves in the syntax as indicated in the structure and c-commands its trace, antecedent-governing it. The object trace is head governed and the structure is licit. In (14b), the object moves in syntax and so subsequent LF-movement of the subject lands in a non-c-commanding position. The subject is thus neither head- nor antecedent-governed, and the structure is out. Adjuncts work in the same way. If the adjunct can move to a c-commanding position by S-Structure, it can license its trace by antecedent-government. LF-movement of the object is allowed, as shown in (14f) because its trace is head-governed. In (14e), the adjunct moves to a non-c-commanding position, and so its trace is not licensed by antecedent- or head-government. If adjunct and subject movement apply in the same structure, ungrammaticality will always result, as shown in (14c) and (14d). Since neither the subject nor adjunct position can be head-governed, both vie for antecedent-government, but only one ec can be c-commanded and antecedent-governed.

(14a) I don't recall $[_{S'}$ who$_i$ $[_S$ t_i bought what]]
(14b) *I don't recall $[_{S'}$ what$_i$ $[_S$ who bought t_i]]
(14c) *I don't recall $[_{S'}$ who$_i$ $[_S$ t_i left why]]
(14d) *I don't recall $[_{S'}$ why$_i$ $[_S$ who $[_{VP}$ left] t_i]]
(14e) *I don't recall $[_{S'}$ what$_i$ $[_S$ Bill $[_{VP}$ sang t_i] why]]
(14f) I don't recall $[_{S'}$ why$_i$ $[_S$ Bill $[_{VP}$ sang what] t_i]][7]

Further ECP LF effects can be seen in languages like French that allow *wh*-in-situ constructions. Consider the examples in (15).[8]

(15a) Jean a dit que Pierre a vu qui
"Jean said that Pierre saw who"
(15b) *Jean a dit que qui est venu
"Jean said that who came"

(15a) is interpreted with *qui* receiving wide scope. On the assumption that this requires the *wh*-operator to move to the matrix COMP at LF then the unacceptability of (15b) once again suggests that the ECP operates after such movement takes place. However, if these data are to fall under the ECP, we must explain why it is that movement through the embedded COMP does not result in a licit structure.[9]

(16) qui$_i$ [Jean a dit [t_i que [t_i est venu]]]

The inability of the trace left by LF-movement to properly govern the subject trace is still more puzzling when one observes that such traces can properly govern in languages like Chinese, as Huang (1982) argued. Thus adjunct traces can be licensed by an intermediate trace in COMP.

(17) Chinese: (Huang)
Ni xiang-zhidao [Lisi weisheme mai-le sheme]
you wonder Lisi why buy what
(17a) Sheme$_i$ [Ni xiang-zhidao [weisheme$_j$ [Lisi t_j mai-le t_i]]]
(17b) *weisheme$_j$ [Ni xiang-zhidao [sheme$_i$ [Lisi t_j mai-le t_i]]]
(17c) [ni renwei [ta weisheme$_i$ meiyou lai
you think he why not come
"Why do you think that he didn't come?"

The difference between (17a) and (17b) can be traced to the fact that in the former case the trace of *what* is properly governed by *buy*, while the trace of *why* must be antecedent-governed. This is possible if there is no further *wh* in COMP, as in (17c), but it is blocked if there is a *wh*-element there.

Problems such as these motivated various COMP indexing procedures to bring these cases under the ECP.[10] It was proposed that it is not the *wh*-element itself that is the antecedent governor but the COMP that it moves into. The latter comes to have the power to antecedent-govern by picking up the index from the *wh*-element it contains as a result of feature percolation. Languages differ in where this index percolation takes place. In Chinese, it takes place at LF and it is the first *wh* in COMP that percolates its features. In English and French, percolation takes place at S-Structure. The relevant LF representations of (17a, b) and (15b) are given in (18):

(18a) $[_{S'}$ $[_{Ci}$ Sheme$_i$] $[_S$ Ni xiang-zhidao $[_{S'}$ $[_{Cj}$ weisheme$_j$] [Lisi t_j mai-le t_i]]]

(18b) $[_{S'}$ $[_{Cj}$ weisheme$_j$] $[_S$ Ni xiang-zhidao $[_{S'}$ $[_{Ci}$ sheme$_i$] [Lisi t_j mai-le t_i]]]

(18c) Qui$_i$ $[_S$ Jean a dit $[_{S'}$ $[_{Cj}$ t_i que$_j$] $[_S$ t_i est venu]]]]

In (18b, c) the COMP is not coindexed with the relevant trace so the structures are ill-formed. With COMP indexing, then, these contrasts can be brought under the purview of the ECP.[11]

Other LF contrasts have been traced to the effects of the ECP. For example, it has been proposed that the ECP restricts Quantifier Raising in examples such as (19).[12]

(19a) Someone expects everyone to dance
(19b) Someone expects everyone will dance

In (19a), it is marginally possible to get the interpretation in which the universally quantified NP *everyone* has scope over the existential *someone*. This seems completely impossible in (19b). This contrast can be laid at the door of the ECP given structures such as (20).

(20a) Everyone$_i$ [someone$_j$ [t_j expects [t_i to dance]]]
(20b) Everyone$_i$ [someone$_j$ [t_j expects [t_i will dance]]]

The trace t_i in (20a) is properly governed by the higher verb *expects* which exceptionally Case-marks it. In (20b), there is no exceptional Case marking and thus the trace t_i fails to be properly governed by the higher verb or by its antecedent *everyone,* on the assumption that its A′-antecedent is simply too far away.

Similar reasoning has recently extended the ECP to cover the lack of reflexives and reciprocals in the subject position of finite clauses, though they are permitted in ECM constructions.[13]

(21a) *The men$_i$ expect that themselves$_i$/each other$_i$ will like jazz
(21b) The men$_i$ expect each other$_i$/themselves$_i$ to like jazz

If we assume that reflexives and reciprocals move at LF and adjoin close to their antecedent, then the trace left by such movement will be subject to the ECP. For example, in (22b) the ECM verb *expect* properly governs t_i. In (22a) t_i has neither a lexical governor nor an antecedent governor. The ECP, thereby, accounts for the contrast in (21).

(22a) The men$_i$ [themselves$_i$ [expect [that [t$_i$ will like jazz]]]]
(22b) The men$_i$ [themselves$_i$ [expect [t$_i$ to like jazz]]]

2.1 *Condition on Extraction Domain (CED) Effects*[14]

Syntactic movement of complements out of adjuncts is unacceptable. Huang (1982) accounted for this in terms of the Condition on Extraction Domains (CED).

(23) CED: no constituent may be extracted out of a domain which is not properly governed.

(23) accounts for the unacceptability of (24) if we assume that the *after* clause is not properly governed by *drink.*

(24) *What did John drink cognac after singing t

It is clear that the CED and the ECP are very close to one another conceptually. However, it is not that clear how or whether to reduce the former to the latter. One relevant issue is whether the CED applies to LF-movement.[15]

(25a) Who drank his cognac after singing what
(25b) Who likes people who live where
(25c) Who thinks that pictures of whom are on sale

The sentences in (25) involve apparent LF-movement out of adjuncts, i.e. non-properly governed domains. This seems to indicate that the

CED does not apply to LF operations. If so, it becomes an open question whether to reduce the CED to the ECP given the latter's application to LF operations. Nonetheless, it still remains curious that both the ECP and the CED should invoke proper government.

As expected, LF extraction of a complement out of an adjunct is acceptable in languages where *wh*-movement does not take place in the syntax. In Japanese, for example, (26) is grammatical.[16]

(26) [Dare-ni atte kara] uti-ni kaetta no?
Who-to meet after house to went back Q
"*Who did you go home after meeting"

It is worth observing that similar facts hold for other adjuncts. Thus syntactic extraction out of a PP in S-Structure adjunct position is prohibited.[17]

(27a) How many boys did she smile at t
(27b) *How many reasons did she smile for

In addition, it is unacceptable to syntactically extract across non-bridge verbs in English.

(28) *What did John guffaw/sigh that Frank kissed t

In most of these cases, LF-movement seems acceptable.[18]

(29a) Who smiled for what reason
(29b) Who guffawed/sighed that Frank saw what

Thus, it appears that the CED correctly rules out the syntactic movement of arguments out of adjuncts but seems to incorrectly prohibit the LF-movement of these elements.

The status of LF-movement of adjuncts out of adjuncts is somewhat less clear. It appears that the movement of some adjuncts at LF is acceptable in Chinese.

(30) [Ni zeme dui ta jiang nasye hua hou] ta cai likai ne
"What manner is such that after you said those words to him in that manner, he left"

However, movement of *naze* "why" out of a *because* phrase in Japanese is very poor.[19]

(31) *?Kimi-wa Mary-ga naze sore-o katta node sonnani okotteru no?
"Why are you so angry [because Mary bought it t]"

That LF extraction of arguments out of adjuncts is better than the LF extraction of adjuncts is plausibly related to the ECP. It is reasonable to suppose that the complement is lexically governed within the adjunct and so extraction is permitted. The adjunct, however, must be antecedent-governed and it is reasonable to assume that the antecedent is too remote to accomplish this. However, it is very unclear why it is that (30) is acceptable while (31) is not. It seems that the unacceptability is a function of the particular adjunct involved.[20]

We return to CED effects in later sections of this review. How to reduce them to the ECP was a motivating factor in subsequent revisions of the Empty Category Principle.

As demonstrated above, the 1981 version of the ECP has considerable empirical support. Nevertheless, the disjunctive character of this definition was theoretically disturbing in the sense that two seemingly unrelated restrictions (head- and antecedent government) were arbitrarily tied together in one definition with no theoretical understanding of why these two principles should be linked. Therefore there was a major push to eliminate this disjunction which took basically two tacks. The first approach exemplified by Kayne (1981), Pesetsky (1982b), Longobardi (1985), Aoun (1981), and Chomsky (1986a) tried to assimilate all cases of the ECP to a version of one of the disjuncts (antecedent government) in the earlier definition. A second approach retains both disjuncts of the ECP but applies them conjunctively, in either the same or different components of the grammar. Thus both disjuncts play a role but the arbitrary linkage into a single condition is removed as each disjunct applies as a separate condition. Advocates of this approach include Stowell (1985), Jaeggli (1982, 1985), Aoun, Hornstein, Lightfoot, and Weinberg (1987), Contreras (1986), Torrego (1985), Chomsky (1986a), Koopman and Sportiche (1986), and Chung and McCloskey (1987). We will discuss both approaches below.

3 Connected Paths

Kayne (1981) proposes a radically different version of the ECP which does not limit it to the distribution of empty categories per se and eliminates the disjunction mentioned above. We will refer to this sort of theory as a "connectedness theory." The basic idea is that linguistically significant relations must be mediated by a path of nodes that link the related elements. The substantive core of the theory consists of the principles for the construction of these paths. ECP effects are analyzed as instances in which these path conditions are violated. The core intuition behind these principles is that licit linguistic relations constitute a restricted set of possible sub-trees that a grammar generates. Linguistic relata must both be members of a common well-formed sub-tree.[21]

(32) *ECP*: An empty category B must have a c-commanding binder A such that there exists a lexical category X such that X governs B and A is contained in some g-projection of X.

(33) *g-projection*
Y is a g-projection of X iff
(a) Y is a projection of X (in the usual sense of X′ theory) or a g-projection of X
or
(b) X is a structural governor and Y immediately dominates W and Z, where Z is a maximal projection of a g-projection of X, and W and Z are in a canonical government configuration.

(34) *Canonical Government Configuration (CGC)*
W and Z are in a CGC iff
(a) V governs NP to its right in the grammar of the language in question and W precedes Z, or
(b) V governs NP to its left in the grammar of the language in question and Z precedes W.

The set of acceptable paths or sub-trees are defined in terms of the notion of "g-projection." Antecedents and their dependents must be members of a common sub-tree that are g-projections of the dependent element. We note that crucial use is made of the notion of lexical government in the guise of the notion "structural governor" in (33). For the dependent element to have a g-projection at all it must be lexically governed.[22] Also note that outside the first g-projection, the one determined by X′ principles and structural government, further g-projections are licensed by being in a CGC with a head rather than being structurally governed by that head. This has the effect that elements that are not structural governors can extend a g-projection once started, though they cannot start one. This distinction is empirically significant. Kayne (1983b) motivates it by observing the following contrast in French.

(35a) *ce qu'elle tient à
that she holds to
"What she is keen on"

(35b) ce qu'elle tient à faire
that she holds to do
"What she is keen to do"

(36a) ce_i [$_{CP}$ t_i que [$_{IP}$ elle I [$_{VP}$ tient [$_{PP}$ à t_i]]]]

(36b) ce_i [$_{CP}$ t_i que [$_{IP2}$ elle I_2 [$_{VP}$ tient [$_{PP}$ à [$_{IP1}$ PRO I_1 [$_{VP}$ faire t_i]]]]]

In (36a) the trace and its antecedent are not in a common g-projection, for in French prepositions are not structural governors. This prohibits the initial PP containing the trace from being a g-projection for it. Thus, the recursive definition of g-projections stops applying at this first phrase. In (36b) t_i has a structural governor, *faire*, and so the VP is a g-projection. In French, canonical government is to the right. Hence, the VP is in a CGC with I so IP1 is a g-projection. Similarly, *à* canonically governs IP1, *tient* PP, I2 VP, and *que* IP2. Therefore, we can construct a g-projection relating the trace inside the VP to its antecedent in CP. Observe that if the CGC requirement were replaced by the requirement that W structurally govern Z, then the g-projection would halt at IP1 since prepositions are not structural governors in French.

With a few ancillary assumptions, essentially the same story extends to account for the *that-t* effects in English.

(37a) [$_{CP}$ Who_i [$_{IP}$ you I [$_{VP}$ think [$_{CP}$ t_i that [$_{IP}$ t'_i I left]]]]]

(37b) [$_{CP2}$ Who_i [$_{IP2}$ you I [$_{VP}$ think [$_{CP1}$ t_i e_i [$_{IP}$ t'_i I left]]]]]

Assume that IP does not block lexical government, that only coindexed C^0s are structural governors for elements they are coindexed with and, following Pesetsky (1982b), that in English, a trace in CP cannot transfer its index to the head if the head is lexical. What this does is prevent t'_i in (37a) from having a g-projection for it has no lexical governor. Consequently, (37a) violates the ECP. (37b), in contrast, is in full conformity. The g-projections of t'_i are CP1, VP IP2 and CP2 and this includes its antecedent *who*$_i$.[23]

The reason we observe no *that-t* effects with objects can once again be traced to the distinction between structural government and the CGC.

(38) [$_{CP2}$ Who_i e_i [$_{IP2}$ you I2 [$_{VP2}$ think [$_{CP1}$ t_i that [$_{IP1}$ John I1 [$_{VP1}$ kissed t_i]]]]]]

In (38), the initial g-projection for t_i is VP1 where it is structurally governed by *kissed*. Thereafter CGC takes over: the following are in a CGC: I1 and VP1, *that* and IP1, *think* and CP1, I2 and VP2, and e_i and IP2. CP2 is a g-projection as well as it is the maximal projection of e_i.

The same logic will apply to handle LF subject/object asymmetries.

(39a) Who believes that Bill bought what
(39b) [$_{CP}$ Who$_i$ what$_j$ [$_{IP}$ t$_i$ I [$_{VP}$ believes [$_{CP}$ t$_j$ that [$_{IP}$ Bill I [$_{VP}$ bought t$_j$]]]]]]
(40a) *Who believes that what fell
(40b) [$_{CP}$ Who$_i$ what$_j$ [$_{IP}$ t$_i$ I [$_{VP}$ believes [$_{CP}$ t$_j$ that [$_{IP}$ t$_j$ I [$_{VP}$ fell]]]]]]

In (39b), t_j is structurally governed by *bought*, initiating the trace's g-projection, and canonical government extends the g-projections to the matrix CP, where the antecedent has moved at LF, in the usual way. In (40a), on the other hand, t_j is not structurally governed at LF, given the lack of indexing transfer to *that*. As noted in section 2, however, deleting the *that* does not appreciably improve (40a). To accommodate this, we need only assume, as we did above, that index transfer must take place at S-Structure in languages like English where selection is at S-Structure. Given this assumption, t_j has no lexical governor at LF either and so no g-projections.

(32) also covers cases of NP-movement given certain natural assumptions.

(41a) [$_{CP}$ [$_{IP}$ John$_i$ [I was] [$_{VP}$ hit t$_i$]]]
(41b) [$_{CP}$ [$_{IP}$ John$_i$ [I was] [$_{VP}$ believed [$_{IP}$ t$_i$ to be a fool]]]
(41c) *[$_{CP}$ [$_{IP}$ John$_i$ [I was] [$_{VP}$ believed [$_{CP}$ [$_{IP}$ t$_i$ was a fool]]]]

The trace in (41a) has a g-projection extending to IP. So too does the trace in (41b) if we assume some version of S′-deletion in these cases. The structural governor in this case is the higher verb *believe*. If S′-deletion is prohibited in (41c) then ECP is violated as t_i does not have a structural governor and so no g-projection relating it to *John*, its antecedent.

A problem, however, arises in cases of super-raising.

(42a) John$_i$ is certain [$_{IP}$ t$_i$ to like ice cream]
(42b) *John$_i$ seems that it is certain [$_{IP}$ t$_i$ to like ice cream]

Certain allows raising as (42a) indicates. As such, there must be g-projections linking the trace to *John*. This presupposes that *certain* is the structural governor for t_i. However, once t_i has a structural governor, then g-projections will link it to *John* in the standard way in (42b). Thus (42b) cannot be ruled out in terms of the ECP given the definitions above.[24]

This analysis has problems handling CED effects. As noted in section 2, adjuncts are islands for overt extraction of complements though LF-movement seems fine. However, given this theory, all extraction of complements out of adjuncts should be fine, at least if the structure is right-branching. The relevant structures are those in (43).

(43) WH_i [. . . [$_{VP}$ V . . .] [adjunct . . . t_i]]

If t_i is structurally governed, then a g-projection is initiated. Furthermore, the g-projection is extended, given that the adjunct is in a CGC with V or I.[25] In contrast, the LF extractability of complements from adjuncts is fully in tune with this analysis.

Longobardi (1985) proposes a modification of (33) that permits the theory to cover the overt CED effects.[26]

(44) A non-properly governed maximal projection is a boundary to the extension of g-projections.

On the reasonable assumption that adjuncts are not properly governed, we can account for the unacceptability of examples such as (45):

(45) *$What_i$ did John drink cognac [$_{PP}$ after singing t_i]

Given (44), there is no g-projection connecting *what* and t_i. The *after* clause, being an adjunct, is not properly governed and so the g-projections that the trace generates stop at the PP boundary.[27]

However, this emendation, though it extends to cover overt extraction from adjuncts, is not cost-free. First, it implies that all LF-movement out of adjuncts, even of complements, should also violate the ECP. However, as noted above this is not obviously correct.

(46a) Who drank his cognac after singing what
(46b) Who likes people who live where
(46c) Who thinks that pictures of what are on sale
(46d) [Dare-ni atte kara] uti-ni kaetta no?
Who-to meet after house went back (Japanese)
"*Who did you go home after meeting t"
(46e) Kimi-wa [$_{NP}$ [[$_{CP}$ dare-ga kai-ta] hon]-o yomi-masi-ta ka?
"Who is such that you read books that he wrote"

The sentences in (46) are quite acceptable, despite the fact that in each case we appear to be extracting a complement out of a non-properly governed constituent. Note that in (46c) *what* is LF-moved out of a left branch. Thus, its acceptability is a problem both for Kayne's (1983b) formulation of the ECP, as well as the one in Longobardi (1985).[28]

Second, in its essentials, Longobardi (1985) returns to Kayne's (1981) analysis. There g-projections were taken to be extendable under co-superscripting which in turn was licensed between lexical heads (excluding P) and what they governed. Kayne (1983b) modified this requirement for reasons given above (see (35)). It is unclear, however, how the problem that motivated Kayne (1983b) to revise the earlier 1981 formulation is to be accommodated if we return to this earlier conception.

The most serious problem, however, is how adjunct movement is to be permitted at all. To get CED effects to fall under the ECP it is assumed that adjuncts are not properly governed. However, if so, the trace of an adjunct cannot initiate a g-projection. Consequently, it can never be in a common g-projection with its antecedent. Thus, if we assume that *after* clauses and *when* occupy the same D-Structure position, then we cannot at once account for the acceptability of (47) and the unacceptability of (45).

(47) When_i did John say [that Bill left for NYC t_i]

If the position occupied by the trace is properly governed then there exists a g-projection extending from the trace to the *wh*-operator in the matrix Comp. However, this would imply that a temporal adjunct generated in the same position should **not** block g-projection extensions and so such adjuncts should be porous. If, conversely, we assume that such positions are not properly governed so that overt extraction is blocked, we imply that simple adjunct movement should also be prohibited, contrary to fact.

The problem is not merely that the connectedness approach to ECP effects is difficult to reconcile with CED effects. This, by itself, could be taken to imply that CED effects should not be reduced to the ECP. Rather, the problem is how non-arguments are to be allowed to sprout g-projections. Recall that a motivating factor for Chomsky's (1981) disjunctive version of the ECP was the asymmetry between arguments and adjuncts. The latter could not meet the head-government disjunct so they had to meet the ECP via antecedent government. However, in the formulation of the ECP above, a precondition for generating a g-projection is being structurally governed and this makes it awkward to accommodate elements that are not (properly) governed at all, i.e. adjuncts.

This might argue for adopting a version of connectedness in which g-projections are calculated without invoking the notion of structural or proper governor. This is what we would get if, for example, we took paths in the sense of Pesetsky (1982b) to define a g-projection.[29] This would solve the problem noted here. However, it disallows an ECP analysis of the data discussed in (35). Furthermore, such an approach would have little to say about CED effects or the prohibition against movement of adjuncts out of *wh*-islands.

(48) *Why$_j$ did John wonder [whether PRO to fix the car t$_j$]]

A theory in which g-projections/paths are calculated without invoking structural government should allow the construction of a path between *why* and its trace. Note that, given that the adjunct trace is on a right branch, it will be in a canonical government configuration with heads up the tree. On the Kayne (1981) or (1983b) accounts the prohibition against this sort of extraction is not problematic since adjuncts have no g-projections as they have no structural governors. In sum, it appears that neither invoking structural government nor dispensing with it yields fully adequate empirical results if ECP effects are to be cashed out in terms of g-projections.

To this point we have reviewed how it is that connectedness theories handle the standard ECP data. However, there are data from multiple-gap constructions that natural extensions of connectedness can account for which are problematic for the standard ECP.

There are three main instances of multiple gap constructions: parasitic gaps, multiple *wh* general questions and crossing structures. The first two were first discussed in Kayne (1983b) and the last was extensively investigated in Pesetsky (1982b).[30] The first two types of structures flesh out what constitutes a connected sub-tree when there is one antecedent for several ecs. The core idea is that the union of the g-projections of all of the ecs bound by the same antecedent must constitute a sub-tree. This is fleshed out in terms of the following definitions.

(49) *A g-projection set G_B of a category B where D governs B*
(49a) for all P, P = a projection of D $\rightarrow$ P is a member of G_B;
(49b) B is a member of G_B;
(49c) if K dominates B and K does not dominate D then K is a member of G_B.
(50) *The Generalized ECP*
Let $B_1 \ldots B_j, B_j + 1, \ldots B_n$ be a maximal set of empty categories in a tree T such that there is an A, such that for all j, B_j is locally bound by A. Then $\{A\}U(UG_{Bj})$, $1 \leq j \leq n$, must constitute a subtree of T.

The basic idea embodied in these definitions is that a given gap can be connected to its antecedent even if it cannot itself sprout a g-projection linking it to the antecedent just in case it connects to a g-projection of an ec with the same antecedent that does have a licit g-projection.

(50) has a very interesting consequence for multiple interrogation

constructions.[31] Recall that superiority effects can be brought under the ECP. This accounts for the contrast in (51):

(51a) I'd like to know who hid what in the closet
(51b) *I'd like to know what who hid in the closet

Within a connectedness account, (51b) is unacceptable because the *who* in situ does not have a g-projection extending from the subject position to COMP, the position it must be related to given the semantics of these constructions.

(52) $[_{CP}$ what$_i$ e$_i$ $[_{IP}$ who$_j$ INFL $[_{VP}$ hid t$_i$ in the closet$]]]$

Note that the subject *who* has no structural governor, given that the null complementizer is not coindexed with it. Thus, there is no g-projection connecting *who* to COMP. Assume, furthermore, that for (50) to form the union of the sets of g-projections, the sets of g-projections must be generated in a "parallel" fashion. What is meant by this is that sets of g-projections generated by syntactic ecs can combine with one another but not with g-projection sets generated by a non-empty category, e.g. the g-projection set generated by *who* in (52).[32]

Given these assumptions, we can use the ECP to account for the fact that superiority violations become ameliorated if another *wh*-in-situ is added. Compare (51b) and (53)

(53) ?I'd like to know what who hid where

In this case we get the g-projection sets going from the *wh*-in-situ expressions to the *wh* in Comp. These g-projection sets are generated in a "parallel" fashion so they can combine. By so combining the subject *who* meets the ECP in (53).

(54)

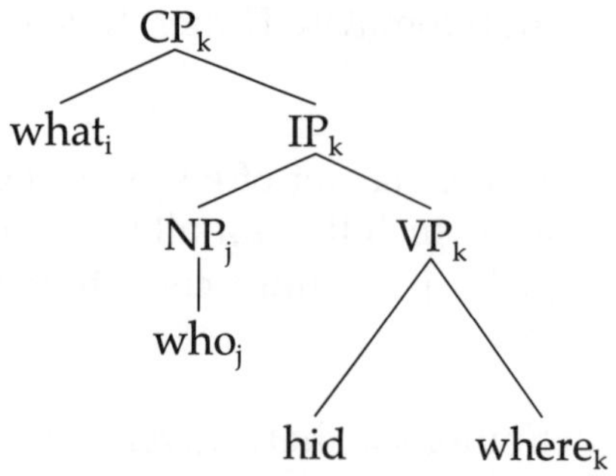

Importantly, if the set of g-projections do not form a sub-tree, improvement does not result.

(55) *I'd like to know where who said that what was hidden

In (55) *what* cannot help *who* meet (50) as the set of its g-projections do not form a sub-tree when combined with the set of the g-projections for *who*.[33]

(56)

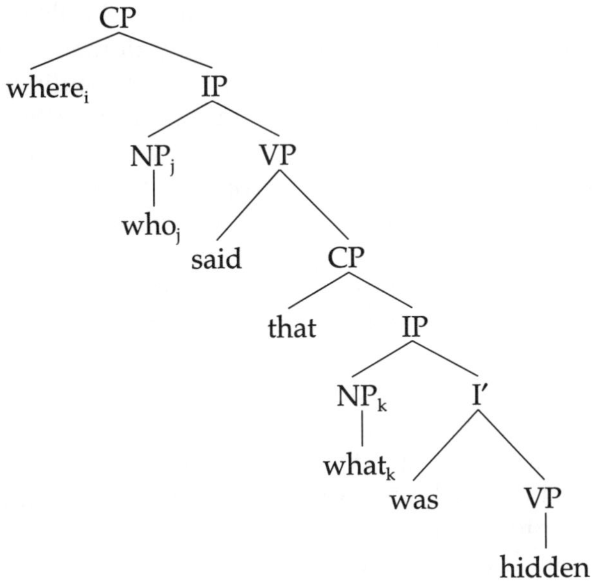

In this section we have examined the contours of an approach to the ECP that takes as its basic notion that antecedents and their dependents should both be parts of certain kinds of sub-trees. This way of looking at things takes the core cases of the ECP to be concerned with antecedent relations. Though head-government is not explicitly rejected as part of the ECP, it plays a relatively small role on its own. However, in the computation of g-projections lexical government in the guise of structural government plays a central role. It would be in the spirit of this approach to the ECP if cases that have been attributed purely to lexical government could be incorporated so that the disjunctive residue of the 1981 version of the ECP could be dispensed with.

4 Extensions to the Standard Definition

In this section, we review the work of Lasnik and Saito (1984) and Chomsky (1986a). These works are more closely linked to Chomsky's

(1981) formulation than were the connectedness approaches discussed above. These works have the common goal of showing that a unified ECP can be supplemented with a reasonable set of parameters to handle both cross-linguistic variation and S-Structure/LF asymmetries. Both approaches use many of the same mechanisms, but there is one important difference between them. Lasnik and Saito (1984) conclude that a structural notion of government of the sort relevant to the theories of Case and theta-marking does not establish a locality domain relevant to the ECP. Under their account, the ECP is a special condition that picks out its own domain of locality. Thus, the program of subsuming the distribution of empty categories under independently needed domains is compromised. Chomsky (1986a) proposes a revision of the notion of government in terms of a *barrier* that purports to establish a unique domain for government here and in other submodules. This approach also has the claimed empirical advantage of unifying the CED discussed above and the Head Movement Constraint of Travis (1984) under the ECP.

Lasnik and Saito (1984) (L&S) argue that cross-linguistic data force two changes in the definition of the ECP. First, they claim that a lexical category can only head govern a category to which it either assigns Case or a theta-role. This disallows lexical government into a complementizer position or into the subject of an exceptional Case marking or raising construction. Their argument involves properties of the adjunct *naze* "why" in Japanese. (57) shows that *naze* can move successive-cyclically at LF, yielding (57b). Movement must be COMP to COMP in order to satisfy antecedent government.

(57a) Bill-wa John-ga naze kubi-ni natta tte itta no?
Bill-top John-nom why was fired COMP said Q
"Why did Bill say John was fired?"

(57b) $[_{CP}$ Bill-wa $[_{CP}$ [John-ga t_i $[_{VP}$ kubi-ni natta] tte t_i] itta] $naze_i$ no $_{CP}]$

In (57b), the italicized trace in the intermediate CP antecedent governs the trace of *naze*. Given a standard definition of government however, this trace cannot be antecedent governed by the *wh* word because it is separated from it by the intervening embedded CP and matrix VP. One could claim that there is a kind of CP deletion or reduction to a non-maximal status in these cases. This would allow the trace in COMP to be head-governed. The alternative is to modify antecedent government so that it ignores VPs and CPs under certain conditions. L&S argue for the latter proposal as follows.

They follow Huang (1982) in claiming that subjacency does not apply at LF. Movement of a complement from a noun complement is grammatical since the trace left by the movement is lexically governed. Movement of *naze* from a similar construction is ungrammatical on the assumption that *naze* can only be antecedent-governed and that the italicized intervening NP and CP maximal projections block antecedent government of the adjunct trace.

(58a) Taroo-ga nani-o te-ni ireta koto-o sonnani okotteru no?
Taro-nom what-acc obtained fact so much be angry Q
"What are you so angry about the fact that Taro obtained (it)"

(58b) *Taroo-ga naze sore-o te-ni ireta koto-o sonnani okotteru no
Taro-nom why it-acc obtained fact so much be angry Q
"Why are you so angry about the fact that Taro obtained it (for some reason)"[34]

(59a) [[$_{NP}$ [$_{CP}$ Taroo-ga t_i te-ni ireta] t_i $_{CP}$] koto-o $_{NP}$] sonnani okotteru] no nani-o_i]

(59b) [[$_{CP}$ Taroo-ga t_i sore-o te-ni ireta] t_i $_{CP}$] koto-o $_{NP}$] sonnani okotteru] no $naze_i$ $_{CP}$]]

If we assume that a verb can lexically govern into the CP position however, we have no explanation for why (60) is bad because *naze* can move to the embedded CP position where it can antecedent-govern the most deeply embedded trace. The italicized trace can be lexically governed from this position and thus considerations of antecedent government become irrelevant.

(60) *Hanako-ga Taroo-ga naze sore-o te ni ireta tte itta? koto-o
Hanako-top Taro-nom why it obtained COMP said fact-acc
sonnani okotteru no
so much angry Q
"Why are you so angry about the fact that Hanako said that Taro obtained it (for some reason)?"

(61) [[$_{NP}$ [$_{CP}$ Hanako-go Taroo-ga t_i sore-o te ni ireta] t_i tte $_{CP}$] itta] koto-o $_{NP}$]sonnani okotteru] $naze_i$ no]]

This argues that lexical government into CP must be excluded and that NP (and CP) should constitute barriers to antecedent government. Recall that, in order to allow successive cyclic movement, VPs and CPs under certain conditions, must not block antecedent government. Thus, we see that the disjunctive nature of the ECP forces L&S to block lexical proper government in cases like (60). This, in turn, forces the introduction of a new notion of locality in the definition of the ECP. Cases like these provide partial motivation for a conjunctive interpretation of the

ECP, which we discuss in section 5 below. L&S propose (62) to handle these cases:

(62) A antecedent governs B if
(i) A and B are coindexed;
(ii) A c-commands B;
(iii) there is no X (X = NP or CP) such that A c-commands X and X dominates B unless B is the head of X.[35]

The lack of lexical government for traces in COMP also partially motivates L&S's decision to treat the ECP as an LF filter. The theory requires empty categories to have been marked with a feature indicating that they were properly governed *at some point in the derivation.* This idea is combined with the notion that categories that play no interpretive role at a particular level and do not have to be present to satisfy independently needed grammatical constraints can be freely deleted. This handles cases like (63).

(63a) Who do you believe that John said will be hired?
(63b) [$_{CP}$ Who$_i$ do [you believe [$_{CP}$ e$_i$ that [John said [$_{CP}$ e$_i$ [e$_i$ will be hired]]]]]?

In this structure, the *who* in the embedded subject position first moves to the embedded CP, insuring antecedent government of the subject trace. Lexical government into CP is not possible given (62). But, in order to handle cases like (64), L&S must assume that a *wh* or its trace cannot antecedent-govern when in a CP containing an overt complementizer. If so, the trace in the embedded CP position in (63b) is neither lexically nor antecedent-governed. This incorrectly predicts (63a) to be ungrammatical.

(64) *[Who$_i$ do you think [$_{CP}$ e$_i$ that [e$_i$ left]]]

To handle (63a), L&S assume a strict ordering whereby the trace in COMP in (63b) can assign the proper government feature to the trace in embedded subject position and can then delete before the derivation enters the LF component. L&S assume that because this trace does not contribute to the semantic interpretation of this structure it can delete. Since it deletes, it does not have to satisfy the ECP, which applies at LF. Therefore, the fact that it is not properly governed does not result in ungrammaticality. In (64), the trace in embedded subject position bears a theta-role, is relevant for interpretation, and therefore cannot be deleted. L&S assume that S-Structure argument traces must be marked for proper government at S-Structure. Thus in (64) the subject trace must be marked as not properly governed.[36]

L&S require, in addition to this intricately ordered sequence of rules and conditions, that the ordering apply differently for arguments than for adjuncts. Consider (65):

(65) *[Why$_i$ did [John accept [$_{NP}$ a proposal [$_{CP}$ *e$_i$* [PRO to change the plans e$_i$]]]]

In this structure, the offending italicized trace can be neither lexically nor antecedent-governed. However, it is also not relevant at the LF level for interpretation and so should be able to give the most deeply embedded trace the proper government feature and then delete, incorrectly predicting this to be a licit structure. In order to block this, L&S are forced to claim that adjuncts, unlike arguments, can only receive the proper government feature at LF, forcing the intermediate trace to remain at this level and triggering an ECP violation.[37]

Thus L&S's theory while empirically motivated has two rather unattractive features from a methodological point of view. As indicated even in this short sketch, it is ad hoc with respect to the level at which proper government features get assigned, and it introduces extrinsic ordering into derivations. Even more troubling is the introduction of yet another locality domain which regulates only the distribution of empty categories.

4.1 *Barriers*[38]

Chomsky (1986a) borrows the idea of derivational assignment of proper government features and free deletion throughout the derivation from Lasnik and Saito (1984). However, he rejects the idea that the ECP requires a separate domain for its application. Rather, he provides an ingenious redefinition of the notion of government in terms of *barriers*, which aims to provide the right locality domains for Case assignment, the ECP, and importantly for Subjacency as well. Thus movement and government theory are unified. Moreover, Chomsky (1986a) claims that this unification eliminates the need for a substantive theory of bounding nodes for movement. Barriers suffice to delimit bounding domains. This has important theoretical consequences that we will detail along the way.

Chomsky (1986a) proposes that all maximal projections are not created equal. Maximal projections which are lexically marked (or L-marked) as sisters to lexical items that assign them a theta-role do not create opaque domains for movement or government.[39] A maximal projection which contains some element X and which is not L-marked is a B(locking) C(ategory) for that category. Any category except for IP that is a BC for X also becomes a barrier for X. Barrierhood is also "inherited" by a maximal projection which immediately dominates a blocking category. The antecedent government clause of the ECP is then stated in terms of barriers, and a category cannot be separated from its antecedent by any barriers. Chomsky (1986a) vacillates between trying to reduce the entire ECP to this condition and using this condition in conjunction or disjunction with a condition of lexical government. In *Barriers* a category Y is *lexically governed* by a lexical X^0 that theta marks Y and which is a sister to Y. This is a variant of the Lasnik and Saito (1984) definition discussed above. As a first pass, we will assume a disjunctive definition of the ECP, but now with the disjuncts formulated in terms of barriers.[40]

The complement/adjunct distinction retains the flavor of previous accounts. Complement movement is governed by Subjacency at S-Structure and so movement is local. At LF, however, complements will always be lexically governed and so we expect non-local movement to be possible. This is shown in cases like (58) above.

Movement of an adjunct from a relative clause or noun complement is ungrammatical in Japanese as shown by (58b) and (61) above and by (66) below:

(66) *Taroo-ga sore-o naze watasita otoko-o sitte-iru no?
Taro -NOM it -acc why handed man know Q
"Why do you know the man to whom Taro handed it (for that reason)"

The LF representation of this structure is given in (67)

(67) [[$_{NP}$ [$_{S'}$Taroo-ga sore-o t_i watasita] t_{i} $_{CP}$] otoko-o $_{NP}$] sitte-iru] naze$_i$ no]?[41]

Chomsky (1986a) assumes that the relative clause is not L-marked by the relative head. This being the case, the italicized trace sitting in the embedded CP position is separated from its antecedent *naze* by two barriers; the non-L-marked CP and the relative clause NP that immediately dominates the CP and so becomes an additional barrier by inheritance. It is further assumed that this trace must remain visible at LF, as antecedent government cannot apply for adjuncts, until that level.[42]

The above assumptions are too restrictive, however, in that they will rule out even successive cyclic movement of adjuncts as in (68).

(68) $[_{CP}$ Bill-wa $[_{CP}$ [John-ga t_i $[_{VP}$ kubi-ni natta] tte t_i $_{CP}]$ itta $_{VP}]$ $_{IP}]$ naze$_i$ no $_{CP}]$
"Why did Bill say John was fired"

The italicized trace is separated from its antecedent by a CP, VP and IP. The CP is not a blocking category because it is a complement to the verb "itta" and is L-marked. The intervening VP is not L-marked, so it becomes a blocking category and the immediately dominating IP becomes a barrier by inheritance. Chomsky (1986a) develops a theory of adjunction and redefines the notion of domination, and barrier in terms of "exclusion" to handle these cases. The intuition is that a category can void the barrierhood of a maximal projection that intervenes between it and its antecedent by adjoining to it. A category adjoined to a maximal projection is no longer dominated by that X^{max} given the definition of domination in (69):

(69) X is dominated by Y only if it is dominated by every segment of Y.

Given the adjunction structure (70) for (68), the adjoined trace is not dominated by the VP, therefore the VP is not a blocking category and the IP does not inherit barrierhood.

(70) $[_{CP}$ Bill-wa $[_{CP}$ [John-ga t_i $[_{VP}$ kubi-ni natta] tte t_i $_{CP}]$ itta $_{VP}]$ t_i $_{VP}]$ $_{IP}]$ naze$_i$ no $_{CP}]$

The adjoined trace is separated from the trace in A-position by a VP. To void the barrierhood of this category, Chomsky (1986a) defines government in terms of "exclusion," which voids the barrierhood of an X^{max} if the potential antecedent is adjoined to it. The definition is given in (71).

(71) *Government* X governs Y iff X m-commands Y and there is no W, W a barrier for Y, such that W excludes X.
Exclusion X excludes Y if no segment of X dominates Y.
m-commands X m-commands Y iff X does not dominate Y and every W (W maximal) that dominates X dominates Y.

This series of definitions is potentially too powerful and requires a theory of adjunction. If adjunction were free to apply to any category, then barrierhood could be voided in (67) repeated as (72), with the potential extra adjunction sites italicized.

(72) [[$_{NP}$ [$_{CP}$ Taroo-ga sore-o t_i watasita] $t_{i\ CP}$] $t_{i\ CP}$] otoko-o $_{NP}$] sitte-iru $_{VP}$] $t_{i\ VP}$] $_{IP}$] naze$_i$ no]?

Therefore adjunction to CP must be barred in this case. It is clear that the set of admissible adjunction positions should not be made through a substantive theory of adjunction sites. Recall that one of the main advantages of Chomsky's (1986a) theory is the unification of locality domains for the various subtheories of the grammar and the elimination of a substantive theory of bounding nodes in the movement component. This proposal would lose its attractiveness if the theory simply transferred the site of these substantive claims from the definition of a barrier to the definition of an adjunction site. Chomsky (1986a) claims that one can derive adjunction sites from the theory of theta-role assignment on the assumption that theta-roles cannot be assigned to parts of categories. This bars adjunction to any argument position, because adjunction would prevent the non-adjoined portion of the category from receiving a theta-role. This would disallow adjunction to the CP in (72) and correctly rule out this structure.

This restriction may not be powerful enough to prevent all undesired movements as it predicts that adjunction to a non-argument NP or CP should not yield ungrammatical results. The ungrammaticality of (73a, b) would thus be unaccounted for.

(73a) *Which book$_i$ did you read e_i yesterday an old copy of e_i
(73b) *Which woman$_i$ did you faint [NP the day that John married e_i]

The shifted NP in (73a) is in an A′-position and is not assigned a theta-role, given standard assumptions. The NP *the day that John left* is a non-subcategorized time adverbial that does not receive a theta-role. These examples suggest that the theory of adjunction would have to mention substantive categories and thus would not be reducible to theta theory, as claimed.[43]

The barriers approach can also handle adjuncts and *wh*-in-situ constructions in English. In (74), we see that a complement can move over an adjunct in an embedded position, but an adjunct cannot move over a complement.

(74a) What$_i$ did [$_{IP}$ you wonder [$_{CP}$ how$_j$ [$_{IP}$ PRO to plan e_i e_j]]]
(74b) *How$_j$ did [$_{IP}$ you wonder [$_{CP}$ what$_i$ [$_{IP}$ PRO to plan e_i e_j]]]

This contrast is explained by claiming that the complement trace, having the option of lexical government can move non-locally. The adjunct trace is subject to antecedent government and the intervening IP, which is a BC, transmits barrierhood to the immediately dominating embedded CP, turning it into a barrier by inheritance. This derivation only goes through under the assumption that adjunction to the embedded CP is impossible, as adjunction would void the barrierhood of this category.

In order to handle cases like (75), Chomsky (1986a) adds a notion of SPEC-HEAD agreement.

(75) Who believes $[_{IP}$ $[_{NP}$ whose pictures] to be on sale

This structure would be out on the double question reading indicated in (76) because the NP is not L-marked and is thus a barrier to antecedent government, with the IP becoming an additional barrier by inheritance.

(76) $[_{CP}$ Who$_i$ whose$_j$ $[_{IP}$ e$_i$ believes $[_{IP}$ $[_{NP}$ e$_j$ pictures] to be on sale]]]

This is blocked by assuming that a specifier which "agrees" with the head of an L-marked category also inherits L-marking to the extent that it does not serve as a barrier for antecedent government. Since there is no theta relation between the L-marker and the NP, it is still not lexically governed, given Chomsky's definitions. Since the NP is not a barrier however, the IP does not inherit barrierhood and so antecedent government is possible from outside of the embedded clause.[44]

Without further supplementation, this account has a difficult time explaining the unacceptability of cases like (58) above. The clausal complements of *nouns* are theta-marked by their head nouns and the whole NP is theta-marked by the adjective *okotteru.* To handle these and other cases, the notion of antecedent government is reformulated in terms of *minimality.* The minimality condition is interpreted as constraining the ambiguity of government. Even in cases where no barrier intervenes, government is blocked if there is a closer lexical governor.

4.2 *Minimality*

> In a configuration . . . A . . . $[_{\delta}$ . . . B . . . C.], A does not govern C if δ is the immediate projection of B excluding A.[45]

With this in mind, recall (58). Here the NP dominating the entire noun complement creates a minimality barrier because, even though the NP is L-marked by the matrix adjective, it contains an N^0, which is a closer potential governor for the trace in the embedded CP position, than is the VP adjoined italicized trace.

(77) Taroo-ga nani-o te-ni ireta koto-o sonnani okotteru no
"What were you so angry about the fact that Taro obtained"
$[[_{NP}\ [_{CP}$ Taroo-ga $[_{VP}\ t_i$ te-ni ireta] $t_i]\ _{VP}]\ t_i\ _{CP}]$ koto $_{N}]$-O $_{NP}]\ [_{VP}$ sonnani okotteru] $t_i\ _{VP}]$ no nani-o$_i\ _{CP}]$

Chomsky (1986a) subsumes the *that-t* part of the fixed subject effects under minimality. In (78), the subject trace is dominated by a projection of C, which serves as a minimality barrier. Assuming that empty projections do not count as in (78b), no minimality barrier intervenes, and the structure is licit.

(78a) Who$_i$ do you think $[_{CP}\ e_i\ [_{C}$ that $[e_i$ left]]
(78b) Who$_i$ do you think $[_{CP}\ e_i\ [\ e_i$ left]][46]

Whether or not this idea turns out to be empirically tenable, it appears at odds with the methodological program in *Barriers*. Chomsky must assume that minimality plays no role in defining barriers for movement. The trace in (79) would be separated from the VP-adjoined antecedent by two heads: V and N.

(79) About which authors$_i$ did you $[e_i\ [_{VP}$ read $[_{NP}\ [_{N}$ articles] $[_{PP}\ e_i]]$

Given that barriers for movement are supposed to unify with barriers for government, one wonders why the no-ambiguity constraint should not play a role here as well. This version of minimality is also specifically crafted to disregard specifiers that are not dominated by an immediate projection of a category, even though there is a closer head in these cases as well. Therefore, it is not clear whether minimality is really a no-ambiguity condition at all or whether it simply reduces government to the head–complement relation that was so carefully dispensed with in other sections of Chomsky's book.[47]

The reduction of the ECP to antecedent government crucially depends on the adjunction and SPEC-HEAD mechanisms discussed above. Chomsky (1986a) claims that A′-movement of a complement will always be licensed even without lexical government on the assumption that the complement can always adjoin to the immediately dominating maximal projection. Adjunction is not possible in the case of A-movement as the result would be an improper chain, with a variable c-commanded by a category in an A-position, violating Principle C of Chomsky's Binding Theory.[48] This rules out (80), because the subject trace is not antecedent-governed as it is separated from its antecedent by the matrix VP, which is a barrier.

(80) $John_i[_{VP}$ seemed $[_{IP}$ e_i to be nice]]

These cases are rehabilitated by postulating that the index associated with the real antecedent *John* is passed to the matrix verb *seemed* by SPEC-HEAD agreement. This verb then serves as a surrogate antecedent governor as there are no intervening barriers between it and the embedded subject trace. Government of complements for A-movement involves an extended version of this SPEC-HEAD agreement and thus the two main cases where lexical government plays a role are handled in this system using other means.[49]

Notice that this reduction seems incompatible with the interpretation of barriers in terms of minimality, at least for some cases. In a case like (81), the complement is head-governed under the disjunctive definition. Given minimality and the restriction against adjunction to arguments, the head of the NP will always be a minimality barrier for antecedent government of the complement.

(81) About $whom_i$ did John write $[_{NP}$ a new $[_{N}$ book] e_i]

An interesting result of the *Barriers* program is the elimination of the Head Movement Constraint of Travis (1984) in favor of the independently needed ECP. Chomsky (1986a, 71) expresses this constraint as in (82).

(82) Movement of a zero-level category X^0 is restricted to the position of a head Y^0 that governs the maximal projection XP of X^0, where Y^0 theta-governs or L-marks XP if Y^0 does not equal C^0.

The head-movement constraint forces movement of a head to proceed in an extremely local manner and bars movement of a head over another head as in (83)

(83) *$[_{CP}$ $Have_i$ $[_{IP}$ you $[_{I'}$ $[_{I}$ will] $[_{VP}$ t_i $[_{VP}$ gone]]]]]

This movement is barred because the auxiliary is separated from its potential antecedent governor in the CP by an intervening barrier VP.[50] If the auxiliary first lands in the I position, though, its trace can satisfy the ECP through lexical government. Chomsky has assumed that the inflection marker assigns a theta-role to the VP. If it picks up lexical features from having a lexical category adjoined to this position, it will be a potential L-marker. If there is a modal sitting in this position, though, as in (83), this is impossible. (84), on the other hand, satisfies antecedent government with the indicated structure.

(84) $[_{CP}$ Have$_i$ $[_{IP}$ you $[_I$ e$_i]$ $[_{VP}$ e$_i$ gone$]]]$[51]

As we have seen, Chomsky (1986a) has had to employ a variety of mechanisms to allow the *Barriers* program to work technically. However, it is not clear that a real unification has been achieved. The notion of *barrier* cannot be relevant to the theta-marking component without making the definition circular, since a barrier is defined in terms of theta government. Case assignment is handled in terms of barriers, but given that the system needs the independent notions of L-marking and SPEC-HEAD agreement, the domains for Case assignment (complement and head of an ECM construction) are independently taken care of. Movement and antecedent government are thus the two potential domains of unification, but even they are not governed by the same notions if minimality plays a role for the ECP, but not for Subjacency.

5 A Conjunctive ECP: Head-Government and Generalized Binding

In this section, we discuss a version of the ECP that returns to the ECP's binding-theoretic roots. The 1981 version of the ECP retained vestiges of the binding theory in the notion of antecedent government; the latter being a binding-like relation that holds between an A′-antecedent and a trace but over a more restricted domain than standard binding relations. The asymmetry between arguments versus subjects/adjuncts was stipulated in this version of the ECP in the form of the two disjunctively satisfiable conditions. One of the present theory's aims is to eliminate the disjunctive character of the classical ECP. However, in contrast to some other approaches that have tried to remove one of the conjuncts, this version adopts both halves, postulates that each is relevant for different ECP effects, and suggests that the two conjuncts apply at different levels of the grammar. The return to the claim that *wh*-traces obey the Binding Theory is motivated by the observation that the pre-ECP approach (which treated *wh*-traces as anaphors) works perfectly in accounting for the distribution of the traces of adjuncts such as *how* and *why*. The problem, then, is to revise and extend the Binding Theory so that it more adequately covers the properties of non-adjunct traces, e.g. the traces of *who* and *what*. Thus, the properties of adjuncts and argument traces are distinguished but via a modified theory of binding rather than through the introduction of an additional grammatical relation like antecedent government.

We will present two versions of a conjunctive theory. In this section, we discuss Aoun, Hornstein, Lightfoot, and Weinberg (1987), in the next Rizzi (1990). Aoun, Hornstein, Lightfoot, and Weinberg (1987) combines a condition on head-government that applies to the distribution of phonetically overt ecs and replaces antecedent government with a version of the Binding Theory generalized to apply to ecs left by LF-movement.[52] This approach returns two earlier theoretical intuitions to center stage: (i) phonetically overt ecs must meet a special condition of proper government but within domains characteristic of other conditions such as Case marking and theta-marking i.e. domains of standard government, and (ii) the distribution of *wh*-traces is a function of the Binding Theory. This combination has several key features. First, it conceptually ties the existence of "antecedent-binding" effects within a given language to its binding properties more generally. For example, it provides a natural account for why it is that "antecedent government" relations have as their domain essentially clauses and noun phrases. These are the domains over which binding relations are checked and if antecedent government is essentially A′-binding it is no surprise that it operates over the same domains.[53] Empirically, this leads us to expect "antecedent-binding" effects and regular binding effects will be linked in a given language. We shall see that there is evidence that supports this view. Second, this sort of theory states that syntactic movement and LF-movement, though similar, are not subject to identical wellformedness conditions. In fact, this account argues that the variety of subject/object asymmetries that have been traced to the ECP do not constitute a unitary class; some (the *that-t* effect) are due to the head-government requirement and some (superiority effects) are due to Generalized Binding. The lexical government condition (85) holds on the PF side of the grammar and so concerns itself with syntactic gaps that are phonetically null.[54] (86) holds on the LF side of the grammar and concerns itself with all expressions that have antecedents, including traces left by LF-movement operations.

(85) *Lexical Government*

(85a) An indexed ec must be properly governed, i.e. governed by a lexical head.

(85b) A governs B iff all maximal projections dominating B also dominate A and for B = Y^{max} if A governs B then A governs the head of B (i.e. Y^0).[55]

(86) *Generalized Binding*
Where X = A or A′

(86a) An X-anaphor must be X-bound in its domain.

(86b) An X-pronoun must be X-free in its domain.

(86c) R-expressions must be A-free.

Binding domains are determined as in (87).

(87) The domain of an expression A is the smallest NP or clause that contains an accessible SUBJECT for A, where a SUBJECT is the most prominent nominal expression in the NP or clause.[56]

In addition, there is an articulated theory of *wh*-traces that distinguishes the traces left by adjuncts (e.g. *how* and *why*) and those left by arguments (e.g. *who* and *what*).[57] The traces of the latter are deemed to be more "referential" than those of the former. This intuition is implemented by having Principle C be a crucial determinant in computing a domain for these traces. The domains for the traces of adjuncts are computed without reference to Principle C.

(88) For A an argument trace, B is an accessible SUBJECT for A iff coindexing A and B would not violate Principle C.[58]

(85) is relevant to several phenomena including complementizer deletion and the *that-t* effect.[59] (85) requires all syntactically created ecs to be properly governed. This implies that the site of a deleted complementizer must be lexically governed.

(89a) It was apparent (that) Bill loved Mary
(89b) It was apparent right after I introduced them *(that) Bill loved Mary
(89c) The book (that) Bill wrote arrived yesterday
(89d) The book arrived yesterday *(that) Bill wrote
(89e) *(That) Bill loved Mary was obvious to all
(89f) Mary believes, but John doesn't, *(that) Bill is smart

In (89a) the complementizer is governed by the adjective *apparent* and in (89c) it is governed by *book*.[60] However, in (89b, d, e, f) the clause containing the complementizer is not proximate to a lexical head, and complementizer deletion is forbidden. (85) can be extended to cover the absence of complementizer deletion in gapping constructions if we assume that a gapped head is not lexical.[61]

(90) John thinks that Bill came early and Sam, *(that) Frank came late

This same assumption accounts for the array of data in (91).

(91) Whose picture did he take?
(91a) He took my mother's picture

(91b) He took my mother's
(91c) [$_{NP}$ my mother$_i$ [$_{N'}$ picture t_i]]

The question in (91) is ambiguous. It can be asking about the "possessor" or thematic subject of the picture. The answer (91a) retains this ambiguity. However, (91b) only carries the possessor interpretation. It is not interpreted as saying "He took a picture of my mother." If the subject of an NP can carry the theme reading only if moved from postnominal position (as in (91c)) then the indicated trace in (91c) will not have a proper governor if the head deletes, in violation of (85). This will block the thematic interpretation in (91b).[62] It will also account for the contrasts in (92).[63]

(92a) It isn't likely that John will sneeze during the aria but it is (likely) that Frank will cough
(92b) John$_j$ isn't likely [t_j to sneeze during the aria] but Frank$_i$ is likely [t_i to cough]
(92c) *John$_j$ isn't likely [t_j to sneeze during the aria] but Frank$_i$ is GAP [t_i to cough]

(92a) has no ecs that require proper government and so gapping the head in the second conjunct is permissible. In (92c), in contrast, a gapped head will leave the embedded subject trace without a proper governor and hence the contrast between (92b) and (92c).[64]

The unacceptability of the gapped cases suggests that a disjunctive ECP is empirically inadequate. In (91c), for example, we have an antecedent governor locally available, namely *my mother$_i$* in the SPEC position. Nonetheless, if the head is deleted then we lose the thematic interpretation. If the ECP allowed the trace to be properly governed by meeting either disjunct, we should expect (91c) to be ambiguous.

To this point we have considered how (85) bears on the distribution of NP-traces. (85) also extends to cover *that-t* effects.

(93a) Who$_i$ did John believe (*that) t_i saw Bill
(93b) Who$_i$ did John believe (that) Bill saw t_i
(93c) Who$_i$ did John believe [$_{CP}$ t_i that [$_{IP}$ t_i saw Bill]]
(93d) Who$_i$ did John believe [$_{CP}$ t_i e_i [$_{IP}$ t_i saw Bill]]

Assume, as we did above, that a non-lexical head can properly govern a trace if and only if it is coindexed with it.[65] Assume also, that index transfer is only permitted to a non-phonetic C^0 in English.[66] This forbids the trace in [SPEC CP] in (93c) from transferring its index to *that*. But, this leaves this trace without a proper governor and so in violation of (85). "Deleting" the complementizer dephoneticizes it and so permits index transfer to occur as in (93d). The irrelevance of the presence of the complementizer in (93b) is due to the fact that the trace is properly governed by *saw*.[67]

LF-movement operations are not subject to (85) as they leave no phonetic gaps.[68] They fall under the Generalized Binding Conditions in (86)–(88). Superiority effects, for example, are accounted for as follows:

(94a) Who bought what
(94b) $[_{CP}$ [what$_j$ [who$_i$]]$_i$ $[_{IP}$ t$_i$ AGR$_i$ bought t$_j$]]
(94c) *What did who buy
(94d) $[_{CP}$ [who$_i$ [what$_j$]]$_j$ $[_{IP}$ t$_i$ AGR$_i$ bought t$_j$]]

Both *who* and *what* leave argument traces and so fall under (88). The LF representations are in (94b) and (94d). We assume that the *wh*-in-situ adjoins to a *wh*-expression already in CP.[69] Note too that we have assumed that AGR and the subject are coindexed under agreement. Consider (94b) first. The trace t_j has no domain. The reason is that there is no coindexing between t_j and either candidate SUBJECT that does not violate Principle C. Coindexing t_i and t_j is a clear violation of Principle C, and coindexing AGR and t_j leads to a violation given that AGR is in turn coindexed with t_i. Thus, t_j has no domain and so does not have to meet the requirements of (86).[70] In contrast t_i does have a domain, i.e. the matrix clause. Note that t_i has an accessible SUBJECT that it can be coindexed with, i.e. AGR. Clearly, agreement does not induce a Principle C violation, so this coindexing endows t_i with a domain (i.e. the matrix clause) within which it must be bound. In (94b), t_i meets this requirement. The traces in (94d) have the same properties. The subject trace t_i has the matrix clause as a domain and the object trace t_j has no domain at all. However, in this case, t_i is not bound as the adjoined *who* fails to c-command it. This leads to a violation of Principle A of Generalized Binding.

A Principle A violation also lies behind the prohibitions against leaving adjuncts in-situ in English or extracting them out of *wh*-islands.

(95a) Why did John buy what
(95b) *What did John buy why
(95c) *Why$_i$ did John wonder [whether Bill quit t$_i$]
(96a) $[_{CP}$ [what$_j$ [why$_i$]]$_i$ $[_{IP}$ John$_k$ AGR$_k$ $[_{VP}$ buy t$_j$] t$_i$]]
(96b) $[_{CP}$ [why$_i$ [what$_j$]]$_j$ $[_{IP}$ John$_k$ AGR$_k$ $[_{VP}$ buy t$_j$] t$_i$]]
(96c) Why$_i$ did John wonder $[_{CP}$ whether [IP Bill quit t$_i$]]

The domain of an adjunct trace is the smallest clause with a SUBJECT. In contrast to argument traces, Principle C is **not** invoked in determining the domain of an adjunct. This means that in (96a–c), t_i, the trace of *why*, must be bound within its immediate containing clause. This requirement is met in (96a) alone. In (96b), the adjoined *why* does not c-command the trace it left behind and in (96c), though it c-commands the trace position, it does not bind it *within* the embedded clause, i.e. its domain. So in these two cases we get a Principle A violation.[71]

Similar *wh*-island effects obtain in Chinese where *wh*-movement operates at LF.

(97a) Ni xiang-zhidao [shei mai-le sheme]
You wonder who buy what
(97b) Ni xiang-zhidao [Lisi weisheme mai-le sheme]
You wonder Lisi why buy what

(97a) is ambiguous in Chinese with either *shei* or *sheme* capable of taking matrix scope. In contrast, (97b) requires that *weisheme* take embedded scope. This is essentially the same fact as (96c) with a wide scope reading of the adjunct prohibited by Principle A of Generalized Binding.

The ambiguity in (97a) is more interesting for it indicates that Chinese does not display superiority effects.

(98a) [$_{CP}$ sheme$_j$ [$_{IP}$ Ni xiang-zhidao [$_{CP}$ shei$_i$ [$_{IP}$ t_i mai-le t_j]]]]
(98b) [$_{CP}$ shei$_i$ [$_{IP}$ Ni xiang-zhidao [$_{CP}$ sheme$_j$ [$_{IP}$ t_i mai-le t_j]]]]

Note that sentences such as (99) are also well-formed.

(99) Zhangsan$_i$ shuo [taziji$_i$ hui lai]
Z say himself will come
"Zhangsan says himself will come"

Here we have an apparent violation of the Nominative Island Condition in Chinese. (99) is accounted for if we assume that Chinese has no AGR. This is a plausible assumption given the absence of any overt agreement morphology in Chinese. If there is no AGR in Chinese, then the domain for the embedded anaphor *taziji* is the matrix clause, and we correctly predict the possibility of anaphor binding between the matrix subject and embedded subject positions. Note that the absence of AGR also accounts for the lack of superiority effects in Chinese. Neither *sheme* nor *shei* have domains in (98). Recall, that in (94c, d) it was only the presence of AGR that endowed subjects with domains, for they were accessible SUBJECTS for them. In the absence of AGR we should find no superiority effects.

Despite the absence of superiority effects, however, we do find subject/object asymmetries resurfacing in cases of overt movement as occurs in Topicalization constructions.

(100a) John [$_{CP}$ dui Bill hen xihuan Mary] hen shangxin
John to Bill very like Mary very sorry
"John is sorry that Bill likes Mary"
(100b) ?Mary$_i$, John [$_{CP}$ dui Bill hen xihuan t$_i$] hen shangxin
"Mary, John is sorry that Bill likes"
(100c) *Bill$_i$, John [$_{CP}$ dui t$_i$ hen xihuan Mary] hen shangxin
"Bill, John is sorry likes Mary"

The postverbal trace in (100b) is properly governed by the verb *xihuan.* In contrast, there is no proper governor for t_i in (100c) and a violation of (85) ensues.[72]

The contrast between overt and covert movement constitutes rather strong evidence in favor of the conjunctive approach to the ECP noted above. Given the absence of AGR in Chinese, we expect to see no subject/object asymmetries for LF-movement. This, however, should have no effect on overt movement such as topicalization, as (85) should still be operative.

The conjunctive combination of head-government for overt traces and Generalized Binding for all traces is supported by super-raising phenomena as well.

(101a) John$_i$ is certain [t$_i$ to like ice cream]
(101b) *John$_i$ seems [$_\alpha$ it is certain [t$_i$ to like ice cream]]

The trace in both (101a and b) is head-governed. Nonetheless, this does not suffice to license (101b). This indicates that head-government alone is not enough, as a disjunctive version of the ECP would lead us to expect. The present theory traces the unacceptability of (101b) to a violation of Principle A of the binding theory. The NP-trace must be A-bound within its domain. Its domain is the clause marked α. Observe that it has an accessible SUBJECT for t_i as coindexing *it* and the NP-t would not violate Principle C given the anaphoric nature of NP-traces. Thus, t_i must be bound within domain α, but it isn't. As expected, failure to meet one part of the ECP leads to unacceptability.

Some have argued that the violation in (102a) is "worse" than the binding violation we see in (102b).

(102a) **The men were believed t were happy
(102b) *The men believed each other were happy

The greater unacceptability of (102a) can be explained if we assume that only well-formed A-chains have theta-roles. This makes (102a) both a Binding Theory and a Theta Criterion violation while (102b) only violates the Binding Theory. Note that this would account for the strong unacceptability of (101b) as it too would violate the Theta Criterion.[73]

In this section, we have explored the main features of a conjunctive approach to the ECP that incorporates a theory of Generalized Binding as a wellformedness condition on traces at LF and a head-government condition that regulates the distribution of phonetically overt gaps. In many respects, this theory returns to earlier intuitions concerning the anaphoric properties of *wh*-traces and the special requirements that overt gaps must meet. The two central contentions are that the notion "antecedent government" is best viewed as a binding relation and not as a special case of government and that the pair of requirements that characterize the 1981 version of the ECP must be conjunctively rather than disjunctively satisfied.

6 Relativized Minimality

Chomsky's (1986a) definition of minimality is the conceptual starting point for Rizzi's (1990) work on the ECP. Recall that Chomsky defined the antecedent government portion of the ECP as subject to a no-ambiguity constraint. A category could not be antecedent-governed if another potential (antecedent or lexical) governor intervened. The intervening governor could create its own minimality barrier. Rizzi's (1990) definition of antecedent government uses a notion of barrierhood where any X^{max} that is not directly selected by a [+V] category is a rigid barrier.[74] However, Rizzi (1990) relativizes the notion of "minimality barrier" in the sense that a category intervening across a non-rigid barrier can block antecedent government but *only* if it is of the same type as the antecedent whose government is being blocked. If the category is the antecedent in an A′-chain, the intervening category must be in an A′-specifier position. Blockers in an A-chain must be in an A-specifier position, blockers in an X^0 chain formed by e.g. head-movement must be X^0 categories.[75]

Rizzi combines this idea with a purely structural notion of head-government given in (103). This definition is applied conjunctively with the definition of antecedent government.

(103) X head-governs Y iff
(i) X is of the category (A, N, P, V, AGR, T);
(ii) X m-commands Y;
(iii) no barrier intervenes;
(iv) relativized minimality is respected.[76]

Furthermore, proper head-government is limited to categories that are within "the immediate projection of the head" (Rizzi (1990, 31)).

Rizzi (1990) also reduces the scope of the antecedent government condition of the ECP.[77] Rizzi claims that the guiding principle underlying the ECP is (104). Thereby, antecedent government becomes irrelevant for complements:

(104) A referential index must be licensed by a referential theta-role. (Rizzi 1990, 86)

Antecedents are normally connected to their variables by coindexation. If coindexation occurs, the relationship between antecedent and empty category only needs to meet the standard requirements that the antecedent c-command the empty category that it licenses and share the same referential index. Structures like (105) are thus licit given only this condition. Other principles must be invoked to rule them out. We return to these.

(105a) *Who$_i$ do you wonder whether e_i likes the movies
(105b) *John$_i$ seems it is certain e_i to win the race

Rizzi (1990) follows Aoun (1981), Aoun, Hornstein, Lightfoot, and Weinberg (1987), and Cinque (1984, 1990b) in claiming that in the normal case, adjuncts are non-referential.[78] Therefore, they cannot be connected to their antecedents through the licensing condition given in (104). The variable they are associated with, being non-referential, does not have a referential theta-role, and the chain containing it will not be licensed by (104). In order to be interpreted however, the ecs must be linked (either directly, or through a chain) to an antecedent. As binding is unavailable, they must be so linked via antecedent government and so are subject to relativized minimality.

Rizzi (1990) argues for this account in two ways. First, it is claimed that the lexical government conjunct of the ECP can pick up the cases of illicit argument movement no longer covered by antecedent government. Second, it is claimed that the remaining cases are handled in a more elegant way than in other systems.

Given the relativization of minimality and the divergent ways that arguments and adjuncts become licensed, the antecedent government portion of Chomsky's (1986a) ECP cannot handle Fixed Subject Effects, subject/object asymmetries, and cases of super-raising. However, a conjunctive version of the ECP requiring ecs to be lexically governed takes up the slack in most of these cases. Consider Fixed Subject Effects.

In (106) the subject e_i is referential and thus not subject to antecedent government or minimality. It is excluded by (103). As the class of lexical governors excludes C^0, (106) is out because the subject trace is not properly head-governed.

(106) Who$_i$ do you believe [$_{CP}$ e$_i$ that [$_{IP}$ e$_i$ [AGR [left]]]

The contrast between (106) and (107) is handled by claiming that the empty complementizer position in (107) actually contains an instance of agreement. It is a case of agreement between the *wh* or trace specifier of CP and its head C^0; an instance of SPEC-HEAD agreement as shown in (107b)

(107a) Who do you think left
(107b) Who$_i$ do [you think [$_{CP}$ e$_i$ AGR [$_{IP}$ e$_i$ left]]

A good deal of Rizzi (1990, chapter 2) presents both theory-internal and overt morphological evidence for this version of lexical government. On the morphological side, a variety of languages that exhibit overt agreement between specifier and head in the CP position are discussed, attesting to the reality of SPEC-HEAD agreement in COMP as a grammatical process. Rizzi (1990) also surveys a variety of languages that exhibit *that-t* effects except in cases where there is overt morphological agreement between the specifier and the head of the CP. The paradigm (108) from French illustrates this point with case neutral *que* obligatorily changing to *qui* showing nominative agreement.

(108a) L'homme$_i$ que je crois [$_{CP}$ e$_i$ que [$_{IP}$ Jean connaît e$_i$]]]
The man that I think that John knows
(108b) L'homme que je crois [$_{CP}$ e$_i$ qui/*que [$_{IP}$ e$_i$ viendra]]]
The man that I think that will come

Note, that in order to generalize this account to long movement in questions, Rizzi (1990) has to stipulate that AGR, unlike other proper governors must bear an independent relationship (agree with) the category that it properly governs. This is highly reminiscent of the index-transferring conventions discussed above. In (109), there is no overt complementizer and we assume that agreement appears in the head of

CP position. Without the coindexing convention, the subject trace would be properly governed.

(109) Who$_i$ do you wonder [what$_j$ AGR$_j$ [e$_i$ saw e$_j$]]]

Examples like (110) from Chinese cause some potential complications for the theory. Recall that in (110) the subject trace can receive wide scope and therefore must be properly head-governed.

(110a) Ni xiang-zhidao shei weisheme mai le shu
You wonder who why bought the book
(110b) Shei$_i$ [Ni xiang-zhidao [weisheme$_j$ [e$_i$ e$_j$ mai le shu]]

It cannot be head-governed by agreement in CP as there is a non-agreeing element in the specifier position. The impossibility of movement from the subject position at S-Structure as shown in (100c) in the previous section, prevents head-government from applying at this level. One possibility would be to move the INFL node into C^0 at LF. This would allow the subject to be properly head-governed in (110). The problem, however, is reconciling this analysis with Rizzi's claim that the head-government condition of the ECP applies at LF. If this is correct, then we predict incorrectly that S-Structure movement from the subject position should also be rehabilitated by subsequent head movement of the INFL. One could adopt the Lasnik and Saito (1984) approach and indelibly mark the subject position as not properly head-governed at S-Structure. However, reintroducing these devices would tend to compromise the elegance of Rizzi's solution. Rizzi is not free to move the head-government condition to the pre-LF-level because head-government is the only condition relevant for capturing subject/object asymmetries at LF in his system.[79]

Super-raising cases get a somewhat less satisfactory treatment. In (111), the subject, being an argument, can transmit a referential index.

(111) John$_i$ seems [it$_j$ is certain [e$_i$ to leave]]

Therefore, the subject trace is exempt from any condition of antecedent government in terms of the ECP. Rizzi (1990) follows Aoun, Hornstein, Lightfoot, and Weinberg (1987) in claiming that these cases are to be handled as Theta Criterion violations. Recall that Aoun, Hornstein, Lightfoot, and Weinberg (1987), ruled these structures out in terms of Generalized Binding, their replacement for the antecedent government portion of Chomsky's ECP. Construction of an A-chain is licit so long as these binding principles are respected. A theta-role can only be borne by a licit A-chain.[80] Since the chain in (111) violates the Binding Theory, it cannot bear a theta-role and the structure is out.

Rizzi (1990) cannot adopt this simple notion of chain. Rather, it is stipulated that a chain must obey conditions of antecedent government even if the links in that chain are not subject to this condition. There seems to be no independent justification for this claim. Nonetheless, given this assumption, (111) will be out by the Theta Criterion if the intervening *it* in subject position blocks antecedent government of the most deeply embedded subject trace. We will see why the intervening specifier blocks this relationship presently as we turn to Rizzi's notion of antecedent government (Rizzi 1990, 6).

(112) X antecedent-governs Y iff
  (i) X and Y are coindexed;
  (ii) X c-commands Y;
  (iii) no barrier intervenes;
  (iv) relativized minimality is respected.

Relativized minimality is respected if there is no c-commanding intervening "typical potential antecedent" between the real antecedent and its trace. A typical potential antecedent is a category in a position to which the trace could have moved violating no conditions, but which, in the structure in question, is not coindexed with the relevant trace. To be specific: an A-bar specifier position blocks antecedent government in an A′-chain, an A-specifier blocks the relation for A-movement and an intervening head will rule out further head-movement. One can see that this idea immediately gives us the effect of the Head Movement Constraint discussed above and will disallow long movement of adjuncts. We see that the traces in (113) are separated from their antecedents by an intervening head and A′-specifier respectively. Both thus violate relativized minimality.

(113a) [Have_j [you [$_I$ will [$_{VP}$ [e_j [gone]]]]

(113b) *How_j did you wonder [who_i AGR [e_i to see e_j]]

Recall that an X^{max} does not count as a barrier if it is selected by a [+V] category. Assuming that [+I] and [+C] categories are non-distinct from V, there are no barriers, intervening between the real antecedent and its trace. Therefore the intervening typical potential antecedent head and A′-specifier are the only things that rule out these structures.[81] With respect to the ECP, this has the advantage over Chomsky's (1986a) system of handling these cases without the devices of adjunction and gamma marking. Note, however, that it vitiates the program of reducing the domain relevant to the ECP with locality domains that are independently motivated with respect to other subtheories of the grammar. The domain of "government" which is relevant for antecedent government can disregard many maximal projections so long as they are in the domain of [+V] elements. This significantly extends the notion needed for Case or theta-marking.[82]

When it comes to dealing with adjuncts, the internal elegance of this program is quite impressive. The relativized minimality requirement accounts for a variety of otherwise recalcitrant cases in a uniform and simple manner. Rizzi discusses a contrast taken from Obenauer (1976, 1985) in (114) which illustrates the simplicity of the system. (114) shows that the object argument can move over a *beaucoup* phrase. This is predicted since the argument phrase is not subject to relativized minimality via the antecedent government condition. It is therefore only subject to head-government and it is properly governed by the verb. Movement over *beaucoup* is impossible with the non-selected specifier *combien* even though movement is possible from both positions if no *beaucoup* blocker intervenes.

(114a) [[Combien de livres]$_i$ a-t-il [[$_{SPEC\ VP}$ beaucoup] consulté] e$_i$]
How many of books has he a lot consulted
"How many books did he consult a lot?"
(114b) *[[Combien]$_i$ a-t-il [[$_{SPEC\ VP}$ beaucoup] consulté [$_{NP}$ e$_i$ [de livres]]
(114c) [[Combien de livres]$_i$ a-t-il consulté e$_i$]
(114d) [[Combien]$_i$ a-t-il consulté [$_{NP}$ e$_i$ [de livres]]

Beaucoup serves as a blocker since it appears in the Specifier of VP position, which is a position to which quantifiers can move as shown in (115). Since there is an A′-specifier intervening between the trace and its real antecedent in this A-bar dependency, antecedent government is blocked.[83]

(115) J'ai beaucoup consulté [e$_i$ [de livres]]
I a lot consulted of books
J'ai consulté beaucoup de livres
"I consulted a lot of books"

In this section, we have seen that relativizing the notion of minimality has very desirable effects when dealing with the locality restrictions on adjuncts. However, we have argued that there are some problems with the theory. First, the government notion relevant for antecedent government is rather more expansive than the one required for government in other domains. This makes it hard to see how the desirable end of unifying the domains of grammatical principles is to be achieved. Second, government seems relevant to operations that do not obviously form a natural class. For example, why is it that A-chain composition and adjunct-ec licensing are both subject to antecedent government? Last of all, the absence of any principle save head-government to account for subject/object asymmetries at LF makes it hard to see how this account could account for the differences observed between LF and overt movement in languages such as Chinese without invoking many of the notions that the system was designed to avoid.

7 Conclusion

We have reviewed some of the major approaches to ECP effects. Our attention has been necessarily selective. However, it should be clear just how productive it has been to investigate the theoretical properties and expand the empirical reach of Chomsky's original 1981 proposal. What started out as a way of handling certain "residues" of the Nominative Island Condition has provided rich explanations regarding subject/object asymmetries, adjunct/argument asymmetries and much more.[84] Furthermore, behind the apparent competing theoretical proposals there seem to have emerged certain points of consensus on what the "right" version of the ECP should look like. Many believe that the original disjunctive 1981 version of the theory should be abandoned and should be replaced with a conjunctive version involving both a head-government clause and some sort of long-distance binding/antecedent government relationship. Where there is controversy is over the precise nature of the two conditions. Is antecedent government distinct from A'-binding? Does head-government apply at PF, LF or S-Structure? What is the best way to state the minimality requirement? In terms of relativized minimality, a minimal binding requirement or Chomsky's (1986a) version? These technical issues are important, but they should not obscure the fact that the theories surveyed above share much in common.

Where the approaches differ in a more fundamental way is in their response to a primary motivation behind the original 1981 proposal; the desire to find a unified domain (or set of domains) for the application of grammatical principles. We believe that it should be a desideratum on an adequate theory that the domain of application of ECP principles not be *sui generis*. Specifically, this means focusing in on the theoretical status of antecedent government. This relation just looks too similar to Subjacency on the one hand or simple A′-binding on the other to be entirely different from both! This theoretical perception is reflected in two approaches that have been pursued to "regularize" antecedent government. Connectedness theories and *Barriers*-like theories have focused on unifying the domain of antecedent government with that of Subjacency. Binding-like approaches have attempted to reduce antecedent government to a species of A′-binding. Our own preferences as regards the desirable direction in which to move have no doubt emerged in this review. However, a primary concern here has been to refocus attention on this wider theoretical concern.

Related Material in Other Chapters

Since the late 1970s the theory of government and in particular the ECP have taken on an increasingly central role in the Principles and Parameters approach, in that process often taking over functions that were previously performed by other principles. This is particularly true for the theory of binding and to some extent the theory of bounding as well. From that point of view the reader may want to review the presentation of the Binding Theory in chapter 4, in particular as it pertains to anaphors and LF-movement, the movement approaches to long-distance binding, and the relationship between binding and traces.

Chapter 3 on Logical Form overlaps with the current chapter in discussing movement in the LF component and how it is constrained by the theories of government and bounding. Chapter 1 introduces the basic notions of X-bar theory that support the different definitions of government discussed in the current chapter. The discussion of morphosyntax in chapter 6 in several places appeals to the ECP, in particular to the role it plays in constraining the movement of lexical X^0 categories. Chapter 7 of the book analyzes how ECP effects are captured in Chomsky's new Minimalist Program.

NOTES

1 See chapter 4 for details.
2 Languages like Italian are superficial counterexamples to this generalization.
3 Returning to (3) above, (3d) is out because the trace in subject position is separated from the matrix verb by the S′ containing a *wh* word that is not a lexical governor. The contrast in (3a) and (3b) is handled by claiming that raising adjectives, like verbs, can be subcategorized to delete an intervening maximal projection. The

adjective in (3b) cannot delete the intervening S′ and so the subject trace is not properly governed.

4 Jaeggli (1982) and Rizzi (1982) showed that similar facts hold in Spanish and Italian.

5 The mechanisms for achieving this result are discussed below.

6 This data is controversial. For example, Lasnik and Saito (1984) claim that cases like (13b) with *who* in place of *what* are acceptable. For alternative judgments see Aoun, Hornstein, and Sportiche (1981), Kayne (1983b) and Aoun, Hornstein, Lightfoot, and Weinberg (1987).

7 The facts here are more complicated. First, Kayne (1983b) pointed out that superiority effects are canceled when the *wh*-elements involved are "det N" as opposed to simple *wh* structures.

(i) Which woman do you think which man loved
(ii) Who thinks Mary left for which reason

Secondly, Hendrick and Rochemont (1982) point out that the ECP does not subsume cases like (iii) and (iv):

(iii) *What did John persuade who to buy
(iv) *What did you expect who to see

In both of these cases, the trace of each *wh*-movement is head-governed, straightforwardly in (iii) and, assuming S′ deletion needed to assign Case to the subject, in (iv). See Pesetsky (1987) and Hornstein and Weinberg (1991) for attempts to deal with this contrast in terms of the ECP.

8 These examples were noted in Aoun, Hornstein, and Sportiche (1981).

9 This is also a problem for (13b) above given that deletion of the *that* does not appreciably improve the sentence.

(i) *Who believes what fell

10 See Aoun, Hornstein, and Sportiche (1981), Lasnik and Saito (1984), Aoun (1985, 1986), and Aoun, Hornstein, Lightfoot, and Weinberg (1987).

11 Aoun (1986) and Aoun, Hornstein, Lightfoot, and Weinberg (1987) tie percolation to where it is that selection is checked in a given language. If we assume that in English and French it is checked at SS and in Chinese at LF we get the right results.

12 See Aoun and Hornstein (1985).

13 See Chomsky (1986b), following Lebeaux (1983) and Kayne (1983b).

14 These were first discussed systematically by Huang (1982). Similar notions were proposed in Belletti and Rizzi (1981) as well. See Browning (1989) for arguments that the CED should not be reduced to the ECP.

15 For Huang (1982), the CED was an S-Structure condition. Examples (25a) and (25c) are from Chomsky (1986a), example (25b) is from Higginbotham (1987a).

16 These data are presented in Lasnik and Saito (1984).

17 From Kayne (1981).

18 These judgments are not firm and there seems to be considerable disagreement as to their acceptability with the indicated multiple question reading. Juan Uriagereka informs us that these seem not to have a multiple interrogation reading in Spanish.

19 The Chinese data is from Aoun, Hornstein, Lightfoot, and Weinberg (1987) The

Japanese data is from Fukui (1988). It should be remarked that there is something odd with putting a *because* phrase within a *because* phrase.

20 There are other possibilities. So the adjunct in Chinese may be an S′ complement while the one in Japanese is within S. If so, there may be a local antecedent in the former for the trace but not for the latter. There may also be a more intimate connection between COMP and *why*-like adjuncts than *how*-like adjuncts. It has been proposed in Rizzi (1990, 47) that *why* is generated in COMP. It may be that the absence of *why* in these cases is due to the absence of a COMP position. *How* is not similarly generated in COMP.

21 These definitions are taken from Kayne (1983b). We will deal with the ECP as specific to ecs for expository convenience. It is unclear whether Kayne (1983b) intended to eliminate the disjunction in the 1981 version of the ECP (see p. 166). However, it is clear that the head-government notion plays a relatively little role in the standard connectedness literature.

22 Structural governors differ from lexical governors. The latter is a more inclusive class. Languages can differ in whether, for example, prepositions are structural governors.

23 This also accounts for the *que/qui* alternation in French (see Kayne (1981)). Transferring an index is possible in French, and this underlies the *que/qui* rule. What's in the text is a modern update of Pesetsky's (1982a) condition on index transfer in the new PS format with CPs and IPs.

There is another approach to the *that-t* effect within the connectedness literature due to Pesetsky (1982b). He treats these as instances of violations of a crossing constraint. The main idea is that when there are multiple A′-antecedent/dependent pairs they must nest rather than cross. Pesetsky (1982b) proposes an A′-relation linking Infl to Comp that results in a crossing relation whenever there is movement across an overt complementizer. For this to work technically, Pesetsky (1982b) must assume that I′ is a maximal projection for the purposes of computing paths. No other X′ category is similarly maximal.

(i) *Who$_i$ did John say [$_{CP}$ t$_i$ that$_j$ [$_{IP}$ t$_i$ [$_{I'}$ I$_j$ [$_{VP}$ left]]]]

In (i), there is a postulated path between *I* and *that* and one between t_i and *who*. The former includes the nodes {I′, IP and CP} while the latter includes {IP, CP, . . . }. The important point is that the two paths overlap at more than one node but neither contains the other. Thus we have a crossing violation.

This analysis has several interesting consequences. First, it implies that there should not be any main clause complementizer-trace effects. The reason is that the path between C and I will contain the path between the subject and the matrix COMP. Koopman (1983), however, argues that lack of *do*-support for subject questions should be traced to the ECP (see Aoun, Hornstein, Lightfoot, and Weinberg (1987) and Rizzi (1990) as well).

(ii) *Who did leave

Second, it implies that the multiple questions given in (iii) contrast significantly in acceptability.

(iiia) Who believes pictures of what to be selling well
(iiib) Who believes (that) pictures of what are selling well

(iiic) Who expected whose book to be a success
(iiid) Who expected whose book would be a success

As far as we can tell, these sentences are on a par. However, only (iiia, c) are postulated to have a path from C to I, so only they should induce ECP effects. Pesetsky (1982b, 611) claims that sentences like (iiib) only carry an echo interpretation, but we find no significant difference between the indicated examples.

There is a similar contrast with *wh*-in-situ constructions in French. Aoun (1985, 62–3) observes the following contrast:

(iva) *Jean veut que qui vienne
(ivb) Jean veut que le portrait de qui soit vendu

If crossing lay behind the ECP we should expect these sentences to be on a par as both cases are finite and so presumably involve a C to I path.

One last point: the acceptability of reflexives and reciprocals within subject NPs is also problematic for crossing if these involve LF movement if these types of dependencies are to be handled in terms of connectedness (see section 2 above and Kayne (1983b)).

(vi) The men think that books about each other/themselves will sell well

A current analysis involves the movement of *each* and the reflexive out of the containing subject NP to the higher clause (see Chomsky (1986b), Lebeaux (1983), Heim, Lasnik, and May (1991)). This, however, induces a crossing violation, so the sentences in (vi) should be unacceptable.

24 Nothing, in principle, forbids invoking the Binding Theory to rule out cases of super-raising. However, Kayne (1983b, examples (82) and (83)) does suggest treating NIC effects in terms of the ECP as in (41c).

25 Observe that the prohibition against extraction from a subject will not be similarly problematic. The reason is that subjects are not in a CGC with INFL, so g-projections cannot extend beyond the subject node.

26 Longobardi (1985) points out that this is a direct way of incorporating Huang's (1982) CED condition within a connectedness framework.

27 Longobardi (1985) argues for the proposal that only complements are properly governed. This is similar to the notion of theta-marking that gets employed in Chomsky (1986a).

28 This problem might be solved within Kayne's (1983b) account if I^0 moved to C^0 at LF. If this were to occur, then subjects would be in a CGC with INFL at LF though not at S-Structure. It seems unlikely, however, that the subject would be a complement of I^0 even after movement. Consequently, Longobardi's (1985) theory would still disallow LF-movement of the *wh*-in-situ. Note that this sort of movement is illicit in Pesetsky (1982b). He claims that these sorts of constructions are ill-formed under a multiple question reading. See note 23 for further discussion.

29

Definition of Paths
Suppose *t* is an empty category locally A′ bound by *b*. Then
(i) for A the first maximal projection dominating *t*
(ii) for B the first maximal projection dominating *b*

(iii) the *path between t and b* is the set of nodes P such that P = {xI(x = A) v (x = B) v (x dom A and x not dom B)}
(Pesetsky (1982b, 289, ex. 69))

30 Pesetsky (1982b) places a condition on structures with multiple antecedent/trace relations; one must be a sub-tree of the other. For reasons of space we concentrate on the former type of multiple-gap construction. However, we note that it is somewhat unclear where crossing is prohibited. Huang (1982) points out that there are sentences in Chinese such as (i) which have the two LF structures displayed in (ii):

(i) Ni xiang-zhidao [shei mai-le sheme]
you wonder who buy what
(iia) Sheme_j [ni xiang-zhidao [shei_i [t_i mai-le t_j]]]
(iib) Shei_i [ni xiang-zhidao [sheme_j [t_i mai-le t_j]]]

Note that the second structure violates crossing in Chinese, yet the sentence with the indicated interpretation is acceptable. See note 23 for further discussion of LF-movement and its relations to crossing effects.

31 These conditions also apply to parasitic gap constructions. For discussion see Kayne (1983b).

32 This could *not* be reformulated as requiring the ECP to apply at both LF and S-Structure and to be stated entirely in terms of ecs available at that level. The reason is that the ec in (52) meets connectedness requirements at S-Structure. Furthermore, after LF-movement the structure we would obtain is (i), which also meets (50) if we combine the g-projection sets generated by t_i and t_j.

(i) . . . [$_{CP}$ what_i, who_j e_i [$_{IP}$ t_j INFL [$_{VP}$ hid t_i in the closet]]]

Thus, the condition on combining g-projection sets must have information on whether the trace was formed by LF-movement or syntactic movement if it is to be stated in terms of ecs.

33 These judgments are from Kayne (1983b). It appears that some speakers do not find much of an improvement. There is still some question as to why the sentences are not *fully* acceptable given that they meet the ECP as formulated in (50). Furthermore, there appear to be some cases that are not improved even for speakers that follow Kayne. Recall that Lasnik and Saito (1984) appears to accept sentences such as

(i) I'd like to know who said that who bit Bill

However, if we change *who* to *what* the sentence becomes quite a bit worse:

(ii) I'd like to know who said that what bit Bill

Now consider the sentences in (iii):

(iiia) *I'd like to know who what bit
(iiib) *I'd like to know who what bit where

There is no perceptible improvement even when we add another *wh*-operator. This suggests that the amelioration Kayne observed is related to the dialectal variation mentioned with regard to Lasnik and Saito (1984).

34 Fukui (1988) claims that these violations are even more pronounced if we try to move from a relative clause.

35 From Lasnik and Saito (1984, 248).

36 The proper government feature must be treated as indelible, in the sense that a structure marked [–proper government] at S-Structure cannot be rescued by deletion of subsequent material. For example, the *that* complementizer in (64) is arguably not relevant to the structure's LF and so presumably could be deleted. If proper government marking were not indelible, *that* deletion would predict the absence of any *that-t* effects.

37 L&S's discussion of fixed subject violations is somewhat more problematic. The theory developed so far treats adjuncts and subjects on a par as amenable only to antecedent government and therefore disallowing wide scope over a complementizer filled with another *wh*-element. Adjuncts obey this prediction, but subjects in Chinese do not, as shown in (iii)

(i) Ni xiang-zhidao shei mai le sheme
You wonder who buy ASP what

(ii) What(x) [you wonder [who(y) [y bought x]]]

(iii) Who(y) [you wonder [what(x) [y bought x]]]

Since subjects pattern like objects in this regard, L&S claim that they must be subject to *lexical* government and follow Huang (1982) in proposing that INFL in Chinese can function as a lexical governor. Thus antecedent government is irrelevant in (i) and (ii) because the subject and object are both locally properly governed by the verb and INFL respectively. But see section 5 for a discussion of subject/object asymmetries in Chinese Topicalization constructions.

38 Much of this discussion is borrowed from and expands on ideas in Lightfoot and Weinberg (1988).

39 Various extensions of the *Barriers* theory have been explored. For example, Diesing (1992) shows how to account for the unacceptability of extractions from definite NPs. She makes two assumptions: (i) Definites adjoin to VP at LF; (ii) Subjacency applies at LF. By (i), the VP-adjoined definite is a barrier as it is not L-marked. Consequently, IP is a derived barrier. Given (ii), therefore, *wh*-chains with links inside definite NPs violate Subjacency.

40 The notion of what should count as a barrier has occupied the field since Chomsky (1986a). Fukui (1986) and Fukui and Speas (1986) claim that a barriers system should capitalize on the distinction between functional and lexical categories. This is pursued in various ways in Baker and Hale (1990) and Raposo and Uriagereka (1990).

41 This example is from Fukui (1988, 509).

42 This example shows why Chomsky (1986a) must also invoke his "inheritance clause" for *Barriers*. The relative NP is L-marked by the matrix verb. It is not an intrinsic barrier. It is only a barrier by inheritance.

43 These examples were first discussed in Weinberg (1988).

44 As pointed out in Lightfoot and Weinberg (1988), this addition introduces its own problems. It is too strong in that it allows S-Structure as well as LF-movement from subject position:

(i) *Which President did you consider [$_{IP}$ [$_{NP}$ a story about] to be in bad taste.

45 The use of "immediate projection" in the definition of minimality barrier is designed to allow movement from the specifier position in a case like

(i) Which men think that $[_{IP}[_{NP}$ which women's pictures] would be on sale.

Antecedent government of the specifier "which women's" would be blocked by the noun, a closer governor, except that the specifier is only dominated at the NP level, not by the "immediate projection" of the N.

46 As noted in *Barriers*, Barss has pointed out a flaw in this argument given Chomsky's assumption that c-command need not be involved in antecedent government and the use of VP adjunction. This allows the subject trace to first lower to the VP of the embedded clause, antecedent-governing the position, and then raise to the CP, with subsequent deletion of the VP-adjoined trace. One could try to build c-command into the definition of antecedent government, but this drives a further wedge between the theory of movement and government, as pointed out by Lightfoot and Weinberg (1988).

47 Observe that (77) is *not* ambiguous as regards what the potential *proper* governor of the trace in COMP is; only the antecedent is a potential proper governor as the A^0 *okkoteru* does not theta-mark the trace in COMP, so it is not a potential lexical governor for this trace. As such, the structure is not really ambiguous as regards potential proper governors. This fact weakens the stated motivation behind the minimality condition, for the condition seems to be crucial even when there is no ambiguity as regards an element's proper governor.

48 This assumes that the binding theory applies both at LF and before the deletion of the intermediate trace.

49 Super-raising is prohibited in this system as index transfer cannot take place across the intervening CP.

(i) $John_i$ $seems_i$ $[_{CP}$ that $[_{IP}$ it is certain $[_{IP}$ t_i to like ice cream]]]

50 Adjunction of an X^0 to an X^{max} is disallowed, so there is no voiding of the barrier by adjunction.

51 This approach has been generalized and refined by Pollock (1989), Belletti (1990), Kayne (1989b), and Uriagereka (1988).

52 The theory of Generalized Binding originates with Aoun (1981) and is developed in Aoun (1985, 1986).

53 As mentioned, L&S explicitly state that the relevant domains for computing antecedent government is the NP and the clause. Chomsky (1986a) tries to derive this result by allowing adjunction to all maximal projections except NP, IP and CP, i.e. NPs and clauses. In both cases, the domain is specially singled out.

54 A conjunctive theory of the ECP need not claim that (85) applies on the PF side of the grammar. S-Structure is also a possibility, as is LF. We mention several reasons for a PF application of (85) below. For a full discussion see Aoun, Hornstein, Lightfoot, and Weinberg (1987) and Hornstein and Lightfoot (1991), Lightfoot (1992). See Rizzi (1990) for arguments that both conjuncts apply at LF.

55 The idea that if X governs Y then X head-governs the head of Y is due to Belletti and Rizzi (1981).

56 This will include the Agreement marker AGR, subjects of clauses [NP, S] and subjects of NP [NP, NP]. The nominal nature of agreement is commonly assumed. This notion of domain is essentially the one proposed in Chomsky (1981).

57 The properties of *where* and *when* are extensively discussed in Aoun, Hornstein, Lightfoot, and Weinberg (1987). Languages differ as to how these are categorized. English and Chinese seem to treat them like arguments. Thus, within Generalized Binding, their traces are treated as similar to those left by *who* and *what*. These

traces seem more "referential" in a sense discussed below. Aoun (1981, 1985, 1986) supports the intuition concerning referentiality by observing that there exist deictic pronouns for places, times, persons, and things, but not for reasons and manners.

58 We assume that no SUBJECT is accessible to itself. The definition of accessibility also makes reference to the i-within-i principle to allow for the binding of reciprocals and anaphors in picture NPs in embedded subject positions. The current notion that these expressions move at LF no longer makes the i-within-i principle necessary, if we assume that the trace left behind is referential, like the traces of *who* and *what*, and we assume that domination implies c-command, as in Reinhart (1983a). These assumptions suffice to account for the acceptability of the examples in (i).

(ia) The men$_i$ thought that pictures of each other$_i$ were on sale
(ib) They$_i$ thought that pictures of themselves$_i$ were on sale
(ic) Who thought that pictures of who/what were on sale

For discussion see Hornstein and Weinberg (1991).

59 This insight is due originally to Stowell (1981) and Kayne (1981). Similar data hold in the Kobe dialect of Japanese (see Saito (1984)).

60 This assumes a Det N′ analysis for restrictive relative clauses. If we assume that appositive relatives are of the structure [NP Clause] then we can also account for why these forbid complementizer deletion.

(i) This book, *(that) Bill just gave to Mary, is a rare collector's item.

A similar account extends to noun complement constructions if, following Stowell (1981), we give them an analogous structure. Contrast the relative clause (iia) and the noun complement (iib) with respect to complementizer deletion.

(iia) The claim (that) Bill made
(iib) The claim *(that) Bill made a fortune

61 Recall that (85) applies on the PF side of the grammar and so it is not surprising that gapped heads should be ineligible as proper governors. For a discussion of the distinction between movement and deletion gaps see Aoun, Hornstein, Lightfoot, and Weinberg (1987).

That (85) holds on the PF side of the grammar is supported by observations originally made in Saito (1984). He points out that Right Node Raising (RNR) impacts on the possibility of complementizer deletion but not on binding domains (see (89ff)).

(i) John wants and Jim expects [him to win]

In (i), Principle B of the Binding Theory must apply to the structure preceding, where *him* is c-commanded by both *John* and *Jim*, given that it is disjoint from both. Whether the Binding Theory holds at S-Structure or LF, then, there needs to be a condition like (85) that regulates the deletability of complementizers and applies to a level of representation after S-Structure and after RNR has applied, namely to some level of representation on the PF side of the grammar.

Lightfoot (1992) notes that further support for this position is provided in Rizzi (1990, section 2.3). There it is pointed out that reconstruction can feed the binding conditions and antecedent government but not head-government. This follows if the latter is a PF condition while both the former apply at LF. Incidentally, the fact that both antecedent government and binding are subject to reconstruction effects is what we would expect if antecedent government were really binding, as proposed here.

62 These data support the position that head-government should not be an LF condition. For instance, the gapped head receives an interpretation at LF, i.e. it functions "as if" it were really there. Consequently, it is hard to see why gapped heads should not pattern exactly like lexical ones *at LF*.

Note that this analysis ties the gapping of the noun to the thematic interpretation by way of the postnominal trace. This implies that this process should be rather free in the absence of such traces. This seems to be correct as (91a) indicates. Note that it can also carry the reading in which *my mother* refers to the creator of the picture. Other roles are also permitted as (i) indicates:

(ia) Which newspaper is this?
It's yesterday's

63 Similar contrasts hold with verbs:

(ia) It wasn't believed that Bill was smart but it was that Frank was handsome
(ib) *Bill wasn't believed to be smart but Frank was to be handsome

An interesting fact is that if we gap the verb and the auxiliary then these sorts of structures substantially improve:

(ii) Bill was believed to be handsome and Frank to be smart

One possibility is that this more extensive gapping also "removes" the NP-trace and hence (ii) does not run afoul of (85).

64 Note that if we gap *likely* in (92a) we cannot then delete the complementizer, though this is permitted if gapping does not take place.

65 Here "lexical" is meant to contrast with "functional." Note that this same assumption will bring head-movement under (85), at least in the case of V-raising. Verbs raise to I^0 and then to C^0. These are both functional categories and so will be able to properly govern ecs they are coindexed with. This forces head-movement to be extremely local and forbids heads from "skipping" across other heads. (i) is a violation of head-government, given that the functional heads *might* and *have* are not coindexed with the ec. *Been* in Comp is so indexed but it is too far away.

(i) $[_{CP}$ been$_i$ $[_{IP}$ John $[_{I'}$ $[_{I^0}$ might$]$ $[_{VP}$ have $[_{VP}$ t_i $[_{VP}$ arrested$]]]]]]$

66 The technology in Aoun, Hornstein, Lightfoot, and Weinberg (1987) assumes a different phrase structure for the clause. It exploits COMP indexing to get the proper government effects noted here and a doubly filled COMP filter regulates index percolation. The doubly filled COMP filter is here equivalent to the restriction that index transfer is not permitted between a trace and a lexical head.

67 It is unclear whether adjuncts must meet the head-government requirement. Aoun, Hornstein, Lightfoot, and Weinberg (1987) remain agnostic on whether they fall under (85). Rizzi (1990) suggests that they are head-governed by functional heads. Not much seems to hang on either decision. In contrast, there are relatively clear empirical consequences of extending (85) to cover *wh*-traces in COMP. We can accommodate bridge verb effects by saying that only bridge verbs can properly

govern into COMP. This will account for why both complementizer deletion and overt *wh* extraction is not permitted in these contexts in English.

(i) *What did John chortle that Bill ate t
(ii) John chortled *(that) Bill ate a hamburger

In addition, there are reasons to follow Kayne (1981) in assuming that prepositions are not generally proper governors. This assumption, coupled with (85) can account for why it is that syntactic extraction out of adjuncts fails in English.

(iii) Which book did John read a magazine [without PRO reviewing t]

On the assumption that Subjacency must be obeyed in (iii) then there must be an intermediate trace either adjoined to *without* or in a CP position before *PRO.* In either case, this trace will not meet (85), so the extraction should be ill-formed. Note that this should not affect the LF-movement of arguments. As noted in section 2, this appears to be correct.

(iv) Who left the opera without PRO hearing what

68 This accounts for why head-government is irrelevant to LF-movement as L&S point out.

69 The analysis given here differs in detail from the one in Aoun, Hornstein, Lightfoot, and Weinberg (1987). This is because we are not here employing COMP indexing. The technical adjustments we have made to translate into the CP/IP framework is that *wh*s that move at LF adjoin to a *wh*-operator already in CP. We assume that the index of the adjoined structure bears the index of the original *wh*-operator. This prevents the adjoined *wh*-expression from c-commanding, and hence binding, its trace. Several other technical adjustments are surely required and there are other ways to make readjustments, but we will ignore these possibilities here.

70 The logic of this account is identical to the logic that lies behind the *PRO* theorem. In both cases, lack of a domain frees an expression from the strictures of the binding theory.

71 The same logic extends to prohibit adjuncts from extracting out of relative clauses. Bringing noun complements within the purview of this theory, however, is quite a bit more complicated. It involves extending to notion SUBJECT to include the head of a noun complement construction. For discussion see Weinberg (1988). The non-extractability of adjuncts out of adjuncts is also problematic, though recall that the data as regards this process is somewhat ambiguous. If extraction should prove to be impossible, as seems likely, this might be accounted for by having adjuncts be bare IPs. This would prevent movement through COMP and hence always lead to a Principle A violation.

72 The "?" in (100b) is accounted for in terms of Subjacency.

73 See Aoun, Hornstein, Lightfoot, and Weinberg (1987, note 24) for further discussion.

74 Given this assumption, it is unclear how to prevent extraction of adjuncts out of structures such as (i) if adjectives are [+V]:

(i) *How$_i$ did you become [eager [PRO to fix the car t$_i$]]

75 Baker and Hale (1990) extend the relativization to functional and lexical categories. See Uriagereka (1988) for a similar suggestion.

76 From Rizzi (1990, 6). This choice of lexical governors is empirically justified throughout Rizzi's book. One wonders about its conceptual naturalness, though. The class of proper governors now consists of a subset of non-lexical and lexical categories, with no unifying feature. Crucially, tense and agreement, but not C^0, must count as lexical governors in this system.

77 This is Rizzi's (1990) final conclusion. The book actually consists of three different proposals for the ECP. The first chapter explores a disjunctive ECP. The second chapter explores a conjunctive definition with a fairly traditional notion of antecedent government. The third chapter restructures the notion of antecedent government so as to apply in the core case to adjuncts alone.

78 Rizzi's (1990) notion of referentiality is somewhat different in the sense that it is tied to receiving a theta-role. See Rizzi (1990, chapter 3) for details.

79 See Lightfoot (1992) for a discussion of Rizzi's (1990) placement of head-government at LF. See note 60 as well.

80 The notion that only licit A-chains can bear theta-roles is also proposed in Haïk (1986).

81 Traces in both these structures also meet the head-government condition, which is conjunctively applied. The trace of *have* is governed by the inflectional element *will* and the trace of *how* is governed by either *T* or perhaps even *V*.

82 Cinque (1990b) provides a theory of islands that incorporates Rizzi's story into Bounding Theory. Therefore there may be some unification with respect to the theories of antecedent government and movement.

83 These facts are also accounted for in terms of the Minimal Binding Requirement (MBR) advocated by Aoun and Li (1989, 1993). The MBR is very close in spirit and detail to relativized minimality as both focus on the role of the first potential antecedent in determining wellformedness. The MBR requires an ec to be bound by the closest potential antecedent. The MBR also accounts for certain effects first discussed by May (1985):

(i) What did everyone buy
(ii) Who bought everything

May observed that (i) is ambiguous with either *what* or *everyone* taking wide scope. This ambiguity is absent in (ii). It only has the reading where *who* has wide scope. May (1985) traces this to the ECP arguing that adjoining *everything* to IP would induce an ECP violation in Pesetsky's (1982b) terms. Aoun and Li reanalyze these data in terms of the MBR. Were *everyone* to adjoin to IP or CP so as to have scope over *who*, the trace it left behind or the trace of *who* would not be bound by the first potential binder.

Note that Rizzi's minimality requirement does not extend to cover these cases. The traces at issue are theta bearers and so are not subject to antecedent government or minimality.

See Hornstein (1991) for a revision of the MBR within a Generalized Binding framework that extends it to cover island effects in existential *there* constructions.

84 This process is far from moribund. Currently, there are proposals for using the ECP to account for incorporation phenomena, LF head-movement, and clitic placement. See Baker (1988a), Baker and Hale (1990), Kayne (1989b), Cole, Hermon, and Sung (1990), Baltin (1991), and Uriagereka (1988), among many others.

6

Morphosyntax

Randall Hendrick
University of North Carolina at Chapel Hill

Contents

Prelude

The present chapter covers topics in morphosyntax that have a relatively long history of research in Generative Grammar as well as topics that have gained widespread attention only relatively recently. Among the first are compounding, derivation, inflection, cliticization, and causatives. The chapter begins with a discussion of the difficult theoretical question of whether words have internal structure and, to the extent that they do, how their component parts are best characterized. Some theories assume that a word like *refusal* contains two morphological units, the morphemes *refuse* and *al* and that both the form and the meaning of a complex word are composed of the forms and meanings of its component morphemes. Other theories that are discussed assume instead that both the lexicon and morphology are word- or stem-based and that Universal Grammar makes available morphological and/or phonological rules that create new words (or stems) from already existing words (or stems) by applying appropriate operations on the information (syntactic, semantic, syntactic, morphological) associated with the input items.

Related to these questions are the controversies whether there is one component of the grammar (specifically, the lexicon) that is privileged in that it contains all formation operations for new words which would preclude the option of syntactic word formation or whether some types of word formation must apply in the lexicon whereas others can apply in the syntax. Discussed as well is the view that all word formation might be done in the syntax.

The chapter proceeds to discuss the properties of clitics and distinguishes between approaches that treat them syntactically, construct them pre-syntactically in the lexicon, or account for their distribution post-syntactically. In this connection approaches to morphology and syntax in terms of parallel but independent representations are presented as well.

Following treatments of agreement and passive morphology, the chapter sets off on a detailed discussion of the formal, distributional, and argument structure properties of compound and derived nominals. Again we meet lexical, syntactic, and mixed approaches to these types of complex words and the advantages and disadvantages of each kind of approach are brought out. Important topics in this area include the inheritance of argument structures, whether the notion *head* plays a role in morphology and which elements of complex words are heads, and whether parts of words are visible to syntactic operations, e.g. the Binding Theory.

The last section of the chapter deals with the relationship between the morphological and the syntactic properties of derived and compound verbs. Besides causatives, the section deals with noun incorporation and applicatives, which are topics that have only recently received a lot of attention. The issue of the mode of generation and representation of the complex verbs of these constructions (i.e. lexical vs. syntactic) arises here as well.

1 Introduction

1.1 *Preliminaries*

Morphology concerns the structure of words. A theory of morphology will specify a set of morphological primitives and their principles of distribution (or in somewhat different terminology the appropriate rules and representations for this domain). Morphosyntax asks whether the morphological primitives and their principles of distribution are distinct from the primitives and principles needed in syntax. One might answer that morphosyntax is trivial: morphology concerns the structure of words as distinct from syntax that addresses the structure of phrases. On the other hand one could claim that there is some nontrivial interpenetration of morphology and syntax, with syntactic principles determining, perhaps only in part, the structure of words. The point then would be to find a principled answer for the ways that word structure seems to be sensitive to syntactic principles. To put the question in a current and popular formulation, the issue at stake is whether the word is the syntactic "atom" or whether a smaller unit, the morpheme, is.

There is no Principles and Parameters approach to morphology or morphosyntax as such, and the issues to be addressed here cut across all theories of Universal Grammar. For this reason I have not attempted a review of the extensive work published in this domain. Instead I have contented myself with identifying some of the principal areas of research and debate by considering what I take to be representative works.[1] In addition, I have taken a narrow construction of morphosyntax and have completely ignored the phonological implications of the interaction between morphology and syntax. Surely letting phonology care for itself in this fashion is a limitation, since the truth of phonology likely bears on syntactic truth.

When linguists approach morphosyntax they often do so with two cardinal points on their compasses. The first concerns what structure words have, and the second concerns how the structure of words correlates with the structure of the grammar as a whole. It is to these cardinal points I turn in the remainder of this section.[2]

1.2 The Structure of Words

Everyone agrees that at least some words have internal structure. Compounds are good candidates for words with internal structure since a compound like *lighthouse* is composed of two forms that are "free" in the sense that they appear elsewhere as independent words. However, it is less clear what the internal structure of a simple word like *gardens* or *refusal* is. Specifically are there two morphemes here, *garden* and an affix *-s*, that combine compositionally to yield the meaning of the form *gardens*. The question is to what extent such affixal morphology patterns like compounding, as Aronoff (1988) notes.

The response to this question is fraught with descriptive and theoretical obstacles of considerable complexity. One difficulty in an assessment of the similarity of structure in compounds and affixal morphology is pinning down what structure compounds in fact have, a topic we return to in section 5. One might think that the way to make headway on the question of affixes and word structure is to determine what the morpheme is. That the structuralists found this such a vexed question should dispel any illusion we might have about the ease of such a course.

Affixes are commonly taken to be morphemes. The definition of the morpheme as the minimal unit of sound and meaning derives from the post-Bloomfieldian American Structuralists.[3] This view takes the morpheme to be a distributional class that identifies a set of phonological forms in complementary distribution (morphs) that share some aspect of meaning. The lexicon on this view is simply a list of morphemes. A somewhat different view, also advocated by some of the structuralists, takes the morpheme to be a distributional class but denies any necessary relation to meaning. This amounts to saying that the morpheme is not the minimal sign and opens the possibility at least that the lexicon is to be conceived of not as a list of morphemes but a list of words. In current theorizing some researchers, notably Aronoff (1976, 1992) and S. Anderson (1982b) conceive of the lexicon and morphology as word- or stem-based. Inflectional morphology such as the plural in *gardens* does not involve two morphemes but the word *garden* with a plural feature that is spelled out in the appropriate fashion by a phonological rule. The more traditional view that bases the lexicon and morphology on affixes as morphemes is used in generative theory to some advantage by Lieber (1980, 1992), Selkirk (1982), Williams (1981b) and a number of others developing that position. Still another view of morphemes takes them to be the smallest unit of syntax and simply lists the morphs in the lexicon. From this stance a word like *gardens* is broken into two morphemes *garden+s* where *s* is the realization of the PLURAL morpheme. Since the affix is syntactically active in agreement processes and elsewhere, the syntax determines the hierarchical relation of that morpheme in the word; yet that relation is independent of the phonological realization of the affix. Something like this is the view of Chomsky (1965) and Chomsky and Halle (1968); an updated version is defended in Halle (1990) and more recently in Halle and Marantz (1992). In the more traditional view of Lieber (1992) it is the lexical subcategorization properties of the affix alone that determines the hierarchical relation and the phonological shape of the affix is in principle available in that process.

Theories that are morpheme-based will insist that the form *gardens* is composed of two morphemes. Word-based theories however might see only one morphological unit here, on a par with *garden,* the added material being the reflex of a morphological feature [+PLURAL]. At least three considerations could be invoked to justify a structural role for the plural affix. One would be that the plural participates in a hierarchical relation. This is the tack that is taken when the notion head is identified with the selectionally dominant element and an affix is claimed to be the head of the form it adjoins to in this sense. In *refusal,* the affix *-al* might be taken to determine the nominal character of the derived form and thus qualify as its head. A second motivation for structure here would be that some generalization required reference to the string *refuse-al* or *garden-s*. Williams (1981b) invokes both these considerations when he attempts to justify the claim that the right-most morpheme is the head of a word. A third structural argument would be to show that some generalization required that two elements or features have the same distribution and hence behave as a single (structural) unit.

There is by now a rather large generative literature on the morpheme and headedness that rivals its structuralist predecessor in scope and subtlety. Williams's proposal for identifying the right-hand member of a word as its head has been subject to a number of criticisms. A number of counterexamples have been provided in Lieber (1984), Hoeksema

(1985), Thomas-Flinders (1982) and conceptual difficulties have been discussed in Zwicky (1985), Hudson (1987), Hoeksema (1985) and Thomas-Flinders (1982).[4] Efforts have been made to revise the right-hand head rule to meet the challenge of these criticisms. Selkirk (1982) limits the right-hand head rule to non-inflectional morphology. Di Sciullo and Williams (1987) attempt to preserve the basic intuition that morphological heads are determined at least in part by the linear order of morphemes. Their proposal is to relativize the right-hand head rule by offering what appears to be a notational variant of Lieber's (1980, 1983) percolation convention. They suggest relativizing the notion of head to a feature so that one morpheme might be the head for F_1 while another morpheme is the head for F_2. The claim is that the right-most member of a morphological object specified for feature F_n is the head for F_n.[5]

Aronoff (1988) finds this defense of the right-hand head rule unsatisfying. However, on the face of it, the proposal is not implausible. Williams (1982a) has argued that prenominal modifiers generally must have right-hand heads. Further, the percolation convention recalls pied-piping where typically a phrase inherits its [+*wh*] feature from its head; and yet there are instances where a non-head that bears the [+*wh*] feature is sufficient to make an entire phrase behave as though it had that feature. Similar examples play a major role in syntactic theories like GPSG that make extensive use of features and feature percolation; see Gazdar, Klein, Pullum, and Sag (1985).

One can of course accept the various criticisms of the right-hand head rule without giving up the claim that words have morphemes as structural heads.[6] Such a possibility prompts us to ask whether any empirical residue to the notion head remains once we jettison the restriction on linear order. Matthews (1974) suggests that the choice between treatments of inflection as morphemes or as features on words is a matter of taste, implying that they are notational variants. Indeed, theorists that make extensive use of features are often forced to elaborate their views in ways that look remarkably similar to theories positing morphemic heads. S. Anderson (1986, 1992), for example, is led to introduce an element of hierarchy into the verbal agreement features of Georgian to distinguish the features relevant to object agreement from those determining subject agreement. These features are not terminal symbols themselves and do not dominate morphemes. Yet the distance between giving features a bracketing structure and the traditional view of an affix as a morpheme seems small. Surely this murky issue deserves some careful thought and clarification.

I am somewhat optimistic about the ability of further research to discriminate between these conceptions empirically. Halle (1990) argues that there is some reason to doubt the featural approach to inflectional morphology because S. Anderson (1986) has shown that it requires a distinct morphological notion of disjunctive rule application, and this special notion recapitulates the idea of a position that morphemes compete to fill.

Moreover, an inflectional affix might be unspecified for a category feature, allowing a sister constituent to determine that property, and yet the affix could still have a set of other features characteristics of heads. This is the contention of Lieber (1992). If inflectional categories never behave as heads, the morphemic theory is endangered since it appears to have no principled explanation for this fact. Although a thorough cross-linguistic investigation is in order, preliminary evidence suggests that the view of inflectional categories as heads has some plausibility. Breton inflectional affixes, specifically the plural affixes, appear to determine the morphological class of a word in this way.[7] The behavior of the Breton plural parallels the phenomena exhibited by Dutch affixes described in Hoeksema (1985).

The point of view that morphemes are syntactic primitives, bundles of grammatical features ultimately associated with morphs drawn from the lexicon, is quite close to Lieber's (1992) view that all morphs are morphemes and are lexically listed. Marantz (1992) tries to distinguish these two conceptions. He argues that the Potawatomi agreement prefix /k–/ and /n–/ would be treated as distinct morphemes because they are associated with different grammatical features as in (1) and (2).

(1) /k–/, [+2nd person], [____[V . . .]]
(2) /n–/, [+1st person], [____[V . . .]]

On his view, Lieber's framework is unable to capture the generalization that these morphemes are mutually exclusive and compete for the same position. It is for this reason, among others, that Halle and Marantz (1992) borrow from S. Anderson (1986, 1992) the conception of disjunctive rule ordering in morphology. Unlike Anderson, however, they are willing to view bundles of grammatical features as morphemes that are syntactically active, for example, constituting syntactic heads of phrasal projections.

1.3 *The Structure of Words and the Organization of a Grammar*

Before Chomsky (1965) introduced a lexicon to the Standard Theory, all derivational and inflectional morphology was of necessity done syntactically. Chomsky (1970) argued that a conceptually simple and explanatory model of grammar could be attained by keeping the base component (comprised of rewriting rules and a lexicon) and the transformational component distinct (i.e. "modular") and by assigning at least some derived nominals (e.g. *destruction*) to the lexicon rather than allowing them to be derived transformationally. Other nominals, the gerundive nominals (e.g. *singing songs*), were argued to be properly syntactic and non-lexical. The reasons that Chomsky cited for this proposal included the idiosyncratic semantic relation between a verb and its corresponding derived nominal as well as the relative non-productive character of the relation between them.[8] Other relevant considerations were the structural similarity between derived nominals and simple nouns that went unexplained on the transformational analysis. Gerunds, in contrast, are semantically regular, highly productive, and exhibit the internal structure of verb phrases rather than noun phrases.[9] The claim that at least some derived nominals are lexically listed rather than transformationally derived is the "lexicalist hypothesis," a contention so widely accepted that I will refer to it as the lexicalist position.[10]

After we admit the lexical character of some derived nominals like *refusal* we can still ask why derived nominals are lexically listed. One response is to say that the lexicon is the repository of idiosyncratic and unpredictable facts about a language. As a consequence, because the relation between *refuse* and *refusal* is unproductive and semantically idiosyncratic it properly belongs in the lexicon. Let us call this response the weak lexicalist hypothesis. One could of course look for some deeper generalization to explain why *refuse* and *refusal* are unproductive and idiosyncratic, and this leads to a second theoretical position. Some believe to have found an answer to this question by assigning all derivational morphology to the lexicon, or at least nearby in a closely connected module called a morphological component. On this view derived nominals are not transformationally related to their base because they are lexically derived; in contrast inflectional morphology is treated non-lexically. Let us call this second position the "split morphology" hypothesis, following Perlmutter (1988). These two theoretical positions are conceptually distinct and at least in principle have different empirical consequences. The weak lexicalist hypothesis could admit some transformational derivation, whereas that possibility is denied by the split morphology hypothesis.

These positions are typically not distinguished, and some of the important works in this domain can be plausibly read either way. Chomsky (1970) for example can be read either way. Similarly even S. Anderson (1982b) seems somewhat ambiguous on this topic. I say this because Anderson places derivational morphology to a morphological component and inflectional morphology to the syntactic component, yet there is no independent characterization of the derivational/inflectional split. What is inflectional is whatever happens to be syntactically relevant and what is "inflectional" in one language might be classified as derivational in another by this diagnostic.[11] A similar comment could be directed to the distinction between inflection and derivation drawn in Lieber (1992).

There is yet a third variant of the lexicalist position. This view tries to explain why derived nominals are not transformationally related by denying transformations the ability to analyze word internal morphology at all.[12] I will call this view the strong lexicalist hypothesis. It is first advocated in Jackendoff (1972) and is defended most recently and vigorously by Selkirk (1982), Lapointe (1980, 1988) and Di Sciullo and Williams (1987). There are variants of the strong lexicalist hypothesis. Selkirk (1982) and Di Sciullo and Williams (1987) permit syntactic rules to refer to morphological features. Lapointe (1980, 1988) denies that syntactic rules ever refer to anything besides the features that define syntactic categories.

These three ways of developing the lexicalist position limit the scope of morphosyntax. There simply is no morphosyntax if the strong lexicalist hypothesis is correct. Instead there is an important morphological component within the lexicon. If the split morphology hypothesis is right, morphosyntax is a theory of inflectional morphology and the morphological component is devoted to derivational morphology. The weak lexicalist hypothesis gives the widest berth to morphosyntax, allowing it to effect morphology generally regardless of its classification in inflectional or derivational terms, although it still places idiosyncratic and unproductive relations in the lexicon. The morphological component is weakened correspondingly. Linguists working within the weak lexicalist hypothesis are divided as to whether a distinct set of morphological principles are still required (cf. Baker (1988a), Sproat (1985a)) or whether syntactic principles suffice to explain the totality of what travels under the rubric of morphology (cf. Lieber (1992)).

2 Clitics

Clitics have the distinguishing property that they are phonologically dependent on an adjacent "host" morpheme, thus failing to constitute an independent word, yet they seem, at least on the face of it, to be syntactically active. Sometimes the unique character of clitics is captured by distinguishing the "syntactic" and the "phonological" word. In free morphemes like *garden* these two notions coincide. In clitics however we encounter syntactic "words" that are phonological "non-words."[13] It is common, following Zwicky (1977), to distinguish simple clitics and special clitics. Simple clitics like the English contracted auxiliary lean on their host and preserve the linear order of their non-cliticized counterpart.[14]

(3) Jane is happy
(4) Jane's happy

Special clitics not only lean on a host but appear in a position other than the one favored by their non-cliticized counterpart. The French clitic *en* offers an example of a special clitic.

(5) Max a lu la préface de ce livre
Max has read the preface of this book
"Max has read the preface of this book"

(6) Max en a lu la préface
Max of-it has read the preface
"Max has read the preface of it"

The bulk of syntactic work on clitics has targeted special clitics. Three general stances have been taken to these clitics. One treats them syntactically, a second constructs them pre-syntactically in the lexicon, and a third accounts for their distribution post-syntactically.

In early generative studies clitics were taken to be fundamentally syntactic. It was recognized early on by Perlmutter (1971) that clitics did not form a single grammatical class: some languages have pronominal clitics, some languages have AUX-clitics, still others have determiner clitics, and so on. While little attention was paid to the phrasal status of clitics, pronominal clitics were taken to be pronominal NPs that in some languages were subject to special syntactic rules accounting for their placement. This can be seen in the classic studies of clitics in Perlmutter (1971) and Kayne (1975). There is a large literature that continues this tradition of syntactic analysis, and we will touch on its development in a Principles and Parameters setting below. For the moment it is sufficient to identify this general line of thought as an attempt to deny that clitics have any special properties other than their obvious phonological ones and account for their distribution by independently necessary syntactic principles. It is generally recognized (cf. S. Anderson (1988b)) that, of all the phenomena loosely labeled morphological, clitics are the best candidates for morphosyntax in that they appear most amenable to syntactic analysis.

Yet while syntactic treatments of cliticization have a venerable tradition, other non-syntactic approaches exist and have substantial influence. One such approach grows out of the work of Zwicky (1977), Kaisse (1985), Klavans (1985), and Nevis (1985). These linguists develop a special set of constraints or parameters defining the behavior of clitics. Klavans (1985) has been particularly influential in this regard. For Klavans, individual clitics are classed in a language-particular fashion by the phrase relevant to their positioning, the anchor that hosts the clitics (which can either be a head of phrase or a left phrasal boundary or a right phrasal boundary), the left to right order of the clitic relative to its anchor and the direction that it leans phonologically. The Australian language Ngiyambaa, for example, has a set of clitics exemplified by **=ndu** in (7) that, Klavans argues, are positioned relative to S, that must appear after their hosting anchor (the left phrasal boundary in this case), and that is an enclitic to that domain. In this way they favor the second position in a sentence familiar from Wackernagel's Law.

(7) girbadja=yanbi:=ndu mamiyi
kangaroo=ADD=2.NOM catch.PAST
"As for a kangaroo, you caught one"

(8) nhila pama-ng nhingu pukpe-wu ku?a=ngu wa:
he-NOM man-ERG him.DAT child-DAT dog=DAT.3SNG give
"The man gave the dog to the child"

(9) nhila pama-ng nhingu pukpe-wu ku?a wa:=ngu
he-NOM man-ERG him.DAT child-DAT dog give=DAT.3SNG
"The man gave the dog to the child"

The clitic **=ngu** from another Australian language Nganchara in examples (8)–(9) on the other hand is positioned with respect to the S domain but is anchored by the right-most phrasal boundary of that category. Because the clitic is unspecified as to whether it positions itself to the left or right of its anchor both (8) and (9) are grammatical. It is significant that clitics are positioned relative to phrases. This claim, if true, would make clitics recalcitrant to a syntactic movement analysis, at least if one accepts the typology of movement operations offered in Baltin (1982) or Chomsky (1986a), where heads cannot be adjoined to phrases. In a deep sense clitics begin to look like phrasal affixes (cf. S. Anderson (1988a) and Carstairs (1981)) subject to morphological principles distinct from recognized syntactic ones. A variant of this view is outlined in Kaisse (1985). What is perhaps unexplained in this approach is why a clitic takes a phrasal boundary to determine its landing site but can only position itself with respect to the word closest to that boundary and not the boundary itself. /phonology?

Sadock (1991) proposes a theory of grammar, dubbed autolexical syntax, in which there are a number of independent levels of structure. These levels, which include a syntactic and a morphological level, are not related derivationally but there must be a relation between the levels that satisfies at least one of two general conditions. One condition (the Linearity Constraint) requires that two lexical items projected on two levels have the same linear order on both levels. The second condition (the Construction Integrity Constraint) requires that a lexical item A that has a sister B on one level can at another level have a different sister C only if there is a dominance relation between B and C. For example structures like (10) where on the syntactic level the Latin conjunction *que* is NP initial but on the morphological level it ends up attached to an adjectival complement of the noun.

(10)

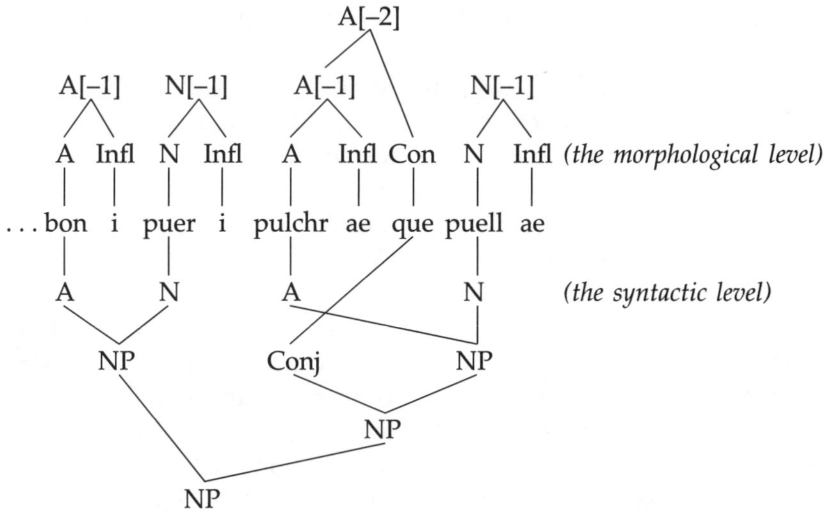

This form is legitimate because although it fails to satisfy the Linearity Constraint (the linear order of the elements Conj, A on the syntactic level is distinct from that on the morphological level), it manages to satisfy the Construction Integrity Constraint since Conj is a sister to the NP on the syntactic level that dominates the element A that it becomes a sister to at the morphological level. Sadock's proposal resembles a number of other proposals for generating parallel structures, such as those offered for Romance causatives in Zubizaretta (1985), and Di Sciullo and Williams (1987), or the verb movement structures explored in Haegeman and van Riemsdijk (1986). Sadock (1991) argues that the autolexical treatment of clitics is empirically equivalent to Klavans's theory.

The autolexical syntax appears to be simultaneously too weak and too strong when measured against the French clitic *en*. It is too weak in that it is unable to give a principled explanation for the fact that the clitic cannot be separated from the NP it modifies by an indefinite number of NPs, i.e. it can be separated by at most one NP.[15] Contrast (11) with (12).

(11) Max en$_i$ a lu [$_{NP}$ la préface [e]$_i$]
Max of-it has read the preface
"Max has read the preface of it"

(12) *j'en$_i$ ai lu [$_{NP}$ la critique de [$_{NP}$ la préface [e]$_i$]]
I of-it have read the critique of the preface

The proposal is too strong in that it is unable to account for the distribution of *en* in raising to subject structures. Ruwet (1972) points out that *en* appears on the embedded verb in raising to subject structures.

(13) la porte de la cathédrale semble être fermée
the door of the cathedral seems to-be closed

(14) la porte semble en être fermée
the door seems of-it to-be closed

(15) *la porte en semble être fermée
the door of-it seems to-be closed

(14) appears to violate both the Linearity Constraint (*en* should be adjacent to the noun *porte* which it modifies) and the Construction Integrity Constraint (*en* does not dominate *semble* which is adjacent to *porte*) yet it is grammatical. (15) obeys the Linearity Constraint (*en* and *porte* are adjacent) and is ungrammatical nonetheless.

Marantz (1988a, 1988b) and Sproat (1988a) develop a particularly interesting theory of clitics that resembles Klavans's in being non-syntactic and in giving special prominence to positioning clitics relevant to phrases. Like Sadock they do not identify the syntactic morpheme and the phonological morpheme; rather morphemes pair these dual representations. However, the two representations are subject to a tighter correspondence. The interest of this theory of clitics is that it offers a generalization between the behavior of clitics, their preference for second position (rather than, say, third position) and the "bracketing paradoxes" discussed in section 5 where there is some syntactic reason for bracketing a word like *ungrammaticality* as in (16) but phonological reason for bracketing it otherwise as (17).

(16) [[un grammatical] ity]
(17) [un [grammatical ity]]

By bringing together these phenomena, Marantz's and Sproat's treatment of clitics diverges from Klavans's and Sadock's theories. S-Structure, in Marantz's view, encodes only hierarchical relations. All adjacency relations are imposed on S-Structure in the mapping to Phonological Form. The operation responsible for adjacency is understood to be associative but not commutative.[16] In addition, the Projection Principle is extended into the phonological side of the grammar requiring that a hierarchical relation be preserved in the mapping of S-Structure to Phonological Form, although Marantz allows a hierarchical relation to be traded for (or expressed by) an adjacency relation at Phonological Form. To the extent that prefixes and suffixes depend on an adjacency relation to a stem they are able to be rebracketed, and it is this rebracketing that produces the so-called "bracketing paradoxes." If a clitic like the English possessive *'s* is made adjacent at Phonological Form to a phrase boundary it can then be rebracketed to appear inside that phrase again by associativity. Finally, if a clitic is affixed to a head (by the operation Morphological Merger) it is claimed to be able to appear either as a proclitic or an enclitic.[17] What is ruled out is clitics that disturb an adjacency relation: for example a clitic that has an adjacency relation with X will not appear in the structure X]*[Y* CL* Z where Y also has an adjacency relation with Z.[18] In this way a preference for second position comes about. This treatment of cliticization explains why the Papago AUX clitic appears in second position in (18).

(18) [$_{V'}$ pi o iam-hu cikpan] g Huan
NEG AUX there work ART John
"John is not working there"

Sproat (1988a) points out that it is not obvious that the preference for second position is a consequence of the mapping from S-Structure to Phonological Form since verb-second phenomena exist in German and Breton and this preference of verbs is presumably syntactic.[19] He recognizes that cliticization in Warlpiri and Serbo-Croatian, which show a preference for second position, is syntactic as well. Typically such second position effects are achieved by raising a verb or clitic to C with another element to the specifier of CP, leaving the element in C in second position. Nevertheless, the success of the Phonological Form mapping at explaining the behavior of the Papago clitic auxiliary is impressive and may not be easily duplicated by syntactic movement since Sproat claims (citing Pranka (1983)) that the Papago negative *pi* in

(18) is unable to escape V′ and there is no apparent syntactic rationale for such a restriction. If the syntax is unhelpful in positioning the Papago negative, it seems equally true that the phonological mapping analysis fails to give an illuminating account to the placement of the French clitic *en* (or its Italian counterpart *ne*). On the surface it would thus seem unlikely that restrictions on the mapping to Phonological Form will explain all the properties of clitics, and that those properties have no single location or statement in a grammar, emerging instead from statements spread throughout several components of the grammar.

Grimshaw (1982) gives a lexical account for the distribution of the French reflexive clitic pronoun, *se*. In Grimshaw's treatment clitics are licensed in a preverbal syntactic structure by a phrase structure rule. The pronominal properties of the clitics then allow them to serve as the object of an appropriate transitive verb. Reflexive clitics however are not pronominal in this sense; instead they are the reflex of a lexical function that alters the argument structure of a verb, changing it from a transitive to an intransitive form. However that may be, it remains unclear whether the lexical approach can generalize in a direct way to account for the distribution of the prepositional clitic *en*, or the appearance of the clitic on auxiliary verbs.[20]

The syntactic approach to clitics has developed in two main directions. One view takes the clitic to have moved from its D-structure position via move alpha. More concretely cliticization is an instance of head-to-head-movement, constrained by the Head Movement Constraint of Travis (1984) or the ECP as developed in Chomsky (1986a). This view, first suggested in Baltin (1982), has been extended most successfully in Kayne's work on Romance. A second line of thought treats the clitics as generated in place by the base component and standing in some relation to the position typically occupied by non-clitic arguments (Jaeggli (1982), Borer (1984a), Aoun (1985), Suñer (1988), Dobrovie-Sorin (1990)). Most often this position takes the form of treating the clitic as an agreement marker (Borer (1984a), Suñer (1988)) identifying a phonologically null pronominal in argument position. Both of these lines of development deny any special syntactic status to clitics, and position clitics relative to heads of phrases rather than relative to phrasal boundaries.

It is extremely difficult to distinguish the clitic and agreement analyses.[21] One would think that the clitic analysis, because it involves movement, would entail a gap in argument position, while the agreement approach would allow another NP to co-occur with it. For that reason a considerable body of work has emerged on so-called clitic doubled structures, structures that contain both a clitic and a coindexed lexical NP (e.g. . . . $CLITIC_i$ . . . NP_i . . .) as illustrated by the Spanish (19).[22]

(19) Marta le$_i$ dió un beso a Juan$_i$
Marta him gave a kiss to Juan
"Marta gave a kiss to Juan"

On the movement analysis, since one expects the clitic to co-occur with a gap, one might not expect to find clitic-doubling structures. However, clitic-doubling constructions might reasonably involve inserting an extra clitic pronoun. In Kayne (1984), such an analysis is given to the French Complex Inversion structure, a structure where a lexical subject co-occurs with a subject clitic, as exemplified in (20).

(20) Pourquoi les chats ont-ils une telle faim?
why the cats have-they a such hunger
"Why are the cats so hungry?"

On the agreement analysis, one expects such doubling, and it is constructions which lack such doubling that are problematic. One could explain the absence of doubling by appealing to various syntactic properties of the clitic. Jaeggli (1982), following a suggestion of Kayne's, proposes that the clitic absorbs Case; this leads to the prediction that doubling should only appear in structures with an added Case assigner to satisfy the Case requirements of the added lexical NP; thus in (19) the preposition *a* is inserted to provide *Juan* with Case. Aoun (1985) suggests that the clitic absorbs the theta-role that the lexical NP would require, predicting that any doubled lexical NP in clitic-doubling constructions should behave as an adjunct. Suñer (1988) attributes the properties of the clitic-doubling construction to a requirement that the clitic and its double match in grammatical features. Much of the difference between these conceptions concerns how *wh*-movement interacts with clitic doubling, and the situation is complicated by substantial variation even among the Romance languages. See Dobrovie-Sorin (1990).

Everett (1989) synthesizes the various syntactic approaches to clitics to produce a typology. Clitics are classified as to whether they require Case or not and whether they require a theta-role or not. Clitics that require both Case and theta-roles are clitics of the standard French type. Clitics that require Case but not thematic roles are the clitic-doubling constructions familiar in Romance and other languages such as Yagua. Clitics demanding a theta-role but not Case are formatives that appear to change the argument structure of a verb like the English passive *-en* that prevents an agent theta-role from being assigned to [NP,IP]. Clitics that are insensitive to both theta-roles and Case are similar to the English agreement elements.

The behavior of subject–verb agreement in English tempts us to reserve the term *agreement* for elements that are insensitive to theta-roles and, because they are not arguments, insensitive to notions of binding relevant to the Binding Theory or theories of quantification such as the Bijection Principle (cf. Koopman and Sportiche (1982/3)). Binding would then emerge as a diagnostic for whether a particular formative was an instance of agreement or a clitic.[23]

Another way to distinguish the movement and agreement analyses would be to show that the relevant structures exhibit a sensitivity to syntactic principles typical of movement. The Subjacency Condition and the ECP seem to be reasonable diagnostics.[24]

I have already mentioned the importance of Baltin's (1982) suggestion that clitics are positioned by movement of a head to another head position. There is some good reason to believe that the placement of the clitic *en* is syntactic. Van Riemsdijk and Williams (1986) note that the cliticization of *en* obeys the Subjacency condition. Thus, the sentence in (12) repeated as (22) is ungrammatical where *en* is related to an empty category embedded within two bounding nodes.

(21) Max en_i a lu $[_{NP}$ la préface $[e]_i]$
Max of-it has read the preface
"Max has read the preface of it"

(22) *j'en_i ai lu $[_{NP}$ la critique de $[_{NP}$ la préface $[e]_i]]$
I of-it have read the critique of the preface

Furthermore, Couquaux (1981) shows that *en* can float off subjects just in unaccusative structures, parallel to what Burzio (1986) argues is true for the corresponding Italian clitic. Thus, the grammaticality of (23) comes from the application of head-movement of the clitic in the D-structure (24) containing a small clause. The ungrammaticality of (25) is due to a failure of c-command and proper government of the relevant trace.

(23) la préface en est trop flatteuse
the preface of-it is too flattering

(24) [e] est $[_{AP}$ [la préface en] trop flatteuse]

(25) *l'auteur en espère devenir célèbre
the author of-it hopes to-become famous

(26) [l'auteur $[e]_i$] [en_i espère [PRO devenir célèbre]]

Kayne (1989b) has continued this project of assimilating the placement of Romance clitics to head-movement and shows that it correlates with other syntactic generalizations.

Italian but not French allows "clitic climbing," the ability of a clitic to escape its D-structure clause.

(27) Gianni li vuole vedere
Gianni them wants to-see
"Gianni wants to see them"
(28) *Jean les veut voir
Jean them wants to-see

Kayne correlates this difference with three other seemingly independent differences between Italian and French: (i) Italian but not French is a null subject language, as (29) shows, and (ii) Italian but not French allows adverbs to intervene between clitics and infinitivals as in (30), and (iii) Italian allows clitics to be postverbal in infinitives but French does not, as illustrated in (31)–(32).

(29) piove (Italian)
*pleut (French)
rains
(30) *Jean a promis de les bien faire (French)
Jean has promised for/to them well do
(31) Parlargli sarebbe un errore (Italian)
to speak-him would be a mistake
(32) *Parler-lui serait une erreur (French)
to-speak-him would be a mistake

Kayne reduces these phenomena to how strong the inflectional I node is: in Italian it is strong in the sense of being an L-marker and voiding the barrierhood of the VP. This allows null subjects (as discussed in chapter 4) in examples such as (29), permitting verb raising over VP-adjoined adverbs to I in infinitives, and clitic movement to I in infinitives as in (31). The French I is weak and does not L-mark its VP in infinitives; as a result, raising of verbs and clitics out of VP is precluded. Since only in Italian is the VP not a barrier, only in Italian can a clitic climb to escape its clause.[25]

The behavior of clitic climbing is important to anyone interested in understanding the nature of cliticization. To the extent that clitic climbing shows syntactic properties, as Kayne argues, it would seem appropriate to subsume it under Move-α. The debate whether clitics are moved pronominals or base-generated agreement markers is in danger of being overtaken by recent work surveyed in chapter 1 that has suggested recognizing agreement as a distinct structural head of phrase, AGR. If that view is correct, it would be equally possible to dislocate

AGR or a pronominal by Move-α. The debate between the clitic pronoun and agreement analyses will not be able to appeal to movement as a distinguishing property but will need to look elsewhere, perhaps in the interaction of agreement with theta theory and Binding Theory to distinguish the two conceptions.

I have been focusing attention on special clitics. Simple clitics have received somewhat less attention, but they essentially raise the same issues and evoke similar responses that special clitics do. The contraction of the English auxiliary is given a post-syntactic treatment in Kaisse (1985), and a prosodic explanation in Selkirk (1984). Shlonsky (1990) argues that the Hebrew complementizer *se*, which is a simple clitic, adjoins syntactically to an adjacent inflected verb because it interacts with the ECP and subject extraction.

As Di Sciullo and Williams (1987) observe, it is hard to escape the conclusion that all versions of the lexicalist position need to treat at least some of the elements traditionally identified as clitics non-lexically. This is true because clitics like *en* can appear on hosts that they are not complements or specifiers of. On the common assumption that lexical operations are local in the sense that they only effect arguments of the lexical item, clitics require a non-lexical account. Moreover, we can add to this consideration our own observation that these clitics seem sensitive to syntactic principles like the ECP and the Subjacency condition. It remains unclear whether some clitics such as the simple clitics and perhaps some special clitics (such as Marantz's and Sproat's Papago example), are also positioned by principles mapping S-Structure to Phonological Form. Because syntactic treatments of cliticization have considerable appeal, syntactic cliticization becomes in many ways a yard stick to measure syntactic accounts of word structure.

3 Agreement

Until recently the role of agreement in Government and Binding Theories has been rather limited. In Chomsky (1981) agreement is taken to be a feature [± AGR] that is in close association with the feature [± TENSE]. These features together constitute the inflectional node I(NFL). The feature AGR is syntactically operative, interacting with both Binding Theory and Case Theory. AGR is responsible for assigning the Case to the subject. In addition it helps determine a governing category for the purposes of the Binding Theory by serving as an accessible SUBJECT.

The agreement relation is standardly taken to be related to anaphoric processes more generally, and for this reason it is formalized as a relation of coindexing. This convention recalls the use of indices in the Binding Theory that determines the anaphoric properties of pronouns in sentence grammar. There is some speculation whether this indexing is induced by all agreement inflection or just agreement with person (and number) features (cf. Borer (1984a)). By the same token, the question has been raised whether the indexing relation is the same type involved in other anaphoric relations or whether it is distinct. If agreement is the same relation, one would formalize it as the same process of coindexing represented by subscripts, but if it is a different process, one might use coindexing by superscripts to distinguish the process. Chomsky (1981) treats agreement with superscripts in part because it fails to serve as an antecedent for the Binding Theory. Yet this concern can be avoided if we assume that I is a non-argument position and the Binding Theory refers to binding only by arguments. Safir (1987) argues that facts about the distribution of expletives can be achieved by using the same mechanism or indexing employed in other anaphoric relations. Borer (1986a) presents further arguments for the same conclusion.[26]

As our discussion in the preceding section revealed, it is difficult to distinguish agreement from clitic pronouns. There we observed examples of elements traditionally identified as clitics being analyzed as agreement markers. It is worth noting in passing here that there are also instances of agreement markers that some have suggested are in fact clitics. In the Celtic languages strong (or synthetic) person and number agreement is in complementary distribution with overt NPs. This fact of distribution leads S. Anderson (1982b), Rouveret (1990), and Baker and Hale (1990) to treat agreement in these languages as an incorporated or cliticized pronoun. This view is criticized in Jensen and Stong-Jensen (1984), Stump (1984), Hendrick (1988), and Andrews (1990). McCloskey and Hale (1984) and Andrews (1990) offer a lexical account for the Celtic pattern of agreement that employs the notion of morphological blocking from Aronoff (1976), while Hendrick (1988) suggests that other syntactic principles such as the Avoid Pronoun Principle and the ECP interact to give agreement its distribution. This debate arises in part because of the anaphoric properties of agreement, and one of the crucial issues is whether the agreement marker has the binding properties of pronominals. S. Anderson (1982b) for example argues that the Breton agreement affix behaves as a pronominal heading an A-chain, and Stump (1984) and Hendrick (1988) argue that the agreement affix is insensitive to the Binding Theory. The same issue is raised in the context of other theories of universal grammars; see for example the discussion of Chichewa agreement in Bresnan and Mchombo (1987) or Arabic agreement in Fassi Fehri (1988).

Superficially at least one can point to examples of agreement between a head and any of the positions admitted by X-bar theory. A proper theory of agreement would place some empirical limits on what could and could not be a natural agreement relation. However such a theory has been slow to emerge, although the situation appears to be changing currently. One path attempts to restrict agreement to a particular structural relation.[27] In Chomsky (1986a) heads agree with their specifiers or with their complements. But even more restrictive hypotheses are possible. Chomsky (1986a) has explored the idea that functional categories C and I are regular in terms of X-bar theory and constitute heads of phrases. The subject NP emerges from this analysis as the specifier of IP. Koopman (1987) posits that all agreement relations are SPEC-head agreement. This proposal certainly makes sense for subject–verb agreement. Current research aims to assess whether it generalizes successfully to object agreement where it is less traditional to think of an object as a specifier and where some languages identify classes of objects (e.g. specific and non-specific) that behave differently for agreement purposes.

Chomsky's treatment of verb inflection requires some syntactic operation to position the inflection on the verb that ultimately hosts it on the surface. Others have accomplished the same task with syntactic features that affix to the verb. See, for example, S. Anderson (1988a) or Williams (1981b), who take similar positions but for different reasons. That inflectional features might head a syntactic phrase of their own runs counter to the spirit of either the strong lexicalist hypothesis or to that version of the split morphology hypothesis that denies inflection has any structural relation in words, let alone sentences.

Most of the agreement phenomena that have been examined involve a controller of the agreement position in an A-position. Georgopoulos (1985) and Chung and Georgopoulos (1988) have shown however that the distribution of realis/irrealis mood in Palauan correlates with whether a subject or non-subject is extracted.[28] Irrealis is reserved for non-subject gaps. In Georgopoulos's view the realis/irrealis alternation functions as a type of A-bar agreement. The Palauan system recalls the situation in Catalan described by Picallo where the subjunctive (irrealis) does not allow long-distance extraction of subjects though indicative (realis) does. Haïk (1990) attempts to explain the distribution of irrealis and its variation cross-linguistically by integrating INFL into Binding Theory with the variation in the distribution of irrealis stemming from whether INFL is pronominal, anaphoric, and so on. Unlike Georgopoulos, the distribution of irrealis for Haïk is not a fact of agreement but of binding and mood.[29]

4 Passive Morphology

The treatment of the English passive sketched in Chomsky (1981) gives the characteristic morphology of the passive participle an essential role in making NP-movement both possible and necessary.

(33) Jane$_i$ is believed [t$_i$ to be crazy]

The passive, it is claimed, fails to assign objective Case, making NP movement necessary, and fails to theta-mark the subject, making NP movement possible. What is it about the passive verb that leads to this constellation of properties? One view expressed in different ways in Chomsky (1981), Marantz (1984), Bresnan (1982b), is that the passive participle is lexically formed and in the process loses its ability to theta-mark the subject, its external argument. For Bresnan, this is the consequence of lexical rules that change the argument structure of a verb. Marantz on the other hand denies that lexical operations have the power to alter argument structures. His passive affix is lexically listed not to project a logical subject. When it becomes the head of the passive participle by affixation to the verb, this property of lacking a logical subject predominates. In Chomsky and Marantz's view, Burzio's Generalization (Burzio (1986)) then insures that the verb is not a Case assigner either.

This account, which gives a role to the lexical formation of the passive participle, can be contrasted with the view advocated in Jaeggli (1986), Baker (1988a), and Baker, Johnson, and Roberts (1989). The position of these latter studies is that the passive affix *-en* is itself assigned the verb's external theta-role and makes it unavailable for assignment to the subject position. Baker (1988a) argues that the passive affix receives the external theta-role because it is a structural subject, being generated in INFL, and attempts to justify the claim by showing that the affix is active in both binding relations, (34), and control relations, (35).

(34) Such a privilege cannot be kept to oneself
(35) It was decided to shave oneself

The *by*-phrase on this account doubles the agent theta-role assigned to the affix. Baker further assumes that a category cannot assign Case to itself. Hence the passive affix cannot receive Case in INFL but must get Case from V. This gives an explanation for Burzio's Generalization. Baker's treatment is thoroughly syntactic: there is a syntactic motivation for what makes movement possible and a syntactic motivation for what makes movement necessary. Baker, Johnson, and Roberts (1989) pursue this view arguing in the spirit of Postal (1971) that the affix *-en* interacts with Binding Theory, showing weak crossover effects.

If the passive affix is syntactically a subject it should serve as an antecedent for binding and for control. Yet the English examples cited above seem rather limited, and they quickly degenerate if they do not involve generic statements.

(36) *It was decided to shave himself/yourself
(37) Such a privilege cannot be kept to ?herself/*each other

Moreover, the resistance of subject control verbs to passivization (Visser's Generalization) is well known.[30] In contrast to English, the "passive" in North Russian described in Timberlake (1976) behaves unambiguously as if it was a structural subject. Its passives permit reflexives readily, control **PRO** with ease, and interact with Burzio's Generalization to license Case on a direct object without forcing movement to subject position, resulting in transitives that have the appearance of "impersonal passives."

(38) *Binding*
Bylo zapisanos'v skolu-to u menja
was-3.n registered.ps.prt.-REFL in school by me
there was signing myself up at school by me
"It has been signed up by me at school"

(39) *Passives and Control of Infinitive*
U nego bylo vzjatos' skosit' gectar
by him was-3.n taken.ps.prt.-REFL to mow lawn
by him was undertaken to mow the lawn

(40) *Impersonal Passive*
S molodyx god vezde zito
with young years everywhere live-ps.prt.
there's been living everywhere since youth

The fact that the passive in North Russian seems more active syntactically leads Marantz (1988b) to insist on a difference between the English and North Russian passive: the former is lexically formed and unable to project an external theta-role, the latter assigns its external theta-role to the passive affix which behaves generally as a structural subject. Baker's UTAH[31] leads him, in Marantz's view, to obscure the differences between the two languages, in an attempt to treat the agent-external argument in a uniform way cross-linguistically.

The objection that the English construction in (36)–(37) is more limited than the North Russian construction is less decisive perhaps than it appears at first glance. Rizzi's work on Italian null objects shows that pronominals can be restricted to a generic or arbitrary reference in a way that is superficially similar to the interpretation claimed for the passive affix. In any event it is worth noting the existence of languages such as North Russian that offer plausible candidates of passive affixes that are syntactically active, as in Baker's analysis, even if one chooses not to count English *-en* among them.

There is some reason to reconsider the putative link between the passive morphology and Case marking that Burzio's Generalization expresses. The behavior of Ukrainian (Sobin (1985)), Norwegian (Hestvik (1986)), Breton (Hendrick (1988)) and Chichewa (Bresnan and Kanerva (1989)) all challenge this traditional account of the link between the passive morphology and Case marking. For example, Hestvik (1986) shows that Norwegian verbs can assign Case even in the passive.[32]

(41) Bordet$_j$ ble laft en duk pa t$_j$
the-table was put a cloth on

Such examples argue against saying, with Baker (1985), that the passive affix is assigned Case, or with Marantz that the passive morpheme is unable to assign objective Case since if it did *en duk* would violate the Case filter. Hestvik (1986), Borer (1986a), Hendrick (1988), and Bresnan and Kanerva (1989) all offer modifications of Burzio's Generalization that make the necessity of NP movement not an issue of Case theory but an issue of the fact that clauses must have subjects in some sense. The English passive involves movement of the object because there is no other way to provide a subject. The Norwegian facts show that when other elements can appear in subject position the object is free to remain in its D-structure position. Åfarli (1989), however, attempts to reconcile the Norwegian facts with the general spirit of Baker's analysis by parameterizing whether the passive morpheme requires Case. The Norwegian affix does not make such a requirement allowing the verb to Case-mark even in the passive.

5 Compound and Derived Nominals

5.1 Synthetic Compounds

Let us limit our attention in this section to the behavior of compounds comprised of two nominals. Compounds, as I indicated in section 1, are generally recognized to have internal structure. There is a debate in the literature on what that structure is, however. Williams (1981b) points out that there are phonological reasons for assigning *hydroelectricity* the bracketing [*hydro* [*electricity*] although if one thinks about the meaning of the compound one might want to assign the structure [[*hydro electric*] *ity*]. Such "bracketing paradoxes," as they have come to be called, can be resolved in a number of ways. One can deny that compounds have a compositional semantic structure, as Williams (1981b) does, making do with the phonological bracketing exclusively.[33] This requires some mechanism for capturing the notion-related word, and Williams offers such a device, although it is criticized in Thomas-Flinders (1982) and Hoeksema (1985). Alternatively, one can maintain the compositionality of the meaning of compounds and question the phonological bracketing, as Fabb (1988) and Hoeksema (1985) do. Let us proceed here on the assumption that these paradoxes are more than illusory.

Compounds such as *doorknob* or *coffee pot,* which are composed of two underived (or primary) nouns, are ubiquitous in English and there are no apparent limitations to creating new parallel examples. Let us call these root compounds. It is possible to distinguish a second class of compounds such as *truck driver,* typically called synthetic compounds, in which one of the members is a derived category. In this example both constituents of the compound may appear elsewhere in the language as free forms, but this is not true of all synthetic compounds. Sometimes one member of a synthetic compound may not appear as a free form in the language, e.g. *red haired – *haired.*

One of the principal issues in the discussion of compounds is whether root and synthetic compounds should be given a uniform structure, like (42), or whether synthetic compounds have a structure like (43) with root compounds having the structure [N N] of (42). A third possibility is to embrace both structures: Pesetsky (1985) could assign both structures to synthetic compounds with (42) as its S-Structure and (43) being its derived structure at LF after the affix is raised by QR. Or one could take (42) to be the structure of the compound at Phonological Form with (43) its structure at S-Structure, as Sproat (1985a) or Marantz (1988b) do.[34] Lieber (1992) takes the surface structure of synthetic compounds to be as in (42), suggesting that they derive by leftward N^0 movement, from a D-structure like (43) with a post-verbal complement.

(42)

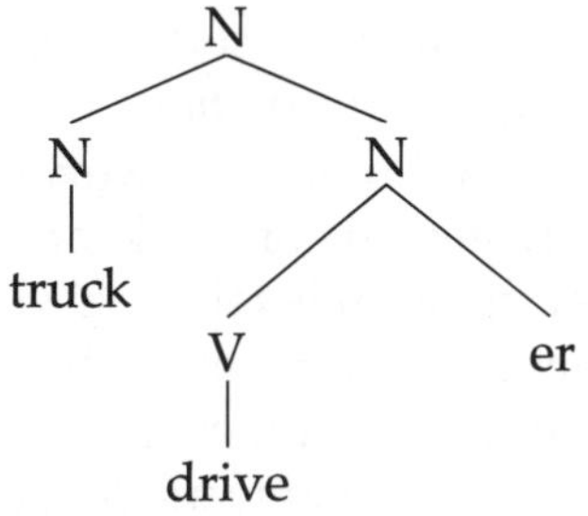

(43)

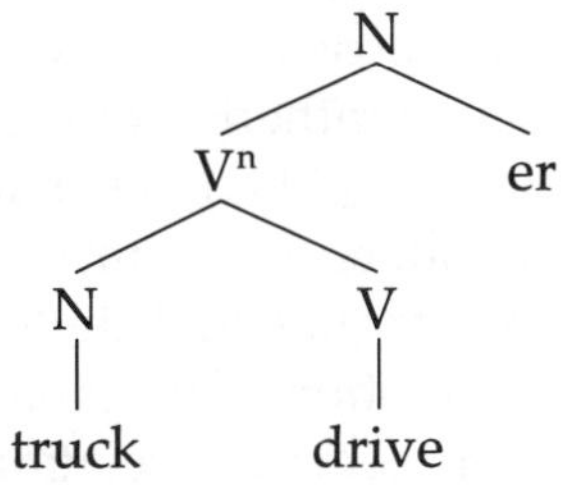

Synthetic compounds are apparently subject to more restrictions than root compounds. For example, Lieber (1983) reports a contrast between *peacemaker* and **peacethinker*. The impossible compound *peacethinker* derives, Lieber suggests, from the fact that *think* cannot take an internal argument (**think* peace) as opposed to *peacemaker*, where *make* does take an internal argument (*make* peace). How then can a theta-role be discharged in a compound? Lieber argues that the more restricted character of synthetic compounds follows from the structure in (43) in conjunction with a principle that requires verbs and prepositions to satisfy their argument structure and that forces sisters of verbs and prepositions to serve as their arguments.[35] Indeed, since nominals cannot have argument structure in Lieber's theory, they do not inherit such structure. As a consequence, (42) is precluded from being a structure for *truck driver* in Lieber's (1983) analysis. In essence Lieber is extending the Projection Principle into the lexical formation of compounds.[36]

Sproat (1985a) advocates a similar structure for synthetic compounds. His treatment diverges from Lieber's in that he forms such compounds syntactically. The Projection Principle applies directly to these forms and no appeal is made to a morphological component. The satisfaction of the verb's argument structure is tied in an interesting way to Higginbotham's (1985) semantics. Arguments within synthetic compounds satisfy the verb's argument structure through theta-identification, a mechanism used in the relation between, for example, a head noun and a modifier, while objects in argument position satisfy the argument structure by theta-marking. Sproat's perspective on argument satisfaction within synthetic compounds recalls the syntactic approach to clitics discussed in section 2 that allowed a clitic to absorb a theta-role and prevent the projection of an NP in argument position.

For Lieber the verbal projection in (43) is V^0; others, however, have given it a phrasal status. Botha (1980) in an analysis of Afrikaans treats synthetic compounds as phrasal. A similar position is taken in Marantz (1989). From this perspective the argument structure of verbs is preserved in synthetic compounds because they are syntactically formed, and the Projection Principle holds at the various syntactic levels.

Selkirk (1982) and Booij (1988) defend the structure in (42) for synthetic compounds. The challenge for these approaches is to account for the semantic relation that apparently restricts synthetic compounds, making forms like *peacethinker* impossible. Selkirk (1982) has a special rule for compounds that allows non-head members of a compound to receive any non-subject theta-role. Booij (1988) argues that the correct theory of inheritance (or percolation) in the derivation of nominals like *driver* from verbs like *drive* will account for this semantic relation. We will return to inheritance in derived nominals below. In Lieber (1992) a different position is sketched from that of Lieber (1983). Lieber (1992) accepts (42) to be the correct structure of synthetic compounds, arguing that this order is syntactically derived from a structure like (43) with a theme in postverbal position in accord with Baker's UTAH. The motivation for this syntactic movement is to guarantee that N^0 does not receive Case from the verb: Lieber assumes that heads of phrases cannot be Case-marked.[37]

For many speakers of English the constituents of compounds are not active anaphorically. So for example in our synthetic compound *truck driver, truck* is not a legitimate antecedent (cf. Postal (1969)).[38]

(44) *Truck$_i$ drivers fill them$_i$ up with diesel

Lieber (1992) studies a less restrictive dialect that permits anaphora into such structures. The fact that members of compounds are unavailable for anaphoric purposes in the restrictive dialect is sometimes attributed to the strong lexicalist hypothesis that prevents syntactic processes from making reference to constituents of words. One of the allures that Lexical Phonology holds is that one of its fundamental tenets, the bracket erasure convention which eliminates the internal bracketing of words produced by affixation or compounding, would seem to have the strong lexicalist hypothesis as a corollary. In this sense Lexical Phonology/Morphology might reasonably claim an advantage in explaining the anaphoric inertness of elements within compounds (cf. Simpson 1983a).

Sproat (1985a, 1988b) offers another explanation for facts like (44). Sproat argues that there is an independently needed principle that prevents maximal projections in general from appearing internal to an English word, although non-maximal phrases do appear word internally. A similar position is taken in Simpson (1983b). Sproat then contends, in the spirit of Postal (1969), that only an argument (i.e. a maximal projection) can be the antecedent for another argument. From this perspective the failure in (44) is that a non-maximal projection is made to serve as an antecedent of a pronoun. Sproat presents evidence from Warlpiri to suggest that maximal projections can appear word-internally in that language and, in corroboration of his conjecture, such word-internal maximal projections can serve as antecedents.

Lieber (1992) doubts the correctness of Sproat's explanation. Inspired by Finer's (1985) study of switch reference affixes as having indices that participate fully in the binding theory, Lieber argues that the noun *self* that appears in compounds such as *self-love, self-contempt* is constrained by the Binding Theory. It is important, Lieber argues, that all speakers share the judgment that coreference is unavailable between *self* and *his* in (45), although that interpretation is possible in (46).

(45) His$_i$ [$_{N'}$ [$_N$ self$_i$ [$_N$ [$_N$ admire] er]]]
(46) His$_i$ [$_{N'}$ [$_N$ self$_i$ [$_N$ admiration]]

Lieber's idea is that the agentive affix *-er* serves as a subject and establishes N′ as a governing category in which *self* must find an antecedent. Only *-er* can serve that function. The Binding Theory will also require that the index of *-er* be disjoint from that of the pronoun *his*, yielding the consequence that *self* and *his* must be disjoint. Because the agent affix is absent in (46), nothing prevents *his* from binding the reflexive. The ability of this analysis to explain the distribution of *self* shows in Lieber's view that sublexical elements can be anaphorically active in English. Yet, while Sproat's analysis has difficulty explaining the facts in (45)–(46), Lieber remains hard-pressed to explain why in the restrictive dialect of Postal and others nouns such as *truck* are anaphorically inert and ignore the Binding Theory.

5.2 *Derived Nominals and Adjectives*

Our discussion of compounding above has focused on (i) how deverbal nouns in synthetic compounds compose with a noun that receives a thematic role of the verb; and (ii) whether constituents of a compound appear anaphorically inert. In section 1 we mentioned the puzzle of how closely compounding and affixation resemble one another. At that point attention was focused on the internal structure of forms composed by affixation. At this juncture we can raise the question anew, this time with respect to the properties of synthetic compounds touched on above.

Let us dispense with anaphoric properties of derived nominals. On this score, derivation seems to behave similarly to compounding. Sproat (1988b) argues that derived nominals like *Reaganite* behave substantially as expected on his proposal that non-maximal projections cannot serve as antecedents, and Lieber (1992) believes that *Reagan* remains anaphorically active. More important, perhaps, are issues bearing on argument structure. There is an impressive body of research that recognizes a set of lexical morphological rules as having the ability to manipulate the argument structure of verbs. In large part the impetus for this research stems from Wasow's (1977) isolation of an adjectival passive distinct from the (transformational) verbal passive. The adjective *unpersuaded* is derived from the verb *persuade*.[39]

(47) Mary was/seemed (un)persuaded of her guilt

The recognition that the subject of the passive adjective corresponds to an internal argument of the verb *persuade* makes it plausible to hypothesize a lexical rule that changes the argument structure of that verb as the passive adjective is derived; see Wasow (1977), Williams (1981b), Bresnan (1982b).

A number of important studies have been conducted on whether argument structure is preserved with derivational morphology. Levin and Rappaport (1986) build a careful case that in adjectival passive participles like (47) the verb *persuade* of necessity projects its argument structure in conformity with general principles and that no specific lexical rule manipulates its argument structure. This claim runs directly counter to earlier studies that admit such lexical rules. Assume for the purposes of discussion that the lexical entry of *persuade* is (48) where it is noted that *persuade* takes two arguments, and one of those arguments is identified (by underscoring) as being realized external to the maximal projection of *persuade*. All other arguments will appear internal to that maximal projection. This is essentially the view advocated in Williams (1981b).

(48) persuade, V, (<u>agent</u>, theme)

Earlier analyses of this construction (Wasow (1977), Williams (1981b), Bresnan (1982b), Borer (1984b)), have isolated the following properties of adjectival passives:

(49a) The verb contains the passive affix *-ed;*
(49b) the verb changes its category to an adjective;
(49c) the verb's external argument is suppressed;
(49d) neither the verb nor the resulting adjective assigns Case;
(49e) the [NP, VP] position is eliminated.

One could imagine a lexical rule that effected these changes to yield the lexical item in (36).

(50) persuaded, A, (<u>theme</u>)

Levin and Rappaport argue that the adjectival passive is constructed by a simple rule that simply takes a verbal participle and changes its category to that of an adjective

$$[_A \; \underset{[+\text{PARTICIPLE}]}{\text{V}} \;]$$

This rule may be nothing more than the affixation of the particle *-ed*. None of the properties in (49) need to be encoded in this rule; rather they all follow from more general principles. The suppression of the verb's external argument and its lack of Case marking are a consequence of the affixation of the particle *-ed,* just as in the verbal passive. The suppression of the [NP, VP] position and the externalization of the verb's internal argument is a consequence of the category change from V to A. With Borer (1984b), Levin and Rappaport attribute the suppression of the [NP, VP] position to the change in category: they assume that adjectives have as a general property the requirement that they have an external argument. The thematic role typically assigned to the internal argument directly theta-marked by the verb must, therefore, be realized as the external argument of the derived adjective rather than, for example, appearing as an argument indirectly theta-marked by a preposition.

Cinque (1990a) casts some doubt on at least part of this analysis.[40] Cinque defends the position that there are ergative (or unaccusative) adjectives, that is to say, adjectives that theta-mark their "object" (i.e. [NP, AP]) but not their subject ([NP, IP]). In Italian such adjectives admit *ne* cliticization, as (51) illustrates, a phenomenon which is taken to be a diagnostic for ergative structures like (52) following Perlmutter (1978) and Burzio (1986).

(51) Ne sono note solo alcune [delle sue poesie]
of-them are well-known only some (of his poems)

(52) Ne$_i$ sono affondate [due t$_i$]
of them are sunk two

Cinque's claim undermines the explanation for why the argument directly theta-marked by the verb becomes an external argument in Levin and Rappaport's treatment of the adjectival passive. The difficulty is that, if Cinque is correct, adjectives do not require that they be predicated of an argument. Cinque suggests that Levin and Rappaport's results can be maintained if we assume that an element can only directly theta-mark a sister. In derived categories like the adjectival passive the verb will be unable to directly theta-mark an NP (although an underived adjective like that in (52) will) and as a consequence the only way that the verb's argument structure will be satisfied is by predicating the adjective of an external argument. Cinque's account immediately explains the fact that ergative verbs produce unergative adjectives.

Inheritance of argument structure has been studied extensively with respect to derived nominals. (I discuss inheritance in derived verbs below.) The general issue is whether derived nominals show in their ability to take arguments any systematic relation with their related verb or whether their behavior is chaotic. For a skeptical view of inheritance generally see Hoekstra and van der Putten (1988). Implicitly denying the importance of inheritance, M. Anderson (1983–4), Higginbotham (1983), and Dowty (1991) take the view that nouns have no obligatory arguments. Nevertheless, the prevailing view seems to be that there is some systematic relation between the argument structure of a verb and its corresponding nominals. Some such relation is certainly suggested in Chomsky (1970) where *refuse* and *refusal* share a lexical entry with a fixed argument structure and a neutral value for the nominal and verb features. Continuing this line of thought, Cinque's investigation of ergative adjectives gives a structural account of inheritance by permitting theta-marking only between X^0 and a sister. Adjectives derived from ergative verbs do not inherit the verb's ergative argument structure on this view. Cinque conjectures that argument structures are inherited in derived nominals because they do not have the structure [$_N$ X [$_V$ Y] Z] but share a lexical entry undefined for category as Chomsky (1970) originally proposed.

Partisans of treating synthetic compounds in the same way formally as root compounds require some type of inheritance in nominals like [$_N$ [$_V$ *drive*] *er*] and have little use for theories like Cinque's that give an explicitly structural account of inheritance by identifying theta-marking with being the sister of a head. Besides Selkirk (1982) and Booij (1988), inheritance in derived nominals is also treated in Randall (1984).[41] Randall (1984) argues that the inheritance of theta-roles interacts in a special way with a thematic hierarchy. Given the hierarchy: theme > agent > source, instrument, goal, affixes that block projection of one of these roles will block the projection of all others lower on the hierarchy.

The affix *-er* blocks the inheritance of an agent as (53a) suggests; on Randall's proposal, *-er* should also then block the inheritance of goals. This claim will explain the ungrammaticality of the noun phrase in (53b).

(53a) *a flyer of kites by experts
(53b) *a flyer of planes to France

However, Sproat (1985a) criticizes Randall's suggestion. Nominals like *destruction* can block the projection of the internal theme, as in (54), and yet still can co-occur plausibly with arguments lower on Randall's hierarchy. Phrases like (55) and (56) exemplify this fact.

(54) the destruction
(55) John's destruction of the jungle fort with a machete
(56) the destruction of the jungle fort with a machete

Hoeksema (1992) raises similar difficulties with the behavior of adjectives derived by affixation of *-able*.[42] Interestingly Sproat's example (55) only has an event interpretation where *destruction* refers to the action of destroying and does not lend itself to a description of the results of the destruction. The traditional distinction between event and result nominals (cf. Comrie and Thompson (1985)) has become increasingly important to thinking about argument inheritance.[43]

We have just seen that, while the verb *destroy* requires an obligatory internal argument, the corresponding nominal appears to behave differently in that it can appear either with or without its argument.

(57) the army destroyed the country
(58) *the army destroyed
(59) the army's destruction of the country
(60) the destruction

At first glance, this situation appears chaotic and seems to falsify any claim that the argument structure of the verb is inherited by the derived nominal. However, Lebeaux (1986) observes that the agent of the derived nominal cannot appear unless the theme is present as well; thus (61) is ungrammatical where *army* is understood as the agent of *destruction* and not its theme.

(61) the army's destruction

There have been several attempts to make sense of this phenomenon. Lebeaux gives an account of these facts from the perspective of Pesetsky's proposal for raising affixes at LF. Safir (1987) meets the challenge that this problem presents with a principle guaranteeing that external arguments can only be assigned after internal arguments are assigned. More recently Grimshaw (1990) has suggested that the observed contrast is ultimately related to aspect. In a move that recalls the more traditional distinction between result and event nominals, Grimshaw recognizes two classes of nominals, result nominals and complex event nominals. Only the latter have an argument structure, where an argument structure is composed of thematic information and aspectual information. Nominals with argument structure fail to co-occur in the plural or with determiners like *a*, they cannot appear as predicate nominals. Nominals like *destruction* happen to be ambiguous between result and complex events. When arguments are inherited, we are dealing with complex events.[44] This proposal has the advantage of explaining why aspectual modifiers like *constant* or *frequent* only appear with arguments, and the observation that adverbs can marginally co-occur with event nominals (see Comrie and Thompson (1985)).[45]

(62) *the constant destruction
(63) the army's constant destruction of the city

Hoeksema (1985) offers an analysis of Dutch derived nominals that shares with Grimshaw the intuition that aspect is central to an understanding of the behavior of derived nominals. Like Grimshaw, Hoeksema recognizes the importance of the determiner to the nominals and correlates it with aspect and the traditional distinction between event and result nominals. Rather than appealing to the lexical structure of thematic and aspectual information to explain these facts, Hoeksema pursues a (model-theoretic) semantic account that licenses event nominals only with "activity" readings in the sense of Dowty (1979).

A somewhat different picture of the pretheoretical distinction between event and result nominals emerges from Sproat (1985a). Lieber (1983) posits that a verb's arguments cannot percolate through a nominal. Such a restriction seems necessary to explain the ungrammaticality of examples like *tree eating of pasta* noted by Selkirk (1982), where some of the verb's arguments are satisfied in the compound and others are satisfied outside of the compound. Selkirk (1982) explains this fact by appeal to a special law that requires all non-subjects' arguments to be satisfied within the first projection of the category in order to exclude such examples. Yet Sproat (1985a) contests these generalizations and argues that a verb's argument structure can percolate beyond a nominal affix. The examples in (64)–(67) are cited as illustrations of such argument inheritance.

(64) John is a putter of books onto tables
(65) *John is a putter onto tables
(66) John is a maker of cookies
(67) *John is a maker

Here the obligatory arguments of *put* and *make* must appear despite the presence of the nominalizing affix *-er*. These facts lead Sproat to contend that there is no need for a special principle of argument projection within the lexicon distinct from the Projection Principle. The problematic cases like (68), parallel to *tree eater of pasta,* are a consequence of the Projection Principle.

(68) book putter on tables

The Projection Principle is interpreted as requiring that all of the verb's arguments are projected at the same structure level, within X^0 or within X′.

Examples like (66) are problematic for Grimshaw's treatment of derived nominals. The *-er* nominals like *maker* cannot be complex event nominals yet they apparently have obligatory argument structures nevertheless. They are also problematic for Cinque's discussion of ergative derived nominals and adjectives. Cinque's requirement that argument inheritance requires a sister relation between a verb and its argument seem to be superficially falsified by Sproat's examples in (64)–(67), on the assumption that the relevant structure is $[_N [_V$ *put*$]$ *er*$]$.[46]

Sproat offers a different view of event and result nominals. Instead of distinguishing them on the basis of obligatory arguments, Sproat divides them by their ability to take instrumental or locational modifiers, items that, he claims, modify events. Thus, it is significant for Sproat that instrumentals can appear with *destruction* but not *-er* nominals.

(69) the destruction of the jungle fort with a machete
(70) *the destroyer of the jungle fort with a machete

6 Derived and Compound Verbs

6.1 Noun Incorporation

Let us, along with Baker (1988a) and Sadock (1991), take noun incorporation to be a phenomenon where a noun enters into a compound with another formative and yet remains syntactically active. Perhaps the strongest cases for such structures can be made for West Greenlandic (Sadock (1980, 1986, 1991)), Southern Tiwa (Allen, Gardiner, and Frantz (1984), Sadock (1985)) and Mohawk (Postal (1962)). The West Greenlandic example in (71) from Sadock (1991) illustrates this type of construction; here *nassata* "baggage" is an incorporated noun.

(71) . . . kisiannimi usi nassata-qar-punga
but in-fact baggage-have-INDIC/1S
"but I just remembered I have some luggage"

Sadock has argued that the incorporated noun retains its referential properties, and that the incorporated noun has the ability to "strand" other material in its syntactic phrase. Baker adds to these considerations the claim that incorporation exhibits the standard ECP effects in that there is a subject–object asymmetry with objects incorporating but not subjects and adjuncts. Apparent exceptions to this generalization come from unaccusative intransitives, but these exceptions can be analyzed with the S-Structure subject as a D-structure object, preserving the generalization of the ECP limiting incorporation. Baker also argues that incorporation has binding-theoretic consequences, eliminating the phrasal projection of the object as a governing category for any stranded material such as a possessive.

Baker argues that noun incorporation is the result of head-to-head-movement. In this way he proposes to treat noun incorporation much in the way that Kayne would treat clitics. Indeed Baker points out that all the properties of noun incorporation are shared with the clitics *ne* in Italian or *en* in French.[47] Baker's theory clearly predicts that structures of Exceptional Case Marking should permit noun incorporation. Unfortunately no such examples have yet been uncovered. One of the principal difficulties of Baker's analysis is that it has no strong explanation for why possessives or some other element inside an NP fail to incorporate. The system of barriers offered in Chomsky (1986a) make the specifier of NP available for possible extraction by letting N′ rather than NP constitute a barrier for the Minimality Condition. Yet possessives apparently fail cross-linguistically to incorporate.[48] Baker deals with this problem by stipulating that maximal projections are inherent barriers. This stipulation seems unlikely, given the fact that clitics like the French *en* can be extracted out of NPs as we saw in section 2. Baker's theory would have cliticization and noun incorporation as fundamentally the same syntactic phenomenon. However, an element is not extracted out of an NP to incorporate as it can to cliticize, and this leaves a troubling gap in the evidence available to support a head-movement approach to noun incorporation. However that may be, Baker's treatment of incorporation receives rather striking confirmation from the study of Greek adverbial incorporation in Rivero (1992). Rivero shows that in Greek adverbs strictly subcategorizing a verb are able to incorporate into that verb, while true adverbial adjuncts are unable to do so. This is exactly what one would expect from Baker's theory.

While Sadock and Baker agree that an incorporated noun remains syntactically active, they disagree on how to represent such structures. Like Baker, Sadock also wants to provide a uniform account for noun incorporation and cliticization. He gives structures like (72) where on the syntactic level *nassata-qua-punga* is a verb but on the morphological level it is composed of a noun, verb, and tense-agreement inflection.

(72)

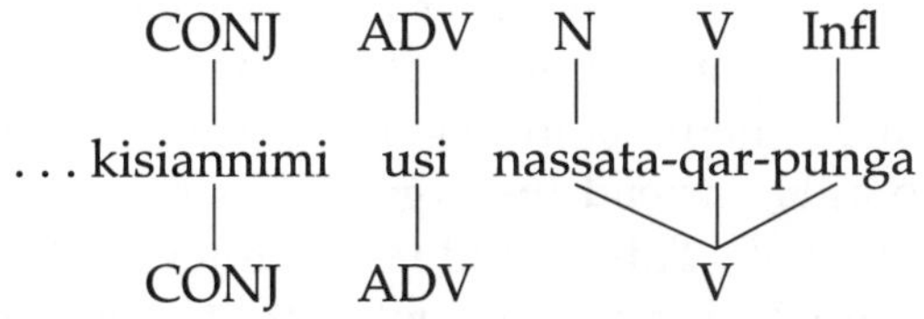

It is unclear that Sadock's autolexical account explains in a restrictive fashion the facts surrounding noun incorporation. For example, it does not seem well suited to dealing with different classes of intransitives that behave asymmetrically in noun incorporation structures. Nor is it able to give a principled explanation for why possessives fail apparently to incorporate cross-linguistically.

A number of researchers defend the point of view that noun incorporation is non-syntactic. Di Sciullo and Williams (1987), Mithun (1984, 1986) and Rosen (1989) all view noun incorporation as a lexical process. Rosen's analysis is perhaps the most carefully worked out alternative to a syntactic treatment of noun incorporation. Rosen distinguishes two basic types of noun incorporation, "classifier noun incorporation" and "compound noun incorporation." The principal difference between these two types is that compound noun incorporation treats the incorporated noun as satisfying the argument structure of the verb it compounds with, recalling our discussion of synthetic compounds above. Because the internal theta-role of the verb is discharged, one will not find stranded material or a lexical NP in object position. Niuean, described in Seiter (1980), is taken to be a language with compound noun incorporation. In languages with classifier noun incorporation the incorporated noun only provides some general grammatical features of the object and crucially does not discharge the verb's internal theta-role. As a result a lexical NP is free to appear in object position effectively doubling the incorporated noun. Stranded material around a null argument is also possible. Mohawk is cited as representative of languages utilizing classifier noun incorporation.

Rosen's treatment is by her own admission inconclusive on the viability of a syntactic treatment of noun incorporation in Southern Tiwa or Western Greenlandic. Her arguments do suggest, however, that Baker's discussion of noun incorporation paints the phenomenon with too broad a syntactic brush. Rosen shows that there are languages with noun incorporation that do not behave exactly as Western Greenlandic or Southern Tiwa. A compounding approach to noun incorporation may be required for some languages (e.g. Niuean) as even Baker and Sadock admit. However, identifying some instances of noun incorporation as compounding does not lead necessarily to a lexical treatment since, as our discussion of synthetic compounding revealed, it is possible to advocate a relatively syntactic analysis of compounds as in Sproat's treatment. Head-movement, as in Baker's treatment, may not play a part in such compounds; instead the argument structure of the verb would be satisfied within V^0. This would be done without admitting a distinct lexical word formation component with its own properties. Here we seem to face a problem very much like the question touched on briefly in section 2 of whether cliticization involves a base-generated agreement element directly discharging a theta-role or syntactic head-movement. Clearly much rides on how one chooses to analyze compounds and clitics.

6.2 *Causatives*

There is a long tradition in generative grammar of treating causatives as biclausal at D-structure and then transforming that biclausal structure into an essentially monoclausal one.[49] In languages such as French and Spanish it is not obvious that this process of clause union is anything more than syntactic. However, in many languages there is a clear morphological dimension associated with the construction as well. Baker (1988a) cites the following Chichewa examples from Trithart (1977).

(73) Mtsikana ana-chit-its-a kuti mtsuko u-gw-e
girl AGR-do-make-ASP that waterpot AGR-fall-ASP
"the girl made the waterpot fall"

(74) Mtsikana anan-gw-ets-a mtsuko
girl AGR-fall-made-ASP waterpot
"the girl made the waterpot fall"

Baker proposes to treat this process in formally the same manner that he dealt with noun incorporation, and for that reason labels the phenomenon verb incorporation. The only difference between noun incorporation and verb incorporation is that in this case a verb undergoes head raising to the causative verbal affix *-ets*. In essence (75) represents the derivation of (74).

(75) [mtsikana I [ets-a] [C [mtsuko I [$_V$ gw]]]]

Baker points to the apparent existence of ECP effects in causatives as evidence favoring his position; specifically the incorporation of the embedded verb is unable to apply from subjects or adjuncts.[50]

Baker's treatment is in many respects quite similar to that presented in Marantz (1984). Neither Baker nor Marantz allow a lexical operation to change the argument structure of a verb; the syntax is responsible for the adjunction of the affix and the added argument in (74). Their principal difference resides in the fact that Marantz's principle of Morphological Merger is invoked to do the work that head-movement does for Baker. It remains unclear what, if any, empirical properties distinguish merger and head-movement.

Besides causatives that are biclausal syntactically until S-Structure where they are collapsed by merger, Marantz also admits a second kind of causative that behaves as though it is monoclausal. In Marantz's treatment such causatives undergo merger at D-structure rather than S-Structure. The intrinsic difference between these two kinds of causatives is revealed by their interaction with Binding Theory. In causatives that are merged at S-Structure, the subject of the embedded clause, the causee, will serve as a specified subject blocking binding of the object of the embedded clause from outside that clause.

(76) *Mi ni-m-big-ish-ize Ali ru:hu-y-a
I 1sS-OP-hit-CAUS-ASP Ali myself
"I made Ali hit myself"

(77) Mi m-phik-ish-ize ruːhu-y-a chaːkuja
I 1sS-cook-CAUS-ASP myself food
"I made myself eat food"

In causatives that are merged at D-structure, the causee loses its subject properties and will not block binding of the object of the embedded clause. Malayalam is an example of such a language. The Malayalam reflexive *swa-* must have a subject as an antecedent. Yet in the causative, the causee is unable to serve as an antecedent, suggesting that it is not a subject.

(78) Amma kuttiyekkonte aanaye swantam wittil wecc null-icc-u
The mother made the child pinch the elephant at the mother's/ *child's house.

We expect the behavior of reflexives to pattern with that of passives: causatives that are biclausal at S-Structure should permit the causee to promote to become the subject of the matrix clause, but the object of the embedded verb will be unable to passivize to become the subject of the matrix clause without violating Principle A of the Binding Theory. Causatives that are merged at D-structure should potentially allow the object of the embedded clause to passivize because the embedded clause is no longer a governing category after it loses its subject.

Baker's analysis of causatives gives a biclausal analysis to all causatives. Structures that Marantz analyzes as causatives involving D-structure merger, Baker treats not as raising a V but raising VP to specifier of CP as illustrated in (79).

(79) $[_{IP}$ N V $[_{CP}$ $[_{VP}$ V NP$]_i$ $[_{IP}$ NP I t_i]]]]

In the specifier of CP the object is free from the effects of the specified subject and can reflexivize or passivize. Whether a language utilizes (75) or (79) for its causative structures is ultimately related to patterns of Case marking in the language: languages with structures like (79) must have verbs with the ability to assign two structural Cases, otherwise the embedded subject will violate the Case filter. What are, in Marantz's analysis, two kinds of causatives formed at different grammatical levels are thus treated as causatives with two distinct S-Structures in Baker's analysis.

The approach to causatives outlined by Marantz and Baker has been criticized for its implications for the Romance causative.[51] The French causative in (80) looks as though it does not involve verb-raising, yet it shows many of the properties of being monoclausal.

(80) Elle fera manger ce gâteau à Jean
she will-make to-eat that cake to Jean
"She will have Jean eat that cake"

For Marantz the Romance causatives involve two clauses that are merged at D-structure and then "split" into two clauses again at S-Structure. Baker analyzes the Romance causatives as moving VP to SPEC of CP and then incorporating the embedded V into the causative *faire* at LF rather than at S-Structure. The approach to causatives outlined here has been criticized as being overly abstract. However in many respects it continues the tradition set out in Rouveret and Vergnaud (1980) that treats the causatives as syntactically biclausal and derives their monoclausal properties from a special restructuring of non-adjacent constituents.

More recently Li (1990a) has offered a treatment of causatives that shares with Baker's analysis a syntactic derivation of causatives by head-movement. It differs in that it does not assume a biclausal structure for causatives; instead, following Burzio (1986), causative verbs embed VPs. And, more importantly, rather than being constrained by the ECP, it is constrained by an extended version of the Binding Theory developed in that work.

A more serious challenge to Baker's treatment of verb incorporation comes from the Chinese resultative compounds explored in Li (1990b). (81) is an example of a resultative compound.

(81) Baoyu qi-lei-le neipi ma
Baoyu ride-tired-asp that horse
"Baoyu rode that horse (and as a result it/Baoyu got) tired"

There does not appear to be any clear sense in which *lei* "tired" is an argument of *qi* "ride" in such structures, making a head-movement analysis unavailable.

As in our examination of noun incorporation, lexical approaches have been suggested for structures of verb incorporation. Grimshaw and Mester (1985) offer an account of complex verbs in Eskimo that makes use of lexical word formation rules that have the power to change argument structures of verbs. Jensen and Johns (1989) analyze Eskimo causatives from a lexical point of view but attempt to make do with feature inheritance and avoid argument-changing rules.

Others have suggested analyses in which a string of morphemes is given two simultaneous structures. For example Zubizaretta (1985) analyzes the Romance causative giving the French (64) the structure in (66).

(82) NP V [S [VP V NP PP]]

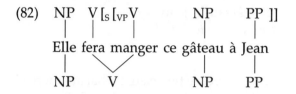

Elle fera manger ce gâteau à Jean

NP V NP PP

The top structure accounts for the fact that the two verbs behave inflectionally as independent words. The bottom structure expresses the intuition that *faire* is like a causative affix and has the ability to trigger deletion, or internalization of a verb's arguments much as other affixes (e.g. the passive affix) do in the theory of Williams (1981b). A similar proposal, called "co-analysis", is sketched in Di Sciullo and Williams (1987), and it resembles the autolexical proposal of Sadock (1991) as well.

6.3 *Applicatives*

Applicative constructions involve verbal affixes that have the property of increasing the number of internal arguments that the verb selects. This pattern is exemplified by the Kichaga sentences below, adapted from Bresnan and Moshi (1990).

(83) N-a-i-ly-a k-elya
FOC-1s-PR-eat-FV 7-food
"He/she is eating food"

(84) N-a-i-lyi-i-a m-ka k-elya
FOC-1SG-PR-eat-AP-FV 1-wife 7-food
"He is eating food for/on his wife"

The verbal affix *-i-* allows the verb *ly(i)* to have an argument in addition to its theme. The applicative construction resembles the Double Object construction in English and Chinese, although no affix accompanies the extra object in these languages.[52]

(85) Jane cooked Jill some food

(86) wo song le Lisi yi ben shu
I give ASP Lisi one copy book
"I give Lisi a book"

Baker (1988b), drawing heavily on the analysis presented in Marantz (1984), treats applicative constructions as preposition incorporation structures. A sentence like (84) would have a D-structure like (87), ignoring the various tense and agreement affixes on the verb.

(87)

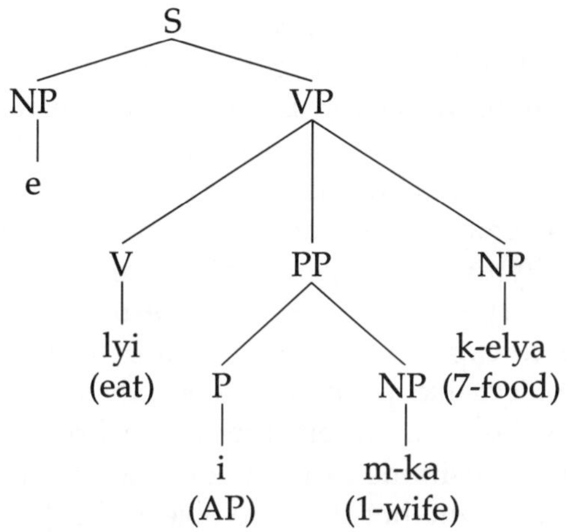

The applicative affix *-i-* is analyzed here as comparable to a preposition that undergoes head-movement affixing it to the verb. The benefactive or goal that is the object adjacent to the verb (the so-called first object) is structurally Case-marked by the V–P complex. Languages are then parameterized as to whether the second object (the theme) receives inherent Case or structural Case. Chichewa adopts the first value for this parameter, while Kinyarwanda and Kichaga adopt the second. One of the consequences of this type of analysis is that the first object takes over the direct object properties typically exhibited by the structurally Case-marked theme in [$_{VP}$ V–NP–PP] structures. For instance, the first object will passivize and control any available object agreement. Languages differ in how they treat the second object because of the parameter regarding how the second object receives Case. In some languages the second object behaves asymmetrically from the first object, failing to passivize for instance; these are the languages like Chichewa that give the second object inherent Case. Languages like Kichaga however assign structural Case to both objects with the result that the second object shows all the object properties of the first object; for example, it can passivize as easily as the first object.

In Baker (1988b) this analysis is extended to account for asymmetries between goals and instruments on the one hand and benefactives on the other when they function as first objects in the applicative construction. Baker treats these asymmetries as reflections of how theta-marking is accomplished structurally. Unlike the other theta-roles, the benefactive role is assigned directly by a preposition, and this fact is held responsible for the more restricted behavior of benefactives regarding object agreement and adjacency to the verb.

Bresnan and Kanerva (1989) and Bresnan and Moshi (1990) present important evidence that strongly suggests that the Marantz/Baker account of applicatives is insufficient. In their study of Chichewa locative inversion structures Bresnan and Kanerva discover an asymmetry between theme and instrument that is surprising on Baker's account that treats them in a parallel fashion. Moreover, Bresnan and Moshi show that Kichaga, a language that admits two structural Cases in Baker's terms, treats the benefactive as parallel to the theme and instrument for the purposes of some phenomena such as passive, yet nevertheless the benefactive behaves differently than the theme or instrument in that it must be adjacent to the verb. This is an unexpected result for Baker's analysis that would lead us to expect both theme and benefactive objects to share all relevant object-like properties since they are Case-marked in exactly the same fashion. As an alternative Bresnan and Moshi cross-classify argument positions in terms of whether they are semantically restricted [±r], and whether they are object-like, [±o]. The first object of a double object construction is a restricted object rather than an unrestricted object which typically shows up in transitive constructions. A markedness hierarchy is defined over these features such that the restricted object is most highly marked. This correlates with the word order position of benefactives relative to themes.

Baker's proposal for applicatives bears an affinity to treatments of the English Double Object Construction proposed in Kayne (1984). For Kayne, the double object construction also involves restructuring of the preposition with the verb, an operation something like incorporation, although the preposition is phonologically null in English.

(88) $[_{VP} [_{VP} V [_{P} \emptyset] NP_1] NP_2]]$

Baker suggests that the English construction should be treated as incorporating a phonologically null preposition.[53]

Larson (1988) has extended Kayne and Baker's proposal further to explain why the second object fails to bind the first object in the double object construction, a fact noted in Barss and Lasnik (1986). Unlike Barss and Lasnik, who argue that Binding Theory is sensitive to linear order, Larson attributes this fact to the failure of NP_1 to c-command NP_2. He gains this result by positing the structure in (89):

(89)

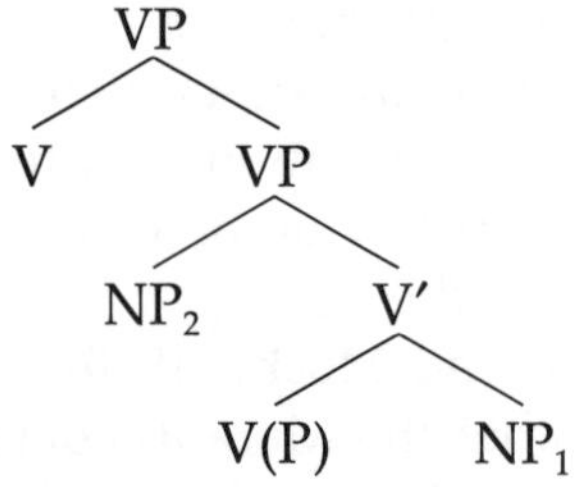

In this structure NP_1 cannot bind NP_2 because there is a failure of c-command. To achieve the desired word order, the embedded verb raises to the empty verb to provide NP_2 with Case. This is a controversial proposal and has sparked considerable debate; see for example Jackendoff (1990) and Larson (1990). This analysis of the double object construction might allow one to distinguish the two objects structurally independently of how they are assigned Case. Its more articulated structure might then provide a way to distinguish objects with different theta-roles in applicatives to meet the challenge of the Bantu evidence uncovered by Bresnan and Moshi (1990) and Bresnan and Kanerva (1989).

7 Conclusion

We have surveyed a number of areas where superficially morphological phenomena seem to interact with syntactic phenomena.[54] In each of these domains we encounter theoretical choices about morphosyntax. On the one hand we can adopt the strong lexicalist hypothesis and construe syntax to be a theory of phrases and not words. To the extent that words have structures, they are determined by a separate set of rules and principles that we can loosely call a morphological component. These rules will have the power to alter the argument structure of lexical items to account for phenomena like causatives, noun incorporation, and so on. On the other hand we can take syntax to be a theory of morphemes and constituent structure, both within phrases and heads. On this view the motivation for a separate morphological component is undermined and there is little use for morphological rules that manipulate argument structure. The relation between the structure of phrases and that of heads will be mediated by syntactic principles like head-movement and the Projection Principle, or perhaps by other non-lexical structures, whether those are phonological or morphological representations. As I hope to have shown, each of these possibilities has plausibility, and yet we have not encountered any knock-down arguments. Often syntactic approaches fail to explain fine-grained distinctions in constructions cross-linguistically, as in Baker's analysis of noun incorporation; for their part, non-syntactic approaches often do not address broad similarities between the structure of heads and that of phrases, as our discussion of clitics and synthetic compounds suggests. In many respects we require further empirical work to determine whether constructions like noun incorporation look syntactic in the same sense that cliticization does.

A large number of phenomena remain to be considered and integrated into a theory of Universal Grammar. One need only look, for example, at the pretheoretical overviews of morphology in Shopen (1985) to appreciate the work that could and should be done expanding the empirical range of our theoretical concerns.[55] And there are a number of language-specific facts about morpheme ordering such as clitic orderings in Romance or the fixed ordering of causative and augmentative or exhortative affixes in Quechua that do not follow from syntactic principles so far as I can see.[56] A careful examination of these phenomena might reveal reasons to prefer lexical/morphological operations or post-S-Structure rules of the sort envisaged by Emonds (1985) or by Halle and Marantz (1992). The correct analysis for these facts may deepen our understanding of the interaction between morphology and syntax, shedding further light on the divergent syntactic and lexical approaches to some of the other phenomena touched on in this chapter, or perhaps outdating them altogether.

Related Material in Other Chapters

Since practically every syntactic function that can be performed by simplex words can be performed by internally complex ones as well, the content of the present chapter touches on many issues discussed elsewhere in this book. The principles of X-bar theory discussed in chapter 1 are important for syntactic approaches to word formation and also for those theories, whether syntactic or lexical, that make use of the notion head in morphology and allow heads to "percolate" categorial and thematic information to their mother nodes. The Case-theoretic notions discussed in chapter 1 are relevant for syntactic theories of word formation as well in that the issue arises whether some X^0 elements need to be Case-marked or not. Case theory of course also plays a role in the treatment of passive morphology.

The theory of argument structures and the locality conditions on theta-marking discussed in chapter 2 are directly relevant for the wellformedness conditions on complex words and probably will have to play different roles depending on whether word formation is syntactic or lexical, post-syntactic, or some mixture of these.

If word formation is at least partly syntactic, then it can be expected to interact with the principles of the Binding Theory presented in chapter 4. This chapter contains proposals along these lines in connection with its discussion of clitics, agreement, and the referential opacity of words. Chapter 4 discusses approaches that differentiate binding theoretically between expressions as a function of whether they are maximal projections or lexical.

The Empty Category Principle of chapter 5, finally, is relevant to the syntactic theories of word formation. To the extent that morphologically related complex words enter into paradigms that are similar to unquestionably syntactic paradigms whose structure is governed by constraints on syntactic representations or operations including the ECP, the syntactic approach to word formation finds strong support.

Chapter 7 briefly thematizes the issue of whether within the Minimalist Program words should be created in the lexicon and inserted into the syntactic tree as a whole (as proposed by Chomsky) or whether the parts of words can combine post-lexically (as proposed by Halle and Marantz).

NOTES

1 No doubt my discussion is colored by my better acquaintance with work in a Principles and Parameters setting. Reviewing the works discussed in these areas will present the reader with further valuable scholarship on the subject.

I should also mention that I will not directly address the substantial issues concerning Case and Case theory since they are discussed in chapter 1 of this book.

2 There a number of excellent overviews of this preliminary ground. See, for example, Matthews (1974), S. Anderson (1988b), Scalise (1984), Jensen (1990), Hammond and Noonan (1988a), and Spencer (1991).

3 Matthews (1974) and S. Anderson (1988b) provide overviews of the different perspectives on the morpheme that we inherit.

4 Hoeksema (1985), for example, notes that in Dutch *ver-* is a left-hand head combining with *plicht* "obligation" to form *verplicht* "oblige." Similarly, Berber contains a prefix head *nn-* that forms denominal verbs, e.g. *anuddem* "sleep" and *n-nuddem* "to doze off"; see Guerssel (1986).

5 The illustration provided by Di Sciullo and Williams is the Spanish diminutive: *chica* "girl," *chiquita*. The diminutive affix *-ita* is unspecified for syntactic category and the stem continues to determine the syntactic category of the diminutive form.

6 After all, some syntacticians believe that linear order is irrelevant syntactically, e.g. Marantz (1984), or irrelevant at some syntactic levels, e.g. Gazdar, Klein, Pullum, and Sag (1985).

7 Breton contains both masculine and feminine nouns. Gender is realized in the effect of consonant mutation. In the singular feminine nouns undergo mutation of the initial consonant after the definite article, while masculine nouns do not. The situation in the plural is virtually inverted: a subset of the masculine nouns (the masculine human nouns) undergo mutation after the article, while feminine nouns do not.

Gender is also signaled by its effect on a postnominal adjective. A feminine singular noun forces mutation on the consonant of a following adjective, but masculine singular nouns do not. In the plural only masculine human nouns trigger mutation of the consonant of a following adjective.

One class of exceptions to this system is of special interest here. There are several plural suffixes in Breton. The affix *-ed* is reserved for animates. However, it so happens that a handful of masculine human nouns select *-(i)où* as their plural suffix rather than *-ed*. For example we find *testoù* (witnesses), *tadoù* (fathers), *priedoù* (spouses). What is significant here is the fact that these masculine humans that are subcategorized by the plural *-(i)où* also fail to trigger mutation on a following consonant. Thus we find *tadoù mat* rather than *tadoù vat* (good father). *Tad* is masculine because it shows the masculine pattern of mutation with an article in the singular. However just in the plural it no longer behaves as masculine in that it fails to mutate to *dadou* and it fails to trigger consonant mutation on a following adjective. If *-où* is the head of *tadoù* and bears independent features for humanness as well as plurality this state of affairs follows directly. If the plural markers are simply phonological realizations of the feature plural, the behavior of *où* on masculine nouns is mysterious. The affix *-où* corresponds to a set of morphological features, [+human], [+plural] that dominate over the features of the stem that they are affixed to. We have here an example of multiple features acting as a unit and being selectionally dominant.

8 Early discussions of lexicalism treat the notion of productivity as self-evident. Aronoff (1976) attempts to clarify the notion as a ratio between actual occurring words and words made possible by a word formation rule. To the extent that an operation seems to have more exceptions than instances of application, it is unproductive. Others, such as Wasow (1977), seem to equate productivity with the (virtual) lack of exceptions. Lieber (1992) on the other hand defends a notion of productivity that is based on the ability to coin an unlimited number of new words by an operation rather than on the presence or absence of exceptions.

9 See Reuland (1983) and Abney (1987) for a discussion of gerundive nominals in a Principles and Parameters setting.

10 See chapter 1 for more discussion. The increasing importance of the lexicon placed on the research agenda a series of questions that we are still in the process of answering to this day in both phonology and syntax. How or to what extent are verbs and their corresponding derived nominals "related"? What are the principled limitations to that relation? How can we account for the morphophonemic changes that accompany this derivation?

11 S. Anderson (1988a) addresses this issue and suggests several other phenomena that correlate with the inflection/derivation split, such as the presence of portmanteau morphs. Emonds (1985) also attempts to give a principled distinction between these classes.

12 This contention is sometimes referred to as the Lexical Integrity Hypothesis.

13 S. Anderson (1988a) posits that the phonological distinctiveness of clitics can be narrowed down to a lack of prosodic structure that forces them to lean on a host.

14 A more exotic example is the Kwakwala determiner system described in S. Anderson (1984) that cliticizes out of its NP onto a preceding word.

15 This fact is noted in van Riemsdijk and Williams (1986).

16 That is to say $(a*b)*c = a*(b*c) \neq b*c*a$ where * denotes "is adjacent to."

17 The Morphological Merger Principle stipulates that at any level of syntactic analysis (D-structure, S-Structure, phonological structure), a relation between X and Y may be replaced by the affixation of the lexical head of X to the lexical head of Y.

18 X*[CL*Y*Z or X*CL]*Y*Z would satisfy the requirements, however.

19 S. Anderson's (1988a) treatment of INFL as a phrasal clitic/affix claims to have the verb-second phenomenon as a consequence. Although the verb-second phenomena in German can be accounted for by raising a finite verb to C, the verb-second

phenomena in Breton appear different, and in Hendrick (1994) I have argued that the Breton finite verb adjoins to AGRP. This analysis of Breton resembles Anderson's view that the verbal inflection is affixed to the clause.

20 Zubizaretta (1985) points out that this proposal does not fare well with asymmetries between dative and accusative reflexive clitics in the French causative construction.

21 Zwicky and Pullum (1983) attempt to use morphophonemic characteristics to decide between competing analyses of inflectional elements and clitics.

22 This example is borrowed from Fontana and Moore (1992).

23 For example, the contrast in River Plate Spanish between (i) and (ii), noted by Jaeggli, would suggest that a clitic was involved in such structures rather than agreement. (ii) is a strong crossover violation since the trace of *wh*-movement is bound by a (clitic) pronoun to its left.

(i) el hombre a $quien_i$ vi $[e]_i$
the man to whom saw-1SNG
"The man I saw"

(ii) *el hombre a $quien_i$ lo_i vi $[e]_i$
the man to whom him saw-1SNG
"The man whom I saw"

24 One might also appeal to the Binding Theory on the assumption that agreement markers do not induce A-binding.

25 It is also worth noting that negatives interact with the ECP to limit the distribution of clitics. The relevant generalization here is that clitics do not appear to the left of the negative. This is true in simple clauses like the French (i)–(ii).

(i) Jean ne les voit pas
John NEG them sees NEG

(ii) *Jean les ne voit pas

And the same is true of the Italian clitic climbing construction in (iii)–(v).

(iii) Gianni vuole non vederli
Gianni wants not see-them

(iv) *Gianni li vuole non vedere
Gianni them wants not see

(v) Gianni non li vuole vedere
Gianni not them want to-see

On the assumption that the negative heads a phrase but is not an L-marker, the NEGP will be a barrier preventing movement of the clitic outside of it by the ECP.

A potential area to test Kayne's discussion of clitic climbing is Hungarian; see Farkas and Sadock (1989).

26 But Ristad (1989) raises a potential problem for this view by arguing that treating local agreement relations with the same formal device used in syntactic binding results in a grammar that is computationally intractable. This issue is complicated by differing interpretations one can give to results concerning computational intractability; see for example Chomsky (1989, 1992).

27 But see Keenan (1974) and Gazdar, Klein, Pullum, and Sag (1985) for a different approach that limits agreement to the relation between functions and arguments. It is not clear that agreement can be limited to relations between a head and its

specifier and complement; see Aissen (1990) for some challenging agreement phenomena.

28 A somewhat more complicated system of "*wh*-agreement" exists in Chamorro, as described in Chung and Georgopoulos (1988).

29 See chapters 1 and 7 for discussion of Pollock's split Infl hypothesis and the analysis of agreement in Chomsky's (1992) minimalist program.

30 See Bresnan (1982b).

31 Baker's UTAH claims that universal principles map elements with the same thematic relations onto the same structural positions in D-structure. The agent role, for example, might be assigned universally to the position [NP, IP].

32 Hendrick (1988) offers independent evidence that Breton behaves similarly.

33 See Andrews (1990).

34 But see Spencer (1988) for a critique of this latter position.

35 A similar proposal is outlined in Selkirk (1982). Her principle requires that all non-subject arguments of a head appear within the first projection immediately dominating the head.

36 Others, notably Borer (1984b) in a study of deverbal adjectives, have taken it as crucial that lexical word formation does not respect the Projection Principle.

37 As I pointed out above, the goal of Lieber (1992) is to eliminate any need for morphological principles distinct from those independently required in the syntactic or phonological components. There should be no principles that treat word-internal phenomena differently from other syntactic phenomena. One potential difficulty for this line of thought is the fact that Lieber's analysis of synthetic compounds still needs to stipulate that Case Theory applies differently within the word than outside it (cf. Lieber (1992, 60)).

38 R-expressions seem to behave somewhat differently however.

(i) His_i mother dislikes Reagan_i bashers
(ii) Reagan_i bashers seem to truly hate him_i
(iii) *He_i hates Reagan_i bashers.

See Sproat (1988b) for some discussion of this fact.

39 It is generally accepted that *persuaded* here is adjectival because it appears in a context that admits only adjectives: after the verb *seem* and after the negative prefix *un*.

40 See Grimshaw (1990) for other difficulties posed by obligatory *by*-phrases in examples like (i).

(i) This event was followed by another
(ii) *This event was followed

41 For a less sympathetic view of inheritance in nominals see Rappaport (1983) and Dowty (1991).

42 The sentence *that property is definable in first-order logic*, for example, is problematic since *-able* suppresses the theme of the verb and yet the locative is still inherited apparently.

43 For the most part researchers have claimed that inheritance, to the extent it exists, can best be captured by generalizations over thematic relations, but several interesting problems for this view are raised in Hoeksema (1992). Hoeksema also gives several cases from German, where nominals exhibit aspect-like distinctions.

44 Grimshaw's proposal thus differs from that of M. Anderson (1983–4) that makes

the ability of a noun to assign a theta-role a function of whether it is abstract or concrete.

45 It is worth noting that Grimshaw's proposal also interacts with the theory of synthetic compounds. She hypothesizes that the distinction between root and synthetic compounds is a distinction in whether the head of the compound is a complex event nominal, that is, whether it has an argument structure in her sense. Synthetic compounds then will not appear in the plural. On this account *truck driver* will not be a synthetic compound though *truck driving* is. And as a consequence the internal argument should only be obligatory with N-V-*ing* and not N-V-*er*. The examples in (64) and (66) may pose difficulties for this claim.

46 And if the relevant structure is otherwise, if for example the agentive *-er* was an affix that embedded under it a VP and was affixed to the verb in the mapping to Phonological Form, we would need some principled explanation for why a similar explanation could not be given to the adjectival passives. That is to say, why couldn't the affix *-ed* embed a VP under it in a similar fashion.

47 The only difference between noun incorporation and cliticization is phonological, not syntactic. Presumably the incorporated noun may have a prosodic independence that is unavailable to clitics.

48 Tzotzil, as described in Aissen (1987), seems to allow possessives to incorporate, but they first raise in her Arc Pair Grammar to become the first object in a double object construction. At issue is whether there are any languages where possessives incorporate directly.

49 See for example Aissen (1974), Kayne (1975), and Shibatani (1976) for an entry into that tradition.

50 I have ignored here variation in Case marking between causatives cross-linguistically although this topic is of some importance to Baker's treatment.

51 See Sadock (1990).

52 The Chinese example here is adapted from Zhang (1990).

53 On this score Kayne and Baker diverge from Marantz who does not give a unified account for applicative constructions like (84) and their English counterparts. Marantz claims that it is crucial that the Bantu applicatives involve a visible and productive affix, while the English construction does not. The English construction is simply lexically listed in Marantz's view.

54 At the same time we have left unexplored other areas. For example, we have not discussed the interaction of affixes that appear to change grammatical functions such as the passive and the causative. Baker (1985) argues that such interactions favor a syntactic approach because such an approach explains why they "mirror" the application of syntactic operations. Di Sciullo and Williams (1987) and Grimshaw (1986) show however that lexical approaches can apparently explain these orderings in a principled fashion equally well.

55 Issues of tense and aspect outlined in Chung and Timberlake (1985) are particularly noteworthy in this regard.

56 Muysken (1988) points out that in Quechua the exhortative and augmentative affixes always occur before the causative, as in (i), although from the compositional semantic point of view there is reason to think that they should embed the causative.

(i) thuni - ya - ra - chi- pu - q
fall apart AUGM EXH CAU BEN AGR
"Throwing over . . ."

7

The Minimalist Program

Alec Marantz
MIT

Contents

Prelude

This chapter, as its first section headline indicates, leads us from a discussion of the Government–Binding (GB) version of the Principles and Parameters approach to the Minimalist Program (MP). It simultaneously serves as an interpretation of Chomsky (1989, 1992) and as an introduction to chapter 8, which at the time of writing is the most recent original development of the Minimalist Program by Chomsky.

The chapter discusses how the MP conceptualizes grammatical representations and their wellformedness. The system reduces the set of four levels of representation D-structure, S-Structure, Logical Form (LF), and Phonological Form (PF) of standard GB theory to the two *interface levels* LF and PF. LF interfaces with semantic–conceptual systems of cognition and PF is connected to articulatory–perceptual modules. As a function of this reduction of the number of levels, the structure of the remaining levels and in particular their interface character (i.e. their role in connecting linguistic representations to interpretation elsewhere in cognition) takes on paramount importance. This is reflected by the following: every principle that constrains derivations either applies at LF, at PF, or at every step of the derivation where it is relevant. Consequently, all the benefits of principles and constraints that applied at D-structure or S-Structure but not throughout the derivation in the classical GB system now have to be captured in a different manner, either by the relevant constraints being reformulated as wellformedness conditions on derivations as a whole or by their becoming conditions on the wellformedness of one of the interfaces.

Another important departure of the MP from earlier versions of generative syntax concerns the notion that the grammaticality of one derivation may depend on the properties of another derivation. In particular, the MP invokes a number of *economy principles* such as "Shortest Move," "Procrastinate," and "Greed" that compare derivations involving the same lexical resources and discard all but the most economical derivations.

I would like to thank audiences and classes in Amsterdam and Seoul and at MIT for their help in clarifying what needed to be said in this chapter. In addition, I am indebted to Morris Halle and Gert Webelhuth for their comments on earlier drafts. I alone am responsible for any misinterpretations of the Minimalist Program contained in these pages; in no way does this chapter reflect any official or authorized view of the theory or of syntax in general. In addition, to the extent that I have correctly explained aspects of the Minimalist Program, my exposition should not be taken as endorsement of ideas or analyses.

0 From Government–Binding to Minimalism

The minimalist program (MP) continues the trend in syntactic theory begun in the late 1970s: the move from specific grammatical rules that describe particular syntactic constructions to general principles that interact to explain syntactic phenomena. This latest version of Chomsky's Principles and Parameters (P&P) approach to grammar grows out of a consideration of the interaction of mechanisms like Move-α and of principles like the Case Filter. In standard Government–Binding theories, operations such as Move-α apply freely. A single derivation resulting from the free application of such operations is evaluated in isolation; if it does not violate any principles, it is a grammatical derivation. In addition, only in a metaphoric sense do operations apply for a reason: an NP may move "to get Case" and thus pass the Case Filter, but this only means that the NP does move and does get Case. The notion that if the NP didn't move, it wouldn't get Case, plays no role in evaluating the grammatical derivation. Moreover, no comparison of the ways that an NP in a given position in a given structure might move "to get Case" is relevant to the grammaticality of any particular movement the NP may undergo.

A number of conceptual issues lead from standard GB theories to the MP. First, certain locality principles seem to have a "least effort" flavor to them. Both NP- and *wh*-movement seem to target the first potential position up from the source position of movement, from a slightly abstract point of view (see the discussion of "Shortest Move" in section 1 below for some relevant examples). NP-movement in passive and raising moves what appears to be the highest NP in a structure to the first A-position above this NP (the subject position); when this closest A-position is filled, movement to a still higher position is blocked. Here, only the shortest possible move, the one requiring the least effort, is allowed. Similarly, *wh*-movement moves a *wh*-constituent to the first available and appropriate A-bar position, usually the local spec of CP. Superiority effects (see e.g. (1c) below) suggest that the highest among a set of *wh*-phrases – the one closest to the spec of CP position – must move; *wh*-island effects suggest that when the closest spec of CP position is filled, movement of a *wh*-phrase beyond this position is blocked in some manner. In the Superiority case, the *wh*-constituent that would make the least overt effort to get to spec of CP must be the one that moves; in the *wh*-island case, the *wh*-constituent seems to be penalized for making the effort to skip the closest possible landing site – the local spec of CP.

Second, operations other than simple (and shortest) movement seem to be "last resort" options, applicable only when other options are prohibited. For example, the insertion of dummy "do" in *do*-insertion contexts in English happens only when other possibilities for realizing tense and agreement are blocked. Both "least effort" and "last resort" notions involve implicit or explicit comparison of derivations. "Least effort" implies the comparison of other amounts of effort a constituent might have made, given a particular configuration. If a filled subject position blocks NP movement to a higher A-position of a constituent c-commanded by the subject, the effort of moving to this filled subject position is being compared with the effort of moving even farther. "Last resort" implies the exhaustion of other possible resorts a derivation might have for avoiding the violation of some principle or filter.

Least effort and last resort suggest a striving for the cheapest or minimal way of satisfying principles. The MP relies explicitly on such "economy principles" in evaluating derivations. Another aspect to the MP is the move toward a minimum of principles and grammatical constructs themselves. Within P&P syntax, an increasing load has been placed on wellformedness conditions at the so-called "interface" levels of PF and LF. PF is assumed to be the structure that interfaces with the perceptual system in speech recognition and with the articulatory system in speech production. LF interfaces with a speaker's general knowledge and with extralinguistic cognitive systems (the systems involved in relating an LF to "meaning" in the intuitive sense). Despite the emphasis on interface conditions, pre-Minimalist systems relied as well on D- and S-Structure conditions and principles. For example, D-structure (DS) was often taken as the projection of lexical properties, including theta-role assignment and subcategorization. Principles of Binding Theory were taken to apply crucially at S-Structure (SS). The notion of PF and LF wellformedness can be linked to "visible" aspects of language – the possibility of phonetic and semantic interpretation; DS or SS wellformedness have no corresponding concreteness. On the LF side, the principle of Full Interpretation might rule out the presence of "excess" constituents in a structure, such as unbound variables or NPs without theta-roles. On the PF side, Full Interpretation might reject representations containing symbols with no phonetic realization. To the extent that ungrammatical derivations could be ruled out by general interface conditions at PF and LF, the grammar itself might be simplified, e.g. through the elimination of the independent levels of DS and SS and of principles that might have applied at these levels.

Conceptually, then, the major changes in the move to the MP are these: constituents move for a reason, not freely; grammaticality depends on a comparison of derivations, not on the evaluation of a particular derivation in isolation; principles apply only at the interface levels of PF and LF or everywhere – DS and SS do not figure into the system. Below I will describe the implementation of these changes. However, this description will not provide anything like a complete technical introduction to Chomsky (1992). The original paper should be consulted for complete details.

1 Principles

In considering the principles that constrain derivations in the MP, it is important first to separate those that apply at the interface levels PF and LF from other principles. Other principles must apply everywhere that they are relevant in a derivation, since there are no other levels of grammar distinguished within this framework. In a conceptually clean version of minimalism, no operations occur explicitly in the course of a derivation to avoid a violation of a principle at one of the interfaces. Individual constituents might have particular needs that motivate them to move, however, and failure to meet these needs can lead to a derivation that is uninterpretable at one of the interfaces. For example, NPs have Case features that they must "check" in a derivation, and NPs will move to check these features. Failure to check a Case feature can lead to an uninterpretable structure at PF or at LF. (See sections 3 and 4 below for some comments on the technical aspects of feature checking.) A structure that fails to meet an interface condition at PF or LF is said to have "crashed." A derivation that crashes at an interface level has "failed to converge" at that level. Section 3 below will discuss the (morphological) features that require checking and the manner in which derivations crash or converge at the interface levels.

The evaluation of a structure at the interface levels for interpretability or crashes does not involve the comparison of the derivation of this structure with other possible derivations. Crashes, then, are local in the computational system. On the other hand, Economy Principles that operate across the grammar often involve the comparison of alternative derivations. The three major economy principles to be discussed here are Shortest Move, Greed, and Procrastinate. Although it might be possible to reduce some of the Economy principles to more general principles, Chomsky emphasizes that the particular forms these principles take in constraining the syntax cannot follow from general, extralinguistic notions of economy. There are many ways a general desire to do the least possible, for example, could play out in the syntax. The particular grammatical Economy principles are just some of the infinite number of possible principles consistent with general economy considerations.

Shortest Move is the most technically specific Economy principle and takes over much of the work performed by Relativized Minimality (Rizzi 1990), Subjacency, and the Head Movement Constraint in earlier versions of P&P theory. The basic idea is that a constituent must move to the first position of the right kind up from its source position. Ideally, a head-movement constraint violation like (1a), a super-raising violation like (1b) and a superiority violation like (1c) would all violate the Shortest Move economy principle.

(1a) *Have John will t left by the time we get there?
(1b) *John is likely for it to seem t to have left
(1c) *What did you persuade who to buy t?

The application of "Shortest Move" needs to be relativized to the type of constituent moving and to the relevant landing site. Heads, for example, should be prohibited by Shortest Move from skipping over any head position "between," in the relevant sense, the position they start in and the targeted landing site. So in (1a), the head "have" cannot skip the head position occupied by "will" to move to a higher head position, perhaps the position of C in the example. For constituents undergoing movement to an A-position, only intervening A-positions count. In (1b), "John" skips the subject A-position occupied by "it" to get to the subject position of "is likely." Similarly, A-bar movement of *wh*-constituents must not skip over A-bar specifier positions. We will return to the question of what counts as a possible intervening A-position for NP-movement in section 4.1 below.

Note too that an explicit account of Shortest Move will need to include more than just a notion of "intervening possible landing site" if it is to account for, e.g., Superiority examples like (1c). Here, we must move the higher of two *wh*-phrases in a derivation in which we derive an LF that yields a pair-seeking question, "For which person X and which thing or things Y did you persuade X to buy Y?" We want to be comparing two derivations with the same lexical items and the same interpretation. In one, the one yielding the grammatical, "Who did you persuade to buy what?" we move the higher *wh*- overtly and do whatever LF operations are necessary to create the multiple *wh*-interpretation with the lower *wh*-. In the other, the one that yields the word order in (1c), we have moved the lower *wh-* overtly. In neither case would the overt movement of the *wh-* cross a filled A-bar specifier position, nor is the overt movement by itself ungrammatical. We want the fact that moving the higher *wh-* involves a shorter move, measured in nodes crossed or some equivalent metric, to make this overt movement less costly than the movement of the lower *wh*-phrase. Since many analyses of multiple *wh-* constructions involve LF movement of the in situ *wh-* constituent(s), we need to make sure that the relative cost of the LF operations on the lower *wh-* added to the overt movement of the higher *wh-* is still less than the overt movement of the lower *wh-* and the LF operations on the higher *wh-*. Here the application of the Shortest Move principle involves a global comparison of different possible derivations, not a local application of a principle at one point in a derivation.

The application of Shortest Move, e.g. in the super-raising case in (1b), does not involve a comparison among "converging" derivations. Instead, the structure generated in the course of producing (1b) loses out to a more economical derivation that fails to converge. The structure generated in (1b) does in fact converge, since it would have all the relevant features checked off before the interface levels. However, *John* skips the position of the lower subject *it* when raising to the higher subject position. *John* could certainly make a shorter move by moving to the lower subject position. This more economical derivation, involving the shortest move that *John* could make from the most deeply embedded clause, would either be impossible – the landing site for the Shortest Move is already filled by *it* – or would fail to converge. Nevertheless, the more economical, but independently ill-formed, derivation blocks the (converging) derivation of (1b). Thus, in a sense, obeying Shortest Move takes precedence over convergence at the interface levels. Or, to put it differently, the evaluation of Shortest Move involves a comparison among all possible derivations, not just those that converge. If the Shortest Move dooms a derivation to crash at an interface, then there is no grammatical derivation using the lexical resources involved in the relevant comparison set of derivations.

Although the MP has no specific level of SS, there is a point in the computation of a grammatical representation where the derivation splits and heads toward the two interface levels, PF and LF. This point, called "Spell-Out," determines which movements will affect the pronunciation of a sentence – those that occur before Spell-Out – and which won't – those that occur after Spell-Out, on the way to LF. The assumption here is that the operations that occur between "Spell-Out" and PF are not of the same sort as those that operate within the computational system on the road to LF. Or, to put it differently, the computational system (whose operations are described in section 2 below) runs on the line to LF, with the derivation from Spell-Out to PF subject to the rules and operations of a separate, phonological component.

(2)

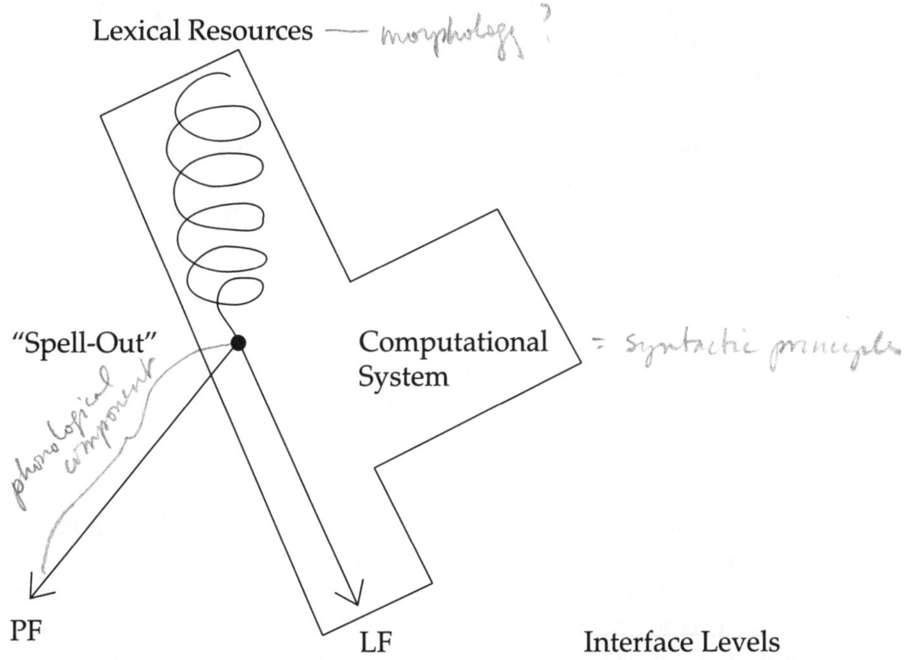

"Procrastinate" is a principle that prefers derivations that hold off on movements until after Spell-Out, so that the results of such movements do not affect PF. Procrastinate is evaluated over convergent derivations; in effect, then, a derivation may violate Procrastinate in order to converge. In English, for example, main verbs do not raise to Tense before Spell-Out, and thus are pronounced within the VP, after certain VP adverbials and after negation (see section 4.2 below). This behavior of English contrasts with French, in which main verbs do raise to Tense before Spell-Out. English verbs are thus obeying Procrastinate, waiting until after Spell-Out to raise to Tense, which they must do by LF to check off their tense features. French verbs must violate Procrastinate to insure convergence. The assumption is that French tense features, unlike their English counterparts, are "strong" and visible at PF if not checked off. English tense features are "weak" and thus invisible at PF if not checked off. Because the English tense features are weak, English may wait to check off the tense features on main verbs until LF and Procrastinate says that if you can wait, you must wait.

Greed is perhaps the most problematic of the economy principles in the MP. The intuitive force of Greed is clear, but the examples in which it should apply seem to be explained by other principles. The principle of Greed states that a constituent may not move to satisfy the needs of some other constituent; movement is motivated for selfish reasons, to satisfy the needs of the moving constituent. For example, a constituent should not move to a position in order to check off features of a node in a checking relation with that position; the constituent should move only to check off its own features.

The problem for Greed is to make the theory of features and feature-checking clear enough to be able to decide where one is failing to be Greedy but nevertheless is satisfying other principles. Greed may have relevance for cases like those in (3) in which an NP has moved from a Case position.

(3a) *John seems [t is leaving]
(3b) *John seems to t [that Bill is leaving]
(3c) *John was said to t [that Bill is leaving]

The idea here is that NP-movement (raising, passive) from a Case position is to be ruled out by Greed. An NP in a Case position already has its Case (and phi-features – person, number and gender features) checked; further movement would only help check off the features of a higher Case position, i.e. further movement would be altruistic rather than greedy. To make Greed account for the ungrammaticality of (3), one must be explicit about what counts as feature-checking. If feature-checking in effect renders the relevant features invisible, then Greed would not be needed to rule out NP-movement from a Case position – since the NP in the Case position has all its relevant features checked in this position, whether the NP is greedy or altruistic, it has no features that can do any (further) checking. Then raising in, say, (3a) could not check features at the higher Case position since *John* has no features to check that haven't already been checked off in the lower Case position.

In languages like French with past passive participle agreement, it appears as if NPs may check at least their phi-features in more than one position. As the underlying object raises to the subject of the auxiliary verb in French passives, it appears to land in a specifier position to check gender and number phi-features with the passive participle. The agreement morphology that contributes the phi-features to the passive participle is visible on the verb in (4).

(4) Les filles sont [t [rencontrées au cinéma]].
the girls are met-fem-pl at the movie theater

The underlying object in (4) must check phi-features again in spec of AGRsP as the subject of the sentence (see the structure in (6) below; AGRsP is the functional phrase above T(ense)P within CP, while AGRoP is the functional phrase above VP). The fact of multiple agreement with the same argument in a single clause suggests that features do not disappear from NPs when they are checked, or at least that phi-features do not disappear. On the other hand, Case features are crucial to the examples in (3). We shall see in connection with the discussion of infinitivals in section 6 below that Greed, like Procrastinate, appears to be limited to deciding among competing derivations that converge at the interfaces. Since movements like the ungrammatical A-movements in (3) are motivated to insure convergence, if an NP could in fact carry multiple Case features or check Case more than once, Greed shouldn't prevent these movements in (3).

2 Derivations and the Computational System

In older versions of P&P Grammar, there was a clear notion of the "starting point" of a derivation. For example, in some theories, the operation of the phrase structure rules (or principles of the Base) would be followed by the insertion of lexical items into a tree generated by these PS rules to produce a DS. A similar view identifies the starting point as a set of items drawn from the lexicon. Combining this set into a single constituent structure tree satisfying X-bar theory and the subcategorization features of the lexical items would yield a DS. The MP gives up any notion that the starting point of the derivation is a single-constituent structure tree; instead the MP claims that syntactic structures are built through generalized transformations that may insert already formed trees into trees. However, although derivations have no DS starting point, still the principle that derivations must compete (since a grammatical derivation is the most economical one from a set of competing derivations) requires some sort of "base" – something shared by competing derivations. It is tempting to try comparing derivations whose LFs have the same interpretation, but the notion of "same interpretation" or even "same LF" is difficult to make precise.

Chomsky relies instead on the notion that competing derivations are those that make use of the same lexical resources. There is a sense, then, in which MP derivations start from a set of lexical resources (see (2) above). Computation, as we will see immediately, involves putting lexical items together and competition among derivations involves comparison of computations on the same set of lexical items. I depart here from Chomsky's (1992) exposition of tree-building to provide an account of the mechanisms that I find more intuitive.

Consider the construction of a sentence to take place in a working area onto which one has already spilled some of the contents of the lexicon. The lexical items in the working area are all those that the computational system will have access to in the course of the derivation; moreover, the economy principles will compare derivations using this same set of lexical items. We will understand the lexicon to contain unlimited tokens of each lexical entry (e.g. as many tokens of the lexical item *John* as one wants); thus, the set of items in the working area may include more than one token of a lexical entry. The lexical items in the working area are completely formed words, fully inflected for case, agreement, tense, etc., a point we will return to below. A move in this working area consists of taking some piece already in the area and adding on to it in some way, perhaps by adding another piece in the area. The expanded constituent now becomes available, like all the lexical items already in the area, for further expansion or combination. At some point, the point of "Spell-Out" in (2), one may decide to take a constituent from the working area and submit it to the LF and PF components for interpretation. In the case of a grammatical representation of a sentence, the constituent removed from the working area will be a CP (or IP) containing all the lexical items originally spilled onto the working area and will (eventually) meet the interface conditions at LF and PF.

The crucial notion of competition or comparison of derivations in the MP is relativized to the derivations one might perform with a single set of lexical items in the working area. For example, suppose that there is a general economy principle of "laziness" that prefers doing nothing computationally over doing something. Clearly, if this were the most highly valued principle, we'd never produce constructions that are well-formed at the interface levels of PF and LF since the laziest thing to do with a set of lexical items is to leave them alone, in an unstructured pile, in the working area. Suppose, then, the need to create a structure well-formed at the interface levels (the desire for convergence at the interfaces) is stronger or more highly ranked than laziness. Then the computational system should do the minimal amount of work with the lexical items in the working area to insure convergence. In principle, then, one would compare all the different derivational paths one could take with the lexical items to find the laziest path that yields convergence. The derivation on this path would win the competition among derivations for this particular set of lexical items and be the only grammatical derivation for this set.

In the working area (i.e. before Spell-Out), any operation on a constituent must expand the constituent structurally, to create a larger constituent. (This expansion or "extension" requirement will need an exception, to be discussed below, to allow head-movement.) The basic operation is one of Projection, in the sense of X-bar theory, where an X projects an X′ or an X′ projects an XP (in the further development of the MP described in chapter 8, Chomsky abandons X-bar theory and proposes a conceptually simpler system of syntactic composition). The computational system targets some constituent in the working area and projects from this constituent. Within this framework, the question of whether adjunction structures may be created in the working area becomes one of whether X can project to X, X′ to X′, and XP to XP. When projecting, one has the option of including an empty category as sister to the constituent being projected, i.e. as a sister to the targeted constituent. This empty category must immediately be filled by either another constituent from the working area or by a constituent from within the targeted constituent itself. If we fill the empty category with another constituent from the working area, we have performed a generalized transformation, one that puts together what have otherwise been separate derivations. If we fill the empty category with a constituent from within the category that we are expanding, we have movement, a singulary transformation. However, movement in the MP is equivalent only to copying, not to copying and deletion. Chains formed by movement consist, then, in a sequence of copies of the "source" constituent. Where the chain is pronounced and where it is interpreted is a matter for independent principles to decide. One possible empirical advance of the MP is in its treatment of "reconstruction effects" (see section 5 below). The analysis of chains just described allows for reconstruction without any special operation; unless something else is said, a "moved" constituent exists at its source location as well as at the head of the chain of movement.

At least one sort of movement that we would wish to occur before Spell-Out cannot be thought of as expanding a targeted constituent. Suppose, as in (5), we do head-movement of the head X of an XP to adjoin to the head Y of YP, where XP is the sister of Y in Y′. This movement might expand Y through adjunction, but it could not expand Y′, which would be the minimal constituent one could target to move X to Y.

(5)

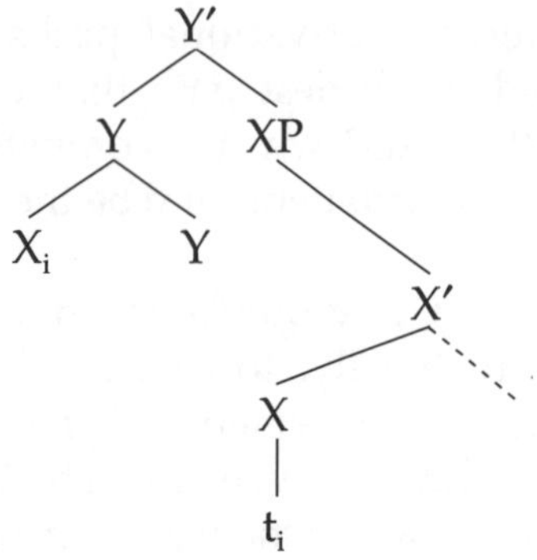

It is possible to say, as Chomsky suggests, that adjunction before Spell-Out need not expand a targeted constituent. This would allow head-movement before Spell-Out. However, if adjunction need not expand a targeted constituent, then the principle of expansion cannot insure a strictly cyclic derivation prior to Spell-Out. Without the necessity to expand the target, head-movement could reach down and move a head deeply embedded in a targeted constituent and adjoin it to another head also deeply embedded. In fact, nothing essential to the basic computational mechanisms here would prevent downward movement and adjunction of a head.

At any point in the computation, one may take the contents of the working area and submit it to the PF and LF components. As noted above, this splitting of the derivation on the separate paths to the interfaces is known as "Spell-Out." After Spell-Out, the generalized transformation of the computational system is no longer active. Thus, if the contents of the working area have not been combined into a single structure at Spell-Out, nothing in PF or LF will be able to put the pieces together, and the unjoined set of items will presumably not be well-formed (as a constituent) at the interfaces. If a derivation is to meet interface conditions, then, all the contents of the working area – all the lexical items – must be combined prior to Spell-Out.

If operations in the working area are limited to the projection and expansion of constituents, we insure that derivations will appear to obey a strict cycle condition. One cannot go back inside a constituent and do further expansion, nor is downward movement a possibility. Questions arise about operations – limited to singulary transformations – in the PF and LF components. Clearly movement at LF must occur within constituents already built in the working area. For example, in English main verbs will raise to Tense and to AGR at LF in the MP (see below); this raising occurs within already constructed AGRPs and TP. Relative to operations already performed before Spell-Out, then, movement at LF will violate a strict cycle condition. If, however, we adopt the same project and expand formalism for movement at LF as for movement before Spell-Out, then still at LF downward movement will be impossible since movement will always attach some constituent from within a target phrase to a constituent containing the target phrase (head-movement will still require special consideration). However, one must still ask whether any independent principles are required to insure a bottom-up derivation at LF for upward movement operations. Will problems arise, for example, if we allow LF-movement in a higher clause followed by LF-movement in an embedded clause?

On the PF side of the grammar after Spell-Out, operations are assumed not to conform to the basic mechanisms of the computational system. Importantly, then, movement to feature-checking positions does not occur on the way to PF after Spell-Out. If features are unchecked at Spell-Out, they remain so at the PF interface and will cause a derivation to crash, if they are visible at PF ("strong").

3 Features and Convergence

At the heart of the MP are what Chomsky calls "morphological features." These include features associated with tense, case, and agreement. Items from lexical categories such as V, N, and Adj, are fully inflected in the lexicon. The addition of, e.g., tense and agreement morphology (such as phonologically overt affixes) to a Verb in the lexicon involves the simultaneous addition of tense and agreement features, features that play a role in the computational system of language but which play no role at the PF or LF interfaces. These features, then, if potentially visible to these interfaces, must be eliminated prior to PF and LF. Failure to eliminate morphological features prior to an interface at which they are visible causes a derivation to crash (fail to converge) at this interface.

The functional categories of AGR and T in this system are the locus of tense and agreement features that may check off or eliminate the corresponding features on a Verb that moves up and adjoins to these categories. AGR and T also contain Case and phi-features that they may check off against features of NPs (DPs) that raise to their specs. In the MP, these functional nodes never contain items from the lexicon; they are not the positions in which inflectional affixes are inserted. Rather, inflectional affixes are attached to items of the lexical categories in the lexicon. The functional nodes of AGR and T serve only to carry the morphological (inflectional) features necessary to check off the features on Ns and Vs.

The hierarchical structure of a CP will look something like that shown in (6) (NEGP will not be discussed in this chapter). Chomsky leaves open what principles determine the hierarchical ordering of the various XPs in (6) as well as the question of whether this hierarchical ordering might vary from language to language. In addition, there may be additional functional projections between VP and CP or above CP.

(6)

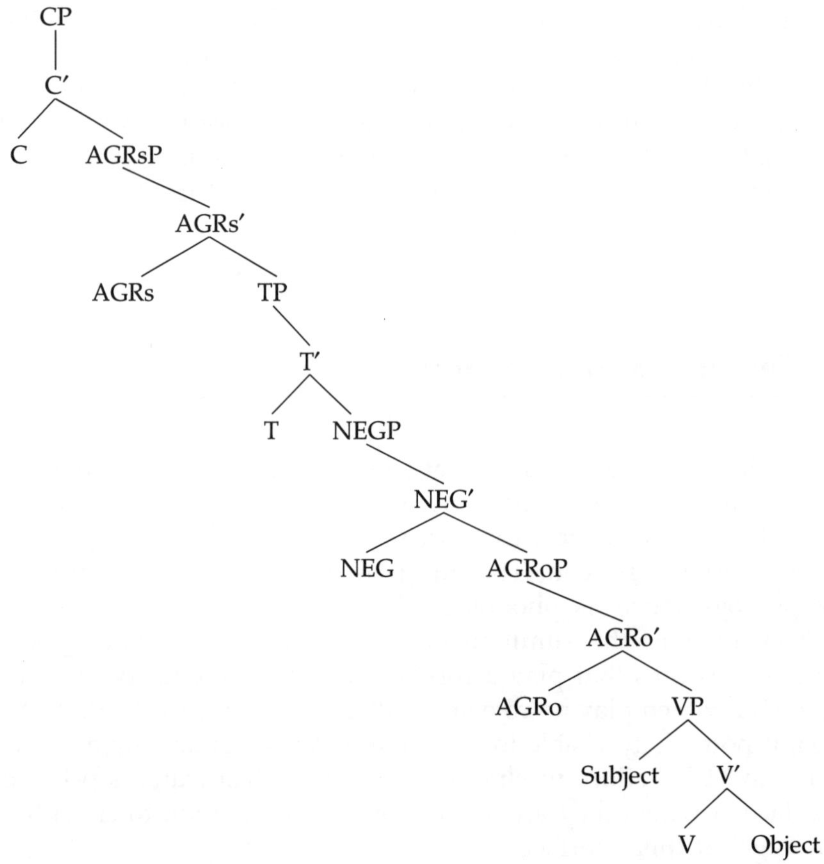

The AGRP above T(ense)P is labeled AGRs for "subject agreement" and the AGRP above VP AGRo for "object agreement." However, Chomsky claims that there is no difference between the sorts of features found at these two AGR positions and hence no difference in the category labels of the two positions. That is, there is no intrinsic difference between the features of AGRs and AGRo, only a positional difference between the two AGR nodes. The contrast between the NOM Case usually licensed by AGRs and the ACC Case associated with AGRo results from the raising of T to AGRs and V to AGRo; the Cases are associated with features of T and V respectively. This is not to say that the AGR features in AGRs and AGRo will be identical in every sentence. The AGR features in AGRs will include the phi-features (person, number, gender) of the subject DP that is raised to spec of AGRs while the AGR features in AGRo will include the phi-features of the object DP that is raised to spec of AGRo. However, the phi-features themselves – i.e. the AGR features – will come from the same pool of features and will not be identifiable as subject or object AGR features except by the location of the AGR node in which they reside.

To check its AGR and Tense features, the V will raise to AGR, to T, and to AGR, either before Spell-Out or at LF. The corresponding tense and agreement features on T and on the AGRs are known as the "V" features of T and AGR, i.e. the features that check off the features of the V. These functional nodes, as well as the Verb, also have "N" features, or features that check off features on NP (DP) arguments. The "Case Filter" of the earlier P&P theory divides into two parts in the MP. First, Ns in the lexicon (and/or perhaps Ds) must be assigned morphological case features before they are inserted into structures via generalized transformations. This requirement insures that DPs will have a need to move to a position to check off these morphological features prior to an interface level at which the features might be visible and cause a derivation to fail to converge. The second part of the Case Filter, that the Case features on DPs be checked off in the syntax, is now part of a much wider and more central system in the MP. Head-movement of Verbs to inflectional nodes as well as the movement of DP arguments to Case positions are now motivated by this generalized form of the Case Filter – i.e. the requirement that morphological features get checked off before the interface levels.

On the MP program, there is only one, generalized, relation that allows one element to license another, by checking off the latter's features. This basic relation derives from what Chomsky takes to be the basic relation of Agreement – the relation between a head and its specifier. Unlike in previous versions of the theory, no licensing takes place between a head and its complement; the relation of "government" plays no direct role in this theory. The licensing or "checking" domain of a head H includes the specifier of H, a head position adjoined to H, a position adjoined to the maximal projection of H, and a position adjoined to the specifier of H. Chomsky's definitions of structural relations puts all these positions in the "checking domain" of H. For the basic cases we will discuss here, the important positions in the checking domain of H are the specifier of H, where DPs will check Case and phi-features against H, and the position adjoined to H, since the Verb will adjoin to functional heads to have its (V) features checked by these heads.

4 Parameters and Basic Word Order

4.1 *Deriving Basic Clause Structure*

Within the MP, differences between languages are attributed to differences between the features of lexical items in the languages and specifically between the features of lexical items belonging to the functional categories AGR and Tense. Recall that Vs and Ns are taken from the lexicon fully inflected with inflectional affixes. The functional nodes in the syntax are not associated with affixes (nor with any phonological content whatsoever) but simply with certain features – Tense, Case, and Agreement features among others. Nevertheless, specific bundles of these features of the category AGR and T are lexical items and differences between the sets of bundles available in the lexicon account for cross-linguistic syntactic differences between languages in the MP.

Consider, then, how a basic sentential structure is derived for English within this framework. We might be deriving a simple transitive sentence, such as, "Hortense touched the porcupine." Subject and object DPs would be initially inserted via generalized transformations within the VP (see (6) above). That is, assume that two DPs, "Hortense" and "the porcupine," have been created with lexical items from the working area and redeposited in the working area. We target a (fully inflected) V, "touched," from the working area, project a V′ with an empty complement position to the V and immediately replace the empty complement with one of the previously constructed DPs, "the porcupine," which will be the object. Next we target the V′, project VP with an empty spec of VP position and replace this empty spec of VP with the other DP previously constructed, "Hortense," which is now the subject. The V will contain ACC Case features to check against the object DP at LF, as well as past Tense features to check against T. It also must have AGR features of both subject and object DPs to check against the AGRs that it will adjoin to.

Case features and phi-features (person, number, gender) would be associated with each DP argument. Chomsky leaves somewhat open where these features of the DP come from, i.e. which lexical items contribute these features to the DP as a whole. One possibility is that the features of the DP are features of the head D of the DP and that other constituents within the DP that bear affixes with, say, Case, gender or number features from the lexicon must check these features against the features in D at some point in the derivation. Another possibility is that the Case and phi-features of the DP are inherited in some manner from the features of the head N of the NP that serves as complement to D.

At some point in the derivation of our basic transitive sentence, an AGR from the working area would be targeted and would project an AGR′ and the VP would be inserted as the sister to the AGR. In our example, for the derivation to converge, the AGR would need to contain the phi-features of "the porcupine." This AGR is identified as AGRo by its position governing VP, but not by any of its intrinsic features. As explained above, features of the functional categories are said to be either "strong" or "weak" with respect to their visibility at the PF interface. "Strong" AGR features are visible at PF if they are not checked off before the interface. "Weak" features are not visible. Visibility at PF does not correspond directly to any notion of "rich phonological content" since the functional nodes do not in any case contain any phonological material – no affixes. Whether an AGR or a T node has strong or weak features, a phonologically null constituent will, in general, appear at that node. In English, the "N-features of AGR" – the person, number, and gender features that AGR will check off against the corresponding features on a DP in spec of AGRP – are weak and therefore may appear (invisibly) at PF without causing a crash (without disturbing convergence). The principle of Procrastination demands that movement wait until after Spell-Out as long as waiting is compatible with convergence. Since an object DP need not move to spec of AGRP to check off the weak features there until after Spell-Out, Procrastinate demands that it not move before Spell-Out. Thus objects in English do not visibly move to the spec of AGRP position. Since this position is not filled before Spell-Out, it is not projected. Recall that if the spec of AGRP were projected, it would be filled by an empty category that would immediately need to be replaced with a constituent from the working area (in a generalized transformation) or with a constituent from within AGR′ (a singulary transformation). There is no entity in the MP consisting of a position that is projected but not filled (although a position might of course be filled by an empty category, such as PRO or *pro*).

After we have created AGRP, a Tense is taken from the working area and projects a T′ into which the AGRP containing the VP is inserted as a complement to T. The T in our example must contain the "V-feature" past tense to check against the past tense feature on the verb, "touched." The N-features of T in English – Nominative Case features in the case of finite tense – are strong. Thus, unless the (subject) DP raises to check the Nom features before Spell-Out, the derivation will crash at PF. However, the assumption is that the N-features of T, like the Case (N-)features of V, are checked in conjunction with AGR. Therefore, T will raise to a higher AGR and check its N-features against a DP in spec of AGRP. For reasons discussed in Chomsky (this volume), the subject raising to spec of this higher AGRP need not and will not pass through the spec of TP position, which will therefore not be projected.

Note again here that head-movement prior to Spell-Out causes a small technical problem for a strict interpretation of the principle that all operations prior to Spell-Out expand the constituent that they target. If we wish to move and adjoin a T from the TP serving as complement to the higher AGR in (6), we must target AGR′, for only the AGR′ contains both the AGR and T heads involved in the movement. But, adjoining the head T of the TP to the head AGR of the AGR′, as we must in English, does not technically expand the targeted AGR′. The AGR head itself may only be targeted when AGR′ is projected. It may be that adjunction in general must be allowed before Spell-Out and allowed to violate the "always expand the targeted constituent" principle. Alternatively, the definitions of "targeting and expanding" a constituent would have to be redefined to allow for head-movement and adjunction as a type of expansion.

Making the N-features (Case features) of T strong in English is a way to implement the Extended Projection Principle (EPP) of earlier approaches, i.e. the requirement that sentences have (overt) subjects. Within Chomsky's particular set of assumptions here, it is not possible to capture the EPP for English by making the N-features of AGR strong. Recall that AGRs and AGRo are not distinguished by their intrinsic features. If the N-features of AGR are strong, then the N-features of the AGR above VP will be strong, in addition to the N-features of the AGR above TP. Thus, if the N-features of AGR were strong in English, objects as well as subjects would have to raise to spec of AGRP before Spell-Out and we would expect to pronounce the object (higher than and) before the verb.

Following along our sample derivation of "Hortense touched the porcupine," to produce a structure like (6) above, we target the higher AGR′, project AGR(s)P, and move the subject from within the VP to the spec of AGRP position. Assume that we have already adjoined T to AGR and that the combination of AGR and T may check the Case and phi-features of the subject DP "Hortense." The movement of the subject from spec of VP to spec of AGRP crosses two potential spec positions, spec of the lower AGRP and spec of TP. However, neither of these positions has been projected, and neither will be projected prior to Spell-Out. Therefore, this movement does not violate the Shortest Move economy principle. To be more accurate about the determination of grammaticality here: we evaluate a derivation in which we move the subject from spec of VP to spec of AGRP against other alternative derivations from the same lexical resources in the working area. Since the distance of movement is computed relative to projected positions of the same sort as the end-point of movement, there is no alternative derivation that gets the subject to spec of AGRP in which the subject takes a shorter movement.

After Spell-Out, "at LF" (i.e. in the computation of LF), the object, "the porcupine," will move to spec of the lower AGR(o)P to check its Case and phi-features. Here it is assumed that the ACC Case feature is associated with the V but checked by the V in combination with AGR, just as NOM is associated with finite Tense but checked by Tense in combination with AGR. The movement of the object to spec of AGRoP crosses a projected spec position, the spec of VP which is occupied by the tail of the A-chain of the subject "Hortense" (i.e. by the trace of the subject). Unless some other consideration applies here, this movement over a projected spec position should be a violation of Shortest Move, here clearly connected to Relativized Minimality. A derivation in which the object moves to spec of VP position on its way to spec of AGRoP (and covers or adjoins to the trace of the subject) would eventually violate other principles or at least be uninterpretable at LF. However, when considering whether a movement would violate Shortest Move, all that matters is that there is a shorter movement available, not that taking this shorter move in some derivation from the same lexical resources could lead to convergence. Shortest Move, unlike Greed and Procrastinate, is ranked higher than convergence in comparing derivations from the same lexical resources (see the discussion of (1b) above).

So how is a violation of Shortest Move avoided when the object moves to spec of AGRoP? At LF, the verb in English will raise to AGR, with the AGR+V combination raising to the T+AGR combination created before Spell-Out. The V has the N-features of (accusative) Case that it will check off, in combination with AGR, against a DP in spec of AGR(o)P. In addition, it has Tense features and AGR features of the subject, which it will check off when it gets to the highest AGR node. Chomsky defines a notion of equidistance that allows the spec of XP and the spec of a YP that is a complement to X to be equidistant from an element inside Y′ just in case Y adjoins to X, as shown in (7a).

(7a)

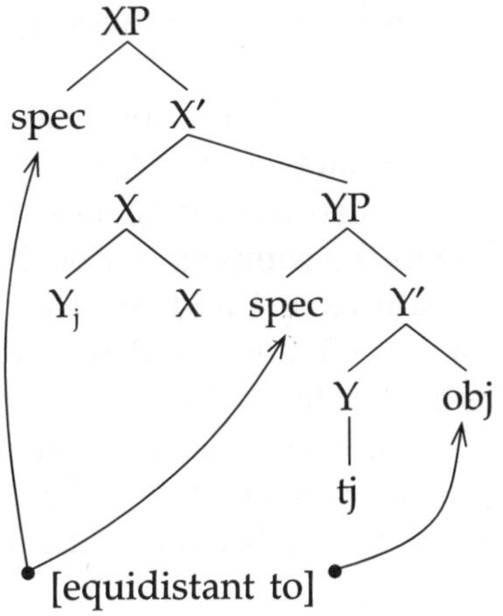

(7b)

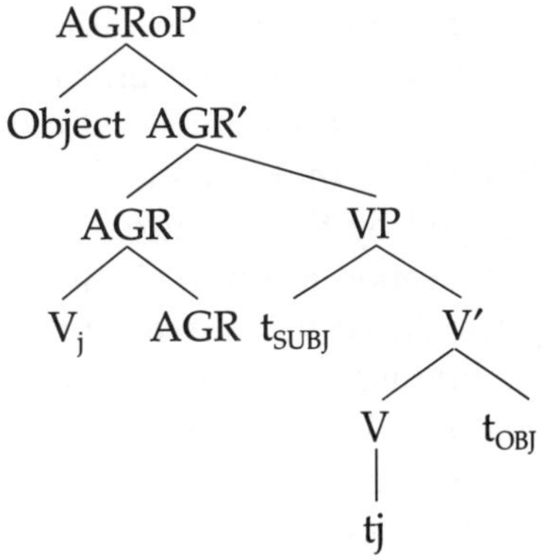

In the situation of interest, (7b), the spec of AGRoP and the spec of VP are equidistant to the complement of V after V raises and adjoins to AGR. Since these specs are equidistant from the object, a derivation in which the object raises over spec of VP to spec of AGRP does not lose out for economy reasons to a derivation in which the object lands in the spec of VP.

The sample derivation discussed above began with the assumption that we had all the proper lexical items in our working area to allow for convergence. In particular, the subject N (or D) "Hortense" was assumed to have NOM Case from the lexicon, the Case that would be checked by the N-features of T in combination with the AGR above TP. The object N (or D), "porcupine" or "the," was assumed to have ACC Case from the lexicon, i.e. the Case that would be checked by N-features of V in combination with the AGR above VP. Suppose, however, that the N in the object DP came from the lexicon with nominative Case and the N in the subject DP came with accusative Case. Could there be a convergent derivation in which the complement to V ends up in spec of the higher AGRP and the specifier of VP ends up in the spec of the lower AGRP, a derivation in which we derive "The porcupine touched Hortense," with the meaning of "Hortense touched the porcupine"?

For the core case of English sentences containing main verbs, such a derivation would not be grammatical. Recall that for the object to raise over the spec of VP at all and not violate Shortest Move, the verb must raise to AGR and the object must land in the spec of the lower AGRP. The strong N-features of T in English require that the DP that ends up in spec of the higher AGRP move to this position before Spell-Out. However, main verbs (i.e. verbs that are not auxiliary verbs) do not raise before Spell-Out in English. Since main verbs do not move before Spell-Out, the object may not raise over a (filled) spec of VP position before Spell-Out and thus may not fill the spec of the higher AGRP before Spell-Out, as required if the underlying object were to have NOM Case checked and end up as the surface subject.

Of course we must ask why it is that main verbs do not raise before Spell-Out in English. Could we violate whatever principle is being obeyed by their failure to raise in order to insure convergence, should we happen to put a DP with NOM Case in the complement position of a transitive VP? We assume that the V-features of T and AGR are weak in English. Thus the verb need not raise to T and AGR to check its features before Spell-Out and, by Procrastinate, it therefore may not raise. However, we have seen that Procrastinate can be violated to insure convergence, as when the subject raises to spec of AGRP before Spell-Out in English. Therefore, perhaps the verb could raise before

Spell-Out in English to allow a NOM DP to escape the VP and head toward spec of the higher AGRP to have its Case checked.

Other considerations rule out such derivations of our "inverse" sentence, "The porcupine touched Hortense," although it is not clear which principles should be considered crucial to derive this result. Recall that movement of a head Y to the head X where YP is complement to X makes the spec of YP and the spec of XP equidistant from material in the complement of Y, as shown in (7a). If we further move X (with Y adjoined) to the head Z of ZP where XP is the complement to Z, we make spec of ZP and spec of XP equidistant from material in the complement to X. However, although the spec of ZP and the spec of XP are equidistant from material below X′ and the spec of XP and the spec of YP are also equidistant from material below Y′, the spec of ZP and the spec of YP are not equidistant from the complement of Y; equidistance is not transitive in this way. Thus an object may move over the spec of VP if the V raises to AGRoP, but it may only move as far as the spec of AGRoP from the complement of V position in one step if spec of VP is filled; no matter how high the AGR to which V is adjoined may move, the spec of VP will be equidistant at most with the spec of AGRoP to the object in the complement of V position.

As a result of the definition of equidistance, if we tried to move a NOM marked object up to spec of the higher AGR(s)P, it would by necessity move through the spec of the lower AGR(o)P. In the simple situation under consideration, where we derive "The porcupine touched Hortense," this lower spec of AGRP is a Case-checking position, a position for checking the ACC Case assumed to be on the (underlying) subject DP, "Hortense." Thus Greed might prevent the object from leaving this spec of AGRP position to move onto the higher spec of AGRP position and check NOM Case, assuming that Greed in general prevents movement from a Case-checking position to another Case-checking position. Alternatively, there might be reasons why the subject DP "Hortense" should be prevented from moving into spec of the lower AGRP at LF, covering the trace of the object. In short, the "reverse" derivation in which a subject moves to spec of AGRoP and the object moves into spec of AGRsP is prohibited if principles prevent the object from moving through the spec of AGRoP on its way to AGRsP, since Shortest Move requires this movement.

4.2 *Parametric Differences*

Recall that Chomsky assumes that the significant parametric differences between languages are limited to lexical differences, specifically, differences in the features of the lexical elements that occupy the functional category nodes. For basic parametric differences in constituent (word) order, Chomsky looks to the AGR and T nodes and their N-features and V-features. The N-features are those that are checked off against a DP in spec of AGRP (or, potentially, spec of TP) and the V-features are those that are checked off against a V that adjoins to a functional head. These features may be either weak – invisible at PF even if unchecked – or strong – visible at PF if unchecked – in a language. For AGR and T independently, there are four different combinations possible of weak and strong N- and V-features (i.e. strong N with strong V, strong N with weak V . . .). Since the strength of N- and V-features on AGR is at least conceptually independent of their strength on T, the four combinations of features on AGR can combine freely with the four combinations on T to yield 16 possible language types defined by the strength of their morphological features in AGR and T. We saw that English has strong N-features on T but weak V-features. The strong N-features require a DP (subject) to move to spec of AGRsP before Spell-Out; the weak V-features permit the V to stay in VP before Spell-Out. Both the N- and V-feature of AGR must be weak. If the V-features were strong, the verb would have to raise out of the VP before Spell-Out. If the N-features of AGR were strong, the object would have to raise to spec of AGR(o)P before Spell-Out.

In French, main verbs do raise to Tense before Spell-Out in finite clauses. Evidence for this difference between English and French comes from, e.g., the relative positions of tensed main verbs and VP-adjoined adverbs, as in (8). English leaves the main tensed verb inside the VP before Spell-Out, and thus to the right of the adverb. French raises the verb to T before Spell-Out, and it is pronounced to the left of the adverb.

(8a) Elmer lave souvent son chat
Elmer washes often his cat
(8b) Elmer often washes his cat

Thus the V-features of either AGR or T or both must be strong in French, in contrast to English. Since objects do not raise out of the VP before Spell-Out in French, the N-features of AGR must be weak, as in English. In adopting this account of the differences between French and English, Chomsky is building on the pioneering work of Emonds and the recent analysis of Emonds's (1978) insights in Pollock (1989).

Chomsky also suggests that the N-features of AGR and T might be weak in verb-initial languages such as Irish. With weak N-features on all functional heads, the subject and object of verbs in these languages could remain in the VP until after Spell-Out. If the V-features of T and/or AGR were strong, the verb would be forced to raise from the VP prior to Spell-Out in these languages, yielding a VSO order of major constituents. The relative positioning of VP adverbs, negative morphemes and the inflected verb in various languages has been widely studied within the MP recently.

5 Copy Theory of Movement

In addition to the various changes to standard P&P theories we have described above, Chomsky's MP adds an explicit endorsement of the copy theory of movement. Thus, when a singulary transformation replaces a projected empty category in position X with a constituent from position Y, both position X and position Y – both members of the chain created by "movement" – contain a copy of the "moved" constituent. After Spell-Out, on the way to both PF and LF, the grammar must decide which members of the chain are pronounced and which are interpreted. In standard cases of A- or A-bar movement, e.g. passive or *wh*-movement, the constituent whose copies form the chain is pronounced at the head of the chain, in either the Case(-checking) position for A-movement or the A-bar operator position for A-bar movement. Similarly, any thematic role associated with the constituent is usually assigned to the copy at the tail of the chain, so in a sense the constituent is interpreted in this position.

The copy theory of movement and the adoption of generalized transformations provides an approach to various types of "reconstruction effects." For example, in standard cases of A-bar reconstruction effects, the proper application of standard Binding Theory requires putting back some or all of an A-bar moved constituent. Treating (9a) with standard Binding Theory at LF necessitates finding the reflexive back in the trace position, as in (10a). Under a copy theory, although the whole moved constituent is pronounced at the head of the chain (with perhaps PF deletion of the material in the copy of the moved constituent at the tail of the chain), at LF we may delete all but the *which* at the head of the chain and nothing but the *which* at the tail of the chain, deriving (in 10a) a possible input to interpretation and producing a suitable candidate for Binding Theory. In the case in (9b), where complete reconstruction would produce a Condition C violation (cf. (9c)), we may choose a different sort of deletion pattern at LF, as shown in (10b). Here we delete all the material at the tail of the chain and retain the material in the operator at the head of the chain.

(9a) Which pictures of himself did Mary say John saw t
(9b) Which pictures of John_i did Mary say he_i saw t
(9c) *Mary said he_i saw those pictures of John_i
(10a) Which_x, Mary said John saw [x pictures of himself]
(10b) Which x, x a picture of John, Mary said he saw x

Chomsky also suggests that adopting generalized transformations will allow him to incorporate insights about the interaction of adjunction and Binding Theory from Lebeaux (1988). Consider the basic contrast in (11); in (11a) coreference between *John* and *he* is allowed, in contrast to (11b) where a similar coreference relation seems ill-formed.

(11a) Which claim that John_i made did he_i regret?
(11b) ?*Which claim that John_i runs did he_i deny?

Assume that the *that* clause in (11b) is the complement to the N *claim*. Assume also that relative clauses, like *that John made* in (11a), are adjoined to DP (or NP). Finally, assume that adjunction falls outside the requirement that an operation in the computational system before Spell-Out must always expand the targeted constituent. Thus relative clauses, as adjuncts, may be added to a DP after this DP has already been incorporated into a sentence via a generalized transformation, and even after this DP has undergone movement. Putting these assumptions together with the copy theory of movement, one may explain the contrast in (11). In (11a), the relative clause is adjoined to *which claim* after this constituent has raised to spec of CP. Thus the copy of the *which claim* in the position c-commanded by *he* in (11a) does not contain *John*, and no Condition C violation is expected. On the other hand, a complement to N must be incorporated into the structure when the N′ is projected. Thus in (11b), the complement *that John runs* must be part of the copy of the constituent *which claim that John runs* in the trace position c-commanded by *he*. We expect then a Condition C violation in (11b) but not in (11a), since there is a derivation of (11a) in which *he* does not c-command (a copy of) *John* at LF.

There is some tension between the explanation of reconstruction effects in (9) and the anti-reconstruction effects in (11). Following the analysis of (9b) above, we might be able to delete most of the trace copy of *which claim that John runs*, leaving *which x, x a claim that John runs* in the operator position and removing *John* from a position c-commanded by *he* at LF. Chomsky discusses approaches to the contrast between reconstruction and anti-reconstruction effects in Chomsky (1992).

6 Some Residual Issues

Although recovering within the MP all the data previously accounted for in earlier versions of P&P syntax is beyond both Chomsky (1992) and this summary, I will briefly discuss here a few remaining issues and constructions. First, although main verbs do not raise from the VP to AGR or T prior to Spell-Out in English, auxiliary verbs do. To account for the behavior of English auxiliary verbs, one might give them strong N-features for the phi-features of subjects or strong Tense features. In either case, the strong features on auxiliaries would force their movement before Spell-Out, in contrast to main verbs. However, Chomsky proposes instead that the behavior of English auxiliaries might be principled and follow from their lack of semantic content. "Have" and "be" in particular, used as auxiliaries, bear tense affixes and appear in connection with participles to express tense and aspect, but carry no particular semantic value in themselves. If "have" and "be," being semantically vacuous, were truly invisible after Spell-Out in the LF part of the grammar, they could not be raised to Tense and AGR to check off features there. Movement prior to Spell-Out of these verbs would then be forced, in violation of Procrastination, since Procrastination only compares derivations that converge at LF and PF. In addition, Greed will be violated by the pre-Spell-Out movement of auxiliaries. Since the auxiliaries are invisible at LF, any morphological features they carry would presumably be invisible as well. Therefore, when the auxiliary verbs move prior to Spell-Out to insure convergence, they are acting altruistically to check off the features of AGR and T, not with Greed to check off their own features.

This solution to the problem of distinguishing main and auxiliary verbs, together with other assumptions of the MP, leaves Chomsky without an account of *do*-insertion (to replace that from Chomsky's earlier "Economy" framework (1989)). We know that auxiliary verbs raise before Spell-Out over *not* to T and AGR in negative sentences like (12a) and over the subject to C in inversion contexts like (12b).

(12a) John is not leaving here soon enough for me
(12b) Is John leaving here at all?

Assume that a tensed main verb agreeing with a subject would need to move to T and AGR to check features by LF. If something prevented the main verbs from moving to T and AGR after Spell-Out, Procrastinate could be violated to assure convergence, and main verbs like auxiliaries should raise before Spell-Out to the AGRs and T in negated sentences – (13a) – and on to C in inversion contexts – (13b). Compare the Procrastination-violating movement of auxiliary verbs prior to Spell-Out to insure convergence.

(13a) *John leaves not until he's told
(13b) *Leaves John before the food arrives?

A number of possible MP approaches to *do*-insertion suggest themselves (and see Watanabe (1993)). Given the assumption that we compare only derivations using the same lexical resources and the assumption that all inflected verbs and all functional nodes are lexical items, we cannot compare derivations of constructions like (13) with constructions containing "do," as in (14). The lexical resources in (13) and (14) are different and thus the derivations of these structures should not compete.

(14a) John does not leave until he's told
(14b) Does John leave before the food arrives?

Therefore, the key to explaining the *do*-insertion facts in the MP as presented has two parts. First, we must make sure that the most economical derivations involving the lexical resources in (13) fail to converge. For example, if Shortest Move were to be violated by the movements of the main verbs in (13) (but not by the parallel movement of auxiliary verbs in (12)), then we're in business, since Shortest Move generally takes precedence over convergence. It is not immediately clear, however, how the derivation of the structures in (13) might violate Shortest Move.

To complete the account of *do*-insertion, there is no problem allowing the derivations of the structures in (14), which should be economical given the choice of lexical resources they use. Rather, the second problem in explaining *do*-insertion is to rule out the use of "do" outside of *do*-insertion contexts, e.g. in (15).

(15) *John does leave before he's told. (non-emphatic: unstressed *does*)

Here again we cannot compare the derivation in (15) to the derivation of "John leaves before he's told," since these employ different lexical resources. A new account of *do*-insertion within the MP needs to find an alternative way to account for the apparent "last resort" character of the use of "do."

Another difference between standard P&P theories and the MP involves the treatment of Exceptional Case Marking (ECM) constructions. On the view of Case checking outlined above, structural Case is never checked under government but only in a spec-head relation with AGR and T or V. To have ACC Case checked, then, objects in English must raise from the VP at LF and land in spec of AGRoP. Similarly, in ECM constructions such as (16), the lower subject must raise at LF out of the lower clause and to the position in the higher spec of AGRoP marked by the ACC in (16).

(16) I [ACC [believe [John_i [to have been chosen t_i for the job]]]]

Although this "raising to object" takes place at LF, not before Spell-Out, raising to object should have recognizable consequences since such principles as those of binding theory apply at LF. Lasnik (1993a) explores some of these, reviving arguments from Postal (1974).

In ECM constructions like (16), interesting issues arise around the overt presence of *John* in spec of AGRsP of the lower clause, raised from the trace position in lower VP (the lower object position). Since *John* doesn't check its Case or phi-features until it moves up to spec of the higher AGRoP at LF (the "ACC" position in (16)), the movement from its base position within the lower VP to spec of AGRsP in its own clause seems unmotivated, a violation of Procrastinate. Apparently Procrastinate is not being violated to insure convergence since it does not appear that strong features are being checked in the lower spec of AGRsP.

To explain the behavior of ECM and raising constructions, a revised theory of infinitivals has been articulated (see Chomsky and Lasnik (1991)). The infinitival Tense of control constructions, those with subject PROs, are assumed to check Case on PRO in spec of AGRsP, perhaps NOM Case, but to be restricted to checking the features only of PRO. So a PRO that reaches the spec of AGRsP of such a control infinitival must stay there, with all its features checked, and a non-PRO that reaches this spec will fail to have its features checked and will cause a crash. Subject position of an infinitival in control constructions (and in any construction that permits an "arbitrary" PRO subject) is thus just like the subject position of a tensed clause, with the exception that only PRO is allowed to occupy this position.

On the other hand, the Tense of an infinitival clause like that in (16), an infinitival Tense of an ECM or raising construction, must check some features against any DP in spec of AGRsP, be it PRO or overt.

These features must be strong to insure movement of the subject to this position before Spell-Out, in violation of both Procrastination and Greed. However, whatever these strong features are, they must not check off the Case and phi-features of a subject, which must move on from the subject position of the embedded infinitival to spec of a higher AGRsP or AGRoP. In raising to subject constructions, the further movement to spec of AGRsP takes place before Spell-Out in English; in the ECM constructions, as we have seen, the further movement to spec of AGRoP takes place at LF. These strong features of non-finite Tense in raising and ECM constructions might be called "Extended Projection Principle" features, because, like the earlier EPP, they insure that sentences will have an "overt" subject (phonologically overt, trace, *pro*, or PRO).

Note that the movement of the subject out of the lower VP in the ECM construction in (16) had to be forced by (strong) features that needed checking in the landing site of the movement. In general, movement is not optional in the MP and overt movement is always forced by strong features. This implies that overt *wh*-movement in English must be forced by strong *wh*-features in C, for example.

If all movement is forced and no movement is optional, the MP faces a challenge in apparent optional movement of constituents, e.g. in Scrambling in Japanese and other languages with apparent freedom in word order. Some differences in constituent order might be accounted for through the imaginative use of some of the functional heads in (6). For example, suppose that all the N features of T and AGR are potentially weak in Japanese. Then no DP need raise from the VP to check Case or phi-features prior to Spell-Out. Now if some of these N-features are optionally strong, movement of some of the constituents from VP but not others could be forced. For example, the N-features of V might optionally be strong, forcing movement of V to AGRo and movement of the object to spec of AGRoP prior to Spell-Out. If all other relevant features are weak, the object will appear to have scrambled over the subject. The optionality in Scrambling on this account would not be in the movement itself but in the choice of lexical items, a choice between a lexical item with strong or weak features. Other approaches to Scrambling within the MP are of course conceivable and are being explored in the literature.

7 Reactions and Extensions

In previous versions of P&P syntax, functional heads such as Tense (or Infl) were often the sites of lexical insertion of actual affixes – lexical items with phonological as well as morphological features. Certain types of word formation, then, were accomplished via syntactic operations on syntactic heads (see Marantz (1984) and Baker (1988a), for example). Attempts were made to explain aspects of the internal structure of words through their construction via syntactic operations.

Under the MP, all inflected words are formed in the lexicon. The question arises, then, whether all explanations of the distribution of morphemes within words should be left to whatever principles govern affixation in the lexicon. In addition, Chomsky explicitly limits the computational system to the path from lexical resources to LF. If any operations on tree structures occur between Spell-Out and PF, they would seem to fall outside the mechanisms, if not the principles, characteristic of the computations in the syntax proper.

In proposing and detailing the theory of "Distributed Morphology," Halle and Marantz (1992) suggest that functional heads like Tense and AGR should in fact serve as the locus of lexical ("Vocabulary") insertion and that all word formation should occur in the syntax, as a result of the syntactic combination of heads. In addition, we argue that the operations taking place in a derivation between Spell-Out and PF are of the same sort and obey the same principles as the operations in the rest of the syntax. The last section of Halle and Marantz (1992) lays out what is at stake in the differences between the assumptions of the MP and those of Distributed Morphology.

Between the introduction of the MP and the writing of this chapter, a large research effort has applied the core of the program to a wide range of languages, with various modifications and extensions of MP ideas and principles. Some energetic work within the MP has centered on the analysis of ergative languages and ergative constructions. For example, Murasugi (1992) modifies principles and assumptions of the MP to allow the subject to land in the spec of AGRoP and the object in the spec of AGRsP in ergative languages. Bobaljik (1993) provides an alternative analysis of ergativity more consistent with the MP as described here.

Much recent MP research has concentrated on the overt appearance of various arguments in the specifier positions above VP. For example, Carnie and Bobaljik (Carnie 1993) propose that the subject in Irish raises to spec of TP before Spell-Out, rather than remaining within the VP. VSO order results when the verb raises to AGRs. Comparative research on the Germanic languages has explored "object shift" and other apparent movements that place arguments to the left of adverbs and other constituents thought to mark the left edge of the VP. Recall that the verb must raise to AGRo to allow the object to move past the spec of VP position and escape the VP; this raising makes the spec of VP and spec of AGRoP equidistant to the object in complement to V position. If the object is to leave the VP prior to Spell-Out, the verb must also raise prior to Spell-Out, i.e. overtly. One apparent consequence of the MP, then, is to predict a correlation between overt movement of the V from the VP and "object shift" – overt movement of the object out of the VP (see Bures (1992) and Jonas and Bobaljik (1993)).

Longer works that propose significant modifications and/or extensions of the MP include Branigan (1992), Watanabe (1993), Lasnik (1993a), Kitahara (1994b), and Zwart (1993). For a collection of recent papers that include applications of the MP as well as extensive bibliographic references, see Bobaljik and Phillips (1993) and Phillips (1993).

8 The End of Syntax

In closing, I would like to discuss a certain radical flavor to the MP in Chomsky (1992) and in his Bare Phrase Structure theory of chapter 8. In contrast to the wide-ranging discussion of somewhat intricate data from a number of languages found in Chomsky (1981), for example, Chomsky's latest papers (1992, this volume) treat very little data, and the discussion of data itself is somewhat programmatic. We should not interpret this move to minimalist syntax as a rejection of the enormous volume of extraordinary work within the P&P approach since the early 1980s. On the contrary, this detailed and highly successful work on a wide range of languages has inspired Chomsky to envisage the end of syntax per se. From one point of view, explanations in current syntactic work are emerging at the interfaces with phonology, and, perhaps more extensively, with semantic interpretation (as this is commonly understood). The syntactic engine itself – the autonomous principles of composition and manipulation Chomsky now labels "the computational system" – has begun to fade into the background. Syntax reduces to a simple description of how constituents drawn from the lexicon can be combined and how movement is possible (i.e. how something other than the simple combination of independent constituents is possible). The computational system, this simple system of composition, is constrained by a small set of economy principles, which Chomsky claims enforce the general requirement, "do the most economical things to create structures that pass the interface conditions (converge at the interfaces)."

The end of syntax has no immediate consequences for the majority of syntacticians, since most of us have been investigating the interfaces whether we acknowledge this or not. After all, word order is phonology and we have always investigated "sentences" (strings or structures of terminal nodes) under particular interpretations, i.e. with particular assumptions about their LF interface. Chomsky's vision of the end of syntax should have the positive consequence of forcing syntacticians to renew their interface credentials by paying serious attention to the relevant work in phonology and semantics. We should not interpret the diminished role of the computational system within the MP grammar as somehow an abandonment of a previously "autonomous" syntax. The question of the autonomy of syntax has had different content at different times, but whatever the meaning of "autonomous," syntax in the MP is as autonomous, or non-autonomous, as it ever was. As always, syntax – here the computational system – stands between the interfaces and is neither a phonological nor a semantic component. And, as always, syntax trades in representations that are themselves neither phonological nor semantic. A vision of the end of syntax – the end of the sub-field of linguistics that takes the computational system, between the interfaces, as its primary object of study – this vision encompasses the completion rather than the disappearance of syntax.

Related Material in Other Chapters

Several other chapters contain information relevant and related to the material discussed in the present chapter. Chapter 1 deals with the assumptions about phrase structure and Case in standard GB theory. It also discusses the Projection Principle which is intimately tied to the concept of a derivation involving mappings between levels of representation. The chapters on LF, the Binding Theory, and the ECP contain much valuable data analyzed within pre-minimalist versions of the Principles and Parameters approach that at the time of writing still awaits treatment within the Minimalist Program (MP). Many binding-theoretic facts are particularly relevant in this respect because parts of the Binding Theory (e.g. the licensing of parasitic gaps) have traditionally been thought to involve S-Structure conditions, i.e. conditions that cannot be incorporated into the MP in their original form. The material contained in the chapter on the ECP is important as well in that the MP discards the notion of head-government that was central to the definition of proper government in Chomsky (1981). It remains to be shown that all the classical ECP cases analyzed in terms of head-government can be reduced in an equally satisfactory manner to the principles of the MP, in particular the "Shortest Move" constraint.

The concerns of the present chapter also overlap with several topics covered in chapter 6 (Morphosyntax), including the treatment of agreement, clitics, and phenomena such as passive, applicatives, etc. That chapter also contains a detailed discussion of the relative merits of various versions of the lexicalist hypothesis which determines the degree to which syntactic word formation is possible.

Chapter 8 by Noam Chomsky develops the Minimalist Program further.

8

Bare Phrase Structure

Noam Chomsky
MIT

Contents

Prelude

In this chapter, Noam Chomsky continues to develop his most recent version of the Principles and Parameters approach to syntactic theory, now usually referred to as the *Minimalist Program.* This work was not originally solicited as part of the textbook portion of the book but was written as a regular contribution to the current linguistic research community. It was agreed that the remainder of the book creates a productive environment in which to publish "Bare Phrase Structure" and that this arrangement provides a unique opportunity to allow the readers of the previous seven chapters to move from originally written but primarily didactically structured materials to authentic and current research in syntax of the highest caliber. The reader with no or little exposure to the primary linguistic literature so far should have the realistic expectation that some of the material in this chapter will prove difficult reading, at least on their first pass through. Those readers are invited, in fact urged, to consult any supporting materials in making their way through this chapter. It would be a good idea to have worked through the previous chapters of the book and to have read the two papers Chomsky (1989, 1992) as well as Chomsky and Lasnik (1991). If the reader has further questions at this point, it would be fruitful to discuss them with peers and instructors. At this level of inquiry, discussions of this sort constitute research, and all those contributing knowledge and insights to that discourse may consider themselves as being at the frontier of the scientific study of syntax.

1 Some Leading Ideas in the Study of Language

This chapter[1] is an extension of earlier works (Chomsky 1989, 1992) that were concerned with two related questions: (1) What conditions on the human language faculty are imposed by considerations of virtual conceptual necessity? (2) To what extent is the language faculty determined by these conditions, that is, how much special structure does it have beyond them? The first question in turn has two aspects: what conditions are imposed on the language faculty by virtue of (A) its place within the array of cognitive systems of the mind/brain, and (B) general considerations of simplicity, elegance, and economy that have some independent plausibility?

Question (B) is not precise, but not without content, as in the natural sciences generally. Question (A) has an exact answer, but only parts of it can be surmised, given what is known about related cognitive systems. To the extent that the answer to question (2) is positive, language is something like a "perfect system," meeting external constraints as well as can be done. The "minimalist" program for linguistic theory seeks to explore these possibilities.

Any progress toward this goal will deepen a problem for the biological sciences that is already far from trivial: how can a system such as human language arise in the mind/brain, or, for that matter, in the organic world, in which one seems not to find systems with anything like the basic properties of human language? That problem has sometimes been posed as a crisis for the cognitive sciences. The concerns are appropriate, but their locus is misplaced; they are a problem for biology and the brain sciences, which, as currently understood, do not provide any basis for what appear to be fairly well-established conclusions about language.[2] Much of the broader interest of the detailed study of language lies right here, in my opinion.

The leading questions that guide the minimalist program came into view as the Principles and Parameters (P&P) model took shape. A look at recent history may be helpful in placing these questions in context; needless to say, these remarks are schematic and selective, and benefit from hindsight.

Early Generative Grammar faced two immediate problems: to find a way to account for the phenomena of particular languages ("descriptive adequacy"), and to explain how knowledge of these facts arises in the mind of the speaker-hearer ("explanatory adequacy"). Though it was scarcely recognized at the time, this research program revived the concerns of a rich tradition, of which perhaps the last major exponent was Otto Jespersen.[3] Jespersen recognized that the structures of language "come into existence in the mind of a speaker" by abstraction from presented experience, yielding a "notion of structure" that is "definite enough to guide him in framing sentences of his own," crucially "free expressions" that are typically new to speaker and hearer. These properties of language determine the primary goals of linguistic theory: to spell out clearly this "notion of structure" and the procedure by which it yields "free expressions," and to explain how it arises in the mind of the speaker – the problems of descriptive and explanatory adequacy, respectively. To attain descriptive adequacy for a particular language L, the theory of L (its grammar) must characterize the state attained by the language faculty. To attain explanatory adequacy, a theory of language must characterize the initial state of the language faculty and show how it maps experience to the state attained. Jespersen held further that it is only "with regard to syntax" that we expect "that there must be something in common to all human speech"; there can be a "universal (or general) grammar," though "no one ever dreamed of a universal morphology."

In the modern period, these traditional concerns were displaced, in part by behaviorist currents, in part by various structuralist approaches, which radically narrowed the domain of inquiry while much expanding the data base for some future inquiry that might return to the traditional – and surely valid – concerns. To address them required a better understanding of the fact that language involves infinite use of finite means, in one classic formulation. Advances in the formal sciences provided that understanding, making it feasible to deal with the problems constructively. Generative Grammar can be regarded as a kind of confluence of long-forgotten concerns of the study of language and mind and new understanding provided by the formal sciences.

The first efforts to address these problems quickly revealed that traditional grammatical and lexical studies do not begin to describe, let alone explain, the most elementary facts about even the best-studied languages. Rather, they provide hints that can be used by the reader who already has tacit knowledge of language, and of particular languages. This is hardly a discovery unique to linguistics. Typically, when questions are more sharply formulated, it is learned that even elementary phenomena had escaped notice, and that intuitive accounts that seemed simple and persuasive are entirely inadequate. If we are satisfied that an apple falls to the ground because that is its natural place, there will be no serious science of mechanics. The same is true if one is satisfied with traditional rules for forming questions, or with the lexical entries in the most elaborate dictionaries, none of which come close to describing simple properties of these linguistic objects.

Recognition of the unsuspected richness and complexity of the phenomena of language created a tension between the goals of descriptive and explanatory adequacy. It was clear that to achieve explanatory adequacy, a theory of the initial state must hold that particular languages are largely known in advance of experience. The options permitted in universal grammar (UG) must be highly restricted; limited experience must suffice to fix them one way or another, yielding a state of the language faculty that determines the varied and complex array of expressions, their sound and meaning, in a uniform and language-independent way. But this goal receded still further into the distance as generative systems were enriched in pursuit of descriptive adequacy, in radically different ways for different languages. The problem was exacerbated by the huge range of phenomena discovered when attempts were made to formulate actual rule systems.

This tension defined the research program of early Generative Grammar – at least, the tendency within it that concerns me here. From the early 1960s, its central objective was to abstract general principles from the complex rule systems devised for particular languages, leaving rules that are simple, constrained in their operation by these UG principles. Steps in this direction reduce the range of language-specific constraints, thus contributing to explanatory adequacy. They also tend to yield simpler and more natural theories, laying the groundwork for an eventual minimalist approach. These two aspects of inquiry are logically independent: it could turn out that an "uglier" and richer version of UG reduces permissible variety, thus contributing to the primary empirical goal of explanatory adequacy. In practice, however, the two enterprises have proven to be mutually reinforcing, and have progressed side by side.

These efforts culminated in the P&P model, which constituted a radical break from the rich tradition of thousands of years of linguistic inquiry, far more so than early Generative Grammar, which could be seen as a revival of traditional concerns and ways of addressing them (which is why it was more congenial to traditional grammarians than to modern structural linguists). The basic assumption of the P&P model is that languages have no rules at all in anything like the traditional sense, and no grammatical constructions (relative clauses, passives, etc.) except as taxonomic artifacts. There are universal principles and a finite array of options as to how they apply (parameters). Furthermore, it may be that Jespersen's intuition about syntax-morphology can be captured, with parameters limited to the lexicon, indeed to a narrow part of it: functional categories. So I will henceforth assume.

The P&P model is in part a bold speculation rather than a specific hypothesis. Nevertheless, its basic assumptions seem reasonable in the light of what is currently at all well understood, and do offer a natural way to resolve the tension between descriptive and explanatory adequacy.

If these ideas prove to be on the right track, there is a single computational system C_{HL} for human language and only limited lexical variety. Variation of language is essentially morphological in character, including the critical question of which parts of a computation enter the phonological component, a question brought to the fore by Jean-Roger Vergnaud's theory of abstract Case and James Huang's work on *wh-* constructions.

This account of the P&P approach overstates the case. Languages may vary in parts of the phonology that can be determined by readily available data; and in "Saussurean arbitrariness," that is, the sound–meaning pairing for the substantive part of the lexicon. We put these matters aside, along with many others that appear to be computationally irrelevant, that is, not entering into C_{HL}: among them, variability of semantic fields, selection from the lexical repertoire made available in UG, and non-trivial questions about the relation of lexical items to other cognitive systems.

Like the earliest proposals in Generative Grammar, formulation of the P&P model led to a huge expansion in empirical materials, by now from a wide variety of typologically different languages. The questions that could be clearly posed and the empirical facts with which they deal are novel in depth and variety, a promising and encouraging development in itself.

Insofar as the tension between descriptive and explanatory adequacy is reduced in this way, the problem of explanation becomes far harder and more interesting. The task is to show that the apparent richness and diversity of linguistic phenomena is illusory and epiphenomenal, the result of interaction of fixed principles under slightly varying conditions. And still further questions arise, namely, those of the minimalist program. How "perfect" is language? One expects "imperfections" in the formal part of the lexicon. The question is whether, or to what extent, this component of the language faculty is the repository of departures from virtual conceptual necessity, so that the computational system C_{HL} is not only unique but optimal. Progress toward this further goal places a huge descriptive burden on the answers to the questions (A) and (B): the interface conditions, and the specific formulation of general considerations of simplicity. The empirical burden, already severe in any P&P theory, now becomes extraordinary. The problems that arise are therefore extremely interesting. It is, I think, of considerable interest that we can at least formulate such questions today, and even approach them in some areas with a degree of success. If the thinking along these lines is anywhere near accurate, a rich and exciting future lies ahead for the study of language and related disciplines.

2 The Minimalist Program

All these investigations have been based on several underlying factual assumptions. One is that there is a component of the human mind/brain dedicated to language – the language faculty – interacting with other systems. A more specific assumption is that there are just two such interacting systems: an articulatory–perceptual system A–P and a conceptual–intentional system C–I.[4] The particular language L is an instantiation of the language faculty with options specified. L must therefore provide "instructions" to be interpreted at these two interface levels. L is then to be understood as a generative system that constructs pairs (π, λ) that are interpreted at the A–P and C–I interfaces, respectively. π is a PF representation and λ an LF representation, each consisting of "legitimate entities" that can receive some interpretation at the relevant level (perhaps interpretation as gibberish). A linguistic expression of L is at least a pair (π, λ) of this sort – and under minimalist assumptions, at most such a pair, meaning that there are no "levels of linguistic structure" apart from the two interface levels PF and LF; specifically, no levels of D-structure or S-Structure.

We say that a computation (derivation) *converges at* one of the interface levels if it forms an interpretable representation in this sense, and *converges* if it converges at both interface levels, PF and LF; otherwise it *crashes*. We thus adopt the (non-obvious) hypothesis that there are no PF–LF interactions;[5] similarly, that there are no conditions relating lexical properties and interface levels, such as the Projection Principle. The notion "interpretable" raises non-trivial questions, to some of which we return.

It seems that a linguistic expression of L cannot be defined just as a pair (π, λ) formed by a convergent derivation. Rather, its derivation must also be *optimal*, satisfying certain natural economy conditions, e.g. conditions of locality of movement, no "superfluous steps" in derivations, etc. Less economical computations are "blocked" even if they converge.

Current formulation of such ideas still leaves substantial gaps. It is, furthermore, far from obvious that language should have anything like the character postulated in the minimalist program, which is just that: a research program concerned with filling the gaps and asking how positive an answer we can give to question (2) of the first paragraph: how "perfect" is language?

Suppose that this approach proves to be more or less correct. What could we then conclude about the specificity of the language faculty (modularity)? Not much. It could be that the language faculty is unique among cognitive systems, or even in the organic world, in that its principles satisfy minimalist assumptions. Furthermore, the morphological parameters could be unique in character. Another source of possible specificity of language is the conditions imposed at the interface, what we may call "bare output conditions." These will naturally reflect properties of the interface systems A–P and C–I (or whatever they turn out to be), but we have no idea in advance how specific to language these properties might be; quite specific, so current understanding suggests.

In brief, the question of the specificity of language is not directly addressed in the minimalist program, except to indicate where it should arise: in the nature of the computational procedure C_{HL}; in the properties of the bare output conditions and the functional component of the lexicon; and in the more obscure but quite interesting matter of conceptual elegance of principles and concepts.

It is important to distinguish the topic of inquiry here from a different one: to what (if any) extent are the properties of C_{HL} expressed in terms of output conditions, say filters of the kind discussed in Chomsky and Lasnik (1977) or chain-formation algorithms in the sense of Rizzi (1986b) in syntax, or conditions of the kind recently investigated for phonology in terms of optimality theory (Prince and Smolensky 1993, McCarthy and Prince 1993)? A related question is whether C_{HL} is derivational or representational in character: does C_{HL} involve successive operations leading to (π, λ) (if it converges), or does C_{HL} select two such representations and then compute to determine whether they are properly paired (or select one and derive the other)? The questions are rather subtle; typically, it is possible to recode one approach in terms of the other. But the questions are nevertheless empirical, turning basically on explanatory adequacy. Thus filters were justified by the fact that simple output conditions sufficed to limit the variety and complexity of transformational rules, advancing the effort to reduce these to just Move-α (or Affect-α, in the sense of Lasnik and Saito 1984) and thus to move toward explanatory adequacy. Similarly, Rizzi's proposals about chain-formation were justified in terms of the possibility of explaining empirical facts about Romance reflexives and other matters.

My own judgment is that a derivational approach is nonetheless correct, and the particular version of a minimalist program I am considering assigns it even greater prominence. There are certain properties of language, which appear to be fundamental, that suggest this conclusion. Under a derivational approach, computation typically involves simple steps expressible in terms of natural relations and properties, with the context that makes them natural "wiped out" by later operations and not visible in the representations to which the derivation converges. Thus in syntax, head-movement is narrowly "local," but several such operations may leave a head separated from its trace by an intervening head, as when N incorporates to V leaving the trace t_N, and the $[_V$ V–N] complex then raises to I leaving the trace t_V, so that the chain (N, t_N) at the output level violates the locality property satisfied by each individual step. In segmental phonology, such phenomena are pervasive. Thus the rules deriving the alternants *decide–decisive–decision* from an invariant underlying lexical form are straightforward and natural at each step, but the relevant contexts do not appear at all in the output; given only output conditions, it is hard to see why *decision,* for example, should not rhyme with *Poseidon* on the simplest assumptions about lexical representations and optimal output conditions. Similarly, intervocalic spirantization and vowel reduction are natural and simple processes that derive, say, Hebrew *ganvu* ("they stole") from underlying *g–n–B,* but the context for spirantization is gone after reduction applies; the underlying form might even all but disappear in the output, as in *hitu* ("they extended"), in which only the /t/ remains from the underlying root /ntC/ (C a "weak" consonant).[6]

In all such cases, it is possible to formulate the desired result in terms of outputs. E.g., in the head-movement case, one can appeal to the (plausible) assumption that the trace is a copy, so the intermediate V-trace includes within it a record of the local N → V raising. But surely this is the wrong move. The relevant chains at LF are (N, t_N) and (V, t_V), and in these the locality relation observed by successive raising has been lost. Similar artifice could be used in the phonological examples, again improperly, it appears. These seem to be fundamental properties of language, which should be captured, not obscured. A fully derivational approach captures them, and indeed suggests that they should be pervasive, as seems to be the case.

I will continue to assume that the computational system C_{HL} is strictly derivational and that the only output conditions are the bare output conditions determined externally at the interface.[7]

We hope to be able to show that for a particular language L, determined by fixing options in the functional part of the lexicon, the phenomena of sound and meaning for L are determined by pairs (π, λ) formed by maximally economical convergent derivations that satisfy output conditions. The computation C_{HL} that derives (π, λ) must, furthermore, keep to natural computational principles (e.g. locality of movement) and others that are also minimalist in spirit. A natural version of this requirement is that the principles of UG should involve only elements that function at the interface levels, specifically, lexical elements and their features, and local relations among them. Let's adopt this proposal, sharpening it as we proceed.

In pursuing a minimalist program, we want to make sure that we are not inadvertently "sneaking in" improper concepts, entities, relations, and conventions. I assume that an item in the lexicon is nothing other than a set of lexical features, or perhaps a further set-theoretic construction from them (e.g. a set of sets of features), and that output conditions allow nothing beyond such elements. The point of the occasional forays into formalism below is to ensure that C_{HL} keeps to these conditions, introducing no further elements, expressing only local relations, and deriving stipulated conventions where valid. Naturally the more spare the assumptions, the more intricate will be the argument.

3 The Computational System

A linguistic expression (π, λ) of L satisfies output conditions at the PF- and LF-interfaces. Beyond that, π and λ must be *compatible*: it's not the case that any sound can mean anything. In particular, they must be based on the same lexical choices. We can, then, think of C_{HL} as mapping some array of lexical choices A to the pair (π, λ). What is A? At least, it must indicate what the lexical choices are and how many times each is selected by C_{HL} in forming (π, λ). Let us take a *numeration* to be a set of pairs (*l*, *n*), where *l* is an item of the lexicon and *n* is its index, understood to be the number of times that *l* is selected. Take A to be (at least) a numeration N; C_{HL} maps N to (π, λ). The procedure C_{HL} selects an item from N and reduces its index by 1, then performing permissible computations. C_{HL} does not converge unless all indices are zero.

If an item is selected from the lexicon several times by C_{HL}, the choices must be distinguished; for example, two occurrences of the pronoun *he* may have entirely different properties at LF. *l* and *l'* are thus marked as distinct for C_{HL} if these are two selections by C_{HL} of a single lexical item.

We want the initial array A not only to express the compatibility relation between π and λ but also to fix the *reference set* for determining whether a derivation from A to (π, λ) is optimal, i.e., not "blocked" by a more economical derivation. Selection of the reference set is a delicate problem, as are considerations of economy of derivation generally. For the moment, let us take N to determine the reference set, meaning that in evaluating derivations for economy we consider only alternatives with the same numeration. At least this much structure seems to be required; whether more is needed is a hard question. We return to the matter in section 7.

Given N, C_{HL} computes until it converges (if it does) at PF and LF with the pair (π, λ). In a "perfect language," any structure Σ formed by the computation – hence π and λ – is constituted of elements already present in the lexical elements selected for N; no new objects are added in the course of computation (in particular, no indices, bar-levels in the sense of X-bar theory, etc.). Let us assume that this is true at least of the computation to LF; standard theories take it to be radically false for the computation to PF.[8]

Output conditions show that π and λ are differently constituted. Elements interpretable at the A–P interface are not interpretable at C–I, or conversely. At some point, then, the computation splits into two parts, one forming π and the other forming λ. The simplest assumptions are (1) that there is no further interaction between these computations and (2) that computational procedures are uniform throughout. We adopt (1), and assume (2) for the computation from N to λ, though not for the computation from N to π; the latter modifies structures (including the internal structure of lexical entries) by processes sharply different from those that take place before entry into the phonological component. Investigation of output conditions should suffice to establish these asymmetries, which I will simply take for granted here.

We assume, then, that at some point in the (uniform) computation to LF, there is an operation Spell-Out that applies to the structure Σ already formed. Spell-Out strips away from Σ those elements relevant only to π, forming Σ_P and leaving Σ_L, which is mapped to λ by operations of the kind used to form Σ. Σ_P is then mapped to π by operations unlike those of the N → λ mapping.

We assume then that each lexical entry is of the form {P, S, F}, where components of P serve only to yield π (phonological features), components of S serve only to yield λ (semantic features), and components of F (formal features, e.g. the categorical features [±N, ±V]) may enter into computations but must be eliminated (at least by PF) for convergence. Since we take computation to LF to be uniform, there is no way to stipulate that elements of F are eliminable only after Spell-Out. But the mapping to PF has different properties and may contain rules that eliminate F-features in ways not permitted in the N → λ computation.

The lexical entry for "book," for example, might contain the phonological feature [begins with stop] stripped away by Spell-Out and mapped to PF, the semantic feature [artifact] that is left behind by Spell-Out, and the formal feature [nominal] that is both carried over by Spell-Out and left behind, interpreted at LF, and eliminated in the course of computation to PF, though relevant to its operation.

Let us assume further that Spell-Out delivers Σ to the module Morphology, which constructs word-like units that are then subjected to further processes that map it finally to π. To fix terminology, let us continue to call the subsystem that maps the output of Morphology to PF the *phonological component* and the subsystem that continues the computation to LF after Spell-Out the *covert component*. Other terms are familiar, but have had misleading connotations. I will have little to say about the phonological component here, except with regard to the matter of ordering of elements in the output (section 6).

The simplest assumption is that Spell-Out can apply anywhere, the derivation crashing if a "wrong choice" is made. After Spell-Out, neither the phonological nor covert component can have any further access to the lexicon, a requirement for any theory, on the weakest empirical assumptions (otherwise sound–meaning relations would collapse). It is unnecessary to add stipulations to this effect. Because of the way C_{HL} is constructed, to which we return, an element selected from the lexicon cannot be embedded; hence the issue is narrow, arising only at the root of a phrase marker. If the phonological component adds a lexical item at the root, it will introduce semantic features, and the derivation will crash at PF. If the covert component does the same, it will introduce phonological features, and the derivation will therefore crash at LF.

Questions remain about lexical items lacking semantic or phonological features: can these be added at the root by the phonological or covert components, respectively? Empirical consequences seem to arise only in connection with functional elements that have "strong features" in the sense of Chomsky (1992), that is, those that must be "satisfied" before Spell-Out. Suppose that root C (complementizer) has a strong feature that requires overt *wh*-movement. We now want to say that unless this feature is checked before Spell-Out it will cause the derivation to crash *at LF*, to avoid the possibility of accessing C after Spell-Out in the covert component. Slightly adjusting the account in Chomsky (1992), we now say that a checked strong feature will be stripped away by Spell-Out, but is otherwise ineliminable.

4 Phrase Markers in a Minimalist Framework

The development of X-bar theory in the late 1960s was an early stage in the effort to resolve the tension between explanatory and descriptive adequacy. A first step was to separate the lexicon from the computations, thus eliminating a serious redundancy between lexical properties and phrase structure rules and allowing the latter to be reduced to the simplest (context-free) form. X-bar theory sought to eliminate such rules altogether, leaving only the general X-bar-theoretic format of UG. The problem addressed in subsequent work was to determine that format, but it was assumed that phrase structure rules themselves should be eliminable.

In the papers on economy and minimalism cited earlier, I took X-bar theory to be given, with specific stipulated properties. Let's now subject these assumptions to critical analysis, asking what the theory of phrase structure should look like on minimalist assumptions and what the consequences are for the theory of movement.

At the LF interface, lexical items and their constituent features must be accessed.[9] Accordingly, such items and their (semantic and formal) features should be available for C_{HL}. It is also apparent that some larger units constructed of these items are accessible, along with their types; noun phrases are interpreted differently from verb phrases, etc. Of the larger units, only maximal projections seem to be relevant to LF-interpretation. If so, output conditions make the concepts minimal and maximal projection available to C_{HL}, and on minimalist assumptions, nothing else apart from lexical features. Minimal and maximal projections must be determined from the structure in which they appear without any specific marking; as proposed by Muysken (1982), they are relational properties of categories, not inherent to them. There are no such entities as XP (X^{max}) or X^0 (X^{min}, terminal element) in the structures formed by C_{HL}, though we may use these as informal notations, along with X′ (X-bar) for any other category. Given a phrase marker, a category that does not project any further is a maximal projection XP and one that is not a projection at all is a minimal projection X^0; any other is an X′, invisible at the interface and for computation.[10]

We also hope to show that computation keeps to local relations of XP to terminal head. All principles of UG should be formulated in these terms, and only such relations should be relevant at the interface for the modules that operate there.[11]

Given the numeration N, C_{HL} may select an item from N (reducing its index) or perform some permitted operation on the structures it has already formed. One such operation is necessary on conceptual grounds alone: an operation that forms larger units out of those already constructed, call it *Merge*. Applied to two objects α and β, Merge forms the new object γ. What is γ? γ must be constituted somehow from the two items α and β; the only alternatives are that γ is fixed for all α, β or that it is randomly selected, neither worth considering. The simplest object constructed from α and β is the set $\{\alpha, \beta\}$, so we take γ to be at least this set, where α and β are the *constituents* of γ. Does that suffice? Output conditions dictate otherwise; thus verbal and nominal elements are interpreted differently at LF and behave differently in the phonological component (see note 9). γ must therefore at least (and we assume at most) be of the form $\{\delta, \{\alpha, \beta\}\}$, where δ identifies the relevant properties of γ; call δ the *label* of γ.

The label must be constructed from the two constituents α and β.

Suppose these are lexical items, each a set of features.[12] Then the simplest assumption would be that the label is either (1a), (1b), or (1c):

(1a) the intersection of α and β
(1b) the union of α and β
(1c) one or the other of α, β

The options (1a) and (1b) are immediately excluded: the intersection of α, β will generally be irrelevant to output conditions, often null; and the union will be not only irrelevant but contradictory if α, β differ in value for some feature, the normal case. We are left with (1c): the label δ is either α or β; one or the other *projects* and is the *head* of γ. If α projects, then γ = {α, {α, β}}.

For expository convenience, we can map γ to a more complex object constructed from additional elements such as nodes, bars (primes, XP, etc.), subscripts and other indices. Thus we might represent γ informally as (2) (assuming no order), where the diagram is constructed from nodes paired with labels and pairs of such labelled nodes, and labels are distinguished subscripts:

(2)

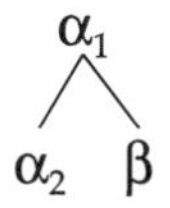

This, however, is informal notation only: empirical evidence would be required for postulation of the additional elements that enter into (2) beyond lexical features, and the extra sets.

The terms *complement* and *specifier* can be defined in the usual way, in terms of γ. The head–complement relation is the "most local" relation of an XP to a terminal head Y, all others within YP being head-specifier (apart from adjunction, to which we return); in principle there might be a series of specifiers, a possibility that seems to be realized (section 7). The principles of UG, we assume, crucially involve these local relations.

Further projections satisfy (1c), for the same reasons. We call these projections of the head from which they ultimately project, restricting the term *head* to terminal elements and taking *complement* and *specifier* to be relations to a head.

If constituents α, β of γ have been formed in the course of computation, one of the two must project, say α. At the LF interface, γ (if maximal) is interpreted as a phrase of the type α (e.g. as a nominal phrase if its head *k* is nominal), and it behaves in the same manner in the course of computation. It is natural, then, to take the label of γ to be not α itself but rather *k*, the head of the constituent that projects, a decision that also leads to technical simplification. Assuming so, we take $\gamma = \{k, \{\alpha, \beta\}\}$, where k is the head of α and its label as well, in the cases so far discussed. We keep to the assumption that the head determines the label, though not always through strict identity.

The operation Merge, then, is asymmetric, projecting one of the objects to which it applies, its head becoming the label of the complex formed. There can be no non-branching projection. In particular, there is no way to project from a lexical item α a subelement $H(\alpha)$ consisting of the category of α and whatever else enters into further computation, $H(\alpha)$ being the actual "head" and α the lexical element itself; nor can there be such "partial projections" from larger elements. We thus dispense with such structures as (3a) with the usual interpretation: *the, book* taken to be terminal lexical items and D+, N+ standing for whatever properties of these items are relevant to further computation (perhaps the categorial information D, N; Case; etc.). In place of (3a) we have only (3b):

(3a)

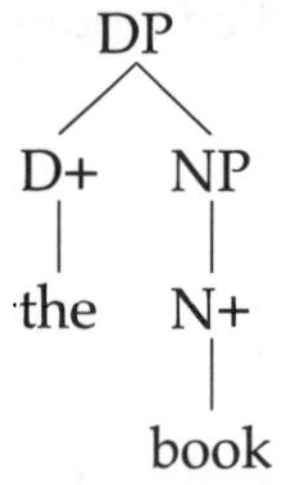

(3b)

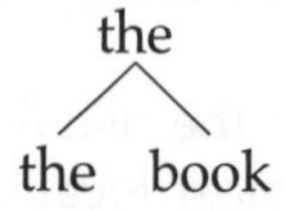

Standard X-bar theory is thus largely eliminated in favor of bare essentials.

Suppose that the label for $\{\alpha, \beta\}$ happens to be determined uniquely for α, β in language L; we would then want to deduce the fact from properties of α, β, L; or, if it is true for α, β in language generally, from properties of the language faculty. Similarly, if the label is uniquely determined for arbitrary α, β, L, as may be the case.

Suppose that we have the structure that we represent informally as (4), with x, y, z, w terminals:

(4)

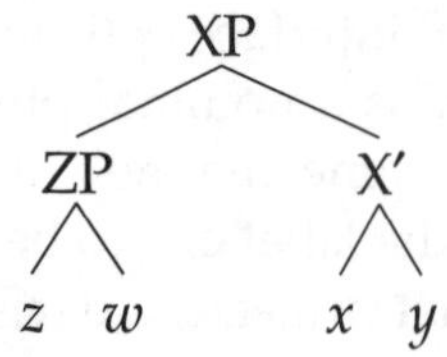

Here ZP = $\{z, \{z, w\}\}$, X′ = $\{x, \{x, y\}\}$, XP = $\{x$, {ZP, X′}}. Note that w and y are both minimal and maximal; z and x are minimal only.

The functioning elements in (4) are at most the nodes of the informal representation: that is, the lexical terminals z, w, x, y; the intermediate element X′ and its sister ZP; and the "root element" XP standing for the full structure formed. In the formal representation, the corresponding elements are z, w, x, y; $\{x, \{x, y\}\}$ = P and its sister $\{z, \{z, w\}\}$ = Q; and the root element $\{x$, {P, Q}}. These alone can be functioning elements; call them the *terms* of XP. More explicitly, for any structure K,

(5a) K is a term of K;
(5b) if L is a term of K, then the members of the members of L are terms of K.

Terms correspond to nodes of the informal representations, where each node is understood to stand for the sub-tree of which it is the root.

In (4), x is the head of the construction, y its complement, and ZP its specifier. Thus (4) could be, say, the structure VP with the head *saw*, the complement *it*, and the specifier *the man* with the label *the*, as in:

(6)

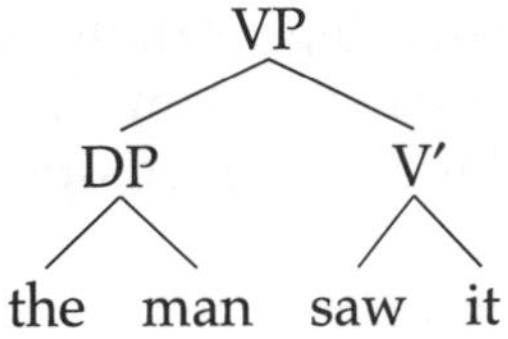

Here V′ = VP = *saw* and DP = *the*.

Note that this very spare system fails to distinguish unaccusatives from unergatives, a distinction that seems necessary in the light of differences of behavior that have been discovered. The simplest solution to the problem would be to adopt the proposal of Hale and Keyser (1993) that unergatives are transitives; I will assume so.

The structure (6) will yield the sentence "the man saw it" when further inflectional elements are added by Merge and the specifier of the VP is raised (assuming this particular form of the predicate-internal subject hypothesis, as I will throughout). This example involves the second operation that forms phrase markers, the operation Move (Move-α). Given the phrase marker Σ with terms K and α, Move targets K, raises α, and merges α with K to form the new category γ with the constituents α, K. This is the operation of *substitution*, a term borrowed from earlier theory that is now somewhat misleading, though we continue to use it. As matters now stand, either K or α could project. The operation forms the chain (α, t); α c-commands t, which is a copy of α.[13]

We return to adjunction. The only other operation is Delete (Delete-α), which leaves the structure unaffected apart from some indication that α is not "visible" at the interface.

In the case of (6), *the man* raises overtly (pre-Spell-Out), targeting the highest AGR-phrase, while *it* raises covertly, targeting the lowest AGR-phrase, each of the raised elements becoming the specifier of the targeted category. As noted, there is another option: the raised phrase itself might have projected, so that the targeted AGR-phrase would become the specifier of the raised nominal phrase, which would now be a D′, not a DP, since it projects to a higher phrase. In pre-minimalist work, this obviously unwanted option was excluded by conditions on transformations and stipulated properties of X-bar theory. But we no longer can – or wish to – make recourse to these, so we hope to show that the conventional assumption is in fact derivable on principled grounds – that it is impossible for Move to target K raising α, then projecting α rather than K. For the case of substitution, the result is immediate within the minimalist framework under the strong formulation of the principle Greed of Chomsky (1992), which licenses movement of α only as a step towards satisfying one of its own properties. If α raises and merges with K, then projecting, α is now an X′ category, not X^{max}. Therefore it can neither enter into a checking relation nor be moved further, being invisible to the computational system C_{HL}. Accordingly, the raising cannot satisfy Greed, and the unwanted option is excluded.

I will assume that Greed holds in this strong form:

(7) Move raises α to a position β only if morphological properties of α itself would not otherwise be satisfied in the derivation.[14]

Thus Greed cannot be overridden for convergence. We cannot, for example, derive (8a) by raising, violating Greed to satisfy EPP (the strong DP-feature of INFL), and (ii) cannot be interpreted as something like (iii), with covert raising:

(8a) *it is believed [a man to seem to *t* that . . .]
(8b) *there seem to a lot of us that . . .
(8c) it seems to a lot of us that . . .

Similarly, DP cannot raise to [SPEC, VP] to assume an otherwise unassigned θ-role. There can be no words HIT or BELIEVE with the θ-structure of *hit*, *believe* but no Case features, with *John* raising as in (9) to pick up the θ-role, then moving on to [SPEC, INFL] to check Case and agreement features:

(9a) John [$_{VP}$ *t'* [HIT *t*]]
(9b) John [$_{VP}$ *t'* [BELIEVE [*t* to be intelligent]]]

The only possibility is direct raising to [SPEC, INFL] so that the resulting sentences "John HIT" and "John BELIEVES to be intelligent" are deviant, lacking the external argument required by the verb.[15] We thus have a partial analogue to the P&P principle that there is no raising to a theta-position. And we can assume that for substitution at least, it is the target that projects. We will see that there are independent reasons for the same conclusion.

Raising of α targeting K is barred by (7) unless some property of α is satisfied by its moving to, or through, this position, and that property would not have been satisfied had this operation not applied; there is no movement to or through a position unless that operation is necessary, in this sense. Consistent with Greed, such movement would be permitted if there were no other way for α to reach a position where its features would eventually be satisfied. Suppose (as we assume) that movement is constrained by a "minimal link condition" (MLC), meaning that α must make the "shortest move" in a sense that must be defined. That could in principle require movement through a position that satisfies no properties of α. The situation should not arise in the kind of case just discussed: a substitution operation that "creates" a new position, [SPEC, K], by raising of α. It might well occur, however, in the case of adjunction satisfying the MLC.

Suppose that the structure K targeted by Move is a proper substructure of Σ. Thus suppose the operation is covert raising of the object to [SPEC, AGR_O] for Case and object agreement. Prior to this operation we have (in informal notation) the structure (10a) embedded in the larger structure (10b):

(10a)

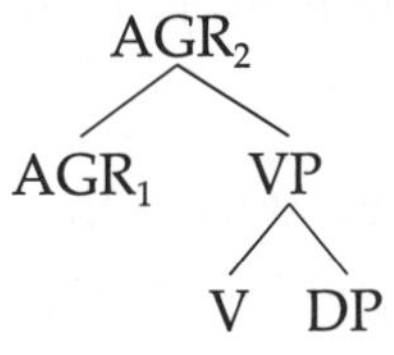

(10b)

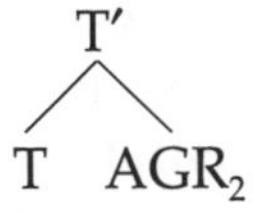

Here T' is {T, {T, K}}, where K (namely (10a)) is {AGR, {AGR, VP}}, VP = {V, {V, DP}}. If we target K, merging DP and K and projecting AGR as intended, we form (11), with the raised DP the specifier of AGR-P (AGR^{max}):

(11) AGR-P

DP AGR_2

Here AGR-P is {AGR, {DP, K}} = L, and the term T′ immediately dominating it is {T, {T, L}}, not {T, {T, K}} as it was before Move raised DP. Note that labels do not change, only constituents, if it is the target that projects, not the raised category.[16]

It remains to extend the discussion to adjunction, forming a two-segment category.[17] That adjunction and substitution both exist is not uncontroversial; thus Lasnik and Saito (1992) adopt only the latter option while Kayne (1993) adopts (virtually) only the former. Nevertheless, I will assume here that the distinction is necessary; that is, that specifiers are distinct in properties from adjuncts and, generally, A- from A′-bar positions.[18]

We have so far considered operations that form Q = {*k*, {α, K}}, where *k* is the head (= the label) of the projected element K. But we now have a second option, in which Q is a two-segment category, not a new category. Plainly we need a new object constructed from K but not identical with its head *k*. The minimal choice is the ordered pair <*k*, *k*>. We thus take Q = {<*k*, *k*>, {α, K}}. Note that <*k*, *k*>, the label of Q, is not a term of the structure formed. It is not identical to the head of K, as before, though it is constructed from it in a trivial way.

Suppose that we adjoin α to K where K is embedded.[19] For substitution, we were able to derive the conventional assumption that the target projects, not the raised element. The argument given does not carry over to adjunction, but let us adopt the convention for the moment, returning to the matter. Thus when α is adjoined to K, the resulting structure is necessarily [K, K] = {<*k*, *k*>, {α, K}}, which replaces K in a structure containing K. Recall that it is the *head* that projects; the head either *is* the label or, under adjunction, determines it.

Adjunction differs from substitution, then, only in that it forms a two-segment category rather than a new category. Along these lines, the usual properties of segments vs. categories, adjuncts vs. specifiers, are readily formulated.

The bare theory outlined here departs from conventional assumptions in several respects. One is that an item can be both an X^0 and an XP. Does this cause problems? Are there examples that illustrate this possibility? I see no particular problems, and one case comes to mind as a possible illustration: clitics. Under the DP hypothesis, clitics are Ds. Assume further that a clitic raises from its theta-position and attaches to an inflectional head. In its theta-position, the clitic is an XP; attachment to a head requires that it be an X^0 (on fairly standard assumptions).

Furthermore, the movement violates the head-movement constraint (HMC, a tentative posit that we hope to derive), indicating again that it is an XP, raising by XP-adjunction until the final step of X^0-adjunction. Clitics appear to share XP and X^0 properties, as we would expect on minimalist assumptions.

If the reasoning sketched so far is correct, phrase structure theory is essentially "given" on grounds of virtual conceptual necessity in the sense indicated earlier. The structures stipulated in earlier versions are either missing or reformulated in elementary terms satisfying minimalist conditions, with no objects beyond lexical features. Stipulated conventions are derived (with a gap yet to be filled, for adjunction). Substitution and adjunction are straightforward. We return to further consequences.

5 Properties of the Transformational Component

We have so far considered two operations, Merge and Move, the latter with two cases, substitution and adjunction. The operation Merge is inescapable on the weakest interface conditions, but why should the computational system C_{HL} in human language not be restricted to it? Plainly, it is not. The most casual inspection of output conditions reveals that items commonly appear overtly "displaced" from the position in which they are interpreted at the LF interface.[20] This is an irreducible fact of human language, expressed somehow in every theory of language, however the displacement may be concealed in notation; it is also a central part of traditional grammar, descriptive and theoretical, at least back to the Port Royal Logic and Grammar. The only question is: what is the nature of these transformational devices (whether one chooses to call them that or not)? On minimalist assumptions, we want nothing more than an indication at LF of the position in which the displaced item is interpreted; that is, chains are legitimate objects at LF. Since chains are not introduced by selection from the lexicon or by Merge, there must be another operation to form them: the operation Move.

So you need move at least at LF

In the early days of Generative Grammar, speculation about this matter invoked parsing and semantic considerations – improved parseability on certain assumptions, the separation of theme–rheme structures from base-determined semantic (theta-) relations, etc. See Miller and Chomsky (1963), Chomsky (1965) for review, The minimalist framework, with the disparity it imposes between theta-role assignment and feature-checking, requires such an operation, as Kenneth Wexler has observed. Our concern here is to ask how spare an account of Move the facts of language allow.

This question was a second focus of the effort to resolve the tension between descriptive and explanatory adequacy, alongside of the steps that led to X-bar theory. A central concern was to show that the operation Move-α is independent of α; another, to restrict the variety of structural conditions for transformational rules. These efforts were motivated by the dual concerns discussed earlier: the empirical demands posed by the problems of descriptive and explanatory adequacy, and the conceptual demands of simplicity and naturalness. Proposals motivated by these concerns inevitably raise the new leading problem that replaces the old: to show that restriction of the resources of linguistic theory preserves (and we hope, even enhances) descriptive adequacy while explanation deepens. The efforts have met with a good deal of success,[21] though minimalist assumptions would lead us to expect more.

Consider first the independence of Move-α from choice of α. While this currently seems a reasonable supposition, it has so far been necessary to distinguish various kinds of movement: XP-movement from X^0-movement; and among XPs, A-movement from A′-movement. Various kinds of "improper movement" are ruled out, essentially by stipulation; e.g. head-raising to an A′-position followed by raising to SPEC. A further goal would be to eliminate any such distinctions, demonstrating on general grounds, without any special assumptions, that the "wrong kinds" of movement crash; not an easy problem.

Some of the general constraints introduced to reduce the richness of descriptive apparatus (hence the variety of transformations) also have problematic aspects. Consider Emonds's structure-preserving hypothesis (SPH) for substitution operations. As has been stressed particularly by Jan Koster, it introduces an unwanted redundancy in that the target of movement is somehow "there" before the operation takes place; that observation provides one motive for non-derivational theories that construct chains by computation on LF (or S-Structure) representations. The minimalist approach overcomes the redundancy by eliminating the SPH: with D-structure gone, it is unformulable, its consequences derived – we hope to show – by the general properties of Merge and Move.

It has also been proposed that something like the SPH holds of adjunction: thus, heads adjoin to heads and XPs to XPs. This extended SPH introduces no redundancy, and is not affected by the minimalist program, though we would like to deduce it from more elementary considerations.

The descriptive facts are not entirely clear, but they might be something like this. Suppose that only YP can adjoin to XP, and that pre-Spell-Out, only Y^0 can adjoin to X^0, though covert operations may adjoin YP to X^0; e.g. VP-adjunction to causative V. We then have two problems: (1) to explain why the SPH holds at all, and (2) if it does, why it differs before and after Spell-Out, apparently violating the (optimal) uniformity assumption on C_{HL}.

The answer to the second problem may lie in the nature of the Morphological component. Recall that at Spell-Out, the structure Σ already formed enters Morphology, a system which presumably deals only with word-like elements, which we may take to be X^0s – that is, either an item α selected from the lexicon (hence with no constituents) or such an item with an element β adjoined to it (hence $\{<\alpha, \alpha>, \{\alpha, \beta\}\}$):

(12) Morphology gives no output (so the derivation crashes) if presented with an element that is not an X^0.

On this natural assumption, the largest phrases entering Morphology are X^0s, and if some larger unit appears within an X^0, the derivation crashes. The pre- vs. post-Spell-Out asymmetry follows.

It remains to explain why Y^0 adjoins only to X^0; e.g. why can a verb not raise from VP and adjoin to an XP, escaping HMC (a tentative posit, which we hope to derive), and then move on to adjoin to an INFL element? Recall that one case of Y^0-adjunction to XP is legitimate, we assume: namely, if Y^0 is also a YP, as in the case of clitics. The question arises for non-maximal Y^0.

Consider more closely the case we want to exclude, say, extraction of V from VP, adjoining to the higher AGR-P:

(13)

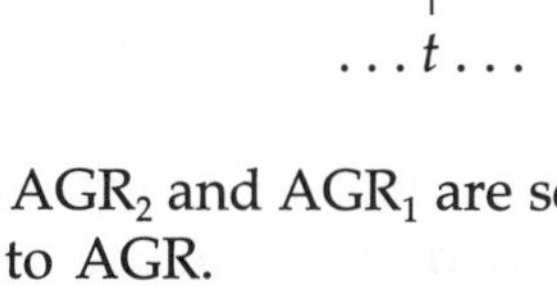

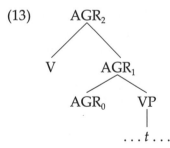

Here AGR_2 and AGR_1 are segments of a category formed by adjunction of V to AGR.

In (13), the V head of the chain (V, *t*) is V^{max} (VP), by definition. But its trace is not. A natural requirement is that chains meet the uniformity condition (14), where the "phrase structure status" of an element is its (relational) property of maximal, minimal, or neither:

(14) A chain is uniform with regard to phrase structure status.

Adjunction of non-maximal α to XP is therefore blocked, including (13). The argument carries over to substitution: quite generally, we cannot raise non-maximal α targeting K, where K then projects. For example, D cannot raise from (non-trivial) DP to [SPEC, INFL] (subject) position, leaving the residue of the DP. These consequences of the SPH for substitution and adjunction have commonly been stipulated; they follow from (14), within the bare theory.

We have seen that when Move raises α targeting K to form a new category L (substitution), then the target K must project, not α. The uniformity condition provides an independent reason for this conclusion when α is maximal. If α raises and projects, it will be an X′, not an X^{max}, so the chain will violate (14). There is also an independent reason for this conclusion when α is non-maximal. Suppose that (15) is formed by Move, raising α to attach to target K, forming L, a projection of α:

(15)

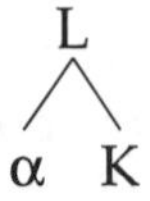

Since α is non-maximal, the operation is head-movement. By HMC, it cannot have crossed any intervening head, from which it follows that K can only be the projection of α itself. Suppose that such "self-attachment" is ruled out on principled grounds (we return to the matter directly). If so, it must be the target that projects.

Note that this argument holds both for substitution and adjunction. We therefore have several independent arguments that the target projects under substitution, and an argument that the same is true for adjunction when the raised element is non-maximal.

Consider more closely the general case of adjunction, as in (15), with L a segment. Suppose that L is projected from α, the case we wish to exclude. We have to determine what is the head of the chain formed by the adjunction operation: is it α, or the two-segment category [α, α]? The latter choice is ruled out by (14). But the former leaves us with a category [α, α] that has no interpretation at LF, violating FI (the same problem would have arisen, this time for α, had we taken the head of the chain to be [α, α]).[22] Again, we conclude that the target must have projected.

The asymmetry of projection after movement thus seems to have solid grounds: it is only the target that can project, whether movement is substitution or adjunction.

One strand of the argument was based on the assumption that self-attachment is impermissible, as in (16):

(16)

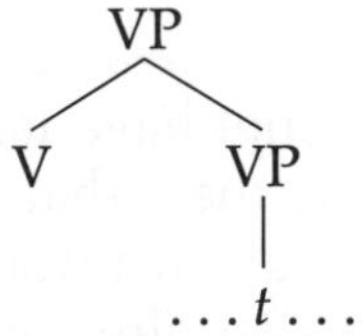

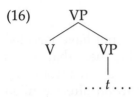

Thus suppose we have the VP "read the book" and we adjoin to it the head "read" forming the two-segment category [*read* [*t the book*]]. Under the intended interpretation of (16), with the target projected, we have formed the object (17), where γ is the target VP = {*read*, {*read, the book*}} (omitting further analysis):

(17) {<read, read>, {read, γ}}

Suppose, however, that we had projected the adjunct V ("read") in (16), yielding (18):

(18)

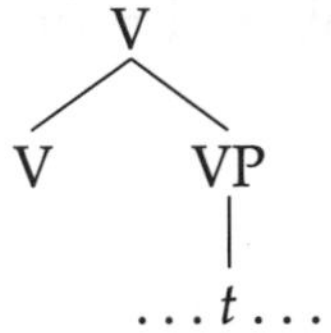

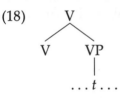

But this too is an informal representation of (17), just as (16) is, though the intended interpretations differ: in (16) we have projected the target, in (18) the adjunct. Furthermore, the latter interpretation should be barred.

Note that the problem is not limited to adjunction. Suppose that we raise the head N of NP to [SPEC, NP]. Then in exactly the same way, we will construct the same formal object whether we think of NP or SPEC as projecting.

We might conclude that this is exactly the right result, with such ambiguity interpreted as a crashed derivation. Then such operations of "self-attachment" (whether adjunction or substitution) are barred outright, as appears to be the case, incidentally filling the gap in the argument that the target projects under head-raising.

Let's turn now to the case of raising of V (= V_2) in a Larsonian shell, as in (19):

(19)

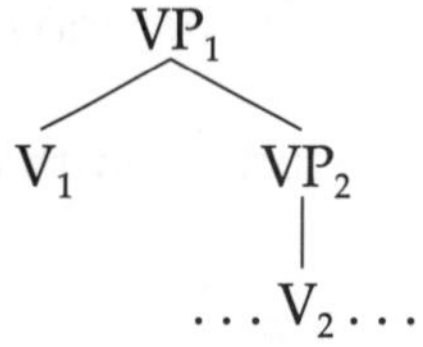

Since self-attachment is ruled out, the operation cannot have targeted VP_2, either as adjunction or substitution. It must be, then, that VP_1 is not a projection of the raised verb V_2 but rather a VP distinct from VP_2, as stipulated in earlier accounts. Thus V_2 raises to an already filled position occupied by a "light verb" *v* that has been selected from the lexicon and heads its own projection, VP_1. V_2 adjoins to *v* forming [*v* V_2 *v*]; the V_1 position is not "created" by the raising operation. That conclusion, in fact, is independently imposed by economy conditions, which permit the raising of V_2 only to satisfy its morphological properties (Greed). Raising of V is legitimate only if the operation is necessary for satisfaction of some property of V. That would not be the case if VP_1 were a projection of V_2, but can be if it is a projection of V_1, to which V_2 adjoins, the complex then raising to satisfy morphological properties of V_2.

We now have several conclusions about chains. Consider again the basic structure (20), where α is the head of the chain CH = (α, *t*):

(20)

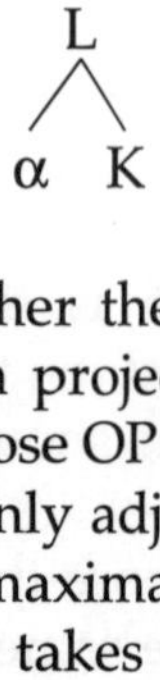

Whether the operation OP forming CH is substitution or adjunction, L is a projection of K, not α. If OP is substitution, then *t* is an X^{max}. Suppose OP is adjunction. If K is maximal, then α is maximal; pure heads can only adjoin to pure heads. If K is non-maximal, then α too must be non-maximal if OP is overt (pre-Spell-Out), though it can be maximal if OP takes place in the covert component, not entering Morphology. We eliminate the SPH for adjunction as well as for substitution. Furthermore, a number of the cases of "improper movement" are eliminated, carrying us a step forward toward a bare principle Move with no breakdown into various kinds of movement.

We have so far side-stepped a problem that arises in the case of normal head-adjunction. Take K to be a non-maximal head in (20) and α to be a head. Since K projects to L, α is maximal. Thus α is both maximal and minimal. If that is true of *t* as well (e.g. the case of clitic-raising), then CH satisfies the uniformity condition (14). But suppose *t* is non-maximal, as in the case of V-raising to INFL or to V. Then under a natural (though not necessary) interpretation, (14) is violated; CH is not a legitimate object at LF, and the derivation will crash. That is obviously the wrong result. We might therefore assume that at LF, word-like elements are "immune" to the algorithm that determines phrase structure status:

(21) At LF, X^0 is submitted to independent word-interpretation processes WI,

where WI ignores principles of C_{HL}, within X^0.[23] WI is something like a covert analogue of Morphology, except that we expect it to be compositional, unlike Morphology, on the assumption that the N $\rightarrow$ LF mapping is uniform throughout.

Suppose that K in (20) is a maximal head and α a pure (non-maximal) head; thus a case of head-adjunction in which the target happens to be a maximal projection. The status of this case depends on the precise interpretation of (21). But the question need not concern us, since the case cannot arise: for reasons of c-command, a pure head α must raise from within the target K.

Suppose that (20) is formed by adjunction, so that L and K are segments, with L = K. So far, there are two ways in which (20) could have been formed: by strict merger of α, K (without movement), or by raising of α, forming the chain CH, α then merging with K. In either case, we form the structure $\gamma = \{<k, k>, \{\alpha, K\}\}$ with the three terms α, K, γ, *k* the head of K. Each of these is a category that is "visible" at the interface, where it must receive some interpretation, satisfying FI. The adjunct α poses no problem. If it heads CH, it receives the interpretation associated with the trace position; if it is added by strict merger, it would presumably be a predicate of K (e.g. an adverbial adjunct to a verb). But there is only one role left at LF for K and γ. Note that the label <*k*, *k*> is not a term, hence receives no interpretation.

If γ is non-maximal, the problem is obviated by (21) under a natural interpretation of WI. This should suffice to account for, say, noun-incorporation to verbs or verb-incorporation to causatives; the same would extend to VP-incorporation to V if the LF interface permits such word structures (unlike Morphology). Furthermore, the target K in such cases often lacks any independent function, e.g. an affix lacking a theta-role. In these cases, only α or the chain it heads is interpreted, and FI is satisfied.[24]

Suppose γ is non-minimal. We now have two terms, γ and K, but only one LF role. The structure is still permissible if K lacks a theta-role, as in the case of covert adjunction to an expletive (independently of (21)). The only other possibility is that the adjunct α is deleted at LF, leaving just K. When would this take place?

One case is when α is the trace of successive-cyclic movement of the type that permits intermediate trace deletion, say, along the lines sketched by Chomsky and Lasnik (1991) in terms of a principle of economy of deletion for non-uniform chains; for example, *wh*-movement to [SPEC, CP] with intermediate adjunction, as in (22):[25]

(22) which pictures of John's brother did he expect that [*t*′ [you would buy *t*]]

Another case is full reconstruction at LF, eliminating the adjunct entirely, thus a structure of the type (23) interpreted only at the trace:

(23) $[_{YP}$ XP $[_{YP} \ldots t \ldots]]$

It follows that "Scrambling" is permissible only if it is interpreted by reconstruction, as is argued to be the case by Saito (1989, and subsequent work). Similarly, it would follow that such constructions as (24) must be Condition (C) violations (under the relevant interpretation), and we predict a difference in status between (25) and (22), the latter escaping the violation because the head of the chain is not an adjunct:

(24a) meet John in England, he doesn't expect that I will
(24b) pictures of John, he doesn't expect that I will buy
(25) pictures of John's brother, he never expected that you would buy

The conclusions are plausible as a first approximation, though we enter here into a morass of difficult and partially unsolved questions of a kind discussed by Barss (1986), Freidin (1986), Lebeaux (1988), and earlier work; see Chomsky (1992) for some discussion.

On strictly minimalist assumptions, these should be the only possibilities for adjunction; namely, (26):

(26a) word formation
(26b) semantically vacuous target (e.g. expletive-adjunction)
(26c) deletion of adjunct (trace deletion, full reconstruction)

In particular, apart from (26c), there will be no adjunction to a phrase that assigns or receives a semantic role (e.g. a theta-role assigner or an argument, a predicate or the XP of which it is predicated). Since (26c) is irrelevant to strict merger, the options for the current counterpart to "base adjunction" are even narrower. We consider adjoined adverbials further in section 7.[26]

Adjunction is therefore an option, but a limited one with rather special properties, under natural minimalist assumptions.

In these terms, we might return to the problem of improper movement. We want to show that the wide variety of such cases are excluded on principled grounds. Some fall into place. Thus, standard cases such as (27) cause no problem in the minimalist framework:

(27) *John is illegal [$_{IP}$ t_2 [$_{IP}$ t_1 to leave]]

The complement of *illegal* permits PRO ("it is illegal to leave") so that (null) Case is assigned to the subject of the infinitive and further raising is barred by Greed, under the strong interpretation (7) (see Martin 1992).

Consider cases of the type (28), with t_2 adjoined to IP in (28a) and in [SPEC, AGR-P] in (28b):

(28a) *John seems [that [t_2 [it was told t_1 [that . . .]]]]
(28b) *why do you wonder whether John said that Bill [t_2 [left t_1]]

Here we do not want to permit the intermediate (offending) trace t_2 to delete, unlike (22). The distinction suggests a different approach to intermediate trace deletion: perhaps it is a reflex of the process of reconstruction, understood in minimalist terms as in Chomsky (1993). The basic assumption here is that there is no process of reconstruction; rather, the phenomenon is a consequence of the formation of operator-variable constructions driven by FI, a process that may (or sometimes must) leave part of the trace – a copy of the moved element – intact at LF, deleting only its operator part. The reconstruction process would then be restricted to the special case of A′-movement that involves operators.[27] Some other cases of improper movement also can be eliminated along lines considered here, e.g. XP-movement passing through or adjoining to a pure Y^0 position, the trace then deleting. The general topic merits a comprehensive review.

So far, we have kept to the minimalist assumption that the computational procedure C_{HL} is uniform from N to LF; any distinction pre- and post-Spell-Out is a reflex of Morphology within the phonological component. I have said nothing so far about the "extension condition" of Chomsky (1992), which guarantees cyclicity. The condition is motivated for substitution pre-Spell-Out by relativized minimality effects (in the sense of Rizzi (1990)) and others, and does not hold post-Spell-Out if the Case-agreement theory of the minimalist approach is correct.

It also cannot hold for adjunction, which commonly (as in head-adjunction) targets an element within a larger projection. We would like to show that these consequences are deducible, not stipulated.[28]

With regard to Merge, there is nothing to say; it satisfies the extension condition by definition.[29] Questions arise only in connection with Move. Move targets K, raising α to adjoin to K or to be the specifier of K, K projecting in either case. K may be a substructure of some structure L already formed. That is a necessary option in the covert component but not allowed freely pre-Spell-Out; as a result of other conditions, we hope to show.

There are several cases of pre-Spell-Out cyclicity to consider. One is of the type illustrated by such standard examples as (29):

(29) *who was [$_\alpha$ a picture of t_{wh}] taken t_α by Bill

This is a CED violation if passive precedes *wh*-movement, but it is derivable with no violation (incorrectly) if the operations apply in countercyclic order, with passive following *wh*-movement. In this case, natural economy conditions might make the relevant distinction between the competing derivations. Passive is the same in both; *wh*-movement is "longer" in the wrong one in an obvious sense, object being more "remote" from [SPEC, CP] than subject in terms of number of XPs crossed. The distinction should be captured by a proper theory of economy of derivation – though the general problem is non-trivial.[30]

The relativized minimality cases fall into three categories: (a) head movement (the HMC); (b) A-movement; (c) A′-movement. In each case, we have two situations to rule out: (I) skipping an already filled position; (II) countercyclic operations, i.e. movement that skips a "potential" position that is later filled. Situation (I) may fall under the Minimal Link Condition (MLC) (no innocuous assumption). As for (II), category (a) is not a problem; as we have seen, head-insertion is necessarily by pure merger, which satisfies the extension condition. The remaining cases to be excluded are countercyclic derivations in which an XP is raised to some SPEC crossing the position of a lower SPEC that is introduced later by movement. It is not easy to construct examples that are not ruled out in one or another independent way, but a closer look is plainly necessary.

It may be, then, that there is no need to impose the extension condition of Chomsky (1992) on overt operations. Furthermore, neither the phonological nor covert component can access the lexicon for reasons already discussed. The Morphology module indirectly allows variation before and after Spell-Out, as does strength of features. It seems possible to maintain the preferred conclusion that the computational system C_{HL}

is uniform from N to LF, in that no pre- vs. post-Spell-Out distinction is stipulated.

6 Order

Nothing has yet been said about ordering of elements. There is no clear evidence that order plays a role at LF or the computation from N to LF. Let us assume not. It must be, then, that ordering is part of the phonological component, a proposal that has been put forth over the years in various forms. It seems natural to suppose that ordering applies to the output of Morphology, assigning a linear (temporal, left-to-right) order to the elements it forms, all of them X^0s though not necessarily lexical elements.

The standard assumption has been that order is determined by the head parameter: languages are head-initial (English) or head-final (Japanese), with further refinements possible. Fukui has proposed that the head parameter provides an account of optional movement, which otherwise is excluded under economy conditions, except in special cases when alternative derivations are equally economical. He argues that movement that maintains the ordering of the head parameter is "free"; other movement must be motivated by Greed ("last resort"). Thus in head-final Japanese, leftward movement (Scrambling, passive) is optional, while in English such operations must be motivated by feature-checking; and in head-initial English rightward extraposition is free, though barred in Japanese.[31]

Kayne has advanced a radical alternative to the standard assumption, proposing that order reflects structural hierarchy universally (Kayne, 1993). Specifically, he proposes the Linear Correspondence Axiom (LCA), which states that asymmetric c-command imposes a linear ordering of terminal elements; any phrase marker that violates this condition is barred. From his specific formulation of LCA, he draws the further conclusions that there is a universal SPEC-head–complement (SVO) ordering, and that specifiers are in fact adjuncts. A head–complement structure, then, is necessarily an XP, which can be extended – exactly once, on Kayne's assumptions – to a two-segment XP. The proposal is very much in the spirit of the minimalist program. Let's consider how it might be incorporated into the bare phrase structure theory just outlined. That is not an entirely straightforward matter, because the bare theory lacks much of the structure of the standard X-bar theory that Kayne adopts and partially reduces to LCA.[32]

Kayne offers two kinds of arguments for LCA: conceptual and empirical, the latter extended in subsequent work (see particularly Zwart 1993). The conceptual arguments show how certain stipulated properties of X-bar theory can be derived from LCA. The empirical arguments can largely be carried over to a reformulation of LCA within the bare theory, but the conceptual ones are problematic. First, the derivation of these properties relies crucially not just on LCA, but on features of the standard X-bar theory that are abandoned in the bare theory. Second, the conclusions are for the most part already derivable in the bare theory without LCA, though in somewhat different form.

Kayne adopts the standard X-bar-theoretic assumptions (30), illustrated for example in (3), above:

(30) Certain features (categorial features) project from a terminal element to form a head, then on to form higher categories with different bar levels.

The conceptual arguments and the conclusions about ordering crucially rely on these assumptions, which are abandoned in the bare theory.

To illustrate, consider two elementary structures central to Kayne's account (his (4), (13), notations modified):

(31a) (31b)

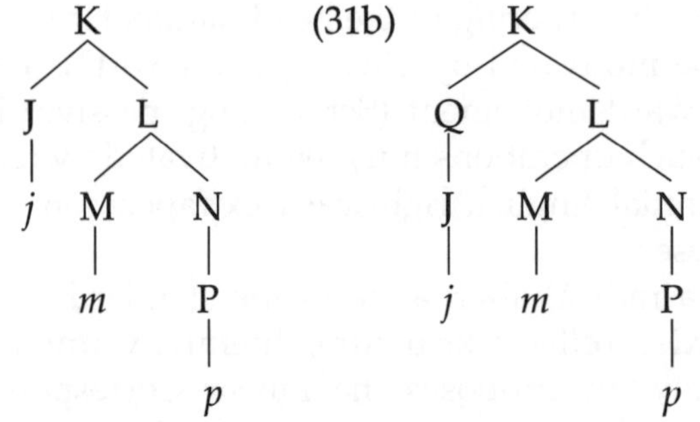

Putting aside the status of K for the moment, consider first (31a). Here *j, m, p* are terminals, selected from the lexicon. They project to J, M, P, respectively, the X^0 categories that are the actual heads. P then projects to the X^{max} category N, which combines with M to form the higher projection L. The categories are J, M, P (heads) and L, N (maximal projections); a tacit assumption is that projection to higher categories in (30) is optional. The c-command relation is stipulated to hold only of categories (not terminals). Asymmetric c-command (ACC) holds between J and M (irrelevantly, also J and N, P); and between M and P. Accordingly, the terminals dominated by these categories are assigned the linear ordering *j–m–p*, and the structure is admissible under LCA.

In (31b) there is a new category Q, an X^{max} projected from the head J. J does not c-command at all; Q c-commands M (and N, P) and L c-commands J, asymmetrically in both cases. The ACC relations do not yield a linear ordering: ACC (Q, M) entails that *j* precedes *m*, which precedes *p* as before; ACC (L, J) entails that *m* precedes *j*.

Therefore (31a) is admissible under LCA and (31b) is not. Turning to K, in (31a) the structure remains admissible under LCA whether K is a new category or a segment of the two-segment category [K, L]; ACC holds the same way in either case. The case of (31b) is different, however. Its inadmissibility follows from the fact that L asymmetrically c-commands J. But if c-command is restricted to categories as Kayne proposes, excluding segments of categories along with terminals, then L will no longer c-command J if [K, L] is a two-segment category. Hence (31b) is inadmissible only if K is a new category; if Q is adjoined to L, (31b) is admissible. The segment–category (adjunct, specifier; A- vs. A′-position) distinction can be maintained in the case of (31a), where *j* projects only to a head, but not in the case of (31b), where *j* projects to an X^{max}; in the latter case we have only adjunction and the distinctions disappear.

This seems an odd result, for several reasons. On conventional assumptions, the admissible structure (31a) should be inadmissible however interpreted; we do not expect non-maximal heads to be specifiers or to be adjoined to maximal projections. Furthermore, it is strange that the only admissible case of the segment–category distinction (and the related ones) should be for a dubious structure such as (31a). Finally, there are real questions as to whether it is possible to eliminate what seem to be fairly significant distinctions between specifiers and adjuncts, A- and A′-positions.

Turning to the bare theory, the counterpart to both (31a) and (31b) is (32):

(32)

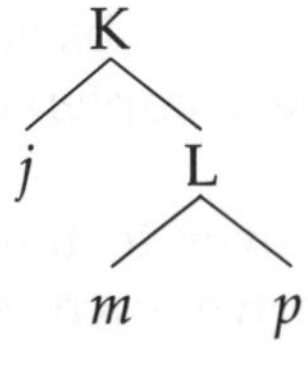

Here L is either *m* or *p* , K is either *j* or L, and K may be either a segment of [K, L] (*j* an adjunct in an A′-position) or a separate category (*j* a specifier in an A-position). The heads are the terminal elements *j*, *m*, *p* themselves; there are no head projections. There are no bar-levels, only lexical elements and sets constructed from them. Assuming that L is not formed by adjunction, whichever of *m*, *p* is not projected to L is an X^{max} as well as a head. (32) cannot be interpreted as intended for (31a), with $[_J j]$ a head adjoined to the maximal projection $[_L M\ N]$. Rather, if L projects to K, then *j* is a single-terminal maximal projection, either specifier or adjunct of the head–complement construction L. And if *j* projects to K, it is either a head with complement L, or L is adjoined to *j* (which is a bare head or both maximal and minimal, depending on higher structure.

The disparity between the systems mounts when we consider richer structures. Thus Kayne (still adopting standard X-bar conventions) compares (31) with an alternative in which the head $[_M m]$ is replaced by the X^{max} $[_{MP}[_M m]]$, inadmissible under LCA. But in the bare theory it again reduces to (32).

Despite the disparity, let us ask how a modified LCA might be added to the bare theory. There is no category–terminal distinction, so either may c-command. Turning to (32), suppose that K is a separate category and L projects, so that *j* is a specifier in an A-position. ACC holds of (*j*, *m*), (*j*, *p*), so that *j* must precede *m* and *p*. But it would hold of (*m*, *p*) only if the single-terminal *p* (the complement of the head *m*) were replaced by a complex category. Hence we have the order SPEC-head–complement, though only for non-trivial complement.

Suppose that instead of terminal *j* we had branching J, with constituents α, β. L is an X′, neither maximal nor minimal, so it does not c-command.[33] Therefore the ACC relations are unchanged.

Suppose that K is a separate category and *j* projects. ACC holds as before; *j* is now the head of K with complement L.

Suppose that K is a segment, either *j* or L. There is no particular problem, but adjunct–target order (to which we return) will depend on the precise definition of c-command.

In brief, LCA can be adopted in the bare theory, but with somewhat different consequences. The segment–category distinction (and the related ones) can be maintained throughout. The intended interpretation of (31) is unformulable, correctly it seems. We draw Kayne's basic conclusion about SVO order directly, though only if the complement is more complex than a single terminal.

The conceptual arguments for LCA do not carry over to the bare theory. Thus Kayne shows how it is possible to derive such X-bar-theoretic stipulations as (33):

(33a) the complement of a head cannot be a head
(33b) a category cannot have two heads
(33c) every phrase must be headed

He notes further that (33c) entails that coordination cannot be of the form [XP YP] but must have a coordinate element as head ($[_\alpha$ XP [and

YP]], etc.); correctly again. But as noted, derivation of these and other consequences crucially requires not only LCA but also (30), assumptions abandoned in the bare theory; and in the latter the conclusions of (33) follow trivially without LCA, though with a slightly different formulation for (33a) and (33b) ((33c) is unchanged): (33a) the complement of a head *can* be a head, which will be an X^{max}; (33b) a category *can* have two heads, one a bare head that projects, the other an X^{max}.

Let us return now to (32), taking L = *m* with the single-terminal complement *p*, both minimal and maximal. Since neither *m* nor *p* asymetrically c-commands the other, no ordering is assigned to *m*, *p*; the assigned ordering is not total, and the structure fails LCA. That leaves two possibilities. Either we weaken LCA so that non-total orderings (but not "contradictory" orderings) are admissible under certain conditions, or we conclude that the derivation crashes unless the structure $\alpha = [_L\ m\ p]$ has changed by the time LCA applies so that its internal structure is irrelevant; perhaps α is converted by Morphology to a "phonological word" not subject internally to LCA, assuming that LCA is an operation that applies after Morphology.

Consider the first possibility: is there a natural way to weaken LCA? One obvious choice comes to mind: there is no reason for LCA to order an element that will disappear at PF, for example, a trace. Suppose, then, that we exempt traces from LCA, so that (32) is legitimate if *p* has overtly raised, leaving a trace that can be ignored by LCA. The second possibility can be realized in essentially the same manner, by assuming that LCA may (but need not) delete traces. Under this interpretation, LCA may eliminate the offending trace in (32), if *p* has raised.[34]

In short, if the complement is a single-terminal XP, then it must raise overtly. If XP = DP, then its head D is a clitic, either demonstrative or pronominal, which attaches at a higher point (determined either generally, or by specific morphological properties, depending on how cliticization works).[35] If XP = NP, then N must incorporate to V (and we must show that other options are blocked). Clitics, then, are bare Ds without complements, and noun-incorporation must be restricted to "non-referential NPs" (as noted by Hagit Borer), assuming the referential, indexical character of a noun phrase to be a property of the D head of DP, NP being a kind of predicate. Within DP, the N head of NP must raise to D (as argued for different reasons by Longobardi).[36]

We therefore expect to find two kinds of pronominal (similarly, demonstrative) elements, weak ones that are morphologically marked as affixes and must cliticize, and strong ones with internal structure, which do not cliticize; thus in French, the determiner D (*le*, *la*, etc.), and the complex element *lui-même*. In Irish the weak element is again D, and the strong one may even be discontinuous, as in *an teach sin* ("that house," with determiner *an-sin*; Andrew Carnie, pc). A phenomenon that may be related is noted by Esther Torrego. In Spanish, in (34a) the Case-marker *de* can be omitted, but not in (34b):

(34a) cerca de la plaza ("near the plaza")
(34b) cerca de ella ("near it")

Deleting *de* in (34a), D = *la* can incorporate in *cerca* satisfying the Case Filter, but that is impossible in (34b) if the strong pronominal *ella* is not D but a more complex word, from which the residue of D cannot be extracted.

Since the affixal property is lexical, weak pronominals cliticize even if they are not in final position; e.g. a pronominal object that is a specifier in a Larsonian shell. If focus adds more complex structure, then focused (stressed) weak pronominals could behave like complex pronominals. If English-type pronouns are weak, they too must cliticize, though locally, not raising to INFL as in Romance (perhaps as a reflex of lack of overt verb-raising). The barrier to such structures as "I picked up it" might follow. English determiners such as "this," "that" are presumably strong, with the initial consonant representing D (as in "the," "there," etc.) and the residue a kind of adjective, perhaps. Various consequences are worth exploring.

While apparently not unreasonable, the conclusions are very strong: thus every right-branching structure must end in a trace, on these assumptions.

What about ordering of adjuncts and targets? In Kayne's theory, adjuncts necessarily precede their targets. Within the bare theory, ordering depends on exactly how the core relations of phrase structure theory, *dominate* and *c-command,* are generalized to two-segment categories.

Consider the simplest case, with α attached to K, which projects:

(35)
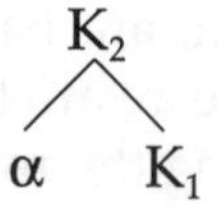

Suppose that K_2 is a new category, α the specifier. Take *dominate* to be an irreflexive relation with the usual interpretation. Then (35) (= {*k*, {α, K}}, *k* the head of K) dominates α and K; informally, K_2 dominates α and K_1.

Suppose however that the operation was adjunction forming the two-segment category [K_2, K_1] = {<*k*, *k*>, {α, K}}. Are α and K_1 dominated by the category [K_2, K_1]? As for c-command, let us assume that α c-commands outside of this category; thus if it heads a chain, it c-commands its trace, which need not be in K_1 (as in head-raising).[37] But what about further c-command relations, including those within (35) itself?

The core intuition underlying c-command is that

(36) X c-commands Y if (i) every Z that dominates X dominates Y and (ii) X and Y are disconnected.

For categories, we take X and Y to be disconnected if $X \neq Y$ and neither dominates the other. The notions *dominate* and *disconnected* (hence *c-command*) could be generalized in various ways for segments.

Let us restrict these relations to *terms*, in the sense defined earlier: in the case of (35), to α, K (= K_1), and the two-segment category [K_2, K_1]. K_2 has no independent status. These decisions comport reasonably well with the general condition that elements enter into the computational system C_{HL} if they are "visible" at the interface. Thus K_1 may assign or receive a semantic role, as may α (perhaps heading a chain), but there is no "third" role left over for K_2; the two-segment category will be interpreted as a word by Morphology and WI (see (21)) if K is an X^{min}, and otherwise falls under the narrow options discussed earlier.[38]

If that much is correct, we conclude that in (35), [K_2, K_1] dominates its lower segment K_1, so that the latter does not c-command anything (including α, not dominated by [K_2, K_1] but only contained in it).

Turning next to c-command, how should we extend the notion "disconnected" of (36b) to adjuncts? Take adjunction to a non-maximal head (Kayne's (16), reduced to its bare counterpart):

(37)

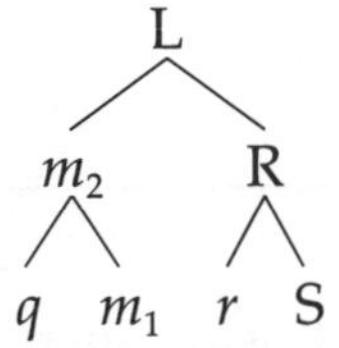

Here q is adjoined to the head m to form the two-segment category [m_2, m_1], a non-maximal X^0 projecting to and heading the category L, which has label m. R is the complement of m and r its head, and S (which may be complex) is the complement of r. What are the c-command relations for the adjunct structure?

The lowest Z that dominates q and [m_2, m_1] is L; therefore q and [m_2, m_1] asymmetrically c-command r and S, however we interpret "disconnected." What are the c-command relations within [m_2, m_1]? As noted, m_1 does not c-command anything. The other relations depend on the interpretation of "disconnected" in (36b). Kayne interprets it as "X excludes Y." Then q (asymmetrically) c-commands [m_2, m_1] so that

q precedes m_1; and in general, an adjunct precedes the head to which it is adjoined. If X, Y are taken to be "disconnected" if no segment of one contains the other, then q c-commands m_1 but not $[m_2, m_1]$, and again q precedes m_1.[39] If "disconnected" requires still further dissociation of X, Y – say, that neither is a segment of a category that contains the other – then no ordering is determined for q, m_1 by LCA.

If m_1 is not a head but the complex category $[_m m$ P], so that q is an X^{max} for reasons already discussed, then q c-commands the constituents of m_1 under all interpretations of "disconnect," and the adjunct precedes the target (whether q is internally complex or not).

Left open, then, is the case of adjunction of a head to another head, i.e. ordering within words. Whether order should be fixed here depends on questions about inflectional morphology and word formation.

Summarizing, it seems that Kayne's basic intuition can be accommodated in a straightforward way in the bare theory, including the major empirical conclusions, specifically, the universal order SVO and adjunct-target (at least for XP-adjuncts). In the bare theory, LCA gains no support from conceptual arguments, and therefore rests on the empirical consequences. We take LCA to be a principle of the phonological component that applies to the output of Morphology, optionally ignoring or deleting traces. The specifier–adjunct (A–A') distinction can be maintained, and there may be multiple specifiers or adjuncts, though the options for adjunction are very limited for other reasons. There are further consequences with regard to cliticization and other matters, whether correct or not, I do not know.

7 Some Residual Problems

In discussing the options for adjunction, we had put aside such structures as (38), with an adverbial adjoined to the two segment category [XP, XP], projected from α:

(38)

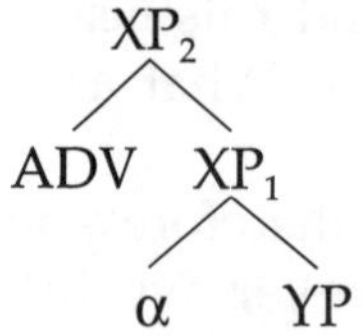

The construction is barred if XP has a semantic role at LF; say, if XP is a predicate (AP or VP), as in (39):

(39) John [$_{VP}$ often [$_{VP}$ reads $\left\{\begin{array}{l}\text{books}\\ \text{to his children}\end{array}\right\}$]]

Such structures as (38) could have been derived either by Merge or Move. The latter possibility can perhaps be ruled out in principle, under Greed; adverbs seem to have no morphological properties that require movement. The empirical evidence also seems to indicate that they do not form chains. Thus, an adverb in pre-IP position cannot be interpreted as if it had raised from some lower position.[40]

The only option, then, is Merge. The question is whether we have "base adjunction," in the EST sense, at least above the level of word formation. So far, it is barred if XP is semantically active, as in (39). The sentences themselves are fine, but the structures assigned to them by (39) are not.

Adverbials can, however, be adjoined to such phrases as AGR-P or IP, or to any X′. Adjunction to X′ by merger does not conflict with the conclusion that X′ is invisible to C_{HL}; at the point of adjunction, the target is an XP, not X′.

Such constructions as (39) have played a considerable role in linguistic theory since Joseph Emonds's studies of differences between verb-raising and non-raising languages (French, English). The basic phenomena, alongside of (39), are illustrated by (40) (both well-formed in French):

(40a) John reads often to his children
(40b) *John reads often books

A proposal sometimes entertained is that V raises from the underlying structure (39) to form (40a), but such raising is barred in (40b) for Case reasons; accusative Case is assigned to *books* by *read* under an adjacency condition of the kind proposed by Timothy Stowell. French differs in the adjacency property or in some other way.

Apart from the fact that the source construction (39) is barred for the reasons discussed,[41] the general approach is problematic on minimalist assumptions. This framework has no natural place for the assumed condition of adjacency. Furthermore, it takes Case to be assigned by raising to [SPEC, AGR] so that adjacency should be irrelevant in any event. It is also unclear why the verb should raise at all in (40), or where it is raising to. It seems that either the standard analysis is wrong, or there is a problem for the minimalist framework.

In fact, the empirical grounds for the analysis are dubious. Consider such adverbial phrases as *every day* or *last night*, which cannot appear in the position of *often* in (39):

(41) *John every day reads to his children

Nevertheless, we still find the paradigm of (40):

(42a) John reads every day to his children
(42b) *John reads every day books

It seems, then, that the paradigm does not involve verb-raising.

Furthermore, similar phenomena appear when raising is not an option at all, as in (43):

(43a) John made a decision (last night, suddenly) to leave town
(43b) John felt an obligation (last night, suddenly) to leave town

Here the adverbial may have matrix scope, so that it is not within the infinitival clause. It can appear between the N head and its complement, though the N cannot have raised in the manner under discussion.

In general, it is doubtful that raising has anything to do with the relevant paradigms.

The phenomena suggest a Larsonian solution. Suppose that we exclude (39) from the paradigm entirely, assuming that *often* appears in some higher position and thus does not exemplify (38) with XP = VP. The structure underlying (40), (41) is (44):

(44)

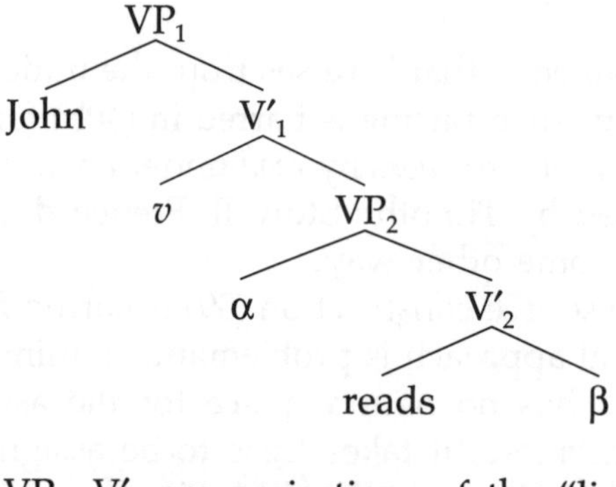

Here VP_1, V'_1 are projections of the "light verb" *v*; and VP_2, V'_2 are projections of *read*. Whether the latter raises or not depends on whether *v* is selected in the initial numeration. Unless *read* raises, the derivation crashes because its features (specifically, its tense and agreement features) are not satisfied; by HMC, it must raise to *v*. The phenomenon is structurally similar to ECM, with a phrase moving so that further movement can satisfy Greed; see below.[42]

Suppose that α in (44) is the adverbial *often*. Then if β = *to the children*, there is no problem. But if β = *books*, the derivation will crash; *books* cannot raise to [SPEC, AGR] to have its Case checked because of the intervening α. The relativized minimality violation cannot be overcome by V-raising, which will not create a large enough minimal domain. Note the crucial assumption that the subject *John* is in [SPEC, VP], the strong version of the VP-internal subject hypothesis that we have been assuming throughout; otherwise that position would be an "escape hatch" for raising of *books*.[43]

Under this analysis, the basic facts follow with no special assumptions. There is a Case solution, but it does not involve adjacency. The problem of optional raising is eliminated, along with those raised by (42), (43).

Questions remain about other matters, among them: What is the basis for the French–English distinction? Why do the *wh*-variants of the adverbials in question behave like adjuncts, not arguments? What about CED effects in the case of such adjuncts as ADJ in (45), which is in a complement position if "base-generated" adjuncts are barred?

(45) they [read the book $[_{ADJ}$ after we left]]

Another question has to do with the scope of adverbials in ECM constructions. Consider the sentences (46):

(46a) I tell (urge, implore) my students every year (that they should get their papers in on time, to work hard)
(46b) I would prefer for my students every year to (get their papers in on time, work hard)
(46c) I believe my students every year to (work hard, have gotten their papers in on time)

Under the Larsonian analysis just outlined, *every year* should have matrix scope in (46a), and (46c) should have the marginal status of (46b), with embedded scope if interpretable at all. The differences seem to be in the expected direction, though they are perhaps not as sharp as they might be. We would incidentally expect the distinction to be obviated in a verb-raising language such as Icelandic, as appears to be the case (Diane Jonas, pc).

Questions also arise about the relevance of the specifier-adjunct distinction to Case and agreement. In Chomsky (1992), I took the checking domain to include adjuncts as well as specifiers, in the light of Kayne's theory of participial agreement. The assumption was that in passive and unaccusative, the object passes through the [SPEC, AGR_o] position (A-movement), checking agreement with the participle, and then raises to subject, driven by Case; and in operator-movement, the object adjoins to the AGR phrase (A′-movement), again checking agreement in the checking domain of AGR, then raising ultimately to [SPEC, CP], driven by the operator-feature. In particular, Kayne found dialect differences associated with the two kinds of participial agreement.

Dominique Sportiche and Philip Branigan have observed that the operator-movement case is problematic because of such long-distance movement constructions as (47):[44]

(47) la lettre [qu'il a [$_{\text{AGR-P}}$ t′ [$_{\text{AGR-P}}$ dit [que Pierre lui a [envoyé t]]]]]

Raising of the operator from *t* to *t′* (perhaps with intermediate steps) and then to [SPEC, CP] is legitimate successive-cyclic A′-movement, and should yield participial agreement with *dit* in the higher clause, incorrectly. That suggests that agreement (hence, presumably, Case as well) should be restricted to the specifier position, so that (47) would be ruled out as a case of improper movement if MLC requires lower adjunction on the way to *t′*. Assuming that the conclusion generalizes properly, we have another reason for the segment–category (specifier–adjunct, A–A′) distinction, as well as for a requirement of successive-cyclic movement. The dialect differences noted by Kayne remain unexplained, however.

Under either analysis, the example illustrates that agreement can be assigned without Case. The same is true of such simple adjectival constructions as (48):

(48) John is [$_{\text{AGR-P}}$ *t′* AGR [$_{\text{AP}}$ *t* intelligent]]

Here *John* raises from the predicate-internal subject position *t* to [SPEC, AGR] (*t′*) for agreement with the adjective (raised to AGR), then raises onto the subject position ([SPEC, AGR_{S}]) for Case checking, with agreement checked independently by AGR_{S}, so that there is double agreement.[45]

The counterpart would be a structure in which Case is assigned without agreement, that is, a structure of the form (49), in which α checks the Case of DP, which then raises to [SPEC, AGR] for agreement:

(49) [DP AGR [. . . . [*t* α . . .]]]

This possibility is illustrated by transitive expletives (TEs), as analyzed by Jonas and Bobaljik (1993), Jonas (forthcoming). Icelandic has structures of the following type (English words):

(50) [$_{\text{AGRS-P}}$ there [$_{\text{AGRS}}$ painted [$_{\text{TP}}$ a student [$_{\text{AGRO-P}}$ [the house VP]]]]]

The meaning is something like "a student painted the house," or the intelligible but unacceptable English counterpart (51):

(51) there painted the house a student (who travelled all the way from India to do it)

In (50), the expletive is in [SPEC, AGR_S] (subject) position; *painted* is the verbal head of VP adjoined to intermediate inflectional nodes and finally to AGR_S; *a student* is raised to [SPEC, Tense], with its Case checked by the trace of the raised Tense that heads TP; *the house* is raised (object-raising) to [SPEC, AGR_O] where its Case and agreement are checked, and the VP contains only traces. Positions are motivated by placement of adverbs and negation in the overt forms. In the covert component, *a student* adjoins to the expletive for checking of its subject-agreement features, as in expletive constructions generally (we are assuming). The usual definiteness effect holds. Possibly this reflects the fact that AGR, an inherently "weak" element, requires a "strong" element as its specifier – hence a definite (or specific) DP, either a full DP or the expletive; others remain in [SPEC, TP] by Procrastinate. A similar argument might bear on the tendency for object-raising to prefer definites; AGR, being weak, attracts the definite to its SPEC, leaving indefinites behind by Procrastinate.[46]

We thus have the full range of expected cases: agreement and Case are fully dissociated,[47] and there is good reason to suppose that AGR (i.e. a set of phi-features) appears twice and Tense once in a proliferated INFL system of the type proposd by Jean-Yves Pollock, a conclusion strengthened by examples such as (51) that couple object-raising with expletives and thus require three pre-VP positions for arguments.

These TE constructions at once raise two questions:

(52a) Why do languages differ with regard to TEs, some (Icelandic) allowing them, others (English) not?
(52b) Are such structures permitted by economy principles?

Question (52a) presupposes some analysis of simple expletive constructions such as (53):

(53a) there arrived a man
(53b) there is a book missing from the shelf

Since subject–verb agreement holds between the verb and the post-verbal DP (*a man, a book*), the latter must have raised covertly to [SPEC, AGR_S], on our assumptions, much as it does overtly in "a man arrived." The fact that the overt raising option exists alongside of (53a) raises no problem; they arise from different numerations, so that if reference sets for economy comparisons are determined by the initial numeration, as proposed earlier, the options are not comparable in terms of economy of derivation. Covert adjunction to the expletive must be driven by some unsatisfied feature, either Case or agreement or both. Suppose that partitive Case can be assigned by unaccusatives, along lines disussed by Adriana Belletti. Then covert raising in (53) would be motivated by agreement, as we have assumed for TEs.[48]

Assuming that much, why does English lack TEs? Example (51) suggests that the lack of TEs may be a rather superficial phenomenon. As noted, the sentence is unacceptable (as is (53a), to some degree) though intelligible, and with other lexical choices the construction ranges in acceptability, as Kayne has observed, improving as the subject becomes "heavier":

(54a) there entered the room a man from England
(54b) there hit the stands a new journal
(54c) there visited us last night a large group of people who travelled all the way from India

Such constructions have been thought to result from an extraposition operation, but that is unformulable in our terms, which allow only one possibility: that they are TEs, with the subject in [SPEC, T] at LF, but on the right overtly. The overt position could be the result of a process in the phonological component, perhaps motivated by properties of theme–rheme structures, which, as often noted, involve "surface" forms in some manner.[49] Prominence of the theme might require that it be at an "extreme" position: to the right, since the left-most position is occupied by the expletive subject. Icelandic might escape this condition as a reflex of its internal-V-second property, which requires a method for interpreting internal themes. The lexical restrictions in English presumably reflect the locative character of the expletive. If speculations along these lines prove tenable, question (a) of (52) may not arise: the TE option may be general.

Question (b) of (52) is harder, leading into a thicket of complex and only partly explored issues. Note first that no problem is raised by the fact that TEs alternate with non-expletive constructions; they arise from different numerations. But it is not obvious that constructions of the form (55), with subject SU in [SPEC, T] at Spell-Out, should be allowed at all:

(55) Expletive AGR [SU [T XP]]

If TEs of the form (55) are legitimate, we should expect to find such structures as (56) in Icelandic, with *seem* raising to AGR_S and SU raising from *t* to [SPEC, TP] (as demonstrated by placement of adverbials and negation).

(56) there seems [$_{TP}$ [$_{SU}$ a man] [$_{IP}$ *t* to be in the room]]

Assuming these to be legitimate,[50] we then have to explain why (57) is barred in English:

(57) *there seems (to me, often) [$_{IP}$ a man to be in the room]

Note that we do not have a direct contradiction. Thus for UG reasons, every language might bar (57) while permitting (56), with the associate having raised to SPEC-TP of the matrix at Spell-Out. Both English and Icelandic would then have only (56), the surface form appearing in English as (58), given the speculative answer to (52a):

(58) there seems to be in the room [a man (who travelled all the way from India)]

Assuming this to be the correct resolution of the problem, we then ask why the structure illustrated in (56) is permitted but that of (57) barred. We cannot appeal to numeration in this case, because it is the same in the two examples.

We also have to explain why the form (59) is permitted, with *there* raising from the position of *t*, where it satisfies the Extended Projection Principle (EPP) in the lower (infinitival) clause:[51]

(59) there seems [*t* to be [a man in the room]]

The problem becomes harder still when we add ECM constructions. In these, the embedded subject *does* raise overtly to a position analogous to *t* in (59), where it is barred (see (57)); and it cannot remain *in situ* as it does in (59):

(60a) I believe [John to be [*t* in the room]] (. . . to have been killed t)
(60b) *I believe [α to be [John in the room]] (. . . to have been killed John)

Within the minimalist framework, we expect the answers to these problems to come from invariant UG principles of economy.

The questions have to do with overt movement; hence the relevant principle should be Procrastinate, which favors covert movement. Recall that Procrastinate selects among convergent derivations. Overt movement is permitted (and forced) to guarantee convergence.

To begin with, let's compare the effects in the contrasting cases (57) and (60). In each case, the reference set determined by the initial numeration includes a second derivation; in the case of (57), the one that yields (59); in the case of (60a), the analogous one that yields (60b) with α the trace of raised *I*. Our goal is to show that in the case of ((57), (59)), economy considerations compel raising of *there* from the embedded clause, while in the case of (60), on the contrary, the same considerations block raising of *I* from the embedded clause, requiring raising of *John* to satisfy EPP (that is, the strong DP-feature on the embedded INFL).[52] The options available suggest that the difference lies in theta theory.

Consider first (57) and (59).[53] Consider the structure that is common to the two derivations. In each, at some stage we construct γ = (61), with the small clause β:

(61) $[_\gamma$ to be $[_\beta$ a man in the room$]$ $]$

The next step must fill the specifier position of γ to satisfy EPP. Given the initial numeration, there are two relevant possibilities:[54] we can raise *a man* to [SPEC, γ] or we can insert *there* in this position. The former choice violates Procrastinate; the second does not. We therefore choose the second option, forming (62):

(62) $[_\gamma$ there to be $\beta]$

At a later stage in the derivation we reach the structure (63):

(63) $[_\delta$ seems $[_\gamma$ there to be $\beta]$ $]$

Convergence requires that [SPEC, δ] be filled. Only one legitimate option exists: to raise *there*, forming (59). We therefore select this option, not violating Procrastinate, which does not arise.

Why, then, does the same argument not favor (60b) over (60a)? The common part of the derivations is (64):

(64) $[_\gamma$ to be $[_\beta$ John in the room$]$ $]$

Again, we have two ways to fill [SPEC, γ], insertion of *I* being preferred if it yields a convergent derivation. Suppose we insert *I*, then raising it to form (60b). Recall that we cannot raise *I* to the VP-internal subject position [SPEC, *believe*]; as already discussed, that violates Greed (see (9)). Therefore the LF output violates the Theta Criterion; the argument chain (*I*, *t*) lacks a theta-role. Note that we must assume now that the derivation crashes; if not, it will converge as gibberish, blocking the desired derivation of (60a).

We therefore conclude that violation of the Theta Criterion prevents convergence (see note 22), although the need for a theta-role is not a formal property, like Case, that permits "last resort" movement. The conclusions are delicate. It remains to investigate further cases and consequences.

Much the same reasoning applies to such structures as (65):

(65) β is believed [α to be [DP XP]]

Before Spell-Out, both positions α and β must be occupied. Hence DP must have raised successive-cyclically, yielding (66) (DP = *John*, XP = *in the room*):

(66) John is believed [*t′* to be [*t* in the room]]

Suppose that the numeration included the expletive *there*. Then (65) would yield the possible outcome (67a) but not (67b) (DP = *a man*, XP = *in the room*; (67a) analogous to (59), (67b) to (57)):

(67a) there is believed [t to be [a man in the room]]
(67b) *there is believed [a man to be in the room]]

Note that (67b) contrasts with (60a), in which overt raising of DP is required.

Suppose that the numeration included expletive *it* instead of *there*. The analogue of (67a) is now impossible because *it*, unlike *there*, is not an LF-affix, so that the features of DP of (65) cannot be checked. Suppose however that instead of such DP we had a phrase that required no such feature-checking, say, a CP instead of [DP XP] in (65), as in (68):

(68) β is believed [α to have been proven [$_{CP}$ that . . .]]]

Then we have the possible outcome (69a) but not (69b):

(69a) it is believed [*t* to have been proven [that . . .]]
(69b) *it is believed [[that S] to have been proven *t*]

With a different numeration, lacking *it*, the embedded CP could have raised to matrix subject position, giving (70):

(70) [that . . .] is believed [*t′* to have been proven *t*]

Hence it is not raising of the CP that is blocked in (68).[55]

Suppose that we have the numeration N that yields (71), with successive-cyclic raising, *t* and *t′* being traces of *John*:

(71) it seems that [John was believed [*t′* to be [*t* in the room]]]

An alternative derivation with the same numeration yields (72), *t* and *t′* traces of *John*:

(72) *John seems that [it was believed [*t′* to be [*t* in the room]]]

The two derivations have the common part (73):

(73) [$_{\alpha}$ to be [$_{\beta}$ John in the room]]

The next step is to fill [SPEC, α], either by raising of *John* (violating Procrastinate unless this is necessary for convergence) or by insertion of *it*. By the earlier reasoning, insertion of *it* is required, yielding only the incorrect output (72) and blocking the correct alternative (71). It must be, then, that the derivation of (72) does not converge, even though all formal properties are satisfied. (72) is an example of super-raising, violating relativized minimality; in the current framework, the Minimal Link Condition (MLC). The conclusion seems to be, then, that violation of this condition – and presumably, of the conglomerate of properties that fall under ECP generally – causes the derivation to crash. The natural conclusion is that a chain that violates ECP is not a legitimate object at LF; in the framework of Chomsky and Lasnik (1991), a chain with a trace marked * is not a legitimate object. If so, then there is no convergent derivation of (72), and (71) is left as the only convergent derivation, as required.[56]

One aspect of question (52b) still remains unanswered: why is the permitted TE structure (55), repeated here as (74a), not blocked by the alternative (74b), in accord with the reasoning just reviewed?

(74a) Expletive AGR [SU [T XP]]
(74b) Expletive AGR [*t* [T [. . . SU . . .]]]

In other words, why is (50), repeated here as (75a), not blocked by (75b), with *there* inserted in the [SPEC, TP] position instead of *the student* raising to this position in violation of Procrastinate?

(75a) [$_{\text{AGRS-P}}$ there [$_{\text{AGRS}}$ painted [$_{\text{TP}}$ a student [$_{\text{AGRO-P}}$ [the house VP]]]]]
(75b) [$_{\text{AGRS-P}}$ there [$_{\text{AGRS}}$ painted [$_{\text{TP}}$ *t* [$_{\text{AGRO-P}}$ [the house [$_{\text{VP}}$ a student . . .]]]]]

A possible argument is that the [SPEC, TP] position must remain open for the subject *a student*, after object-raising. But that is not compelling. First, the trace of *there*, serving no function at LF, might well be deleted or replaced, so that [SPEC, TP] would remain open; see note 53. Second, the same question arises if there is no object-raising.

Consider the structure (76) that is common to the two competing derivations:

(76) [$_{\text{TP}}$ T AGR-P]

The object may or may not have raised to SPEC of the AGR-P complement of T. The next step is to fill [SPEC, TP]. Given the numeration, the choice, as before, is between raising of the subject *the students* or insertion of the expletive *there* by Merge. The former violates Procrastinate. Therefore, insertion of *there* is preferred – *if* it will lead to a convergent derivation. In the cases discussed earlier, that was indeed the case: *there* was able to raise to SPEC of the matrix clause, satisfying EPP. But in this case the matter is different, because of intrinsic properties of *there*. Note that *there* bears Case but lacks intrinsic agreement, the latter determined not by *there* but by its associate, which raises to adjoin to it. Raising of the associate is driven by agreement, not Case, under the assumptions of the previous discussion (following Belletti). Accordingly, if *there* is already in a Case position, it is prevented from raising by Greed; all its features are already satisfied. Hence if *there* is in [SPEC, TP], it cannot raise, and the derivation will crash.[57] Therefore given (76), the only convergent derivation results from raising of the subject *the students*, overriding Procrastinate and yielding (75b). Insertion of *there* yielding the alternative (75b) is not an option.

The assumptions here are those of Chomsky (1992), repeated earlier. The principle of Greed (last resort) overrides convergence; Procrastinate selects among convergent derivations. In addition, we have several conclusions about expletive constructions, theta theory, economy, and convergence. These are strong assumptions, with varied empirical consequences. So far, they seem both conceptually plausible and supported by sometimes rather intricate argument.

The basic assumption about reference sets that underlies the preceding discussion is that they are determined by the initial numeration, but determined stepwise; at a particular point in the derivation, we consider the continuations that are permitted, given the initial numeration; the most economical derivation blocks the others. On that assumption, we explain the full set of cases – although, it must be stressed, it is no trivial matter to generalize the reasoning to more complex cases, and the assumptions to which we have been led are far from solid.

Recall that the bare phrase structure theory allows multiple SPECs in principle. Is this option realized? If so, we will have the structure (77):

(77)

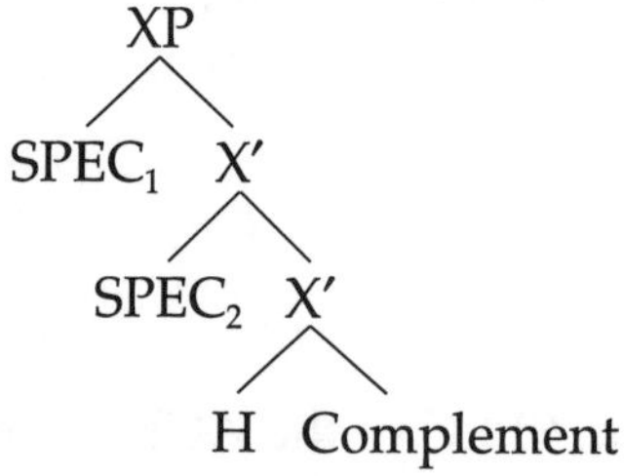

Here we may assume $SPEC_1$ and $SPEC_2$ to be equidistant targets for movement, being within the same minimal domain.

Such ideas and phenomena related to them have been investigated in recent work (Miyagawa 1993a, b, Koizumi 1993, Ura 1993). If a language permits (77), then it should allow multiple assignment of Case and agreement from the same head, since SPEC is available for checking of these features.[58] Suppose that the head H has a strong DP-feature. Then Case must be checked pre-Spell-Out at least at $SPEC_2$, satisfying the strong feature of H. But $SPEC_1$ is still an available position, and could be filled by covert movement, so that the same Case is checked again by H. Furthermore, $SPEC_1$ allows an escape hatch for super-raising. Finally, it permits Scrambling with A-position properties (binding, obviating weak crossover effects, etc.), unlike Scrambling to an A′-position which, under earlier assumptions, involves full reconstruction.

Ura has found that these properties correlate in a wide range of languages, lending strong empirical support to the conclusion that (77) is indeed an option that a language may have. A language might allow this option for some heads but not others (perhaps C but not AGR), in which case other properties follow, all matters now under investigation.

A major question left unresolved is the exact nature of the Minimal Link Condition (MLC). Specifically, we want MLC to deal with relativized minimality cases without any reference, direct or oblique, to the three categories: (a) HMC, (b) A-movement, and (c) A′-movement. Let's review the kinds of problems that arise.

MLC imposes a "shortest move" requirement. Exactly how should we interpret that? We might understand MLC to mean that Move-α must attach α to the nearest target in the already formed structure in a way that does not cause the derivation to crash.[59] One natural strategy for implementing this idea would be to rely on the fact that multiple SPECs are allowed in principle. Whether the "nearest target" is a head H or an X^{max} HP, the operation of substitution can always create a new equidistant SPEC, moving α to occupy it. MLC is therefore satisfied, and no new reason is added for the derivation to crash. If this operation turns out to satisfy Greed in the manner already discussed (and, perhaps, other conditions, if any are relevant), the derivation allows what appears to be a relativized minimality violation, as just discussed. If not, the derivation is illegitimate; whether it crashes depends on how we understand the status of illegitimate multiple SPEC. Hence substitution satisfies MLC.[60] We can therefore restrict attention to adjunction; the task is to show that "improper movement" crashes, bearing in mind that a wide range of cases are admitted in principle when we keep to bare minimalist assumptions.

What is the "nearest target"? Recall that self-attachment is ruled out for α a head. The nearest target for α is therefore the head H that immediately c-commands α, or its (equidistant) specifier (or HP itself, if that too is equidistant). These are the nearest targets for non-minimal α as well if adjunction is barred within a minimal domain, as might be the case.[61]

Consider non-maximal α (a pure head). Recall that substitution (i.e. raising to SPEC or to a new head position) is ruled out; only adjunction is an option. Adjunction of α to X^{max} (either [SPEC, H] or HP) causes the derivation to violate (14) (uniformity), therefore to crash. That leaves only the possibility that α adjoins to H, yielding HMC in this case. Adjunction of α to H does not cause the derivation to crash on the assumption that α can still raise for feature-checking, either by excorporation or pied-piping of H.[62]

For α maximal, MLC requires that α adjoin to H, to HP, or to [SPEC, H]. It remains to show that all of these are cases of "improper movement" that crash, if α ends up in an A-position.

These remarks are intended only to sketch out the issues that remain when the operation Move is freed from any specific conditions. Whether the facts of the matter are consistent with that goal is at the moment unclear, though parts of the problem seem to be within reach.

To summarize, it seems that we can hope to eliminate the theory of phrase structure almost entirely, deriving its properties on highly principled grounds. Many consequences follow for the theories of movement and economy when these conclusions are combined with other minimalist assumptions. We are left with hard and challenging questions, of a new order of depth, and prospects for a theory of language with properties that are quite surprising.

NOTES

1 Most of what follows is based on lecture-seminars at MIT in the fall of 1993. Thanks to the participants for their many suggestions and criticisms in what was (as usual) a cooperative effort, insufficiently acknowledged. Thanks particularly to Samuel Epstein, John Frampton, Sam Guttmann, and Howard Lasnik for comments on an earlier draft.

2 For some discussion of this issue, see Chomsky (1994), referring to (though not mentioning) Edelman (1992) and commentary on it. The terms "mind" and "mental" are used here innocuously, as when we informally class certain phenomena, and whatever is involved in accounting for them, as "optical" or "chemical."

3 For some discussion, see Chomsky (1977a), chapter 1.

4 The assumption that articulation and perception involve the same interface (phonetic representation) is controversial, the obscure problems relating to the C–I interface even more so. The term "articulatory" is too narrow in that it suggests that the language faculty is modality-specific, with a special relation to vocal organs. Work of the past years in sign language shows that this traditional assumption is too narrow. I will continue to use the term, but without any implications about specificity of output system, while keeping to the case of spoken language.

5 Which is not, of course, to deny that a full theory of performance might involve operations that apply to the (π, λ) pair.

6 The work in optimality theory mentioned above does not consider such problems. In Prince–Smolensky, there seems no barrier to the conclusion that all lexical inputs yield a single phonetic output, namely, whatever the optimal syllable might be (perhaps /ba/). That would be ruled out by Prince–McCarthy's "containment condition" (suggested in passing in Prince–Smolensky as a "non-obvious assumption" that they have "found essential" (1993, 80)). But it is hard to see how this can be sustained in segmental phonology (as in the cases mentioned) without implausible and widely varying assumptions about parseability. It seems likely that these approaches will have to postulate intervening levels within the phonological component, raising the question how they differ from rule-based approaches. They may well differ, at least in the domain of prosodic processes (which are hard to separate from segmental ones). At present, it seems to me likely that Bromberger and Halle (1991) are correct in holding that phonology, unlike the rest of C_{HL}, is rule-based, perhaps apart from some specific subdomain.

7 Recall that the ordering of operations is abstract, expressing postulated properties of the language faculty of the brain, with no temporal interpretation implied.

8 Indications of syllabic and intonational structure are not contained in lexical items, nor is, apparently, much of the output phonetic matrix.

9 The PF level is too primitive and unstructured to give meaningful output conditions

itself, but the phonological component does select items of particular kinds to be mapped to the PF output, thus indirectly posing what amount to output conditions for the computation to LF. In speaking of PF output conditions, we really mean those determined by the operations of the phonological component, which indirectly reflect the actual A–P interface conditions.

10 See also Fukui (1986), Speas (1986), Oishi (1990), Freidin (1992), among others. From a representational point of view, there is something odd about a category that is present but invisible; but from a derivational perspective, as Epstein observes, the result is quite natural, these objects being "fossils" that were maximal (hence visible) at an earlier stage of derivation.

11 In our terms, head–head selection is a head–complement relation, and chain-links are reflexes of movement. Further questions arise about Binding Theory and other systems.

12 Nothing essential changes if a lexical entry is a more complex construction from features.

13 I put aside here the question whether chains are formed by successive applications of Move, or by a single Form-Chain operation that could be "successive-cyclic," as suggested in Chomsky (1993). I also dispense with a more precise account of Move along the following lines: given the phrase marker Σ, select K, α s.t. the root of K dominates or c-commands α; form γ by merging α, K (what we call "targeting K and raising α"); define the chain CH = (α_1, α_2) relationally as the pair $<\alpha, \alpha>$, with the usual properties relative to γ. Note that there is no ambiguity in defining a chain this way, given that there are no "copies" other than those formed by movement, given that independent selections of a lexical item are distinguished, as noted.

14 See Lasnik (1993b) for argument for a weaker version.

15 On the nature of this deviance, see section 7. For different approaches to the question, see Brody (1993), Boscovic (1993). Note that the same economy considerations bar raising-to-object, even if the object is a specifier in a Larsonian shell.

16 Problems could arise if X′ were targeted and the raised category were to project, but neither contingency is possible.

17 I put aside here the question of multiple-segment categories beyond two. Nothing essential changes if these exist.

18 Take A-positions to be those narrowly L-related in the sense of Chomsky (1992), A′-bar positions those non-L-related, and the status of broadly L-related yet to be determined. Note that the specifier–adjunct distinction does not quite correlate with the A–A′ distinction.

19 The normal case, and in fact the only case when heads are adjoined, since the target head H is always within the higher projection H′.

20 Technically, this is not quite correct; see note 9.

21 Not entirely, however. A look at the earliest work from the mid-1950s will show that many phenomena that fell within the rich descriptive apparatus then postulated, often with accounts of no little interest and insight, lack any serious analysis within the much narrower theories motivated by the search for explanatory adequacy and remain among the huge mass of constructions for which no principled explanation exists – again, not an unusual concomitant of progress.

22 A non-trivial question is whether violation of this principle (say, violation of the Theta Criterion) causes the derivation to crash or yields a convergent derivation interpreted as gibberish. We have no performance tests to differentiate the cases. There are other empirical differences, in principle. Thus if the derivation converges,

it could block others under economy conditions. Such arguments are hard to construct; we return to one in section 7. The discussion of reconstruction as a process driven by FI in Chomsky (1992) suggests another line of argument, which would support the conclusion that a derivation crashes if it violates FI.

23 We evade here a certain ambiguity about adjunction to α that is simultaneously X^{max} and X^{min}. Is it X^0-adjunction? X^{max}-adjunction? Either, freely? The unanswered questions carry over to subsequent discussion. Specific answers are readily formulated; the question is which ones are factually correct. Note also that there may be a crucial difference between V-raising to INFL and V-raising to V. In the former case, the INFL element may be "invisible" at LF (see next note), so chain-uniformity will not be violated, on an appropriate interpretation.

24 K presumably does not function at LF, having mediated the relation between SPEC and raised head. See Chomsky (1992). A question arises about implementation; deletion raises technical issues in our terms (including a question of self-adjunction). Suppose, for concreteness, that checked functional features are simply understood to be "invisible" to operations of the interface.

25 See note 13. Note that the concept of uniformity here is different from uniformity of phrase structure status discussed earlier.

26 Condition (26b) partially generalizes a conclusion in Chomsky (1986), based on a suggestion by Kyle Johnson: that there be no adjunction to arguments (partially, because of (26c)). The motives required that the conclusion be generalized in very much this way, as has been pointed out a number of times.

27 That reconstruction should be barred in A-chains is thus plausible on conceptual grounds. It has some empirical support as well. Thus, under the relevant interpretation, (i) can only be understood as a Condition (B) violation though under reconstruction the violation should be obviated, with *him* appearing in the position of *t*, c-commanded by *me*; that the latter c-commands α is shown by such Condition (C) violations as (ii):

(i) John expected [him to seem to me [$_\alpha$ *t* to be intelligent]]
(ii) Mary seems to him [*t* to like John]

That the raised subject does not fully reconstruct is shown by standard binding-theoretic facts as well as by the quasi-agentive status commonly conferred in "surface subject" position; e.g., in (iii):

(iii) PRO to appear [*t* to be intelligent] is harder than one might think

We assume here that the quasi-agentive role is a by-product of the raising, motivated on other grounds. Note further that on these assumptions, *there*-adjunction does not reconstruct.

28 See Kitahara (1994a, c) for an economy-based account that yields these consequences within standard X-bar theory, involving structures that are not permitted in the bare theory outlined here.

29 One could define Merge differently, of course, allowing "internal merger." But there is no conceptual advantage in that; in fact, the definition is more complex.

30 See Collins (1994). For a different approach to (29) in terms of economy, see Kitahara (1994c).

31 Fukui (1993); see also Ueda (1990). Note that this proposal requires that ordering be imposed within the N $\rightarrow$ LF computation.

32 I depart from Kayne in understanding linear ordering to be literal precedence, not simply a transitive, asymmetric, total relation among terminals. That is clearly the intended interpretation, but Kayne's more abstract formulation allows very free temporal ordering even if LCA is satisfied. Thus if a class of phrase markers satisfies LCA, so will any interchange of sisters (as Samuel Epstein notes), meaning that consistent with LCA a language could, for example, have any arrangement of head–complement relations (e.g., *read-books* or *books-read* freely). Kayne considers one case of the problem (fully left-to-right or fully right-to-left), but it is more general.

33 Note that L is part of the structure, however; otherwise we would have a new kind of structure, inadmissible in our terms. Thus the branching structure remains, and *m*, *p* do not c-command out of L.

34 On the latter interpretation, we must assume that Morphology precedes LCA, so as to prevent the use of XP-adjunction to X^0 as an "escape hatch" in the syntax, its effects disappearing by LCA before they cause Morphology to crash.

35 Note that V-raising (as in French) does not affect the conclusion that the clitic must raise overtly. If D remains in situ, then whether the trace of V is ignored or deleted by LCA, it will still be a terminal complement, either to V itself or to some intervening element, and the derivation will crash.

36 Presumably the affixal character of N is a general morphological property, not distinguishing nouns with complements from those without (which must raise).

37 The assumption is not entirely obvious; see Epstein (1989) for a contrary view. Much depends on resolution of questions involving reconstruction after adjunction and word-internal processes at LF.

38 Suppose that, as has been proposed, the upper segment enters into calculating subjacency, scope, or other properties. Then we would hope to show that these effects receive a natural expression in terms of containment and domination, notions still available even if the upper segment is "invisible" for C_{HL} and at the interface.

39 That *q* c-commands [m_2, m_1] is required in Kayne's theory for reasons that do not hold in the bare theory, where the assumption plays no role.

40 Operator-phrases formed from adverbials can of course be moved, e.g. "how often." Here it is the *wh*-phrase that moves to satisfy a formal feature.

41 Note that although (39) is barred, *often* could be adjoined to V′, under present assumptions.

42 A number of questions arise here that we have left unsettled. Thus, HMC has only been stipulated, and we have to determine just how it and other MLC cases interact with Greed.

43 Recall that if the VP-internal subject is missing, the position cannot be filled by raising of DP to pick up the unassigned theta-role. See (9).

44 Branigan (1992). See Friedemann and Siloni (1993) for a reanalysis of the phenomenon with a broader data base, within a minimalist framework that distinguishes a participial phrase from AGR_o.

45 See Cardinaletti and Guasti (1991) for further evidence for a structure like (48). Raising to SPEC of the lower AGR is necessary for convergence if agreement features of the adjective must be checked, and is permitted, since the features of the subject can be checked there as well without causing the derivation to crash, as it would with a transitive verb.

46 The observations, if valid, might be assimilated to the apparent tendency for rich overt inflectional morphology (Case and agreement) to appear either in SPEC or

related head (noun or verb) but not both. Such properties are natural if Case and agreement are manifestations of basically the same relation. See Chomsky (1991, 1992).

47 That is, they are different manifestations of the same relation with different features, phi-features vs. Case features; see last note.

48 See Lasnik (1993b) for a somewhat different analysis and discussion of internal problems in the account in Chomsky (1992). Also Groat (1993). Note that we must assume that inherent Case-assignment satisfies agreement, perhaps by raising to SPEC of a functional category that assigns it (or that is associated with the Case-assigner).

49 On movement operations within prosodic phrases, see Truckenbrodt (1993), Zubizarreta (1993).

50 Apparently, that is the case; Jonas, pc.

51 Note that we want to distinguish "there be NP" constructions with strong existential import from the expletive constructions with small clause, which are much weaker in this respect, differing in other properties as well. E.g. the sentence (53b) may be true even if there is no book, just a space on the shelf where a book should be. Similarly, "John has a tooth missing" does not entail the existence of a tooth. A fuller analysis of expletive constructions and the like will also bring in focal stress and other relevant questions that have yet to be examined properly, to my knowledge.

52 Procrastinate then blocks further overt movement of *John* (for Case and agreement) to [SPEC, AGR_o], though overt movement would be required, to satisfy EPP, in "John is believed to be intelligent."

53 Covert raising of *a man* to matrix subject is required in (59) for convergence. This operation could involve replacement of the trace of *there*, which plays no LF role, or might simply skip this position if that trace is deleted, EPP having been satisfied.

54 Technically, there are others, but they will crash or violate Greed – or so it must be demonstrated; not a trivial problem in general.

55 The assumption here is that "I believe [[that he was here] to have been proven]," while not felicitous, is better than (55b). That is not obvious. See Koster (1978).

56 Discussion of the *it*-expletives thanks to John Frampton.

57 We assume, then, that the associate has its agreement checked directly from the head. Raising of *there* with adjoined associate is barred by Greed even if the features of the associate would be checked thereby, since *there* itself lacks agreement features.

58 The Cases assigned are always the same, but agreement may vary. This may reflect the fact that Case is an inherent feature of the Case-checker (thus, transitive verbs check accusative, finite tense checks nominative), but there is no reason to view the phi-features of AGR the same way: perhaps AGR in these cases simply checks such features, whatever they are, lacking phi-features of its own. Note that we have tentatively reached a similar conclusion for expletive *there*; it does not have arbitrary phi-features, but lacks them. There are various technical problems overlooked here.

59 Another possibility, discussed in lectures some years ago, is that raising α over X to position Y could be blocked because raising X would be a shorter move, an approach that requires suspending Greed in evaluating the raising of X. Such an account might be framed in terms of the notion of "shallowness" introduced in Oka (1993). There are other possibilities that merit consideration.

60 We need not be concerned with substitution that literally replaces the target K. That is excluded by recoverability of deletion; furthermore, substitution for K is meaningless if α is within K, as in all cases other than pure head-adjunction, where substitution is also barred by the uniformity condition (14) and other requirements.

61 Also to be considered is targeting an adjunct. Considerations are similar.

62 Suppose H is not morphologically marked as accepting head-adjunction. We would then have to assume that adjunction of α to H creates a violation within Morphology that is distinct from a crashed derivation, again distinguishing word-internal process. Note that adjunction of α to H is not motivated by Greed, but that is irrelevant for adjunction, as discussed.

Postscript

Chapter 8 concludes this book's survey of the Principles and Parameters approach to syntactic theory. The editor hopes that all those who read this book have gotten from it what they set out to find. It is also hoped that the content of this book has (further) stimulated the reader's interest in linguistics in general and syntax in particular. Besides providing information, if we have succeeded in bringing across some of the excitement of being a linguist in these interesting times, it has served a paramount purpose. The reader will have many questions at this point. Perhaps she wants to know more about some topic that was discussed in these chapters all too briefly; or she wants to learn what was written on this same topic in the time gap that invariably lay between the completion of the individual chapters and the production and sale of the book. This intellectual curiosity and the manners in which we try to satisfy it in essence make up what it means to do linguistics and to enjoy the intellectual fascination of this field.

Bibliography

Abney, Steven Paul (1987) *The English Noun Phrase in its Sentential Aspect*, Ph.D. dissertation, MIT.

Adams, Marianne (1987) "From Old French to the theory of pro-drop," *Natural Language and Linguistic Theory* 5, 1–32.

Åfarli, Tor A. (1989) "Passive in Norwegian and English," *Linguistic Inquiry* 20, 101–8.

Aissen, Judith (1974) *The Syntax of Causative Constructions*, Ph.D. dissertation, Harvard. [Published (1979), New York: Garland.]

Aissen, Judith (1987) *Tzotzil Clause Structure*, Dordrecht: D. Reidel.

Aissen, Judith (1990) "Toward a theory of agreement controllers," in B. Joseph and P. Postal (eds), *Studies in Relational Grammar* 3, Chicago: University of Chicago Press.

Akmajian, Adrian and Frank Heny (1976, c1975) *An Introduction to the Principles of Transformational Syntax*, Cambridge, Mass.: MIT Press.

Allen, Barbara J., Donna B. Gardiner, and Donald G. Frantz (1984) "Noun incorporation in Southern Tiwa," *International Journal of American Linguistics* 50, 292–311.

Allen, Margaret Reece (1978) *Morphological Investigations*, Ph.D. dissertation, University of Connecticut.

Anderson, Mona (1979) *Noun Phrase Structure*, Ph.D. dissertation, University of Connecticut.

Anderson, Mona (1983–4) "Prenominal genitive NPs," *The Linguistic Review* 3, 1–24.

Anderson, Stephen (1982a) "Types of dependency in anaphors: Icelandic (and other) reflexives," *Journal of Linguistic Research* 2.2, 1–22.

Anderson, Stephen (1982b) "Where's morphology?" *Linguistic Inquiry* 13, 571–612.

Anderson, Stephen (1984) "Kwakwala syntax and the government-binding theory," in Eung-Do Cook and Donna B. Gerdts (eds), *The Syntax of Native American Languages* (Syntax and Semantics, vol. 16), Orlando: Academic Press, 21–75.

Anderson, Stephen (1985) "Typological distinctions in word formation," in Shopen (ed.), 3–56.

Anderson, Stephen (1986) "Disjunctive ordering in inflectional morphology," *Natural Language and Linguistic Theory* 4, 1–31.

Anderson, Stephen (1988a) "Inflection," in Hammond and Noonan (eds), 23–43.

Anderson, Stephen (1988b) "Morphological theory," in Frederick J. Newmeyer (ed.), *Linguistic Theory: Foundations* (Linguistics: The Cambridge Survey, vol. 1), Cambridge: Cambridge University Press, 146–91.

Anderson, Stephen (1992) *A-morphous Morphology*, Cambridge: Cambridge University Press.

Andrews, Avery D. (1976) "The VP complement analysis in modern Icelandic," in *Proceedings of the Sixth Annual Meeting*, NELS, Amherst, Mass.: GLSA, University of Massachusetts, Amherst. [Published (1990), in Maling and Zaenen (eds), 165–85.]

Andrews, Avery D. (1982a) "Long distance agreement in Modern Icelandic," in Pauline

Jacobson and Geoffrey K. Pullum (eds), *The Nature of Syntactic Representation*, Dordrecht: D. Reidel, 1–33.

Andrews, Avery D. (1982b) "The representation of case in Modern Icelandic," in Bresnan (ed.), 427–503.

Andrews, Avery D. (1990) "Unification and morphological blocking," *Natural Language and Linguistic Theory* 8, 507–57.

Aoun, Joseph (1979) "On government, case-marking, and clitic placement," unpublished manuscript, MIT.

Aoun, Joseph (1981) *The Formal Nature of Anaphoric Relations*, Ph.D. dissertation, MIT.

Aoun, Joseph (1985) *A Grammar of Anaphora*, Cambridge, Mass.: MIT Press.

Aoun, Joseph (1986, c1985) *Generalized Binding: The Syntax and Logical Form of WH-Interrogatives*, Dordrecht: Foris.

Aoun, Joseph, Elabbas Benmamoun, and Dominique Sportiche (1992) "Agreement, word order and conjunction in some varieties of Arabic," unpublished manuscript, University of Southern California and University of California at Los Angeles.

Aoun, Joseph and Norbert Hornstein (1985) "Quantifier types," *Linguistic Inquiry* 16, 623–37.

Aoun, Joseph and Norbert Hornstein (1991) "Bound and referential pronouns," in Huang and May (eds), 1–23.

Aoun, Joseph, Norbert Hornstein, David Lightfoot, and Amy Weinberg (1987) "Two types of locality," *Linguistic Inquiry* 18, 537–77.

Aoun, Joseph, N. Hornstein, and D. Sportiche (1981) "Some aspects of wide scope quantification," *Journal of Linguistic Research* 1.3, 69–95.

Aoun, Joseph and Yen-hui Audrey Li (1988) "Minimal disjointness," in Hagit Borer (ed.), *Proceedings of the the Seventh West Coast Conference on Formal Linguistics, 1988*, Stanford, Calif.: Stanford Linguistics Association, by The Center for the Study of Language and Information, 29–39. [Published (1990), *Linguistics* 28.2, 189–203.]

Aoun, Joseph and Yen-hui Audrey Li (1989) "Scope and constituency," *Linguistic Inquiry* 20, 141–72.

Aoun, Joseph and Yen-hui Audrey Li (1993) *Syntax of Scope*, Cambridge, Mass.: MIT Press.

Aoun, Joseph and D. Sportiche (1981) "On the formal theory of government," *The Linguistic Review* 2, 211–36.

Aronoff, Mark (1976) *Word Formation in Generative Grammar*, Cambridge, Mass.: MIT Press.

Aronoff, Mark (1988) Review of Anna-Maria Di Sciullo and Edwin Williams, *On the Definition of Word*, *Language* 64, 766–70.

Aronoff, Mark (1992) "Stems in Latin verbal morphology," in Mark Aronoff (ed.), *Morphology Now*, Albany: State University of New York Press, 5–32.

Authier, J.-Marc (1991) "V-governed expletives, case theory, and the Projection Principle," *Linguistic Inquiry* 22, 721–40.

Bach, Emmon (1964) *An Introduction to Transformational Grammars*, New York: Holt, Rinehart and Winston.

Bach, Emmon (1968) "Nouns and noun phrases," in Emmon Bach and Robert T. Harms (eds), *Universals in Linguistic Theory*, New York: Holt, Rinehart and Winston, 90–122.

Bailyn, J. (1991) "LF movement of anaphors and acquisition of embedded clauses in Russian," unpublished manuscript, Cornell University.

Baker, C. L. (1970) "Notes on description of English questions: the role of an abstract question morpheme," *Foundations of Language* 6, 197–219.

Baker, C. L. (1979) "Syntactic Theory and the Projection Problem," *Linguistic Inquiry* 10, 533–82.

Baker, Mark (1985) "The mirror principle and morphosyntactic explanation," *Linguistic Inquiry* 16, 373–415.

Baker, Mark (1988a) *Incorporation: A Theory of Grammatical Function Changing*, Chicago: University of Chicago Press.

Baker, Mark (1988b) "Theta theory and the syntax of applicatives in Chichewa," *Natural Language and Linguistic Theory* 6, 353–89.

Baker, Mark and Kenneth Hale (1990) "Relativized minimality and pronoun incorporation," *Linguistic Inquiry* 21, 289–97.

Baker, Mark, Kyle Johnson, and Ian Roberts (1989) "Passive arguments raised," *Linguistic Inquiry* 20, 219–51.

Baltin, Mark (1982) "A landing site theory of movement rules," *Linguistic Inquiry* 13, 1–38.

Baltin, Mark (1987) "Do antecedent-contained deletions exist?" *Linguistic Inquiry* 18, 579–95.

Baltin, Mark (1991) "Head movement in logical form," *Linguistic Inquiry* 22, 225–49.

Barlow, Michael and Charles A. Ferguson (eds) (1988) *Agreement in Natural Language: Approaches, Theories, Descriptions*, Stanford, Calif.: Center for the Study of Language and Information.

Barss, Andrew (1986) *Chains and Anaphoric Dependence: On Reconstruction and its Implications*, Ph.D. dissertation, MIT.

Barss, Andrew, Ken Hale, Ellavina Tsosie Perkins, and Margaret Speas (1991) "Logical form and barriers in Navaho," in Huang and May (eds), 25–47.

Barss, Andrew and Howard Lasnik (1986) "A note on anaphora and double objects," *Linguistic Inquiry* 17, 347–54.

Barwise, Jon and Robin Cooper (1981) "Generalized quantifiers and natural language," *Linguistics and Philosophy* 4, 159–219.

Battistella, Edwin (1987) "Chinese reflexivization," paper presented at the 2nd Harbin Conference on Generative Grammar, Heilongjiang University, Harbin, China; manuscript, University of Alabama at Birmingham. [Published (1989), *Linguistics* 27.6, 987–1012.]

Battistella, Edwin (1989) "Chinese reflexivization: a movement to INFL approach," *Linguistics* 27, 987–1012.

Bayer, Josef (1983) "COMP in Bavarian syntax," *The Linguistic Review* 3, 209–74.

Belletti, Adriana (1988a) "The case of unaccusatives," *Linguistic Inquiry* 19, 1–34.

Belletti, Adriana (1988b) "Generalised V-movement: on some differences and similarities between French and Italian," paper presented at GLOW 1988, Budapest.

Belletti, Adriana (1990) *Generalized Verb Movement: Aspects of Verb Syntax*, Turin: Rosenberg and Sellier.

Belletti, Adriana and Luigi Rizzi (1981) "The syntax of 'ne': some theoretical implications," *The Linguistic Review* 1, 117–54.

Belletti, Adriana and Luigi Rizzi (1988) "Psych-verbs and theta-theory," *Natural Language and Linguistic Theory* 6, 291–352.

Benmamoun, Elabbas (1992) *Functional and Inflectional Morphology: Problems of Projection, Representation and Derivation*, Ph.D. dissertation, University of Southern California.

Bennis, Hans (1986) *Gaps and Dummies*, Dordrecht: Foris.

Bennis, Hans and Liliane Haegeman (1984) "On the status of agreement and relative clauses in West Flemish," in W. de Geest and Y. Putseys (eds), *Sentential Complementation: Proceedings of the International Conference at UFSAL, Brussels, June, 1983*, Dordrecht: Foris, 33–53.

Bennis, Hans and Teun Hoekstra (1984/5) "Gaps and parasitic gaps," *The Linguistic Review* 4, 29–87.

Besten, Hans den (1981) "A case filter for passives," in Adriana Belletti, Luciana Brandi, and Luigi Rizzi (eds), *Theory of Markedness in Generative Grammar*, Pisa: Scuola Normale Superiore di Pisa.

Besten, Hans den (1983) "On the interaction of root transformations and lexical deletive rules," in Werner Abraham (ed.), *On the Formal Syntax of the Westgermania*, Amsterdam: John Benjamins, 47–131.

Besten, Hans den and Corretje Moed-van Walraven (1986) "The syntax of verbs in Yiddish," in Haider and Prinzhorn (eds), Dordrecht: Foris, 111–35.

Bobaljik, Jonathan (1993) "Ergativity and ergative unergatives," in Phillips (ed.), 45–88.

Bobaljik, Jonathan and Colin Phillips (eds) (1993) *Papers on Case and Agreement I* (MIT Working Papers in Linguistics, vol. 18).

Booij, Geert (1988) "The relation between inheritance and argument linking: deverbal nouns in Dutch," in Everaert, Evers, Huybregts, and Trommelen (eds), 57–73.

Borer, Hagit (1984a) *Parametric Syntax: Case Studies in Semitic and Romance Languages*, Dordrecht: Foris.

Borer, Hagit (1984b) "The projection principle and rules of morphology," in Charles Jones and Peter Sells (eds), *Proceedings of NELS 14: 1984*, Amherst, Mass.: GSLA, University of Massachusetts at Amherst, 16–33.

Borer, Hagit (1986a) "I-subjects," *Linguistic Inquiry* 17, 375–416.

Borer, Hagit (ed.) (1986b) *The Syntax of Pronominal Clitics* (Syntax and Semantics, vol. 19), Orlando: Academic Press.

Boscovic, Z. (1993) "D-structure, theta criterion, and movement into theta-positions," unpublished manuscript, University of Connecticut and Haskins Laboratories.

Botha, Rudolph (1980) "Word-based morphology and synthetic compounding," *Stellenbosch Papers in Linguistics*, no. 5.

Bouchard, Denis (1982) *On the Content of Empty Categories*, Ph.D. dissertation, MIT. [Published (1984, c1983), Dordrecht: Foris.]

Bowers, John (1987) "Extended X-bar theory, the ECP, and the Left Branch Condition," in Megan Crowhurst (ed.), *Proceedings of the West Coast Conference on Formal Linguistics, Volume 6, 1987*, Stanford: Stanford Linguistics Association, 47–62.

Bowers, John (1989) "The syntax and semantics of predication," unpublished manuscript, Cornell University.

Branigan, Philip (1992) *Subjects and Complementizers*, Ph.D. dissertation, MIT.

Bresnan, Joan (1972) *Theory of Complementation in English Syntax*, Ph.D. dissertation, MIT. [Published (1979), New York: Garland.]

Bresnan, Joan (1977) "Transformations and categories in syntax," in Robert E. Butts and Jaakko Hintikka (eds), *Basic Problems in Methodology and Linguistics*, Dordrecht: D. Reidel, 261–82.

Bresnan, Joan (ed.) (1982a) *The Mental Representation of Grammatical Relations*, Cambridge, Mass.: MIT Press.

Bresnan, Joan (1982b) "The passive in lexical theory," in Bresnan (ed.), 3–86.

Bresnan, Joan and Jonni M. Kanerva (1989) "Locative inversion in Chichewa: a case study of factorization in grammar," *Linguistic Inquiry* 20, 1–50.

Bresnan, Joan and Sam A. Mchombo (1987) "Topic, pronoun, and agreement in Chichewfla," *Language* 63: 741–82.

Bresnan, Joan and Lioba Moshi (1990) "Object asymmetries in comparative Bantu syntax," *Linguistic Inquiry* 21, 147–85.

Brody, Michael (1993) "θ-theory and arguments," *Linguistic Inquiry* 24, 1–23.

Bromberger, Sylvain and Morris Halle (1991) "Why phonology is different," in Asa Kasher (ed.), *The Chomskyan Turn*, Oxford: Blackwell, 56–77.
Browning, M. A. (1989) "ECP ≠ CED," *Linguistic Inquiry* 20, 481–91.
Bures, T. (1992) "There is an argument for a cycle at LF here," *Papers from the Twenty-eighth Regional Meeting Chicago Linguistic Society.*
Burzio, Luigi (1986) *Italian Syntax: A Government–Binding Approach*, Dordrecht: D. Reidel.
Burzio, Luigi (1988) "On the non-existence of disjoint reference principles," paper presented at a colloquium, annual meeting of the Linguistic Society of America.
Cardinaletti, A. and M. T. Guasti (1991) "Epistemic small clauses and null subjects," unpublished manuscript, University of Venice and University of Geneva.
Carnie, A. (1993) "Nominal predicates in Irish," in Phillips (ed.), 89–129.
Carrier, Jill and Janet H. Randall (1992) "The argument structure and syntactic structure of resultatives," *Linguistic Inquiry* 23, 173–234.
Carstairs, Andrew (1981) *Notes on Affixes, Clitics and Paradigms*, Bloomington: Indiana University Linguistics Club.
Cheng, Lisa Lai-Shen (1991) *On the Typology of Wh-Questions*, Ph.D. dissertation, MIT.
Choe, Jae W. (1987) "LF movement and pied-piping," *Linguistic Inquiry* 18, 348–53.
Chomsky, Noam (1957) *Syntactic Structures*, The Hague: Mouton.
Chomsky, Noam (1965) *Aspects of the Theory of Syntax*, Cambridge, Mass.: MIT Press.
Chomsky, Noam (1970) "Remarks on nominalization," in Roderick A. Jacobs and Peter S. Rosenbaum (eds), *Readings in English Transformational Grammar*, Waltham, Mass.: Ginn and Co., 184–221. [Reprinted in Chomsky (1972c), 11–61.] (All page references are to Chomsky 1972c.)
Chomsky, Noam (1972a) "Deep structure, surface structure and semantic interpretation," in Chomsky (1972c), 62–119.
Chomsky, Noam (1972b) "Some empirical issues in the theory of transformational grammar," in Chomsky (1972c), 120–202.
Chomsky, Noam (1972c) *Studies on Semantics in Generative Grammar*, The Hague: Mouton.
Chomsky, Noam (1973) "Conditions on transformations," in Stephen R. Anderson and Paul Kiparsky (eds), *A Festschrift for Morris Halle*, New York: Holt, Rinehart and Winston, 232–86.
Chomsky, Noam (1976) "Conditions on rules of grammar," *Linguistic Analysis* 2, 303–51.
Chomsky, Noam (1977a) *Essays on Form and Interpretation*, Amsterdam: Elsevier North-Holland.
Chomsky, Noam (1977b) "On WH-movement," in Peter W. Culicover, Thomas Wasow, and Adrian Akmajian (eds), *Formal Syntax*, New York: Academic Press, 71–132.
Chomsky, Noam (1979) Transcripts of the lectures delivered at the Scuola Normale Superiore, Pisa. [Published as Chomsky (1981).]
Chomsky, Noam (1980) "On binding," *Linguistic Inquiry* 11, 1–46.
Chomsky, Noam (1981) *Lectures on Government and Binding: The Pisa Lectures*, Dordrecht: Foris. [7th edn (1993), Berlin: Mouton.]
Chomsky, Noam (1982) *Some Concepts and Consequences of the Theory of Government and Binding*, Cambridge, Mass.: MIT Press.
Chomsky, Noam (1986a) *Barriers*, Cambridge, Mass.: MIT Press.
Chomsky, Noam (1986b) *Knowledge of Language: Its Nature, Origin, and Use*, New York: Praeger.
Chomsky, Noam (1989) "Some notes on economy of derivation and representation," in Itziar Laka and Anoop Mahajan (eds), *Functional Heads and Clause Structure* (MIT

Working Papers in Linguistics, vol. 10), Cambridge, Mass.: Department of Linguistics and Philosophy, MIT. [Published (1991), in Freidin (ed.), 417–54.]
Chomsky, Noam (1991), *see* Chomsky (1989).
Chomsky, Noam (1992) "A minimalist program for linguistic theory," *MIT Occasional Papers in Linguistics,* 1. [Published (1993), in Kenneth Hale and Samuel Jay Keyser (eds), *The View from Building 20: Essays in Linguistics in Honor of Sylvain Bromberger,* Cambridge, Mass.: MIT Press, 1–52.]
Chomsky, Noam (1994) *Language and Thought,* Wakefield, Rhode Island: Moyer Bell.
Chomsky, Noam (this volume) "Bare phrase structure", pp. 383–439.
Chomsky, Noam and Morris Halle (1968) *The Sound Pattern of English,* New York: Harper and Row. [1st MIT Press Paperback edn (1991), Cambridge, Mass.: MIT Press.]
Chomsky, Noam and Howard Lasnik (1977) "Filters and control," *Linguistic Inquiry* 8, 425–504.
Chomsky, Noam and Howard Lasnik (1991) "Principles and parameters theory," to appear in Joachim Jacobs, Arnim von Stechow, Wolfgang Sternefeld, and Theo Vennemann (eds), *Syntax: Ein internationales Handbuch zeitgenössischer Forschung = An International Handbook of Contemporary Research,* Berlin: Walter de Gruyter.
Chung, Sandra and Carol Georgopoulos (1988) "Agreement with gaps in Chamorro and Palauan," in Barlow and Ferguson (eds), 251–67.
Chung, Sandra and James McCloskey (1987) "Government, barriers and small clauses in Modern Irish," *Linguistic Inquiry* 18, 173–237.
Chung, Sandra and Alan Timberlake (1985) "Tense, aspect, and mood," in Shopen (ed.), 202–58.
Cinque, Guglielmo (1984) "A-bar bound *pro* vs. variable," unpublished manuscript, University of Venice.
Cinque, Guglielmo (1990a) "Ergative adjectives and the lexicalist hypothesis," *Natural Language and Linguistic Theory* 8, 1–39.
Cinque, Guglielmo (1990b) *Types of A′-Dependencies,* Cambridge, Mass.: MIT Press.
Clark, Robin (1992) "Scope assignment and modification," *Linguistic Inquiry* 23, 1–28.
Clements, George N. (1975) "The logophoric pronoun in Ewe: its role in discourse," *Journal of West African Languages* 10, 141–77.
Cole, Peter (1987) "The structure of internally headed relative clauses," *Natural Language and Linguistic Theory* 5, 277–302.
Cole, Peter, Gabriella Hermon and Li-May Sung (1990) "Principles and parameters of long-distance reflexives," *Linguistic Inquiry* 21, 1–22.
Cole, Peter and L.-M. Sung (1991a) "Head movement and long-distance reflexives," paper presented at the Third North American Conference on Chinese Linguistics, Cornell University.
Cole, Peter and L.-M. Sung (1991b) "Long distance reflexives and islandhood in Chinese," unpublished manuscript, University of Delaware.
Collins, Chris (1994) "Economy of derivation and the Generalized Proper Binding Condition," *Linguistic Inquiry* 25, 45–61.
Comrie, Bernard and Sandra A. Thompson (1985) "Lexical nominalization," in Shopen (ed.), 349–98.
Contreras, Heles (1986) "Chain theory, parasitic gaps and the ECP," unpublished manuscript, University of Washington, Seattle.
Contreras, Heles (1987) "Small clauses in Spanish and English," *Natural Language and Linguistic Theory* 5, 225–43.
Couquaux, Daniel (1981) "French predication and linguistic theory," in Robert May and Jan Koster (eds), *Levels of Syntactic Representation,* Dordrecht: Foris. 33–64.

Culicover, Peter W. and Wendy Wilkins (1986) "Control, PRO, and the Projection Principle," *Language* 62, 120–53.
Déprez, Viviane M. (1990) *On the Typology of Syntactic Positions and the Nature of Chains: Move α to the Specifier of Functional Projections*, Ph.D. dissertation, MIT.
Di Sciullo, Anna-Maria and Edwin Williams (1987) *On the Definition of Word*, Cambridge, Mass.: MIT Press.
Diesing, Molly (1990) "Verb movement and the subject position in Yiddish," *Natural Language and Linguistic Theory* 8, 41–79.
Diesing, Molly (1992) *Indefinites*, Cambridge, Mass.: MIT Press.
Dobrovie-Sorin, Carmen (1990) "Clitic doubling, *Wh*-movement, and quantification in Romanian," *Linguistic Inquiry* 21, 351–97.
Dobrovie-Sorin, Carmen (1992) "What does QR raise?" unpublished manuscript, Université Paris 7.
Dowty, David (1979) *Word Meaning and Montague Grammar: The Semantics of Verbs and Times in Generative Semantics and in Montague's PTQ*, Dordrecht: D. Reidel.
Dowty, David (1991) "Thematic proto-roles and argument selection," *Language* 67, 547–619.
Edelman, Gerald M. (1992) *Bright Air, Brilliant Fire: On the Matter of the Mind*, New York: Basic Books.
Emonds, Joseph (1970) *Root and Structure-Preserving Transformations*, Bloomington, Ind.: Indiana University Linguistics Club.
Emonds, Joseph (1976) *A Transformational Approach to English Syntax: Root, Structure-Preserving, and Local Transformations*, New York: Academic Press.
Emonds, Joseph (1978) "The verbal complex V′–V in French," *Linguistic Inquiry* 9, 151–75.
Emonds, Joseph (1980) "Word order in generative grammar," *Journal of Linguistic Research* 1.1, 33–54.
Emonds, Joseph (1985) *A Unified Theory of Syntactic Categories*, Dordrecht: Foris.
Enç, Mürvet (1989) "Pronouns, licensing and binding," *Natural Language and Linguistic Theory* 7, 51–92.
Engdahl, Elisabet (1986) *Constituent Questions: The Syntax and Semantics of Questions with Special Reference to Swedish*, Dordrecht: D. Reidel.
Epstein, Samuel David (1989) "Adjunction and pronominal variable binding," *Linguistic Inquiry* 20, 307–19.
Evans, Gareth (1980) "Pronouns," *Linguistic Inquiry* 11, 337–62.
Everaert, Martin (1980) "Inherent reflexive verbs and the 'Zich'/'Zichzelf'-distribution in Dutch," *Utrecht Working Papers in Linguistics* 10, 1–48.
Everaert, Martin (1988) *The Syntax of Reflexivization*, Ph.D. dissertation, University of Utrecht. [Published (1986), Dordrecht: Foris.]
Everaert, Martin, Arnold Evers, Riny Huybregts, and Mieke Trommelen (eds) (1988) *Morphology and Modularity: In Honour of Henk Schultink*, Dordrecht: Foris.
Everett, Daniel L. (1989) "Clitic doubling, reflexives, and word order alternations in Yagua," *Language* 65, 339–72.
Evers, Arnold (1981) "Two functional principles for 'move V'," *Groninger Arbeiten zur Germanistischen Linguistik* 19, 96–110.
Fabb, Nigel (1988) "English suffixation is constrained only by selectional restrictions," *Natural Language and Linguistic Theory* 6, 527–39.
Fanselow, Gisbert (1989) "Konkurrenzphänomene in der Syntax: eine nicht-pragmatische Reduktion der Prinzipien B und C der Bindungstheorie," *Linguistische Berichte* 123, 385–414.

Farkas, Donka F. and Jerrold M. Sadock (1989) "Preverb climbing in Hungarian," *Language* 65, 318–38.
Farmer, Ann Kathleen (1984) *Modularity in Syntax: A Study of Japanese and English*, Cambridge, Mass.: MIT Press.
Fassi Fehri, Abdelkader (1988) "Agreement in Arabic, binding and coherence," in Barlow and Ferguson (eds), 107–58.
Fiengo, Robert and James Higginbotham (1981) "Opacity in NP," *Linguistic Analysis* 7, 395–421.
Fiengo, Robert, C.-T. James Huang, Howard Lasnik, and Tanya Reinhart (1988) "The syntax of Wh-in-situ," in Hagit Borer (ed.), *Proceedings of the Seventh West Coast Conference on Formal Linguistics, 1988*, Stanford, Calif.: Stanford Linguistics Association, by The Center for the Study of Language and Information, 81–98.
Fillmore, Charles J. (1968) "The case for case," in Emmon Bach and Robert T. Harms (eds), *Universals in Linguistic Theory*, New York: Holt, Rinehart, and Winston, 1–88.
Finer, Daniel L. (1985) "The syntax of switch-reference," *Linguistic Inquiry* 16, 35–55.
Fodor, J. A. (1970) "Three reasons for not deriving 'kill' from 'cause to die'," *Linguistic Inquiry* 1, 429–38.
Fontana, Josep M. and John Moore (1992) "VP-internal subjects and se-reflexivization in Spanish," *Linguistic Inquiry* 23, 501–10.
Freidin, Robert (1978) "Cyclicity and the theory of grammar," *Linguistic Inquiry* 9, 519–49.
Freidin, Robert (1986) "Fundamental issues in the theory of binding," in Barbara Lust (ed.), *Studies in the Acquisition of Anaphora*, vol. 1, Boston: D. Reidel, 151–88.
Freidin, Robert (ed.) (1991) *Principles and Parameters in Comparative Grammar*, Cambridge, Mass.: MIT Press.
Freidin, Robert (1992) *Foundations of Generative Syntax*, Cambridge, Mass.: MIT Press.
Freidin, Robert and Howard Lasnik (1981) "Disjoint reference and Wh-trace," *Linguistic Inquiry* 12, 39–53.
Friedemann, M. and T. Siloni (1993) "AGR_{OBJECT} is not $AGR_{PARTICIPLE}$," unpublished manuscript, University of Geneva.
Fukui, Naoki (1986) *A Theory of Category Projection and Its Applications*, Ph.D. dissertation, MIT.
Fukui, Naoki (1988) "LF extraction of *naze*: some theoretical implications," *Natural Language and Linguistic Theory* 6, 503–26.
Fukui, Naoki (1993) "Parameters and optionality in grammar," *Linguistic Inquiry* 24.
Fukui, Naoki and Margaret Speas (1986) "Specifiers and projection," in Naoki Fukui, Tova R. Rapoport, and Elizabeth Sagey (eds), *Papers in Theoretical Linguistics* (MIT Working Papers in Linguistics, vol. 8), 128–72.
Gazdar, Gerald, Ewan Klein, Geoffrey K. Pullum, and Ivan Sag (1985) *Generalized Phrase Structure Grammar*, Cambridge, Mass.: Harvard University Press.
George, Leland M. and Jaklin Kornfilt (1981) "Finiteness and boundedness in Turkish," in Frank Heny (ed.), *Binding and Filtering*, Cambridge, Mass.: MIT Press, 105–27.
Georgopoulos, Carol (1985) "Variables in Palauan syntax," *Natural Language and Linguistic Theory* 3, 59–94.
Gilligan, Gary Martin (1987) *A Cross-Linguistic Approach to the Pro-Drop Parameter*, Ph.D. dissertation, University of Southern California.
Giorgi, Alessandra (1983–4) "Toward a theory of long distance anaphors: a GB approach," *The Linguistic Review* 3, 307–61.
Giorgi, Alessandra and Giuseppe Longobardi (1991) *The Syntax of Noun Phrases: Configuration, Parameters, and Empty Categories*, Cambridge: Cambridge University Press.

Grewendorf, Günther and Wolfgang Sternefeld (eds) (1990) *Scrambling and Barriers*, Amsterdam: John Benjamins.
Grimshaw, Jane (1979) "Complement selection and the lexicon," *Linguistic Inquiry* 10, 279–326.
Grimshaw, Jane (1982) "On the lexical representation of Romance reflexive clitics," in Bresnan (ed.), 87–148.
Grimshaw, Jane (1986) "A morphosyntactic explanation for the mirror principle," *Linguistic Inquiry* 17, 745–9.
Grimshaw, Jane (1990) *Argument Structure*, Cambridge, Mass.: MIT Press.
Grimshaw, Jane and Ralf-Armin Mester (1985) "Complex verb formation in Eskimo," *Natural Language and Linguistic Theory* 3, 1–19.
Groat, E. (1993) "English expletives: a minimalist approach," in H. Thráinsson, S. Epstein, and S. Kuno (eds), *Harvard Working Papers in Linguistics* 3.
Gruber, Jeffrey S. (1965) *Studies in Lexical Relations*, Ph.D. dissertation, MIT. [Distributed (1970), Bloomington: Indiana University Linguistics Club.]
Gruber, Jeffrey S. (1976) *Lexical Structures in Syntax and Semantics*, Amsterdam: North-Holland.
Guerssel, Mohamed (1986) "On Berber verbs of change," *Lexicon Project Working Papers* 9.
Guilfoyle, Eithne Henrietta Hung, and Lisa Travis (1990) "Spec of IP and Spec of VP: two subjects in Malayo-Polynesian languages," manuscript, McGill University and Brandeis University. [Published (1992) "Spec of IP and Spec of VP: two subjects in Austronesian languages," *Natural Language and Linguistic Theory* 10, 375–414.]
Haan, Ger de (1979) *Conditions on Rules: The Proper Balance between Syntax and Semantics*, Dordrecht: Foris. [2nd edn (1981).]
Haegeman, Liliane (1990) "Understood subjects in English diaries: on the relevance of theoretical syntax for the study of register variation," *Multilingua* 9, 157–99.
Haegeman, Liliane (1991) *Introduction to Government and Binding Theory*, Oxford: Basil Blackwell. [2nd edn (1994).]
Haegeman, Liliane and Henk van Riemsdijk (1986) "Verb projection raising, scope, and the typology of rules affecting verbs," *Linguistic Inquiry* 17, 417–66.
Haegeman, Liliane and Raffaella Zanuttini (1990) "Negative concord in West Flemish," unpublished manuscript, Université de Genève.
Haider, Hubert (1981a) "Dependenzen und Konfigurationen," *Groninger Arbeiten zur Germanistischen Linguistik* 21, 1–59.
Haider, Hubert (1981b) "Empty categories and some differences between English and German," *Wiener Linguistische Gazette* 25, 13–36.
Haider, Hubert (1985, c1984) "The case of German," in Jindrich Toman (ed.), *Studies in German Grammar*, Dordrecht: Foris, 65–101.
Haider, Hubert (1986) "V-second in German," in Haider and Prinzhorn (eds), 49–75.
Haider, Hubert and Martin Prinzhorn (eds) (1986) *Verb Second Phenomena in Germanic Languages*, Dordrecht: Foris.
Haïk, Isabelle (1986) *The Syntax of Operators*, Ph.D. dissertation, MIT.
Haïk, Isabelle (1990) "Anaphoric, pronominal and referential Infl," *Natural Language and Linguistic Theory* 8, 347–74.
Hale, Kenneth (1978) "On the position of Warlpiri in a typology of the base," manuscript, MIT. [Distributed (1981), Bloomington: Indiana University Linguistics Club.]
Hale, Kenneth (1983) "Warlpiri and the grammar of non-configurational languages," *Natural Language and Linguistic Theory* 1, 5–47.
Hale, Kenneth and S. J. Keyser (1993) "On argument structure and the lexical expression

of syntactic relations," in Kenneth Hale and Samuel Jay Keyser (eds), *The View from Building 20: Essays in Linguistics in Honor of Sylvain Bromberger*, Cambridge, Mass.: MIT Press, 53–109.

Halle, Morris (1973) "Prolegomena to a theory of word formation," *Linguistic Inquiry* 4, 3–16.

Halle, Morris (1990) "An approach to morphology," in Juli Carter, Rose-Marie Déchaine, Bill Philip, and Tim Sherer (eds), *Proceedings of NELS 20*, vol. 1, Amherst, Mass.: GSLA, University of Massachusetts at Amherst, 150–84.

Halle, Morris and Alec Marantz (1992) "Distributed morphology and the pieces of inflection," manuscript, MIT. [Published (1993), in Kenneth Hale and Samuel Jay Keyser (eds), *The View from Building 20: Essays in Linguistics in Honor of Sylvain Bromberger*, Cambridge, Mass.: MIT Press, 111–76.]

Hammond, Michael and Michael Noonan (1988a) "Morphology in the generative paradigm," in Hammond and Noonan (eds), 1–19.

Hammond, Michael and Michael Noonan (eds) (1988b) *Theoretical Morphology: Approaches in Modern Linguistics*, San Diego: Academic Press.

Harada, Shin-Ichi (1977) "Nihongo ni henkei wa hituyoo da," *Gengo* 6.10, 88–95; 6.11, 96–103.

Harbert, Wayne (1984) "The SSC and empty categories," *Cornell Working Papers in Linguistics* 6, 105–20.

Harbert, Wayne (1986) "Markedness and the bindability of subject of NP," in Fred R. Eckman, Edith A. Moravcsik, and Jessica R. Wirth (eds), *Markedness*, New York: Plenum, 139–54.

Harbert, Wayne (1991) "Binding, SUBJECT, and accessibility," in Freidin (ed.), 29–55.

Harlow, Stephen (1981) "Government and relativisation in Celtic," in Frank Heny (ed.), *Binding and Filtering*, Cambridge, Mass.: MIT Press, 213–54.

Heim, Irene (1982) *The Semantics of Definite and Indefinite Noun Phrases*, Ph.D. dissertation, University of Massachusetts, Amherst. [Published (1988), New York: Garland.]

Heim, Irene, Howard Lasnik, and Robert May (1991) "Reciprocity and plurality," *Linguistic Inquiry* 22, 63–101.

Hellan, Lars (1986, c1985) "The headedness of NPs in Norwegian," in Muysken and van Riemsdijk (eds), 89–122.

Hellan, Lars (1988) *Anaphora in Norwegian and the Theory of Grammar*, Dordrecht: Foris.

Hendrick, Randall (1988) *Anaphora in Celtic and Universal Grammar*, Dordrecht: Kluwer Academic Publishers.

Hendrick, Randall (1991) "The morphosyntax of aspect," *Lingua* 85, 171–210.

Hendrick, Randall (1994) "Head raising and the Celtic copula," in David Lightfoot and Norbert Hornstein (eds), *Verb Movement*, Cambridge: Cambridge University Press.

Hendrick, Randall and Michael Rochemont (1982) "Complementation, multiple WH and echo questions," unpublished manuscript, University of North Carolina, Chapel Hill and University of California, Irvine.

Hermon, Gabriella (1990) "Syntactic theory and language acquisition: a case against parameters," *Studies in the Linguistic Sciences* 30, 139–63.

Hestvik, Arild (1986) "Case theory and Norwegian impersonal constructions: subject–object alternation in active and passive verbs," *Nordic Journal of Linguistics* 9, 181–97.

Hestvik, Arild (1990) *LF-Movement of Pronouns and the Computation of Binding Domains*, Ph.D. dissertation, Brandeis University.

Higginbotham, James (1980a) "Anaphora and GB: some preliminary remarks," in John T. Jensen (ed.), *Cahiers Linguistiques d'Ottawa* 9, 223–36.

Higginbotham, James (1980b) "Pronouns and bound variables," *Linguistic Inquiry* 11, 679–708.

Higginbotham, James (1981) "Reciprocal interpretation," *Journal of Linguistic Research* 1.3, 97–117.

Higginbotham, James (1983) "Logical form, binding, and nominals," *Linguistic Inquiry* 14, 395–420.

Higginbotham, James (1985) "On semantics," *Linguistic Inquiry* 16, 547–93.

Higginbotham, James (1987a) "The autonomy of syntax and semantics," in Jay L. Garfield (ed.), *Modularity in Knowledge Representation and Natural-Language Understanding*, Cambridge, Mass.: MIT Press, 119–32.

Higginbotham, James (1987b) "On semantics," in Ernest Lepore (ed.), *New Directions in Semantics*, London: Academic Press, 1–54.

Higginbotham, James and Robert May (1981) "Questions, quantifiers and crossing," *The Linguistic Review* 1, 41–79.

Hoeksema, Jack (1985) *Categorial Morphology*, New York: Garland.

Hoeksema, Jack (1992) "Categorial morphology and the valency of nouns," in Mark Aronoff (ed.), *Morphology Now*, Albany: State University of New York Press, 83–106.

Hoekstra, Teun (1984) *Transitivity: Grammatical Relations in Government–Binding Theory*, Dordrecht: Foris.

Hoekstra, Teun (1988) "Small clause results," *Lingua* 74, 101–39.

Hoekstra, Teun and René Mulder (1990) "Unergatives as copular verbs; locational and existential predication," *The Linguistic Review* 7, 1–79.

Hoekstra, Teun and Frans van der Putten (1988) "Inheritance phenomena," in Everaert, Evers, Huybregts, and Trommelen (eds), 163–86.

Hoji, Hajime (1985) *Logical Form Constraints and Configurational Structures in Japanese*, Ph.D. dissertation, University of Washington.

Holmberg, Anders (1986) *Word Order and Syntactic Features in the Scandinavian Languages and English*, Ph.D. dissertation, Stockholm University.

Hornstein, Norbert (1977) "S and X′ convention," *Linguistic Analysis* 3, 137–76.

Hornstein, Norbert (1991) "Expletives: a comparative study of English and Icelandic," *Working Papers in Scandinavian Syntax* 47, University of Lund, 1–92.

Hornstein, Norbert and David Lightfoot (1981) Introduction, in Norbert Hornstein and David Lightfoot (eds), *Explanation in Linguistics: The Logical Problem of Language Acquisition*, London: Longman, 9–31.

Hornstein, Norbert and David Lightfoot (1987) "Predication and PRO," *Language* 63, 23–52.

Hornstein, Norbert and David Lightfoot (1991) "On the nature of lexical government," in Freidin (ed.), 365–91.

Hornstein, Norbert and Amy Weinberg (1991) "The necessity of LF," *The Linguistic Review* 7, 129–67.

Horvath, Julia (1986) *Focus in the Theory of Grammar and the Syntax of Hungarian*, Dordrecht: Foris.

Huang, C.-T. James (1982) *Logical Relations in Chinese and the Theory of Grammar*, Ph.D. dissertation, MIT.

Huang, C.-T. James (1983) "A note on the binding theory," *Linguistic Inquiry* 14, 554–61.

Huang, C.-T. James (1984) "On the distribution and reference of empty pronouns," *Linguistic Inquiry* 15, 531–74.

Huang, C.-T. James (1989) "Pro-drop in Chinese: a generalized control theory," in Jaeggli and Safir (eds), 185–214.

Huang, C.-T. James (1991) "Modularity and Chinese A–not-A questions," in Carol Georgopoulos and Roberta Ishihara (eds), *Interdisciplinary Approaches to Language: Essays in Honor of S.-Y. Kuroda*, Dordrecht: Kluwer, 305–32.

Huang, C.-T. James (1993) "Reconstruction and the structure of VP: some theoretical consequences," *Linguistic Inquiry* 24, 103–38.

Huang, C.-T. James and Robert May (eds) (1991) *Logical Structure and Linguistic Structure: Cross-Linguistic Perspectives*, Dordrecht: Kluwer.

Huang, C.-T. James and C.-C. J. Tang (1991) "The local nature of the long-distance reflexive in Chinese," in Jan Koster and Eric Reuland (eds), *Long-Distance Anaphora*, Cambridge: Cambridge University Press, 263–82.

Huang, Shuan-Fan (1981) "On the scope phenomena of Chinese quantifiers," *Journal of Chinese Linguistics* 9, 226–43.

Hudson, Richard A. (1987) "Zwicky on heads," *Journal of Linguistics* 23, 109–32.

Huybregts, M. A. C. (1979) "On bound anaphora and the theory of Government–Binding," paper presented at NELS X, University of Ottawa.

Iatridou, Sabine (1986) "An anaphor not bound in its governing category," *Linguistic Inquiry* 17, 766–72.

Iatridou, Sabine (1990) "About Agr(P)," *Linguistic Inquiry* 21, 551–77.

Iatridou, Sabine and Anthony Kroch (1992) "The licensing of CP recursion and its relevance to the Germanic verb-second phenomenon," *Working Papers in Scandinavian Syntax* 50.

Itô, Junko (1986) "Head movement at LF and PF," in N. Hasegawa and Y. Kitagawa (eds), *University of Massachusetts Occasional Papers in Linguistics* 11, 109–38.

Jackendoff, Ray (1969) *Some Rules of Semantic Interpretation for English*, Ph.D. dissertation, MIT.

Jackendoff, Ray (1972) *Semantic Interpretation in Generative Grammar*, Cambridge, Mass.: MIT Press.

Jackendoff, Ray (1975) "Morphological and semantic regularities in the lexicon," *Language* 51, 639–71.

Jackendoff, Ray (1977) *X′ Syntax: A Study of Phrase Structure*, Cambridge, Mass.: MIT Press.

Jackendoff, Ray (1990) "On Larson's treatment of the double object construction," *Linguistic Inquiry* 21, 427–56.

Jaeggli, Osvaldo (1982) *Topics in Romance Syntax*, Dordrecht: Foris.

Jaeggli, Osvaldo (1985) "On certain ECP effects in Spanish," unpublished manuscript, University of Southern California, Los Angeles.

Jaeggli, Osvaldo (1986) "Passive," *Linguistic Inquiry* 17, 587–622.

Jaeggli, Osvaldo and Kenneth J. Safir (eds) (1989a) *The Null Subject Parameter*, Dordrecht: Kluwer.

Jaeggli, Osvaldo and Kenneth J. Safir (1989b) "The null subject parameter and parametric theory," in Jaeggli and Safir (eds) (1989a), 1–44.

Jensen, John T. (1990) *Morphology: Word Structure in Generative Grammar*, Amsterdam: John Benjamins.

Jensen, John T. and Alana Johns (1989) "The morphosyntax of Eskimo causatives," in Donna B. Gerdts and Karin Michelson (eds), *Theoretical Perspectives on Native American Languages*, Albany: State University of New York Press, 209–29.

Jensen, John T. and Margaret Stong-Jensen (1984) "Morphology is in the lexicon!" *Linguistic Inquiry* 15, 474–98.

Jespersen, Otto (1924) *The Philosophy of Grammar*, New York: Henry Holt and Co. [University of Chicago Press edn (1992), Chicago: University of Chicago Press.]

Johns, Alana (1992) "Deriving ergativity," *Linguistic Inquiry* 23, 57–87.

Johnson, Kyle (1988) "Clausal gerunds, the ECP, and government," *Linguistic Inquiry* 19, 583–609.

Johnson, Kyle (1991) "Object positions," *Natural Language and Linguistic Theory* 9, 577–636.

Jonas, D. (forthcoming) "The TP parameter in Scandinavian syntax," in C. Hedlund and A. Holmberg (eds), *Göteborg Working Papers in Linguistics.*

Jonas, D. and J. Bobaljik (1993) "Specs for subjects: the role of TP in Icelandic," in Bobaljik and Phillips (eds), 59–98.

Jones, Douglas (1993a) "A-binding and scrambling in Hindi: reflexives vs. reciprocals," paper presented at the Workshop on Theoretical Issues in Ergative Languages, Rutgers University.

Jones, Douglas (1993b) *Binding as an Interface Condition: An Investigation of Hindi Scrambling,* Ph.D. dissertation, MIT.

Kaisse, Ellen M. (1985) *Connected Speech: The Interaction of Syntax and Phonology,* Orlando: Academic Press.

Kameyama, Megumi (1984) "Subjective/logophoric bound anaphor *zibun*," in Joseph Drogo, Veena Mishra, and David Testen (eds), *CLS 20: Papers from the Twentieth Regional Meeting,* 228–38.

Kang, Beom-Mo (1988) "Unbounded reflexives," *Linguistics and Philosophy* 11, 415–56.

Karttunen, Lauri (1977) "Syntax and semantics of questions," *Linguistics and Philosophy* 1, 3–44.

Katada, Fusa (1991) "The LF representation of anaphors," *Linguistic Inquiry* 22, 287–313.

Katz, Jerrold J. and Paul M. Postal (1964) *An Integrated Theory of Linguistic Descriptions,* Cambridge, Mass.: MIT Press. [1st MIT Press paperback edn (1978).]

Kayne, Richard (1975) *French Syntax: The Transformational Cycle,* Cambridge, Mass.: MIT Press.

Kayne, Richard (1981) "ECP extensions," *Linguistic Inquiry* 12, 93–133. [Reprinted in Kayne (1984).]

Kayne, Richard (1983a) "Chains, categories external to S, and French complex inversion," *Natural Language and Linguistic Theory* 1, 107–39.

Kayne, Richard (1983b) "Connectedness," *Linguistic Inquiry* 14, 223–49. [Reprinted in Kayne (1984).]

Kayne, Richard (1984) *Connectedness and Binary Branching,* Dordrecht: Foris.

Kayne, Richard (1985, c1984) "Principles of particle constructions," in J. Guéron, H.-G. Obenauer, and J.-Y. Pollock (eds), *Grammatical Representation,* Dordrecht: Foris, 101–40.

Kayne, Richard (1989a) "Facets of Romance past participle agreement," in Paola Beninca (ed.), *Dialect Variation and the Theory of Grammar,* Dordrecht: Foris, 85–103.

Kayne, Richard (1989b) "Null subjects and clitic climbing," in Jaeggli and Safir (eds), 239–61.

Kayne, Richard (1993) "The antisymmetry of syntax," unpublished manuscript, CUNY Graduate Center.

Keenan, Edward L. (1974) "The functional principle: generalizing the notion of 'subject of'," in Michael W. LaGaly, Robert A. Fox, and Anthony Bruck (eds), *Papers from the Tenth Regional Meeting Chicago Linguistic Society,* 298–309.

Kikuchi, A. (1987) "Comparative deletion in Japanese," unpublished manuscript, Yamagata University.

Kim, Dae-Bin (1992) *The Specificity/Non-Specificity Distinction and Scrambling Theory,* Ph.D. dissertation, University of Wisconsin, Madison.

Kiss, Katalin É. (1987) *Configurationality in Hungarian,* Dordrecht: D. Reidel.

Kiss, Katalin É. (1991) "Logical structure in syntactic structure: the case of Hungarian," in Huang and May (eds), 111–47.

Kitagawa, Yoshihisa (1985) "Small but clausal," in William H. Eilfort, Paul D. Kroeber, and Karen L. Peterson (eds), *CLS 21, Part 1: Papers from the General Session at the Twenty-first Regional Meeting, Chicago Linguistics Society*, 210–20.

Kitagawa, Yoshihisa (1986) *Subjects in Japanese and English*, Ph.D. dissertation, University of Massachusetts at Amherst. [Published (1994), New York: Garland.]

Kitahara, H. (1994a) "Relativized minimality, superiority, and the Proper Binding Condition," unpublished manuscript, Harvard University.

Kitahara, H. (1994b) *Target α: A Unified Theory of Movement and Structure-Building*, Ph.D. dissertation, Harvard University.

Kitahara, H. (1994c) "Target α: deducing strict cyclicity from principles of derivational economy," to appear in *Linguistic Inquiry*.

Klavans, Judith L. (1985) "The independence of syntax and phonology in cliticization," *Language* 61, 95–120.

Koizumi, M. (1993) "Topicalization in English as adjunction to PolP," *Proceedings of NELS* 24.

Koopman, Hilda (1983) "ECP effects in main clauses," *Linguistic Inquiry* 14, 346–50.

Koopman, Hilda (1984) *The Syntax of Verbs: From Verb Movement Rules in the Kru Languages to Universal Grammar*, Dordrecht: Foris.

Koopman, Hilda (1987) "On the absence of case chains in Bambara," manuscript, University of California, Los Angeles. [Published (1992), *Natural Language and Linguistic Theory* 10, 555–94.]

Koopman, Hilda and D. Sportiche (1982/3) "Variables and the bijection principle," *The Linguistic Review* 2, 139–60.

Koopman, Hilda and Dominique Sportiche (1985) "Theta theory and extraction," abstract in *GLOW Newsletter* 14, 57–8.

Koopman, Hilda and Dominique Sportiche (1986) "A note on long extraction in Vata," *Natural Language and Linguistic Theory* 4, 357–74.

Koopman, Hilda and Dominique Sportiche (1988) "Subjects," unpublished manuscript, University of California, Los Angeles.

Koopman, Hilda and Dominique Sportiche (1989) "Pronouns, logical variables, and logophoricity in Abe," *Linguistic Inquiry* 20, 555–88.

Koopman, Hilda and Dominique Sportiche (1991) "The position of subjects," *Lingua* 85, 211–58.

Koster, Jan (1978) "Why subject sentences don't exist," in S. Jay Keyser (ed.), *Recent Transformational Studies in European Languages*, Cambridge, Mass.: MIT Press.

Koster, Jan (1984) "On binding and control," *Linguistic Inquiry* 15, 417–59.

Koster, Jan (1987a, c1986) *Domains and Dynasties: The Radical Autonomy of Syntax*, Dordrecht: Foris.

Koster, Jan (1987b) "The relation between pro-drop, scrambling, and verb movements," *Groningen Papers in Theoretical and Applied Linguistics* 1.

Kroch, Anthony S. (1974) *The Semantics of Scope in English*, Ph.D. dissertation, MIT. [Published (1979), New York: Garland.]

Kuroda, S.-Y. (1988) "Whether we agree or not: a comparative syntax of English and Japanese," *Lingvisticae Investigationes* 12, 1–47.

Laka Mugarza, Miren Itziar (1990) *Negation in Syntax: On the Nature of Functional Categories and Projections*, Ph.D. dissertation, MIT.

Lakoff, George (1968) "Instrumental adverbs and the concept of deep structure," *Foundations of Language* 4, 4–29.

Lakoff, George (1971) "On generative semantics," in Danny D. Steinberg and Leon A. Jakobovits (eds), *Semantics*, Cambridge: Cambridge University Press, 232–96.
Lapointe, Steven (1980) *A Theory of Grammatical Agreement*, Ph.D. dissertation, University of Massachusetts, Amherst. [Published (1985), New York: Garland.]
Lapointe, Steven (1988) "Toward a unified theory of agreement," in Barlow and Ferguson (eds), 67–87.
Larson, Richard K. (1985) "On the syntax of disjunction scope," *Natural Language and Linguistic Theory* 3, 217–64.
Larson, Richard K. (1988) "On the double object construction," *Linguistic Inquiry* 19, 335–91.
Larson, Richard K. (1990) "Double objects revisited: reply to Jackendoff," *Linguistic Inquiry* 21, 589–632.
Larson, Richard K. (1991) "*Promise* and the theory of control," *Linguistic Inquiry* 22, 103–39.
Larson, Richard K. and Robert May (1990) "Antecedent containment or vacuous movement: reply to Baltin," *Linguistic Inquiry* 21, 103–22.
Lasnik, Howard (1981) "On two recent treatments of disjoint reference," *Journal of Linguistic Research* 1.4, 48–58.
Lasnik, Howard (ed.) (1989a) *Essays on Anaphora*, Dordrecht: Kluwer.
Lasnik, Howard (1989b) "A selective history of modern binding theory," in Lasnik (ed.), 1–36.
Lasnik, Howard (1991) "On the necessity of binding conditions," in Freidin (ed.), 7–28.
Lasnik, Howard (1992) "Case and expletives: notes toward a parametric account," *Linguistic Inquiry* 23, 381–405.
Lasnik, Howard (1993a) "Lectures on minimalist syntax," *University of Connecticut Occasional Papers in Linguistics*, vol. I, distributed by MIT Working Papers in Linguistics.
Lasnik, Howard (1993b) "Case and expletives revisited," unpublished manuscript, University of Connecticut.
Lasnik, Howard and Mamoru Saito (1984) "On the nature of proper government," *Linguistic Inquiry* 14, 235–89.
Lasnik, Howard and Mamoru Saito (1992) *Move α: Conditions on its Application and Output*, Cambridge, Mass.: MIT Press.
Lasnik, Howard and Tim Stowell (1991) "Weakest crossover," *Linguistic Inquiry* 22, 687–720.
Lasnik, Howard and Juan Uriagereka (1988) *A Course in GB Syntax: Lectures on Binding and Empty Categories*, Cambridge, Mass.: MIT Press.
Lebeaux, David (1983) "A distributional difference between reciprocals and reflexives," *Linguistic Inquiry* 14, 723–30.
Lebeaux, David (1984–5) "Locality and anaphoric binding," *The Linguistic Review* 4, 343–63.
Lebeaux, David (1986) "The interpretation of derived nominals," in Anne M. Farley, Peter T. Farley, and Karl-Erik McCullough (eds), *CLS 22, Part 1: Papers from the General Session at the Twenty-Second Regional Meeting Chicago Linguistic Society*, 231–47.
Lebeaux, David (1988) *Language Acquisition and the Form of the Grammar*, Ph.D. dissertation, University of Massachusetts, Amherst.
Lee, Young-Suk (1993) *Scrambling as Case-Driven Obligatory Movement*, Ph.D. dissertation, University of Pennsylvania.
Lee, Young-Suk and Beatrice Santorini (1990) "Towards resolving Webelhuth"s paradox:

evidence from German and Korean," manuscript. [Published (1994), in Norbert Corver and Henk van Riemsdijk (eds), *Studies of Scrambling: Movement and Non-Movement Approaches to Free Word Order Phenomena*, Berlin: Mouton.]

Levin, Beth and Malka Rappaport (1986) "The formation of adjectival passives," *Linguistic Inquiry* 17, 623–61.

Lewis, David (1975) "Adverbs of quantification," in Edward L. Keenan (ed.), *Formal Semantics of Natural Language*, Cambridge: Cambridge University Press, 3–15.

Li, Audrey (1992) "Indefinite Wh in Mandarin Chinese," *Journal of East Asian Linguistics* 1, 125–56.

Li, Yafei (1990a) "On V–V compounds in Chinese," *Natural Language and Linguistic Theory* 8, 177–207.

Li, Yafei (1990b) "X^0–binding and verb incorporation," *Linguistic Inquiry* 21, 399–426.

Lieber, Rochelle (1980) *On the Organization of the Lexicon*, Ph.D. dissertation, MIT. [Published (1990), New York: Garland.]

Lieber, Rochelle (1983) "Argument linking and compounds in English," *Linguistic Inquiry* 14, 251–85.

Lieber, Rochelle (1984) "Grammatical rules and sublexical elements," in David Testen, Veena Mishra, and Joseph Drogo (eds), *Papers from the Parasession on Lexical Semantics: Chicago Linguistics Society*, 187–99.

Lieber, Rochelle (1992) *Deconstructing Morphology: Word Formation in Syntactic Theory*, Chicago: University of Chicago Press.

Lightfoot, David (1992) "Government: the long and the short of it," *Journal of Linguistics* 28, 185–97. [Review of Rizzi (1990).]

Lightfoot, David and Amy Weinberg (1988) Review of Noam Chomsky, *Barriers*, *Language* 64, 366–83.

Longobardi, Giuseppe (1985) "Connectedness and island constraints," in J. Guéron, H.-G. Obenauer, and J.-Y. Pollock (eds), *Grammatical Representation*, Dordrecht: Foris, 169–85.

Longobardi, Giuseppe (1991) "In defense of the correspondence hypothesis: island effects and parasitic constructions in logical form," in Huang and May (eds), 149–96.

Mahajan, Anoop Kumar (1990) *The A/A-bar Distinction and Movement Theory*, Ph.D. dissertation, MIT.

Malatin, Philip S. (1991) *Finnish Verbal Morphology and Functional Syntactic Categories*, MA thesis, University of North Carolina at Chapel Hill.

Maling, Joan (1984) "Non-clause-bounded reflexives in Modern Icelandic," *Linguistics and Philosophy* 7, 211–41.

Maling, Joan and Annie Zaenen (eds) (1990) *Modern Icelandic Syntax* (Syntax and Semantics, vol. 24), San Diego: Academic Press.

Manzini, M. Rita (1983a) "On control and control theory," *Linguistic Inquiry* 14, 421–46.

Manzini, M. Rita (1983b) *Restructuring and Reanalysis*, Ph.D. dissertation, MIT.

Manzini, M. Rita and Kenneth Wexler (1987) "Parameters, binding theory and learnability," *Linguistic Inquiry* 18, 413–44.

Marácz, László (1989) *Asymmetries in Hungarian = Assymmetrieen in het Hongaars*, Ph.D. dissertation, University of Groningen.

Marácz, László and Pieter Muysken (eds) (1989) *Configurationality: The Typology of Asymmetries*, Dordrecht: Foris.

Marantz, Alec (1979) "Assessing the X-bar convention," unpublished manuscript, MIT.

Marantz, Alec (1984) *On The Nature of Grammatical Relations*, Cambridge, Mass.: MIT Press.

Marantz, Alec (1988a) "Apparent exceptions to the projection principle," in Everaert, Evers, Huybregts, and Trommelen (eds), 217–32.
Marantz, Alec (1988b) "Clitics, morphological merger, and the mapping to phonological structure," in Hammond and Noonan (eds), 253–70.
Marantz, Alec (1989) "Projection vs. percolation in the syntax of synthetic compounds," unpublished manuscript, University of North Carolina at Chapel Hill.
Marantz, Alec (1991) "Case and licensing," ESCOL (Proceedings of the Eastern States Conference on Linguistics) 1991.
Marantz, Alec (1992) "What kind of pieces are inflectional morphemes?" paper presented at the Berkeley Linguistics Society.
Martin, R. (1992) "On the distribution and case features of PRO," unpublished manuscript, University of Connecticut.
Matthews, P. H. (1974) *Morphology: An Introduction to the Theory of Word-Structure*, Cambridge: Cambridge University Press. [2nd edn. (1991) *Morphology*.]
May, Robert (1977) *The Grammar of Quantification*, Ph.D. dissertation, MIT. [Published (1990), New York: Garland.]
May, Robert (1985) *Logical Form: Its Structure and Derivation*, Cambridge, Mass.: MIT Press.
May, Robert (1988a) "Ambiguities of quantification and *Wh*: a reply to Williams," *Linguistic Inquiry* 19, 118–35.
May, Robert (1988b) "Bound variable anaphora," in Ruth M. Kempson (ed.), *Mental Representations: The Interface Between Language and Reality*, Cambridge: Cambridge University Press, 85–104.
McCarthy, John and Alan Prince (1993) *Prosodic Morphology I*, unpublished manuscript, University of Massachusetts at Amherst and Rutgers University.
McCawley, James D. (1970a) "English as a *VSO* language," *Language* 46, 286–99.
McCawley, James D. (1970b) "Where do noun phrases come from?" in Roderick A. Jacobs and Peter S. Rosenbaum (eds), *Readings in English Transformational Grammar*, Waltham, Mass.: Ginn and Co., 166–83.
McCawley, Noriko Akatsuka (1972) *A Study of Japanese Reflexivization*, Ph.D. dissertation, University of Illinois at Urbana–Champaign.
McCloskey, James (1979) *Transformational Syntax and Model Theoretic Semantics: A Case Study in Modern Irish*, Dordrecht: D. Reidel.
McCloskey, James and Kenneth Hale (1984) "On the syntax of person–number inflection in Modern Irish," *Natural Language and Linguistic Theory* 1, 487–533.
Miller, G. and N. Chomsky (1963) "Finitary models of language users," in R. Duncan Luce, Robert R. Bush, and Eugene Galanter (eds), *Handbook of Mathematical Psychology*, vol. II, New York: Wiley.
Mitchell, Erika (1991) "Evidence from Finnish for Pollock's theory of IP," *Linguistic Inquiry* 22, 373–9.
Mithun, Marianne (1984) "The evolution of noun incorporation," *Language* 60, 847–94.
Mithun, Marianne (1986) "On the nature of noun incorporation," *Language* 62, 32–7.
Miyagawa, S. (1993a) "Case, agreement, and ga/no conversion in Japanese," in *Proceedings of the Third Southern California Japanese/Korean Linguistics Conference*, Stanford: CSLI.
Miyagawa, S. (1993b) "LF case-checking and Minimal Link Condition," in Phillips (ed.).
Mohanan, K. P. (1982) *Grammatical Relations and Anaphora in Malayalam*, Master's Thesis, MIT.
Mohanan, K. P. and Tara Mohanan (1990) "Dative subjects in Malayalam: semantic

information in syntax," in Manindra K. Verma and K. P. Mohanan (eds), *Experiencer Subjects in South Asian Languages*, Stanford: Center for the Study of Language and Information, Stanford University, 43–57.

Mohanan, Tara Warrier (1990) *Arguments in Hindi*, Ph.D. dissertation, Stanford University.

Montalbetti, Mario M. (1984) *After Binding: On the Interpretation of Pronouns*, Ph.D. dissertation, MIT.

Murasugi, Kumiko (1992) *Crossing and Nested Paths — NP Movement in Accusative and Ergative Languages*, Ph.D. dissertation, MIT.

Muysken, Pieter (1982) "Parametrizing the notion 'head'," *Journal of Linguistic Research* 2.3, 57–75.

Muysken, Pieter (1988) "Affix order and interpretation: Quechua," in Everaert, Evers, Huybregts, and Trommelen (eds), 259–79.

Muysken, Pieter and Henk van Riemsdijk (eds) (1986, c1985) *Features and Projections*, Dordrecht: Foris.

Napoli, Donna Jo (1979) "Reflexivization across clause boundaries in Italian," *Journal of Linguistics* 15, 1–28.

Nevis, Joel Ashmore (1985) *Finnish Particle Clitics and General Clitic Theory*, Ph.D. dissertation, Ohio State University. [Published (1988), New York: Garland.]

Nishigauchi, Taisuke (1984) "Control and the thematic domain," *Language* 60, 215–50.

Nishigauchi, Taisuke (1990) *Quantification in the Theory of Grammar*, Dordrecht: Kluwer.

Obenauer, Hans-Georg (1976) *Études de syntaxe interrogative du français: quoi, combien et le complémenteur*, Tübingen: Niemeyer.

Obenauer, Hans-Georg (1985) "On the identification of empty categories," *The Linguistic Review* 4, 153–202.

Oishi, M. (1990) "Conceptual problems of upward X-bar theory," unpublished manuscript, Tohoku Gakuin University.

Oshima, S. (1979) "Conditions on rules: anaphora in Japanese," in George Bedell, Eichi Kobayashi, and Masatake Muraki (eds), *Explorations in Linguistics: Papers in Honor of Kazuko Inoue*, Tokyo: Kenkyusha, 423–48.

Ottósson, Kjartan G. (1989) "Structural and lexical Case in Icelandic," unpublished manuscript, University of Maryland, College Park.

Ouhalla, Jamal (1991) *Functional Categories and Parametric Variation*, London: Routledge.

Park, Sung Hyuk (1986) "Parameterizing the theory of binding: the implication of *caki* in Korean," *Language Research* 22, 229–54.

Perlmutter, David M. (1971) *Deep and Surface Structure Constraints in Syntax*, New York: Holt, Rinehart and Winston.

Perlmutter, David M. (1978) "Impersonal passives and the unaccusative hypothesis," in Jeri J. Jaeger et al. (eds), *Proceedings of the Fourth Annual Meeting of the Berkeley Linguistics Society, February 18–20, 1978*, 157–89.

Perlmutter, David M. (1988) "The split morphology hypothesis: evidence from Yiddish," in Hammond and Noonan (eds), 79–100.

Pesetsky, David (1982a) "Complementizer-trace phenomena and the Nominative Island Condition," *The Linguistic Review* 1, 297–343.

Pesetsky, David (1982b) *Paths and Categories*, Ph.D. dissertation, MIT.

Pesetsky, David (1985) "Morphology and logical form," *Linguistic Inquiry* 16, 193–246.

Pesetsky, David (1987) "'Wh'-in-situ: movement and unselective binding," in Eric J. Reuland and Alice G. B. ter Meulen (eds), *The Representation of (In)definiteness*, Cambridge, Mass.: MIT Press, 98–129.

Pesetsky, David (1989) "Language-particular processes and the earliness principle," unpublished manuscript, MIT.

Phillips, Colin (ed.) (1993) *Papers on Case and Agreement II* (MIT Working Papers in Linguistics, vol. 19).

Pica, Pierre (1987) "On the nature of the reflexivization cycle," *Proceedings of NELS 17*, vol. 2, Amherst Mass: GSLA, Department of Linguistics, University of Massachusetts, 483–99.

Picallo, M. Carme (1984–5) "Opaque domains," *The Linguistic Review* 4, 279–88.

Platzack, Christer (1982/3) "Transitive adjectives in Swedish: a phenomenon with implications for the theory of abstract case," *The Linguistic Review* 2, 39–56.

Platzack, Christer (1983) "Existential sentences in English, German, Icelandic and Swedish," in Fred Karlsson (ed.), *Papers from the Seventh Scandinavian Conference of Linguistics: Hanasaari, Finland, December 17–19, 1982*, Helsinki: University of Helsinki, Department of General Linguistics, 80–100.

Platzack, Christer (1986) "COMP, INFL and Germanic word order," in Lars Hellan and Kirsti Koch Christensen (eds), *Topics in Scandinavian Syntax*, Dordrecht: D. Reidel, 185–234.

Platzack, Christer and Anders Holmberg (1989) "The role of AGR and finiteness in Germanic VO-languages," *Working Papers in Scandinavian Syntax* 43, 51–76.

Poeppel, David and Kenneth Wexler (1993) "The full competence hypothesis of clause structure in early German," *Language* 69, 1–33.

Pollard, Carl, and Ivan A. Sag (1987) *Information-Based Syntax and Semantics*, vol. I: *Fundamentals*, Stanford: Center for the Study of Language and Information.

Pollock, Jean-Yves (1989) "Verb movement, universal grammar, and the structure of IP," *Linguistic Inquiry* 20, 365–424.

Pollock, Jean-Yves (1992) Review of Adriana Belletti, *Generalized Verb Movement: Aspects of Verb Syntax*, *Language* 68, 836–40.

Postal, Paul M. (1962) *Some Syntactic Rules in Mohawk*, Ph.D. dissertation, Yale University. [Published (1979), New York: Garland.]

Postal, Paul M. (1969) "Anaphoric islands," in Robert I. Binnick, Alice Davison, Georgia M. Green, and Jerry L. Morgan (eds), *Papers from the Fifth Regional Meeting of the Chicago Linguistic Society*, 205–39.

Postal, Paul M. (1971) *Cross-Over Phenomena*, New York: Holt, Rinehart and Winston.

Postal, Paul M. (1974) *On Raising: One Rule of English Grammar and its Theoretical Implications*, Cambridge, Mass.: MIT Press.

Postal, Paul M. and Geoffrey K. Pullum (1988) "Expletive noun phrases in subcategorized positions," *Linguistic Inquiry* 19, 635–70.

Pranka, Paula Marie (1983) *Syntax and Word Formation*, Ph.D. dissertation, MIT.

Prince, Alan and P. Smolensky (1993) *Optimality Theory*, unpublished manuscript, Rutgers University and University of Colorado.

Progovac, L. (1991) "Relativized SUBJECT, long-distance reflexives, and accessibility," unpublished manuscript, Indiana University.

Radford, Andrew (1988) *Transformational Grammar: A First Course*, New York: Cambridge University Press.

Randall, Janet H. (1984) "Thematic structure and inheritance," *Quaderni di Semantica* 5, 92–110.

Raposo, Eduardo (1985–6) "Some asymmetries in the binding theory in Romance," *The Linguistic Review* 5, 75–110.

Raposo, Eduardo and Juan Uriagereka (1990) "Long-distance Case assignment," *Linguistic Inquiry* 21, 505–37.

Rappaport, Gilbert C. (1986) "On anaphor binding in Russian," *Natural Language and Linguistic Theory* 4, 97–120.

Rappaport, Malka (1983) "On the nature of derived nominals," in Lori Levin, Malka

Rappaport, and Annie Zaenen (eds), *Papers in Lexical–Functional Grammar*, Bloomington: Indiana University Linguistics Club, 113–42.
Reinhart, Tanya (1976) *The Syntactic Domain of Anaphora*, Ph.D. dissertation, MIT. [Reprinted with corrections and revisions (1984).]
Reinhart, Tanya (1981) "Definite NP anaphora and c-command domains," *Linguistic Inquiry* 12, 605–35.
Reinhart, Tanya (1983a) *Anaphora and Semantic Interpretation*, London: Croom Helm.
Reinhart, Tanya (1983b) "Coreference and bound anaphora: a restatement of the anaphora questions," *Linguistics and Philosophy* 6, 47–88.
Reinhart, Tanya (1986) "Center and periphery in the grammar of anaphora," in Barbara Lust (ed.), *Studies in the Acquisition of Anaphora*, vol. 1, Boston: D. Reidel, 123–50.
Reinhart, Tanya (1991) "Elliptic conjunctions – non-quantificational LF," in Asa Kasher (ed.), *The Chomskyan Turn*, Cambridge, Mass.: Basil Blackwell, 360–84.
Reinhart, Tanya and Eric Reuland (1989) "Anaphoric territories," manuscript. [Published (1991), *Groninger Arbeiten zur Germanistischen Linguistik* 34, 155–99.]
Reis, Marga (1985a) "Mona Lisa kriegt zuviel: vom sogenannten 'Rezipientenpassiv' im Deutschen," *Linguistische Berichte* 96, 140–55.
Reis, Marga (1985b) "Satzeinleitende Strukturen im Deutschen: über COMP, Haupt- und Nebensätze, *w*-Bewegung und die Doppelkopfanalyse," in Werner Abraham (ed.), *Erklärende Syntax des Deutschen*, Tübingen: Narr, 271–311.
Reuland, Eric (1983) "Governing *-ing*," *Linguistic Inquiry* 14, 101–36.
Reuland, Eric (1986, c1985) "A feature system for the set of categorial heads," in Muysken and van Riemsdijk (eds), 41–88.
Richards, Norvin (1993) "Head binding," paper presented at the eleventh annual meeting of the West Coast Conference on Formal Linguistics.
Riemsdijk, Henk van (1978) *A Case Study in Syntactic Markedness: The Binding Nature of Prepositional Phrases*, Lisse: The Peter de Ridder Press. [2nd edn, Henk van Riemsdijk (1982, c1981), Dordrecht: Foris.]
Riemsdijk, Henk van (1983) "The case of German adjectives," in Frank Heny and Barry Richards (eds), *Linguistic Categories: Auxiliaries and Related Puzzles*, vol. I, Dordrecht: D. Reidel, 223–52.
Riemsdijk, Henk van and Edwin Williams (1981) "NP-structure," *The Linguistic Review* 1, 171–217.
Riemsdijk, Henk van and Edwin Williams (1986) *Introduction to the Theory of Grammar*, Cambridge, Mass.: MIT Press.
Ristad, Eric (1989) "Complexity," unpublished manuscript, MIT.
Ritter, Elizabeth (1991) "Two functional categories in noun phrases: evidence from modern Hebrew," in Susan D. Rothstein (ed.), *Perspectives on Phrase Structure: Heads and Licensing* (Syntax and Semantics, vol. 25), San Diego: Academic Press, 37–62.
Rivero, María-Luisa (1992) "Adverb incorporation and the syntax of adverbs in Modern Greek," *Linguistics and Philosophy* 15, 289–331.
Rizzi, Luigi (1982) *Issues in Italian Syntax*, Dordrecht: Foris.
Rizzi, Luigi (1986a) "Null objects in Italian and the theory of *pro*," *Linguistic Inquiry* 17, 501–57.
Rizzi, Luigi (1986b) "On chain formation," in Borer (ed.).
Rizzi, Luigi (1990) *Relativized Minimality*, Cambridge, Mass.: MIT Press.
Rizzi, Luigi (1994) "Residual verb second and the WH-criterion," in Adriana Belletti and Luigi Rizzi (eds), *Parameters and Functional Heads: Essays in Comparative Syntax*, New York: Oxford University Press.
Rizzi, Luigi (to appear) "Early subjects and null subjects," in Barbara Lust, G. Hermon,

and J. Kornfilt (eds) *Syntactic Theory and First Language Acquisition*, vol. 2: *Binding Dependencies and Learnability*, Hillsdale, NJ: Lawrence Erlbaum.

Roberts, Craige (1985) "On the assignment of indices and their interpretation in binding theory," in Stephen Berman, Jae-Woong Choe, and Joyce McDonough (eds), *Proceedings of NELS 15: 1985*, Amherst, Mass.: GSLA, University of Massachusetts at Amherst, 362–76.

Roberts, Ian G. (1985) "Agreement parameters and the development of English modal auxiliaries," *Natural Language and Linguistic Theory* 3, 21–58.

Rochemont, Michael S. (1978) *A Theory of Stylistic Rules in English*, Ph.D. dissertation, University of Massachusetts, Amherst. [Published (1985), New York: Garland.]

Rodman, Robert (1976) "Scope phenomena, 'movement transformations,' and relative clauses," in Barbara H. Partee (ed.), *Montague Grammar*, New York: Academic Press, 165–76.

Rögnvaldsson, Eiríkur (1984) "Icelandic word order and *það*-Insertion," *Working Papers in Scandinavian Syntax* 8.

Rögnvaldsson, Eiríkur and Höskuldur Thráinsson (1990) "On Icelandic word order once more," in Maling and Zaenen (eds), 3–40.

Rosen, Sarah Thomas (1989) "Two types of noun incorporation: a lexical analysis," *Language* 65, 294–317.

Rosenbaum, Peter S. (1967) *The Grammar of English Predicate Complement Constructions*, Cambridge, Mass.: MIT Press.

Ross, John Robert (1967) *Constraints on Variables in Syntax*, Ph.D. dissertation, MIT. [Distributed (1968), Bloomington: Indiana University Linguistics Club.]

Rothstein, Susan Deborah (1983) *The Syntactic Forms of Predication*, Ph.D. dissertation, MIT. [Distributed (1985), Bloomington: Indiana University Linguistics Club.]

Rouveret, Alain (1990) "X-bar theory, minimality, and barrierhood in Welsh," in Randall Hendrick (ed.), *The Syntax of the Modern Celtic Languages* (Syntax and Semantics, vol. 23), San Diego: Academic Press, 27–79.

Rouveret, Alain and Jean-Roger Vergnaud (1980) "Specifying reference to the subject: French causatives and conditions on representations," *Linguistic Inquiry* 11, 97–202.

Rozwadowska, Božena (1988) "Thematic restrictions on derived nominals," in Wendy Wilkins (ed.), *Thematic Relations* (Syntax and Semantics, vol. 21), San Diego: Academic Press: 147–65.

Ruwet, Nicolas (1972) *Théorie syntaxique et syntaxe du français*, Paris: Éditions du Seuil.

Růžička, Rudolf (1983) "Remarks on control," *Linguistic Inquiry* 14, 309–24.

Sadock, Jerrold M. (1980) "Noun incorporation in Greenlandic: a case of syntactic word formation," *Language* 56, 300–19.

Sadock, Jerrold M. (1985) "The Southern Tiwa incorporability hierarchy," *International Journal of American Linguistics* 51, 568–72.

Sadock, Jerrold M. (1986) "Some notes on noun incorporation," *Language* 62, 19–31.

Sadock, Jerrold M. (1990) Review of Mark C. Baker, *Incorporation: A Theory of Grammatical Function Changing*, *Natural Language and Linguistic Theory* 8, 129–41.

Sadock, Jerrold M. (1991) *Autolexical Syntax: A Theory of Parallel Grammatical Representations*, Chicago: University of Chicago Press.

Safir, Ken (1983) "On small clauses as constituents," *Linguistic Inquiry* 14, 730–5.

Safir, Ken (1984) "Multiple variable binding," *Linguistic Inquiry* 15, 603–38.

Safir, Ken (1985a) "Missing subjects in German," in Jindrich Toman (ed.), *Studies in German Grammar*, Dordrecht: Foris, 193–229.

Safir, Ken (1985b) *Syntactic Chains*, Cambridge: Cambridge University Press.

Safir, Ken (1987) "The syntactic projection of lexical thematic structure," *Natural Language and Linguistic Theory* 5, 561–601.

Saito, Mamoru (1984) "Three notes on syntactic movement in Japanese," unpublished manuscript, MIT.
Saito, Mamoru (1985) *Some Asymmetries in Japanese and Their Theoretical Implications*, Ph.D. dissertation, MIT.
Saito, Marmoru (1989) "Scrambling as semantically Vacuous A′-movement," in M. Baltin and A. Kroch (eds), *Alternative Conceptions of Phrase Structure*, Chicago: University of Chicago Press, 182–200.
Saito, Mamoru (1992) "Long distance scrambling in Japanese," *Journal of East Asian Linguistics* 1, 69–118.
Saito, Mamoru and Hajime Hoji (1983) "Weak crossover and move-α in Japanese," *Natural Language and Linguistic Theory* 1, 245–59.
Santorini, Beatrice Elizabeth (1989) *The Generalization of the Verb-Second Constraint in the History of Yiddish*, Ph.D. dissertation, University of Pennsylvania.
Saxon, Leslie (1984) "Disjoint anaphora and the binding theory," in Mark Cobler, Susannah MacKaye, and Michael T. Wescoat (eds), *Proceedings of the West Coast Conference on Formal Linguistics*, vol. 3, Stanford, Calif.: Stanford University, Department of Linguistics, Stanford Linguistics Association, 242–51.
Scalise, Sergio (1984) *Generative Morphology*, Dordrecht: Foris. [2nd edn (1986).]
Schein, B. (1982) "Small clauses and predication," unpublished manuscript, MIT.
Scherpenisse, Wim (1986) *The Connection between Base Structure and Linearization Restrictions in German and Dutch*, Frankfurt am Main: Peter Lang.
Seiter, William J. (1980) *Studies in Niuean Syntax*, New York: Garland.
Selkirk, Elisabeth O. (1982) *The Syntax of Words*, Cambridge, Mass.: MIT Press. [2nd MIT Press Paperback edn (1983).]
Selkirk, Elisabeth O. (1984) *Phonology and Syntax: The Relation between Sound and Structure*, Cambridge, Mass.: MIT Press. [1st MIT Press Paperback edn (1986).]
Sells, Peter (1986) "Coreference and bound anaphora: a restatement of the facts," in Stephen Berman, Jae-Woong Choe, and Joyce McDonough (eds), *Proceedings of NELS 16*, GSLA, Department of Linguistics, University of Massachusetts, 434–46.
Sells, Peter (1987) "Aspects of logophoricity," *Linguistic Inquiry* 18, 445–79.
Sengupta, Gautam (1990) *Binding and Scrambling in Bangla*, Ph.D. dissertation, University of Massachusetts, Amherst.
Shibatani, Masayoshi (ed.) (1976) *The Grammar of Causative Constructions* (Syntax and Semantics, vol. 6), New York: Academic Press.
Shibatani, Masayoshi (1990) "Japanese," in Bernard Comrie (ed.), *The World's Major Languages*, New York: Oxford University Press, 855–80.
Shlonsky, Ur (1989) "The hierarchical representation of subject–verb agreement," unpublished manuscript, University of Haifa, Israel.
Shlonsky, Ur (1990) "Pro in Hebrew subject inversion," *Linguistic Inquiry* 21, 263–75.
Shopen, Timothy (ed.) (1985) *Language Typology and Syntactic Description*, vol. III: *Grammatical Categories and the Lexicon*, Cambridge: Cambridge University Press.
Siegel, Dorothy (1979) *Topics in English Morphology*, New York: Garland.
Sigurðsson, Halldór Ármann (1986) "Moods and (long-distance) reflexives in Icelandic," *Working Papers in Scandinavian Syntax* 25, 1–53. [Published (1990) "Long-distance reflexives and moods in Icelandic," in Maling and Zaenen (eds), 309–46.]
Sigurðsson, Halldór Ármann (1989) *Verbal Syntax and Case in Icelandic: In a Comparative GB Approach*, Ph.D. dissertation, University of Lund.
Sigurðsson, Halldór Ármann (1991) "Icelandic case-marked PRO and the licensing of lexical arguments," *Natural Language and Linguistic Theory* 9, 327–63.
Simpson, Jane (1983a) *Aspects of Warlpiri Morphology and Syntax*, Ph.D. dissertation,

MIT. [A revised version appears as (1991) *Warlpiri Morpho-Syntax: A Lexicalist Approach*, Dordrecht: Kluwer.]

Simpson, Jane (1983b) "Discontinuous verbs and the interaction of morphology and syntax," in Michael Barlow, Daniel P. Flickinger, and Michael T. Wescoat (eds), *Proceedings of the West Coast Conference on Formal Linguistics*, vol. 2, Stanford: Stanford Linguistics Association, 275–86.

Sinclair, Melinda (1982) "The development of the Specified Subject Condition and the Tensed S-Condition/Propositional Island Condition," *Stellenbosch Papers in Linguistics* 9.

Sobin, Nicholas J. (1985) "Case assignment in Ukrainian morphological passive constructions," *Linguistic Inquiry* 16, 649–62.

Speas, Margaret (1986) *Adjunctions and Projections in Syntax*, Ph.D. dissertation, MIT.

Speas, Margaret (1990) *Phrase Structure in Natural Language*, Dordrecht: Kluwer.

Spencer, Andrew (1988) "Bracketing paradoxes and the English lexicon," *Language* 64, 663–82.

Spencer, Andrew (1991) *Morphological Theory: An Introduction to Word Structure in Generative Grammar*, Oxford: Basil Blackwell.

Sportiche, Dominique (1981) "Bounding nodes in French," *The Linguistic Review* 1, 219–46.

Sportiche, Dominique (1982) "Zibun," *Linguistic Inquiry* 17, 369–74.

Sportiche, Dominique (1988) "A theory of floating quantifiers and its corollaries for constituent structure," *Linguistic Inquiry* 19, 425–49.

Sportiche, Dominique (1992) "Clitic Constructions," unpublished manuscript, University of California at Los Angeles.

Sproat, Richard (1985a) *On Deriving the Lexicon*, Ph.D. dissertation, MIT.

Sproat, Richard (1985b) "Welsh syntax and VSO structure," *Natural Language and Linguistic Theory* 3, 173–216.

Sproat, Richard (1988a) "Bracketing paradoxes, cliticization and other topics: the mapping between syntactic and phonological structure," in Everaert, Evers, Huybregts, and Trommelen (eds), 339–60.

Sproat, Richard (1988b) "On anaphoric islandhood," in Hammond and Noonan (eds), 291–301.

Sprouse, Rex A. (1989) *On the Syntax of the Double Object Construction in Selected Germanic Languages*, Ph.D. dissertation, Princeton University.

Srivastav Dayal, Veneeta (to appear) "Binding facts in Hindi and the scrambling phenomenon," in Miriam Butt, Tracy King, and Gillian Ramchand (eds), *Word Order in South Asian Languages*, Stanford: Center for the Study of Language and Information.

Stowell, Tim (1978) "What was there before there was there," in Donka Farkas, Wesley M. Jacobsen, and Karol W. Todrys (eds), *Papers from the Fourteenth Regional Meeting, Chicago Linguistic Society, April 13–14, 1978*, Chicago: Chicago Linguistic Society, University of Chicago, 458–71.

Stowell, Tim (1981) *Origins of Phrase Structure*, Ph.D. dissertation, MIT.

Stowell, Tim (1983) "Subjects across categories," *The Linguistic Review* 2, 285–312.

Stowell, Tim (1985) "Null operators and the theory of proper government," unpublished manuscript, University of California, Los Angeles.

Stowell, Tim (1991) "Small clause restructuring," in Freidin (ed.), 182–218.

Stowell, Tim (1992) Colloquium presented at the Department of Linguistics, University of Wisconsin–Madison, November 1992.

Stump, Gregory T. (1984) "Agreement vs. incorporation in Breton," *Natural Language and Linguistic Theory* 2, 289–348.

Stuurman, Frits (1985) *Phrase Structure Theory in Generative Grammar*, Dordrecht: Foris.

Suñer, Margarita (1988) "The role of agreement in clitic-doubled constructions," *Natural Language and Linguistic Theory* 6, 391–434.

Takahashi, D. (1993) "Minimize chain links," unpublished manuscript, University of Connecticut.

Tang, Chih-Chen Jane (1985) *A Study of Reflexives in Chinese*, Master's Thesis, National Taiwan Normal University.

Tang, Chih-Chen Jane (1989) "Chinese reflexives," *Natural Language and Linguistic Theory* 7, 93–121.

Taraldsen, Knut Tarald (1980) *On the Nominative Island Condition, Vacuous Application, and the That-Trace Filter*, Bloomington: Indiana University Linguistics Club.

Thiersch, C. (1982) "A note on 'scrambling' and the existence of VP," *Wiener Linguistische Gazette* 27/8, 83–95.

Thomas-Flinders, Tracy (1982) "On the notions 'head of a word' and 'lexically related': evidence from Maricopa verbal morphology," in Daniel P. Flickinger, Marlys Macken, and Nancy Wiegand (eds), *Proceedings of the First West Coast Conference on Formal Linguistics*, Stanford, Calif.: Linguistics Department, Stanford University, 168–78.

Thráinsson, Höskuldur (1976a) "Reflexives and subjunctives in Icelandic," *Proceedings of NELS* 6, 225–39.

Thráinsson, Höskuldur (1976b) "Some arguments against the interpretive theory of pronouns and reflexives," in J. Hankamer and J. Aissen (eds), *Harvard Studies in Syntax and Semantics*, 573–624.

Thráinsson, Höskuldur (1979) *On Complementation in Icelandic*, New York: Garland.

Thráinsson, Höskuldur (1986a) "On auxiliaries, AUX and VPs in Icelandic," in Lars Hellan and Kirsti Koch Christensen (eds), *Topics in Scandinavian Syntax*, Dordrecht: D. Reidel, 235–65.

Thráinsson, Höskuldur (1986b) "V1, V2, V3 in Icelandic," in Haider and Prinzhorn (eds), 169–94.

Thráinsson, Höskuldur (1987) "What is a reflexive pronoun?" unpublished manuscript, University of Iceland.

Thráinsson, Höskuldur (1991) "Long distance reflexives and the typology of NP's," in Jan Koster and Eric Reuland (eds), *Long-Distance Anaphora*, Cambridge: Cambridge University Press, 49–76.

Tiedeman, Robyne (1990) "An S-structure/LF asymmetry in subject extraction," *Linguistic Inquiry* 21, 661–7.

Timberlake, Alan (1976) "Subject properties in the North Russian passive," in Charles N. Li (ed.), *Subject and Topic*, New York: Academic Press, 545–70.

Torrego, Esther (1985) "On empty categories in nominals," unpublished manuscript, University of Massachusetts, Boston.

Travis, Lisa deMena (1984) *Parameters and Effects of Word Order Variation*, Ph.D. dissertation, MIT.

Trithart, Mary Lee (1977) *Relational Grammar and Chichewa Subjectivization Rules*, Bloomington: Indiana University Linguistics Club.

Truckenbrodt, H. (1993) "Towards a prosodic theory of relative clause extraposition," unpublished manuscript, MIT.

Ueda, Masanobu (1990) *Japanese Phrase Structure and Parameter Setting*, Ph.D. dissertation, University of Massachusetts, Amherst.

Ueyama, Ayumi (1990) "Scrambling in Japanese as a uniform chain," paper presented at the Workshop on Scrambling, Tilburg University.

Ura, H. (1993) "Super-raising and the feature-based X-bar theory," unpublished manuscript, MIT.
Uriagereka, Juan (1988) *On Government*, Ph.D. dissertation, University of Connecticut, Storrs.
Vikner, Sten (1985) "Parameters of binder and binding category in Danish," *Working Papers in Scandinavian Syntax* 23, 1–58.
Vikner, Sten (1990) *Verb Movement and the Licensing of NP Positions in the Germanic Languages*, Ph.D. dissertation, Université de Genève. [Published (1994) *Verb Movement and Expletive Subjects in the Germanic Languages*, New York: Oxford University Press.]
Vikner, Sten and Bonnie Schwartz (1994) "The verb always leaves IP in V2 clauses," in Adriana Belletti and Luigi Rizzi (eds), *Parameters and Functional Heads: Essays in Comparative Syntax*, New York: Oxford University Press.
Wasow, Thomas (1977) "Transformations and the lexicon," in Peter W. Culicover, Thomas Wasow, and Adrian Akmajian (eds), *Formal Syntax*, New York: Academic Press, 327–60.
Watanabe, Akira (1991) "Wh-in-situ, subjacency and chain formation," unpublished manuscript, MIT.
Watanabe, Akira (1992) "Subjacency and S-structure movement of Wh-in-situ," *Journal of East Asian Linguistics* 1, 255–91.
Watanabe, Akira (1993) *AGR-Based Case Theory and its Interaction with the A-bar System*, Ph.D. dissertation, MIT.
Webelhuth, Gert (1984/5) "German is configurational," *The Linguistic Review* 4, 203–46.
Webelhuth, Gert (1987) "A universal theory of scrambling," in *Proceedings of the 10th Conference on Scandinavian Linguistics*, Bergen, Norway: Department of Linguistics, University of Bergen, 284–98.
Webelhuth, Gert (1990) "Diagnostics for structure," in Grewendorf and Sternefeld (eds), 41–75.
Webelhuth, Gert (1992) *Principles and Parameters of Syntactic Saturation*, New York: Oxford University Press.
Webelhuth, Gert (1993) "A necessary condition for the postulation of functional heads," unpublished manuscript, University of North Carolina at Chapel Hill.
Webelhuth, Gert and Farrell Ackerman (1993) "Passive auxiliaries and raising verbs as predicate operators," unpublished manuscript, University of North Carolina and University of California at San Diego.
Wegener, Heide (1985) "'Er bekommt widersprochen': Argumente für die Existenz eines Dativpassivs im Deutschen," *Linguistische Berichte* 96, 127–39.
Weinberg, Amy Sara (1988) *Locality Principles in Syntax and in Parsing*, Ph.D. dissertation, MIT.
Wexler, Kenneth and M. Rita Manzini (1987) "Parameters and learnability in binding theory," in Thomas Roeper and Edwin Williams (eds), *Parameter Setting*, Dordrecht: D. Reidel, 41–89.
Williams, Edwin (1975) "Small clauses in English," in John P. Kimball (ed.), *Syntax and Semantics*, vol. 4, New York: Academic Press, 249–73.
Williams, Edwin (1977) "Discourse and logical form," *Linguistic Inquiry* 8, 101–39.
Williams, Edwin (1980) "Predication," *Linguistic Inquiry* 11, 203–38.
Williams, Edwin (1981a) "Argument structure and morphology," *The Linguistic Review* 1, 81–114.
Williams, Edwin (1981b) "On the notions 'lexically related' and 'head of a word'," *Linguistic Inquiry* 12, 245–74.

Williams, Edwin (1982a) "Another argument that passive is transformational," *Linguistic Inquiry* 13, 160–3.
Williams, Edwin (1982b) "The NP cycle," *Linguistic Inquiry* 13, 277–95.
Williams, Edwin (1983) "Against small clauses," *Linguistic Inquiry* 14, 287–308.
Williams, Edwin (1984) "Grammatical relations," *Linguistic Inquiry* 15, 639–73.
Williams, Edwin (1986) "A reassignment of the functions of LF," *Linguistic Inquiry* 17, 265–99.
Williams, Edwin (1987a) "Implicit arguments, the binding theory, and control," *Natural Language and Linguistic Theory* 5, 151–80.
Williams, Edwin (1987b) "NP trace in theta theory," *Linguistics and Philosophy* 10, 433–47.
Williams, Edwin (1988) "Is LF distinct from S-structure?: a reply to May," *Linguistic Inquiry* 19, 135–46.
Williams, Edwin (1989) "The anaphoric nature of θ-roles," *Linguistic Inquiry* 20, 425–56.
Williams, Edwin (1994) *Thematic Structure in Syntax*, Cambridge, Mass.: MIT Press.
Woolford, Ellen (1991) "VP-internal subjects in VSO and nonconfigurational languages," *Linguistic Inquiry* 22, 503–40.
Yang, Dong-Whee (1983) "The extended binding theory of anaphors," *Language Research* 19, 169–92.
Yokoyama, Olga Tsuneko (1980) "Studies in Russian functional syntax," in Susumo Kuno (ed.), *Harvard Studies in Syntax and Semantics*, vol. 3, 451–774.
Yoon, J.-M. (1989) "On the nature of long-distance binding in Korean," unpublished manuscript, University of Illinois.
Yoon, Jeong-Me (1991) *The Syntax of A-Chains: A Typological Study of ECM and Scrambling*, Ph.D. dissertation, Cornell University.
Zaenen, Annie (1985) *Extraction Rules in Icelandic*, New York: Garland.
Zaenen, Annie and Joan Maling (1990) "Unaccusative, passive, and quirky case," in Maling and Zaenen (eds), 137–52.
Zaenen, Annie, Joan Maling, and Höskuldur Thráinsson (1985) "Case and grammatical functions: the Icelandic passive," *Natural Language and Linguistic Theory* 3, 441–83.
Zagona, Karen T. (1982) *Government and Proper Government of Verbal Projections*, Ph.D. dissertation, University of Washington, Seattle.
Zanuttini, Raffaella (1991) *Syntactic Properties of Sentential Negation: A Comparative Study of Romance Languages*, Ph.D. dissertation, University of Pennsylvania.
Zaring, Laurie Ann (1985) *The Syntactic Role of Verbal Inflection in French and Brazilian Portuguese*, Ph.D. dissertation, Cornell University.
Zhang, Shi (1990) "Correlations between the double object construction and preposition stranding," *Linguistic Inquiry* 21, 312–16.
Zubizarreta, Maria Luisa (1985) "The relation between morphophonology and morphosyntax: the case of Romance causatives," *Linguistic Inquiry* 16, 247–89.
Zubizarreta, Maria Luisa (1993) "Some prosodically motivated syntactic operations," unpublished manuscript, University of Southern California.
Zwart, J.-W. (1993) *Dutch Syntax: A Minimalist Approach*, Ph.D. dissertation, University of Groningen.
Zwicky, Arnold M. (1977) *On Clitics*, Bloomington: Indiana University Linguistics Club.
Zwicky, Arnold M. (1985) "Heads," *Journal of Linguistics* 21, 1–29.
Zwicky, Arnold M. and Geoffrey K. Pullum (1983) "Cliticization and inflection: English *n't*," *Language* 59, 502–13.

Index